A World Record of
Major Conflict Areas

A World Record of Major Conflict Areas

David Munro
and
Alan J Day

St_J

St James Press

Chicago and London

© 1990 Edward Arnold Publishers Ltd

First published in Great Britain 1990 by Edward Arnold
Published in North America by St. James Press,
233 East Ontario Street, Chicago, Illinois 60611, USA.

ISBN 1–55862–066–4

Typeset in 10/11 pt Palatino by Anneset, Weston-super-Mare, Avon
Printed and bound in Great Britain by Butler and Tanner Ltd,
Frome, Somerset
Maps drawn by Elizabeth Clark and Anona Lyons

Contents

I Africa
1. Sudan 3
2. Ethiopia 14
3. Western Sahara 24
4. Angola/Namibia 34
5. Mozambique 51
6. South Africa 63

II Middle East
1. Palestine/Israel 83
2. Lebanon 104
3. Iraq and the Gulf 121
4. Kurdistan 134

III Asia/Far East
1. Afghanistan 147
2. Kashmir 163
3. Sikh Nationalism 173
4. Sri Lanka 181
5. Cambodia 197
6. Korea 210
7. East Timor 223

IV Americas
1. Nicaragua 235
2. El Salvador 249
3. Colombia 261
4. Peru 273
5. Falklands/Malvinas 285

V Europe
1. Baltic Republics 301
2. Armenia/Azerbaijan 310
3. Romania 321
4. Kosovo 334
5. Cyprus 345
6. Northern Ireland 358

General Bibliography 374

Preface

The 20th century has seen two world wars, but by mid-1990 the once-confident prediction of the inevitability of a third was no longer being made. Instead, the Cold War had ended and peace and reconciliation had broken out in the traditional theatres of East–West confrontation. Meanwhile, however, war and conflict had continued on a massive scale in various parts of the globe since 1945, involving such factors as territorial and boundary disputes, guerrilla insurgencies, struggles against residual colonialism or external hegemony, and racial or religious antagonisms. Even though converging superpower interests had, by the late 1980s, brought a number of these conflicts to the point of a settlement, most remained highly sensitive, while many others showed no signs of being resolved. Indeed, as this book went to press, Iraqi forces invaded Kuwait, thereby precipitating another major international crisis in one of the world's most notorious flashpoints (as described in section 2.3).

The purpose of the present volume is to describe and elucidate, in an easy reference format, some 28 current conflicts in different parts of the world. Each situation covered has not only a deep-rooted historical background but also an important contemporary international dimension involving intense diplomatic activity as well considerable media interest. The authors are acutely conscious of the time-sensitivity of the data presented. As the latest Gulf crisis shows, political conflicts are notoriously liable to undergo unpredicted changes, especially in the new era of rapid international change unleashed by the collapse of communism in Eastern Europe in 1989. Information in the current volume covers developments up to mid-1990, and every effort has been made to ensure that rapidly-evolving situations are dealt with in a way which makes the data given useful for understanding of the background of the conflict in question.

The broad arrangement of the book is geographical, in that there are five sections covering, respectively, Africa, the Middle East, Asia and the Far East, the Americas, and Europe. Within these sections, chapters on specific conflicts follow a standard structure, beginning with a map and a profile of the relevant country or territory, followed by an Introduction describing the historical background and current status of the conflict, together with a Chronology of Events setting out the critical stages of each situation with emphasis on recent developments. Then follow three directory sections giving cogent entries in alphabetical order covering (i) important personalities (Who's Who), (ii) geographical locations (Key Places), and (iii) other ingredients of the conflict such as organizations, treaties and declarations, ethnic groups and political terms (Key Words). Thus the aim is to provide for the user not only a broad picture of conflicts covered but also handy reference entries on their key human, geographical and political ingredients.

DMM/AJD, August 1990

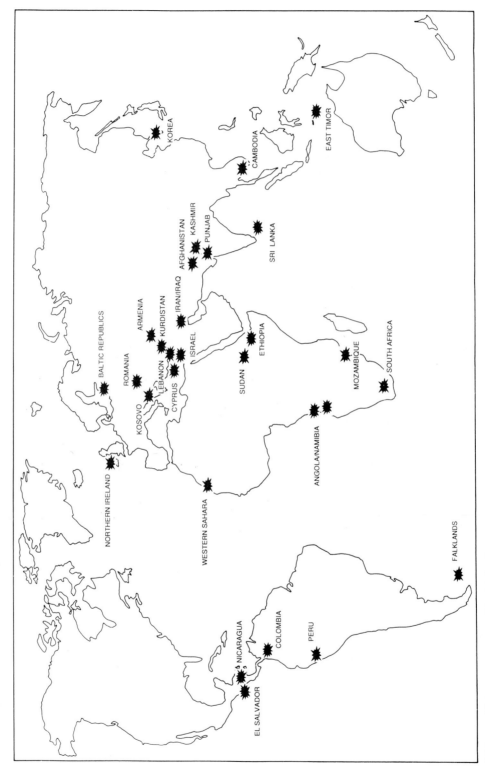

Major conflict areas represented in this book

I Africa

1
Sudan

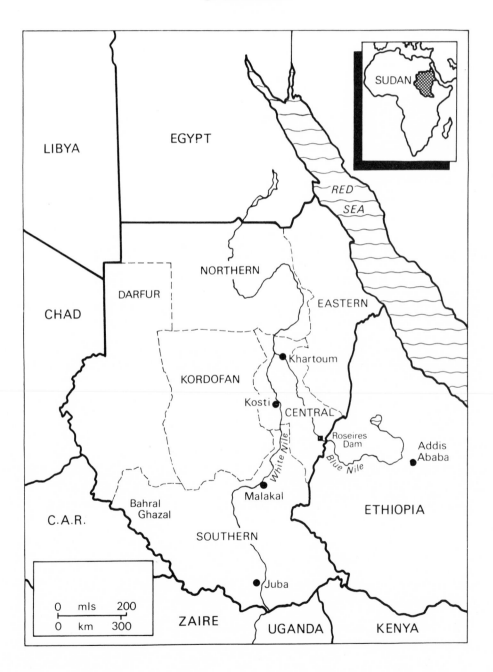

■ Profile

- **Area:**　2 505 810km² (largest country in Africa)
- **Population (1988):**　24million
- **Ethnic groups:**　Arab 46%, Nilotic 25%, Azande 6%, Nuba 6%, Beja 5%
- **Official language:**　Arabic
- **Commonly spoken languages:** Nubian, Ta Bedawie and various dialects of Nilotic, Nilo–Hamitic and Sudanic languages
- **Religions:**　Sunni Muslim 70% (mostly in the north), local beliefs (animist) 20%, Christian 5% (mostly in the south)
- **Life expectancy (1985):**　47 years for men, 50 years for women
- **Infant mortality rate:**　112 per 1000 in 1985
- **Literacy:**　20%
- **Currency:**　Sudanese pound
- **Timezone:** GMT +2
- **Capital:**　Khartoum
- **Chief cities:**　Omdurman (526 300), Khartoum (476 200), Khartoum North (341 100), Port Sudan (206 700)

■ Introduction

The roots of Sudan's present internal conflict are to be found in ethnic and religious divisions aggravated historically by slavery and the impact of British colonial rule. Black Nubian slaves from what is now Sudan were prized by the ancient Egyptians, Greeks and Romans, a tradition which the later Arab and Turkish Muslim rulers of Egypt kept up with enthusiasm. Arab migration from Arabia and Egypt led to the Islamicization of northern and central Sudan by the mid-14th century, when the last independent Christian Nubian kingdoms disappeared. Miscegenation of Arabs and Negroes blurred the racial divide in these areas, but blacks continued to be taken as slaves, particularly from the non-Muslim south. When Mohammed Ali Pasha of Egypt conquered Sudan in 1820–22, one of his main objectives was better access to the lucrative trade in black slaves. Not until the British arrived on the scene in the 1860s was the slave trade gradually curtailed, although even today "chattel slavery" persists in the south.

Sudan received its first British anti-slavery expedition in 1869, the year of the completion of the Suez Canal. The latter event's strategic implications governed subsequent British policy towards the region, but Britain also took seriously its self-assumed "civilizing" mission, as exemplified in the career of Gen. Charles Gordon. Appointed governor-general of Sudan in 1874 (by an Egyptian government already under British influence), Gordon not only campaigned effectively against the Muslim-run slave trade but also promoted his own brand of evangelical Christianity among the non-Muslim blacks. By the time British forces established full control of Egypt in 1882, Sudanese Muslims led by the Mahdi were in open revolt against British-inspired interference with their Islamic way of life. The insurgency continued for nearly two decades, during which Gordon met his celebrated death at Khartoum in 1885. Although British military might eventually prevailed at Omdurman in 1898, the Mahdist revolt remained a potent symbol for Muslims aspiring to restore the supremacy of Islam in a country containing many non-Muslims and governed by Christian Europeans.

An important feature of British policy under the Anglo-Egyptian Condominium established over Sudan in 1899 was the gradual extension of its borders southwards. The resolution in Britain's favour of the 1898–99 Fashoda confrontation with France meant that the vast Upper Nile region, inhabited mainly by non-Muslim blacks, was confirmed as part of the Condominium. Moreover, before and after World War I portions of black-populated British East Africa were transferred to Sudan. When British diktat obliged Egypt, on its achievement of independence in 1922, to withdraw from the Condominium in favour of a Sudanese Muslim administration under British tutelage, non-Muslim blacks in the south staged their first major revolt. It was quickly suppressed but had the effect of persuading Britain to adopt a new policy of separating the south from the north with a view to the former becoming part of an East African Federation (with Uganda and Kenya).

Under the new British approach the south was closed to Muslim traders and Muslim priests, the teaching of Arabic was banned and English was fostered. Moreover, Christian missionaries sought to further their cause among blacks by stressing the role of Muslims in the slave trade. They made only limited headway against the animist beliefs prevalent among the southern tribes, but such teaching had the effect of keeping the blacks' ancestral fears of northerners very much alive. Britain abandoned the policy of southern separation after World War II, but by then the north-south divide had become rooted in a country whose boundaries were drawn by the colonialists, not by its inhabitants. The southerners did not of course form a united people, being themselves divided into four main language groups and into many tribes within those groups; in consequence, inter-tribal strife has remained a serious problem in the region. Nevertheless, black southerners shared a basic animosity towards the Muslim slavers of the north and, coached by the missionaries, were aware of northern assumptions of racial superiority over all the blacks of the south.

Britain's policy reversal from 1945, to one favouring independence for a united Sudan, reflected its calculation that a Muslim Sudan minus the south would lack economic viability and thus be susceptible to incorporation into Egypt. The latter had resumed joint responsibility for Sudan in 1936; after World War II it argued that Sudan belonged to the Egyptian crown. The Egyptian claim was rejected by Britain and formally renounced by Cairo after the overthrow of the monarchy in 1952, but Britain remained suspicious. From 1953 the British concentrated on preparing a Sudanese elite for independence, but in this drive to "Sudanization" virtually no black southerners were admitted to the hierarchy. For their part, northern leaders combined traditional Muslim contempt for the peoples of the south with a realization that the southern region, containing the head-waters of the Nile and much fertile agricultural land, was indispensable to an independent Sudan. The stage was therefore set for confrontation when rebellion again broke out in the south in 1955, even before Sudan achieved independence in January 1956. Sudan became Africa's largest country but was a classic case of a new state inheriting boundaries which took no account of population realities.

The first phase of the civil war was to last for 17 years, during which successive governments in Khartoum, both civilian and military, committed huge resources in an effort to subdue the southern revolt. The estimated death toll resulting directly or indirectly from the conflict reached over half a million. Not until the accession to power of General Nimeiri in 1969 was there a sustained effort to find a negotiated settlement on the basis of a compromise by both sides. The outcome was the 1972 Addis Ababa Agreement providing for a federal solution under which an autonomous Southern Region was created in return for the southerners accepting a ceasefire and abandoning secessionist aims. For a while this settlement, heralded as a model for African states beset with tribalism, kept the peace. By the early 1980s, however, serious strains had resurfaced, as the Nimeiri regime ran into economic failure and became increasingly autocratic, while the Southern Region administration itself succumbed to the familiar African woes of corruption and inter-tribal strife.

The catalyst for the resumption of open hostilities was provided by two fateful decisions by Nimeiri in 1983. The first was the redivision of the Southern Region, in breach of the 1972 accord, into its three constituent provinces. This was seen in the south as a "divide and rule" manoeuvre intended to strengthen the central government in its perceived designs on "southern" water and also on the oil reserves recently discovered in the region by Chevron. The result was the formation by pre-1972 secessionist activists of the Sudanese People's Liberation Movement (SPLM), whose military wing, the SPLA, embarked upon armed struggle against the central government with backing from the radical regimes of neighbouring Ethiopia (*see section 1.2*) and Libya. Later in the year support for the SPLM among southern blacks, themselves continually rent by tribal conflict, was greatly increased by Nimeiri's second disastrous decision, namely the imposition of Islamic Sharia law throughout Sudan. Whereas the pre-1972 southern insurgency had included a strong secessionist dimension, the SPLM's key demand was for the reinstatement of the Addis Ababa accord, including autonomy for the Southern Region within Sudan and the non-enforcement of Sharia law in the south.

Nimeiri's intention in introducing Sharia law was to counter the appeal of Sudanese opposition elements propagating the doctrines of Islamic fundamentalism. However, such was the chaos to which his policies reduced the country that he was deposed by a military coup in 1985, leading to the installation of a civilian government a year later. Hopes then rose for a negotiated settlement of the civil war raging in the south, especially since Libya withdrew its support for the SPLM on the overthrow of Nimeiri and the new government relaxed the harsher applications of Sharia law in the south. In the event, efforts to find a settlement met with no success, with the result that military rule was reimposed in Khartoum in June 1989. The new regime declared itself ready for yet another attempt to end the war, but subsequent peace talks failed to bridge the gulf between the two sides. Perhaps significantly for the future course of the dispute, Sudanese military leaders were by now openly countenancing the south's secession as the only realistic solution, whereas the SPLM continued to favour the preservation of Sudan as one country.

■ Chronology of events

1821 With a view to establishing an Egyptian–Arab empire Mohammed Ali Pasha of Egypt extends his control of the Nile Valley southwards into Sudan.

1881 The religious rebel leader Mohammed Ahmed Abdulla, known as the "Mahdi" calls for the reformation of Islam and incites the people of Sudan to rebel against Egyptian rule.

1882 In the scramble for Africa Britain gains effective control over Egypt but decides it cannot hold Sudan against the Mahdists. General Gordon is sent to Khartoum to supervise the evacuation of Sudan.

1885 Anglo–Egyptian control over Sudan is broken with the fall of Khartoum and the death of General Gordon.

1896 Egyptian and British forces under General Kitchener set out to reconquer Sudan.

1898 The Sudan finally comes under Anglo–Egyptian control when the last of the Mahdists are defeated at the battle of Omdurman. The capture of the town of Fashoda in SE Sudan by French forces gives rise to a serious international crisis that almost results in war between Britain and France.

1899 The Anglo–Egyptian Agreement establishes a protectorate with British administration over both Egypt and the Sudan, although Britain does not claim sovereignty over either territories.

1916 On the death of Sultan Ali Dinar, Darfur becomes a province of Sudan.

1922 Britain abolishes the protectorate and recognizes Egypt as a sovereign independent state. Sudan remains under British administration.

1924 Egyptian troops and civil personnel leave the Sudan. In an attempt to stem the tide of nationalism, "native administration" is introduced in northern Sudan. A rebellion of the Dinka people in the south prompts the government to launch a new "Southern Policy" aimed at the eventual separation of the three non-Muslim southern provinces from the rest of Sudan. The setting up of a system of "closed districts" accentuates the north–south divide.

1936 Egypt resumes its position as joint administrator of the Sudan.

1943 Local government by "native administration" is extended to central government with the launching of an Advisory Council for Northern Sudan.

1948 The Advisory Council is replaced by a Legislative Assembly for the whole of Sudan.

1953 A year after the revolution in Egypt that brought Nasser to power the right of Sudan to determine its own future is established with the signing of an Anglo–Egyptian Agreement.

1954 Following an election, Ismail el-Azhari, leader of the National Unionist Party, becomes the first Sudanese Prime Minister in January.

1955 A mutiny amongst southern troops at Juba in the province of Equatoria sparks off a revolt in the Southern Region. Over 300 northern officials and civilians are killed before order is restored. Deciding not to hold a referendum on self determination, the Sudanese parliament declares the Sudan an independent republic on 19 December.

1956 On 1 January Sudan celebrates its independence from Egypt and Britain.

1958 Following a disastrous harvest the leading members of the coalition government cannot agree on the need for foreign aid. A February election results in a further stalemate and in November the Prime Minister joins with the army in staging a military coup. Under the leadership of General Ibrahim Abboud, parliamentary rule is suspended and aid from the USA and Soviet Union is negotiated.

1964 Military action against rebels in the south forces thousands of southerners to live as refugees across the border in neighbouring countries. Missionaries, considered to have been part of the divisive "Southern Policy" of the British, are expelled in February. This action, coupled with a growing opposition to the corrupt and undemocratic military regime, leads to a general strike in October. General Abboud is forced to resign and the country returns to civilian rule.

1965 Parliamentary elections are held in April and a coalition government is elected. The new leaders of Sudan declare a general amnesty in the southern provinces and open up a dialogue between northern and southern politicians. This does not prevent further rebel activity around Juba.

1969 The inability of successive coalition governments to resolve ethnic differences and economic stagnation results in a second military coup on 25 May. Under the left–wing leadership of Jaafar Mohammed Nimeiri, parliamentary democracy is again abolished and all opposition political parties are outlawed. The new one-party state changes its name to the Democratic Republic of the Sudan. Banks and businesses are nationalized in a programme of "Sudanese socialism" and a Ministry for Southern Affairs is created.

1972 In March the government and the southern rebels reach a peace agreement. The Addis Ababa Accord effectively brings to an end 17 years of civil war. In exchange for a ceasefire, greater autonomy is granted with the setting-up of a Regional People's Assembly based in Juba.

1983 In September President Nimeiri embarks on a programme of Islamic reform. The application of Sharia law with its stiff penal code and the introduction of new business loan procedures under the principle of murabaha prove unpopular, particularly in the non-Muslim Southern Region. A decree dividing the south into three provinces further helps to revive the civil war.

1985 The Sudanese government is unable to pay the interest on loans totalling $9 billion and a crisis occurs when the USA cuts off aid in February. US Vice-president George Bush visits Sudan in March and a month later while Nimeiri is out of the country, senior military officers led by General Suwar el-Dahab, stage a coup. The country is placed in the hands of a 15–member Transitional Military Council which appoints a civilian cabinet that paves the way for democratic elections. Attempts are made to reconcile the differences between north and south, but the civil war continues. The SPLA forces of Col. John Garang now control two of Sudan's three southern provinces. Meanwhile, over two million Sudanese are faced with starvation as a result of drought and famine.

1986 Sadiq el-Mahdi is elected Prime Minister of a coalition government in April. He will not negotiate with the Sudan People's Liberation Army (SPLA) which he claims is being used by neighbouring Marxist Ethiopia. Libya increases financial and military aid to Sudan. In return for Libyan support in the fight against the SPLA, el-Mahdi allows Libyan–backed Chadian rebels to operate in Western Sudan. While SPLA forces lay siege to the towns of Juba, Wau and Malakal, the UN attempts to supply aid to victims of famine in the south.

1987 SPLA forces prevent food from reaching the town of Malakal, capital of Upper Nile province, and the capture of Kurmuk and Gizen takes the battle into northern Arab provinces.

1988 Believing Western aid agencies and the Christian Church to be in collusion with the southern rebels, Islamic fundamentalists attack Western Christians in Khartoum killing five Britons. Hunger and disease cause the death of over 250 000 people in the southern war zone as drought conditions are compounded by scorched–earth policies applied by both sides. An agreement reached between the SPLA and leaders of the Democratic Unionist Party in November fails to gain the support of other parties in the coalition government.

1989 In the face of heavy military defeats in the south the reshuffled coalition cabinet offers a peace plan to the SPLA rebels. Although the plan is rejected, the rebel leader Col. John Garang announces a one-month ceasefire to allow international aid to reach over 100 000 people dying of starvation. The government of Sadiq el-Mahdi is deposed during a coup in July that brings the country under military rule once more. Ceasefire offers are again made by the new leader, Lieut. General Omar Hassan el-Beshir, but his ability to negotiate a political solution in the south is limited by the influence of Islamic fundamentalists in the north. Peace talks are held in Addis Ababa in August, but no agreement is reached. Later in the year, a further round of negotiations is secured by the mediation of ex–US President Jimmy Carter who brings both sides together again in Nairobi. On 2 November these talks also break down with the government refusing to address the question of Sharia law.

1990 With the failure of peace talks in 1989, the new decade begins with an SPLA offensive against Juba where over 100 000 townspeople and 200 000 refugees are caught in the crossfire. An attempt to oust President el-Beshir fails and the civil war continues.

■ Who's who

Abboud, Lt. General Ibrahim Military Chief of Staff who overthrew the first parliamentary government of Sudan in a bloodless coup that took place in November 1958. Failing to return the country to civilian rule as he had promised, he was forced to relinquish power in 1964.

Alier, Abel A national Vice–president of Sudan in the Nimeiri regime who was appointed President of the High Executive Council for the South following the peace settlement that temporarily ended the civil war in 1972.

Azhari, Ismail el- Leader of the National Unionist Party, Azhari became the first Prime Minister of Sudan in 1954. Although his party had been supported by the Egyptian government, he steered Sudan towards self determination under the terms of the Anglo–Egyptian Agreement of 1953 and avoided union with Egypt. Shortly after independence was achieved in 1956 the Azhari regime was replaced by a coalition government led by Abdulla Khalil.

Beshir, General Omar Hassan el- Muslim leader of the 15–member military junta that replaced the democratic government of Prime Minister Sadiq el-Mahdi in June 1989. Tired of unsuccessful military action against the SPLA rebels in Southern Region, he has attempted to negotiate a political settlement to the civil war in Sudan while maintaining the Islamic law of Sudan.

Chuol, William Abdullah Leader of the Anya Nya II guerrilla group formed during the 1980s in opposition to the SPLA. After Chuol was killed in August 1986 fighting the SPLA, his Anya Nya II movement collapsed.

Dhahab, General Abd el-Rahman Suwar el- Leader of the 1985 military coup that toppled the government of President Jaafar Nimeiri. Following the coup he chaired a 15–member Transitional Military Council that was responsible for appointing a civilian cabinet and framing a new constitution in the run-up to elections held a year later in 1986. A supporter of the fundamentalist National Islamic Front.

Garang, Colonel John Leader of the Sudan People's Liberation Army since 1982.

Khalifa, Omar Sudanese athlete who launched the Sport Aid campaign to relieve famine victims in 1986 by visiting 12 European countries and the UN in New York.

Khalil, General Abd al-Mazid Hamid Sudanese Vice–president in the Nimeiri regime and Defence Minister after 1985. In 1989 he resigned from the Council of Ministers when his call for a reduction in Islamic fundamentalism was ignored.

Kong, Major Gordon Military commander of the southern separatist movement known as Anya Nya II. Succeeded by William Abdullah Chuol.

Lagu, Joseph Leader of Anya Nya until the peace settlement of 1972 when he became a Major–General in the Sudanese army from which he had fled as a Captain in the 1960s.

Mahdi, Sadiq el- Former Prime Minister of Sudan and leader of the traditional Mahdist Umma Party, deposed during a military coup in June 1989. Educated at Oxford University in England, Sadiq el-Mahdi was a great-grandson of the Mahdi who opposed the Anglo–Egyptian takeover of Sudan in the 1880s. While in exile in London following the 1969 Nimeiri coup he founded the Sudanese National Front. He came to power following elections in 1986 but proved incapable of holding together a coalition government and of defeating the SPLA rebels in the south.

Mirghani, Ahmed el- Spiritual leader of the Khatmiya Muslim sect and brother of Mohammed Osman el-Mirghani. Appointed to the Supreme Council in 1986.

Mirghani, Mohammed Osman el- Leader of the Democratic Unionist Party who attempted to reach a settlement with Col. Garang in 1988.

Nimeiri, Jaafar Mohammed Former president of Sudan who came to power in 1969 following a military coup that resulted in the abolition of parliament and the outlawing of party politics. His decision to introduce authoritarian Islamic rule in September 1983 encouraged rebel insurgency in southern Sudan. Civil war, drought and famine led to his eventual overthrow while out of the country in April 1985.

Tayib, Ummar, Mohammed el- Former head of the State Security Service sentenced to 20 years' imprisonment in December 1986 for his complicity in the airlift of Ethiopian Jews to Israel during 1984–85.

Turabi, Hasan el- Influential leader of the National Islamic Front and brother–in–law of former Prime Minister Sadiq el-Mahdi.

■ Key places

Bahr al-Ghazal   One of the three constituent provinces of Southern Region separated from and then reunited with Equatoria and Upper Nile in 1985. Area 77 625km²; population (1983) 2 265 500. The chief town is Wau.

Bentiu   An oil-rich area in the Upper Nile province of S Sudan; situated to the west of the White Nile where it turns east towards Malakal. A major attempt by Chevron to extract oil was shelved following the outbreak of civil war.

Blue Nile or **Bahr el Azraq** (Arabic)   A river which rises in the mountains of Ethiopia at an altitude of 500m and flows 2000km NNW to meet the White Nile at Khartoum.

Equatoria or **El Istiwaiya** (Arabic) The southernmost province of Sudan and one of the three constituent provinces of Southern Region, bisected by the White Nile which flows northwards from Uganda; area 76 495 km²; population (1983) 1 406 000. The administrative centre and only town of any size is Juba. Most of the province is devoted to agriculture, with cereals and cotton the dominant crops. There are some remnants of tropical forest between the Zaire border and the Southern National Park which straddles the northern frontier of the province. Equatoria is a focal point for resistance against the Khartoum government by SPLA rebels.

Fashoda   former name (until 1905) of the town of Kodok in Upper Nile province, SE Sudan; situated on the White Nile, north–east of Malakal. The capture of this town by French troops caused an international incident in 1898.

Jonglei Canal   A canal in S Sudan linking Jonglei on the White Nile with the Sobat river to the north east. The completion of this project, designed to drain swamplands and increase water flows lower down the Nile, was postponed as a result of the outbreak of civil war.

Juba   Chief town and administrative centre of Southern Region; situated on the White Nile at the centre of Equatoria province. The population of the town is estimated to be 100 000.

Kapoeta   A town in E Equatoria province, Southern Region, S Sudan; situated 240km east of Juba. Captured by SPLA rebel forces in 1988 and used by them as a headquarters until retaken by government forces.

Khartoum   Capital city of Sudan; situated at the junction of the Blue and White Niles; population (1983) 476 200. The city is connected by road and rail to the suburbs of North Khartoum (pop. 1983 341 100) over the Blue Nile and Omdurman (pop. 1983 526 300) over the White Nile. Founded in the 1820s, Khartoum became an important trade link between the Arab countries of North Africa and other African states. An oil pipeline links Khartoum with its Red Sea port at Port Sudan (pop. 1983 206 700).

Kosti or **Kusti** A town with an estimated population of 65 000 in Blue Nile province, central Sudan; situated on the White Nile, 240km S of Khartoum. Site of a proposed refinery for oil from the south.

Lalugo   A refugee camp near Juba in Equatoria province, Southern Region. Occupied by people displaced from surrounding villages by the SPLA rebels.

Roseires   A reservoir on the Blue Nile close to the Ethiopian frontier. Supplying 70% of Sudan's hydropower, the Roseires dam is a strategic target within striking distance of the SPLA who were able to capture Kurmuk which lies only 100km to the south.

Southern Region   A region of S Sudan created in 1972; area 246 389km²; population (1983) 5 271 000. The 1980 Decentralization Act established a regional administration comprising a locally elected assembly and a governor appointed by the president. In 1983 President Nimeiri aroused southern opposition by dividing the region into the three provinces of Equatoria, Upper Nile and Bahr al-Ghazal. Two years later the provinces were reunited as Southern Region and put under the rule of a military governor based in Juba.

Torit A town in Equatoria province, S Sudan; situated 160km south–west of Juba. It fell to SPLA rebels in March 1989 after a year–long siege.

Upper Nile or **A'Ali en Nil** (Arabic) One of the three constituent provinces of Southern

Region on the frontier with Ethiopia; area 92 269km²; population (1983) 1 600 000. The chief town is Makala.

White Nile or **Bahr el Jebel** (Arabic) A river that rises in Lake Victoria, Uganda, and flows northwards into Sudan where it travels a distance of 1700km before meeting the Blue Nile at Khartoum. Between the Ugandan frontier and Khartoum the river falls a total of 600 metres.

■ Key words

Addis Ababa Agreement A peace agreement signed in 1972 by President Nimeiri and representatives of the South Sudan Liberation Movement, a political arm of Anya Nya. The accord temporarily brought to an end 17 years of civil war in southern Sudan and resulted in a plan to introduce regional autonomy with the formation of a High Executive Council and Regional People's Assembly in the south.   Following the peace accord many Anya Nya guerrillas, including their leader Joseph Lagu, were integrated into the Sudanese army.

Ansars An Islamic religious sect responsible for planning an unsuccessful attempt to overthrow President Nimeiri in 1976. Although many Ansars were tried and executed, President Nimeiri opened the way for reconciliation with his political opponents when he met with the Ansar leader Sadiq el-Mahdi at Port Sudan in July 1977. As leader of the Umma Party, el-Mahdi became Prime Minister in 1986.

Anya Nya ("venom of the viper") A name given to the separatist guerrilla army fighting in south Sudan during the first phase of the civil war between 1955 and 1972. This group later developed into the SPLA military force which took up the civil war again in the 1980s.

Anya Nya II A guerrilla movement founded in the 1980s by Abdullah Chol who was opposed to total secession of Southern Region from Sudan

and prepared to co-operate with the government of President Nimeiri against the SPLA. The group eventually collapsed when Chol was killed while fighting the SPLA.

Azande An ethnic group of SW Sudan allied to the Niger–Congo "Sudanic" people of West Africa.

Decentralization Act An act passed in 1980, creating five northern and one southern region in Sudan.

Decisive Justice Courts Emergency courts set up in northern Sudan under Sharia law to enforce a strict penal code that included amputations for theft and public lashings for the possession of alcohol.

Democratic Unionist Party A generally pro-Egyptian political arm of the Khatmia sect and a member of the coalition government of Sudan until the military take-over in July 1989. Opposed to the rigorous application of Islamic law its leader, Mohammed Osman el-Mirghani, attempted to draw up a political settlement with SPLA rebels in November 1988.

Dinka Largest of the many Nilotic Negro tribes of southern Sudan. Membership of the rebel SPLA is largely drawn from these people who have been subjected to renewed slavery by Arabs from the north.

dura or **sorghum**   The principal food crop of Sudan.

Khatmiya   A Muslim religious sect.

Koka Dam Declaration   A statement made in Ethiopia by Col. Garang, leader of the SPLA, boycotting the April 1986 elections unless the government will agree to a national constitutional conference.

Mahdi   An Arabic word meaning "the expected one". The title was first used in 1881 by Mohammed Ahmed ibn Abdalla who led a nationalist revolt against the British that culminated in the fall of Khartoum in 1885.

murabaha   An Islamic principle applied to financial deals in Sudan by President Nimeiri in September 1983. Under the Civil Transactions Act, which ran to 849 articles, lenders of capital were required to share the risks of a venture rather than receive an interest payment on a loan.

National Islamic Front   A fundamentalist Sudanese Islamic party in favour of imposing Sharia laws. Led by Hasan al-Turabi, it controls newspapers and student unions, maintains strong links with Saudi Arabia and Egypt and enjoys   support from middle and high ranking army officers.

Nuer   A Nilotic ethnic group occupying most of Upper Nile province in S Sudan. Like the Dinka they have been subjected to starvation and slavery by both sides in the civil war.

Operation Lifeline   Codename for the UN–organized supply of aid to the starving people of southern Sudan. The operation was initiated in April 1989 in an attempt to supply 100 000 tons of food to drought-stricken areas.

Operation Rainbow   The name given to the UN relief operation sponsored by 11 countries in an attempt to supply food aid to famine stricken regions of Sudan in 1986.

September Laws   The name given to the Islamic Sharia laws imposed by President Nimeiri in September 1983.

Sharia   Islamic laws introduced into Sudan in 1983 by President Nimeiri. Their repeal coupled with the abolition of extreme forms of punishment that include whipping and hand amputation are key SPLA demands to end the civil war.

Shilluck   A Nilotic ethnic group of southern Sudan, related to the Dinka and Nuer people.

Southern Policy   An administrative policy introduced into southern Sudan by the British following the Dinka rising of 1924. As a means of preventing the spread of nationalism, a system of closed districts was devised that virtually cut off the south from the north. Muslims and Arabic–speaking people of northern origin were removed from the south, travel between regions was restricted and those who had adopted Arabic customs were persuaded to change to English or local tribal ways. The ultimate aim was to transfer the non- Muslim southern region of Sudan to neighbouring territories that would ultimately form a British–controlled East African Federation. Accentuating the divide between north and south, this policy eventually culminated in the civil war that followed independence in the 1950s.

South Sudan Liberation Movement   The political arm of the Anya Nya separatist guerrilla force in Southern Sudan, formed prior to the signing of a peace agreement that temporarily ended the 17–year civil war.

Steering Committee for National Dialogue   A 106–man body set up in 1989 to draw up proposals for solving the conflict in Sudan. After meeting for six weeks it suggested a federal constitution, an elected legislature, an independent judiciary and a president elected by universal suffrage.

Sudan Aid   A campaign launched in 1986 by the Sudanese athlete Omar Khalifa to provide relief for victims of famine in Sudan.

Sudan People's Liberation Army (SPLA)   A secessionist rebel force opposed to the Muslim dominated Khartoum government. Led since 1982 by Col. John Garang, it has engaged in military action against government forces in southern Sudan since 1984. The SPLA is mainly drawn from Dinka people in the south, but the organization also includes militia units from the Nuer, Shilluk and other Nilotic tribes.

Sudanization   An Anglo–Egyptian policy designed to prevent the spread of nationalism by introducing native Sudanese administrators, first into local government in the 1920s and later into central government in the 1940s.

Transitional Military Council   The interim 15–member military government set up under the leadership of General Suwar el-Dhahab formed after the 1985 coup that toppled President Nimeiri. The military council suspended the regional assemblies and placed each region under the rule of a military governor.

Umma Party   A right–wing Muslim political party led by Sadiq el-Mahdi until his overthrow in July 1989. Following the overthrow of the Nimeiri regime in 1985 the Umma Party won 99 of the 301 seats on the National Assembly, drawing most of its support from the Ansar Muslim sect in the White Nile area and from the western provinces of Darfur and Kordofan.

zakat   An Islamic system of taxation established by President Nimeiri in 1983 but abolished two years later when it proved unworkable.

■ Further reading

Mohamed Omer Beshir, *The Southern Sudan: From Conflict to Peace*, Barnes and Noble, New York, 1976

Robert Collins, *The Southern Sudan in Historical Perspective*, Shiloh Center for Mid–Eastern and African Studies, 1975

Charles Gurdon, *Sudan at the Crossroads*, Menas, Wisbech, 1984

A. Halsa et al., *The Return to Democracy in Sudan*, Geneva, 1986

P.M. Holt,   *A Modern History of the Sudan*, Grove, New York, 1979 (3rd edn.)

Bona Malwal, *People and Power in Sudan: The Struggle for National Stability*, Ithaca Press, London, 1981

Minority Rights Group, Report No. 78, *The Southern Sudan*, London, 1988

J. Rogge, *Too Many, Too Long; Sudan's Twenty-year Refugee Dilemma*, Rowman and Allanheld, New Jersey, 1985

John O. Voll, *The Sudan*, Westview Press, Boulder, 1985

Dunstan M. Wai, *The African–Arab Conflict in the Sudan*, Africana Publishing Co., New York, 1981

2
Ethiopia

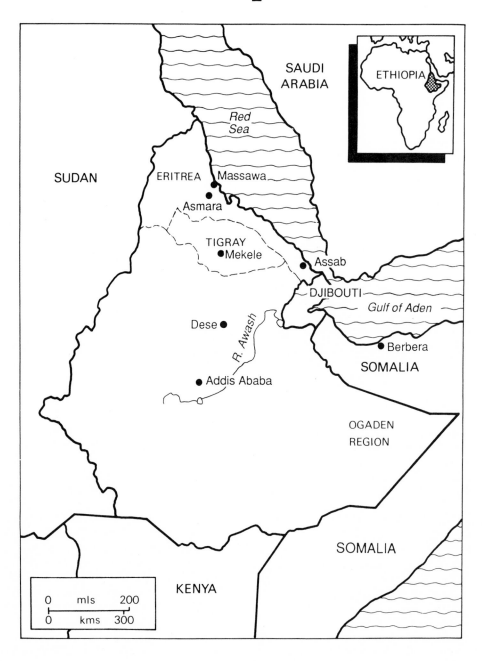

■ Profile

Official name (since 1987):   The People's Democratic Republic of Ethiopia

- **Area:**   1 221 900km²
- **Population(1986):**   46 million
- **Ethnic groups:**   Oromo 40%, Amhara 25%, Tigray 12% and Sidama 9%
- **Languages:**   Over 80 languages and dialects including Amharic (official), Orominga, Tigrinya, Somali, Arabic, English
- **Religion:**   Muslim 45%, Christian 40%
- **Life expectancy:** 44.5 years
- **Infant mortality rate:**   145 per 1000
- **Currency:**   Ethiopian Birr of 100 cents
- **Timezone:**   GMT +3
- **Capital:**   Addis Ababa
- **Administrative divisions:**   15 regions
- **Capital:**   Addis Ababa
- **Chief cities:**   Addis Ababa (1 412 500), Asmera (275 000), Dire Dawa (98 000), Nazret (76 000)

■ Introduction

Ingredients of Ethiopia's internal strife include ethnic and religious divisions, separatist claims, territorial disputes, ideological conflict, regional rivalries and contending superpower interests. In the north, government forces are fighting an interminable war against mainly Muslim separatist movements in Eritrea and Tigray provinces, whose demands range from greater autonomy to outright independence. In the east, ethnic Somalis have been fighting for the "self-determination" of the Ogaden region, which is claimed by neighbouring Somalia. In the south, the Oromo people also nurture separatist aspirations. As if all this were not enough, Ethiopia's endemic poverty periodically deteriorates into wholesale famine, aggravated by the ceaseless hostilities and the resultant refugee problem.

Traditionally said to have been founded in the 10th century BC by a son of King Solomon of Israel and the Queen of Sheba, Abyssinia (as Ethiopia was known in the West until recent times) was converted to Coptic Christianity in the 4th century AD. The rise of Muslim Arab power on the Red Sea and the Gulf of Aden gradually deprived the Abyssinians of access to the coast, a process consolidated by the Ottoman conquest of Eritrea in the 16th century. Not until the European "scramble for Africa" in the late 19th century did Abyssinia emerge from its inland obscurity, when its independence was threatened by Italy's acquisition of Eritrea and the dismemberment of Somaliland between Britain, Italy and France. Under the vigorous leadership of Emperor Menelek II, Abyssinia rose to the challenge by defeating the Italians at Adowa in 1896. Prior to that historic victory, Menelek had imposed Abyssinian rule over the Somali-populated Ogaden, which was recognized as part of the Emperor's domains in subsequent border demarcation treaties with Britain and Italy.

Fascist Italy's revenge for Adowa, the military conquest of Abyssinia in 1935–36, proved to be shortlived. In World War II all the Italian possessions in Africa were captured by the British, who by 1941 controlled the entire Horn of Africa. Having restored Emperor Haile Selassie to the throne of what now became generally known as Ethiopia, the British for some years retained effective control of Eritrea and the Ogaden (as well as British and former

Italian Somaliland). Not until 1950, by decision of the United Nations, was Eritrea awarded to Ethiopia (which thus regained access to the sea), on the understanding that it would enjoy autonomy within a federal structure. As regards the Ogaden, Britain floated the idea of including it in a "greater Somalia", but this was dropped in the face of Ethiopian and international opposition. In 1955 the region formally reverted to Ethiopian sovereignty, so that the new state of Somalia established in 1960 consisted only of the former British and Italian Somaliland colonies.

These dispositions ensured that Ethiopia faced not only a Muslim revolt in Eritrea but also Somali irredentism in respect of the Ogaden. An Eritrean liberation movement emerged in 1956 and secured backing from Arab states, especially those of anti-Western disposition. Moves by Ethiopia in 1962 to impose central control over the province, in breach of its undertakings to the UN, only served to escalate the insurgency, which many Eritrean Christians also joined. The Ogaden dispute was less active in the 1960s, in part because Somalia and Ethiopia were both signatories of a 1964 OAU resolution enjoining respect for boundaries drawn in the colonial era. However, the left-wing military regime which came to power in Somalia in 1969 pledged itself to "fight for the unity of the Somali nation". According to Somalia, the Ogaden Somalis were one of the three parts of the Somali nation (of five) remaining outside the Somali state. The other two are the Somalis of eastern Kenya and the Issas of Djibouti (once French Somaliland), although Somalia has not actively prosecuted these claims in recent years.

In pursuit of its regional aims, post-1969 Somalia established close relations with the Soviet Union, whereas pro-Western Ethiopia received material aid from the United States. This predictable alignment was transformed by the overthrow of Emperor Haile Selassie in 1974 and the eventual seizure of power by military officers of Marxist-Leninist persuasions. Somalia took the opportunity of Ethiopia's internal unrest to back a major offensive by Somali separatists in the Ogaden in 1977–78, but it was defeated by the Ethiopians thanks to massive Soviet and Cuban assistance. Somalia

responded by cutting its Soviet ties, ejecting the Soviet navy from its new base at Berbera and turning for assistance to the United States. By 1980 Washington's new alliance with Somalia, under which the US navy acquired the Berbera base, became a cornerstone of the US military build-up in the Indian Ocean. Meanwhile, the Soviet bloc had withdrawn its support for Eritrea's separatists and had swung the full weight of its influence behind the Marxist regime in Addis Ababa.

After 1978 the Ogaden rebels ceased to be a major threat to Ethiopia, which took the offensive on the eastern front by backing Somali groups seeking to overthrow the regime in Mogadishu. Consequential border tensions and military clashes brought the two countries to the brink of war in 1982, although thereafter, through OAU and Italian mediation, the situation eased. A meeting between the two Presidents in January 1986 accelerated this process, which culminated in a joint agreement in April 1988 to demilitarize the Ethiopian/Somali border and to cease fomenting insurgency against one another. In the north, however, the Eritrean separatists stepped up their operations in the 1980s, to an extent that the writ of the central government virtually ceased to run outside the larger towns. From the late 1970s, moreover, Ethiopia faced another serious revolt, in Tigray province, immediately to the south of Eritrea, and a lesser rebellion among the Oromo (Galle) people in the southern provinces of Shoa, Hararghe, Bale and Sidamo. In both cases, the guerrilla movements involved had close contacts with the Eritrean separatists.

Throughout the 1980s the war in the north followed the familiar pattern of such internal conflicts. Despite repeated offensives, government forces were unable to establish effective control of the countryside and sustained mounting casualties. Facing increasing demoralization and unrest among its troops, under pressure from Moscow to reach a settlement and beleaguered by economic failure, the Addis Ababa regime had little option but to enter into negotiations with the Eritrea and Tigray rebels. Yet the prospects for a settlement did not appear promising, in part because of the government's adamant opposition to any form of separatism but also because of continuing major policy and ideological differences among the various guerrilla movements themselves. The collapse of communism in Eastern Europe in 1989 presented a new challenge to the Addis Ababa regime, especially since under Mikhail Gorbachev the Soviet government had become less committed than its predecessors to backing "fraternal" regimes in Africa. Ethiopia responded by resuming diplomatic relations with Israel, which was more than willing to assist Ethiopia in its confrontation with Arab states over Eritrea because of its strategic interest in preventing the Red Sea from becoming an entirely Arab lake.

■ Chronology of events

1896 By defeating the Italians at the Battle of Adowa, Emperor Menelik II ensures the independence of the Ethiopian Empire at a time when the countries of Europe are carving up the map of Africa.

1897 Ethiopia signs a treaty with Britain establishing a boundary between Ethiopia and British Somaliland. This treaty accepts the fact that certain Somali tribes people in the Haud plateau will come under Ethiopian jurisdiction. A joint boundary commission agrees the line of demarcation in 1932–35.

1908 Ethiopia signs an agreement with Italy establishing the frontier between Ethiopia and Italian Somaliland on the basis of a line running more or less parallel to the coast and 225km from it. With no boundary commission to demarcate a precise frontier on the map, the border area remains in dispute despite a statement in the treaty that confirms the Ogaden region as belonging to Ethiopia.

1930 Haile Selassie becomes Emperor of Ethiopia, but his hold over the country is threatened by Italian imperial interests in neighbouring Somaliland and Eritrea.

1936 Ethiopia is overrun by the Italians and Haile Selassie is forced into exile.

1941 Allied forces defeat the Italians. The Emperor Haile Selassie returns to Ethiopia and the former Italian colony of Eritrea is placed under British administration.

1950 In December the General Assembly of the United Nations passes a resolution (390A) agreeing that Eritrea should become an autonomous region federated with Ethiopia.

1952 On 15 September Ethiopia, supported by the Western powers, takes over the administration of Eritrea which becomes an autonomous region within the federation of Ethiopia and Eritrea.

1955 The constitution of Ethiopia is revised in order to create a more democratic form of government consisting of an appointed Senate and an elected Lower House. In the south east, the Ogaden desert region held by the British since the Italian defeat of 1941, is returned to Ethiopia.

1960 The former colonial territories of British and Italian Somaliland are united to form the independent state of Somalia. The Somali–populated Ogaden region, however, remains under Ethiopian control.

1962 On 14 November Ethiopia unilaterally imposes direct control over Eritrea. This action is opposed by a secessionist movement, the Eritrean Liberation Front, which launches a guerrilla campaign against the Ethiopian government.

1971 Serious drought in the northern provinces of Wollo and Tigray highlights the need for land reform and the introduction of modern agricultural methods. Haile Selassie tries to cover up the seriousness of the situation and offers to reform Ethiopia's system of government by 1974.

1974   Reforms are slow in coming and civil unrest breaks out in February as prices soar and a further drought takes its toll. In September the 44–year reign of Haile Selassie finally comes to an end when his government is deposed during a military coup. State power falls into the hands of a Provisional Military Administrative Council which begins to reshape Ethiopia into a socialist state. Banks and businesses are nationalized and a programme of land reform is initiated.

1976   Ethiopian forces launch a major offensive against the Eritrean rebels following an escalation of guerrilla activities. At the request of   revolutionary Arab states the operation is called off in June. In December Ethiopia signs a military assistance agreement with the Soviet Union and expels all US military missions.

1977   Ethiopia's third government leader since the 1974 coup, General Aman Michael Andom, is shot by members of a radical Marxist faction led by the 32–year-old Mengistu Haile Mariam who is installed as Ethiopia's Head of State. A period of mass arrests and executions known as the "red terror" effectively eliminates all opposition to the military government in Addis Ababa. Taking advantage of the power vacuum in Ethiopia, the left–wing military regime in neighbouring Somalia backs the rebel Somali groups in the Ogaden who launch a major armed offensive against Ethiopian government forces. As a consequence of this, the Soviet Union withdraws its support for Somalia in November and is ejected from its modern naval facility on the Horn of Africa.

1978   Now backed by Soviet supplies and supported by 15 000 Cuban soldiers, Ethiopian forces launch major counter–offensives in Eritrea and the Ogaden. They recapture most of the rebel–controlled territory, but in the process thousands die and hundreds of thousands are made homeless.

1980   Ethiopia and Sudan sign a treaty of friendship in an attempt to close the frontier to Eritrean rebels, but tension between Ethiopia and Somalia grows.

1981   At the OAU 18th Assembly of Heads of State and Government held in Nairobi in June a resolution is passed confirming the Ogaden as "an integral part of Ethiopia".

1982   Fighting on the Somali border intensifies in mid–June as Ethiopian forces penetrate Somalia.

1983   Full scale war between Ethiopia and Somalia is averted when Italy mediates to bring both sides together at a meeting in Djibouti in January.

Ethiopian troops launch a further attack on rebel forces in Eritrea and Tigray.

1984 In August the UN Children's Fund makes public its projections of large-scale famine, predicting that seven million people could face starvation in Ethiopia. A request is now made for foreign aid and a massive relief operation begins. In September the government celebrates the tenth anniversary of the fall of Haile Selassie by forming a Communist Party under the leadership of Mengistu. A new ten–year plan proposes policies of resettlement and "villagization" which are likened to the collectivist farming policies imposed on the Russian peasantry by Stalin in the 1930s.

1985   Over 600 000 people are moved from the arid northern Highlands to more fertile land further south. The callous way in which the resettlement scheme is carried out causes a storm of international protest.

1986   Following a meeting between the presidents of Ethiopia and Somalia a joint-committee is formed to improve relations between the two countries and to resolve the Ogaden dispute.

1987   The EPLF rebels gain effective control of northern Eritrea, cutting off the Ethiopian governments access route to the Red Sea port of Massawa. Between October and March of the following year at least 90 trucks carrying relief supplies to drought–stricken villages in the north are attacked by EPLF guerrillas who suspect they are being used as cover for government troop supplies.

1988   In March a sustained attack by well–organized and heavily–armed EPLF rebels results in the collapse of Ethiopian government positions along a wide front. The following month, rebels in the provinces of Tigray and Eritrea join forces to form a military alliance. On 6 April President Mengistu orders all relief agencies except UNICEF out of the provinces of Tigray and Eritrea. Faced with stiff rebel opposition in the north the Ethiopian government decides to "normalize" the situation in the south by agreeing in April to demilitarize the Ethiopian–Somali border. The governments of Ethiopia and Somalia also agree to refrain from supporting guerrilla groups in each others' countries.

1989   TPLF rebels in the northern province of Tigray launch a major offensive against demoralized government troops who are driven out of the province after suffering heavy losses. In May disenchanted army units take part in an attempt to oust President Mengistu who is then forced to initiate talks with the rebels in Tigray and Eritrea. In December Israel offers military aid to Mengistu while the superpowers attempt to negotiate a "peace corridor" through the northern war zones of Ethiopia in order to supply food aid via the Red Sea port of Assab to an estimated four million people again threatened by drought and starvation.

1990   As the long–running civil wars in Ethiopia continue to drain the country's economy President Mengistu announces sweeping reforms in March in an attempt to bring rebel groups into the political process.

■ Who's who

Afewerki, Issaias   Secretary–general of the Marxist–Leninist Eritrean People's Liberation Front.

Barre, Major–General Mohammed Siyad   Military commander who took power in Somalia following a coup in October 1969. As President of Somalia he suspended the constitution and formed a Supreme Revolutionary Council to rule the country which he renamed the Somali Democratic Republic. His expulsion of the Russians from their new naval base in the Horn of Africa and his support for irredentist Somali rebels in the Ogaden led to full–scale open warfare between Somalia and Ethiopia during 1977–78. In the face of mounting opposition from dissident Somali groups President Barre has been brought to the negotiating table in an attempt to resolve the Ogaden border dispute with Ethiopia.

Haile Selassie   (1891–1975) Emperor of Ethiopia from 1930 until his overthrow in 1974. As Prince Ras Tafari, he established his claim to the throne by leading a revolution against the pro-German Emperor Lij Yasu in 1916. Appointed regent to Menelik's daughter, the Empress Zawditu, he set about westernizing the institutions of Ethiopia. In 1930 he inherited the throne on the death of Empress Zawditu, but was forced into exile following the Italian campaign of 1935–36. When Ethiopia was liberated by the British in 1941 he was returned to power. Although he played a crucial role on the international stage, as in the establishment of the Addis Ababa-based Organization of African Unity (OAU) in the 1960s, he was unable to prevent famine and corruption in his own country. Both of these factors led to his downfall in 1974, but his unique status has been preserved by groups, such as the Rastafarians, who revere his name.

Menelik II   Emperor of Ethiopia from 1889 until his death in 1913, he was allegedly descended from Menelik I, by tradition son of King Solomon and the Queen of Sheba. Under his influence Ethiopia emerged from medieval isolation and fought off European colonial interests. He was succeeded by his pro-Muslim grandson Lij Yasu who was deposed in 1916 by Haile Selassie and the Christian nobility of Ethiopia.

Mengistu Haile Mariam   Marxist leader of Ethiopia who became president in 1977 following a power vacuum that was caused by left–wing military and civilian infighting in the three years after the coup that deposed Haile Selassie in 1974. As Secretary General of the Worker's Party of Ethiopia and Commander in Chief of the Revolutionary Armed Forces

President Mengistu has established his supreme authority in Ethiopia and embarked on a policy of economic socialism.

Tedla, Major–General Adis   Appointed Chief of staff in the cabinet reshuffle that followed the attempt to oust President Mengistu in May 1989.

Tewelde, Gherezghiher   Foreign relations representative of the Eritrean Liberation Front which announced its attempts to form an alliance with other Eritrean resistance groups in 1988.

Zenawi, Meles   Chairman of the Marxist Tigrayan People's Liberation Front.

■ Key places

Abyssinia   A name once widely used but never officially adopted for the country of Ethiopia. It is derived from the Arabic "El Habesha" which describes a mixed race of black and white people. Ethiopia, the name of the country today, takes its name from "Ityopya" a word of the official Amharic language that is popularly thought to be derived from the Greek for "people with sunburnt faces".

Addis Ababa or **Adis Abeba** ("new flower") Capital of Ethiopia, situated in the Shoa uplands at an altitude of 2400m. Founded by Menelik II in 1887, it replaced Intotto as capital of the Ethiopian Empire two years later in 1889. The city, which has a population (1984) of 1,412,000, is the headquarters of the Organization of African Unity (OAU) and the UN Economic Commission for Africa. Since 1917 Addis Ababa has been linked by rail with the port of Djibouti.

Afabet   The largest town in Sahel province, N Eritrea, 70km south–east of Nafka. In 1979 it became the main Ethiopian military headquarters and supply depot in N Eritrea. Government forces occupied the town until driven out during the EPLF offensive of March 1988.

Asmera or **Asmara**   Capital of the region of Eritrea in the N Ethiopian Highlands, 65km south–west of the Red Sea port of Massawa; population(1984) 275 000.

Assab   A Red Sea port in the province of Eritrea, linked by road to Addis Ababa; population (1984) 21 000. Assab is a vital port

of entry for relief supplies heading for the highlands of Tigray and Eritrea via the town of Dese.

Awash   A river that rises in the central highlands of Ethiopia S of Addis Ababa and flows north–east to Lake Abbé on the Djibouti frontier. The Awash is considered by Somalis to have marked the eastern limit of Ethiopian sovereignty prior to the colonial division of the territory at the end of the 19th century.

British Somaliland   A British protectorate established over an area of 176 000 km² on the Somali coast in 1884 with an administrative centre at Hargeisa. Between 1901 and 1910 the British were harassed in this region by a self-proclaimed messiah known as the "Mad Mullah". Occupied by Italy in 1940, the protectorate returned to British administration in 1941. In 1960 it united with the former Italian Somaliland to form the independent state of Somalia.

Dese   Capital town of the province of Wollo which lies just to the south of Tigray; population (1984) 69 000. A key location in the distribution of relief aid to the people of Tigray, the town is situated at the junction of the roads linking the Red Sea ports of Massawa and Assab with Addis Ababa.

Eritrea or **Er'tra**   A region of N Ethiopia occupying a strategic position on the coast of the Red Sea where it stretches for a distance of 1070km from Bab el Mandeb on the Djibouti frontier to Ras Kasar on the border with Sudan; area 117 600km²; population (1984) 2 615 000; capital Asmera. Massawa and Assab on the

Red Sea coast of Eritrea are Ethiopia's only ports. The people of Eritrea, who are 50 per cent Muslim and 50 per cent Christian, regard themselves as separate from the Amhara of central Ethiopia, their regional identity being strengthened by the Italians who ruled the area as a political entity between 1880 and 1941. After nine years of British administration the UN General Assembly agreed that Eritrea would become an autonomous region federated with Ethiopia. When Ethiopia annexed the region in 1962, secessionist rebels launched a guerrilla campaign against the Ethiopian government. By 1988 the EPLF had effectively defeated government forces in Eritrea and had severed Addis Ababa's link with the Red Sea. In September 1987 Eritrea was designated in the new constitution as one of five so-called autonomous regions.

Haud or **Reserve Area**   A plateau of the Ogaden region lying on the border between Ethiopia and the former British Somaliland, claimed by the government of Somalia since independence in 1960.

Horn of Africa   That part of the African continent between the Gulf of Aden and the Indian Ocean occupied by Djibouti, Somalia and the Ogaden region of SE Ethiopia.

Italian Somaliland   A former Italian Trust territory extending to 502 300km² on the Somali coast with an administrative centre at Mogadishu. Italy gained a foothold in Somaliland in 1889, leased territory in 1892 and purchased coastal stations from the Sultan of Zanzibar in 1905. Twenty years later in 1925 Italy acquired Jubaland from Kenya and after the Italian–Ethiopian conflict of 1936 extended its control over the Ogaden region to create an enlarged Italian East Africa. With the defeat of Italy in 1941 the region came under British military administration. In 1950 Italian rule was restored for a further ten years prior to union with British Somaliland to form the independent state of Somalia in 1960.

Massawa   Ethiopia's principal port on the Red Sea coast of Eritrea, cut off from Addis Ababa and eventually captured by EPLF and TPLF rebel

forces in February 1990; population (1984) 27 000.

Mekele   Capital of the region of Tigray in the northern highlands of Ethiopia; population (1984) 62 000. Occupied by Ethiopian government forces until their defeat at the hands of the rebel TPLF in 1989.

Nafka   A town in N Eritrea forming part of a military front line developed by Ethiopian government forces in 1979. Ethiopian positions along the entire Nafka front collapsed in 1988 when EPLF rebels launched a major offensive.

Ogaden   A desert area inhabited by Somali people and administered by Ethiopia as part of the provinces of Hararge, Sidamo and Bale. Since independence in 1960, successive governments of Somalia have claimed this territory which they refer to as Western Somalia. The basis of this claim rests on the fact that prior to the development of British and Italian colonial interests at the end of the 19th century, Ethiopian sovereignty did not extend further east than the line of the Awash river which marks the north–western boundary of the Ogaden.

Tigray or **Tigré**   An administrative region in the northern highlands of Ethiopia; area 65 900km²; population (1984) 2 410 000; capital Mekele. With Eritrea, this arid region has most often experienced drought and crop failure and has consequently been subjected to government resettlement and villagization schemes. Although the predominantly Christian Tigrayans are akin to the Amhara race that dominates the rest of the country, they speak a different language and consider themselves a distinct political entity. In an attempt to gain more regional autonomy a Marxist-Leninist rebel group with popular support launched an armed campaign against the Ethiopian government in 1975. In 1989 this group successfully managed to overwhelm government troops and drive them out of the region. In September 1987 Tigray was designated in the new constitution as one of five so-called autonomous regions.

■ Key words

Afar Liberation Front   A minority group seeking autonomy for the nomadic Afar or Danakil people occupying the territory between the Shoa hill country and the Red Sea. They mainly carry out resistance activities against the government of Ethiopia in the eastern province of Wollo.

Amhara   One of the principal ethnic groups of Ethiopia occupying the central highlands. The official language of Ethiopia is Amharic.

belg   The name given to the light rains that occur in Ethiopia between February and April.

Derg   Former name for the Provisional Military Administrative Council.

Eritrean Liberation Front (ELF)   When Ethiopia annexed Eritrea in 1962 the Eritrean Liberation Front, a guerrilla force of 40 000 men, formed the main rebel opposition force in the armed struggle for independence. After early successes the ELF eventually split into a number of factions before being pushed out of the main towns of Eritrea in 1977 by Soviet–backed government forces.

Eritrean Liberation Front–Popular Liberation Forces (ELF–PLF)   A breakaway faction of the ELF.

Eritrean People's Liberation Front   The principal rebel force fighting for the independence of Eritrea. Formed in 1970 as a breakaway faction of the ELF, it operates without international support under a Marxist ideology. By 1987 the well equipped and highly organized EPLF had regained control of northern Eritrea from the Red Sea to the Sudanese border and in 1988 it launched a major offensive that succeeded in driving government troops back in the direction of Addis Ababa. In alliance with the Tigray People's Liberation Front it has taken the armed conflict closer to the capital and forced the Ethiopian government to the negotiating table.

Eritrean Relief Association (ERA)   Controlled by the EPLF, the Eritrean Relief Association is the principal voluntary agency distributing relief supplies to starving people in drought–stricken Eritrea. The organization, which was formed in 1976, also supports health and education projects as well as rural land development schemes in rebel–controlled areas of the northern highlands.

Ethiopian People's Revolutionary Democratic Front (EPRDF)   An anti-government rebel organization comprising the EPLF, TPLF and the Ethiopian People's Democratic Movement.

irredentism   The doctrine of "redeeming" territory from foreign rule upheld by Somali rebel groups fighting to regain the Ogaden from Ethiopian control.

meher   The name given to the "big" rains that fall in Ethiopia from the beginning of June to the end of September. The failure of the meher rain can result in serious drought and crop failure.

Oromo   The principal ethnic group of Ethiopia, the Oromo or Galle people comprise about 40% of the total population of the country. They are an agricultural and pastoral people of Hamitic origin. Since the late 1970s the Oromo Liberation Front, a resistance group seeking to obtain regional autonomy for the Oromo people, has led armed opposition to the Ethiopian government in Shoa, Hararghe, Bale and Sidamo.

peace corridor   A land bridge through the northern war zones of Ethiopia, linking Addis Ababa with the drought–stricken regions of Tigray and Eritrea. Both Soviet and Western powers pressed President Mengistu to allow aid supplies to be delivered along a "peace corridor" to an estimated four million people facing starvation at the end of 1989.

Provisional Military Administrative Council (PMAC) or Derg   Later renamed the Provisional Military Government of Socialist Ethiopia (PMGSE), the PMAC was a co-ordinating committee set up by the armed forces to govern Ethiopia following the coup that toppled Hailie Selassie in September 1974. The PMAC was responsible for initiating a programme of nationalization and land reform aimed at creating a socialist state. Opposition to the PMAC was swiftly dealt with during the period known as the "red terror" from November 1977 until March 1978 when an estimated 10 000 people were executed following mass arrests. The function of the PMAC came to an end in 1987 with the adoption of a new constitution and the introduction of an 813–member civilian legislature.

red terror A period of mass arrests and executions from November 1977 to March 1978 instigated by the ruling military officers of Ethiopia in an attempt to eliminate opposition to their programme of nationalization and land reform. An estimated 10 000 people were killed during the so-called "red terror".

Relief Society of Tigray (REST) The principal relief agency operating in the province of Tigray since 1978. Run by the TPLF rebels, it attempts to provide a wide range of medical, educational and agricultural facilities throughout the province.

Shengo The parliament or national legislature of Ethiopia established by the new constitution of 1987.

Somali Abo Liberation Front A Somali rebel group largely operating in Bale province.

Somali Fatherland Liberation Front A Somali rebel group founded in 1977 with the aim of uniting the Ogaden with the rest of Somalia.

Tigray People's Liberation Front (TPLF) A rebel group in the northern region of Tigray that recognises the Eritrean claim for independence but claims only regional autonomy for Tigray. The Marxist TPLF has been engaged in armed resistance since 1975 and in 1989 succeeded in driving government forces out of the region.

villagization The transition to a fully "socialised" economy, outlined by President Mengistu in his 10–year Development Plan in 1984, involved a programme of land reform that included population resettlement and "villagization" or farm collectivization.

Western Somalia Liberation Front (WSLF) The principal militant irredentist Somali group in the Ogaden. Formed in 1975 and backed by Somalia, it joined with other Somali guerrilla groups in engaging Ethiopian forces in open warfare during 1977–78. By the end of 1980 WSLF rebels had returned to the use of guerrilla tactics following the withdrawl of support from Somalia and their expulsion from most of the Ogaden right up to the Somalia border.

Workers' Party of Ethiopia (WPE) The sole legal political party of Ethiopia, created as a Marxist party dedicated to the building of "scientific socialism" in 1984. Led by President Mengistu, it was elected to the new civilian legislature following Ethiopia's first parliamentary election in June 1987.

■ **Further reading**

C. Clapham, *Transformation and Continuity in Revolutionary Ethiopia*, Cambridge University Press, Cambridge, 1988

F. Haliday and M.E. Molyneux, *The Ethiopian Revolution*, NLB, London, 1981

Paul Henze, *Rebels and Separatists in Ethiopia*, Rand, 1985

Minority Rights Group, Report No. 5, *Eritrea and Tigray*, London, 1983

D. Pool, *Eritrea: Africa's Longest War*, Anti-Slavery Society, London, 1982

P. Schwab, *Ethiopia: Politics, Economics and Society*, Westview Press, Boulder, 1985

Richard Sherman, *Eritrea: The Unfinished Revolution*, Praeger, New York, 1980

3
Western Sahara

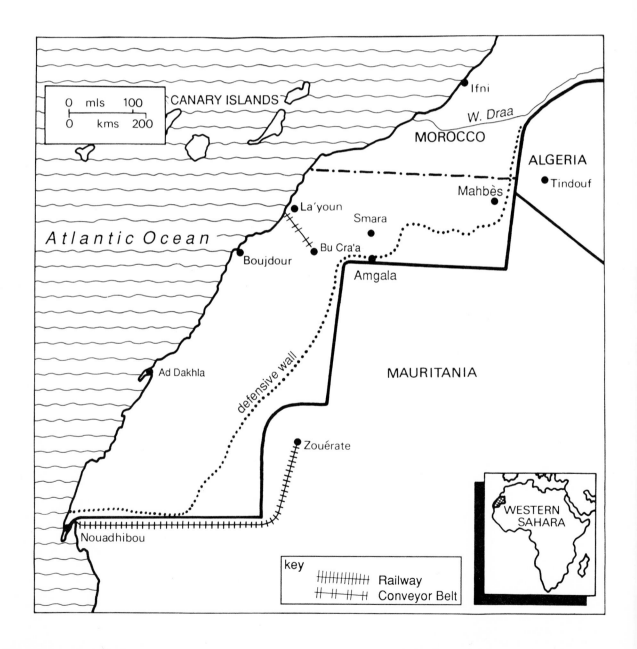

CANARY ISLANDS

0 mls 100
0 kms 200

Ifni

W. Draa

MOROCCO

ALGERIA
• Tindouf

Mahbès

La'youn

Smara

Bu Cra'a

Atlantic Ocean

Boujdour

Amgala

Ad Dakhla

MAURITANIA

defensive wall

Zouérate

Nouadhibou

WESTERN
SAHARA

key

┼┼┼┼┼┼┼┼ Railway
┼─┼─┼─┼ Conveyor Belt

■ Profile

- **Area:** 266 769km²
- **Population (1988):** 181 400
- **Ethnic groups:** Arab and Berber
- **Language:** Hassaniya and Moroccan Arabic
- **Religion:** Sunni Muslim
- **Timezone:** GMT (Summer time, GMT +1)
- **Currency:** Moroccan dirham of 100 centimes
- **Capital:** La'youn
- **Chief towns:** La'youn (96 800), Ad Dakhla (17 800), Smara (17 800)

■ Introduction

Of Moorish Berber stock, the nomadic Sahrawi people of Western Sahara were Arabized from the 13th century by invading Bedouin tribes. The sultans of Morocco claimed suzerainty over the region, although the Sahrawis exercised broad autonomy through councils (yemaa) of chiefs and elders. Spain's interest in the area dated from the establishment of its rule over the Canary Islands in the 15th century. But not until the era of European colonization in the 19th century did Spain move to take control of the African coast opposite the Canaries. Having defeated Morocco in a brief war in 1860, Spain in 1884–86 established a protectorate over Rio de Oro (southern Western Sahara) by agreement with the local emir. It then joined with France in carving up Morocco itself into Spanish and French protectorates, as part of which process Saguia el-Hamra (northern Western Sahara) was allocated to Spain in 1904. The Sultan of Morocco had no option but to accept these European dispositions. He nevertheless continued to regard Western Sahara (and vast adjoining areas besides) as part of his historic domains. On achieving independence from France in 1956, Morocco quickly regained sovereignty over most of Spanish Morocco (1956–58) and eventually over the Spanish-ruled enclave of Ifni (1969). But the Franco regime insisted on retaining not only the enclaves of Ceuta and Melilla (on the Mediterranean coast) but also the whole of Western Sahara,

where Spanish and French forces crushed an early revolt in 1958. For its part, independent Morocco laid claim not only to Western Sahara but also to the whole of Mauritania and to the iron-rich Tindouf region of western Algeria. These latter "greater Morocco" aspirations were later abandoned, whereupon Morocco, Algeria and Mauritania agreed to co-operate in bringing an end to Spanish rule in Western Sahara.

In the 1960s the Spanish authorities sought to deflect UN calls for self-determination in Western Sahara by setting up (1967) a territorial Yemaa in which the Sahrawi people were supposed to enjoy home rule. In 1970 Spanish forces suppressed another revolt in the territory, but the tide of anti-colonialism was running strongly by then. In the mid-1970s the newly-founded Polisario Front took up the struggle against Spanish rule, initially from bases in Mauritania but later from Algerian territory. Significantly, the Moroccan–Algerian axis had by now collapsed, as the Rabat government opted for a pro-US alignment while Algeria joined the radical Arab camp backed by Moscow. From mid-1974 Morocco renewed its claim to Western Sahara, whose newly-discovered phosphate riches it was anxious to add to its own. Mauritania quickly lodged its own claim, while Algeria became the champion of an independent Western Sahara as demanded by Polisario. Just about the only concurrence between the three countries was that a Spanish census of 1974 giving the territory's population as 74 000 was far too low, especially if Sahrawi exiles were included in the total.

In August 1974 Spain declared its readiness to hold a referendum in Western Sahara to determine the wishes of its people. But this consultation was postponed indefinitely (and has yet to take place) when, in December 1974, Morocco and Mauritania secured the backing of the UN General Assembly for submitting their conflicting claims to the International Court of Justice (ICJ). It later transpired that in a move worthy of European colonialism at its most cynical the two governments had at the same time made a secret agreement to partition Western Sahara after Spain's withdrawal. That this would be sooner rather than later became clear by mid-1975, as Polisario guerrilla warfare reduced the territory to paralysis and Spain itself entered a period of uncertainty arising from Franco's long death agony. In October 1975 the ICJ gave its advisory opinion that neither Morocco nor Mauritania had any real claim to sovereignty over Western Sahara and that its people should therefore exercise the right of self-determination. Undeterred, Morocco and Mauritania concluded the Madrid Agreement on 14 November 1975 (six days before Franco's death) under which Spain agreed to withdraw from the territory and to hand it over to Morocco and Mauritania.

On the speedy completion of the Spanish departure (by mid-January 1976), Morocco and Mauritania moved swiftly to partition Western Sahara on the old dividing line between Rio de Oro in the south (renamed Tiris el-Gharbia by Mauritania) and Saguia el-Hamra in the north. The reaction of Polisario and Algeria was one of outrage at what they regarded as latter-day colonialism, a view for which they obtained substantial support from other Third World states. A somewhat unconvincing ratification of the Madrid Agreement by the Western Sahara Yemaa was immediately followed in February 1976 by Polisario's declaration of an independent Sahrawi Arab Democratic Republic (SADR). The stage was therefore set for a classic national liberation struggle, in which the old European colonial masters had been replaced by home-grown varieties.

Under their partition agreement, Morocco and Mauritania had envisaged joint exploitation of Western Sahara's phosphate reserves, mostly located in the Moroccan sector. Military successes by Polisario rendered this impossible, with the result that the ongoing war in the territory brought Mauritania to the verge of bankruptcy. Following the inevitable military coup in Nouakchott in July 1978, the new regime in August 1979 signed a peace agreement with the SADR renouncing any Mauritanian claim to Western Sahara, from which Mauritanian forces were withdrawn by the end of the month. But expectations that Polisario would obtain the vacated southern Western Sahara proved wide of the mark: Moroccan forces swiftly took control of the former Mauritanian sector, which was renamed Oued Addahab.

As the sole administering power in Western Sahara, Morocco now bore the full brunt not only of Polisario's guerrilla struggle but also of an Algerian-led campaign to isolate it diplomatically. By 1982 the radical majority of OAU member states were ranged against Morocco and its supporters (not all of them conservative) in favour of admitting the SADR to membership. Various mediation attempts in the 1980s, by the OAU, the UN and other bodies, foundered on the refusal of Morocco to negotiate with Polisario and on the latter's insistence on a Moroccan withdrawal. Meanwhile, Morocco concentrated on building a defensive wall along the eastern and southern frontiers of Western Sahara. That its completion in 1987 did not stop continuing Polisario raids was a grave disappointment to Morocco, which at last began to show interest in a negotiated settlement. Also important was the new determination of the superpowers in the late 1980s to resolve regional disputes in which opposing US and Soviet involvement had been an aggravating factor.

A rapprochement in Moroccan/Algerian relations led in August 1988 to acceptance by both Morocco and Polisario of a UN-sponsored ceasefire formula under which a referendum would be held to determine the wishes of the Western Sahara people. This was followed in January 1989 by the first publicly-acknowledged meeting between King Hassan of Morocco and Polisario officials. However, Polisario's suspicions about Morocco's real intentions were rekindled by the King's reluctance to continue the dialogue process and also by the formation in February 1989 of the Arab Maghreb Union by Algeria, Morocco, Libya, Tunisia and Mauritania. For Polisario, this rush to reconciliation by the states of the region was unlikely to assist the creation of a new state, given that Western Sahara remained under Moroccan control. It was hardly surprising, therefore, that the ceasefire should break down in October 1989, when Polisario launched a new offensive against Moroccan positions. As the fighting resumed, the prospects of a referendum being held in Western Sahara and of a lasting settlement being found seemed as distant as ever.

◾ Chronology of events

1767 Spain signs a treaty of friendship with Morocco.

1830 An insult to the French Consul in Algiers results in the occupation of Algiers by France.

1860 A dispute over the Spanish enclave of Ceuta in North Africa causes a brief war between Spain and Morocco. In March, the Spanish defeat the Moroccans at Los Castillejos and capture the city of Tetuan. Under the terms of the peace agreement that followed, the Ceuta enclave was enlarged, Spain received an indemnity of 100 million pesetas and Morocco granted to Spain the small territory of Ifni on the Atlantic coast opposite the Canary Islands.

1884 Spain claims a protectorate over the Rio de Oro, a coastal zone to the south of Morocco.

1900 In June, France and Spain agree on the boundaries between their Saharan possessions.

1912 Morocco becomes a protectorate of France, but Spain maintains two protectorates in the north and south of the country.

1934 The Spanish territory to the south of Morocco is divided into two sectors, the northern Saguia el Hamra and the southern Rio de Oro. These enclaves are administered jointly with Ifni but remain separate from the adjacent Spanish protectorate in southern Morocco.

1956 In March the French government recognises the independence of Morocco which stakes an immediate claim to the Spanish possessions in NW Africa as well as to territory in SW Algeria, Mauritania and French Sudan (present–day Mali). Spain endorses the independence of Morocco and hands over the northern part of the protectorate it established in 1912.

1958 Following anti-colonial attacks on Spanish possessions, Spain hands over the southern part of its protectorate in Morocco but holds on to the enclaves of Ceuta, Melilla and Ifni. Saguia el Hamra and Rio de Oro are united into a single Spanish province which is named Spanish Sahara.

1967 The UN urges Spain to hold a referendum in order to allow the people of Spanish Sahara to determine their own future.

1969 In June the coastal enclave of Ifni is handed over to Morocco.

1970 Morocco drops its claim to Mauritania.

1972 Morocco drops its claim to Algerian territory.

1973 In August an armed struggle against Spanish rule is launched from bases in Algeria by the Polisario liberation group.

1974 Relations between Spain and Morocco deteriorate. With phosphate exports from Spanish Sahara on the increase, Morocco feels its economy under threat. Anti–colonial feeling runs high as both Morocco and Mauritania press their claims to the Spanish territory and reject repeated calls for a referendum. A fishing dispute heightens the tension. In October the government of Morocco initiates a debate in the UN General Assembly. The UN Special Committee on Colonialism agrees to send a mission to the Sahara.

1975 The UN mission, backed by the International Court of Justice, suggests that the majority of Saharans favour independence. King Hassan of Morocco responds in October by ordering 350 000 unarmed civilians to take possession of Spanish Sahara. The four–day "Green March" is brought to a halt on 9 November and five days later an agreement between Spain and Morocco is signed in Madrid. On 31 December the Western Sahara ceases to be a Spanish province and is handed over to a joint Moroccan–Mauritanian administration.

1976 In January Spanish troops leave the Sahara and Moroccan forces move in. Large numbers of Saharans flee to Algeria where support for the Polisario liberation movement is stepped up. On 27 February the Polisario declares the establishment of the Sahrawi Arab Democratic Republic (SADR) and a government in exile is formed in Algeria. Morocco breaks off diplomatic relations with Algeria in March and a month later Morocco and Mauritania partition the Western Sahara. The Moroccan sector, which contains most of the mineral wealth, is divided into three provinces and military garrisons are lodged in the main urban settlements to protect them against an increasing number of Polisario guerrilla attacks. The rebels are still able to penetrate the unprotected desert areas which are occupied by nomadic tribesmen.

1977 Morocco and Mauritania form a joint defence committee in May as the phosphate mines of Morocco, Mauritania and Western Sahara become a focus for guerrilla attacks. Operations at the important Bu Cra'a mines cease when the conveyor belt link with the coast is sabotaged. The death of French nationals in the Mauritanian mining town of Zouérate prompts a series of air attacks by France against Polisario positions.

1978 Morocco announces a $292 million Saharan development programme designed to settle the nomads and establish a sedentary economy. Meanwhile, the worsening

economic situation in Mauritania comes to a head in July when a coup topples the government of Moktor Ould Daddah. Polisario immediately ceases hostilities against Mauritania whose new President resolves to sue for peace. In September King Hassan agrees to mediation in the dispute by a committee of "wise men" who are the heads of state of five African countries.

1979 In January the Polisario launch a major attack on the town of Tan–Tan deep inside Morocco. King Hassan forms a National Defence Council to formulate defence policy. At the OAU summit in Khartoum in July a resolution is passed calling for a referendum on self-determination in Western Sahara. The Polisario breaks its ceasefire with Mauritania which now decides to withdraw from the conflict and renounce all claims to Western Sahara. A peace treaty is signed in August and Morocco immediately steps in to take over the former Mauritanian share of the territory (known as Tiris el Gharbia) which becomes the Moroccan province of Oued Addahab. In September Morocco receives offers of military aid from Egypt and the USA and in November a major offensive is launched south of the Oued Draa river bed.

1980 Polisario armed forces continue to attempt to drive a wedge between Morocco and Western Sahara by attacking targets as far north as the Oued Draa river bed. Morocco responds by starting to build a massive defensive wall which is designed to hinder the movement of the rebels. By July a total of 40 countries recognise the SADR. In September the OAU "wise men" meet in Freetown, Sierra Leone in an attempt to find a solution to the problem.

1981 At the OAU Nairobi summit in June, King Hassan proposes a referendum in Western Sahara but refuses to negotiate with the Polisario. The Polisario leadership replies by agreeing to a UN/OAU supervised referendum but first requires the withdrawal of Moroccan troops and direct negotiations with Morocco. Equipped with more sophisticated tanks and missiles, Polisario forces launch more devastating attacks into Morocco and Western Sahara.

1982 At an OAU summit in Tripoli one–third of the membership walk out after the SADR is elected to membership by a majority vote. Moroccan forces secure control over the "useful triangle" and the phosphate mines at Bu Cra'a reopen.

1984 Morocco will not comply with a 1983 OAU resolution that it should negotiate a peace settlement with Polisario officials and as a consequence Mauritania recognises the SADR in February. A third section of the Moroccan wall is completed in May. Despite this, Polisario forces launch the "Greater Maghreb" offensives against the Moroccan defensive line south–west of Zag.

1985 Two further sections of the Moroccan wall are completed in January and August. A total of 200 000km² in the Western Sahara is now enclosed by this defensive line. Zaire boycotts the 21st OAU summit of heads of state when Polisario leader Abd al-Aziz is elected a vice–president.

1986 UN-sponsored indirect talks between Moroccan and Polisario officials fail.

1987 The completion of the sixth and final section of the defensive wall in April virtually seals off the Western Sahara. Mauritania is unhappy about the massing of Moroccan troops so close to its frontier and fears that the wall will force Polisario guerrillas to attack Moroccan targets through its territory. Between July and November the Polisario launch major offensives against bases close to the new wall. In November a 10-day ceasefire allows a UN technical mission to visit the Western Sahara.

1988 In May Algeria and Morocco restore diplomatic relations and on 22 June UN Secretary–General Perez de Cuellar visits Western Sahara for the first time. Two months later in August, both Morocco and the Polisario agree to the UN peace proposals. The year ends with the unilateral declaration of a ceasefire by the Polisario Front.

1989 King Hassan of Morocco meets with senior Polisario officials for the first time in January. Both sides agree in principle to holding a referendum on the future of Western Sahara and a general ceasefire is established. In February Morocco signs a regional co-operation pact with Tunisia, Algeria, Libya and Mauritania. A total of 70 countries now recognize the SADR. King Hassan calls off a second follow-up meeting and in October the ceasefire breaks down when impatient Polisario guerrillas attack positions on the Moroccan wall.

■ Who's who

al-Aziz, Mohammed Abd Secretary–General of the Polisario Front since August 1976 and first president of the SADR government–in–exile in Algeria since October 1982. Born in Marrakesh, he made an historic return to the city in April 1989 to hold talks with King Hassan of Morocco.

Beida, Mahfoud Ali Elected Prime Minister of the SADR government–in–exile at the the 7th Congress of the Polisario Front held at the Smara refugee camp in SW Algeria in April 1989.

Bennani, General Abd al-Aziz Succeeded General Dlimi in 1983 as commander of the Moroccan Southern Zone.

Chadli, Colonel Benjedid A former commander of the Oran military district elected to the post of President of Algeria following the death of President Boumedienne on 27 December 1978. Since taking office in 1979 he has been re-elected in 1984 and 1989.

Daddah, President Moktar Ould As first President of Mauritania after it gained independence from France in 1960 he declared a one–party state in 1964. A military coup brought his rule to an end in July 1978, two years after his country had joined with Morocco in administering Western Sahara.

Dlimi, General Ahmed Commander of Moroccan forces in the Western Sahara 1976–83 and an Aide to King Hassan. In January 1983 he was killed in a road accident in Marrakesh.

Hassan, King   Born in July 1929, Hassan II succeeded his father Mohammed V in February 1961 as 17th Sovereign of the Moroccan Alouite dynasty. In 1975 he staked his country's claim to the Spanish Sahara by ordering the Green March, a move that precipitated the joint Moroccan–Mauritanian administration of the Western Sahara. While supporting the idea of a referendum, he persistently refused to negotiate with the Polisario Front. In 1989, however, international pressure forced him to have talks with Mohammed Abd al-Aziz in Marrakesh although he claimed this meeting was to make "contact" rather than to "negotiate".

Salek, President Colonel Moustapha Ould   Leader of the Mauritanian Military Committee for National Salvation following the coup that ousted the one–party government of President Moktar Ould Daddah in July 1978. Recognising that the Western Sahara conflict was draining the economy of Mauritania, he signed a peace treaty with the Polisario Front and withdrew from the Mauritanian administered sector of the territory in August 1979. He was succeeded by President Moaouia Ould Sidi Mohammed Taya who took office in December 1984.

■ Key places

Amgala   A town in the Saguia el Hamra region of N Western Sahara; situated south–east of the town of Smara, close to the Moroccan wall, it was the scene of the first major encounter between Moroccan and Polisario rebel forces in January 1976. Intermittently held by the Polisario, the town was finally taken by Moroccan troops in January 1984.

Boujdour   A coastal district in the Saguia el Hamra region of Western Sahara. Occupied since 1976 by Morocco as a province with an area of 100 120km^2 and a population (1982) of 8 500. Its chief town is Boujdour with a population of 3600.

Bu Cra'a or **Boukraa**   A phosphate mining centre in the "useful triangle" of NW Western Sahara, 120km SSE of La'youn; linked by conveyor belt to the coast; a target for raids by Polisario guerrillas who inflicted a series of defeats on the Moroccan armed forces here during the early years of the conflict.

Dakhla, Ad   A coastal town of Western Sahara; situated on a peninsula that sticks out into the Atlantic Ocean; known as Villa Cisneros until 1976, it lies just to the south of the western end of the 1976 Moroccan–Mauritanian Arbitration line.

Ifni   A former Spanish enclave on the Atlantic coast of North Africa opposite the Canary Islands; area 2140km^2. Seceded by Morocco to Spain in 1860, it was returned to Morocco in 1969.

La Guera or **Lagwira**   A strategically important garrison town in NW Mauritania; situated at the tip of the Ras Nouadhibou peninsula (C. Blanc) to the south of Mauritania's chief port at Nouadhibou.

La'youn or **El Aaiún**   Atlantic coast capital of Western Sahara. As a result of Moroccan investment the city expanded from a small Saharan town with a population of 25 000 in 1970 to a busy provincial capital with 96 800 inhabitants in 1982.

Mahbès   A town in the Saguia el Hamra region of NE Western Sahara; situated on a 500–metre–high plateau overlooking the triangle formed by the meeting of the international frontiers of Algeria, Morocco and Mauritania; the town is a key Moroccan military command post close to the Moroccan wall.

Marrakesh   Imperial city in the Tensift province of central Morocco, situated in the northern foothills of the High Atlas;

population(1982) 439 700; birthplace of the Polisario leader Mohammed Abd al-Aziz and scene of the first meeting between al-Aziz and King Hassan in January 1989.

Nouadhibou   Atlantic seaport and capital of Dakhlet–Nouadhibou region, NW Mauritania; situated on the Cap Blanc peninsula close to the frontier with Western Sahara; founded in 1960 and known as Fort Etienne until 1965, the city has a population of about 22 000; the port is linked by rail to the important iron mines of Zouérate; the fish processing and iron exporting operations based here are vital to the economy of Mauritania.

Oued Addahab   Southern territory of Western Sahara occupied by Mauritania 1976–79, under the name Tiris el Gharbia. In August 1979 Mauritania withdrew from the conflict and the area was declared a province of Morocco; area 50 880km²; population (1982) 21 500.

Oued Draa or **Wad Draa**   A wadi or intermittent river that rises in the Ouarzazate province of S Morocco, south–west of Zagora. It flows south–west and west to meet the Atlantic just north of Tan–Tan. In November 1979 Morocco deployed a large scale expeditionary force south of the Oued Draa river bed. In the following year the Polisario guerrillas attempted to cut off Morocco from the Western Sahara by launching attacks into Moroccan territory between the Oued Draa and the Western Saharan frontier.

Rio de Oro   The southern region of Western Sahara; area 189 934km². Formerly a general title for the Spanish territories of NW Africa, its northern frontiers were defined in 1904 and southern borders in 1912. In 1934 it formed one of two separate Spanish territories divided by the 26th parallel and lying to the south of Morocco. In 1958 Rio de Oro united with the territory of Saguia el Hamra to the north to form the province of Spanish Sahara. The chief town is Ad Dakhla.

Saguia el Hamra or **Sekia el Hamra**   The northern region of Western Sahara; area 82 969km². In 1934 it formed one of two separate Spanish territories lying to the south of Morocco. In 1958 it was united with the territory of Rio de Oro to form the province of Spanish Sahara. La'youn is the chief town.

Smara   Second largest town in Western Sahara; situated 240km east of La'youn; the population increased from a total of 11 000 in 1982 to a figure of 22 000 by the mid–1980s as the conflict forced desert nomads to abandon their traditional pasture land. Smara is the chief town of a province of the same name with an area of 61 760km² and a population (1982) of 20 480. The name of Smara was also adopted by Western Saharan exiles at a refugee camp near Tindouf in Algeria.

Spanish Sahara   The name given to the territories of Saguia el Hamra and Rio de Oro which were united into a single Spanish province in 1958. Following independence on 31 December 1975, the former colony of Spanish Sahara became the Western Sahara.

Tindouf   A Saharan oasis in the Aín–Sefra region of Algeria; situated close to the Western Sahara frontier on the Agadir–Dakar desert route. Used as a base by the Polisario guerrillas in exile. The iron ore reserves near Tindouf were formerly claimed by Morocco.

Tiris el Gharbia   The name given to the southern region of Western Sahara occupied by Mauritania between 1976 and 1979 when it was declared a province of Morocco under the name Oued Addahab.

Zouérate, Zouîrât or **Az Zwirat**   An iron ore mining town in the Tiris Zemmour region of NW Mauritania; linked by rail to the Atlantic port of Nouadhibou; attacked by Polisario guerrillas in 1977 with the death of two and the capture of six French nationals; France subsequently intervened directly at the request of Mauritania by launching air attacks on the Polisario in Algeria.

■ Key words

Arbitration Line   The line demarcating the boundary between the Moroccan and Mauritanian administered sectors of Western Sahara between 1976 and 1979. It stretched from a point on the Atlantic coast just north–east of Ad Dakhla at the 24th parallel inland to a point on the 23rd parallel at 13° W.

Green March   In October 1975 both the UN and the International Court of Justice gave their support to self–determination in Spanish Sahara. The immediate response of King Hassan of Morocco was to order 350 000 unarmed civilians to march south across the border to take possession of the Spanish province. The March began on 6 November and was only called off when King Hassan succeeded in persuading the Spanish to withdraw from the Sahara and hand over the colony to a joint Moroccan–Mauritanian administration.

Maghreb (Arabic "far west")   An area of NW Africa largely occupied by sedentary and nomadic Berbers and Tuareg groups. The term has generally been applied to the area comprising the countries of Morocco, Tunisia and Algeria, but in 1989 an Arab Maghreb Union was formed which also incorporated Libya and Mauritania. In October 1984 the Polisario Front launched the so-called "Greater Maghreb" offensive against Moroccan positions on the Saharan wall.

Moroccan Wall   A series of defensive walls 4000km (2500 miles) in length constructed in six sections by Morocco between 1980 and 1987 in an attempt to prevent the free movement of Polisario Front forces into Western Sahara. Built of sand and stone, the wall is defended by artillery, radar and electronic sensors.

Operation Ouhoud   A major offensive launched by the Moroccan armed forces under General Dlimi in November 1979. Over 6000 troops backed by tanks and air cover were deployed south of the Oued Draa river bed. The operation was named after a famous battle fought by the Prophet Mohammed.

Organization of African Unity (OAU)   A union of 32 African countries whose heads of state came together in May 1963 at a conference in Addis Ababa. The OAU has helped in the search for a solution to the Western Sahara conflict. In 1982 the SADR was elected by a majority vote to membership of the OAU causing a split in the union. In 1983 SADR officials were persuaded not to attend the Addis Ababa summit but a resolution was adopted calling for direct negotiations between Morocco and the Polisario Front.

Ould Delim   A largely pro-Mauritanian ethnic group in S Western Sahara.

Polisario Front (Frente Polisario or fully **Frente Popular para la Liberación de Saguia el Hamra y Rio de Oro)**   A Saharan liberation movement opposed to Spanish colonial rule and hostile to Moroccan and Mauritanian claims over Western Sahara. In February 1976, from a base in Algeria, they declared the Sahrawi Arab Democratic Republic and formed a government in exile under the leadership of Mohammed Abd al-Aziz.

Reguibat   An ethnic group that formerly dominated the central region of Western Sahara. The Polisario Front is largely drawn from the ranks of these people, many of whom have moved across the border into Algeria.

Sahrawi Arab Democratic Republic (SADR)   The official name of the Western Sahara declared in February 1976 by the Polisario Front government in exile. By 1989 a total of 70 countries recognized the SADR.

Tekna   A largely pro-Moroccan ethnic group in N Western Sahara.

Wise Men   A name given to the heads of state of Guinea, the Ivory Coast, Mali, Nigeria, Tanzania and Sudan who were proposed as mediators in the Western Sahara conflict by the President of the OAU in 1978.

■ Further Reading

David Lynn Price, *The Western Sahara*, Sage Publications, London, 1979

Tony Hodges, *Western Sahara: The Roots of a Desert War*, Westport, Connecticut, 1983

Minority Rights Group, Report No. 40, *The Western Saharans*, London, 1984

Toby Shelley, Fighting for a Desert Home, *Geographical Magazine*, 61(4), 1989, pp.46–48

Virginia Thompson and Richard Adloff, *The Western Saharans: Background to Conflict*, Croom Helm, London, 1980

Frank E. Trout, *Morocco's Saharan Frontiers*, Geneva, 1969

4
Angola/Namibia

■ Introduction

The post–1945 decolonization of Africa was a relatively rapid process in respect of French and most British possessions. The Portuguese colonies had to wait until the 1974 revolution in Lisbon had overthrown 40 years of dictatorship and with it the belief that the overseas possessions were inalienable parts of Portugal. Partly because of the delay, Angola's independence a year later was achieved in civil war conditions, which persisted thereafter and became aggravated by the conflict over Namibia to the south. When Rhodesia moved to legal independence from Britain as Zimbabwe in 1980, South African-ruled Namibia was the only remaining colony on the African continent, if Spain's enclaves in North Africa and white-ruled South Africa itself (*see section 1.5*) are excluded. A decade later Namibia was at last permitted to join the community of independent nations on the basis of black majority rule. But the legacy of these long struggles was one of regional instability and violence, particularly in Angola.

Portuguese mariner-explorers opening up the Cape sea route to the East Indies reached Angola in the late 15th century. By the 18th century Portuguese coastal settlements had developed a flourishing trade in African slaves for Brazil and other American colonies. Gradual penetration inland accelerated in the 19th-century European "scramble for Africa", when Angola's borders as a Portuguese colony were established by agreement with neighbouring colonial powers. The enclave of Cabinda to the north was secured for Portuguese Angola in 1885 and later found to be rich in

■ Profile

Angola

- **Area:**   1 246 700km²
- **Population (1988 est.):**   9 390 000
- **Ethnic groups:**   Ovimbundu 37%, Kimbundu 25%, Bakongo 15%, Lunda-Chokwe 8%, Nganguela 6%, Haneca and Humbe 3%, Ovambo 2%, European and Mestico 2%
- **Official language:**   Portuguese
- **Religion:**   Roman Catholic 70%, Protestant 20%, Animist 10%
- **Infant mortality rate:**   167 per 1000
- **Life expectancy:**   42 years
- **Currency:**   kwanza of 100 lwei (since 1977)
- **Administrative divisions:**   18 provinces
- **Timezone:**   GMT +1
- **Capital:**   Luanda
- **Chief cities:**   Luanda (1 200 000), Huambo (62 000), Lobito (59 000), Benguela (42 000)

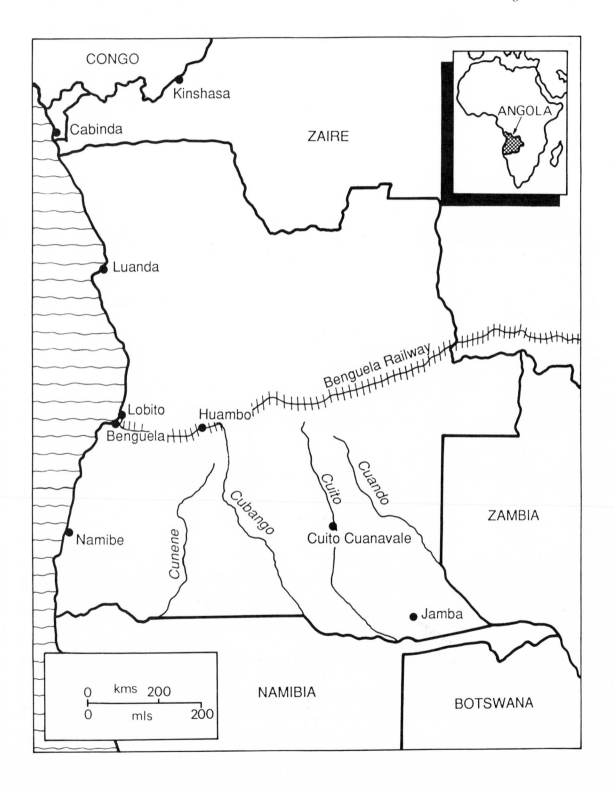

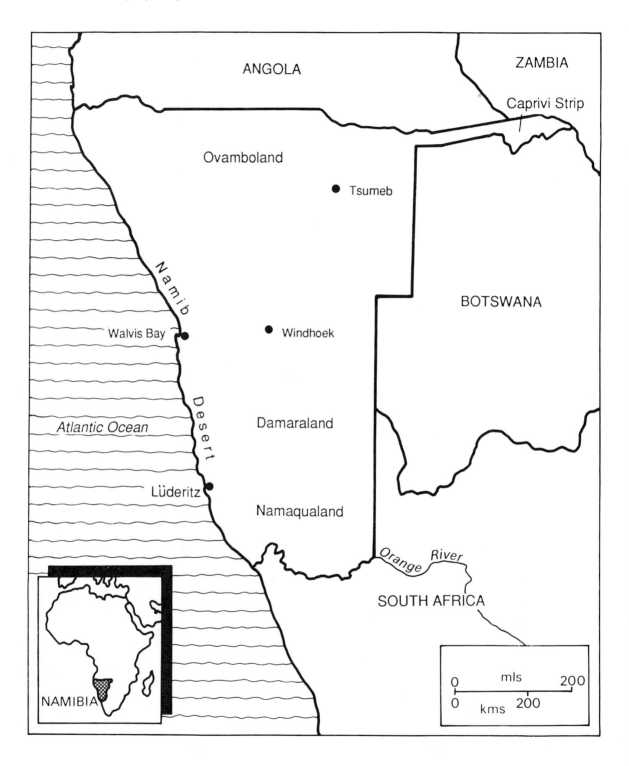

oil. Meanwhile, Germany had found one of its few places in the sun by taking control of the vast region between Angola and South Africa. This became known as South West Africa, which eventually included the narrow Caprivi Strip in the north-east, giving access to the British-controlled Zambezi river. British concern at the perceived German threat to the Cape was apparent in the annexation for South Africa of Walvis Bay, the main port in South West Africa. An incipient Boer–German alliance also caused British alarm, although this was scotched by the British victory in the Boer War (1899–1901). During World War I, South African forces overran the German colony, which was mandated to South African administration by the post-war League of Nations. After achieving independence in 1931, South Africa applied to the League for permission to establish sovereignty over South West Africa, but was refused despite being supported by the territory's Boer and British settlers, by now dominant over those of German origin.

South Africa retained control of South West Africa after World War II, in increasingly acrimonious defiance of the United Nations as successor to the League. The application of apartheid laws to the territory intensified international concern, as did white minority rule. In 1966 the UN General Assembly terminated South Africa's mandate; five years later South Africa's occupation of Namibia (the official UN name from 1968) was declared illegal by the International Court of Justice. Such steps failed to move the Pretoria government, for whom Namibia formed part of a southern African bloc of white rule seeking to resist the wind of change from the north. But cracks were already appearing in this monolith, especially in the Portuguese "overseas provinces" of Mozambique and Angola. Hard-pressed by nationalist guerrilla insurgents, Portuguese military leaders came to view the costly African wars as unwinnable, despite the substantial settler presence in both Angola and Mozambique. When left-wing officers finally deposed the Portuguese dictatorship in 1974, independence for the colonies was a major plank in their programme. The rapid Portuguese withdrawal a year later left Angola with little in the way of effective administration or trained personnel.

However, Angola's main problem at independence was that three different liberation movements, largely tribally-based, were vying for power. Of these, the Popular Movement for the Liberation of Angola (MPLA) secured control of the central government in Luanda and imposed a Marxist-Leninist regime with Soviet, and later Cuban, backing. Given the prevailing global competition between the

---

■ Profile

Namibia

- **Area:** 823 168km^2
- **Population (1986 est):** 1 184 000
- **Ethnic groups:** Ovambo 49%, Kavango 9%, Damara 7%, Herero 7%, Whites 7%, Nama 5%, Coloured 4%, Caprivi 4%, Bushmen 3%, Rehoboth Baster 2%
- **Official languages:** Afrikaans, English
- **Religion:** Christian 96%
- **Infant mortality rate:** 110 per 1000
- **Life expectancy:** black Africans 40 years; white Europeans 69 years
- **Currency:** South African rand
- **Administrative divisions:** 26 districts
- **Timezone:** GMT +2
- **Capital:** Windhoek
- **Chief towns:** Windhoek (114 500), Swakopmund (15 000), Rehoboth (15 000)

superpowers, US support inevitably swung behind the other two movements, the National Front for the Liberation of Angola (FNLA) in the north and the National Union for the Total Independence of Angola (UNITA) in the south. Whereas the FNLA threat evaporated, UNITA proved more resilient. The crucial factor was Pretoria's determination to maintain a buffer zone between Angola and its puppet regime in Namibia, itself under challenge from Angola-based SWAPO guerrillas. A pattern emerged of repeated South African anti-SWAPO incursions deep into Angola combined with UNITA guerrilla warfare against the Luanda regime. The MPLA responded by bringing in Soviet-armed Cuban troops, eventually to the number of some 50 000. One interesting effect was that Cuban troops found themselves protecting vital oil installations in Cabinda run largely by US personnel. Another was that South Africa placed Walvis Bay under the administration of Cape Province, to guard against that port becoming part of an independent Namibia.

Of various peace initiatives, that undertaken by the Western Contact Group (of the United States, Britain, France, Canada and West Germany) came near to success in 1978 with the adoption of UN Security Council Resolution 435. Conditionally accepted by South Africa and SWAPO, this envisaged UN-supervised elections and the withdrawal of South African troops at independence. Hostilities on the ground prevented implementation, however, whereupon South Africa sought to establish an "internal" settlement by holding elections in Namibia and moving to abolish apartheid in the territory. This process was in turn boycotted by SWAPO as being the perpetuation of South African domination by other means. As the conflict dragged on, the key issue became the insistence of South Africa and the United States on a Cuban withdrawal from Angola as a prerequisite for a Namibia agreement. But not until the post-1985 Gorbachev government's reassessment of Soviet global commitments had created a joint determination in Moscow and Washington to resolve regional disputes was the route to a Namibia settlement unblocked. The outcome was the December 1988 New York agreement to implement Resolution 435 on the basis of a South African military withdrawal from Namibia during 1989 and the phased departure of all Cuban troops from Angola by mid-1991.

Namibia duly proceeded to independence in March 1990 under the leadership of SWAPO, whose willingness to include whites and other non-SWAPO representatives in its government set a tone of hopeful reconciliation. Yet not only did underlying tribal hostilities remain acute in Namibia itself, but also the UNITA movement remained unreconciled to the MPLA regime in Luanda and continued to receive US backing. Efforts by other African governments to bring about an accommodation between UNITA and the Angolan regime had made some progress in June 1989 with the signature of the Gbadolite ceasefire agreement, but three months later the Angolan civil war was raging as violently as ever. When in January 1990 UNITA attacks were cited as justification for the temporary suspension of further Cuban troop withdrawals from Angola, the whole 1988 peace package appeared to be in jeopardy. It remained to be seen whether converging superpower interest would prevail upon the parties to sink their differences, possibly on the basis of the integration of UNITA into Angola's state structures.

■ Chronology of events

1482   With the arrival of the explorer Diogo Cao Portugal establishes a trading presence at the mouth of the Congo.

1575   The coastal city of Luanda is founded by the Portuguese.

1842   German missionaries arrive on the coast of South West Africa.

1877   The British annex Walvis Bay.

1883 The British government objects to the purchase of land north of the Orange River by the German merchant, Franz A.E. Lüderitz.

1884 British plans to annex South West Africa are frustrated when Germany issues a proclamation extending protection over the region.

1884–85 Portugal joins other European powers at the Berlin Conference and succeeds in obtaining a "right of occupation" over its territory in Angola.

1885 An agreement is reached between the newly created Congo State and Portugal by which the latter receives the enclave of Cabinda.

1886 In May Portugal and France fix the boundary of the Cabinda enclave and in December Portugal and Germany come to an agreement over the frontier between their respective territories.

1890 Portugal and Britain agree a boundary between Angola and Bechuanaland (then part of South Africa).

1892 Sovereignty over South West Africa is assumed by the German government.

1904–08 A rising of the Herero people involves both Germany and Portugal in a bloody military campaign to restore order.

1905 The frontier between Angola and Northern Rhodesia (Zambia) is agreed.

1915–18 During World War I South West Africa is occupied by South African troops.

1919 On 7 May the League of Nations assigns a mandate over the former German South West Africa to the Union of South Africa. Prime Minister Botha fails in his attempts to have the territory ceded to South Africa.

1920 On 17 December South Africa takes over the administration of South West Africa under the mandate agreement.

1925 The German population in South West Africa become British citizens under a constitution that provides the former German colony with a legislative assembly. German still remains an official language.

1926 Britain and Portugal define the frontier between Angola and South West Africa at the Cunene River.

1931 The opening of the Benguela railway completes the first trans-African railway stretching from Lobito in Angola to Beira in Mozambique via the Belgian Congo and Northern Rhodesia.

1932 In South West Africa the newly–formed Farmers' and Labour Party calls for an end to the mandate   and the setting-up of a separate provincial government.

1933 With the passing of the Colonial Act, the administration of Angola is more closely linked to that of Salazar's Portuguese Republic.

The government of South Africa applies to the Mandates Commission of the League of Nations for the incorporation of South West Africa into South Africa. Critical of South African administration, the Commission refuses to consider the request.

1934 Prompted by Hitler's rise to power in Germany the previous year, the dominant British and Dutch elements in the legislative assembly of South West Africa petition the government of South Africa for admission to the Union as a fifth province.

1946 The old League of Nations is replaced by the United Nations. South Africa claims that the mandate over South West Africa has consequently expired.

1954 The UPNA (later UPA) nationalist movement is created from the ranks of the Kongo ethnic group in northern Angola. This "tribal" organization is headed by Holden Roberto.

1956 The multi–racial MPLA nationalist movement is secretly formed in Luanda. Its manifesto outlines the revolutionary struggle required to bring an end to the colonial system.

1960   The South West African People's Organization (SWAPO) is formed under the leadership of Sam Nujoma who is forced into exile.

1961   A rebellion against Portuguese colonial rule breaks out during February in Angola where an attempt is made to release political prisoners from a gaol in Luanda. A violent uprising of Kongo rebels in northern Angola is brutally suppressed at a cost of some 20 000 lives.

South Africa refuses to submit reports on her administration of South West Africa to the UN which sets up a 24–man Special Committee on South West Africa.

1962   Backed by Zaire, the Angolan National Liberation Front (UPA) lays claim to a monopoly of Angolan nationalism and forms an alliance with a northern ethnic revolutionary group to become the FNLA. Before taking on the Portuguese, Holden Roberto attempts to eliminate the MPLA.

Agostino Neto escapes from imprisonment in Portugal and returns to Africa where he rallies the MPLA leadership in Léopoldville (Kinshasa) and attempts to form a united front with the UPA against the Portuguese.

In South West Africa the Odendaal Commission recommends the establishment of "homelands" in a policy of separate development similar to that operating in South Africa.

1963   Based in Léopoldville (Kinshasa), the UPA establishes a government-in-exile (GRAE) under the leadership of Holden Roberto. The Foreign Minister of this government is Jonas Savimbi. Meanwhile the MPLA takes refuge in Congo–Brazzaville where it makes plans to relaunch the revolutionary struggle in the Angolan enclave of Cabinda.

1964   Barred from operating from Zaire territory, the MPLA move to the western

frontier of newly–independent Zambia where they set up bases from which to attack the sparsely populated eastern plains of Angola.

Believing that Holden Roberto is not only a racist but a tool of the United States, Jonas Savimbi abandons the UPA.

The Organization of African Unity (OAU) calls for an end to Portuguese colonialism and for sanctions against Portugal.

1966   The United Nations revokes South Africa's mandate over South West Africa which is to be governed by an eleven–nation UN–appointed Council until independence. The SWAPO liberation movement begins to launch guerrilla raids into Namibia from bases in Zambia.

In Angola Jonas Savimbi establishes a movement of his own, (UNITA), with a base near the eastern town of Luso. He reaches an understanding with the Portuguese in the struggle against the MPLA.

1967   The United Nations General Assembly calls for sanctions against Portugal as a means of securing the independence of its colonies in Africa.

The first Bantustan "homeland" is declared in South West Africa with the setting up of a tribal authority in Ovamboland.

1968   A resolution of the UN General Assembly changes the name of South West Africa to Namibia. The UN–appointed Special Council recommends that decisive action should be taken to enforce UN Resolutions but this fails to win international support. South Africa proceeds to incorporate Namibia into the Republic.

1969   The South African government passes the South West Africa Affairs Act which abolishes the autonomy of Namibia's legislative assembly and transfers power to Pretoria.

1970   The policy of separate development continues in Namibia with the establishment of a tribal homeland in Okavangoland in August.

1971 The International Court of Justice orders South Africa to end its administration of Namibia, but the South African government refuses to recognize the jurisdiction of the court. A general strike is called in protest against South African occupation.

1972 The general strike continues in Namibia where a state of emergency is declared on 4 February. On the same day the UN Security Council meeting in Addis Ababa initiates consultations on the subject of Namibian independence. South African administration of Namibia continues regardless and a third tribal homeland is set up in East Caprivi where tribal leaders are appointed to a local legislative council.

1973 The UN recognises SWAPO as the "authentic" voice of the Namibian people. Meanwhile, South Africa sets up an Advisory Council in Namibia with representatives from all communites. SWAPO refuses to participate and in December the UN decides to end its attempts to establish meaningful talks with South Africa over the future of Namibia.

1974 Partly inspired by discontent over Portugal's prolonged colonial wars in Africa, a revolution overthrows the regime of the Portuguese dictator Marcelo Caetano. The new government immediately decides to grant independence to the African colonies.

1975 In January Portugal reaches an agreement (the Alvor Accord) with the Angolan FNLA, MPLA and UNITA liberation movements in preparation for independence in November. A transitional government comprising representatives of all three groups is formed. This soon collapses and in the fighting that follows rebel groups vie with each other to gain control of the country before independence. From bases in Zaire Holden Roberto's FNLA moves into northern Angola and captures the town of Caxito, 56km north of Luanda. Meanwhile, on the southern frontier South African forces cross the border from Namibia in support of Jonas Savimbi's UNITA rebels. By October some 5000 South African troops have entered Angola, ostensibly to protect a joint Angolan–Nambian

hydro–electric scheme at Calueque. Arms are supplied to both FNLA and UNITA guerrillas from the United States. In March the left–wing MPLA begins to receive similar support from the Soviet Union and from Cuba. Later in the year Cuban troops begin to arrive in large numbers.

Backed by the Soviet Union and Cuba, the MPLA fights off attempts by UNITA and the FNLA to capture Luanda. On 11 November Portugal cedes power without recognizing an Angolan government and the MPLA steps in to take control. A one-party Marxist state is established under the leadership of Agostinho Neto. Similar governments are declared by the FNLA based in Carmona (Uíge)and UNITA based in Nova Lisboa (Huambo), but attempts by these two groups to form a united front founder as a result of personal and tribal differences.

Faced by increasing international pressure, the South African government convenes the Turnhalle Conference in September in an attempt to bring together leaders of Namibia's 12 ethnic groups to discuss the future of Namibia. SWAPO is not represented at the conference which reconvenes intermittently until November 1977.

1976 The MPLA grip on Angola is strengthened when the United States withdraws support for the UNITA and FNLA rebels and when South African troops retreat back into Namibia. Rent by internal divisions, the FNLA gradually dissolves as a serious opposition to the MPLA. On the other hand the South African–backed UNITA rebels continue to wage a guerrilla war from bases in Namibia.

While the MPLA allows SWAPO guerrillas to move from Zambia and set up bases in southern Angola, the Turnhalle Conference announces that 31 December 1978 is the target date for Namibia's independence. The OAU and UN Council for Namibia, however, will not endorse the independence proposals which include segregated development and the continued presence of South African troops.

1977 The MPLA, which now has control over most of the country, launches an offensive against isolated UNITA rebel groups in the High Plateau. In May an attempted uprising by Interior Minister Nito Alves is quickly suppressed.

South Africa appoints an Administrator–General for Namibia in the run-up to pre-independence elections and an estimated 45 000 South African counter-insurgency troops are mobilized along the northern frontier of Namibia in order to prevent SWAPO raids into the territory from Angola. The Turnhalle Conference is dissolved in November, but the supporters of the South African proposals regroup as a multiracial political alliance of 11 parties calling itself the Democratic Turnhalle Alliance (DTA).

1978 SWAPO intensifies its guerrilla campaign and the leader of the DTA, Chief Clemens Kapuuo, is assassinated. The five Western "Contact Group" members of the UN Security Council present a plan (Security Council Resolution 435) for the peaceful independence of Namibia after lengthy consultations with South Africa, the Front Line States and SWAPO. In defiance of the UN proposal, elections are held in Namibia. These elections, which are largely boycotted, are declared null and void by the UN which continues to negotiate for an agreement that involves a phased withdrawal of South African troops and UN-supervised elections.

1979 President Agostinho Neto of Angola dies and is replaced by the 37–year–old José Eduardo dos Santos.

1981 The United States presents a "linkage" plan that involves linking the withdrawal of Cuban troops from Angola with the independence of Namibia.

1983 In November the South African government encourages the formation of a broad, seven–party political coalition called the Multi–Party Conference.

1984 On 16 February South Africa and Angola sign an agreement in Lusaka under which Angola undertakes to end SWAPO's use of Angolan soil for guerrilla attacks on Namibia in return for the withdrawal of South African troops from Angola. A Joint Monitoring Commission is set up to supervise the arrangement. This accord brings SWAPO and South Africa to the negotiating table. At a meeting in Cape Verde in July Sam Nujoma asks for a fixed date for the implementation of the UN Security Council Resolution 435 in return for a SWAPO ceasefire. The Administrator–General for Namibia, Dr Willie van Niekerk, will not support the plan for Namibian independence until 50000 Cuban troops have been withdrawn. Later in the year Angola and South Africa present proposals linking the implementation of Resolution 435 with Cuban troop withdrawal.

In September the SWANU liberation movement is split over adherence to the Multi–Party Conference. Two months later the SWANU faction opposed to the MPC decides to unite with other anti–MPC parties, SWAPO and the Namibian Council of Churches to form a Peoples' Consultative Conference.

1985 While the United States attempts to mediate between South Africa and Angola in the search for a compromise on Cuban troop withdrawal, the Multi–Party Conference in Namibia presents a plan for a pre-independence transitional government. This new administration is inaugurated in Windhoek on 17 June. In April South Africa removes the last of its troops from Angola, but in July the US Senate votes to renew aid to the UNITA rebels fighting the Luanda government.

In September the situation deteriorates when South African troops cross the border into Angola in pursuit of SWAPO guerrillas.

1986 South Africa agrees to implement the UN plan for Namibian independence provided Cuban troops are withdrawn from Angola. The UN sees these two issues as quite separate problems. In April a conference of Namibian groups opposed to the Transitional Government of National Unity issues the Ai-Gams Declaration calling for an internationally recognized, democratically elected government.

1987　The draft of a constitution for Namibia is drawn up by a Constitutional Council set up by the Transitional Government, but the leader of the South West African National Party announces that the white legislative authority will go ahead with elections in 1988 regardless of the views of the Transitional Government. In July the USA and Angola hold a round of talks.

1988　In March, during further talks with the United States in Luanda, the Angolan government agrees to the withdrawal of Cuban troops. Two months later the first quadripartite meeting involving Angola, Cuba, South Africa and the United States takes place in London to discuss Namibian independence and Cuban troop withdrawal. A second round of talks is held in Cairo in June and at a third round of talks held in New York in July all parties agree to 14 principles for a settlement (New York Principles). A fourth round of talks held in August in Geneva finally results in an agreement to begin the implementation of the UN plan for Namibian independence on 1 November. Later in the month military leaders from South Africa, Angola and Cuba meet on the Angola-Namibia border at Ruacana to sign an agreement that formally ends hostilities between Angola and South Africa. By the end of August all South African troops have left Angola.

A further five rounds of quadripartite talks take place before a timetable for Cuban troop withdrawal is finally agreed. On 13 December Angola, Cuba and South Africa sign the Brazzaville Protocol which paves the way for a tripartite agreement, signed in New York on 22 December, that provides for the implementation of the UN plan for the independence of Namibia from 1 April 1989. Angola and Cuba agree to a phased withdrawal of Cuban troops by 1 July 1991.

1989　A UN Transition Assistance Group begins to arrive in February and on 1 April a ceasefire between SWAPO and South Africa comes into effect. On the eve of the so-called "D"–Day on which the UN plan is due to commence, several hundred SWAPO guerrillas cross the border into Namibia and disrupt the implementation of the peace process. On 8–9 April an Extraordinary Session of the Joint Commission set up under the Brazzaville Protocol meets at Mt Etjo and takes steps to defuse the crisis. It is agreed that under UNTAG supervision, SWAPO forces are to retire to bases in Angola north of the 16th parallel via nine specified assembly points on the Angola–Namibia frontier.

Within six months about 40 000 exiles including Sam Nujoma return to Namibia where registration takes place prior to the holding of elections in November. SWAPO wins a decisive victory in the elections and by the end of the month, after 74 years of armed occupation, South African troops leave Namibia.

With the help of President Mobuto Sese Seko of Zaire, a ceasefire is negotiated between the UNITA rebels and the Angolan government in June (Gbadolite Declaration). When MPLA troops are moved into south–east Angola in mid–August, Jonas Savimbi renounces the ceasefire but does not rule out further peace talks that will lead to an integration of UNITA into the government of Angola.

1990　The Angolan government still faces opposition from UNITA rebels in SE Angola and in January Cuban troop withdrawals are temporarily suspended. Nevertheless, the formal independence of Namibia from South Africa takes place on 21 March. With Sam Nujoma as its first president, Namibia applies to become the 50th member of the Commonwealth.

■ Who's who

Alves, Nito   MPLA Interior Minister who attempted to overthrow the Angolan government in May 1977.

Caetano, Marcelo   Portuguese prime minister (1968–74), ousted during a military coup in April 1974. His overthrow paved the way for the independence of Portuguese colonies in Africa.

Chand, General Prem   Commanding officer of the military component of UNTAG which arrived in Namibia in February 1989.

Crocker, Dr Chester   United States Assistant Secretary for African Affairs responsible for maintaining diplomatic contacts with Angola, Cuba and South Africa between 1981 and 1989 in an attempt to bring about the withdrawal of Cuban troops from Angola and the peaceful independence of Namibia. Crocker formerly held the post of Director of African Studies at the Center for Strategic and International Studies in Washington.

Dreyer, Major–General   Senior officer of SWAPOL and founder of the paramilitary Koevet counter–insurgency unit.

Geingob, Hage   American–educated former Director of the UN Institute for Namibia in Lusaka who returned to Namibia in 1989 to direct SWAPO's election campaign. In February he was elected first prime minister of independent Namibia at the age of 48.

Kangueehi, Kuzeeko   Former deputy leader of SWANU, elected to the leadership at a party congress in September 1984. His election was quickly followed by a vote to withdraw SWANU from the Multi–Party Alliance.

Katjuiongua, Moses   Leader of the SWANU liberation movement until September 1984 when the anti–Multi–Party Conference deputy leader, Kuzeeko Kangueehi, was elected party leader.

Lubowski, Anton   Leading white member of SWAPO, assassinated outside his home in Windhoek on 12 September 1989.

Nascimento, Fortunato Ferreira Lopo de   The first prime minister of Angola following independence from Portugal in 1975.

Neiring, Major-General George   Officer commanding the South West African Defence Force prior to independence.

Neto, (Antonio) Agostinho   An Angolan physician, poet and politician who became the first MPLA president of Angola following independence in 1975. As a doctor he worked for the colonial health service, but his political activities led to his imprisonment on four occasions between 1952 and 1960. Escaping in 1962, he led the MPLA struggle for Angolan independence. Neto died in September 1979 and was succeeded by José Eduardo dos Santos.

Nujoma, Sam   Namibian nationalist leader and president of SWAPO since 1960. Born in 1929, Nujoma worked as a railway steward before becoming a municipal clerk in Windhoek in 1957. Arrested in December 1959, he fled the country in February 1960 after being released pending trial. In 1960 he set up SWAPO's provisional headquarters in Dar es Salaam. Returning to South West Africa in 1966 he was arrested again and formally ordered out of the country. Leading the SWAPO struggle for Namibian independence, Nujoma returned to his native country in 1989. Following elections in February 1990 he was elected president of Namibia.

Pienaar, Louis   The last South African Administrator–General of Namibia prior to independence in 1990.

Pretorius, Kosie   Leader of the white South West Africa National Party and former Chairman of the Executive Committee of the Transitional Government of National Unity.

Roberto, Holden   Angolan nationalist leader, born in N Angola in 1925 and educated in the Congo. After working for the Belgian administration in the Congo he founded the UPA nationalist liberation movement. In 1962 he became leader of the FNLA and declared himself prime minister of the Angolan government in exile. When the USA withdrew its support for the FNLA in 1975, Roberto's liberation movement virtually dissolved and he was forced to leave the country once again.

Santos, José Eduardo dos   Angolan politician who succeeded Agostinho Neto as president of Angola in September 1979 at the age of 37. Born in a shanty town outside Luanda, dos Santos trained as a petroleum engineer in the Soviet Union before joining the MPLA in 1961.

Savimbi, Dr Jonas Malheiro   Angolan nationalist leader, born in 1934, the son of a

railway worker. After obtaining a medical degree in Lisbon he returned to Africa where he joined the UPA liberation movement and became foreign minister in the Angolan government in exile. He fell out with Holden Roberto in 1964 and after a year of postdoctoral study at Lausanne he set up his own UNITA liberation movement. In 1975 he declared himself president of Angola and engaged in a guerrilla war against the Soviet–backed MPLA government.

Toivo ja Toivo, Andimba   Secretary–General of SWAPO.

◼ Key places

Benguela   A town on the Atlantic coast of Angola, 25km S of Lobito; population 41 000. The 2500km Benguela railway links the port of Lobito with central Angola, Zaire and the Zambian city of Ndola. Conceived in 1902 by the British entrepreneur, Robert Williams, as a means of bringing minerals from the interior to the coast of Africa, the Benguela railway transported more than half of Zambia's total copper exports before the line was cut by UNITA guerrillas in 1975. Temperatures along the W coast of Africa are modified by the cool Benguela current which sweeps up from the Antarctic.

Cabinda   An enclave of Angola situated between two arms of the River Congo and separated from the rest of Angola. Its chief town is Cabinda; area 7 270km². Oil is exploited in the offshore Kambala and Livuite fields. For a short while after independence from Portugal Cabinda boasted its own insurgency movement.

Calueque   A joint South African–Angolan hydro-electric scheme centred around the Calenda and Cazambue rapids on the Cunene River, 20km north of the frontier between Namibia and Angola. Following the independence of Angola South African troops

crossed into Angola to protect this installation from attack by guerrillas.

Caprivi Strip or **Caprivi Concession, Caprivi Zipfel** (Afrikaans)   A narrow strip of Namibian territory extending a distance of 450km from the NE corner of Namibia to the southern frontier of Zambia. Named after the German Foreign Minister of the time, the Caprivi Strip was ceded to Germany by Great Britain in 1893 in order that German South West Africa could gain an outlet to the Zambezi River.

Cubango River or **Okavango River**   Rising in the Bié plateau E of Huambo, the Cubango flows south–east to the Namibian frontier and crosses the Caprivi Strip before draining into the extensive Okavango marshes of N Botswana. With a total length of 1 600km it is Africa's third longest river.

Cuito Cuanavale   A small town in the remote forest of Cuando-Cubango province, SE Angola. A frontline outpost in the government offensive against South African–backed UNITA rebels in the south–east of the country. In March 1988 the struggle for Cuito Cuanavale developed into the biggest battle in Africa this century in terms of troop numbers (over 18 000) and firepower.

Cunene River   Rising in W central Angola near Huambo, the Cunene flows S till it meets the Namibia frontier. After passing through a number of cataracts it turns west and flows on along the Namibia-Angola border until it meets the Atlantic 250km south of Namibe.

Damaraland   A region of central Namibia lying between Ovamboland (N) and Namaqualand (S). From a dry, barren coastal plain the land rises to a mountain district with peaks over 2500m. Damaraland is the homeland of the nomadic Damara and Herero peoples. Attempts by the South African government to create a Bantustan "homeland" in Damaraland in 1973 failed when the local council refused the offer of partial self–rule from Pretoria.

Dar es Salaam   ("haven of peace")   Seaport on the E coast of Tanzania, 45km south of Zanzibar; population 757 000. Founded by the Sultan of Zanzibar in 1882, Dar es Salaam was capital of German East Africa from 1891 until 1915 and capital of Tanzania until 1974. Following his escape from South West Africa in 1960, Sam Nujoma, leader of SWAPO set up his headquarters in Dar es Salaam.

Huambo   Known as Nova Lisboa between 1928 and 1978, Huambo is the second largest city in Angola; population 62 000. Huambo is situated on the Benguela railway, at an altitude of nearly 1700m in the central Highlands of Angola.

Jamba   ("elephant")   Headquarters of UNITA leader Jonas Savimbi in the remote SE corner of Angola midway between the Cuando and Cuito rivers.

Katutura   A black African township outside Windhoek, capital of Namibia. In June 1987 74 people were injured during a police raid.

Kinshasa   Known as Leopoldville until 1966, the river port of Kinshasa is the capital of Zaire. Situated on the Congo River opposite Brazzaville, Kinshasa was founded in 1887 by H.M. Stanley. In 1926 it became capital of the Belgian Congo. Population (1984) 2 653 000. The seat of Holden Roberto's 1975 FNLA "revolutionary government–in–exile".

Lobito   A seaport on the Atlantic coast of Angola, 385km south of Luanda. Linked by rail to the copper mines of the interior, Lobito is one of the best natural harbours on the west coast of Africa. Before the Benguela railway was cut by guerrillas in 1975 the port handled 2.6 million tonnes of cargo annually. Population 60 000.

Luanda   Seaport capital and largest city in Angola, situated on the Atlantic coast of NW Angola, 530km south–west of Kinshasa; population (1988) 1 800 000. Founded in 1575, Luanda was the centre of Portuguese colonial administration from 1627 until 1975 when it fell into the hands of the Marxist MPLA liberation movement.

Mavinga   A town in the Cuando-Cubango province of SE Angola, situated on the Cubia River, a tributary of the Cuando. Held by rebel UNITA guerrillas, Mavinga came under heavy attack during a major MPLA offensive in early 1990.

Namaqualand   The traditional land of the Nama people of SW Namibia. Little Namaqualand refers to the copper–mining territory within South Africa extending south from the Orange River and including the town of Springbok, while Great Namaqualand comprises that part of S Namibia to the north of the Orange River and south of Damaraland.

Namibe   A seaport on the Atlantic coast of SW Angola, 200km north of the Namibian frontier. Known as Moc,amedes until 1978

Nova Lisboa   Former Portuguese name for Huambo, 1928–78.

Oshakati   A garrison town in Ovamboland, N Namibia.

Ovamboland   A region of N Namibia, with Angola to the north and Damaraland to the south. The homeland of over half a million people of the Ovambo tribe and centre of operations for both SWAPO and UNITA guerrillas until 1989. In March 1967 Ovamboland was the first "homeland" to be declared by the South African government in South West Africa.

Savimbi Trail   The route used by Jonas Savimbi's UNITA guerrillas when travelling to areas of N Angola from their headquarters at Jamba in the remote SE corner of the country. In September 1988 access to the north was halted when government troops captured five towns on the so-called "Savimbi Trail" (Munhango, Cangumbe, Cangonga, Sautar and Luando).

Tsumeb   A major mining centre NW of Grootfontein, N Namibia; population 13 500. The focal point in 1971–72 of a major strike of contract workers opposed to the contract labour system and the South African occupation of Namibia. The strike not only shut down local diamond, copper, lead and zinc mines but also brought railways and the fishing industry to a standstill.

Walvis Bay   An enclave of South Africa on the Atlantic coast of Namibia, 275km WSW of Windhoek; population 25 000. Incorporated into Cape Colony in 1884, it remained part of South Africa during the German occupation of South West Africa. Administered by South West Africa during most of the period of South African control of that territory, it was restored to South Africa's Cape province in 1977. The ruling SWAPO government claims Walvis Bay should rightfully be part of Namibia.

Windhoek   Capital of Namibia, situated at an altitude of 1650m, 1450km north of Cape Town; population 105 000. An important centre for the diamond and copper mining industries.

■ Key words

Ai-Gams   A grouping of left-wing Namibian political parties including SWAPO. In April 1986 the "Ai-Gams" Declaration rejected the Transitional Government of National Unity formed by the MPC in June 1985 and called for its replacement by an internationally recognized, democratically elected government.

Alvor Accord   An agreement promoted by President Kenyatta of Kenya in January 1975 in an attempt to create a transitional government in Angola as it moved towards independence from Portuguese colonial rule. The three main Angolan liberation movements (MPLA, UNITA and FNLA) were called upon to work together in a tripartite government prior to independence on 11 November 1975, but negotiations collapsed and civil war prevented the agreement from becoming effective,

Bakongo   One of the three largest Bantu ethnic groups in Angola. Mostly living in Cabinda and on the northern frontier with Zaire and the Congo, the Bakongo account for an estimated 15 per cent of the total population.

Brazzaville Protocol   An agreement reached in December 1988 under which Angola, Cuba and South Africa agreed to the phased withdrawal of Cuban troops from Angola and a timetable for the implementation of the UN plan for the independence of Namibia.

Clerk Amendement   A US decision of December 1975, banning military aid to UNITA and FNLA rebel forces in Angola. In 1985 the US government voted to lift the ban.

Constitutional Council   A Council set up by the Transitional Government of National Unity in 1985 for the purpose of drafting a constitution for Namibia.

Contact Group   The name given to the five Western states of the UN Security Council (Canada, France, West Germany, UK and USA) which launched a joint diplomatic effort in 1977 to bring about a peaceful, internationally acceptable transition to independence for Namibia.

Damara   With an estimated population of 89 000 the Damara constitute the third largest ethnic group within Namibia. The Damara are nomads occupying the central part of

Namibia between Ovamboland in the north and Namaqualand in the south.

D-Day   The date on which it was agreed that the UN plan for Namibian independence was to get under way. Originally to be 1 November 1988, the date was changed to 1 April 1989 in order that an agreement could be reached on the phased withdrawal of Cuban troops.

Democratic Turnhalle Alliance (DTA)   A multiethnic coalition of Namibian political parties formed in 1977 after the dissolution of the Turnhalle Conference.

Front for the Liberation of Cabinda (FLEC)   A resistance movement that carries out low–level guerrilla attacks against Angolan government targets in a bid to secure the independence of the northern enclave of Cabinda.

Gbadolite Declaration   A ceasefire between UNITA rebels and the Angolan government concluded in June 1989 at a meeting in the town of Gbadolite in Zaire where President Mobutu Sese Seko acted as mediator. The movement of 3000 MPLA troops to Cuito Cuanavale in SE Angola prompted Jonas Savimbi to renounce the ceasefire two months later.

Geneva Protocol   An agreement reached in Geneva after four rounds of talks involving representatives from South Africa, Angola, Cuba and the United States. The various steps leading towards the implementation of the UN plan for Namibian independence were defined. After another five rounds of talks a further agreement on Cuban troop withdrawal was established and a timetable for military disengagement, elections and independence drawn up under the Brazzaville Protocol.

Herero   A migratory cattle–herding ethnic group of SW Angola and Namibia, the Herero played a significant part in the tribal uprisings against the Portuguese and Germans during the first decade of the 20th century. Brutal suppression by the Germans led to the virtual annihilation of the Herero people.

Interessengemeinschaft   A German–speaking interest group representing white farmers and businessmen in Namibia.

Kavango   With a population of 110 000 in Namibia, the Kavango occupy the territory known as Okavangoland in NE Namibia and N Botswana.

Kimbundu   One of the three largest Bantu ethnic groups in Angola. Concentrated in the area around Luanda, the Kimbundu account for about 25 per cent of the total population.

Koevoet (Afrikaans, "crowbar")   A Namibian Police Counter–Insurgency Unit set up by South Africa in Namibia, but later absorbed into the police following the tripartite agreement of December 1988.   With a reputation for brutality against civilians in its war against SWAPO, it formed the frontline of attack against the SWAPO guerrillas who infiltrated into the territory in early April 1989.

Kwanyama   A sub-group of the Ovambo people that provides the core of the SWAPO leadership.

linkage   A plan proposed by the United States linking military disengagement, and in particular the withdrawal of Cuban troops from Angola, to the independence of Namibia.

Lusaka Agreement   An agreement reached at a meeting held in Lusaka in February 1984 at which South Africa undertook to withdraw its troops from Angola in return for an undertaking by the Angolan government that it would deny SWAPO the right to launch raids into Namibia from Angola.

Mt Etjo Declaration   An Extraordinary Session of the Joint Military Commission set up by the Brazzaville Protocol met at Mt Etjo in Namibia on 13 December 1988. The members of the commission recommended that SWAPO guerrilla forces withdraw under UNTAG supervision from Namibia through designated border assembly points to bases in Angola north of the 16th parallel.

Multi-Party Conference (MPC)   A seven–party political coalition formed by the South African government in Namibia in November 1983. The MPC helped develop proposals for the setting-up of an interim administration announced by South Africa in April 1985.

Support for the MPC caused a rift within the SWANU nationalist liberation movement.

National Front for the Liberation of Angola (Frente Nacional de Libertação de Angola – FNLA)   An Angolan liberation movement formed in March 1962 when the UPA and the PDA united under the leadership of Holden Roberto. The FNLA, which drew its support from tribal elements in northern Angola, largely dissolved as a serious opposition to the MPLA when the United States withdrew its support in December 1975.

National Union for the Total Independence of Angola (Unia Nacional para a Independencia Total de Angola – UNITA)   An Angolan liberation movement founded in March 1966 by Dr Jonas Savimbi who has led the UNITA forces against the Marxist MPLA during the prolonged civil war in Angola. Operating from bases in Namibia and SE Angola, UNITA has received support from the USA and South Africa.

New York Principles   A set of 14 principles leading to a settlement of the Angola–Namibia conflict, agreed at the third quadripartite meeting of representatives from Angola, Cuba, South Africa and the United States held on 11–13 July 1989 in New York.

Odendaal Commission   A commission appointed by the government of South Africa to define the geographic, political and economic aspects of establishing *apartheid* in Namibia.

Operation Hooper   An operation in which South African Defence Force (SADF) units came into direct conflict with MPLA forces in January–February 1988. The resulting defeat inflicted on MPLA troops allowed UNITA troops to consolidate in territory formerly held by the Angolan government.

Operation Modular   A name applied by the South African Defence Force (SADF) to the MPLA offensive against UNITA forces that commenced in August 1987 and brought SADF units into direct conflict with the MPLA.

Ovambo   A migratory cattle–herding ethnic group of northern Namibia and southern Angola. Numbering about one million, the Ovambo constitute about 51 per cent of the population of Namibia. SWAPO draws its support mainly from the Ovambo people.

Ovamboland People's Organization   A Namibian liberation movement that evolved into SWAPO under the leadership of Sam Nujoma in 1960.

Ovimbundu   The largest of the Bantu ethnic groups of Angola, accounting for an estimated 37 per cent of the total population. The Ovimbundu are largely traders and farmers and are responsible for much of the agricultural development of the central highlands.

People's Liberation Army of Namibia (PLAN)   The military wing of SWAPO.

Popular Movement for the Liberation of Angola (Movimento Popular de Libertação de Angola – MPLA)   A Marxist Angolan liberation movement founded in Luanda in December 1956. With broad support in the townships and with the support of Cuba and the Soviet Union, the MPLA under Agostinho Neto was able to fight off opposition from the US–backed UNITA and FNLA liberation movements and take control of Angola when Portugal ceded power in 1975.

Resolution 435   A plan for solving the Namibian problem proposed by the Contact Group and passed by the UN Security Council in 1978. Known as the UN plan, the proposal called for the holding of elections in Namibia under UN supervision and for the cessation of hostilities. The eventual implementation of Resolution 435 took place once agreement had been reached on the withdrawal of Cuban and South African troops from Angola–Namibia.

Ruacana Accord   An agreement signed at Ruacana on the Angola–Namibia border on 22 August 1988 by military representatives of Angola, Cuba and South Africa, bringing to an end hostilities between Angola and South Africa.

South African Defence Force (SADF)   South African regular army units operating against insurgents in Namibia and Angola. The last units of SADF withdrew from Angola in August 1988 and from Namibia in June 1989.

South West Africa National Party (SWANP)
A Namibian political party representing the white community which owns 80 per cent of the land.

South West African National Union (SWANU)   A non-violent nationalist Namibian liberation movement founded in 1959. In 1984 SWANU was split into two separate factions on the subject of adherence to the proposals put forward by the Multi-Party Conference.

South West African Peoples' Organization (SWAPO)   A Namibian liberation movement that evolved from the Ovamboland People's Organization in 1960 under the leadership of Sam Nujoma and Herman Toiva ja Toiva. Exiled from Namibia in 1960, Nujoma established a SWAPO headquarters in Dar es Salaam a year later. Drawing most of its support from the Ovambo people of N Namibia, SWAPO first launched guerrilla raids against South African Defence Forces from bases in Zambia in 1966. When Angola gained its independence in 1975 the MPLA government allowed SWAPO to operate from bases in that country.

South West Africa Police Force (SWAPOL)   A Namibian police force which included units of the infamous Koevet counter-insurgency group until 1989. When SWAPO guerrillas crossed into Namibia after "D–Day" on 1 April 1989 they were engaged in clashes with SWAPOL forces while SADF and SWATF troops were confined to base.

South West Africa Territorial Force (SWATF)   A Namibian defence force operating alongside the SADF, but phased out in the run-up to pre-independence elections in 1989.

Transitional Government of National Unity (TGNU)   A Multi-Party Conference Interim Administration in Namibia set up by South Africa on 17 June 1985. The TGNU cabinet was chaired by former SWANU leader, Moses Katjiuonga.

Turnhalle Conference   A multiracial conference convened by South Africa in September 1975 to discuss the future of Namibia. Delegates from each of Namibia's ethnic groups met intermittently until the conference was dissolved in November 1977.

Typhoon   The name of an élite, 600–strong SWAPO military task force.

UN Angola Verification Mission (UNAVEM)
A unit of 70 military observers and 20 civilian support staff appointed by the UN to monitor the staged withdrawal of some 50 000 Cuban troops from Angola between 1989 and 1991.

UN Transitional Assistance Group (UNTAG)   A United Nations supervisory body deployed in Namibia and Angola in 1989 for the purpose of monitoring the UN plan for Namibian independence. The UNTAG force consisted of 4050 soldiers, 500 military policemen and 100 civilians.

■ Further reading

G.J. Bender, *Angola Under the Portuguese: The Myth and the Reality*, Heinemann Educational, London, 1979

M.R.Bhagvan, *Angola's Political Economy 1975–1985*, Uppsala, 1986

R.H. Green, Kimmo Kiljunen and Marja-Liisa Kiljunen (eds.), *Namibia*, Longman (UK), Harlow, 1981

A.J. Klinghoffer, *The Angolan War*, Westview Press, Boulder, 1980

J. Marcrum, *The Angolan Revolution*, (2 vols.), MIT Press, Massachusetts, 1969 and 1978

D. Soggot, *Namibia: The Violent Heritage*, New York, 1986

K. Somerville, *Angola: Politics, Economics and Society*, Westview Press, Boulder, 1986

5
Mozambique

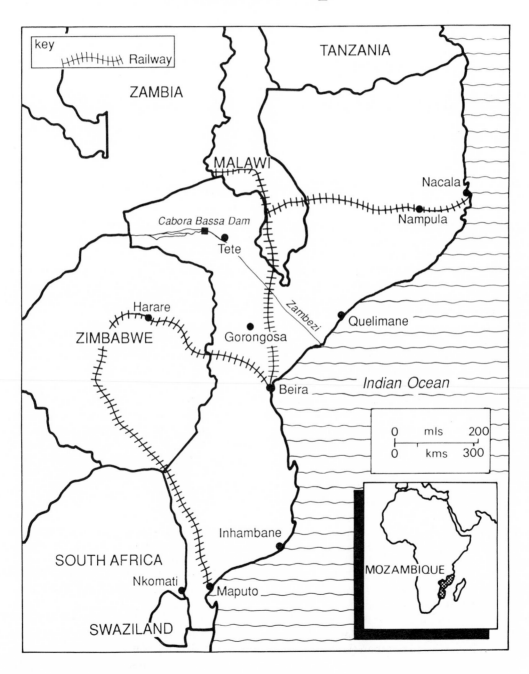

key
⊢⊦⊦⊦⊦⊦⊦⊦⊦ Railway

TANZANIA

ZAMBIA

MALAWI

Cabora Bassa Dam

Tete

Nacala

Nampula

Harare

Zambezi

ZIMBABWE

Gorongosa

Quelimane

Beira

Indian Ocean

0 — mls — 200

0 — kms — 300

Inhambane

SOUTH AFRICA

Nkomati

Maputo

SWAZILAND

MOZAMBIQUE

■ Profile

- **Area:**   799 380km²
- **Population(1987):**   14 591 000
- **Ethnic groups:**   Makonde, Makua, Malawi, Yao, Swahili, Shona, Zulu, Ngoni and Tsonga
- **Languages:**   Portuguese (official), Swahili (N of the Zambezi) and many local dialects
- **Religions:**   Local beliefs 60%, Christian 30%, Muslim 10%
- **Life expectancy:**   48 years
- **Infant mortality rate:**   109 per 1000
- **Currency:**   metical of 100 centavos
- **Timezone:**   GMT +2
- **Capital:**   Maputo
- **Chief cities:**   Maputo (882 800), Beira (269 700), Nampula (182 500)

■ Introduction

On achieving independence in 1975, the black inhabitants of Mozambique had experienced a thousand years of exploitation at the hands of outsiders. Arab traders of gold, ivory and slaves had been present on its coast for 500 years when Portuguese explorers arrived in the late 15th century and quickly established a colony. Penetration inland led to the creation of large feudal estates owned by private Portuguese adventurers subject to minimal government control. By the mid-18th century, use of black labour had developed into an extensive slave trade supplying Boer settlers further south as well as the slave markets of the Americas. When Portugal followed Britain's example by abolishing slavery in 1869, the system of black contract labour which replaced it meant little discernible change for Africans. The same was true of the employment of large numbers of Mozambican blacks in the gold mines of South Africa. Nevertheless, due mainly to the influence of the Catholic Church, exploitation of black labour in the Portuguese colonies never hardened into a legal system of discrimination of the South African type (*see section 1.6*).

In the 19th-century European "scramble for Africa" Portugal sought to extend Mozambique westwards to connect with Angola (*see section 1.4*). This aim was thwarted by the British, who nevertheless recognized the borders of the two Portuguese colonies. Mozambique thus occupied a key strategic position as the coastal outlet of much of British southern Africa. A revolt by Mozambican blacks at the turn of the century led the metropolitan government to begin curbing the feudal powers of the landowners. Change accelerated when a surge of immigration from Portugal in the early 20th century increased Mozambique's white artisan and professional classes. Under the Salazar dictatorship (1932–68) Mozambique and other colonies came to be defined as overseas provinces of Portugal and therefore as inalienable parts of the national territory. An assimiliation policy in the post-war era meant that blacks could aspire to the same citizenship rights as whites, but in practice only a tiny minority attained the required educational and economic standards. Even when citizenship rights were granted to all overseas subjects in 1963, the status of blacks was little changed. In Mozambique pro-independence nationalists had by then united in the Front for the Liberation of Mozambique (Frelimo), which from bases in newly-independent Tanzania launched an armed struggle against Portuguese rule.

Resolved to defend its African "provinces", Portugal sought to stem the tide of black liberation south of the Zambezi by forming an axis with South Africa and the illegal white regime in Rhodesia/Zimbabwe. But the increasingly costly wars in Mozambique and Angola served to alienate the Portuguese military. When left-wing officers seized power in Lisbon in 1974, independence for the African colonies soon followed. In Mozambique, Frelimo came to power with a Marxist programme of the familiar African type, which quickly resulted in a mass white exodus. This not only deprived the country of most of its skilled manpower but also devastated the economic infrastructure, as departing whites destroyed what they could not carry with them, including machinery and livestock. As if this were not enough, independent Mozambique also faced grave external dangers arising from its new status as a front-line state confronting continuing white minority rule in neighbouring Zimbabwe and South Africa. Support for the Zimbabwean liberation struggle exposed Mozambique to several years of military harassment, before the closing of its ports to Zimbabwean trade helped to bring about the surrender of the white regime. However, black majority rule in Zimbabwe from 1980 only increased Mozambique's exposure to the wrath of a Pretoria regime intent on demonstrating that blacks were unfit to govern.

South Africa's policy in Mozambique was destabilization through the agency of the so-called National Resistance Movement (MNR). One aim was to exact a heavy price for the Frelimo government's support for African National Congress (ANC) guerrilla operations in South Africa. More broadly, Pretoria sought to undermine the whole strategy of the Southern African Development Co-ordination Conference (SADCC), through which the black states sought to reduce their economic dependence on South Africa, particularly in transport. In Mozambique's case, South Africa achieved much success, as MNR violence and murder destroyed most of what was left of the country's infrastructure. Forced to the negotiating

table at Nkomati in 1984, Mozambique signed a non-aggression pact with South Africa, agreeing to withdraw active support from the ANC in return for Pretoria's pledge to end its sponsorship of the MNR. Mozambique also agreed to open its economy to South African investment, thus expediting Pretoria's goal of creating a regional "constellation of states" which it would dominate by virtue of its greater economic and military strength.

Mozambique kept its side of the Nkomati bargain, for which it incurred much criticism from other front-line states. The Frelimo government also tacitly admitted the error of its previous Marxist ways by switching to free-enterprise economic policies. However, after a brief interlude, the MNR resumed its campaign of violence and intimidation, reducing the country to such an abject condition that emergency aid appeals had to be launched in the late 1980s. A series of natural disasters added to the misery. While Pretoria deflected Mozambique's protests by claiming that the MNR had become a self-sustaining opposition movement, many observers speculated that the South African military establishment was continuing to run its own show in Mozambique independently of government policy. Whatever the truth of the matter, it was clear that the overthrow of the Frelimo government in Maputo would represent a major victory for South Africa's strategy of breaking the SADCC front and creating a network of client states in southern Africa. Despite Namibian independence and the momentous developments in South Africa in 1989–90, opening the prospect of black aspirations being accommodated in a new constitutional structure, it seemed unlikely that South African regional policy would change in the near future. Mozambique's economic and political prospects therefore remained bleak in the extreme.

■ Chronology of events

1498 The Portuguese navigator Vasco da Gama lands on present-day Mozambique Island on 2 March.

1506 The coastal region of Sofala is occupied and a trading fort is established by Portugal which administers the area as part of Portuguese India.

1752 The Sofala region is separated from Portuguese India and put under separate administration.

1869 Slavery is abolished in the Portuguese overseas possessions.

1891 After Portugal extends its territory inland, an agreement is reached with Britain which defines the frontiers with British South and East Africa. In the same year the Mozambique Company is given a charter of Manica and Sofala regions.

1894–97 A rebellion by Mozambican blacks, in which Lourenço Marques is beseiged, is eventually put down with great bloodshed.

1907 Portuguese East Africa is given colonial status by Portugal with Lourenço Marques (Maputo) as capital.

1942 The Mozambique Company charter expires and the territories of Sofala and Manica revert to the Portuguese government.

1951 Mozambique becomes an Overseas Territory of Portugal.

1955 Mozambique becomes an Overseas Province of Portugal.

1962 Three nationalist groups unite to form the Frelimo movement under the leadership of Eduardo Mondlane. Guerrilla training camps are set up in neighbouring Tanzania.

1963 Portuguese citizenship rights are accorded to all inhabitants of Mozambique and other Portuguese possessions.

1964 Samora Machel crosses the border into Mozambique with a 250–man guerrilla force to begin the armed struggle for independence from Portugal.

1970 In May Samora Machel is appointed President of Frelimo.

1974 A military coup overthrows the government of Portugal and the new administration opens negotiations in Dar es Salaam and Lusaka with a view to ending ten years of conflict and granting Mozambique its independence. After rejecting the idea of a referendum, an agreement is reached and representatives of Portugal and Frelimo form a transitional government under Prime Minister Joaquim Chissano. Immediately after a ceasefire is announced on 7 September white colonials opposed to independence stage a three-day revolt in Lorenço Marques (Maputo).

1975 On 25 June Mozambique gains independence from Portugal under the leadership of President Samora Machel who proceeds to initiate a socialist programme of nationalization and farm collectivization. A National Service of Popular Security is set up in October to ensure that a Marxist ideology is followed and that power will stay "in the hands of the workers". Machel tries to avert an economic crisis by forging close economic links with Tanzania and South Africa, but an attempt to freeze army pay leads to political unrest which culminates in an abortive four–day revolt in December by dissident elements of the police and the armed forces.

1976 The situation in neighbouring Rhodesia results in the closure of the frontier with Mozambique in March and the country is put on a war alert. In order to counter Zimbabwean resistance groups operating inside Mozambique, the Rhodesian Central Intelligence Organization sets up the Mozambique Resistance Movement (later known as the MNR or Renamo) and broadcasts anti–Frelimo propaganda via the "Voice of Free Africa". Relations with

Portugal also deteriorate and by June over 250 000 Portuguese nationals have left the country. After a March summit in Lusaka, Machel allows members of the African National Congress (ANC) to settle in Maputo and to pass through Mozambique en route from Tanzania to South Africa via Swaziland. Marxist policies begin to prove unpopular, particularly amongst the Maku and Makonde people in the northern provinces where an estimated 10 000 people are alleged to have been subjected to "people's tribunals" or forced into "re–education camps".

1977 President Machel attempts to extend international links by including Zambia in the Tanzania–Mozambique Joint Co-operation Committee and by (signing a 20–year friendship treaty with the Soviet Union whose president visits the country in March. Frelimo is declared a Marxist–Leninist organization and People's Assemblies are set up from village to national level. Support for the Zimbabwean Patriotic Front nationalist movement led by Joshua Nkomo and Robert Mugabe proves costly when Rhodesian forces penetrate Mozambique to attack guerrilla training and refugee camps. Over 15 000 are reported to be killed in cross-border raids.

1978 In the space of three years since independence the economy of Mozambique has been devastated by nationalization, corruption, the Rhodesian conflict and the flight of Portuguese capital and skill. Agricultural and industrial ouput in that period have fallen by 70 per cent and 75 per cent respectively.

1979 With Rhodesian support, the Mozambique Resistance Movement, led by former Frelimo freedom fighter André Matsangani, begins to focus on strategic targets. Cross–border raids from Rhodesia effectively cut off Maputo from the fertile agricultural land to the north of the Limpopo river and in March a daring raid successfully destroys fuel storage tanks in the port of Beira. Hardline Marxist policies continue to be pursued by the Frelimo government which sends 1150 detainees from Maputo to "re–education camps" in Niassa province

and closes down churches, on the pretext that the Roman Catholic Church is a force for "political and ideological subversion".

1980 After 15 years of sanctions and civil war Southern Rhodesia gains its independence and changes its name to Zimbabwe. Robert Mugabe, the first Prime Minister of independent Zimbabwe, will not support the Mozambique Resistance Movement which now tries to gain a wider appeal within Mozambique by playing on tribal differences and by encouraging opposition to the Frelimo government's southern bias. Despite the destruction of power lines from the Cabora Bassa dam to the Transvaal, it is clear that the MRM is now receiving support from South Africa. As communications between Maputo and Beira are disrupted by guerrilla raids, Machel begins to blame corruption and inefficiency for the growing economic plight of the country. The problems of Mozambique receive international attention when nearly one million people are faced with starvation following a drought in the central provinces.

1981 Relations with both South Africa and the USA deteriorate rapidly. On 29 January South African commandos kill 12 ANC members in Maputo and in December documents are captured linking South Africa with the Mozambique Resistance Movement. The Frelimo government declares itself "ready for war" as Soviet warships arrive in two of the country's ports. US diplomats are expelled when an alleged "spy ring" is uncovered and President Reagan cuts off the supply of food aid. A co-operation agreement with Portugal is signed in May in an attempt by Machel to improve international relations and gain support for his country's failing economy. In the face of growing MRM guerrilla activity aimed at breaking communications between Zimbabwe and the port of Beira, Frelimo tries to stem rural support for rebels by regrouping people in "communal villages" – a process that is described as the "socializing of the countryside".

1982 The 3000–strong Mozambique Resistance Movement, now known as the Mozambique National Resistance (MNR or Renamo), is operational in seven of the country's eleven provinces, but Beira is once again a principal target. In December a guerrilla raid destroys 28 BP fuel tanks in the port. In order to safeguard the road, rail and oil pipeline between Zimbabwe and Beira, troops are sent from Zimbabwe to help patrol the Beira Corridor.

1983   The civil war reaches every province of Mozambique except Cabo Delgado in the far north as the MNR steps up its raids on roads, railways, power supplies, food stores, factories and mines. In April and May they sweep through the province of Zambezia meeting next to no opposition and in December attacks are launched from bases in South Africa's Kruger National Park. The increasing tension between Mozambique and South Africa leads to a meeting between ministers of the two countries in the border town of Komatipoort, but this does not prevent further attacks on ANC targets in Maputo. In an attempt to woo Western support and investment, President Machel removes some of the hardline Marxist ideologues from his cabinet and in October visits Europe. This is enough to persuade President Reagan to resume supplies of food aid to Mozambique.

1984   A further step towards increasing support for the Frelimo government is taken by President Machel in March when he meets South Africa's Prime Minister, P.W. Botha, in Komatipoort. They sign a treaty of "non-agression and good neighbourliness" that comes to be known as the Nkomati Accord. In exchange for South Africa dropping its support for the MNR, Machel agrees to put an end to the transit of ANC members through Mozambique. The immediate result of this agreement is an increase in business activity between the two countries. At the end of the day, however, South Africa is unable to control MNR activities. The so-called Pretoria Declaration of 3 October lays down preconditions for a ceasefire, but MNR leaders refuse to negotiate a peace settlement. An estimated 100 000 die of famine during 1983–84 and Machel is forced to abandon his communal village policy.

1985   By now the civil war has reached the suburbs of Maputo, the power lines from Cabora Bassa are constantly sabotaged and the distribution of food air proves almost impossible. The presence of 10 000 Zimbabwean troops is not enough to prevent raids in the Beira Corridor and the resulting breakdown in communications hits exports which fall by 22 per cent. Despite a successful offensive against MNR bases in the Gorongosa National Park, South African businessmen lose confidence and withdraw from Mozambique.

1986   The MNR is reckoned to control almost 85 per cent of the country while one–third of the population faces starvation. Morale in the armed forces reaches an all–time low as guerrillas recapture their bases in the Gorongosa National Park from where they succeed in launching raids that cut off water and electricity supplies to Beira. Machel warns President Banda of Malawi that he will attack with missiles if MNR rebels continue to operate from bases inside his country. Banda agrees to deny support to the MNR and deploys troops along the vital rail link to the port of Nacala. Frelimo is accused of violating the Nkomati Accord when six South African soldiers are killed during a border incident. In retaliation the South African government withdraws the right of 53 000 Mozambicans to work in South African mines. On 19 October President Machel is killed in a plane crash.

1987   In an attempt to tackle the economic crisis and to restore morale amongst the armed forces, the incoming president, Joaquim Chissano, devalues the currency by 40 per cent and reshuffles the military leadership. A further purge of Marxist ideologues from the cabinet is accompanied by a cooling of the relationship between Maputo and Moscow. The MNR causes international outrage when 380 civilians are killed in a raid on the village of Homoine near Inhambane in July and a further 400 die during ambushes on the road north of Maputo.

1988   The Frelimo government controls little of the country outside the capital and principal cities of Mozambique, but in June an agreement is signed in Lisbon restoring the 800–km hydropower link from Cabora Bassa to South Africa. Prime Minister P.W. Botha of South Africa meets President Chissano on 12 September and both agree to resume the Nkomati Accord. As an act of good will, Botha offers to fund half the cost of restoring and protecting the power line. In the same month Frelimo hostility towards the church is relaxed after Pope John Paul II makes a four–day visit to Mozambique.

1989 The agreement reached between the MPLA government in Angola and Jonas Savimbi's Unita movement gives rise to hope that a similar settlement can be reached in Mozambique. In June President Chissano tries to open negotiations with MNR leaders who are willing to initiate peace talks, but the peace process receives a set back in July when the MNR headquarters in the Gorongosa area is attacked. However, the following month meetings between senior Mozambican clergymen and rebel leaders take place in Nairobi in an attempt to bring Frelimo and the MNR to the negotiating table and in October the presidents of Kenya and Zimbabwe step in to mediate between the two sides urging them to drop preconditions to peace talks.

1990 Facing growing industrial unrest, Joaquim Chissano proposes sweeping constitutional reforms that include direct elections for a fixed–term presidency and legislature.

■ Who's who

Ataide, João da Silva Appointed Secretary–General of the MNR in January 1987 in succession to Evo Fernandes.

Burlison, John British ecologist captured by the MNR and held by them between December 1981 and May 1982. On his release he was able to report that the MNR guerrillas were well organized and capable of stepping up their damaging raids on strategic targets in their bid to dislodge the Frelimo government.

Chissano, Joaquim Alberto Succeeding to the leadership of Mozambique in October 1986 at the age of 47, he came to power following the death of President Machel who was killed in a plane crash. His attempts to restore a failing economy and improve morale amongst the armed forces led him to order a much–needed shake–up of the military command and other senior government posts in the following year. At the same time, he attempted to allay Western fears about Mozambique's Marxist–Leninist policies. A founder member of the Frelimo liberation movement and secretary to Eduardo Mondlane, Chissano served as Prime Minister in the 1974–75 transitional government and as Foreign Minister throughout the presidency of Samora Michel.

Cristina, Orlando MNR leader killed on his farm in the Transvaal in April 1983. Cristina had been invaluable to the resistance movement in forging links with supporters amongst the international white community.

Dhlakama, Afonso Former Portuguese soldier and Frelimo guerrilla fighter who changed his allegiance to the Mozambique National Resistance in 1977. On the death of Orlando Cristina in April 1983, Dhaklama inherited the post of Supreme Military Commander of the 10 000–strong MNR force. In 1989 the 36–year-old rebel leader agreed to take part in peace talks with the Frelimo government providing the MNR was recognized by Chissano.

Fernandes, Evo Former Secretary– General of the MNR found dead in April 1988. A Portuguese of Goan descent, Fernandes was replaced in January 1987 by João da Silva Ataide.

First, Dr Ruth Director of the Centre of African Studies at Eduardo Mondlane University in Maputo and a prominent member of the South African Communist Party and the ANC. In August 1982 she was killed by a letter bomb in one of a series of attacks on ANC members based in Mozambique.

Flower, Ken Chief of the Rhodesian Central Intelligence Organization responsible, in 1977, for setting up the Mozambique National Resistance as a means of sabotaging attempts by Frelimo to help the Zimbabwean resistance movement.

Fondo, Major–General Domingos Appointed commander of the Border Guard Troops in the military leadership reshuffle of June 1987, he was charged with the task of preventing the infiltration of MNR guerrillas into Mozambique from South Africa and Malawi.

Gersony, Robert Consultant to the US State Department's Bureau for Refugees responsible for exposing the scale of the atrocities committed by MNR guerrillas during a three–month survey in Mozambique in 1988.

Machel, Samora Moises (1933–86) President of Mozambique from independence in 1975 until his death in a plane crash in October 1986. At the age of 20 he crossed the border into Tanzania to join the Frelimo liberation movement and set up the first training camp for resistance guerrillas. A year later he led a 250–man unit into Mozambique to begin the armed struggle against Portuguese colonial rule. In 1968 he became Commander–in–Chief and in May 1970 President of Frelimo. In the post–independence years the country's crippling civil war forced him to turn first to the Soviet bloc for arms and advice, and then to the West.

Mabote, General Sebastiao Army Chief of Staff dismissed by President Chissano and replaced by General Antonio Hama Thai during the military command shake–up in 1987.

Machungo, Mario Appointed Prime Minister of Mozambique in July 1986, a position he retained after the death of President Machel in September of that year.

Matsangani, André A former Frelimo freedom fighter who became leader of the Mozambique Resistance Movement after the country gained its independence.

Mondlane, Eduardo Founder of the Frelimo liberation movement which was established in Tanzania in 1962.

Thai, General Antonio Hama Following a successful offensive against MNR guerrillas in the central province of Zambezia, General Thai was appointed Chief of Staff of the armed forces during President Chissano's military command shake–up in 1987.

Vieira, Sergio Minister of Security in the Mozambique government of Samora Machel. His radically pro–Soviet stance resulted in his dismissal from the cabinet in January 1987 not long after Joaquim Chissano took over the leadership of the country.

■ Key places

Beira Seaport capital of the province of Sofala, central Mozambique; situated on the Mozambique Channel at the mouths of the Buzi and Pungué rivers, 725km NNE of Maputo. Population (1986) 279 600. The Portuguese first established a trading post here in the early years of the 16th century and in 1891 the Mozambique Company developed the site as a natural harbour from which to export produce from the interior. Port facilities, hydro–electric stations, fuel stores and local industries, which include textile manufacture, food processing and hardware production, have been hard hit by MNR guerrilla raids since 1979.

Beira Corridor The name given to the 698–km route between Harare, capital of landlocked Zimbabwe, and the Mozambique port of Beira which is a major trade outlet to the Indian Ocean. A road and railway run almost parallel to each other all the way from Beira to Harare and an oil pipeline runs from Beira to the border town of Mutare. The importance to Zimbabwe of this communication link is demonstrated by that country's willingness to deploy over 10 000 troops to protect the Mozambique stretch of the Beira corridor from MNR sabotage raids.

Cabora Bassa or **Quebrabasa** Africa's largest hydro–electric scheme, created as a result of the damming of the Zambezi river to form a great reservoir that stretches 230km W–E from the Mozambique frontier at Zumbo to the town of Songo, north-west of Tete. The Cabora Bassa Dam was the meeting place on 12 September 1988 of South African Prime Minister P.W. Botha and President Chissano of Mozambique. Here the two leaders agreed to resume the 1984 Nkomati Accord and re-establish the hydropower line to South Africa.

Gorongosa A national park in the water catchment area of the Urema and Mucombeze rivers in Sofala province, central Mozambique. Established in 1940, the park covers an area of 3770km². From a guerrilla base, established here in 1979, the MNR have been able to launch   attacks on strategic targets that include installations in the port of Beira which lies to the south east.

Homoine A small town 25km west of the port of Inhambane in southern Mozambique. Scene of the massacre of 380 civilians during an MNR guerrilla raid in July 1987.

Inhambane Seaport and capital of a province of the same name in southern Mozambique, 370km north–east of Maputo. Population (1980) 56 000.

Komatipoort or **Nkomati** A town at the southern tip of the Kruger National Park in E Transvaal; situated on the river Komati where it passes through a 185–metre–deep gorge close to the frontier between South Africa and Mozambique. On 16 March 1984 the Nkomati Accord was signed here by President Samora Machel of Mozambique and Prime Minister P.W. Botha of South Africa.

Kruger National Park A South African national park stretching along the frontier between E Transvaal and Mozambique from

the town of Komatipoort in the south to the Limpopo river in the north. Established in 1926 and named after former President Kruger(1825–1904), the park covers an area of 19 485 km². Following the independence of Zimbabwe in 1980, MNR guerrillas began to raid strategic targets in southern Mozambique from bases set up with South African support in the Kruger National Park.

Limpopo The Limpopo river rises north of Johannesburg in South Africa and flows in a great sweep around the Transvaal border until it meets the Mozambique frontier at the northern tip of the Kruger National Park. Once inside Mozambique, it flows in a south–easterly   direction through fertile agricultural land before emptying into the sea near the town of Xai–Xai. The Limpopo Railway, stretching 522km from Maputo to the frontier town of Chicualacuala and on as far as Harare (a further 747km), is an alternative route from Zimbabwe to the Indian Ocean. Although much longer than the Harare–Beira route, the Limpopo Railway provides a convenient outlet for goods from southern Zimbabwe and other front–line states including Zambia and Zaire. The transport of goods by this route has been drastically reduced as a result of MNR guerrilla activity.

Maputo Seaport capital of Mozambique, situated in the south of the country on an inlet of the Indian Ocean. First visited by the Portuguese navigator Antonio do Campo in 1502, the trading settlement that developed came to be known as Lourenço Marques, the name of another Portuguese trader and explorer. In 1907 the city became capital of Portuguese East Africa and following independence from Portugal it changed its name to Maputo in 1976. The civil war waged between the Frelimo government and MNR guerrillas after 1975 led to rural depopulation and the swelling of Maputo's population from a figure of 750 000 in 1980 to an estimated total of 882 800 in 1986.

Mutare A mining town and capital of the Zimbabwean province of Manicaland; situated on the frontier between Zimbabwe and Mozambique at the W terminus of an oil pipeline linked to the port of Beira. Formerly known as Umtali, the town has a population of 70 000.

Nacala   A small deep–water port in Nampula province, N Mozambique, linked by rail to the Malawi frontier 615km to the west. In 1986 Malawi deployed troops along the Nacala Railway to protect it from MNR guerrilla raids. A French consortium employing Portuguese and Canadian interests restored large parts of the line which was reopened in May 1989 after Afonso Dhaklama, the MNR leader, declared his insurgents would not attack the Nacala corridor while peace negotiations were in progress. In return for halting attacks on the railway line Dhaklama was allowed to travel through Malawi to Kenya to take part in peace talks.

Nampula   Capital of a province of the same name in N Mozambique; situated on the railway

that links Malawi with the Indian Ocean port of Nacala. Population (1986) 182 500.

Tete   Capital of a province of the same name in NW Mozambique; situated at the head of river navigation on the Zambezi. The town developed as a river outlet for coal, diamonds, gold and other minerals discovered in the interior. Population (1980) 45 000.

Zambezi   One of the principal rivers of SE Africa. Rising in NW Zambia it flows a distance of 2 700km in a great arc through E Angola, W and S Zambia, and central Mozambique before emptying into the Mozambique Channel between Quelimane and Beira. At the Victoria Falls, the river separates Zimbabwe from Zambia to the north. The Zambezi is dammed at Kariba and Cabora Bassa to create major sources of hydro–electric power.

■ Key words

Defence Systems Limited   A private British company using former SAS personnel to train Frelimo government troops to defend strategic targets such as power lines and railroads against MNR guerrilla attacks.

Front Line States   Those southern African states within the sphere of influence of South Africa, namely: Mozambique, Angola, Botswana, Lesotho, Swaziland, Malawi, Tanzania, Zambia and Zimbabwe.

Gersony Report   A report compiled in 1988 by Robert Gersony, consultant to the US State Department's Bureau for Refugee Programs, accusing the MNR guerrillas of systematic and brutal violence against civilians. His three–month survey in Mozambique reassured the US administration that, despite Marxist leanings, the Frelimo government could be supported in its move towards developing ties with the West.

Makua   A Bantu ethnic group occupying that part of Mozambique lying to the north–east of the Zambezi river. Under the Marxist Frelimo government, the Makonde were subjected to extensive "political tribunals" and "re-education".

Malawi   The principal Bantu ethnic group occupying the valley of the Zambezi river.

Mozambique Liberation Front (Frente de Libertação de Moçambique–Frelimo)   A Marxist liberation movement founded by Eduardo Mondlane in 1962 with the aim of freeing Mozambique from Portuguese colonial rule. Its first guerrilla training camp was set up in Tanzania in 1963 by Samora Machel who led armed units across the border into Mozambique in 1964. Following the independence of the country in 1975, Frelimo took control of Mozambique. Two years later Frelimo was reconstituted as the sole legal political party.

Mozambique National Resistance (MNR or Renamo) A right-wing rebel movement opposed to the Marxist Frelimo government of Mozambique. Originally known as the Mozambique Resistance Movement (MRM), the organization was founded in 1977 by the Rhodesian intelligence service as a means of gathering information and sabotaging possible Frelimo support for black resistance groups based in Zimbabwe. The first units were allegedly set up under the direction of the Portuguese Grupos Especiais and the Rhodesian Selous Scouts. Opposed by the government of Robert Mugabe following the independence of Zimbabwe in 1980, the rebels turned to South Africa for support in waging a brutal civil war in Mozambique that has crippled the country's economy and claimed the lives of an estimated 600 000 people in the space of 14 years.

Mozambican Research Center An information office maintained by the MNR movement on Capitol Hill, Washington DC, where the movement has received support from right-wing Congressmen such as Jessie Helms.

National Service of Popular Security A Marxist organization set up by President Machel following independence in 1975 in order to ensure that power stayed in the hands of the workers.

Nkomati Accord An agreement signed on 16 March 1984 by President Samora Machel of Mozambique and Prime Minister P.W. Botha of South Africa who met in the border town of Komatipoort. In exchange for efforts to ensure the withdrawal of South African backing of MNR guerrilla activities, the Frelimo government agreed to abandon its support of the ANC and withdraw the right of transit to ANC members travelling through Mozambique into South Africa via Swaziland.

Pretoria Declaration The name given to a statement made by the South African government on 30 October 1984 in which preconditions for a ceasefire and peace negotiations between MNR guerrillas and Frelimo government forces were laid down. MNR rejection of these conditions clearly showed that the Pretoria government could not control MNR activities as it had promised in the Nkomati Accord.

Railway Security Battalion A special unit of the 30 000–strong Mozambique army set up to ensure the security of vital installations. This was one of the few special forces to maintain discipline during a period of low morale that preceded President Chissano's military command shake–up in June 1987.

red berets Soviet–trained special forces spearheading the Frelimo offensive against MNR guerrillas in northern Mozambique.

Shona The principal Bantu ethnic group occupying the central provinces of Mozambique between Zimbabwe and the coast and north of the Save river.

Southern African Development Co-ordination Conference (SADCC) An organization formed by the nine Front Line African states which united in 1979 to liberate their economies from dependence on South Africa, an aim defined by the Lusaka Declaration of April 1980. As a member of SADCC, Mozambique took responsibility for co-ordinating policy in the transport sector. The headquarters of the SADCC is in Gabarone, Botswana.

Tiger Battalion An elite military force guarding the European Community–backed agricultural project near Maputo.

Tsonga The principal Bantu ethnic group in southern Mozambique to the south of the Save river.

União Nacional Africana da Rombezia (UNAR) A Mozambique secessionist movement founded in the 1960s with the aim of creating a separate state north of the Zambezi river. The organization was later thought to have been backed by former Portuguese colonists living in South Africa.

Yao The principal ethnic group occupying territory in the far north of Mozambique to the east of Lake Nyasa in Niassa province.

■ Further reading

C. Darch, *Mozambique*, Clio, Oxford, 1987

T.H. Henriksen, *Revolution and Counter-revolution: Mozambique's War of Independence 1964–74*, Greenwood, Westport, 1983

A. and B. Isaacman, *Mozambique: From Colonialism to Revolution, 1900–1982*, Westview Press, Boulder, 1983

Keith Middlemas, *Cabora Bassa: Engineering and Politics in Southern Africa*, Weidenfeld and Nicolson, London, 1975

E. Mondlane, *The Struggle for Mozambique*, Zed, London, 1983

B. Munslow, *Mozambique: The Revolution and its Origins*, London and New York, 1983

B. Munslow (ed.), *Samora Machel, an African Revolutionary: Selected Speeches and Writings*, Zed, London, 1985

6
South Africa

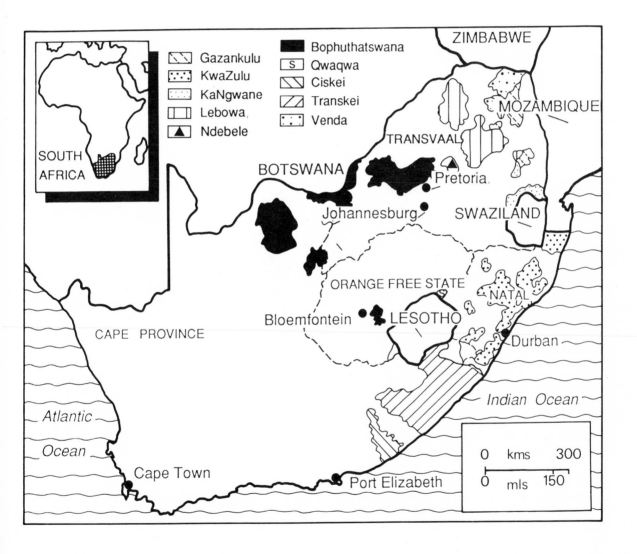

■ Profile

Official name: Republic of South Africa
- **Area:** 1 221 040 km²
- **Population (1988 est.):** 35 million
- **Ethnic groups:** Whites 17.8%, Asians 2.9%, Coloureds 9.4%, Africans 69.9%
- **Official languages:** Afrikaans, English
- **Average monthly household income (rand):** Whites 1958, Asians 1109, Coloureds 680, Africans 352
- **Infant mortality rate (per 1000):** Whites 13, Asians 24, Coloureds 60, Africans 80
- **Life expectancy (years):** Whites 71, Asians 67, Coloureds 61, Africans 48
- **Administrative divisions:** 4 provinces; 6 "national states" and 4 "independent republics"
- **Currency:** rand of 100 cents
- **Timezone:** GMT +2
- **Capital cities:** Pretoria (administrative), Cape Town (legislative), Bloemfontein (judicial)

■ Introduction

South Africa is by no means alone in the modern world in being deeply divided by race. Such divisions are a key factor in the political and social life of many countries and often a source of bloody conflict. Nor is domination by one ethnic group over others uncommon, least of all in black Africa. Nevertheless, the South African situation has special characteristics which combine to make it unique. The dominant race is a white minority and the subject majority mostly black, in a continent whose other black peoples had all achieved independence by early 1990. Most blacks see white supremacy in South Africa as a legacy of the European colonization of Africa, with all the emotional overtones which that episode still generates. Moreover, white domination has been enshrined in a legal system of racial segregation (*apartheid*) that has been applied more rigorously than any other modern institutionalization of racial discrimination. The overall effect has been to make South Africa a major source of regional instability, arising not only from the country's internal strife but also from its confrontation externally with neighbouring black-ruled states seeking the overthrow of the *apartheid* system.

The contention that South Africa is a colonial problem is rejected by most whites, especially by the dominant Afrikaners of Dutch ancestry, once known as Boers. Described as "the white tribe of Africa", the Boers settled the Cape in the 17th century and began migrating northwards in the 18th century, meeting Zulus and other black tribes moving southwards. Afrikaners therefore contend that blacks have no greater historical claim to the South African hinterland than whites of Boer stock. The real colonialists, say the Afrikaners, were the British, who acquired the Cape from the Dutch in the Napoleonic Wars and thereafter sought to dominate Boers and blacks alike. The abolition of slavery in the British Empire in 1834 was particularly resented by Boers long accustomed to using black slaves on their farms. Boer resistance to such British interference precipitated 19th-century treks further north to settle new lands; and if this was at the expense of local tribes, the migration was, in the Afrikaner view, no different from, say, the Arab conquest of North Africa. Afrikaners also lay stress on the Boers' long conflict with the British, whose imperialist designs were sharpened by the discovery of gold and diamonds in Boer lands. The confrontation led to the Boer Wars of 1881 and 1899–1902, from which the British emerged victorious and the Boers an impoverished subject people.

Having secured the whole of South Africa for the Empire, the British later had some success in reconciling the Afrikaners to British rule. But one consequence was that the rights of non-whites, to which the British had hitherto given some recognition, disappeared from the political agenda. When the Union of South Africa achieved full legal independence in 1931, white rule, and the subordination of blacks and other non-whites, were assumed to be the natural order of things, despite the protests of early black nationalist movements. The post-1945 change in the international climate in favour of the freedom of subject peoples left most South African whites unmoved. In 1948 the Afrikaners at last gained revenge for the Boer War by electing (with much non-Afrikaner white support) a National Party (NP) government committed to implementing their vision of the country's future. This was *apartheid*, which meant enforced segregation and "separate development" of whites and non-whites, on the grounds that the economic and social gulf between the races made integration impossible. The flaw was that non-whites, forming the great majority of the population, were never consulted about this scenario. The inevitable result was the development of armed resistance by blacks through their evolving political organizations. Of these, the African National Congress (ANC) became dominant and its activists came in for increasingly harsh treatment from the South African security forces.

As the post-1948 NP government erected the full panoply of *apartheid* laws, the price paid was isolation and ostracism in the international community. South Africa's enforced exit from the Commonwealth in 1961, a year after the infamous Sharpeville massacre, symbolized the country's new pariah status. But the government remained impervious to external criticism and also to the wind of change bringing independence to much of black Africa. During the 1960s and early 1970s South Africa formed the linchpin of continuing white rule south of the Zambezi, in Portuguese Angola and Mozambique, white-ruled Rhodesia (Zimbabwe) and the Pretoria-controlled

former German colony of South West Africa (Namibia). Internally, the logic of *apartheid* was pursued with the creation of several "independent" Bantu homelands which were supposed to cater for black national aspirations (although whites retained the lion's share of land, and economic necessity dictated that most blacks remained in white areas). Externally, South Africa used its superior military and economic strength to harass and destabilize neighbouring black-ruled states harbouring ANC and Namibian guerrillas. When, by 1980, Angola, Mozambique and Zimbabwe had all won independence on the basis of majority rule, South Africa seemed even more determined to defend its remaining redoubts. To this end, it was reported to have developed a nuclear weapons capability, possibly in co-operation with Israel.

Erratic international sanctions failed to inflict any serious damage on South Africa's economy. Britain's post-1979 Conservative government declined to tighten the screw, and South African minerals remained of great strategic importance to the West. The Pretoria regime also had the advantage of being perceived by the US government as a bulwark against Soviet-inspired communist encroachment in southern Africa. Nevertheless, deepening economic recession and the steady withdrawal of Western companies, combined with a growing black insurgency, forced the white establishment to contemplate change. A new constitution in 1984 gave limited political rights to South Africa's Indian and coloured communities, but this "divide and rule" tactic only served to increase the hostility of the excluded blacks. The gradual abolition of "petty *apartheid*" laws likewise failed to ease internal tensions. The reaction of hardline whites was to advocate a strengthening of the "bunker", even to the extent of partitioning the country into separate white and black states. But the white mainstream, faced with the prospect of endless siege conditions, came to understand the potential benefits of a reconciliation of black aspirations with white interests. The conclusion in 1988 of a Namibian independence agreement, on the basis of the withdrawal of Soviet-sponsored Cuban troops from Angola, assisted this evolution in white attitudes. Thus when F.W. de Klerk succeeded to the presidency in 1989 he was able to take the momentous step of announcing the release of long-gaoled ANC leader Nelson Mandela and proposing talks on a new constitutional framework based on racial equality rather than apartheid.

Despite the euphoria generated by Mandela's release in February 1990, it quickly became clear that an internal settlement would not be easy to achieve. Hardline Afrikaners condemned de Klerk's initiative as a sellout of the white heritage and demanded an immediate general election to test white opinion. Among the black population, tribal and political divisions escalated into violent conflict, mainly between ANC supporters and the more conservative Zulu Inkatha movement. Amid the mounting violence, moroever, the South African security forces showed themselves to be as ruthless as ever in dealing with black demonstrators. Much therefore depended on the statesmanship not only of de Klerk but also, more crucially, of Nelson Mandela. Only these two leaders appeared to have the necessary stature to lead their respective peoples towards a new constitutional era for South Africa.

■ Chronology of events

1652   The Dutch East India Company establishes a refreshment station on the site of present-day Cape Town for ships en route to the Spice Islands. Fresh meat is obtained by trading with indigenous Hottentots and Bushmen who occupy the hinterland as far north as the Orange River.

1688–94   The population of Cape Town is augmented by the arrival of several hundred French Huguenot refugees who have escaped from the religious persecutions of Louis XIV.

1770s   Dutch farmers begin to move north-eastwards and encounter Zulus migrating southwards.

1795   The Dutch surrender the Cape to the British in order to prevent it falling into the hands of the French.

1803   Under the terms of the Treaty of Amiens the British return the Cape to the Dutch.

1806   The Dutch again surrender to the British.

1807   The slave trade is abolished throughout the British Empire. This creates a problem in South Africa where slaves have been imported for over a century to work on Dutch cattle farms.

1809   The movement of the Hottentots is legally restricted in order to force them to work for white farmers.

1814   The Treaty of Paris gives Britain outright possession of the Cape in exchange for a payment of 6 000 000 in compensation to the Dutch.

1820   Four thousand British colonists settle on the east coast.

1822   English replaces Dutch as the official language.

1828   The old Dutch judicial system is replaced by a British judiciary.

A missionary, Dr John Philip, advocates the segregation of the Hottentots. Through his efforts, an ordinance is passed removing earlier restrictions placed on Hottentots who are now allowed to buy land.

1834   Slavery is abolished throughout the British Empire and 35 000 slaves are freed in South Africa.

1835–37   Annoyed by restrictions placed on them by the British, 10 000 Dutch farmers set out on the Great Trek in search of freedom and new land. One group led by Andries H. Potgieter crosses the Vaal River into present-day Transvaal, while another group under Piet Retief crosses the Drakensberg mountains into Zululand and Natal.

Ancestors of South Africa's present–day Bantu–speaking population, who had occupied most of South Africa north of the Orange River by the end of the 18th century, continue their migration southwards.

1838 The Dutch Boers led by Andreas Pretorius defeat Dingaan, king of the Zulus, at the Battle of Blood River.

1843 In order to protect the indigenous population, Natal becomes a British colony and Basutoland becomes a native state under British protection. Many Boers again object to British interference and decide to move northwards into Transvaal.

1846 A location commission in Natal sets up preserves for immigrant Zulus in what amounts to a policy of native segregation.

1852 The British government under the Sand River Convention recognizes the independence of the Transvaal.

1853 A new constitution for the Cape Colony extends the franchise to all British subjects, black or white.

1854 The British withdraw from the territory north of the Orange River and the Boer settlers set up the independent Orange Free State.

1856 A South African Republic is created in the Transvaal under Marthinus Pretorius.

1860 The first of a large number of labourers is imported from India to work in the sugar plantations of Natal.

1867 Diamonds are discovered near Hopetown on the Orange River.

1871 The British government angers the Boers by annexing the diamond region of Griqualand West.

1877 In order to get protection against the Zulus, Boer leaders agree to the British annexation of the South African Republic. This action, which is part of a British strategy designed to bring about the federation of the South African colonies, leads to the development of an Afrikaner nationalist movement.

1879 A Zulu war waged against the British ends when a peace agreement is made with Zulu chiefs in September.

Anti–British Boer nationalism is enhanced by the formation of the Afrikander Bond.

1880–81 The Boer farmers of the Transvaal revolt against the British who are defeated at Majuba Hill in February. Independence is restored to the South African Republic (Transvaal) by the Convention of Pretoria.

1884 Nominal British suzerainty over the Transvaal is abandoned.

1886 Gold is discovered in the Witwatersrand region of southern Transvaal and by September Johannesburg is established.

1899–1902 Britain tries to prevent the South African states from uniting under the Boers who then declare war on the British. The Boers eventually concede defeat in the Peace of Vereeniging of 31 May 1902 on being promised representative institutions and compensation.

1902 The first black African political movement is created with the founding of the African People's Organization (APO) by Dr Abdullah Abdurahman.

1906 The British government, accepting that it cannot impose its supremacy over Boer–populated areas, grants self–government to Transvaal and Orange Free State.

1908–09 British and Boer settlers bury their differences and agree to the formation of a Union of South Africa with English and Dutch as the official languages. The rights of South Africa's black and Asian populations are not considered.

1910 The Union of South Africa is created under the premiership of   General Louis Botha. Although formally a Dominion within the British Empire, it is virtually independent. White supremacy is established with the election of an all–white parliament.

1911 Under the Mines and Works Act, black miners are not allowed to obtain certificates of competence for blasting operations and are therefore excluded from higher paid jobs.

1912 The South African Native African National Congress, a forerunner of the African National Congress, is formed to fight for the political rights of black Africans.

1913 An Immigration Act restricting the movement of Asians leads to rioting.

In June the policy of segregation is extended with the passing of a Bantu Land Act which restricts the purchase of land by Bantu–speaking Africans and fixes the boundaries of tribally-occupied "reserves". Because these reserves are not capable of supporting more than half of those living in them, black Africans effectively become a source of cheap labour.

1914 The National Party is founded by Afrikaners opposed to the ruling South Africa Party's "united white nation" policy. It advocates the preservation of Afrikaans– and English–speaking identities.

1920 A native affairs commission is set up to tackle the problems of the African population, a large proportion of which has been detribalized and settled as labourers working for white farmers or mine owners.

1923 Further segregation of black and white communities takes place with the passing of the Natives (Urban Areas) Act. This virtually deprives Africans of the right to live in towns unless their services are required by whites. Africans are obliged to occupy poor quality housing in townships outside the major conurbations.

1924 The National Party begins a nine–year term of government in coalition with the Labour Party. During this period Afrikaans replaces Dutch as the second official language and colour bar legislation is enacted.

1931 The Union of South Africa achieves full legal independence from Britain.

1934 The National and South Africa parties merge to form the United Party, but hardline nationalists led by Dr. D.F. Malan reject the merger.

1936 The Representation of Natives Act allows Africans to retain their vote in Cape Province but only permits them to vote for white representatives in the Union Parliament.

A Bantu Trust and Land Act reinforces and extends the 1913 Act allowing 6 209 857 hectares of land to be added to the African reserves. The land area now assigned to black Africans, who constitute 70 per cent of the population, amounts to only 13 per cent of South Africa's total area.

1939 On the outbreak of World War II, the pro–neutrality Afrikaner minority of the United Party rejoins Dr. Malan's National Party in protest against South Africa's declaration of war on Britain's side. During the war many Afrikaners openly support the Nazi cause.

1948 In a general election held in May, Dr Daniel F. Malan's Nationalist Party sweeps into power on a platform of racial segregation or *apartheid*.

1949 The new government begins to institutionalize the segregation of black and white communities by introducing a series of acts that include measures to prevent mixed marriages, to control African migration, to extend white job reservation and to apply racial segregation to all public places.

1950 The passing of the Group Areas Act legalizes residential segregation by assigning separate areas to the different races of South Africa. This leads to demonstrations and race riots.

1952 The Supreme Court invalidates much of the race legislation of the Nationalist government but has its powers restricted by parliament. Demonstrations continue to encourage the defiance of the race laws.

1953 A Bantu Education Act requires that Africans be educated separately and ensures that they will not be educated for positions in the white–dominated society.

1955 Opposition to *apartheid* is advanced when members of the African National Congress, South African Indian Congress, Coloured People's Political Organization and White Congress of Democrats meet in Kliptown to draw up a "Freedom Charter" laying down the principles for a non–racial, democratic society.

1956 Voting rights granted to Cape Province Africans in 1853 and 1936 are removed and over 60 000 persons are taken off the voters' roll. In August an estimated 100 000 black Africans are ordered to leave their homes in Johannesburg to make way for whites.

In December a National People's Congress is broken up and 156 black leaders, including Nelson Mandela, are arrested and charged with treason. All are acquitted after a trial that lasts five years.

1958 With most of their leaders under arrest, a number of ANC supporters break away to form the Pan–Africanist Congress.

1959 A Promotion of Bantu Self–Government Act attempts to consolidate the 264 separate Bantu national units into a united black African homeland.

1960 On 21 March 69 Africans are killed in the black township of Sharpeville when police open fire on a crowd demonstrating against the pass laws. A month later parliament bans the African National Congress and the Pan–Africanist Congress.

1961 South Africa severs its ties with the British Commonwealth to become an independent republic. The banned ANC and PAC movements launch guerrilla campaigns against white minority rule.

1962 Nelson Mandela is arrested and charged with sabotage and plotting to overthrow the government.

1963 The UN Security Council calls for a ban on the shipment of arms to South Africa until racist policies are brought to an end.

1964 A Bantu Laws Amendment Act helps consolidate existing *apartheid* legislation by empowering the Minister responsible for Bantu administration to declare "prescribed areas" in which the number of black Africans can be regulated.

Nelson Mandela and seven other African leaders are sentenced to life imprisonment after a two–year trial.

1966 President Verwoerd, the architect of "grand apartheid", is assassinated on 6 September.

The former British colony of Basutoland gains full independence as Lesotho.

1968 A Prohibition of Political Interference Act prevents whites, black Africans, coloureds and Asians from participating in each other's political organizations.

Landlocked Swaziland becomes independent within the British Commonwealth under the leadership of King Sobhuza II who attempts to pursue a non–racist policy.

1972 With an economy running out of skilled white workers, Prime Minister Vorster opts for the training of black Africans into semi–skilled positions. This is the first step in the slow erosion of *apartheid*.

1976 Transkei is declared an independent homeland. Meanwhile, in the black township of Soweto, thousands of students demonstrate against a requirement that lessons be taught in Afrikaans. Police shoot dead several students and spark off a nation-wide series of riots that lasts for nearly a year during which 575 black Africans lose their lives. Students, now a major force in South African politics, form a number of groups that are known collectively as the Black Consciousness Movement.

1977 Bophuthatswana becomes an independent homeland of the Tswana people.

Steve Biko, founder of the Black Consciousness Movement, dies in police custody on 12 September. A month later, restrictions are placed on 18 African organizations and two newspapers are banned.

Commonwealth heads of government, meeting at Gleneagles in Scotland, agree to impose economic and sporting sanctions in an attempt to isolate South Africa.

1979 Venda is the third Bantu area to be designated an independent homeland.

1980 At a Transvaal National Party congress on 1 September, Prime Minister P.W. Botha concedes that the black homelands cannot be consolidated to form sufficiently independent economic units since less than 20 per cent of people's income is derived from their own immediate area.

1981 Ciskei is the fourth Bantu area to become an independent homeland.

1982 Black local councils are created under the Black Local Government Act.

1983 In September riots break out in Sharpeville in a year that sees 262 904 arrests for contravention of the pass laws, 105 000 arrests for trespass and nearly 11 000 prosecutions for curfew offences. The riots in Sharpeville ignite three years of violence that leads to the death of an estimated 2 500 black Africans.

The United Democratic Front (UDF) is launched as a political opposition to the proposed creation of a tricameral parliament that still excludes blacks from the political process. This party quickly becomes the largest legal anti-apartheid organization in South Africa.

1984 A new constitution inaugurates limited power–sharing with coloureds and Asians but not with black Africans. Elections for the two non–white chambers take place in August amidst a background of black violence that

reaches a climax on the anniversary of the Sharpeville massacre.

President Samora Machel agrees to curb ANC guerrilla activity from bases sinside Mozambique (Nkomati Accord).

1985 Violence continues and in July a state of emergency is declared. The Urban Areas Act is amended in order to restrict the movement of blacks by preventing them from remaining more than 72 hours in prescribed areas.

Western banks halt all new loans to South Africa and demand repayment of $14 billion in short–term loans. At the same time, at least 39 American firms withdraw from South Africa in the face of growing international opposition to *apartheid*.

1986 In March President P.W.Botha lifts the state of emergency that has existed in South Africa since July 1985. In the period September 1984 – March 1986 over 1000 people have died.

Under pressure from the US Congress, President Reagan abandons the US policy of constructive engagement and announces a package of economic sanctions against South Africa. Britain, which accounts for nearly half of the country's foreign investment, reluctantly joins other Commonwealth countries in adopting sanctions as a means of bringing apartheid to an end.

1988 The UDF and 17 other opposition parties are banned by the government.

1989 In July Mr Botha opens talks with the jailed ANC leader, Nelson Mandela, but a month later Botha is replaced by F.W. de Klerk who says he will allow peaceful anti-apartheid protests. Large demonstrations in all major cities pass without incident. In August the OAU's Harare Declaration sets out the ANC's pro–negotiations stance. In October six ANC leaders, including Walter Sisulu, are released after 25 years in prison. In December Mr. de Klerk invites Nelson Mandela to the President's office for talks.

1990   On 2 February de Klerk legalizes the ANC and many other banned opposition groups. Nine days later international media attention focuses on the release of the 71–year–old ANC leader Nelson Mandela who walks free after 28 years in prison.

Despite the release of Mandela, divisions within the anti-apartheid movement are heightened by violence in Natal where members of the Zulu Inkatha movement clash with supporters of the United Democratic Front.

■ Who's who

Biko, Steve   Student leader of the Black Consciousness Movement. Biko's death from injuries received while in custody raised an international outcry against the racialist policies of the South African government in 1977.

Botha, Pieter Willem   Born in 1916, P.W. Botha was leader of the Nationalist Party between 1978 and 1989. From 1978 until 1984 he was prime minister of South Africa and from 1984 until he retired in 1989 he was state president. During his term of office limited social and political reforms were introduced as a first step towards accommodating the black African majority.

Buthelezi, Chief Gatsha   South African Zulu leader and Chief Executive of the tribal homeland of KwaZulu. A chief of the Buthelezi tribe since 1953, he was elected leader of Zululand in 1970 and Prime Minister of KwaZulu in 1972. As leader of the predominantly Zulu Inkatha anti-apartheid movement he has opposed the use of violence.

de Klerk, Frederik Willem   Born in 1936, F.W. de Klerk became a lawyer before entering politics in 1972. He was Minister of Education during the 1976 Soweto riots. Following the resignation of P.W. Botha, de Klerk was appointed President in 1989. Within months of taking office he legalized the ANC and released from prison a number of black nationalist leaders including Nelson Mandela.

Goldberg, Dean   Leader of the South African Communist Party, arrested on a charge of treason with Nelson Mandela and imprisoned for a period of 22 years between 1963 and 1985.

Hani, Chris   Army commissioner of the ANC's military wing.

Mandela, Nelson Rolihlala   A South African lawyer and politician born in 1918 in Transkei. The son of a chief of the Tembu tribe, Mandela practised law in Johannesburg before becoming national organizer of the ANC. Arrested in 1956 and tried for treason, he was acquitted in 1961 but arrested again a year later and charged with sabotage. In June 1964 he was sentenced to life imprisonment but in February 1990 after 28 years in custody he was released. Nelson Mandela has symbolized the struggle for freedom against white minority rule and *apartheid* by the black majority in South Africa.

Mandela, Winnie   After Nelson Mandela was imprisoned on Robben Island in 1962, the struggle against *apartheid* in South Africa was epitomized by the defiance of his wife, Winnie Mandela.

Manuel, Trevor   Secretary–General of the anti–apartheid United Democratic Front movement in Cape Town.

Mothopeng, Zeph   President of the Pan–Africanist Congress. Born in 1914, Mothopeng is opposed to the multiracial approach of Nelson Mandela.

Nzo, Alfred   Secretary–General and chief spokesman of the ANC.

Ramaphosa, Cyril   Leader of the Mass Democratic Movement and head of the black National Union of Mineworkers. Born in 1953.

Sisulu, Albertina President of the United Democratic Front.

Sisulu, Walter Max Born in 1916, Walter Sisulu worked variously as a gold miner in the Rand and as a baker in Johannesburg before joining the ANC. Between 1949 and 1954 he was Secretary–General of the ANC. Arrested and charged with treason in 1956, he was acquitted in 1961 but again arrested for organizing a national strike. In June 1964 he was found guilty of sabotage and imprisoned for a period of 25 years.

Slovo, Joe Leader of the South African Communist Party and a member of the ANC Committee who returned to South Africa in 1990 after 30 years in exile.

Suzman, Helen An outspoken opposition member of the South African parliament since 1953 and a member of the South African Institute of Race Relations. During the period 1944–52 she lectured in the Department of Economics and Economic History in the University of Witwatersrand.

Tambo, Oliver President of the ANC since 1977. Born in 1917, Tambo worked as a solicitor in Johannesburg between 1951 and 1960. In 1956 he was arrested and charged with treason, but was released a year later. Between 1958 and 1967 he was Deputy President of the ANC. Tambo's leading role in the ANC took a setback in 1989 when he suffered a stroke.

Terreblanche, Eugene Neo–Nazi leader of the far right Afrikaner Resistance Movement.

Tutu, Most Reverend Desmond Mpilo An outspoken member of the anti-apartheid movement in South Africa. Born in Klerksdorp in 1931, Desmond Tutu served as Dean of Johannesburg in 1975–76 before becoming Bishop of Lesotho. He returned to Johannesburg in 1984 where he remained as Bishop for two years until his appointment as Bishop of Cape Town in 1986. In 1984 he was awarded the Nobel Peace Prize.

Verwoerd, Hendrik Frensch Prime minister of South Africa during the period 1958–66, Verwoerd was an advocate of white supremacy and the architect of "grand apartheid." During his term of office South Africa became a republic outside the Commonwealth and race riots led to the banning of black nationalist movements including the ANC. Verwoerd was assassinated in 1966.

Viljoen, Gerrit Born in 1926, Viljoen was appointed Minister of Constitutional Development by President de Klerk in 1989. In this position he became the South African government's chief political negotiator with the black majority. Viljoen was formerly a professor and chairman of the secret Broederbond.

Vorster, Balthazar Johannes Leader of the National Party and prime minister of South Africa after the assassination of Verwoerd in 1966. Born in 1915, he was first elected to parliament in 1953. He later served as Justice Minister (1961–66). During his term of office, Voster began to improve relations with South Africa's black majority. In 1978 he retired on grounds of ill health and served as President until a scandal forced his resignation in 1979.

■ Key places

Agulhas, Cape ("needles") The southernmost point of the African continent, at the tip of Cape Province.

Azania An alternative name for South Africa used by some black Africans.

Bloemfontein ("fountain of flowers") Capital of the Orange Free State and judicial capital of South Africa; population (1985) 233 000 of whom 117 500 are black Africa.

Bophuthatswana Tribal homeland of the Tswana people. Comprising six areas of land in Transvaal and Cape Province, it was in 1977 the second Bantu area to be designated an "independent republic" under the Bantu Constitution Homeland Act of 1971. Its capital is Mmbatho; area 44 000km²; population (1985) 1 627 000. Situated close to Johannesburg, the gambling resort of Sun City is a major source of national income. The mining of platinum, gold, copper, nickel, chromium, manganese, fluorspar, vanadium and asbestos generates the largest income of the four "independent" homelands.

Cape Province The largest of the provinces of South Africa, stretching from the Orange River to the southern tip of the African continent. The provincial capital is Cape Town; area 641 379km²; population (1985) 4 901 200. First settled by the Dutch in 1652, the Cape was eventually ceded to the British in 1814.

Cape Town or **Kaapstad** (Afrikaans) Seaport capital of Cape province and legislative capital of South Africa. Situated at the foot of Table Mountain, Cape Town was established by Jan van Riebeeck in 1652 as a victualling station of the Dutch East India Company. Greater Cape Town, including the suburbs of Belleville, Goodwood and Wynberg, has a population (1980) of 1 911 500.

Ciskei Situated on the SE coast of South Africa between East London and Port Alfred, Ciskei was the fourth tribal homeland to be designated an "independent republic" in 1981. Established with Transkei as a homeland for the Xhosa people, its capital is Bisho; area 7700km²; population (1985) 925 000. Ciskei has laid claim to the territory known as the "white corridor" lying between it and Transkei.

Crossroads The largest of the black African squatter settlements in the south–eastern suburbs of Cape Town; population (1985) 29 200. Attempts have been made to move the residents to the more distant new settlement of Khayelitsha.

Gazankulu A tribal homeland in the Transvaal designated a self–governing "national state"

for the Tsonga people in 1971; population (1985) 495 000.

Johannesburg Founded in 1886 during the great gold rush, Johannesburg is the largest city in South Africa and the financial centre of the Transvaal; population (1985) 1 609 400 of whom 914 000 are black African.

Kaffraria A native reserve for Kaffirs or Bantu–speaking people, situated between the Keiskamma and Kei rivers. Established by the British in 1847, it was joined to Cape Colony in 1866.

KaNgwane A tribal homeland of the Swazi people in Natal, designated a self-governing "national state" in 1971; population (1985) 389 000. The chief town is Eerstehoek.

Khayelitsha A coastal settlement 39km south of Cape Town, built in 1983 to house the occupants of the squatter camps of that city. Attempts to encourage black Africans to move there have proved largely unsuccessful.

Kimberley A major centre of the diamond–mining industry in Cape Province since it was founded in 1871. During the period 1867–90 an estimated six tons of diamonds valued at 39 million was mined in the surrounding area which lies between the Vaal and Orange rivers. The 800m–deep Big Hole is claimed to be the biggest man-made hole in the world.

KwaNdebele A tribal homeland for the Ndebele people in NE Transvaal, designated a self–governing "national state" in 1981. Its chief town is Moutjana; area 2 860km²; population (1985) 233 000.

KwaZulu Known as Zululand until 1972, KwaZulu is a Zulu tribal homeland designated a self-governing "national state" in 1971. With a population (1985) of 3 737 000 it is the largest of the black African homelands.

Lebowa A tribal homeland of the North Sotho people, designated a self-governing "national state" in 1972; population (1985)1 842 000.

Lesotho A land-locked enclave in South Africa formerly known as Basutoland until it gained its independence from Britain in 1966. The Kingdom of Lesotho has an area of 30460km^2 and a population of nearly 1.5 million. The capital city is Maseru.

Lusaka Capital of Zambia and headquarters of the ANC from 1963, three years after it was banned in 1960. Population (1980) 538 000.

Natal Eastern province of South Africa, bounded to the east by the Indian Ocean. Settled by the Dutch Boers in the 1830s, it was annexed by the British in 1843 and established as a separate colony in 1856. Its capital is Pietermaritzburg; area 91 785km^2; population (1985) 2 145 000 of whom 665 300 are Asians and 1 358 000 are black African.

Orange Free State A land-locked South African province lying between the Vaal and Orange rivers. Annexed by the British in 1848, it was given its independence six years later in 1854. In 1900 it was annexed again as the Orange River Colony. The chief city is Bloemfontein; area 127 993km^2; population (1985) 1 863 300 of whom 1 459 800 are black African.

Orange River A major river of southern Africa that rises in the Drakensberg Mountains and flows over 2000km through Lesotho and South Africa to meet the Atlantic Ocean at Alexander Bay on the South Africa–Namibia frontier. The Orange River is joined by the Vaal west of Douglas.

Paarl A town in SW Cape Province, situated on the Great Berg River, 50km ENE of Cape Town at the centre of a famous wine-producing region. Nelson Mandela's last days of imprisonment were spent at the Victor Verster prison near Paarl.

Pretoria Administrative capital of South Africa and capital of Transvaal province, situated at an altitude of 1370m, 48km NNE of Johannesburg. The city was founded in 1855 and named after the Boer leader Andries Pretorius (1799–1853). In 1881 it became capital of the South African Republic.

Rivonia A township in the northern suburbs of Johannesburg, Transvaal province. Headquarters of the banned ANC movement from 1960 until raided by the South African police in 1963.

Robben Island An island in Table Bay, Cape Town, noted for its high security prison where leaders of the ANC, including Nelson Mandela, were jailed in the 1960s.

Qwaqwa A tribal homeland of the South Sotho people designated a self–governing "national state" in 1984. Population (1985) 183 000.

Soweto ("South–West Township") A black African township situated 5km south–west of Johannesburg, Transvaal province. The township's name is linked with the 1976 Soweto student riots in protest at the teaching of all lessons in Afrikaans.

Sharpeville A black African township near Vereeniging, Transvaal province. In March 1960, 69 Africans were killed here by police who opened fire on a crowd demonstrating against the pass laws.

Swaziland The smallest country in southern Africa, situated on the border between South Africa and Mozambique. Occupied by the Swazis since the early 19th century, the country gained full independence as a constitutional monarchy in 1968. Until the signing of the Nkomati Accord in 1974 ANC guerrillas penetrated South Africa via Swaziland from bases in Mozambique.

Transkei In 1976 Transkei became the first tribal homeland to be designated an "independent republic" for the Xhosa people. Comprising three separate areas SW of Durban, Transkei lies between the Kei and Mtamvuna rivers. Its capital is Umtata; area 42 276km^2; population (1985) 2 947 000. In January 1988 Prime Minister Stella Sigcu was ousted in a bloodless coup led by Major-General Bantu Holomisa. The village of Qunu in Transkei was the birthplace of Nelson Mandela.

Transvaal A province of NE South Africa, bounded N by the Limpopo River where it follows the frontier with Mozambique and Botswana. Colonized by Dutch Boers following the Great Trek in the 1830s, Transvaal was annexed by the British in 1877. Four years later, following the first Boer War, it was granted self–government. In 1886 the discovery of gold on the Witwatersrand led to an influx of foreign prospectors and the rapid development of Johannesburg. The capital of the province is Pretoria; area 262 499km²; population (1985) 7 532 000, of whom 270 300 are Asians and 4 674 300 are black Africans.

Upington A city on the Orange River, N Cape Province associated with the "Upington 25" who were convicted under the law of "common purpose" for the murder of a policeman in 1985.

Venda A tribal homeland of the Vhavenda people designated an "independent republic" in 1979. Its capital is Thohoyandou; area 6 500km²; population (1985) 455 000. The principal resources of Venda are coal, graphite, magnesite, phosphate and copper sulphide.

Vereeniging A city in Transvaal province to the south of Johannesburg. In 1902 the Treaty of Vereeniging brought to an end the Boer War.

Witwatersrand or **The Rand** ("ridge of white waters") A series of parallel ridges running E-W for a distance of 100km/60 miles through S Transvaal where they form a watershed between the Vaal and Olifant rivers. The Rand, with Johannesburg at its centre, is the focal point of South Africa's gold–mining industry. Since the gold rush of 1886 half of the world's gold has been mined in this area.

Zululand The former name, until 1972, of the "national state" of KwaZulu.

■ Key words

African National Congress (ANC) Founded in 1912 as the South African Native National Congress, the ANC has the longest record of political activity within the African nationalist movement. The ANC opposed apartheid by constitutional means until 1960 when it turned to more violent action following the Sharpeville massacre. Banned in April 1960, ANC leaders including Nelson Mandela were arrested and imprisoned during 1962–64. Operating from bases in Mozambique and Zambia, its leaders in exile developed a military wing known as Umkhonto we Sizwe. In February 1990 the ANC was legalized once again and its leaders released after more than 25 years of imprisonment.

African People's Organization (APO) A political movement representing the interests of non-white South Africans formed in 1902 by Dr Abdullah Abdurahman.

Afrikaans The native language of the Dutch Boers spoken by over 2.5 million Afrikaners who represent over 60 per cent of the white population of South Africa. Afrikaans replaced Dutch as South Africa's second official language in 1924. A government directive requiring lessons to be taught in Afrikaans sparked off the Soweto riots of 1976.

Afrikander Bond A Dutch nationalist movement established in the Cape Colony in 1879. Opposed to British interference it advocated a policy of "South Africa for the South Africans". In 1910 the movement gained political momentum with the formation of the South Africa Party by Botha and Herzog.

Afrikaner Resistance Movement (Afrikaner Weerstandsbeweging – AWB) A neo-Nazi white Afrikaans movement opposed to any form of racial powersharing or dilution of the apartheid laws. The social and political reforms introduced by the government in the 1980s led to a white right-wing backlash in the form of a defection by Nationalist Party members of parliament and a rise in support for the AWB.

Albany Settlers   The name give to the 4000 British colonists who arrived en masse on the east coast of South Africa in 1820.

Amandla awethu ("power is ours")   A slogan of the black nationalist movement.

apartheid (Afrikaans, "apartness")   The separate development of black, white, Asian and coloured communities in South Africa under a regime in which the politically dominant white population has consolidated its rights and privileges at the expense of others. Between 1913 and 1948 a social and economic colour bar was initiated. Black Africans were forced to live on small "preserves" of land where they became little more than a supply of cheap labour for the white–controlled farms, mines and industries of South Africa. The rise to power of the Nationalist Party in 1948 brought with it a policy of *apartheid* that involved complete social, political and geographical segregation. In the 1950s and 1960s *apartheid* was institutionalized by a series of discriminatory legislation introduced first by Dr Daniel Malan and then by Hendrik Verwoerd.

Azanian Peoples' Organization (AZAPO)   A "black consciousness" African nationalist movement formed in 1979 and led by Curtis Nkondo. An offshoot of the banned Pan–Africanist Congress, AZAPO has been opposed to the multiracial approach of the UDF.

baaskap   An Afrikaans word applied to the system of white supremacy in South Africa.

Bantu   An official name for black South Africans, but more generally applied to a family of central and south African negro peoples that includes the Zulu, Xhosa, Sepedi, Seshoeshoe and Tswana. Since the 1970s the word Bantu has been considered a pejorative term and largely dropped from official use.

Black Consciousness Movement   An alliance of anti–apartheid black African student organizations formed in the aftermath of the 1976 Soweto riots.

black spots   A term describing parcels of land bought freehold by Africans before the Natives' Land Act of 1913. Since then the South African

government has tried to consolidate these "black spots" by resettling over 700 000 black people in tribal "homelands" that are often far distant from their original farms and villages.

Boer A Dutch word for a "farmer" used to described the early Dutch settlers of the Cape.

Broederbond   A secret organization responsible for uniting the Afrikaner leadership and securing its rise to power in 1948.

constructive engagement   The name given to President Reagan's US policy of opposing *apartheid* in South Africa through involvement rather than isolation. Reagan was forced by the US Congress to abandon this approach in 1985.

Freedom Charter   A charter advocating a multiracial, democratic society in South Africa formulated in 1955 at a meeting held in Kliptown.

Gleneagles Agreement   An attempt to isolate South Africa by means of sporting and economic sanctions, formulated in 1977 by Commonwealth heads of government who met at Gleneagles in Scotland.

Group Areas   Urban areas defined for the the exclusive occupation of specific races. In 1950 the Group Areas Act gave legal status to residential segregation and a register was instituted for the classification of the entire adult population according to race. By the mid 1980s 448 group areas had been proclaimed for whites, 313 for coloured people and 116 for Asians.

Harare Declaration   Issued by the OAU in August 1989 (and adopted by the UN General Assembly in December 1989), the Declaration set out the negotiating position of the ANC, calling for non–racial, multi–party democracy, an entrenched Bill of Rights to reassure whites and a mixed economy.

Het Volk   A Dutch nationalist movement established in the Transvaal by Louis Botha, but later incorporated into the South Africa Party in the run–up to the first elections in the Union of South Africa in 1910.

homelands The name given to areas of land allocated to black Africans under the system of "separate development" or *apartheid* introduced in the 1940s and 1950s. The areas set aside for black Africans were called "homelands" to denote the supposed association between tribal groups and their area of origin. Sometimes called Bantustan, these areas have attained a degree of self-government as "national states" and "independent republics", although their status has not been recognized internationally.

Hottentots or **Khoi-Khoi** An ethnic group of SW Africa largely dispossessed of their tribal lands up to the Orange River by Dutch settlers in the 17th and 18th centuries. Before their adoption as farm labourers, the Hottentots grazed sheep and cattle in addition to augmenting their diet by hunting and gathering.

impi A troop of Zulu warriors.

indaba A Zulu word for a conference or negotiations. Particularly applied to recent negotiations between black nationalist leaders and the South African government.

Inkatha Officially described as a cultural movement, Inkatha is a predominantly Zulu nationalist movement opposed to sanctions and guerrilla warfare. Inkatha is led by Chief Gatsha Buthelezi who is Chief Executive Officer of KwaZulu or Zululand. Intercommunal conflict between members of the rival United Democratic Front (which supports sanctions and guerrilla activity) and Inkatha cost the lives of nearly 3000 people in Natal between 1985 and 1990.

Kaffir An Arab word meaning "infidel", used to describe the Bantu–speaking people of South Africa. In 1847 the British defeated the Kaffirs in the War of the Axe and set up the native reserve of British Kaffraria. Between 1850 and 1853 the Great Kaffir War was waged on the eastern frontier of Cape Colony and in 1856 the long–standing Kaffir problem came to a tragic end when nearly two–thirds of the Kaffirs died of starvation after slaughtering their own cattle. The word kaffir is now considered a pejorative term.

kitskonstabels ("instant constables") Members of a security force appointed by the Pretoria government to support councillors elected to represent the black African townships after the 1989 elections. Backed by squads of municipal police and battalions of the South African Defence Force, the kiskonstabels were employed in an attempt to prevent a repetition of the unrest that had engulfed the black African townships during 1984–86.

Mass Democratic Movement (MDM) A loose but broad militant anti-apartheid alliance largely directed by the banned South African Communist Party and ANC during the campaign of defiance waged against white minority rule in 1988–89. The movement claimed to represent the voice of black Africans following the banning of the United Democratic Front in 1988.

Nationalist Party Drawing most of its support from the Afrikaner population, the National Party has been the ruling party in South Africa since it swept to power in the general election of 1948. Although the practice of *apartheid* has been central to nationalist government policy there are elements of the party who believe that some accommodation must be made with the black majority. An attempt to introduce a form of powersharing led to a defection of 17 members of Parliament who formed the Conservative Party.

Nguni A group of Bantu languages that includes Zulu, Xhosa, Swazi and Ndebele.

Orangia Unie A Dutch nationalist movement that was eventually incorporated into the South Africa Party on the creation of the Union of South Africa in 1910.

Ossewa brandwag A semi–secret neo–Nazi paramilitary organization formed by Afrikaner nationalists in 1938. By preserving the spirit of the Great Trek, it hoped to secure political power for the Afrikaners. The Ossewa brandwag supported former Defence Minister Oswald Pirow and his "New Order" in the fight for a Nazi–style Afrikaner republic.

Pan-Africanist Congress (PAC) An African nationalist movement formed in 1958 under Robert Sobukwe at a time when the effectiveness of the ANC opposition to *apartheid* had been reduced by the arrest of its leaders. This organization was banned along with the ANC in April 1960 but legalized 30 years later in February 1990. The PAC is essentially an "Africanist" movement opposed to the multi–racialist approach of Mandela's ANC.

pass laws   Measures designed to control the movement of black Africans in urban areas and the influx from rural areas into townships. Africans outside the "homelands" are required to carry a reference "pass" book which serves as an internal passport. It was during a demonstration against the unpopular "pass laws" that 69 people were killed when police opened fire on an African crowd in Sharpeville in 1960.

Poqo ("we alone")   The military wing of the Pan–Africanist Congress, set up in 1962 for the purpose of launching an armed struggle against *apartheid* and white minority rule.

Reddingdaadsbond   An Afrikaner nationalist organization formed in 1938 with the aim of securing Afrikaner participation in the control and ownership of industry.

Sand River Convention   An agreement reached between the British government and the Boers recognizing the independence of the Transvaal in 1852.

Section 10   A section of the Black (Urban Areas) Consolidation Act of 1945, amended in June 1985, that limits the right of residence of black Africans who are not allowed to remain more than 72 hours in an urban area unless they have lived there since birth or worked there for at least ten years.

Sepedi   With a population of 2 348 000, the Sepedi or North Sotho is the third largest of the South African black ethnic groups. They predominate in the homeland of Lebowa.

Seshoeshoe   Numbering 1 742 000, the Seshoeshoe or South Sotho people are the fourth largest black African group in South Africa.

Soweto "football team"   The name given to the bodyguard of Winnie Mandela, wife of the jailed ANC leader. The so-called "football team" were believed responsible for a number of killings.

Sharpeville Six   A group of six black Africans arrested and charged with murder following the Sharpeville massacre of 1960. Although there was no evidence that they had actually committed murder, their conviction was based on the law of "common purpose".

Sullivan Code   A code of practice defined in 1977 by an American civil rights activist and corporation executive, the Rev. Leon Sullivan, who encouraged American companies in South Africa to oppose *apartheid* in the work place.

Tswana   The fifth largest of the black African ethnic groups of South Africa, numbering some 1 357 000. The independent homeland of Bophuthatswana is largely peopled by the Tswana tribe.

uitlander   An Afrikaans word for a "foreigner" or "outsider" now often used in a derogatory way to describe someone who interferes in the internal politics of South Africa. Foreign white mineworkers in Johannesburg in the 1880s and 1890s were called Uitlanders. It was amongst this group that Cecil Rhodes tried to promote a rebellion against the Boers in 1895.

Umkhonto we Sizwe ("spear of the nation")   The guerrilla wing of the African Nationalist Congress set up in 1961 following the banning of the ANC a year earlier. For many years this group maintained bases in Mozambique, but following an agreement between the governments of South Africa and Mozambique (Nkomati Accord) in 1984 it was expelled from that country.

United Democratic Front (UDF)   A multi-racial nationalist party formed in July 1983 in political opposition to the proposal that coloureds and Asians but not black Africans be represented in a tricameral Assembly. This party, which quickly became the largest legal political opposition to *apartheid* in South Africa, was banned in 1988. UDF opposition to the compromising approach of the Zulu Inkatha movement has resulted in bitter intercommunal violence in Natal since 1985.

Upington Twenty Five   A group of 25 black Africans convicted in April 1988 of murdering a policemen in the township of Upington during demonstrations that took place in 1985. The State prosecution's case was based on the law of "common purpose" which had previously secured the conviction of the celebrated Sharpeville Six. The mere presence of a person in a demonstrating crowd was enough to ensure a conviction on the grounds of complicity or "common purpose" in the case of any death that took place.

Vereeniging, Treaty of   A treaty signed on 31 May 1902 bringing to an end the three–year Boer War of 1899–1902. The Boers accepted British sovereignty in exchange for a degree of self–rule and compensation.

verkramptes   An Afrikaans word used to describe those "unenlightened" members of the white minority, ultra conservative right wing which opposes any form of power–sharing in South Africa.

Voortrekker   The Afrikaans name for those Dutch farmers who took part in the Great Trek of 1835–37. The spirit of the original Voortrekkers is imbued in the ideology of the ruling Afrikaner Nationalist Party.

Xhosa   A Bantu-speaking people of SE Africa, numbering 2 987 000 in South Africa. The principal group within the independent homelands of Ciskei and Transkei.

Zulu   The dominant black African ethnic group in South Africa with a population of 5 682 000. Over two-thirds of the Zulu population live in the KwaZulu homeland (Zululand).

■ Further reading

H. Adams and H. Giliomee, *The Rise of Afrikaner Power*, David Philip, Cape Town, 1979

M. Benson, *Nelson Mandela: The Man and the Movement*, New York, 1986

W.R. Böhning, *Black Migration to South Africa*, Geneva, 1981

T.R.H. Davenport, *South Africa: A Modern History*, Cambridge University Press, Cambridge, 1986 (3rd edn.)

Deon Geldenhuys, *The Diplomacy of Isolation: South African Foreign Policy Making*, Macmillan, Johannesburg, 1984

Muriel Horrell, *Race Relations as Regulated by Law in South Africa*, South African Institute of Race Relations, Johannesburg, 1982

Brian Lapping, *Apartheid: A History*, Grafton, London and New York, 1986

Richard Leonard, *South Africa at War: White Power and the Crisis in Southern Africa*, Paddington Press, 1979

R. Price and C. Rossberg, *The Apartheid Regime: Political Power and Racial Domination*, University of California Press, California, 1980

II Middle East

1
Palestine/Israel

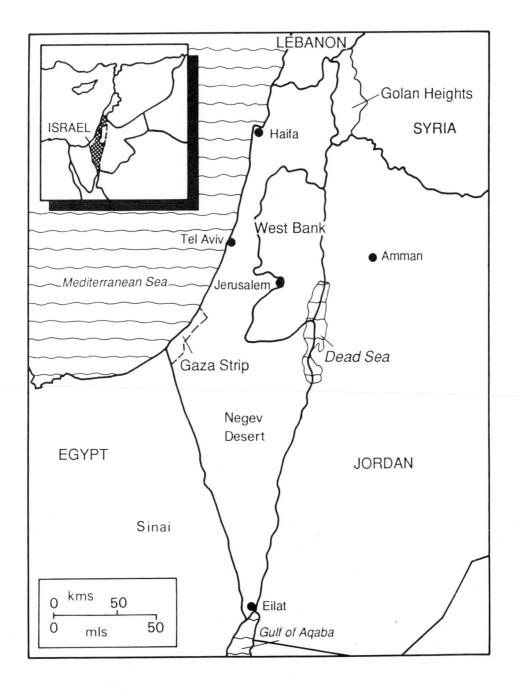

■ Profile

Official name: State of Israel

- **Area:** 20770km²
- **Population (1988 est.):** 44 442 000
- **Ethnic groups:** Jews 83%, Arabs 14%
- **Languages:** Hebrew, Arabic, English
- **Religion:** Judaism 83%, Muslim 13%, Christian 2%, Druse 2%
- **Infant mortality rate:** Jews 8.8 per 1000; Arabs 16.6 per 1000
- **Life expectancy:** 75 years
- **Currency:** new shequel of 100 agorot
- **Timezone:** GMT +2
- **Capital:** Jerusalem (since 1950)
- **Chief cities:** Jerusalem (482 700), Tel Aviv-Jaffa (319 500), Haifa (223 200)

Israeli–occupied Territories

Gaza
- **Area:** 363km²
- **Population:** 564 000
- **Ethnic majority:** Palestinian Arabs 98%
- **Chief town:** Gaza (120 000)

West Bank

- **Area:** 5879km²
- **Population:** 866 000
- **Ethnic majority:** Palestinian Arabs 97%
- **Chief towns:** Nablus, Hebron, Bethlehem, Ramallah Bireh, Jericho

■ Introduction

Of all the world's current conflicts, the one between Arabs and Jews over the land of Palestine is the most intractable and goes back furthest into history. That a succession of Jewish states flourished in the region in the pre-Christian era is clear. Whether they ever ruled the coastal plains of what is now Israel is not. That the Romans had erased the Jewish state of Judea from the map by AD 135 is historical fact. Whether the dispersed Jewish people had a right thereafter to maintain a claim to a homeland in Palestine gets to the nub of the present-day problem. The Arabs contend that Palestine became irreversibly part of the Muslim world when Jerusalem fell to the Arabs in the 7th century. The Jews claim that Jewish residence in Palestine was unbroken through the centuries and stress that Jewish immigration increased from 1517, when the Ottoman conquest ushered in greater religious tolerance. Arabs point out that as late as 1880 Jews were no more than a tiny fraction of Palestine's population and contend that only a 20th-century alliance between Zionism and European imperialism enabled the Jews to challenge the verdict of history. Jews say that the historical case for the creation of the state of Israel was given a hard moral edge by their long experience of antisemitism, culminating in the Holocaust of World War II.

Jews and Arabs agree that the dramatic change in Palestine after 1880 was due to the impact of Zionism. This was (and is) the doctrine that the survival and renewal of the Jewish people could be assured only through the creation of a Jewish state. An idea floated in

Britain that a Jewish homeland might be located in Uganda was never a serious contender. The new Zionists of Eastern Europe, facing growing antisemitism in the host countries, wanted to return to the cradle of Jewish civilization. The problem was that Palestine already had a population of Muslim Arabs with a thousand years of occupancy rights. That the new immigrants to Palestine were mainly Ashkenazic Jews from Russia and Poland provided an added ingredient in the conflict scenario. In the Arab view, Ashkenazis are "European" Jews without roots in Palestine because they are descended from 8th-century Khazar converts to Judaism and not from the original Sephardic Jews of the Middle East. As for Zionism itself, Arab theorists have condemned it as racist, because it excludes non-Jews, and as colonialist, expansionist and even fascist in its methods. For the Jews, Zionism is the national liberation movement of the Jewish people throughout the world, akin to other movements which have fought for the independence or recognition of oppressed peoples.

The critical moment for the Zionists came when the Turks sided with Germany in World War I and were ousted from the Arab Middle East by British and French armies. Anticipating that Britain would be the post-Ottoman power in Palestine, the Zionists persuaded the London government to issue the 1917 Balfour Declaration (which France also endorsed), expressing support for the establishment in Palestine of "a national home for the Jewish people", provided that the rights of "existing non-Jewish communities" were not prejudiced. It quickly became clear that these two propositions would be impossible to reconcile. The declaration sat uneasily with Britain's pledges of support for Arab independence, which had in any case been disregarded in secret allied plans to carve up the Middle East into British and French spheres of influence. Under the post-war settlements, the latter policy generally prevailed. Although Arabia was earmarked for speedy independence, the vast region to the north was divided into British and French mandated territories under the new League of Nations. Britain took the mandate for Palestine, whose terms enshrined those of the Balfour Declaration. Thus, for the first time, the Jews secured an international commitment to the creation of a national home in Palestine. The Arabs faced what they saw as an imperialist/Zionist plot to implant an alien state in their midst.

The unhappy period of the mandate, during which Britain failed to reconcile conflicting national aspirations, was the predictable result. The Jews wanted, at least, a homeland open to all Jews. The Arabs insisted on majority rule in a unitary Palestine, from which further Jewish settlement would inevitably be banned. Amid growing inter-communal clashes, Britain concluded in 1937 that partition was the only viable solution. The idea gained reluctant acceptance from the Jews but was rejected by the Arabs. British restrictions on Jewish entry from 1939 incurred the wrath of the Jews, who accused Britain of reneging on its pledges at a time when European Jewry faced its greatest peril. The violence escalated after World War II, as the Arabs sought to emulate their neighbours in achieving independence and the Jews emerged from the Nazi persecution more convinced than ever of the need for a Jewish state. Ranged on the Jewish side were the United States and the Soviet Union, the former pro-Jewish in any case but also sharing the latter's hostility to British imperialism.

Assailed on all sides, Britain opted to hand over the problem to the United Nations and to make a speedy exit from Palestine. The UN solution was yet another partition plan, giving the Jews rather less than half of Palestine. In a historic UN General Assembly vote in November 1947 the plan secured the necessary two-thirds support, thanks to combined Western and Soviet-bloc support. The Jews thus achieved internationally-recognized statehood, on which there was to be no going back despite the Arabs' total rejection of the UN plan. In May 1948 Arab League armies invaded the newly-declared state of Israel with the aim of establishing an independent and unitary state of Palestine. When the fighting ended early in 1949 the Jews were in possession of over two-thirds of the former mandated territory. Massive and much-disputed displacement of Arabs in the fighting created a festering refugee problem, which worsened as a result of later wars. The resultant borders gained widespread international acceptance, but not from the

Arab states. Their joint policy of refusing to recognize Israel, within any borders, was to be maintained until Egypt broke ranks in 1979.

The advent in 1954 of Nasser's radical nationalist regime in Egypt exacerbated Arab–Israeli tensions and also brought Egypt into direct confrontation with Britain and France over the Suez Canal. This resulted in the 1956 Israeli invasion of Egypt, in collusion (it transpired) with Britain and France, which sent in troops ostensibly to separate the two sides but, in fact, to repossess the canal. Combined US and Soviet pressure ended that adventure and forced Israel to withdraw to the 1949 armistice lines. The consequential eclipse of British and French influence in the Arab world enabled the Soviet Union to fill the vacuum and to promote the radicalization of Arab politics. This, in turn, drew the United States further into the Middle East arena as the main external backer of Israel, for which a powerful American Jewish lobby campaigned tirelessly. A key development in 1964 was the formation of the Palestine Liberation Organization (PLO), whose Charter called for the creation of a Palestinian state in the whole of Palestine. Most Israelis see this Charter as urging Israel's destruction and have refused to negotiate with the PLO.

An arms build-up and increased Palestinian guerrilla operations against Israeli targets heightened the tension. These escalated into the third Arab–Israeli war in June 1967, when the Israelis made pre-emptive strikes against their Arab neighbours, excepting Lebanon. Within a week they had captured Sinai and the Gaza Strip from Egypt, the West Bank and Old Jerusalem from Jordan, and the Golan Heights from Syria. Arab spokesmen later claimed that these conquests had long been planned by the Israelis in accordance with Zionist blueprints. Israel maintained that menacing Arab troop movements and other actions had placed it in mortal danger. Apart from declaring unified Jerusalem as its capital, Israel made no move to annex any of its new conquests. But Israeli hopes of being able to exchange territory for definitive peace treaties were disappointed, for the time being. When Egypt and Syria launched a surprise attack on Israel in October 1973, their main war aim was to recover the Arab territories lost in 1967. They fell well short of

this, but an important outcome of the fourth Arab–Israeli war was that the Egyptians, for the first time, had some military success against Israel. With honour thus restored, Egypt became psychologically better able to move to a political accommodation.

US-mediated disengagement agreements in 1974–75, under which Egypt consolidated its 1973 military gains, heightened the new Egyptian appreciation of the potential benefits of grasping the nettle of peace with Israel. Another key factor was the active diplomacy of the US government, whose strategic interest in resolving the Arab–Israeli conflict had been underlined by its experience of an Arab oil embargo after the 1973 war. The intransigent line adopted by the 1974 Arab League summit in Rabat, where the PLO was proclaimed the "sole legitimate representative" of the Palestinian people, appeared to raise a new obstacle to peace negotiations, as did the 1977 election victory of the right-wing Likud front in Israel. Whereas Labour-led governments had not ruled out territorial concessions in Palestine, Likud maintained that Israel had an inalienable right of sovereignty over the whole "Land of Israel", including the West Bank, where restrictions on Jewish settlement were gradually relaxed from 1977. Ironically, it was the Likud government which achieved rapprochement with Egypt, starting with President Sadat's historic visit in November 1977, continuing with the 1978 Camp David accords and culminating in a peace treaty in March 1979, the first (and so far only) such agreement between Israel and an Arab state. Under the treaty, the whole of Sinai (but not the Gaza Strip) was returned to Egypt by 1982, whereupon bilateral relations were normalized.

The cost to Egypt was almost total isolation in the Arab world, especially when it became clear that the Camp David formula contained nothing of immediate substance for the Palestinians beyond a vague commitment to negotiations on West Bank and Gaza Strip "autonomy" for a five-year transitional period pending final determination of their status. Apart from Egypt, no interested Arab party was prepared to enter into such negotiations, not even moderate Jordan and especially not the PLO (with which Israel refused to talk anyway). Moreover, Israel's Likud government not only made no secret of its aim to annex the West Bank and Gaza at the end of the transitional period but also, in December 1981, added insult to Arab injury by annexing the Golan Heights. US-prompted efforts by Egypt to assume the "Arab role" in autonomy negotiations with Israel accordingly made no progress. They were suspended when in June 1982, less than two months after its final withdrawal from Sinai, Israel launched a full-scale invasion of Lebanon. The Israelis' declared aim was to eradicate the PLO from the Lebanese bases it had been using since its expulsion from Jordan in 1970–71; they also hoped to secure a peace treaty from their troubled neighbour's Christian-dominated government.

The Lebanon incursion ended in disappointment and controversy, calling down much international opprobrium on Israel, none of whose main objectives were lastingly achieved. Moreover, domestic opposition to the operation helped the Labour Party to return to government in July 1984, in coalition with Likud. But the apparent prospect of greater Israeli flexibility did not materialize because Likud blocked Labour proposals for peace talks with the Arabs via a broader international conference rather than through the moribund Camp David formula. Egypt's rehabilitation in the Arab world from 1984 produced some movement in the moderate Arab camp towards a formal recognition of Israel's right to exist (within its pre-1967 borders). Crucially, however, Jordan held back, not least because it could not decide whether to abide by the 1974 Rabat decision that the PLO represented the Palestinian people. As Jordan's relations with the PLO blew hot and cold in the late 1980s, the PLO itself underwent fierce feuding between moderate and hardline factions, each with their government backers in the Arab world. The unexpected development which transformed this confused deadlock was the uprising (*intifada*) launched by Palestinians in the occupied territories late in 1988.

Regarded in the Arab world and elsewhere as an heroic revolt against an oppressive occupier, the *intifada* finally persuaded Jordan to renounce responsibility for the West Bank in favour of the PLO. It also, rather conversely, strengthened the moderate leadership of the PLO. Almost universal condemnation of Israeli anti-insurgency methods not only boosted PLO morale but also persuaded most factions that an opportunity had been created for productive negotiations with Israel. The result was the Palestinian declaration of independence issued in November 1988, followed by a renunciation of terrorism and public acceptance of UN resolutions which themselves acknowledged Israel's right to exist in security. Applauded worldwide as a major breakthrough, this metamorphosis enabled the US government to lift its ban on direct talks with the PLO. But US and other efforts to convince Israel that a real change had occurred ran up against the conviction, not confined to the Israeli right, that the PLO remained dedicated to Israel's destruction, as evidenced by its failure to renounce the 1964 Palestinian Charter. Under strong US pressure, the Israeli government in April 1989 came up with a plan for elections in the occupied territories to establish the "self-governing authority" envisaged (11 years earlier) in the Camp David accords. But the plan provoked controversy, not only on the Arab side (notably because it ruled out PLO involvement) but also within Israel, where it was attacked by Likud hardliners as a sellout and by Labour as too restrictive. The consequential collapse of the national unity coalition and the formation in June 1990 of a Likud-led right-wing government created new uncertainties, which intensified in August when the Iraquis invaded and annexed Kuwait, with the approval of the PLO.

Whether or not the elections plan came to anything, prospects of movement on the basic Arab–Israeli dispute appeared to be in the balance at the start of the 1990s. Optimists pointed to the resolution in 1988–89 of other seemingly intractable conflicts around the world and envisaged a similar breakthrough in the Middle East on the model of the 1979 peace treaty between Egypt and Israel. They also saw the end of the Cold War in Europe and US–Soviet détente as likely to have a positive impact on the Arab–Israeli deadlock. At the very least, maintained this school, Israel's overwhelming military superiority made another war unlikely. Pessimists pointed to the uniquely intractable nature of the territorial confrontation between Arab and Jew, suggesting that a solution would have been found by now if there was one. They also saw the political transformation in Eastern Europe as creating new hazards for Arab–Israeli relations in the shape of increased Jewish immigration to Israel and consequential pressure to expand Jewish settlement of the occupied territories. As for the security dimension, they cautioned that in the age of nuclear and chemical weapons conventional calculations of military strength might become irrelevant. Above all, the pessimists viewed the simultaneous growth of Iraqi power and Islamic fundamentalism in the Arab world as running counter to the willingness of moderate Arabs to reach some sort of lasting accommodation with Israel.

◼ Chronology of events

AD 70   The Jewish state of Judaea is overthrown by the Roman Emperor Titus and the Jewish Temple in the Holy City of Jerusalem is destroyed.

AD 135   After prolonged rebellion against Rome, Jerusalem is raised to the ground and the Jews expelled from Palestine. In the succeeding centuries the Jewish people migrate to all corners of the world.

AD 636   Jerusalem is captured by the Arabs and the Semitic inhabitants of Palestine become part of the Muslim world.

1095–1291   In an attempt to recapture the Holy Land from the Muslims, European rulers launch a series of eight wars or Crusades during which Jerusalem is captured and recaptured several times. The Seljuk Turks eventually retain their grip on Palestine. In the years that follow, the relative tolerance shown to Jewish people encourages the gradual return of some Jews from Europe, where they face a growing tide of persecution.

1492   The expulsion of the Jews from Spain further stimulates the migration of the Jews back to Palestine.

1517   Palestine becomes part of the Turkish Ottoman Empire. Jewish immigration continues.

1880–1914   There is an upsurge in Jewish immigration, particularly following the anti-semitic pogroms that take place in Russia and Poland. In this period the estimated number of Jews in Palestine rises from 25 000 to 90 000, as against an estimated Arab population of some 450 000 in 1914.

1891   Conflict between Arab and Jew increases. Arab leaders in Jerusalem send a petition to Constantinople asking the Turkish authorities to restrict Jewish immigration and land purchase.

1896   The publication of *Der Judenstaat* (Jewish State) by the Hungarian–born Zionist, Theodor Herzl, stimulates the demand for a Jewish homeland and encourages a new wave of Jewish migration to Palestine.
1897   At the first Zionist Congress, Herzl calls for the national reunion of the Jewish people in a "legally assured home in Palestine."

1908   Although the Turkish Sultan will not agree to the setting-up of a Jewish homeland, the wealthy Jews of Western Europe provide finance for the purchase of land in Palestine. The first kibbutz, or co-operative settlement, is established at Kinneret on the SW shore of the Sea of Galilee.

1909   Tel Aviv, the first entirely Jewish town in modern Palestine, is built on the Mediterranean coast to the north of the Arab port of Jaffa.

1914   Turkey allies itself with the central powers at the outset of World War I.

1915–16   Britain and France begin to draw up plans for the post-war dismemberment of the Ottoman Empire into British and French spheres of influence that would recognize the existence of an independent Arab state or confederation.

1917 In an attempt to gain international Jewish support for the allied war effort, the British Foreign Secretary, Arthur Balfour, sends a letter to the prominent Jewish businessman, Lord Rothschild, supporting the Zionist aim of establishing a homeland in Palestine, subject to the interests of non-Jewish communities being safeguarded. In December the British, under General Edmund Allenby, capture Jerusalem from the Turks.

1918 On 30 October an armistice is concluded between Turkey and the Allies at Mudros. The disposal of Turkish territory to the Allies effectively brings to an end the Ottoman Empire.

1920 At a conference of the Allied prime ministers at San Remo in April the British and French agree to the setting-up of mandates over non-Turkish territory. The dismemberment of the former Ottoman Empire is concluded with the signing of the Treaty of Sèvres on 10 August. By this treaty the Sultan relinquishes all claims to non-Turkish territory, Syria becomes a mandate of France and Britain establishes a mandate over Mesopotamia and Palestine.

Arab resentment against the presence of so many Ashkenazic "European" Jews in Palestine leads to a series of attacks on Jewish settlements. The Jews respond by forming their own defence force, the *Haganah*.

1921 In May there are further anti-Jewish riots. The area east of the Jordan River is closed to Jewish settlement and separated administratively from the rest of the Palestine mandate.

1922 The Council of the League of Nations approves the British mandate over Palestine but, in accordance with the Balfour Declaration of 1917, Britain is obliged to secure the eventual establishment of a Jewish homeland. For the first time Jewish national identity is enshrined within an internationally recognized instrument. The Arabs, however, feel betrayed when wartime promises of independence are not fulfilled.

1923 Transjordan is established as an autonomous state under the rule of Emir Abdullah ibn Hussein, son of the sherif of Mecca. The Golan Heights are transferred from the British mandate to French–mandated Syria.

1925 On 1 April the Hebrew University in Jerusalem is opened by Lord Balfour.

1928–29 Large-scale violence between Arab and Jew erupts in Palestine where the Jewish population has reached a total of 150 000 compared with an Arab population of 600 000.

1930 Attempts to restrict Jewish immigration lead to strikes and protests by Jews. Britain is condemned in a report of the League of Nations for providing inadequate police protection during the 1928–29 riots. A further report, known as the Passfield White Paper, stresses the plight of the landless Arab and suggests limiting Jewish immigration and land acquisition.

1933 Arab demands that the sale of Arab lands be forbidden and Jewish immigration restricted are ignored. The Arab executive announces a policy of non-co-operation with the British.

1936 Faced with persecution in Nazi Germany, large numbers of Jewish immigrants swell the total Jewish population of Palestine to 400 000, about 30 per cent of the total. Palestinian Arabs set up an Arab High Committee in order to organize the opposition to Jewish settlement. British troops are unable to prevent inter-communal violence.

1937 In July a royal commission chaired by Lord Peel presents a report suggesting the partition of Palestine into separate Arab and Jewish States. While Jews reluctantly accept this solution as the best available to them, Arabs totally reject the proposals and launch a revolt against both Zionists and the British. Following the assassination of the British district commissioner for Galilee, members of the Arab High Committee are arrested and deported to the Seychelles. Special military courts are set up to deal with terrorists.

1938 As open conflict between Jew and Arab intensifies, the British government abandons partition as a possible solution to the Palestinian problem.

1939 The British government produces a White Paper in which it is proposed that a Palestinian state be set up within 10 years and that Jewish immigration into Palestine should be limited in the future and subject to Arab consent after five years. Both Arabs and Jews reject this solution as one which fails to meet their long–term demands, but for the duration of World War II inter-communal violence is suspended.

1945 In the aftermath of Hitler's holocaust Jews are determined to establish a homeland in Palestine. Supported by the newly-formed Arab League, Palestinian Arabs renew their opposition to the Zionist cause.

1947 In the face of escalating violence, Britain refers the Palestinian problem to the United Nations General Assembly which establishes a Special Committee on Palestine (UNSCOP) in May. The committee submits a majority recommendation that Palestine should be partitioned into separate Arab and Jewish states. The Jews accept the plan as a means of achieving internationally–recognized statehood despite the fact that it will give them less than half of Palestine's territory. The Arabs, on the other hand, totally reject the partition scheme. In December Britain declares that it will terminate its mandate over Palestine on 15 May of the following year.

1948 Determined to establish themselves in the area designated to them, Palestinian Jews announce that they will establish a Jewish state at the termination of the British mandate. Attempts by President Truman of the United States to have the partion plan abandoned fail as fighting between Arab and Jew escalates. On 14 May, a few hours before the termination of the British mandate, the Jewish National Council declares the establishment of the State of Israel. Almost immediately Palestine is invaded on all sides by Arab forces from Egypt, Transjordan, Syria, Lebanon and Iraq. Israeli troops not only repulse the Arab assault but also take control of at least 50 per cent more territory than the total alloted to the Jews under the UN partition plan.

1949 The Arab–Israeli conflict eventually comes to an end when both sides sign a series of Armistices. Israel agrees to surrender captured territory in southern Lebanon, northern Sinai and Gaza, but ends up with control over two-thirds of the territory of Palestine. Although 15 000 Arabs remain within the boundaries of the state of Israel, large numbers of Arabs are displaced. Many of them settle in refugee camps in the West Bank and the Gaza Strip.

1950 The United Nations continues its efforts to bring about a peaceful solution based on the earlier partition plan, but major obstacles to peace emerge in the shape of the resettlement of Arab refugees and the position of frontiers between Israel and its neighbouring Arab states. Arab states refuse to integrate refugees on the grounds that their rightful home is in Palestine, but in April King Hussein decides to incorporate the West Bank and East Jerusalem into the Kingdom of Jordan.

1952 King Farouk of Egypt is overthrown by a group of socialist army officers led by Lieut.–Colonel Gamal Abdel Nasser. Egypt steps up its restriction of Israeli sea trade in the Gulf of Aqaba and its support of *fedayeen* guerrillas operating against Israel from bases in Gaza.

1956 In October Israel invades Gaza and the Sinai peninsula in a move designed to allow Anglo–French forces the opportunity of securing the Suez Canal which Nasser had decided to nationalize. Under pressure from the United States and the Soviet Union, the tripartite offensive is called off and Israel withdraws from Gaza and Sinai. The UN establishes an Emergency Force in both of these areas.

1959 Egypt begins a new blockade of Israeli trade through the Suez Canal.

1964 Arab heads of state meeting in Cairo in January call for the creation of Palestinian Arab representative bodies and at the first meeting of the Palestinian National Council, held in the Jordanian sector of Jerusalem in May–June, a Palestinian National Charter is adopted. Declaring the 1947 UN partition plan illegal, the PNC also announces the formation of the Palestine Liberation Organization (PLO) as the principal anti-Zionist movement responsible for the armed struggle to liberate Palestine.

1965 Although active since the mid–1950s, the al-Fatah guerrilla group is formally established on 1 January under the leadership of Yasser Arafat, Abu Jihad and Salah Khalaf.

1966 Al–Fatah intensifies its attacks on Israeli targets from bases in Jordan and Syria. Israel retaliates by launching a reprisal raid on villages in the West Bank of Jordan. Tension between Israel and Jordan continues to mount when West Bank villagers begin to riot, demanding weapons to defend themselves against further Israeli attacks.

1967 In May President Nasser of Egypt moves 80 000 troops into Sinai and requests the UN to withdraw its Emergency Force. When the Straits of Tiran are closed to all ships flying the Israeli flag and to any vessels carrying strategic goods to Israel, the Israeli government accuses Egypt of an act of aggression in violation of assurances given when Israel withdrew from Sharm el Sheik in 1957. On 30 May, having blockaded the Gulf of Aqaba once again, Nasser signs a mutual defence treaty with Jordan. On 5 June Israel launches air attacks on Egypt, Syria, Jordan and Iraq, and destroys virtually the entire air defences of these countries.

By the time hostilities end six days later, Israel has gained control of the Gaza Strip, West Jerusalem, the Golan Heights and the entire Sinai Peninsula as far as the Suez Canal. By increasing its territory from an area of 20 000km^2 to a total of 70 000km^2, Israel also increases the number of Palestinian Arabs under Jewish rule from 300 000 to about 1 200 000 (compared with a Jewish population of 2 500 000). Despite a UN Security Council resolution (242) opposing "the acquistion of territory by war", Israel refuses to withdraw from the territory occupied during the Six–Day War. The conflict between Arab and Jew is now less concerned with the liberation of Palestine than it is with the recovery of territory lost to Israel.

1968 Yasser Arafat takes the powerful al–Fatah guerrilla group into the PLO.

1969 Yasser Arafat is elected chairman of the PLO.

1970 King Hussein sees the presence of PLO guerrillas in Jordan as a threat to his authority. In September ("Black September") he sends his troops against them.

1971 The PLO, which has been ejected from Jordan, moves its political and military headquarters to Lebanon where it finds support amongst sections of the Muslim community.

1973 Unable to regain by peaceful means territory lost during the Six–Day War, Egypt and Syria launch a major offensive against Israel on 6 October, Yom Kippur (the Jewish Day of Atonement). Although Egypt and Syria make initial advances in Sinai and the Golan Heights, Israel recovers on both fronts and after heavy fighting pushes the attack back beyond the 1967 cease-fire lines. The United States and the Soviet Union step in to help bring about a ceasefire in October. By early November a new UN peace-keeping Emergency Force is deployed on the Suez Front.

1974 US Secretary of State, Dr Henry Kissinger, helps to reduce tension by securing military disengagements.
Divisions within the PLO emerge. Liberal groups headed by Yasser Arafat are prepared to consider a negotiated settlement that would involve the creation of a Palestinian state in the West Bank and Gaza Strip alongside Israel. More radical factions oppose this solution and form a "Rejection Front" that will have nothing less than the complete liberation of Palestine by force.

1975 Dr Kissinger is able to secure a further Egyptian–Israeli military disengagement that results in Israeli forces withdrawing by a further 20–40km along the Sinai front. The Suez canal is reopened in June.

The virtual collapse of central government authority in Lebanon during the 1975–76 civil war gives the PLO the chance to develop its infrastructure and launch attacks across the border into Israel.

1977   The Likud party comes to power in Israel. President Sadat of Egypt initiates a rapprochement with Israel in an attempt to reach a peace settlement.

1978   The PLO condemns Sadat's attempts to reach a settlement with Israel and in March steps up its campaign of guerrilla attacks from south Lebanon. Israel retaliates by launching a full-scale invasion of Lebanon that is designed to root out PLO guerrillas. The subsequent deployment of a UN peace-keeping force (UNIFIL) and the withdrawal of Israeli troops back across the border allows the USA to continue its diplomatic efforts to bring about a peaceful solution to the Arab–Israeli conflict. President Sadat of Egypt and Prime Minister Menachim Begin of Israel meet at Camp David near Washington to work out the basis of a Middle East settlement and a peace treaty between Israel and Egypt.

1979   On 26 March the leaders of Egypt and Israel sign the first-ever Arab–Israeli peace treaty. In exchange for a right of passage through the Suez Canal and recognition of the Gulf of Aqaba and the Straits of Tiran as international waterways, Israel agrees to return the Sinai peninsula to Egypt and begin negotiations that will lead to "full autonomy" for the Palestinian Arabs in the occupied territories of Gaza and the West Bank. The PLO opposes the peace treaty since it neither recognizes the PLO nor provides for Palestinian independence. Opposition to the Egypt–Israel peace treaty brings the PLO into contact with Jordan for the first time since the expulsion of the *fedayeen* in 1971.

1982   Israel completes its withdrawal from Sinai in April, but two months later invades Lebanon in an attempt to eliminate the PLO as a military and political force. For three months PLO leaders are beseiged in Beirut which has been the headquarters for many of the organization's political, social and cultural institutions since 1971. The PLO, led by Arafat, are forced to withdraw from the Lebanese capital in early September.

In September three new peace initiatives are announced. The first, by President Reagan of the United States, suggests self-government for Palestinian Arabs in the West Bank and Gaza in association with Jordan, but rules out the possibility of an independent Palestinian state. The second plan, announced by Arab leaders meeting in Fez, calls for the creation of an independent Palestinian State backed by a UN Security Council guarantee of "peace for all states in the region". The third plan is proposed by President Brezhnev of the Soviet Union who agrees that the Palestinian Arabs have the right to create their own state, provided the border between Israel and her Arab neighbours is declared inviolate.

1983   At the 16th annual meeting of the Palestine National Council in Algiers the Reagan plan is rejected, but the concept of a future confederal relationship between Jordan and Palestine is endorsed. In May there is a major split between Arafat loyalists and pro-Syrian extremist factions of the PLO. After a seige of al–Fatah loyalists in the north Lebanese town of Tripoli, Arafat is forced to leave Lebanon once again and set up his headquarters in Tunis. In May Israel agrees to withdraw from Lebanon following the establishment of a six–mile "security zone" in southern Lebanon to prevent the reinfiltration of Palestinian guerrillas into the area.

1984   Radical opposition to Arafat's leadership of the PLO is consolidated with the formation of the Palestinian National Salvation Front, comprising an alliance of al–Fatah dissidents, as–Sa'iqa, the PFLP–GC and the PPSF.

At the 17th session of the Palestine National Council held in Amman, Arafat is confirmed as PLO leader despite a boycott by hardline Democratic Alliance and National Salvation Front groups. In Israel, Labour returns to government in a national unity coalition with Likud.

1985   In February Jordan and the PLO leadership reach an agreement (the Amman accord) that will give Palestinians self-determination within an Arab confederation comprising Jordan and a Palestinian state.

1986 A year after the Amman accord, King Hussein decides not to continue political co-operation with the PLO leadership. Instead, he pursues a policy of rapprochement with Syria.

1987 Mounting frustration in the Israeli–occupied Territories finally boils over in early December when four Palestinians are killed in a traffic accident in Gaza involving an Israeli army lorry. This incident sparks off a display of defiance by Palestinian youths who shout abuse and throw stones at members of the Israeli Defence Forces. Severe counter-measures are adopted in an attempt to restore law and order.

1988 By mid-January the *intifada* or "uprising" has spread to Jerusalem and the West Bank and within weeks the grass roots uprising has turned into an open revolt involving almost the entire Palestinian community in the occupied territories. A clandestine leadership, calling itself the Unified National Leadership of the Uprising, emerges to organize resistance in the form of strikes and boycotts and to set up "popular committees" capable of maintaining essential supplies to Palestinian towns and camps. The killing, beating and deportation of Palestinian agitators by Israeli security forces focuses international media attention on the Palestinian problem. In April 29 Palestinians die during a single week of rioting.

In June the PLO maintains the political momentum by acknowledging Israel's right to exist. A month later King Hussein announces Jordan's withdrawal from all legal and administrative functions in the West Bank and recognizes the right of an independent Palestinian state to secede from Jordan. In November the 19th session of the Palestine National Council endorses a negotiated two–state solution to the Palestinian problem and approves the declaration of Palestinian independence. When the USA refuses to give Arafat a visa in order to attend a debate at the United Nations in December, the session is transfered to Geneva. At a press conference Arafat recognizes Israel's right to exist in "peace and security" and renounces all forms of terrorism, but warns that the *intifada* will not come to an end until an independent Palestinian state has been set up. Although condemned by the Israeli prime minister, this statement is enough to encourage the United States to open up a dialogue with the PLO.

1989 The *intifada* continues in the Israeli–occupied Territories and, by the end of February, it is estimated that during 15 months of civil unrest 370 people have lost their lives, 8000 have been wounded and 22 000 detained.

At a May summit in Casablanca Arab leaders give their backing to the new PLO strategy despite the fact that Damascus–based Palestinian factions continue to denounce Arafat. The Israeli prime minister refuses to deal with the PLO but proposes elections in the occupied territories to identify Palestinian representatives who might hold talks with the Israeli government. The PLO rejects this idea and the Middle East peace process reaches a stalemate.

1990 The Labour Party coalition with Likud collapses when Prime Minister Yitzak Shamir refuses to move towards talks with Palestinian representatives in Cairo as a prelude to self–rule in the occupied territories.

■ Who's who

Abbas, Muhammed (Abu'l Abbas) Secretary–General of the Palestine Liberation Front and one of the 15 members of the Executive Committee of the PLO since 1984. A supporter of Yasser Arafat, Abbas opposes Syrian attempts to gain control of the PLO.

Afanah, Brigadier Ahmed (Abu'l Mu'tassim) Chief–of–staff of the Palestine National Liberation Army, in command of units of the Palestine Liberation Army remaining loyal to Arafat fighting alongside al–Fatah militia.

Ahmad, Abd ar–Rahim   Secretary–General of the pro–Iraqi Arab Liberation Front which he represents on the 15–man PLO Executive Committee.

al–Qadi, Dr Issam   Secretary–General of the pro–Syrian as–Sa'iqa and leading member of the Syrian Ba'ath Party Pan–Arab Command.

al–Rahman, Ahmed Abd   As head of the Unified Information Department, al–Rahman has become a leading PLO spokesman.

Arafat, Yasser (Abu Ammar)   Elected Chairman of the PLO Executive Committee in 1969, Yasser Arafat is perhaps internationally the best known PLO leader. In August 1989 he was acclaimed as Chairman of the ruling Central Committee of al–Fatah, the dominant group within the PLO. Despite a setback in relations with King Hussein in 1986–87, Arafat favours the confederation of a Palestinian state with Jordan as a solution to the Arab–Israeli dispute.

Awwad, Arabi   A former leader of the Palestine Communist Party, now heading the pro–Syrian Palestine Revolutionary Communist Party which broke away from the PCP in 1987.

Begin, Menachem   Israeli lawyer and politician who was Prime Minister 1977–83. In 1978 he was jointly awarded the Nobel Peace Prize with President Sadat of Egypt for his attempts to bring peace to the Middle East.

Ghusha, Dr Samir   Secretary–General of the Damascus–based Palestine Popular Struggle Front.

Habbash, Dr George   Founder of the Arab Nationalist Movement formed in the early 1950s to promote Arab nationalism and unity. In 1967 he founded and became Secretary–General of the left–wing Popular Front for the Liberation of Palestine. Although Habbash remained in Damascus he refused to align himself with the pro–Syrian anti–Arafat alliance.

Hawatmeh, Nayef   Founder and Secretary–General of the left–wing Democratic Front for the Liberation of Palestine. Although based in Damascus Hawatmeh, who opposes international terrorism, has not aligned himself with the anti–Arafat alliance.

Herzl, Theodore   (1860–1904), Hungarian–born Zionist leader who advocated the formation of a Jewish state in a pamphlet entitled *Der Judenstaat* published in 1896. A year later he convened the first Zionist Congress at Basle.

Jarrar, Sheik Bassam   A spiritual leader of the extremist Islamic Resistance Movement (Hamas) in the West Bank.

Jibril, Ahmed   Secretary–General of the pro-Syrian Popular Front for the Liberation of Palestine–General Command which broke away from the PFPL coalition of George Habbash in 1968.

Jihad, Abu (Khalil al–Wazir)   Former PLO military commander and co–leader of al–Fatah, responsible for turning the spontaneous *intifada* in the Israeli–occupied Territories into a full scale guerrilla war. On 16 April 1988 an Israeli raiding party murdered Abu Jihad at his villa in Tunisia.

Jihad, Umm (Intisar al–Wazir)   Wife of the murdered PLO military commander, Abu Jihad. Elected to the Central Committee of al–Fatah, she is the first woman to achieve high office in the PLO.

Muragha, Colonel Sa'id Musa   Syrian–based leader of the rebels who broke away from Arafat's al–Fatah in 1983 to form Fatah–Intifada.

Nidhal, Abu (Sabri al–Banna)   Founder and leader of the breakaway Fatah–Revolutionary Council (Abu Nidhal Organization), Abu Nidhal is an extremist Palestinian nationalist advocating the liberation of Palestine by means of armed struggle.

Peres, Shimon   Leader of Israel's Labour Alignment and an advocate of Palestinian autonomy in those areas of the West Bank and Gaza not vital to Israel's security. Born in Poland in 1923, his family came to Palestine in 1934. He was appointed head of the Israeli

Naval Service in 1948 and Labour Minister of Defence 1974–77. In 1984 he became Prime Minister for the first 25 months of the government of national unity.

Qaddoumi, Faruq (Abu Lutf)   A leading member of al–Fatah and head of the Political Department of the PLO.

Rabin, Itzhak   Leader of the Israeli Labour Party and Prime Minister 1974–77.

Sayeh, Sheikh Abd al–Hamid   Speaker of the Palestinian parliament, the Palestine National Council.

Shamir, Yitzhak   Leader of Israel's right-wing Likud bloc which is opposed to handing over to the Arabs any of the territories captured during the Six–Day War. Born in Poland in 1915, Shamir was founder and leader of the anti–British Stern Gang in 1937. Exiled to Eritrea, he returned to the newly–established State of Israel in 1948. After holding the office of Foreign Minister he succeeded Menachem Begin as Prime Minister in 1983. A year later he was forced into a coalition government of unity that led to the rotation of the post of Prime Minister. Shamir returned to office as Prime Minister in 1986 for a period of 25 months.

Yassin, Sheik Ahmed   A prominent spiritual leader of the extremist Islamic Resistance Movement (Hamas) in the Gaza Strip.

■ Key places

Aqaba, Gulf of   An inlet of the Red Sea bounded to the west by the Sinai peninsula and to the east by Jordan and Saudi Arabia. The port of Aqaba at the north end of the Gulf gives Jordan access to the Red Sea. Similarly, the port of Eilat gives Israel a southerly outlet. The island of Tiran at the narrow mouth of the gulf where it meets the Red Sea is of strategic importance to navigation in and out of the gulf. The withdrawal of Israeli forces from Sinai in 1957 and 1982 was dependent on guarantees that the Gulf of Aqaba would be recognized as an international waterway.

Camp David   A presidential summer retreat in the Catocin Mountains of Maryland, USA. First used as a summer alternative to the suffocating atmosphere of Washington by Franklin D. Roosevelt who named it Shangri–La. Under President Truman Camp David became the official presidential retreat. Of the many historic meetings to have taken place here, the most celebrated were the encounters between Roosevelt and Churchill in 1943 and Eisenhower and Kruschev in 1959. In September 1978 President Carter of the United States arranged a series of talks at Camp David between the leaders of Israel and Egypt in an attempt to resolve the Arab–Israeli conflict.

The resulting Camp David agreements formed a basis for the 1979 Egypt–Israel peace treaty.

Eilat or **Elat**   A seaport and resort in S Israel on the N shore of the Gulf of Aqaba. Built in 1949 on the site of Biblical Elath, the city has a population of 21 000 today. Eilat, the southernmost town in Israel, is linked to Ashquelon on the Mediterranean by an oil pipeline.

Gaza   A narrow strip of land controlling the northern approaches to the Sinai peninsula where it occupies an area of 363km² on the Mediterranean coast. Formerly part of Egypt, the Gaza Strip was taken by Israel during the Six–Day War in 1967. With a Palestinian Arab population in excess of 550 000, Gaza is one of the most densely populated areas of the world. The chief town, Gaza, has 120 000 inhabitants, but over 50 per cent of the people live in refugee camps which were first established during the Arab–Israeli war of 1948–49. In the 1950s Arab *fedayeen* guerrillas launched frequent attacks into Israel from bases in the Gaza Strip, a situation that prompted the 1956 Israeli invasion of Egypt. An incident in December 1987 sparked off the Palestinian uprising or *intifada*.

Golan   An escarpment stretching for 50km between the mouths of the Hermon and Yarmuk rivers on the frontier between Syria and Israel. Rising to 1204m at Mount Avital, the basalt plateau that forms the Golan Heights commands a strategic position overlooking Upper Galilee. Formerly part of Syria, Golan was captured by Israel during the Six–Day War in 1967. Although 12 000 Druse peasants remained in the Israeli Occupied Territory, nearly all of the Golan's Arab population of 90 000 fled into Syria. Syrian troops managed to retake the Golan Heights for a short while during the Arab–Israeli war of 1973, but they were driven back to within 30km of Damascus by a counter–offensive that added a further 777km² to the area occupied by Israel. A disengagement agreement between Israel and Syria in 1974 resulted in some of this territory being handed back to Syria. Despite the presence of a UN peace-keeping force Israel decided to ensure the security of its northern frontier with Syria, first by settling over 9000 Jews in the Golan area, and second by formally annexing the territory in December 1981. The extension of Israeli jurisdiction over the Golan heights was immediately condemned by the United Nations which declared the move "null and void, without international legal effect."

Jaffa or **Yafo**   With Tel Aviv, Jaffa is the second largest city in Israel; population 319 500. Situated on the Mediterranean coast 60km north-west of Jerusalem, Jaffa was the great landing-place of the Crusaders during the wars to recapture the Holy Land from the Muslims. During the last three decades of the 19th century the population of the town rose from 15 000 to 40 000 as the trade in oranges developed. In later years Haifa superceded Jaffa as Israel's major port. In 1950 Tel Aviv and Jaffa were joined together as one city.

Jerusalem   Capital of the state of Israel and a holy city of Jews, Christians and Arabs, situated in the E Highlands of Judaea. In 1947 the United Nations decided to partition Palestine and make Jersulem an international city, but a year later, when the British mandate came to an end, Israel and Jordan fought each other for control of the city. A ceasefire in 1949 effectively divided the city into eastern and western sectors controlled by Jordan and Israel respectively. In 1950 the Israelis made West Jerusalem their capital. In 1967 Israel annexed East Jerusalem and in 1980 the whole city was declared capital of the state of Israel. Out of a total population of 482 700, there are 130 000 Palestinian Arabs, mostly living in East Jerusalem.

Jordan   A river rising in several headstreams in the Anti-Lebanon mountains near the Lebanon–Syria frontier. Flowing southwards along a rift valley for 320km, it passes through the Sea of Galilee before falling into the Dead Sea. In the south the river separates the East Bank of Jordan from Israeli-Occuppied Territory on the West Bank.

Kinneret   A Jewish settlement on the SW shore of the Sea of Galilee, established in 1908 as the first experimental kibbutz or co-operative farm. The settlement gives its name to a district of N Israel with a population of 62 600.

Negev   (Hebrew, "desert")   An arid desert region in southern Israel, irrigated and occupied by Jewish settlers since 1948. Since the days of the British mandate in Palestine the population of the Negev has risen from 12 000 to 230 000. Beersheba, with a population of 114 600, is the largest settlement.

Palestine   In Biblical times, the land of the Philistines, but in this century applied to the territory W of the River Jordan now occupied by Israel and the West Bank of Jordan. Ruled by the Ottoman Turks for four centuries, Palestine was assigned to Britain as a mandated territory following the break-up of the Arab Levant in 1920. The settlement of Palestine by an increasing number of Jewish immigrants eventually led to conflict between Arab and Jew and the termination of the British mandate in 1948. A UN plan to partition Palestine was pre-empted by the first Arab–Israeli war during which the state of Israel was established. The liberation of Palestine from Jewish rule and the creation of an independent Arab Palestine state have been the aims, first of the Arab High Committee, and then of the PLO which was formally set up in January 1964.

Sinai A peninsula of NE Egypt, lying between the Suez Canal and the Gulf of Aqaba, with the Mediterranean to the north. Covering an area of 58 714km², the Sinai has a population of 176 000. The coastal plain rises to heights of 2 286m at Mt Sinai and 2 637m at Mt Katherina in the Gebel Musa range in the south. In 1956 Israeli troops invaded Egypt, crossing the Sinai as far as the Suez Canal, but in response to US and Soviet pressure they eventually withdrew from the peninsula. When Israel attacked Egypt once again in 1967 the Sinai was recaptured by Israeli Defence Forces who remained in occupation until a phased withdrawal was initiated in 1979. The last Israeli troops left Sinai in April 1982.

Tel Aviv Twinned with the Arab port of Jaffa to the south, Tel Aviv was founded in 1909 as the first Jewish city in Palestine. Following the declaration of the state of Israel in 1948 Tel Aviv became the country's first capital. In 1950 the capital was transferred to West Jerusalem and Tel Aviv was incorporated with Jaffa. Although Jerusalem became the permanent capital most foreign embassies are still located in Tel Aviv–Jaffa.

Transjordan Territory to the east of the River Jordan held under mandate by the British following the break-up of the Ottoman Empire at the end of World War I. Transjordan, which became an independent state in May 1946, changed its name to the Hashemite Kingdom of Jordan in 1951.

West Bank A territory lying to the west of the River Jordan, where it extends over 5 879km² from the lowland rift valley to the Highlands of Samaria and Judaea. In 1948–49 Palestinian Arabs and Israelis fought each other for control of the West Bank, but a ceasefire in April 1949 left the territory in Jordanian hands. The West Bank remained part of Jordan until it was captured by Israeli forces during the Six–Day War in 1967. Still under Israeli occupation, it has a population of 866 000 of whom 97 per cent are Palestinian Arabs. About 88 per cent of the people are residents of towns or villages. The remainder live in refugee camps. The chief towns are Nablus, Ramallah, Hebron and Jericho.

■ Key words

Abu Nidal Organization or **Fatah–Revolutionary Council** A break-away faction of al–Fatah dedicated to the liberation of the whole of Palestine by force. Originally based in Baghdad, the Revolutionary Council first emerged as an extreme dissident group in 1974 when the Palestine National Council suggested the less militant possibility of negotiating a two–state solution to the Palestinian problem. Opposed to Syria's involvement in Lebanon, it began a series of anti-Syrian attacks in 1976 under the name Black June Organization. This group has claimed responsibility for a large number of terrorist attacks aimed at PLO, Arab, Israeli, Syrian and European targets.

al–Asifa The original militia wing of al–Fatah which first carried out guerrilla operations in 1965. After the Israeli occupation of the Gaza Strip and the West Bank in 1967, irregular militia groups based in countries bordering Israel proliferated and al–Asifa intensified its activities.

al–Fatah ("conquest") or **Palestine National Liberation Movement** The largest and most powerful political and military group within the PLO. Active within Palestinian refugee camps in the 1950s, it was formally organized as a clandestine guerrilla group in 1965 under the leadership of Yasser Arafat, Salah Khalaf and Abu Jihad. The movement quickly rose to power after the 1967 Arab–Israeli War. In the space of two years it not only joined the PLO but gained control of the organization when Yasser Arafat was elected Chairman of the Executive Committee in 1969.

Amman Accord An agreement between the PLO and Jordan signed in February 1985. In the search for peace both sides agreed on a plan of action that would give the Palestinians self-determination within an Arab confederation comprising Jordan and a Palestinian state. A year later the agreement was terminated by King Hussein who declared he could not continue to co-operate with the PLO.

Arab High Committee   An organization set up by the Palestinian Arabs in 1936 for the purpose of co-ordinating opposition to Jewish settlement. In 1964 the Committee was replaced by the PLO which was established at a Palestinian Congress in Jerusalem.

Arab Liberation Front (ALF)   A small pro-Iraqi faction of the PLO created by the Ba'ath Party in 1969 to rival the pro-Syrian as-Sa'iqa group.

Ashkenazim   Israeli Jews of European origin as opposed to the Sephardic Jews of Afro-Asian origin.

as–Sa'iqa   A pro-Syrian political and military grouping within the PLO founded in 1966 by Palestinian members of the Syrian Ba'ath Party. Based in Damascus, as–Sa'iqa promotes the Syrian opposition to PLO policy under Arafat's leadership while maintaining a strong position in the Palestine National Salvation Front. Although officially opposed to terrorism, a number of guerrilla attacks have been linked to some as–Sa'iqa members who call themselves Eagles of the Palestine Revolution.

Balfour Declaration   A letter written on 2 November 1917 by the British Foreign Secretary, Arthur Balfour, to the prominent British Jew, Lord Rothschild, in which it was stated that "His Majesty's Government view with favour the establishment in Palestine of a national home for the Jewish people". This communication is still seen by many Palestinians as the root cause of their problems.

Black June Organization   A name used by Abu Nidahl's dissident faction of al–Fatah in 1976 when it began to attack Syrian targets in protest at Syria's involvement in Lebanon.

Black September   The name given to the month of September 1970 when King Hussein ordered the PLO to leave Jordan. In the flight to Lebanon 3000 Palestinians lost their lives. A Black September Organization, thought to have been set up by the security wing of al–Fatah, carried out terrorist reprisals that included the assassination of the Jordanian prime minister in 1971, the attack on Israeli athletes at the 1972 Munich Olympics and the killing of the US ambassador in Khartoum in 1973.

Camp David Agreements   Agreements reached between Israel and Egypt in September 1978 following two years of discussions between President Anwar Sadat of Egypt and Prime Minister Menachem Begin of Israel. A series of talks was held in the United States at Camp David, the summer retreat of President Carter who acted as intermediary. The two countries agreed never to go to war; the Sinai was to be returned to Egypt; and self-determination was eventually to be granted to Palestinians living in the Israeli-Occupied Territories of Gaza and the West Bank.

Central Council   A PLO consultative group which meets every few months to interpret policy, make recommendations to the Palestine National Council (PNC) and oversee the various departments of the PLO. Set up in 1973, it has some 90 members including a 15-man Executive Committee.

Democratic Front for the Liberation of Palestine (DFLP)   A Damascus–based Marxist–Leninist grouping within the PLO, formed in 1969 by the Jordanian Nayef Hawatmeh who had withdrawn from the PFLP which he had co-founded in the previous year. Until 1974 the movement was known as the Popular Democratic Front for the Liberation of Palestine. This organization claims to have been the first to advocate a negotiated settlement of the Palestinian problem that involves the setting up of two states.

Eagles of the Palestine Revolution   A small grouping within the pro-Syrian as–Sa'iqa organization linked with a number of terrorist activities including the attack on a train carrying Soviet Jews through Austria to Israel in 1971 and the occupation of the Egyptian Embassy in Ankara in 1979.

Eretz Israel   The "Land of Israel" as described

in biblical texts and including the West Bank and Gaza.

Executive Committee   A 15-man executive group comprising leading members of the PLO who are responsible for implementing Palestine National Council (PNC) decisions. The heads of the various PLO departments or "ministries" are selected from this group.

Fatah–the Intifada   ("uprising") or **Fatah–Provisional Command**   An extreme dissident faction of al–Fatah which emerged in 1983 in the aftermath of the Israeli invasion of Lebanon. Believing that force is the only way to liberate the whole of Palestine, the Syrian–backed Provisional Command opposes Arafat's attempts to reach a negotiated settlement with Israel.

February 6 Movement   A Sunni Muslim militia led by Palestinian sympathizers based in the Tariq Jdideh district of Beirut.

fedayeen   The name given to Palestinian resistance militias which operated against Israeli targets from bases in Gaza during the 1950s and 1960s. When the Israelis captured Gaza during the Six–Day War of 1967 the fedayeen established bases in Jordan, but in July 1971, after a year of open conflict with the government of King Hussein, they were forced out of that country and into Lebanon.

Force 17   A paramilitary group responsible for looking after the security of al–Fatah personnel and property.

General Union of Palestinian Students   A Palestinian organization set up in the 1950s to act as a means of communication between higher education students studying in over 40 countries. The union is run by an 11-member Executive Committee which is selected from a 33-man Administrative Council. All branches send delegates to a National Conference.

Haganah   A defence force set up by Palestinian Jews following Arab attacks in 1920.

Institution of Social Affairs and Welfare   Originally created in 1965 as an agency to care

for the families of Palestinians killed in action, the institute developed into a social welfare organization providing financial, medical, legal and educational help to the dependents of those who had been killed, wounded or imprisoned.

intifada   The "uprising" or "shaking off" that first emerged in the West Bank and Gaza Strip at the end of 1987 when stone-throwing demonstrators confronted Israeli security forces. Press coverage of the violence that took place in the following months heightened international awareness of the Palestinian problem.

Islamic Resistance Movement or **Hamas** ("zeal")   A Muslim fundamentalist group particularly active in the refugee camps of the Gaza Strip. Hamas is dedicated to the destruction of Israel and the creation of an Islamic state,

Jihaz ar–Rasd   The security and intelligence wing of al–Fatah.

kibbutz   A communal or co-operative settlement in Israel, where it was originally conceived in the early years of the 20th century by Professor Franz Oppenheimer. After a successful experiment initiated in 1908, the first permanent kibbutz farmers were allowed to settle on land at Kinneret on the south-west shore of Lake Tiberias. Initially, the term kibbutz was used to describe a large collective settlement in contrast to the smaller kuutsai; now the term is generally applied to all collectives.

Knesset   The 120-member unicameral parliament of Israel.

Labour Alignment   A coalition of Israel's left-wing political parties (except the Communist Party) which held power from the founding of Israel in 1948 until defeated by the Likud bloc in 1977. The Labour Alignment draws most of its support from the kibbutzim and the middle and upper-middle classes of European or Israeli-born origin.

Likud bloc   An alignment of right-wing political parties in Israel comprising the

Herut ("freedom") Party, the Liberals and the small La'am Party. The Likud draws most of its support from the Sephardic community of oriental Jews who came to Israel after the founding of the state in 1948. The Likud bloc, which allied with the National Religious Party in 1977 to form a government, is opposed to the Labour policy of negotiating with the Palestinians on the basis of "land for peace".

Mossad   The Israeli external security service, responsible for counter-terrorist operations overseas and for the supply of armed guards on all *El Al* airliners.

Operation Peace for Galilee   The codename for the June 1982 Israeli invasion of South Lebanon.

Palestine Communist Party (PCP)   A political organization formed in 1982 by Palestinian members of the Jordanian Communist Party. In 1987 this group aligned itself with Arafat and joined the Palestine National Council. The group does not have a militia.

Palestine Liberation Army (PLA)   The regular army of the PLO, formed in 1964. Although theoretically under the command of the Chairman of the PLO Executive Committee who is its Commander-in-Chief, in practice the PLA is controlled by the government of the country in which its active units are based. Units of the PLA remaining loyal to Arafat have joined forces with al–Fatah militia to form the Palestine National Liberation Army.

Palestine Liberation Front (PLF)   A pro-Iraqi PLO group which broke away from the Popular Front for the Liberation of Palestine – General Command in 1977 in protest at PFLP–GC collusion with Syrian action against Palestinian militia forces in Lebanon. The group gained seats on the Palestine National Council in 1981. A split in the PLF took place during 1983–84 when a faction led by Tala'at Yaqub aligned itself with the pro-Syrian Palestine National Salvation Front. In 1985 this group claimed responsibility for the highjacking of the Italian cruise liner, *Achille Lauro*.

Palestine Liberation Organization (PLO)   A Palestinian Arab organization formed in June 1964. It replaced the largely ineffectual Arab High Committee which had been responsible for the Palestinian struggle in the aftermath of the Arab–Israeli War of 1948–49. The decision to set up the PLO was taken at an Arab summit conference held in January 1964.

Palestine Martyrs' Works Society (SAMED)   Originally set up to provide employment and training for the families of Palestinians killed in action, SAMED has developed into a large profit-making enterprise that is intended to form the industrial and commercial foundation of any future Palestinian state.

Palestinian National Council (PNC)   The principal policy-making body of the PLO. Operating as a "parliament-in-exile", it consists of 400 members elected or selected from the various political and military organizations, from the refugee camps and from the Palestinian communities throughout the world. In addition there are 180 members from the Israeli-Occupied Territories who are not able to attend the annual PNC sessions. Based in the Jordanian capital of Amman, the day-to-day running of the PNC is in the hands of a secretariat known as the office of the Speaker.

Palestine National Fund (PNF)   Based in Amman, the PNF was set up in 1964 to act as an agency responsible for financing PLO activities. The fund, which is handled by an Administrative Council, derives its revenue from the donations of private individuals and Arab states and from the taxation of Palestinian workers.

Palestine National Liberation Army   Units of the Palestine Liberation Army that have amalgamated with al–Fatah militia and have remained loyal to Arafat.

Palestine National Salvation Front   A coalition of extremist pro-Syrian PLO groups opposed to Yasser Arafat's leadership of the PLO. Formed in 1984, it includes al–Fatah dissidents and members of as–Sa'iqa, PFPL–GC and PPSF guerrilla groups.

Palestine Popular Struggle Front (PPSF) An offshoot of the Palestine Liberation Army tthat emerged in the 1960s and later united with al–Fatah in 1971. Based in Damascus, the group eventually broke away from al–Fatah in 1973.

Palestine Red Crescent Society (PRCS) Affiliated to the International Red Cross Society, the Palestine Red Cross Society was set up in 1968 as a medical branch of the PLO. Based in Cairo it offers medical facilities for both Palestinians and non-Palestinians.

Palestinian Revolutionary Communist Party (PRCP) A pro-Syrian Palestinian group based in Damascus where it is headed by a former leader of the palestine Communist Party.

Palestine Trade Union Federation (PTUF) A trade union movement that acts on behalf of Palestinians working throughout the world. Established in the city of Haifa in 1925 as the General Union of Palestinian Workers, the union was brought to life again in 1965 at its first Congress in Gaza.

Partition Plan A UN proposal adopted in November 1947, which called for the division of Palestine into an Arab and a Jewish state and for the designation of Jerusalem as an international city under UN administration. The plan was thwarted by the Jewish declaration of the State of Israel on 14 May 1948,

Peel Commission A Royal Commission set up under the chairmanship of Lord Peel in 1936 to look into the relationship between Jew and arab in Palestine. The report of the commission, published in July 1937, recommended the partition of Palestine into separate Arab and Jewish states.

Popular Front for the Liberation of Palestine (PFLP) A coalition of small guerrilla groups who merged with the Palestinian branch of the Arab Nationalist Movement in December 1967 to form a left-wing party dedicated to social change throughout the region. Although it claims to represent the working class its membership is largely drawn from the intellectual and professional classes. Based in Syria, the PFLP also receives support from

Algeria, Libya and Yemen. Until his death in 1978 Wadi Haddad, Baghdad-based co-founder and deputy leader of the PFLP, directed terrorist attacks and hijackings despite a 1972 announcement from the Front's leader, Dr Habbash, that such operations would no longer be mounted.

Popular Front for the Liberation of Palestine–General Command (PFLP–GC) A pro-Syrian PLOgroup formerly called the Palestine Liberation Front. It merged with other groups to form the Popular Front for the Liberation of Palestine in 1967 but broke away a year later following a series of disputes. Opposed to the negotiated solution proposed by the Arafat leadership of the PLO, the PFLP–GC seeks to liberate the whole of Palestine by force.

Resolution 242 A resolution proposed by Britain and adopted by the United Nations on 22 November 1967 which emphasized "the inadmissability of the acquisition of territory by war and the need to work for a just and lasting peace in which every state in the area can live in security". The resolution was accepted by Israel and the front line Arab states, except Syria.

Resolution 338 A ceasefire resolution proposed by the USA and the Soviet Union and adopted by the United Nations Security Council on 22 October 1973. Recommending the immediate implementation of UN Resolution 242, the two super-powers co-operated in securing the passage of Resolution 338 in an attempt to prevent the escalation of the Arab–Israeli conflict into a broader confrontation.

Sephardim Jews of oriental rather than European origin.

Shebab A name given to the Palestinian youths in the Israeli–occupied Territories who hurled insults and stones at Israeli soldiers during the early days of the *intifada*.

Shin-Beth The Israeli Department of Internal Security, responsible for counter-terrorist measures within Israel. This branch of the intelligence service is noted for its hardline reaction to Palestinian violence and agitation.

Six–Day War   The name given to the hostilities which broke out between Israel and Egypt, Jordan and Syria on 5 June 1967. After six days of fighting all sides accepted a ceasefire called for by the UN Security Council but, by this time, Israel had succeeded in gaining control of Sinai, the Gaza Strip, the Golan Heights and the West Bank of the River Jordan including East Jerusalem.

Sykes–Picot Agreement   A secret agreement concluded in 1916 by Sir Mark Sykes and Georges Picot dividing the former Ottoman Empire into English and French spheres of influence to the south and north of a line roughly following the present-day Syrian border with Jordan and Iraq. The two British mandates of Palestine and Transjordan were established to the south of this line in 1922.

Unified Information Council   A Palestinian media organization based in Tunis where it operates the Palestine News Agency and produces bulletins in Arabic, English and French.

Unified National Leadership of the Uprising (UNLU)   A grass roots leadership that emerged in 1988 to co-ordinate the *intifada*

activities of the Palestinian communities in the Israeli–occupied Territories. UNLU has organized strikes, encouraged non-payment of taxes and called for a boycott of Israeli products. In order to create an alternative administration, "popular committees" have been set up in villages, towns and refugee camps for the purpose of organizing medical care, education and the distribution of food, fuel and other resources.

Vanguard of the Popular War for the Liberation of Palestine   The official title of the political wing of the Syrian–backed as–Sa'iqa organization.

Venice Declaration   A declaration of the European Community of June 1980 endorsing the 1967 UN Security Council Resolution affirming the right of Palestinian people to self-determination while allowing all peoples and states in the Middle East the right to live in peace and security.

Zionism   Founded in 1897 by Theodore Herzl, the Zionist movement sought to establish a Jewish nation in Palestine. The holy hill of Zion in Jerusalem is the focal point of the Jewish religion and is symbolic of the "Promised Land", as well as the Zionist hope of returning to Palestine.

■ Further reading

H. Cobban, *The Palestine Liberation Organization: People Power and Politics*, Cambridge University Press, Cambridge, 1984

A. Frangi (ed.), *The PLO and Palestine*, Zed, London, 1987

M. Gilbert, *The Arab–Israeli Conflict: Its History in Maps*, (4th edn.) Weidenfeld and Nicolson, London, 1984

D. Gilmour, *The Ordeal of the Palestinians 1917–1980*, Sidgwick & Jackson, London, 1980

Chaim Herzog, *The Arab–Israeli Wars: War and Peace in the Middle East*, Random House, New York, 1982

G.R.Keival, *Party Politics in Israel and the Occupied Territories*, Westport, Connecticut, 1983

W.R. Louis and R.W. Stookey (eds.), *The End of the Palestine Mandate*, Tauris, London, 1986

Minority Rights Group, Report No. 24, *The Palestinians*, London, 1987

D. Newman, Civilian and Military Presence as Strategies of Territorial Control: The Arab–Israeli Conflict, *Political Geography Quarterly*, 8(3), 1989

B. Reich, *Israel: Land of Tradition and Conflict*, Praeger, London and New York, 1986

Howard Morley Sachar, *A History of Israel*, (2 vols.), Oxford University Press, Oxford, 1976 and 1986

David K. Shipler, *Arab and Jew: Wounded Spirits in a Promised Land*, Time Books, New York, 1986

Martin Wright (ed.), *Israel and the Palestinians*, Longman (UK), Harlow, 1989

2
Lebanon

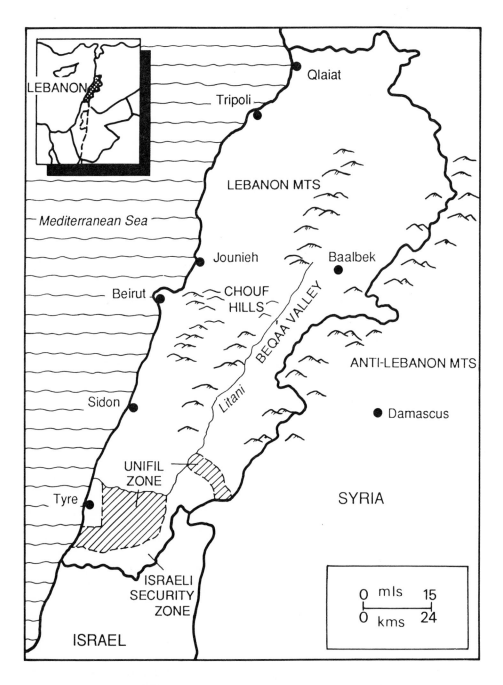

LEBANON

Mediterranean Sea

Qlaiat

Tripoli

LEBANON MTS

Jounieh

Baalbek

Beirut

CHOUF
HILLS

BEQAA VALLEY

Litani

ANTI-LEBANON MTS

Sidon

Damascus

UNIFIL
ZONE

SYRIA

Tyre

ISRAELI
SECURITY
ZONE

ISRAEL

0	mls	15
0	kms	24

■ Profile

Official name: Republic of Lebanon

- **Area:**   10 452km²
- **Population (1984 est.):**   3.5 million
- **Ethnic groups:**   Arab 93%, Armenian 5%, Kurd 1%
- **Languages:**   Arabic, French, English, Armenian
- **Religion:**   *Muslim:* Shia 31.4%, Sunni 21.4%, Druse 5.7%,
  Christian: Maronites 25%, Greek Orthodox 7.1%, Armenian Orthodox 5%,
  Greek Catholic 4.3%
- **Infant mortality rate:**   48 per 1000
- **Life expectancy:**   65 years
- **Currency:**   Lebanese pound of 100 piastres
- **Timezone:**   GMT +2
- **Capital:**   Beirut
- **Chief cities:**   Beirut (702 000), Tripoli (175 000), Zahlé (46 800), Sidon (24 700), Tyre (14 000)

■ Introduction

The roots of Lebanon's present troubles lie mainly in its ethnic and religious diversity, partly in the impact of French colonial rule and partly in the knock-on effects of the Arab–Israeli conflict over Palestine (*see section 2.1*). Situated at one of the world's trading crossroads, ancient Lebanon came successively under Phoenician, Hellenistic and Roman rule. Christianized by the 4th century AD, the country succumbed to rising Arab power in the 7th. The Catholic Maronite sect, however, resisted Islamicization from its strongholds in the mountains and cedar forests north of Beirut. From the 11th century substantial adherence to the heretical Druse offshoot of Islam created another enclosed community in Lebanon. The Ottoman Turkish conquest in the early 16th century dampened down confessional conflict, but Islamic social rigidities enabled the Maronites to prosper economically at the expense of the Muslims. Developing links with Christian Europe, especially Italy and France, the Maronites dominated commerce by the 19th century, as the European powers began to cast covetous eyes on the declining Ottoman Empire.

The establishment of a French protectorate in 1860 followed the classic pattern of an intervention to halt inter-communal warfare. The main beneficiaries of French protection were the Maronites, whose economic ascendancy stimulated increasing Muslim resentment. Half a century later, the mandating of Syria/Lebanon to France after World War I was welcomed by many Christians, as was the French decision of 1926 to separate Lebanon from Syria. In those inter-war years Beirut became a very French city, with French language and culture predominant among the Maronite elite. A French-organized census in 1932 – disputed then and since but still the only such exercise ever held in Lebanon – found that Christians (all denominations) formed a majority of the population. When the World War II defeat of France in 1940 created irresistible pressure for independence, the Maronite leadership was able to control the process. It secured the agreement of moderate Muslim leaders to the unwritten National Pact of 1943 specifying that institutional power in the new state would be shared out between the confessions according to their numerical strength. Thus the President and army commander were always to be Maronites and the Prime Minister always a Sunni Muslim, while the Parliament would have a built-in Christian majority.

For three decades the Lebanese power-sharing arrangement worked reasonably well. As part of the Christian identification with the Arab cause, Lebanon became a member of the Arab League and joined in the 1948–49 war against Israel. The resignation of President Bishara al-Khoury in 1952 was forced by joint Christian and Muslim opposition to corruption. And in its greatest early test, power-sharing emerged strengthened from the crisis of 1958, when Nasserite Muslim leftists tried to overthrow President Camille Chamoun and the latter called in the US Marines. That particular conflict was resolved when Chamoun stood down in favour of Fouad Chehab, who created a new alliance of moderate Christian and Muslim parties backing reconciliation. Under the "Chehabist" compromise, extremists on both sides were kept in check and Lebanon enjoyed unprecedented economic prosperity during the 1960s, becoming the Middle East's main financial and commercial centre. But the clouds of future storms were already gathering.

Although Lebanon kept out of the 1967 and 1973 Arab–Israeli wars, the resultant influx of Palestinian refugees served to destabilize the internal status quo. Doubtful about the commitment of Lebanese Christians to the Palestinian/Arab cause, the Palestinians formed a natural alliance with disadvantaged Shia Muslims and Druses. These communities were already restive at the willingness of more prosperous Sunni Muslims to accept Christian dominance when most assessments agreed that Muslims now formed a majority of the Lebanese population. Early clashes led to the Cairo agreement of 1969 imposing restrictions on Palestinian activities in Lebanon. But the expulsion of the Palestine Liberation Organization (PLO) from Jordan in 1970–71 and the transfer of many PLO guerrillas to Lebanon added a new dimension. Lebanese Christian fears of the PLO becoming a "state within a state" were exacerbated by Israeli reprisal actions against PLO camps providing springboards for guerrilla incursions into Israel. The flashpoint came in 1975, when right-wing Lebanese Christians massacred a coach-load of Palestinians in Beirut, sparking off a civil war

which has continued without much abatement ever since.

Identifying the opposing sides at any given moment of the post-1975 Lebanese conflict has been notoriously difficult. In its first phase, a mainly Muslim alliance of Lebanese leftists and the PLO took the battle to the conservative, mainly Christian, forces of the establishment. The composition and aims of the former were to shift constantly, but its basic demand for constitutional and economic reforms in favour of Muslims remained a constant factor in the struggle, as did, although less so, Christian resistance to change. Also constant has been the "greater Syria" (i.e. including Lebanon) aspiration of the Damascus regime, in terms of control of Lebanase affairs if not of outright takeover. In April 1976 Syrian troops were called in by the Maronite President, Suleyman Franjieh, to prevent the defeat of the Christian forces. Designated the Arab Deterrent Force (ADF) by the Arab League, they have remained in Lebanon ever since, sometimes keeping the Lebanese factions apart. Syria's political objective has been a new constitutional framework for Lebanon giving Muslims a greater role without undermining Christian rights, the whole to have suitable deference to Syrian interests. Its problem has been to persuade the Lebanese factions, particularly hardline Christians, to compromise and also not to alarm an ever-watchful Israel.

Israel's suspicions of Syrian intentions, combined with its longstanding concern over the security threat posed by Lebanon-based PLO guerrillas, determined the course of the second phase of the Lebanese conflict from 1978 to 1985. After occupying southern Lebanon for three months in 1978, Israeli forces left behind a surrogate army of pro-Israeli Christians to police the border area, in which a UN peacekeeping force was also deployed. Nevertheless, Israel remained deeply concerned about the PLO role in Lebanon's steadily growing internal anarchy. Having secured its peace treaty with Egypt, Israel mounted another invasion of Lebanon in mid-1982 intended to eradicate the PLO once and for all. Penetrating to Beirut and beyond, its forces secured the withdrawal of PLO guerrillas and Syrian ADF units from the Lebanese capital. But like many another occupying army, the Israelis found that superior military strength was no guarantee of political success. Israeli connivance in a massacre of Palestinian refugees in Beirut by right-wing Christian Phalangists in September 1982, in retaliation for the murder of President-elect Bashir Gemayel, was condemned internationally and in Israel. A US-sponsored agreement between the Israelis and the new President, Amin Gemayel, for the withdrawal of all foreign forces collapsed in face of Syrian and Muslim Lebanese opposition. In Israel fierce opposition to the Lebanese adventure was strengthened by mounting Israeli casualties. When Israeli forces finally withdrew in mid-1985, the situation in Lebanon was little different from when they invaded: the Syrians controlled northern and eastern Lebanon, PLO guerrillas had returned and the internal conflict still raged.

Since 1985 the underlying Christian/Muslim confrontation has tended to be obscured by more ferocious hostilities between rival groups within the two main camps. On the leftist–Muslim side, Shia energies have been dissipated in bitter feuding between the pro-Syrian AMAL movement and the Teheran-backed Hezbollah militia; and both have periodically clashed with one or other faction of the PLO, with the Druses and with Sunni militias (which in turn have all been prepared to fight each other). The baleful influence of fundamentalist and anti-Western Iran has also been apparent in the high incidence of kidnappings of Western nationals (very few of whom remained in Lebanon). On the Christian side, President Gemayel's hardline Phalangist faction consistently opposed Syrian-sponsored peace initiatives and came into conflict with other Christian groups prepared to accept Syrian mediation. A succession of "peace settlements" involving acceptance of a national unity government proved to be stillborn. In the absence of agreement on the presidential succession in 1988, Gemayel's last act in office was to bequeath further trouble to his country by appointing an interim military government under General Michel Aoun, the Maronite army commander. Condemned as illegal by Muslim groups (who supported the existing, albeit nominal, government headed by a Sunni Muslim), the Aoun regime declared its intention to expel the Syrians from Lebanon. Backed by Syria's arch-enemy, Iraq, Aoun quickly found himself also embroiled in fierce conflict with Christian factions opposed to his hardline policy.

By the end of the decade 15 years of continuous civil war had reduced Lebanon to a state of general anarchy, while the country's infrastructure and once-prosperous economy lay in ruins. Few observers saw any obvious way out of the nightmare, given the intractable positions of key participants and the communal loyalties and fears which underpinned them. Perhaps most depressing of all, there was little sign of the region's powers ceasing to pursue their rivalries on a Lebanese battlefield.

■ Chronology of events

1860–61 Following a massacre of Maronites by Druses, France establishes a protectorate over Lebanon by agreement with the Ottoman government. The largely Maronite Christian area around Mount Lebanon is granted special autonomous status within the Ottoman Empire.

1914 The Ottoman Empire joins the central powers in World War I; Britain and France launch a military campaign to capture Ottoman Arab territories in the Middle East.

1918 The French capture Beirut on 5 October.

1920 The Ottoman Empire is carved up by the League of Nations. France is assigned the mandate for Syria which is divided into three loosely federated Arab states and a separate Christian state called Great Lebanon.

1925 The Islamic Druse community accuses the French of favoritism towards the Christians and begins a two–year revolt.

1926 In May Great Lebanon is proclaimed a semi–autonomous republic by the French.

1932   A French–organized census finds that Christians (all denominations) make up 55 per cent of Lebanon's population.

1941   On 16 November the decision to grant full independence to Lebanon is announced in Beirut.

1943   British and Free–French forces overthrow the Vichy administration and Lebanon finally gains full independence under the presidency of Sheikh Bishara al–Khoury. An unwritten "National Pact", devised by President al–Khoury and Prime Minister Riyadh al–Solh, forms the basis of a system of power sharing between Christians and Muslims in the ratio 6:5. It is agreed that the country's President should be a Maronite Christian, Prime Minister a Sunni Muslim and President of the National Assembly a Shia Muslim.

1946   The evacuation of French troops is completed.

1948–49   Lebanon, as a member of the Arab League, joins the first Arab war against the new State of Israel. Amid the Israeli victory, Lebanon accepts Palestinian refugees who settle in camps in the south.

1958   President Chamoun's pro–Western policies cause friction between Muslims and Christians. When fighting breaks out, the Lebanese government asks the United States to send troops to help restore law and order. Chamoun resigns in favour of Fouad Chetab, who establishes a reconciliation government based on compromise by moderate Christian and Muslim factions.

1964   The Palestine Liberation Organization is founded.

1967   Lebanon keeps out of the Six–Day War between Israel and Arab states, but receives another wave of Palestinian refugees.

1968   Arab terrorists operating from Lebanon attack an Israeli airliner in Athens. Israel responds by carrying out a raid on Beirut airport.

1969   The Lebanese government tries to limit Palestinian *fedayeen* attacks on Israel by reaching a secret agreement with the PLO (the Cairo agreement), placing restrictions on guerrilla activities. This effectively legitimizes the Palestinian presence in Lebanon.

1970–71   The PLO, which is expelled from Jordan, establishes its headquarters in Lebanon. Cross-border raids into Israel by Palestinian *fedayeen* are intensified.

1973   Following Israeli reprisals on villages in south Lebanon, units of the Lebanese army attack Palestinian camps. The situation deteriorates as Christian militia fight Palestinian guerrillas. The government is unable to put an end to the conflict and the Christian Maronites turn to the Kata'eb (Phalange) Party for support against the growing Palestinian threat.

1974   Palestinian guerrillas continue to fight Maronite units. Meanwhile, the Shia Muslim community under the influence of the radical Iranian, Imam Musa Sadr, begins to organize its own AMAL militia groups.

1975   In February violence breaks out during a demonstration in Sidon. Two months later Phalange militia massacre a bus–load of Palestinians in Beirut – an action that sparks off intercommunal unrest throughout the country. By the end of the year full scale civil war is being waged by Christian and Muslim militias, with Arafat's al–Fatah entering the conflict in support of the Muslims.

1976   Right–wing Christian groups, including the Kata'eb and the National Liberal Party of ex–President Chamoun, unite to form the Lebanese Front. Their joint militia, the Lebanese Forces, is led by Bashir Gemayel until his death in 1982. In October, a ceasefire is declared and an Arab Deterrent Force is set up to keep the peace. This force is dominated by Syrian troops. Palestinian guerrillas return from Beirut to southern Lebanon where the Arab Deterrent Force has little influence.

1977–78   Conferences held at Shtoura and Beiteddin call for the disarming of private militias as a prerequisite to reaching a political settlement, but little can be done to put this into effect. The Christian Lebanese Front begins to split up into feuding factions.

1978 Half way through the year fighting erupts between the largely Syrian Arab Deterrent Force and Christian militias. In an attempt to bring an end to the conflict, Arab foreign ministers meet at the Lebanese President's summer palace where they form an Arab Follow–Up Committee composed of Lebanon, Kuwait, Syria and Saudi Arabia. This committee fails to find a solution and does not meet again for three years following an incident in which the Saudi ambassador is shot.

Israel responds to PLO guerrilla attacks across the border by invading Lebanon as far as the Litani River. A ceasefire is agreed in July and Israel hands over key positions to Lebanese Christian militia led by the right-wing army officer, Major Da'ad Haddad. The withdrawal of Israeli forces is supervised by the UN Interim Force in Lebanon (UNIFIL).

1979 The Israeli–backed South Lebanese Army under Major Haddad establishes a so–called "independent, free Lebanon" in the south.

1980 Israeli attacks on Palestinian positions in south Lebanon attract condemnation from the United Nations.

1981 Syrian attempts to restrict the Christian Phalange forces meet with opposition in the south where Major Haddad launches an artillery bombardment on the port of Sidon. Israel intervenes and, following an incident near Zahlé where two Syrian helicopters are shot down, Syria installs a SAM–6 air defence system. All–out confrontation is avoided and the seige of Zahlé is lifted only after intervention by Arab League mediators. Israel continues to attack PLO positions in south Lebanon until a ceasefire is agreed on 24 July.

1982 The July 1981 ceasefire collapses after ten months and in June an attempt to assassinate the Israeli ambassador in London provokes Israel into bombing Palestinian targets in south Lebanon once again. The PLO responds by launching rocket attacks on Jewish settlements in northern Galilee. On 6 June Israeli forces cross the border into Lebanon and push northwards. By mid–June they surround Muslim west Beirut, trapping a Syrian brigade and over 8000 Palestinian fighters including the PLO leader, Yasser Arafat. During July–August the United States helps to negotiate an agreement with Lebanese, Israeli and Palestinian representatives. This leads to the withdrawal from the city of Palestinian fighters and Syrian troops under the supervision of a 2000–strong Multinational Peace–keeping Force comprising US, French and Italian troops.

On 23 August Bashir Gemayel is elected President of Lebanon. Three weeks later, on 14 September, he is killed in a bomb attack at the Kata'eb headquarters – an act that prompts Israeli troops to enter west Beirut on the following day. Within 24 hours of the Israeli move, Christian Phalange militia enter the Palestinian refugee camps of Sabra and Chatila and massacre many of their inhabitants. A week later Gemayel's brother, Amin, is elected President. He begins the difficult process of restoring order and negotiating the withdrawal of all foreign troops from Lebanon.

The year ends with an outbreak of factional feuds. Around Tripoli pro–Syrian militia of the Arab Democratic Party start to fight anti–Syrian Sunni Muslim groups, while in the Chouf mountains south–east of Beirut, Lebanese Forces battle with Druse militia.

1983 In May Israel agrees to withdraw its troops as long as Syria does the same. Syria refuses to withdraw its forces and Israeli troops remain. Two months later, a pro–Syrian National Salvation Front opposing Gemayel is formed. Headed by the Druse leader, Walid Jumblatt, the Front joins with AMAL militia against the largely Christian Lebanese army in west Beirut.

On 4 September the Israeli army begins to withdraw to the Awali River despite pleas from Gemayel to wait until the Lebanese army has regained control of Beirut. The conflict between Lebanese Forces and Druse militia in the Chouf mountains intensifies and US warships anchored offshore begin to shell Druse positions. On 25 September a ceasefire is agreed and between 31 October and 4 November a National Reconciliation Conference is held in Geneva. Suicide attacks on the Multinational Peace–keeping Force result in the deaths of 241 US and 58 French marines.

In north Lebanon fighting breaks out between PLO units loyal to Yasser Arafat and Palestinian dissidents backed by Syria. Arafat and 4000 supporters fall back on Tripoli from where they are evacuated under French naval protection in Greek ships flying the UN flag.

1984   The situation deteriorates as west Beirut falls to Muslim militias in late January. With the Lebanese army losing control and the announcement by President Reagan of a phased withdrawal by the Multinational Peace–keeping Force, the AMAL leader, Nabih Berri, calls for the resignation of President Gemayel. Gemayel refuses to resign but offers to reconvene the Geneva conference and present a power–sharing plan that gives Christians and Muslims equal representation. In March, after visiting Syria, Gemayel cancels the May 1983 accord and announces that he will seek "alternative security arrangements" on the border with Israel. The decision is criticized by some Maronite leaders who also oppose any attempts to increase Muslim influence in the government.

In April a buffer zone is created along the Green Line and in the mountains south–east of Beirut. Rashid Karamé is appointed Prime Minister and a government of National Unity with equal representation for Muslims and Christians is formed in May. General Michel Aoun is appointed commander of the Lebanese army and the disarmament of militias is proposed as part of a new security plan.

The peace is shattered again when fighting breaks out in Beirut between rival Druse and Sunni militias.

1985   Israel begins to withdraw its troops from Lebanon in January, leaving a buffer zone to be policed by the South Lebanese

Army. A month later Palestinian positions in the south are bombed once again by Israeli aircraft. As the internal security situation continues to deteriorate, fighting breaks out between Christians and Muslims in Beirut. The first in a series of kidnappings takes place in March when the fundamentalist Islamic Jihad organization abducts three British and American residents of the city.

In May the Shia Muslim AMAL militia launches a five–week attack on Palestinian refugee camps in an attempt to oust Palestinian guerrillas who have returned to Lebanon. Fighting spreads northwards to Tripoli where the pro–Syrian Arab Democratic Party battles with the Islamic Unification Movement. A Syrian–backed "tripartite accord" among various leaders of Lebanese factions comes to nothing when it is opposed by the President and when the leader of the Lebanese Forces is overthrown by his hardline anti-Syrian rival, Dr Samir Geagea.

1986   The so-called "camp wars" involving conflict between AMAL and Palestinian militia intensify when members of al–Fatah return to Lebanon to help defend the beseiged refugee camps. Meanwhile, abductions continue as the fundamentalist pro–Iranian Hezbollah strengthens its presence in west Beirut and South Lebanon.

1987   Renewed violence in Beirut forces the Lebanese government to ask for Syrian intervention. Syrian troops arrive but fail to gain control of the southern suburbs of Beirut or bring to an end the AMAL seige of the Palestinian camps.

In January the Archbishop of Canterbury's special envoy is abducted while trying to negotiate the release of hostages. He is the first of ten people captured in the city during 1987. In June the political deadlock suffers a   further setback when Prime Minister Rashid Karamé is assassinated.

1988   Najih Berri, leader of the AMAL militia brings to an end the "camp wars" that have cost over 2500 Palestinian lives since 1985. Later in the year political attention focuses on the election of a new president. Syria backs former President Suleiman Franjieh, but he proves unacceptable to the Lebanese Forces which are in a position to prevent a quorum in the National Assembly. Attempts by the United States and Syria to find a compromise candidate fail and on 22 September President Gemayel, at the end of his term of office, appoints General Michel Aoun as Prime Minister. This contravenes the 1943 "National Pact" which states that the Prime Minister must be a Sunni Muslim and, accordingly, General Aoun's premiership is rejected by both Lebanese Muslims and Syria who insist on the appointment of the acting Prime Minister, Selim Hoss. The political situation in Lebanon has now become even more complicated with the creation of two rival administrations.

1989 Divisions within the Shia Muslim community become apparent when fighting breaks out between Amal and Hezbollah militias in early January, but under pressure from Iran and Syria a truce is signed in Damascus by the end of the month. In mid–February a split within the Christian militia forces develops as Aoun's Lebanese army attempts to gain control of East Beirut. In March Aoun attempts to block the Shia Muslim and Druse–controlled ports of southern Lebanon, without first consulting the rival administration based in west Beirut. In the fighting that ensues, Walid Jumblatt's Druse militia bombards east Beirut and Aoun responds by shelling west Beirut. General Aoun blames the Syrians and vows to drive out the 35 000 Syrian troops that are deployed over two-thirds of Lebanon.

The Arab League helps to negotiate a ceasefire which takes effect on 3 May but intercommunal rivalry is inflamed once more when the Grand Mufti of Lebanon, who favoured the Arab League ceasefire, is killed in a bomb attack on 16 May.

In October deputies of the Lebanese parliament, still without a president, meet in the Saudi Arabian resort of Taif and agree to hold presidential elections. A month later, on 5 November, the deputies fly in to the abandoned airbase at Qlaiat and elect René Moawad to the presidency. Seventeen days later Moawad is killed in a bomb blast. He is replaced by the pro–Syrian Maronite agricultural engineer, Elias Hrawi.

1990 The conflict between Aoun's Lebanese army and the Lebanese Forces led by Samir Geagea escalates into bitter fighting once again and Beirut suffers its worst devastion in 15 years of civil war.

■ Who's who

Adwan, George Leader of the al-Tanzim right-wing Maronite movement and a member of the Lebanese Forces Command Council.

al–Amin, Sheikh Ibrahim A spokesman for the fundamentalist Hezbollah movement.

al–Khoury, Sheikh Bishara The first president of independent Lebanon 1943–52.

Anderson, Terry Bureau chief of the American Associated Press News Agency, abducted in Beirut in March 1985. The longest–held captive in the Lebanon.

Aoun, General Michel Appointed commander of the Christian units of the Lebanese national army in June 1984, Michel Aoun claims to be the Christian prime minister of Lebanon. The declared aim of Aoun has been to force the withdrawal of some 35 000 Syrian troops deployed throughout Lebanon, but in January 1990 he became embroiled in a costly feud with Dr Samir Geagea's Phalangist Lebanese Forces in a bid to gain control of the Christian enclaves in and around Beirut. On the day that Lebanese deputies elected René Moawad president in November 1989, Aoun announced the dissolution of parliament and ordered general elections to be held for the first time in 18 years.

Arslan, Faisal   Leader of the Yazbeki branch of the Druse community.

Berjawi, Chaker   Leader of the Sunni Muslim militia in Beirut.

Berri, Nabih   Damascus–based leader of the   AMAL Shia militia and Minister of Justice and of Reconstruction for South Lebanon.

Chamoun, Camille   Maronite president of Lebanon 1952–58, whose term of office ended in political turmoil. Based in the Chouf hills, his Lebanese Front militia was defeated by Gemayel's Christian Phalange in 1980. Chamoun, who was a founder of the National Liberal Party, died in August 1987.

Chebab, General Fouad   President of Lebanon 1958–64. He established the "Chehabist compromise" based on reconciliation between moderate Christian and Muslim leaders.

Daoud, Daoud   AMAL commander in southern Lebanon, often at odds with Nabih Berri.

Fadlallah, Sheikh Mohammed Hussein   A Shia Muslim religious leader believed to be the spiritual leader of the Hezbollah fundamentalist movement.

Franjeih, Suleiman   Pro–Syrian Maronite president of Lebanon 1970–76. During President Franjeih's term of office the country slid into full–scale civil war.

Geagea, Dr Samir   Hard–line Christian Maronite leader of the Phalangist Lebanese Forces since 1986. In January 1990 Geagea's Phalangists engaged in a fierce struggle with General Michel Aoun's units of the Lebanese Army in an attempt to gain control of the Christian sectors of east Beirut.

Gemayel, Amin   Son of the pro–Western Maronite leader, Pierre Gemayel, Amin Gemayel was elected president of Lebanon in September 1982 following the assassination of his brother, Bashir. The end of his term of office left Lebanon without a President and his last–minute appointment of General Aoun as Prime Minister resulted in the creation of rival Christian and Muslim administrations.

Gemayel, Bashir   Son of Pierre Gemayel and brother of Amin Gemayel, Bashir, a former commander of the Lebanese Forces, was elected president of Lebanon in August 1982 but was assassinated in a bomb attack a month later.

Gemayel, Pierre   Christian Maronite founder and co-leader of the Phalange or Kata'eb. Died in 1984.

Haddad, Major Sa'ad   Leader of the pro–Israeli South Lebanese Army until his death in January 1984.

Hoss, Dr Salem   A Sunni Muslim economist who was Prime Minister of Lebanon 1976–80. Hoss was reappointed to the premier's post by President Moawad after the election held in November 1989.

Hrawi, Elias   Christian Maronite President of Lebanon appointed following the assassination of President Moawad in November 1989.

Ibrahimi, Lakhdar   Assistant Secretary-General of the Arab League responsible for persuading Lebanese parliamentarians to agree to the Taif accord that led to the presidential elections of November 1989.

Jumblatt, Kamal   Hereditary chief of the Jumblatt branch of the Druse community until his death in March 1977. As founder of the Progressive Socialist Party, he frequently advocated the setting up of a secular state.

Jumblatt, Walid   Leader of the Progressive Socialist Party and only son of the Druse leader Kamal Jumblatt. A leader of the former Lebanese National Movement and Minister of Public Works and Tourism.

Karamé, Rashid   Sunni Muslim Prime Minister of Lebanon on eight occasions between 1955 and 1970 and again during the 1975–76 civil war. Elected once more in April 1984, he was assassinated three years later in June 1987.

Karameh, Dr Elie President of the Lebanese Phalange Party after the death of Pierre Gemayel in 1984.

Keenan, Brian Anglo–Irish teacher at the American University of Beirut, abducted and held hostage from April 1986 till August 1990.

Khaled, Sheikh Hassan Grand Mufti and spiritual leader of Lebanon's 700 000 Sunni Muslims who was killed with 21 other people in a bomb attack on 16 May 1989. An important link in the dialogue between General Aoun and Prime Minister Hoss, Khaled was in favour of a united Lebanon.

Lahad, Antoine A retired Major–General who succeded Sa'ad Haddad as leader of the South Lebanese Army in January 1984.

Lahoud, General Emile A former director of personnel at the Lebanese Defence Ministry, appointed commander of the Lebanese Army in December 1989 in an attempt by President Hrawi to overthrow the renegade Christian army commander, Michel Aoun. Lahoud is the son of General Jamil Lahoud, a national hero during the former French mandate.

McCarthy, John British World TV News journalist, abducted while on his way to the airport and held hostage in Beirut since April 1986.

Moawad, René A Christian Maronite lawyer from the north Lebanese town of Zghorta who was elected President of Lebanon in November 1989 at the age of 64, but was killed in a bomb attack 17 days later.

Obeid, Sheikh Abdul Karim A leader of the Hezbollah terrorists in southern Lebanon captured and held hostage by the Israelis in June 1989. The Israeli government offered Obeid and 150 Shia Muslim prisoners in return for the release of three Israeli hostages and all the Western hostages.

Qoleit, Ibrahim A Sunni Muslim leader of al–Murabitun.

Sa'ad, Mustafa A Sunni Muslim leader of the Popular Nasserite Organization during the 1975–76 civil war. He was seriously injured after an assassination attempt in 1985.

Saadeh, Dr Georges Leader of the Christian Phalange (Kata'eb party).

Salem, Saeb Former prime minister and head of the Sunni Muslim Rassemblement Islamique. His family controls the Makassed charitable organization and has close links with Saudi Arabia.

Sarkis, Elias President of Lebanon 1976–82. During his term of office the Arab Deterrent Force, composed mainly of Syrian troops, was invited into Lebanon to separate the Christian and Muslim combatants in the civil war.

Sfeir, Bishop Nasrullah Maronite Christian Patriarch of Lebanon whose residence at Bkirke, north of Beirut, was attacked by supporters of General Aoun in November 1989. Forced to move to his summer residence at Diman in north Lebanon, Bishop Sfeir has long been an advocate of mutual understanding between Christian and Muslim communities.

Sutherland, Thomas Dean of the American University of Beirut, abducted and held hostage by the Islamic Jihad organization since June 1985.

Tofaili, Sheikh Subhi Leading figure of the fundamentalist Hezbollah movement based in the Beqa'a Valley.

Waite, Terry Special envoy of the Archbishop of Canterbury abducted in January 1987 while on a mission to negotiate the release of hostages held in Beirut. He was last seen when Druse militia bodyguards left him in the hands of the pro–Iranian Islamic Jihad organization.

■ Key places

Adma   A hilltop village overlooking the port of Jounieh, 15km north-east of Beirut. Used as a commando and helicopter base by General Aoun's Lebanese Army units until driven out by Phalangists in February 1990.

Ain al–Hilweh   A Palestinian refugee camp on the outskirts of Sidon, W Lebanon.

Ain al–Rummaneh   A southern suburb of east Beirut, the scene of bitter fighting in February 1990 between rival Christian units of the Lebanese Forces and the Lebanese army.

Anti–Lebanon or **Jebel esh Sharqi**   A barren mountain range on Lebanon's eastern frontier with Syria. Separated from the Jebel Liban to the west by the fertile Beqa'a Valley, the Anti–Lebanon rises to a height of 2 814m at Mount Hermon.

Awali River   A river in S Lebanon marking the line of the Israeli withdrawal of September 1983.

Baabda   A south–eastern suburb of Beirut and capital of the province of Jebel Lubnan. Held by Christian units of the Lebanese Army, the presidential palace at Baabda is the headquarters of General Michel Aoun.

Baalbek   An ancient town in the Beqa'a Valley at the western edge of the Anti-Lebanon mountains. The Phoenicians built a temple to the sun–god Baal and later the site had associations with the Roman god, Jupiter. Today, Baalbek is an important base for Shia Muslim fundamentalists who are backed by units of the Iranian Revolutionary Guard.

Bayt ad Din or **Beit ed–Dine** ("house of faith")   Site of a grand palace built by Bechir II (1786–1840) in the Lebanese mountains, 25km south-east of Beirut. Now the official summer residence of the President of Lebanon. At a meeting of Arab foreign ministers held here in 1978, an Arab Follow–Up Committee was formed to end the fighting between Syrians and Christians.

Bcharre or **Becharre**   A town in the Ash Shamal province of N Lebanon, 20km south-east of Tripoli. At an altitude of 1400m in the Jebel Liban range, and overlooking the Qadisha Valley, the town is surrounded by Cedars of Lebanon – the emblem of the Lebanese republic. Bcharre was the birthplace of Gibran Khalil Gibran (1883–1931), the best known Lebanese writer.

Beqa'a Valley, El Beqa'a or **Beka'a Valley**   A province of E Lebanon bounded to the north-east and east by the state of Syria and subdivided into the five districts (*cazas*) of Baalbek, Hermel, Zahlé, Beqa'a al Gharbi and Rachaiya. The provincial capital is Zahlé. Other important towns are Hermel and Baalbek. Much of the province lies on a high plateau at an altitude of 800–1500m. The River Litani, which drains the plateau in a NE–SW direction, divides the Lebanon mountains in the west from the Anti-Lebanon mountains in the east.

Beirut or **Beyrouth**   Seaport capital of Lebanon since 1920, Beirut is situated on a promontory that juts out into the Mediterranean, midway along Lebanon's 225km coastline. Once the financial and cultural centre of the country, Lebanon has been ravaged by civil war since 1975 when rival religious and political factions first divided the city into a Christian eastern sector and a Muslim western sector separated by the "Green Line". In the predominantly Shi'ite SW sector of Beirut lie the Palestinian refugee camps of Chatila, Sabra and Bourj el–Barajneh which were created as a result of the evacuation of Palestinians from the city during the Israeli seige of 1982.

Bourj el–Barajneh   A Palestinian refugee camp, situated just to the south of the Sabra and Chatila camps in the south-western suburbs of Beirut. The camp was the scene of a prolonged seige in 1987.

Chatila   A Palestinian refugee camp in the south-western suburbs of Beirut. The scene of a massacre carried out by Christian Phalangists in September 1982.

Chouf or **Shuf** A range of hills to the south-east of Beirut, forming a southern outlier of the Lebanon Mountains. The Chouf hills form part of the traditional Lebanese homeland of the Druse.

Dbyeh tunnel A tunnel on the coastal road linking east Beirut with the port of Jounieh. The scene of heavy fighting in 1989–90 between General Aoun's Lebanese Army and the opposing Lebanese Forces militia.

Deir al–Qamar A town in the Chouf hills, 20km south-east of Beirut. Surrounded by pine trees and vineyards the town is the centre of the largest Christian enclave within a predominantly Druse territory. Deir al–Qamar was the home town of former president, Camille Chamoun.

Green Line A dividing line between Muslim west Beirut and Christian east Beirut established during the 1975–76 civil war.

Hermon, Mount or **Jebel esh Sheikh** ("mountain of the chief") Rising to 2 184m, Mt Hermon is the highest peak of the Anti–Lebanon range in E Lebanon. Ancient Caesarea and Philippi stood at its foot and a Druse shrine is located nearby at Hasbeya.

Janub, Al The southernmost province of Lebanon, bounded on the south by Israel, the west by the Mediterranean and the east by Syria. Sidon is the capital and Tyre, Jezzine and Marjayoun are important towns. One of the country's principal oil refineries is located at Az Zahrani. In 1982 Israeli forces penetrated Al Janub province in an attempt to expel members of the PLO from Lebanon. Two years later an Israeli security zone was established along the frontier between Lebanon and Israel with the aid of South Lebanese forces.

Jounieh or **Jôunié** Mediterranean port, situated 15km north of Beirut. At the centre of an anti–Syrian Christian enclave, Jounieh has been constantly beseiged by Syrian and Druse forces.

Lebanon Mountains or **Jebel Lubnan** A mountain range stretching for a length of about 160km parallel to the Mediterranean coast of Lebanon. Separated by the Beqa'a Valley from the Anti–Lebanon range on the Syrian frontier, the Lebanon Mountains rise to 3087m at Qornet es Saouda. The mountain range gives its name to a province of Lebanon whose capital is Baabda.

Levant A name formerly applied to the east coast of the Mediterranean Sea including present–day Lebanon. Between 1920 and 1943 the French mandated territories of Syria and Lebanon were known as the Levant States.

Litani River Rising near Baalbek in the Anti–Lebanon mountains of NE Lebanon, the Litani River flows in a NE–SW directions through the Beqa'a Valley before turning west on its way to meet the Mediterranean Sea 8km north of Tyre. Its total length is 144km. The west–flowing section of the river was the northern limit of the 1978 Israeli invasion of Lebanon.

Mieh Mieh A Palestinian refugee camp 4km east of Sidon.

Naqoura A small town in Lebanon's southern Al Janub province, situated 4km north of the Israel–Lebanon frontier. UN sponsored talks on the withdrawal of Israeli troops from Lebanon took place here in November–December 1984.

Qlaiat A small town with an abandoned airbase located near the Mediterranean coast of N Lebanon, 5km south of the Syrian frontier. On 5 November 1989, 58 deputies of the Lebanese parliament flew in from exile to Qlaiat in order to elect René Moawad President of Lebanon.

Qornet es Saouda Rising to 3087m in the Lebanon Mountains, Qornet es Saouda is the highest peak in Lebanon.

Rashidiyah A Palestinian refugee camp 4km south of Tyre.

Sabra A Palestinian refugee camp in the south-western suburbs of Beirut. The scene of a massacre by Christian Phalangists in September 1982.

Sidon or **Saïda** ("fishing")   The seaport capital of Al Janub province in S Lebanon, 35km north of Tyre; population 24 700. Situated at the edge of a well–watered coastal plain, the ancient city of Sidon was founded in the third millenium BC. Once noted for the manufacture of glass and purple dyes, the city is now an oil refining centre linked by pipeline to Saudi Arabia.

Taif   A Red Sea resort on the W coast of Saudi Arabia, 64km ESE of Mecca. Scene of an Arab League–sponsored meeting held in October 1989 at which Lebanese politicians agreed to the holding of presidential elections and the formation of a mixed Muslim–Christian government. The agreement reached at Taif was bitterly opposed by the Christian military commander, General Michel Aoun.

Tripoli or **Trâblous**   Seaport capital of the north–western province of Ash Shamal and second largest city in Lebanon; population 175 000. A trade centre for north Lebanon and the coastal cities of Syria, Tripoli is also linked by oil pipeline to Iraq. The city is mostly occupied by Sunni Muslims, but in addition, there are about 15 000 members of the minority Islamic Alawite sect.

Tyre or **Soûr** ("rampart")   A Mediterranean fishing port in S Lebanon's Al Janub province, 25km north of the Israeli frontier; population 14 000. The ancient city was originally built on several islands which were joined together by King Hiram and then linked to the mainland by Alexander the Great. Tyre became the most important commercial centre in the E Mediterranean for land and seaborne trade and was noted for its silk garments, fine glass and purple dye (derived from the murex sea mussel). The introduction of the alphabet into Greece has been attributed to Cadmus of Soûr. Amongst a number of interesting historical monuments ranging from Graeco–Roman to Arab times is one of the largest hippodromes of the Roman period.

Yarze   Headquarters of the Lebanese national army, situated near Baabda in the south-eastern suburbs of Beirut.

Zaghorta   A mountain town in the north-western province of Ash Shamal, 12km south-east of Tripoli. A base of the Maronite Zghorta Liberation Brigade and home of ex–president Suleiman Franjieh.

Zahlé or **Zahlah**   Chief town of the Beqa'a Valley province in E Lebanon; population 46 800. The scene of a major confrontation between Christian militia and Syrian troops in April–June 1981.

■ Key words

Alawites   A minority Islamic group with a population of about 15 000 based in Tripoli.

al–Murabitun   A Sunni Muslim militia group of the Independent Nasserite Organization largely active in Beirut.

AMAL (Afwaj al–Muqawama al–Lubnaniyya)
A Shia Muslim political and militia group, originally a military arm of the Movement of the Deprived led by Imam Musa Sadr. The Islamic AMAL is a breakaway faction of AMAL.

Arab Democratic Party (ADP)   A group operating in north Lebanon and owing allegiance to Colonel Rifa'at al–Asad, brother of President Asad of Syria. The group has its own militia, the Arab Knights, popularly called the Pink Panthers.

Arab Deterrent Force (ADF)   A military force created by the Arab League in October 1976 to keep the peace in Lebanon following the 1975–76 civil war. Several Arab states made brief contributions to this force which was dominated by Syrian troops who entered Lebanon in June 1976.

Arab Follow–Up Committee   When conflict broke out between the Syrian–dominated Arab Deterrent Force and the Christian militias in mid–1978, Arab foreign ministers of Saudi Arabia, Syria, Lebanon and Kuwait met at the Lebanese presidential summer palace at Bat ad–Din to find a way of separating the combatants. After the wounding of the Saudi ambassador in December 1978 the committee did not meet again until the Zahlé crisis of 1981.

Arab Knights or **Fursan al–Arab**   The militia arm of the Arab Democratic Party. Popularly known as the Pink Panthers.

Ba'ath Party or **Arab Socialist Renaissance Party**   Syrian and Iraqi ruling political parties with branches operating in Lebanon.

Beiteddin Conference   A conference convened in 1978 for the purpose of resolving the conflict in Lebanon and disbanding private militias.

Cairo Agreement   An agreement reached in November 1969 between the Lebanese government and the PLO, defining the principles of Palestinian residence in Lebanon and the limits of PLO militia operations.

camp wars   The name given to the conflict within the Shia Muslim community that resulted in the Syrian–backed AMAL militia attacks on pro-Arafat *fedayeen* operating from the Palestinian refugee camps near the cities of Beirut, Tyre and Sidon between 1985 and 1988.

confessions   Religious sects of which there are about 17 in Lebanon. Many Lebanese owe greater allegiance to their sect than to the state of Lebanon, hence the proliferation of independent militia groups.

Druse   An unorthodox and secretive branch of Islam forming a close–knit and largely agricultural community. Numbering about 200 000 in Lebanon, they mainly occupy the Chouf hills. There are two major factions led by the Jumblatt and Arslan families (Yazbeki Druse).

Faithful Resistance   A militant arm of AMAL forming part of the Islamic Resistance that has opposed both Israeli and South Lebanese forces.

February 6 Movement   A Sunni militia group led by Palestinian sympathizers based in the Tariq Jdideh district of Beirut.

fedayeen   Palestinian guerrilla fighters, largely operating against Israeli forces from Palestinian refugee camps in Beirut and south Lebanon.

Front for National Unity   A pro–Syrian group comprising Muslims, independent Christians and left–wing elements formed in 1985. At their first meeting in Shtura they called for a constituent assembly to draft a new Lebanese constitution.

Government of National Unity   A government formed on 10 May 1984 by President Gemayel and led by Prime Minister Rashid Karamé who announced a programme of reform which included equal representation in the Lebanese Parliament for both Muslims and Christians.

Guardians of the Cedars   An extremist Christian Maronite group which advocates the complete expulsion of foreigners, including Palestinians, from Lebanon.

Hezbollah ("party of God")   An Iranian–backed fundamentalist Shia Muslim group largely operating in south Lebanon but with a growing presence in Beirut where it is often in armed conflict with AMAL militia. Striving to remove Israelis from Arab territory, Hezbollah adopts a xenophobic approach that seeks to set up an Islamic republic rather than a Lebanese national entity.

hudna   A word used to describe a lull in fighting during which the citizens of Beirut can restock their provisions.

Independent Nasserite Organization   A political wing of al–Murabitun, formed in 1975 by Ibrahim Qoleilat.

Islamic AMAL   A breakaway faction of the AMAL political and military movement based in Baalbek. This group works closely with Iranian Revolutionary Guards to promote the establishment of an Islamic Republic of Lebanon.

Islamic Grouping or **Rassemblement Islamique**   A Sunni Muslim political organization.

Islamic Jihad   The name given to a number of fundamentalist Islamic groups who carry out attacks in the name of the Islamic Revolution.

Islamic Resistance Movement   A militia group operating against the Israelis in south Lebanon. Identified with Hezbollah, it draws its support from both Sunni and Shia fundamentalist groups.

Islamic Society   A grouping of Sunni fundamentalist factions in alliance with Hezbollah and the Faithful Resistance which together form the Islamic Resistance in south Lebanon.

Islamic Unification Movement or **Tawhid**   A fundamentalist Sunni Muslim group active in Tripoli.

Israeli Security Zone   A strip of Lebanese territory stretching along the Lebanon–Israel frontier from Mt Hermon to the coast. Although Israel withdrew the bulk of its troops from south Lebanon in 1985 a 1000–strong Israeli force was left behind to prevent the infiltration of guerrillas across the border into Israel.

Jundallah   A fundamentalist Sunni Muslim faction of the Islamic Unification Movement. There is also a Shia Muslim Jundallah faction.

Kata'eb or **Phalange**   A Christian paramilitary youth movemement founded in 1936 by Pierre Gemayel at a time when Maronites feared they might be overwhelmed by the Muslim community. Predominantly of Maronite membership, it has functioned as a political party (Social Democratic Party) since 1952. It is now the largest of the Christian militia groups

and the most powerful political grouping in Lebanon.

Lebanese Arab Army   A pro–Syrian armed force of Muslims who deserted from the Lebanese Army during the 1975–76 civil war.

Lebanese Armed Forces (LAF)   The Lebanese regular army.

Lebanese Communist Party   A pro–Soviet group numbering between 1000 and 2000. Founded in 1952, it is the oldest political party in Lebanon.

Lebanese Forces   A Christian Phalange militia led by Dr Samir Geagea who broke away from the Lebanese Front in 1985. This movement came into direct conflict with General Aoun's Lebanese Army in 1989–90.

Lebanese Front   A group of right–wing Christian parties formed in 1976. The group includes Kata'eb, the National Liberal Party, the Guardians of the Cedars, al–Tanzim and the Maronite Monastic Order. During the civil war in 1975–76 its militia fought against the Lebanese National Movement/Palestinian alliance.

Lebanese National Movement (LNM)   A loose coalition of Muslim groups formed in 1969. Although it was backed by a number of Arab governments, the alliance was suspended in 1982 following the Israeli invasion of Lebanon.

Lebanese National Resistance Front   A south Lebanese resistance group operating against the Israelis since the invasion of 1982. Claiming over 1200 attacks, this group is believed to include members of AMAL and the Lebanese Communist Party.

Makassed   An influential charitable welfare organization run by the Salem family.

Marada Brigades or **Zghorta Liberation Army**   A pro–Syrian Maronite militia based in the north–western corner of the Lebanon Mountains at Zghorta.

Maronites   A uniate sect of the Catholic Church forming the largest Christian political and military grouping in Lebanon. The Maronites control parts of east Beirut and a substantial area to the north of Beirut between the Mediterranean coast and the Lebanon Mountains.

Maronite Monastic Order An order of Maronite monks active during the civil war of 1975–76 under the leadership of Father Boulos Na'aman whose hard-line approach earned the disapproval of the Vatican.

Marunistan The name of a proposed Maronite mini–state within Lebanon.

Mughniyah A guerrilla group formed by Imas Mughniyah and based in Baalbek. Thought to be responsible for a large number of kidnappings and hijackings, this group's original aim was to secure the release of 17 Shi'ite terrorists held in Kuwait since 1983.

Mukhabarat The Syrian security police.

Multinational Peace–keeping Force (MNF) A 2000–strong military force comprising contingents from France, Italy and the USA which arrived in Lebanon to help keep the peace and supervise the withdrawal of PLO fighters and Syrian troops from Beirut in August–September 1982. In February 1983 a contingent of 100 soldiers from the UK augmented the force which by then totalled 5700 troops. After a series of attacks in which 241 US and 58 French marines were killed, the MNF withdrew from Lebanon in 1984.

Murabitoun A Nasserite Sunni Muslim militia forming part of the Lebanese National Front alliance of 1969.

National Bloc An independent nationalist Christian group opposed to both pan–Arabists and Christian hegemony.

National Democratic Front A coalition of pro–Syrian left-wing factions formed in 1984 by Walid Jumblatt.

National Guard An Israeli–backed village militia operating alongside the South Lebanese Army.

National Liberal Party A political party founded in 1958 but effectively eliminated in 1980 when its militia wing was defeated by Bashir Gemayel's Maronite Christian Lebanese Forces. The National Liberal party was formerly the principal Christian political group in the Chouf hills.

National Pact An unwritten agreement that formed the basis for a system of power–sharing by Christians and Muslims in Lebanon, devised in 1943 by the country's first president and prime minister. By convention the president is a Maronite Christian, the prime minister a Sunni Muslim and the president of the National Assembly a Shia Muslim.

National Salvation Party A Syrian–backed political opposition to Gemayel's 1984 Lebanon–Israel agreement, led by Walid Jumblatt, ex–President Franjieh and Rashid Karamé.

National Syrian Socialist Party Originally a right–wing party founded in 1932 as the Parti Populaire Syrien in order to promote a united Arab Syrian nation.

October 24 Movement A largely Sunni Muslim militia group that operated in Tripoli until driven out by the Islamic Unification Movement.

Operation Litani Codename for the 1978 Israeli invasion of south Lebanon in pursuit of Palestinian terrorists.

Operation Peace for Galilee Codename for the Israeli invasion of Lebanon in 1982.

Organization for Revolutionary Justice A pro–Iranian guerrilla group operating in the southern suburbs of Beirut.

Organization of Communist Action in Lebanon (OCAL) A radical political party closely linked with the Democratic Front for the Liberation of Palestine.

Progressive Socialist Party (PSP) A Druse political and militia group led by Walid Jumblatt.

Shi'ite or **Shi'at Ali**   A fundamentalist Muslim sect which believes in Ali as the true successor to the Prophet Mohammed. Numbering some 90 million worldwide, this Islamic group is dominant in Iran, Iraq, Bahrain and parts of Lebanon where an estimated 1 100 000 Shia Muslims are to be found between Sidon and Tyre as well as in the Beqa'a Valley. Traditionally playing a minor role in the political life of the country, they became more active in the 1980s. The more orthodox Sunnis did not accept Shi'ism as a legitimate school of Islam until 1959.

Shtoura Conference   A conference convened in 1977 to discuss the Lebanese conflict and the possible disarming of private militias.

Social Democratic Party   A predominantly Maronite political party.

South Lebanese Army   A pro–Israeli Maronite militia operating in south Lebanon against Palestinian guerrillas.

Squad 16   A name given to the red–bereted Lebanese gendarmes.

Sunnis (Sunna, "the tradition of the Prophet")   An orthodox Muslim sect with an estimated following of 700 million people worldwide. In Lebanon Sunni Muslims numbering some 800 000 are mainly located in the coastal cities.

Taif accord   An agreement to hold presidential elections in Lebanon reached in 1989 with the help of mediation by the Arab League committee on Lebanon. The acceptance of the Taif accord by Maronite Phalangists eventually led to a bloody feud between rival Christian factions led by Samir Geagea and Michel Aoun.

Tawhid   The Islamic Unification Party.

UN Interim Force in Lebanon (UNIFIL)   A UN peace–keeping force sent to Lebanon in 1978 to oversee the return to the Lebanese government of territory up to the Litani River that had been occupied by Israeli Forces.

UN Relief and Works Agency (UNRWA)   An organization set up by the UN in 1948 to care for Palestinian refugees.

■ Further reading

H. Cobban, *The Making of Modern Lebanon*, Hutchinson Education, London, 1985

A. Dawisha, *Syria and the Lebanese Crisis*, Macmillan, London, 1980

M. Deeb, *The Lebanese Civil War*, New York, 1980

D. Gilmour, *Lebanon: The Fractured Country*, Martin Robertson, Oxford and New York, 1983

Minority Rights Group. Report No. 61, *Lebanon: A Conflict of Minorities*, London, 1986

A.R. Norton, *Amal and the Shi'a: Struggle for the Soul of Lebanon*, University of Texas Press, 1987

I. Rabanovich, *The War for Lebanon*, Cornell University Press, New York, 1984

J. Randal, *The Tragedy of Lebanon*, Chatto and Windus, London, 1982

Gwyn Rowley, Lebanon: From Change and Turmoil to Cantonization?, *Focus*, 39(3), 1989, pp. 9–16

3
Iraq and the Gulf

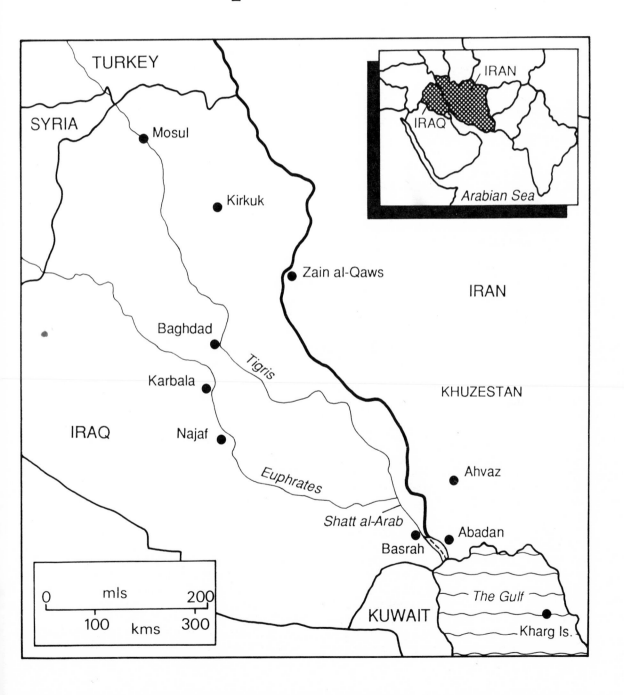

■ Profile

Iran

- **Area:** 1 648 000km²
- **Population (1988):** 53 920 000
- **Ethnic groups:** Persians 63%, Azeris and Turkomans 18%, Kurds 3%, Baluchis 2%, Arab 3%
- **Languages:** Farsi, Turkish, Kurdish, Arabic, English and French
- **Religion:** Shia Muslim 93%, Sunni Muslim 5%
- **Infant mortality rate:** 110 per 1000
- **Life expectancy:** 57 years
- **Timezone:** GMT +3
- **Capital:** Teheran
- **Chief cities:** Teheran (6 042 600), Masshad (1 463 500), Esfahan (971 500)

Iraq

- **Area:** 434 924km²
- **Population(1988)** 17 060 000
- **Ethnic groups:** Arabs 77%, Kurds 19%, Turks 2%, Persians 1%
- **Languages:** Arabic, Kurdish, Turkish
- **Religion:** Shia Muslim 65%, Sunni Muslim 32%
- **Infant mortality rate:** 76 per 1000
- **Life expectancy:** 64 years
- **Timezone:** GMT +3
- **Capital:** Baghdad
- **Chief cities:** Baghdad (4 648 600), Basrah (616 700), Mosul (570 900)

■ Introduction

To the extent that Iran and Iraq are successors to the Persian Empire and Ottoman Mesopotamia respectively, their conflict on the Gulf has deep historical roots, as does Iraq's claim to Kuwait. Iranians like to recall that at various times from the 6th century BC onwards the Persian Empire covered much of the Middle East. Iraq looks back to the Arab expansion of the 7th century AD, when Mesopotamia and Persia were conquered for Islam. Both countries claim descent from the Baghdad-based Abbasid Empire (750–1258), under which the Arab conquerors gradually surrendered power to the Aryan Persians and others. Under the Persian Safavid Empire (1501–1736), ethnic divisions acquired a religious angle when the Safavids espoused the Shia variant of Islam to rally resistance to the rising power of the Sunni Ottoman Turks. The latter nevertheless conquered Mesopotamia, where urban Sunni Arabs became dominant over the rural Shia majority. Wars in the 17th and 18th centuries resulted in periodic shifts in the Turkish–Persian border, which remained especially vague in the southern sector where the Tigris and Euphrates rivers combine to form the Shatt al-Arab waterway.

Russian expansion southwards added a new dimension to the Persian–Turkish border question, in which Britain also became closely interested in the 19th century. Joint Russo–British pressure produced a treaty in 1847, under which Turkey obtained full sovereignty over the Shatt al-Arab in return for territorial concessions to Persia. But continuing problems were exacerbated by Persia's determination to maintain full navigation rights on the waterway and by the Ottoman claim to suzerainty over Arab-populated Khuzestan on the Persian side of the border. The discovery of oil in Persia in 1908 greatly increased the strategic importance of the Shatt al-Arab, not least for Britain and Russia as the aspiring post-Ottoman powers in the region. Renewed Russo–British intervention led to the 1913 Constantinople Protocol confirming Turkish sovereignty over the waterway, although the following year a significant supplementary accord applied the Thalweg principle for the first time by moving the boundary at the Persian river port of Khorramshahr to the median line of the deepest channel. This was the position after World War I when Britain took responsibility for Mesopotamia (Iraq) under a League of Nations mandate, whereas Persia, despite wartime occupation by Britain and Russia, remained independent. Under the mandate, the British protectorate over Kuwait dating from 1899 remained in being.

When the post-1921 modernizing regime of Reza Shah renewed Persia's claim to rights in the Shatt al-Arab, Britain showed little sympathy, an attitude maintained by Iraq after it achieved independence in 1932. By then Iraq too was known to possess large oil reserves and the Shatt al-Arab was its only access to the Gulf from the major port of Basrah. Britain became more interested in a border accommodation from the mid–1930s, partly because it was the principal exploiter of both countries' oil and partly because it sought a pro-British regional alliance. Success came in 1937 with the conclusion of a pact between Persia, Iraq, Turkey and Afghanistan and an accompanying Persian–Iraqi border agreement. The latter reaffirmed the 1913–14 delimitation but at the same time granted Persia additional Thalweg rights in the vicinity of its oil-terminal port of Abadan. Thereafter, Britain's occupation of Iraq and southern Persia during World War II and dominant post- war influence in both countries ensured that the border issue remained dormant. But the gravitation of Iran (as Persia became) towards the United States and the eclipse of British influence in Iraq by the revolution of 1958 combined to revive old antagonisms. Both countries used their large oil revenues to build up their military strength, and Iraq countered US influence in Iran by establishing close relations with the Soviet Union. However, Iraq's attempts to prevent Kuwait achieving separate independence (in 1961), on the grounds that it was historically Iraqi territory, failed in the face of Arab and international opposition.

The unilateral abrogation of the 1937 agreement by the Shah of Iran in 1969 brought the territorial issue to the fore. Additional strains were generated by Iran's backing for Iraq's Kurdish rebels and by its occupation in 1971 of three Gulf islands which Iraq regarded as belonging to the United Arab Emirates. The 1973 Arab-Israeli war then reduced tensions, in that Iran and Iraq, as members of the Organization of Petroleum Exporting Countries (OPEC), were united in applying OPEC's steep oil price increases (and in deriving huge new revenues therefrom). The rapprochement deepened with the signature of the 1975 Algiers Agreement, under which Iraq accepted the application of the Thalweg principle along the whole Shatt al-Arab in return for a cessation of Iranian support for Kurdish rebels in Iraq. But the mutual congratulations on this compromise did not survive the fall of the Shah in 1979 and the coming to power in Teheran of a Shia fundamentalist regime committed to exporting its revolution. In September 1980 Iraq abrogated the Algiers Agreement and invaded Iran to establish its renewed claim to the Shatt al-Arab and to "liberate" not only the three Gulf islands but also Khuzestan, which it called Arabistan.

The Gulf War turned out to be the longest inter-state conflict of the 20th century and the bloodiest since World War II, causing more deaths than all the Arab–Israeli wars. Neither side shrank from indiscriminate missile attacks on civilian centres, and evidence emerged of Iraqi use of chemical weapons against both Iranians and Iraqi Kurds (by now again in revolt with Iranian backing). Iranian efforts to stir up unrest among Iraq's majority Shias had much less success than Iraq's promotion of *mujahedin* opposed to the Teheran regime. With the principal exceptions of arch-enemy Syria and also Libya, Iraq enjoyed the support of most Arab states, one effect of Saudi Arabian and Kuwaiti backing for Iraq being the easing of Baghdad's territorial disputes with those states. Externally, the concurrent Soviet military presence in Afghanistan raised US fears of a Soviet "push to the Gulf", a concern later apparent in the US government's combining of qualified support for Iraq with arms sales to anti-US Iran (albeit with the main intention of securing US hostage releases in Lebanon). As the war continued, however, Western concern focused on the toll exacted on Gulf shipping by both combatants and on the huge destruction of oil installations.

During the 1980s repeated mediation efforts by various parties foundered mainly on Iran's insistence that Iraq's "war guilt" should be proclaimed and the Saddam Hussein regime removed from power. In 1988, however, Iraq began to get the upper hand militarily, in recognition of which Iran accepted a UN-mediated ceasefire on the basis of a return to international boundaries and talks to resolve the dispute that had caused the war. Needless to say, however, these talks quickly became deadlocked over the precise implementation of the ceasefire terms.

It was perhaps inevitable that Saddam Hussein's Gulf ambitions should then revert to Kuwait, especially since alleged Kuwaiti over-production of oil was seen as impeding Iraq's economic recovery. Nevertheless, most observers were caught by surprise when in August 1990 Iraq forces invaded Kuwait, which was promptly annexed to Iraq. The United States responded by leading a massive military build-up in the Gulf to defend Saudi Arabia and to enforce a UN-imposed blockade of Iraq. Faced with almost universal condemnation of its action, not least among other Arab regimes, Iraq moved to secure its eastern flank by making peace with Iran on the basis of the 1975 Algiers Agreement. On its southern border, yet another Middle East war loomed.

■ Chronology of events

1639 The frontier between Persia (Iran) and the Ottoman Empire is vaguely defined for the first time in a treaty signed at Zuhab.

1724 A plan to partition Persia devised by Turkey and Russia is followed by a Turkish invasion of Persia.

1727 Under the Treaty of Hamadan, Turkey acquires the western provinces of Persia.

1746 After further hostilities, the 1639 border treaty is reaffirmed under the Treaty of Kherden.

1812 The city of Mohammerah (Khorramshahr) on the east bank of the Shatt al–Arab is founded by the Arab Muhaisin tribe.

1823 Following two years of warfare between Turkey and Persia, the Treaty of Kherdan is declared invalid under the first Treaty of Erzerum.

1843 Pressure on Turkey and Persia from Russia and Britain results in the formation of a boundary commission comprising representatives of the four powers.

1847 The second Treaty of Erzerum delimits a boundary that partly follows the Shatt al–Arab for the first time. While Turkey retains sovereignty over the waterway, Persia acquires anchorages on the east bank including Abadan and Mohammerah (Khorramshahr).

1850 The frontier demarcated by the boundary commission proves unacceptable to both Turkey and Persia, but the onset of the Russo-Turkish War (1853–56) prevents any further survey work being carried out.

1869 The drafting of a *Carte Identique* or joint map by Britain and Russia still leaves much of the frontier between Turkey and Persia undemarcated, although local inhabitants of the southern border area generally accept that the frontier runs down the centre of the Shatt al–Arab.

1896 Kuwait asserts its independence from the Ottoman Empire.

1899 The ruler of Kuwait signs a protection agreement with Britain.

1907 Persia is divided into Russian and British spheres of influence.

1908 The frontier issue becomes important to Persia when oil is disovered at Masjed Sulaiman and an outlet to the Persian Gulf is required.

1913 Efforts to delimit the frontier between Turkey and Persia are renewed with the signing of a protocol by representatives of the boundary commission meeting in Constantinople.

Under an Anglo–Turkish convention signed on 29 July, Britain secures Turkish recognition of Kuwait's autonomy within an area formed by a 64–km radius around the city of Kuwait.

1914 In demarcating the border the boundary commission moves the frontier opposite the port of Mohammerah (Khorramshahr) to the Thalweg line in the middle of the river.

1920 Iraq becomes a British mandated territory and a port authority is established at Basrah to supervise navigation on the Shatt al–Arab estuary. Persia does not accept Iraq's sovereignty over the waterway, claiming that the frontier should follow the Thalweg line.

1922 The boundary between Iraq and Saudi Arabia is defined under the aegis of Britain, which establishes a neutral zone on the contentious eastern border.

1932 Iraq becomes an independent state and on joining the League of Nations raises the issue of the frontier between Persia and Turkey.

1937 Prompted by the Italian invasion of Abyssinia, Iran and Iraq sign a frontier agreement in Baghdad on 29 June and in Teheran on 5 July. On 8 July Iran, Iraq, Turkey and Afghanistan sign a treaty of friendship and non-aggression known as the Saadabad Pact. The border agreement reaffirms the frontier line established by the boundary commission in 1913–14, but also applies the so-called "Mohammerah Principle" that diverts the border to the Thalweg line in the middle

of the river for a distance of 6.4km opposite the ports of Mohammerah (Khorramshahr), Khosrowabad and Abadan. All vessels are to fly the Iraqi flag and employ Iraqi pilots, except in those areas in which the boundary was determined at the Thalweg.

1955 Iran and Iraq form a military alliance known as the Baghdad Pact.

1958 Following a revolution in which King Faisal II is killed, Iraq abandons the Baghdad Pact.

1959 In November the issue of navigation on the Shatt al–Arab emerges as a major source of contention between Iran and Iraq when Iraq begins to interfere with Iranian vessels.

1961 On 16 February Iran announces that vessels entering or leaving its ports on the Shatt al–Arab will be guided by Iranian, rather than Iraqi pilots. A strike of Iraqi pilots virtually paralyzes the port of Abadan, forcing Iran to accede to the Iraqi position.

Iraq lays claim to all of newly–independent Kuwait, arguing that formerly it had been part of the Mesopotamian province of Basrah, to which it had succeeded on the dissolution of the Ottoman Empire.

1963 Iraq recognizes the sovereignty of Kuwait.

1964 The Islamic scholar, Ayatollah Khomeini, is exiled to France following his criticism of the Shah of Iran.

1969 Claiming that the revenues from ships visiting Iranian ports are not being properly used by Iraq to benefit river navigation, the Shah of Iran declares the 1937 treaty invalid and refuses to pay any further tolls levied on Iranian vessels.

1971 Iran occupies the Tunb Islands and the island of Abu Musa in the Gulf, both held formerly by rulers in the newly created United Arab Emirates. At the same time, Iran continues to support Kurdish rebels in their opposition to the government of Iraq.

1974　Despite a deterioration in the relationship between Iran and Iraq that leads to border fighting, both sides declare a willingness to resolve their frontier dispute peacefully.

1975　Following a meeting in Algiers, Iran and Iraq reach an agreement over the long–disputed boundary between the two countries. Confirming the land boundary fixed in 1913–14, both Iran and Iraq agree to re-demarcate the frontier on the ground and define the southern boundary where it follows the Shatt al–Arab. In June, both sides come together in Baghdad to sign a Treaty Relating to the State Boundary and Good Neighbourliness. In December, an Agreement on Regulations Concerning Navigation on the Shatt was also signed in Baghdad. By surrendering her sovereignty over the waters of the Shatt al-Arab on the eastern side of the Thalweg, or median line along the deepest channel, Iraq obtained from Iran an agreement to withdraw its support for Kurdish rebels opposing the government in northern Iraq.

1978　Ayatollah Khomeini returns to Iran to lead an Islamic fundamentalist revolution against the government of the Shah.

1979　The overthrow of the Shah of Iran and the establishment of an Islamic Republic led by Ayatollah Khomeini is quickly followed by a deterioration in relations between Iran and Iraq. Iraq's media reports ethnic unrest near the Iraqi frontier in the Iranian province of Khuzestan, while Iran's press accuses Iraq of stirring up intercommunal rivalry in Khuzestan and of supporting Iranian Kurdish separatists in Azerbaijan.

On 31 October Iraq demands that Iran evacuates the Tunb Islands and Abu Musa which it had occupied in 1971.

1980　Following repeated border clashes between June and early September, fighting escalates on the Iran–Iraq frontier. On 17 September President Hussein of Iraq abrogates the 1975 Algiers Agreement and declares that Iraq will now exercise full sovereignty over the Shatt al–Arab. Five days later Iraqi troops invade Iran on three fronts, bombing airports and military installations. A day later Iran retaliates by bombing Baghdad and other Iraqi cities. Pushing into Iran, Iraqi forces capture Khorramshahr and take control of more than 10 000km² of Iranian territory. A further Iraqi advance is brought to a halt when it meets stiff opposition at Susangerd. On 20 November Olaf Palme, former Prime Minister of Norway, is appointed as the UN's Special Representative to mediate in the conflict.

In December the United Arab Emirates insist on the restoration of their sovereignty of the Tunb Islands and Abu Musa.

1981　Offers of mediation proposed at an Islamic Summit Conference in January and by the Non–aligned Movement in April are rejected by Iran. In September an Iranian offensive succeeds in pushing the Iraqis back over the Karun River and relieving the beseiged oil town of Abadan.

Iraq revives its claims to the Kuwaiti islands of Warba and Bubiyan.

In December Iraq and Saudi Arabia sign an agreement defining their common border and dividing the neutral zone that had been established in 1922.

1982　Iranian troops continue their counter-offensive and on 24 May Khorramshahr is liberated. A month later Iraq declares a unilateral ceasefire and withdraws from most of the territory taken in 1980–81. On 12 July the UN Security Council calls for an immediate end to all military operations and a withdrawal of forces to internationally recognized boundaries. A day later Iran launches an offensive into Iraqi territory in an attempt to capture the port of Basrah. The Iranian oil installations on Kharg Island, which had first been bombed by Iraq in April, again come under attack in August. In the same month the Iraqi government announces that the Gulf is now a maritime exclusion zone.

1983　In March–April Iraq bombs the oil installations at the Nowruz oilfield and carries out a series of missile attacks on civilian targets. Iran responds by launching offensives into Iraqi territory in Kurdistan.

1984 The sale of French Super Etendard planes and Exocet missiles to Iraq prompts another round of missile attacks on civilian targets. Iran and Iraq also begin to internationalize the conflict by attacking ships in the Gulf. The British merchant vessel *Charming* being the first target in this so-called "tanker war". When Iran attacks Kuwaiti and Saudi tankers in May, Saudi Arabia responds by shooting down an Iranian fighter plane over the Gulf. Although Iran captures the Majnoon Islands in March there are few territorial gains on either side throughout 1984. Iran accuses Iraq of using chemical weapons.

1985 In March the bombing of civilian targets intensifies into the "war of the cities" and Iranian forces begin to push forward to the Tigris. The bombing of civilian targets by both sides ends in June but Iraq continues to bomb industrial targets.

1986 Iran opens up a second southern front in the drive to take Basrah when it lands troops on the Fao peninsula in February. Iran is unable to capture Basrah but in July begins to shell the city almost daily. Meanwhile, Iraq continues to launch devastating air attacks on Iranian oil installations in an attempt to cripple Iran's oil exports. In desperation, Ayatollah Khomeini tries to step up the offensive by calling for mass mobilization and the establishment of provincial war centres.

1987 In January Iran boycotts the Fifth Islamic Summit in protest at Kuwaiti support for Iraq and for several weeks the bombing of cities intensifies once again. The United States expresses concern when Iran begins to test Silkworm missiles in the Straits of Hormuz. Tension in the Gulf is heightened in May when a Soviet freighter is attacked by an Iranian patrol boat and the US frigate *Stark* is attacked by Iraqi planes with the loss of 37 lives.

Relations between Iran and Saudi Arabia deteriorate in July when clashes between Saudi security forces and Iranian pilgrims visiting Mecca result in 400 deaths. An increased US presence in the Gulf prompts the Speaker of the Iranian Parliament to threaten any Gulf country that makes facilities available to the United States. In July the US Navy begins to escort Kuwaiti–registered tankers through the Straits of Hormuz and in August the British, French and Italian governments agree to send minesweepers and naval escort squadrons into the Gulf.

The UN Secretary–General visits Teheran and Baghdad in September in an attempt to secure a ceasefire and efforts are made to impose an arms embargo against Iran. For most of the year world attention is focused on the Gulf where incidents involving attacks on international shipping take place almost daily. During December alone, 34 merchant ships are attacked by Iraqi aircraft or by fast patrol boats manned by Iranian Revolutionary Guards.

1988 Attacks on shipping in the Gulf continue and the "war of the cities" is renewed for a short while in March. In the following month, after two years of occupation by Iranian forces, Iraq recaptures the Fao peninsula, but in north–east Iraq Iranian troops advance into the Kurdish Autonomous Region. Iraq retaliates with the use of chemical weapons that claim the lives of an estimated 5000 people in the town of Halabja. Similar attacks on Kurdish villages in Iran provoke the sending of angry letters of complaint to the UN Secretary–General in May. On 3 July the USS *Vincennes* accidentally shoots down an Iranian civil airbus.

After years of stalemate the UN Secretary-General succeeds in getting both sides to agree to a ceasefire which takes effect on 20 August. A 350–strong UN Iraq–Iran Military Observer Group (UNIIMOG) takes up positions along the border between the two countries and on 25 August peace talks begin. Although these talks soon end in deadlock over the status of the Shatt al–Arab waterway, low-level discussions between Iran and Iraq continue under UN mediation.

1990 In June Iraq denounces Kuwait for forcing down the price of oil by persistently exceeding production quotas agreed by OPEC. A month later President Saddam Hussein of Iraq outlines a list of grievances against Kuwait and reasserts his country's claim to Kuwaiti territory. On 2 August Iraqi troops enter Kuwait, oust the ruling emir and establish a pro-Iraqi government. A few days later, in the face of total international condemnation, Iraq announces the annexation of Kuwait. While economic sanctions are immediately imposed by the UN, the fear of an Iraqi invasion of Saudi Arabia prompts a rapid and massive deployment of US troops to defend the Saudis and protect the oil fields to the south of Kuwait. Expecting a military showdown between Saddam Hussein and the USA, media attention once again focuses on conflict in the Gulf.

■ Who's who

al–Bakr, Ahmad Hassan   The first Ba'athist Prime Minister of Iraq for a period of nine months following the assassination of President Qasim in February 1963. He re-emerged as President of Iraq when the Ba'ath Party returned to power in 1968. Just over 10 years later in 1979 he resigned and was replaced by Saddam Hussein. During his presidency the Shatt al–Arab issue dominated relations between Iran and Iraq.

Aziz, Tariq   Foreign Minister of Iraq engaged in peace talks with his Iranian counterpart following the declaration of a ceasefire in the Iran–Iraq war in August 1988.

Hakim, Hojjatoleslam   Leader of the Supreme Assembly of Islamic Revolution of Iraq which has been banned by the ruling Ba'athist party in Baghdad. Based in Teheran, the SAIRI is a military and political organization whose aim is to overthrow the Ba'athist regime in Iraq.

Hussein, Saddam   The Ba'athist President of Iraq, Saddam Hussein has faced conflict on several fronts since he came to power in 1979. In September 1980 he initiated a war with Iran that eventually cost his country an estimated US $112 000 million, and 350 000 lives. In the north he took on a large–scale rebellion by elements of the Kurdish population and in 1990 he ordered the invasion of Kuwait to the south.

Khagani, Sheikh Mohammed Taher Shobeir   Leader of the Arab Political and Cultural Organization that seeks autonomy for Khuzestan.

Khomeini, Ayatollah Ruhollah   Iranian head of state and spiritual leader of Iran's Shi'ite Muslims from 1979 until his death in 1989. Born in Khumain in NE Iran in 1900, Khomeini became a prominent Islamic scholar and teacher before being exiled to France in 1964 for criticizing the Shah of Iran. In 1978 he returned to Iran to lead a revolution that ousted the Shah of Iran and installed an Islamic fundamentalist government.

Rafsanjani, Ali Akbar Hashemi   Born in 1934 in the SE Iranian town of Rafsanjan, Ali Rafsanjani became a religious leader and fervent supporter of the Islamic revolution which he helped organize while Ayatollah Khomeini was in exile. As a founder member of the Islamic Republican Party and Speaker of the Iranian Parliament, Rafsanjani developed a power base that made him an obvious successor to Ayatollah Khomeini. His pragmatic approach to politics helped open doors to the West and bring about a ceasefire in the Iran–Iraq conflict.

Rajavi, Massoud   Leader of the rebel National Liberation Army of the Iranian People's Mujahedin. Opposed to Khomeini, the Rajavi family escaped to France where they remained in exile, until forced out of the country and back to Iran, where they raised a rebel army to fight the government of the Islamic Republic.

Shah, Mohammed Reza   Shah of Iran who ascended the "peacock throne" in 1941 when his father, Reza Shah, was deposed. Despite a programme of social and economic reforms known as the "Shah's White Revolution" in 1961, the Shah of Iran assumed an authoritarian rule over his country which he rapidly modernized with the aid of vast oil revenues. Political opposition to the Shah's rule culminated in the 1979 Islamic revolution that turned Iran into a theocratic republic.

Shah, Reza   An Iranian officer of the Persian Cossack Brigade who seized power in 1921 and four years later declared himself Shah of Persia as Reza Shah Pahlavi. During his 16–year reign the country began to modernize as the central government asserted its authority over the tribes and provinces of Persia.

Vellayati, Ali Akbar   Iranian Foreign Affairs Minister engaged in face–to–face peace talks with his Iraqi counterpart, Tariq Aziz, after the declaration of a ceasefire in the Iran–Iraq conflict in August 1988.

■ Key places

Abadan   Iranian port and oil–refining centre near the mouth of the Shatt al–Arab waterway; population (1986) 294 000. Beseiged by Iraqi forces which invaded Iranian territory in 1980, Abadan was eventually relieved by Iranian troops in September 1981.

Abu Musa   A small island situated close to the Tunb Islands in the Persian Gulf. Formerly held by the Ruler of Sharjah, the island was occupied by Iran in November 1971.

Ahvaz   Industrial capital of the oil-producing province of Khuzestan in SW Iran. Situated on the River Karun, it has a population (1986) of 58 0000. In March 1985 the phase of the Gulf War known as the "war of cities" began when Iraq bombed the Iranian city of Ahvaz.

Arabistan   The Iraqi name for the Iranian province of Khuzestan.

Arvand River   The Iranian name for the Shatt al–Arab waterway.

Baghdad   Capital city of Iraq, situated on the Tigris; population (1985) 4 648 600.

Basrah   An Iraqi port and oil–refining centre on the Shatt al–Arab waterway, 120km from the head of the Gulf; population (1985) 61 6700. In July 1982 the Iranians launched a major offensive in a bid to capture Basrah.

Bubiyan   A Kuwaiti island at the head of the Persian Gulf, just south of the border between Iraq and Kuwait. In 1981, a year after Iraq reasserted its territorial claims on Iran, Iraq laid claim to the islands of Warba and Bubiyan. Subsequent Kuwaiti support for Iraq during the Gulf War, served to defuse this territorial issue until the annexation of Kuwait by Iraq in 1990.

Dezful   A textile manufacturing town in the Iranian province of Khuzestan, about 200km north of Khorramshahr and 60km east of the Iraqi border; population (1986) 151 400. A hydro–electric dam on the Ab–i–Dez river 32km to the north is a major source of power. In April 1983 Dezful was the first city to be hit by Iraqi missiles in a series of attacks on civilian targets.

Fao or **Al Faw**   An Iraqi oil port on a peninsula at the mouth of the Shatt al–Arab waterway. In February 1986 Fao was captured during the "Dawn Light" offensive by Iranian troops, whose object was to penetrate Iraq's southern battlefront and head for Basrah. After two years of occupation, Iraqi troops recaptured the Fao peninsula in April 1988.

Hormuz, Strait of   A narrow channel of water linking the Persian Gulf to the Arabian Sea and separating the south coast of Iran from the Musandam peninsula of Oman. The importance of this 50–80km–wide passage was fully realized in 1987 when the Iran–Iraq war threatened to cut off the ocean traffic to and from the Gulf oil ports.

Karbala   A province on Iraq's southern frontier with Saudi Arabia; area 5034km²; population (1985) 329 000. The provincial capital, which lies 88km SSW of Baghdad, is also named Karbala. It is a holy city of the Shia Muslims. Karbala and the neighbouring province of Najaf together have the highest concentration of Shia Muslims outside Iran. The export of Islamic revolution from Iran into southern Iraq is viewed by the Iraqi government as a means of exerting old territorial claims.

Kharg Island   A small island in the Persian Gulf, 48km from the coast of Iran. Iran's principal deepwater oil terminal in the Gulf was built on Kharg Island in the 1950s, replacing Abadan which could only be approached through a narrow channel controlled by Iraq. First bombed by Iraq in April 1982, the Kharg Island oil installation came under frequent attack throughout the "tanker war" phase of the Gulf War.

Khorramshahr   Known as Mohammerah until 1924, Khorramshahr is a trading port and oil–refining centre at the junction of the River Karun with the Shatt al–Arab in Iran's south–western province of Khuzestan. Captured by Iraq in November 1980, the town was eventually retaken by Iran in May 1982. In the "war of the cities" Khorramshahr was virtually destroyed.

Khuzestan   A province of SW Iran on the frontier with Iraq; population (1982) 2 197 000; area 67 236km². Iran's richest oil–producing region, Khuzestan is bounded to the west by the Shatt al–Arab and to the south by the Persian Gulf. Ahvaz is the chief town. Between 1890 and 1925 the Khuzestanis enjoyed autonomy under a tribal sheikh who maintained close relations with Britain and Teheran, but in 1925 the Persian ruler, Reza Shah, began to settle Persians amongst the Arab majority in the province. The border disputes between Iran and Iraq have been complicated by Baghdad's periodic support for the autonomy movement in Khuzestan, or Arabistan, as the Iraqis prefer to call it.

Kuwait   An oil-rich Arab state in the northeastern corner of the Arabian peninsula, bounded to the north and west by Iraq, to the south by Saudi Arabia and to the east by the Persian Gulf; capital, Kuwait City. Of a total population (1985) of 1.7 million, 680 000 are Kuwaitis. The majority (70%) are Sunni Muslims. Protected by the British from 1899 until 1961, Kuwait has been ruled by the Sabah family since 1751. The northern frontier with Iraq was established in 1913, but the agreement with Turkey was never ratified. Although Iraq acepted the situation when it gained independence in 1932, it subsequently laid claim to Kuwait in 1961, and again in 1981. At the beginning of August 1990 Iraq finally resorted to military action when it annexed Kuwait.

Najaf   A province of S Iraq bounded to the south by Saudi Arabia; area 27 844km²; population (1985) 472 100. The Shia Muslim shrine of Ali in the provincial capital, Najaf, is a starting point on the pilgrimage route to Mecca.   Together with Karbala it has the largest population of Shia Muslims outside Iran.

Persian Gulf, Arabian Gulf or **The Gulf**   An inlet of the Arabian Sea separating Iran from the Arabian peninsula. The Persian Gulf is linked to the Arabian Sea by the narrow Strait of Hormuz and the Gulf of Oman.

Rumeila Oilfield   An oilfield straddling Kuwait's disputed northern frontier with Iraq. The extraction of oil by Kuwait from the Rumeila field was one of the grievances raised by Saddam Hussein prior to the Iraqi invasion of Kuwait in August 1990.

Shatt al–Arab ("Arab River") **Arvand River** (Iranian)   A waterway stretching 225km from the confluence of the Tigris and Euphrates rivers at Al-Qrna to the head of the Persian Gulf. The river is an important access route to the oil ports and oilfields of both Iran and Iraq. While it is Iraq's only access to the sea, it poses a problem for Iran whose ports are all enclosed by territorial waters claimed by Iraq. For 105km of its length the river forms the long–disputed boundary between Iran and Iraq that contributed to the outbreak of hostilities between these two countries in 1980.

Teheran or **Tehran**   Capital and largest city of Iran, situated in the foothills of the Elbruz mountains at an altitude of 1200–1700m; population (1986) 6 042 600. Teheran succeeded Esfahan as capital of Persia in 1788 and was almost totally rebuilt by Reza Shah after he came to power in 1921.

Tunb Islands   Known to the Arabs as Tunb as–Sughra and Tunb al–Kubra and to the Iranians as Tunb–e Bozorg and Bani Tanb, the two small islands of Greater and Lesser Tunb lie about 110km north of Dubai in the Gulf. On 30 November 1971, two days after the formation of the United Arab Emirates, these islands were forcibly occupied by Iran which had failed to negotiate their peaceful transfer from the Ruler of Ras al–Khaimah.

Warba   A small Kuwaiti island claimed, along with Bubiyan, by Iraq which eventually secured it with the annexation of Kuwait in 1990.

Zain al–Qaws   Strategic heights lying to the south of Qasr–e–Shirin in the Iranian province of Bakhtaran. Situated close to the Iraqi frontier, the heights of Zain al–Qaws and Saif Saaf, totalling an area of 550km^2, have long been a source of dispute between Iran and Iraq. One of the conditions of the 1975 Algiers Agreement was that Iran would return this territory to Iraq. Much of the prewar 1980 shelling of Iraqi towns and villages came from artillery positions on this high ground.

■ Key words

Algiers agreement   An agreement between Iran and Iraq reached at an OPEC meeting held in Algiers in March 1975. In exchange for concessions on the Shatt al–Arab frontier Iran agreed to withdraw its support for the Kurdish separatists in northern Iraq.

Arab Political and Cultural Organization   An alliance of political and cultural groups whose common aim is to gain autonomy for the province of Khuzestan in W Iran.

Armilla patrol   The name given to a squadron of British ships sent to the Persian Gulf in 1980 to provide a low-profile escort for British merchant ships travelling to and from the various ports around the Gulf. In 1987 the patrol was augmented by the arrival of four Royal Navy minesweepers. During the Iran–Iraq war the Armilla patrol escorted about 80 ships a month through the Strait of Hormuz.

Ba'ath Party or **Arab Socialist Renaissance Party**   The ruling political party in Syria and Iraq. Founded in Damsacus in 1946 by the Christian, Michel Aflaq, who advocated Arab nationalism and union among Arab countries. With the departure of the French from the Middle East the movement became a legal political Party. The Ba'ath Party first came to power in Iraq for a short period in 1963. It later regained control in 1968 following the

overthrow of the Arif regime by Ahmad Hassan al–Bakr.

Baghdad Pact   A military alliance between Iran and Iraq established in 1955. Following the revolution that brought down the Hashemite monarchy of Iraq in 1958, Iraq withdrew from the pact. The Baghdad Pact was reconstituted in 1959 as the Central Treaty Organization (CENTO).

Baluchis   One of the five principal ethnic minorities in Iran. A Sunni Muslim semi–nomadic group, with a total population of about 550 000 in Iran, they occupy the south–eastern region of the country on the frontier with Pakistan. Baluchis in Iran, Pakistan and Afghanistan have pressed for autonomy and occasionally have taken up arms in the struggle for an independent homeland.

Carte Identique   A joint map produced in 1869 by Russian and British members of the boundary commission first set up in 1847 to delimit the frontier between Iran and Iraq.

Carter Doctrine   Enuciated by US President Carter in 1980, the doctrine proposed that the Soviet Union, then in military occupation of Afghanistan, should not be permitted to take advantage of the Iran–Iraq war to attempt penetration of the Gulf.

Erzerum, Treaty of   A treaty first signed by Turkey and Persia in 1823 following a two–year conflict between the two countries. A second Treaty of Erzerum, signed in 1847, established Turkish sovereignty over the Shatt al–Arab waterway and set up a boundary commission to delimit the frontier between Persia and Turkey.

Hamadan, Treaty of   A treaty by which the western provinces of Persia were ceded to Turkey in 1727.

Gulf Co-operation Council   An alliance of Gulf states established in May 1981 for the purpose of ensuring stability and security in the Persian Gulf in the light of the Iran–Iraq conflict and the rise in Islamic fundamentalism. The original members of the Council included Bahrain, Kuwait, Oman, Qatar, Saudi Arabia and the United Arab Emirates. The strategic significance of this alliance is reflected by the fact that, with a total population of 14 million, these countries control about one–third of the world's oil reserves.

Kherden, Treaty of   A treaty of 1746 reaffirming the 1639 frontier between Persia and Turkey.

Majlis   The 27–member Parliament of Iran which is dominated by religious mullahs.

maritime exclusion zone   The Iran–Iraq conflict broadened into the Gulf when Iraq announced on 12 August 1982 that the Gulf had become a maritime exclusion zone in which any vessel was liable to come under attack.

mohafaza   A first order administrative region or province, of which there are 18, in Iraq.

Mohammerah principle   An agreement reached in 1914 by the Turkey-Persia boundary commission that involved moving the frontier in the vicinity of the port of Mohammerah (Khorramshahr) from the east bank of the Shatt al–Arab to the *Thalweg* line in the middle of the river. The "Mohammerah principle" was later applied to the ports of Abadan and Khosrowabad.

National Liberation Army (NLA)   The military wing of the Iranian Mujahedin e-Khalq organization opposed to the regimes of both the Shah of Iran and the Ayatollah Khomeini. Led by the Rajavi family, this rebel group claims to have a fighting force of about 15000 combatants. The membership of the NLA is drawn from the educated middle class. The Mujahedin suffered a major defeat near Kermanshah in 1988.

Operation Dawn   The codename for a series of Iranian military offensives. The most famous of these was "Operation Dawn 8", which involved the successful landing of 25 000 troops on the Fao peninsula in February 1986.

Operation Desert Shield   The codename for the massive deployment of US forces in Saudi Arabia following the Iraqi invasion of Kuwait in August 1990.

Operation Praying Mantis   The codename given to the US attack on two Iranian oil platforms in the Gulf carried out on 18 April 1988 in response to the mining of a US Navy frigate four days earlier. These oil platforms were known to be used by Iranian Revolutionary Guards as bases from which to attack merchant shipping.

Operation Ramadan   The codename for the Iranian counter–offensive against Iraqi forces launched in July 1982.

ostan   A first order administrative region or province, of which there are 24, in Iran.

Pan–Arab Charter   An Arab nationalist stance enunciated by Iraq's president, Saddam Hussein, on 8 February 1980. Iraqi claims to the Kuwaiti islands of Warba and Bubiyan and Iraq's subsequent confrontation with Iran have largely been prompted by Ba'athist pan–Arabic nationalism.

Pasdaran   The paramilitary Iranian Revolutionary Guards.

Revolutionary Command Council   A nine–member legislative council through which the Ba'ath Party has ruled Iraq since the 1968 revolution.

Saadabad Pact A treaty of friendship and non-agression signed on 8 July 1937 by Iran, Iraq, Turkey and Afghanistan.

Supreme Assembly of Islamic Revolution of Iraq (SAIRI) A political and military organization established in Tehran in November 1982. Led by Hojjatoleslam Hakim, its aim is to overthrow the ruling Ba'athist regime in Iraq.

tanker war A name given to a phase of the Iran–Iraq conflict which began in March 1984 and during which both sides directed their attacks on shipping and oil installations in the Persian Gulf.

Thalweg line A riverine frontier that follows the median line in the deepest channel of the river rather than either of the river banks. Under agreements of 1914 and 1937, the *Thalweg* line formed the basis of the river frontier established along a stretch of the Shatt al–Arab opposite the Iranian ports of Abadan, Khorramshahr

and Khosrowabad. In 1975 it was applied to the whole waterway under the Algiers Agreement, but this was repudiated by Iraq on the outbreak of war in 1980.

Turkomans One of the five principal ethnic minorities in Iran, mostly living in the north–east on the border with Afghanistan and Soviet Turkmenistan.

United Nations Iran-Iraq Military Observer Group (UNIIMOG) A 350–strong UN observer force sent to positions along the frontier between Iran and Iraq in 1988 to supervise the ceasefire that came into effect on 20 August.

war of the cities A name given to phases of the Iran–Iraq conflict during which both sides launched indiscriminate air attacks on civilian targets in cities. The "war of the cities" began in March 1985 with the bombing of Ahvaz, capital of Khuzestan.

Further reading

J.M. Abdulghani, *Iraq and Iran: The Years of Crisis*, Croom Helm, London, 1984

S. Chubin and C. Tripp, *Iran and Iraq at War*, Tauris, London, 1988

Anthony H. Cordesman, *The Iran–Iraq War and Western Security 1984–87: Strategic Implications and Policy Options*, Jane's Publishing Co., London, 1987

Stephen R. Grummon, *The Iran–Iraq War: Islam Embattled*, Praeger Publishers, New York, 1982

Asaf Hussain, *Islamic Iran: Revolution and Counter–revolution*, Pinter, London, 1985

Tareq Y. Ismael, *Iraq and Iran: Roots of Conflict*, Syracuse University Press, Syracuse, 1982

Robert Litwak, *Security in the Persian Gulf: Sources of Inter–state Conflict*, The International Institute for Strategic Studies, Aldershot, 1981

Will D. Swearingen, Geopolitical Origins of the Iran–Iraq War, *Geographical Review*, 78(4) pp.405–16, 1989

Claudia Wright, Implications of the Iran–Iraq War, *Foreign Affairs*, 59, 1980–81

Martin Wright (ed.), *Iran: Khomeini's Revolution*, Longman (UK), Harlow, 1989

4
Kurdistan

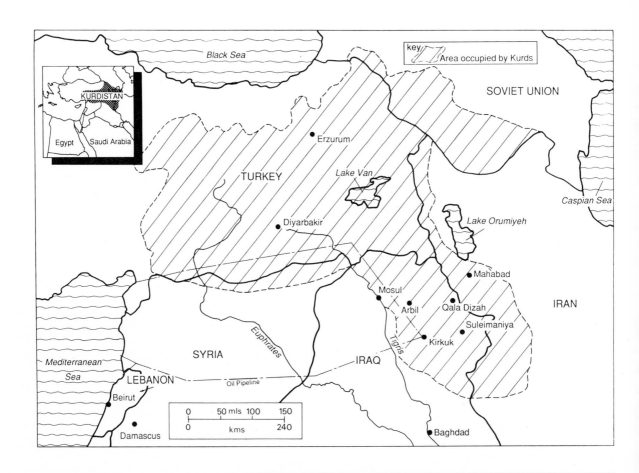

Black Sea

key
Area occupied by Kurds

SOVIET UNION

KURDISTAN

Egypt Saudi Arabia

• Erzurum

TURKEY

Lake Van

Caspian Sea

• Diyarbakir

Lake Orumiyeh

• Mahabad

Mosul •

Arbil •   • Qala Dizah

IRAN

• Suleimaniya

• Kirkuk

Euphrates

Tigris

SYRIA

IRAQ

~ Mediterranean
Sea

LEBANON   Oil Pipeline

Beirut •

| 0 | 50 mls 100 | 150 |
| 0 | kms | 240 |

• Damascus

• Baghdad

■ Profile

- **Area:** c.191 600km²
- **Kurdish population:** 19.7 million
- **Turkey** 9.6 million out of a total population of 52.6 million
- **Iran** 5 million out of a total popuiation of 52 million
- **Iraq** 3.9 million out of a total population of 17.1 million
- **Syria** 0.9 million out of a total population of 11.2 million
- **Soviet Union** 0.3 million out of a total population of 286.7 million

■ Introduction

Probably descended from Aryan tribes that settled west of the Caspian Sea in c.2000 BC, the Kurds popularly trace their ancestry to the Medes, ancient rivals of the Persians. From about AD 600 the term Kurds was applied to the assorted inhabitants of the remote mountainous regions straddling the modern borders of Turkey, Syria, Iraq, Iran (Persia) and the USSR. From the 14th century Kurds moved into eastern Anatolia, coming up against the rising power of the Ottoman Turks to the north and west. The Kurds remained disunited in many respects, and to this day their various dialects do not amount to a common language. But, in time, a shared semi-nomadic culture, blood ties and territorial affiliation created a distinctive Kurdish identity which transcended a predilection for inter-tribal warfare. The vast majority of Kurds became Muslims of the Sunni persuasion, sharing that faith with the Ottoman Turks. The latter, in wars with the Persians, conquered much of the Kurdish lands in the 16th century and appointed Kurdish emirs to rule what became known as Kurdistan. The Persians also used local Kurdish rulers on their side of the border, which was itself the subject of endless dispute.

In the early 19th century moves by both the Ottomans and the Persians to centralize their fraying empires sparked off the first modern Kurdish revolts. Their suppression broke the power of the Kurdish emirs, whose secular authority was dispersed among a host of local chiefs. But such fragmentation was countered by the rise of the Kurdish religious brotherhoods and an awakening of national consciousness, at least among educated Kurds. Pro-autonomy Kurdish rebellions became a recurrent feature of 19th-century history, although Kurdish irregulars happily assisted Turkish repression of Christian Armenians (*see section 5.2*) and other subject peoples. When the empire finally collapsed in World War I (1914- 18), Kurdish leaders at last had an opportunity to press their case. Under the 1920 Treaty of Sèvres the Allies agreed that the Kurdish regions should be prepared for autonomy prior to possible independence. But this unimplemented provision was as close as the Kurds have ever come to national recognition.

Two main factors explain why the Sèvres terms never became a reality. First, Britain and France were determined to carve up the Turkish Empire in their own interests rather than its subject peoples'. Thus the new entities of Iraq and Syria, under British and French mandates respectively, incorporated much Kurdish-populated territory in the north. Second, the Turks staged a remarkable national revival in the early 1920s under the leadership of Kemal Atatürk. The new Turkish Republic's sovereignty over Kurdish eastern Anatolia was established by force of arms and then confirmed by the 1923 Treaty of Lausanne. Persistent revolts by the Kurds in the 1920s failed to change the new territorial dispositions. They meant, and continue to mean, that the Kurds were assigned to various states, the largest concentrations being in Turkey, Iran and Iraq, with lesser numbers living in Syria, the new USSR and Lebanon.

Since the 1920s the two main strands of the Kurds' history have been struggles for autonomy or basic rights within the states in which they live and the never-abandoned hope of achieving a state of their own. Kemalist Turkey was the most determined to quash Kurdish separatism. Secularization and Westernization of the state in the 1920s were particularly harmful to Kurdish religious and national identity. The banning of the dialect spoken by Turkey's Kurds (which is still in force) and of their social and cultural institutions was part and parcel of this drive to modernization. But as much as the Ankara government insisted that the Kurds were "eastern Turks", the Kurds themselves doggedly maintained other aspirations. In the post-1945 era, Turkey's pro-Western alignment inevitably meant that Kurdish separatism took on a leftist, pro-Soviet hue, at least in the perception of the Turkish authorities. There were occasional initiatives to accommodate moderate Kurdish demands, but the overall pattern was one of continued repression of a minority regarded as a potential "fifth column".

Across Turkey's borders with Syria, Iraq and Iran, Kurdish minorities also suffered periodic repression, interspersed with efforts, particularly in Iraq, to establish limited autonomy for Kurds. Remoteness from the centres of government authority gave many Kurds in these countries a degree of physical security. They were also hard to defeat militarily, not least because Kurdish guerrillas in one country could always get arms from the government of another. The various regimes of the region all combined opposition to Kurdish separatism at home with support for Kurdish separatist activities against disliked governments abroad. Both Syria and Iraq used the other's Kurds as surrogates for their own fierce hostilities, as did Iran and Iraq; and the Soviet government played this game when it could. In the most cynical of such manoeuvres, Iran agreed in 1975 to stop backing Iraq's Kurds in return for Iraqi concessions on the Shatt al-Arab waterway dispute. Five years later Iran resumed its support for Iraq's Kurds on the outbreak of the Gulf War, during which the Iraqi regime used chemical weapons against Kurdish strongholds (*see section 2.3*).

Efforts by the various Kurdish movements to establish a genuine cross-border front met with little success. A short-lived Kurdish republic set up in Mahabad (north-eastern Iran) in 1945 received scant support from Kurds in other states. Moreover, its suppression after the Soviet military withdrawal from Iran was achieved by Iranian troops largely made up of pro-government Kurdish contingents. Indeed, each state with a large Kurdish minority has consistently attracted one or more Kurdish factions to the pro-government banner. Amid such persistent disunity, and with the regional borders having achieved a degree of permanence over several decades, the prospects for an independent Kurdistan seemed as bleak as ever at the end of the 1980s. It remained to be seen whether secessionist tendencies in the southern Soviet republics would lead to regional territorial realignments in which Kurdish national aspirations would again come to the fore.

■ Chronology of events

1826 A growing sense of national identity amongst the Kurds leads to the first in a series of 19th century armed revolts against their Ottoman rulers.

1834 The Kurds engage in a second revolt against the Ottoman Turks.

1853–56 Taking advantage of the Russo–Turkish war, the Kurds attempt to gain independence once more.

1920 The disintegration of the Ottoman Empire after World War I raises Kurdish hopes of self-determination. These hopes are encouraged by President Woodrow Wilson of the United States who declares that "non–Turkish minorities of the Ottoman Empire should be assured of an unmolested opportunity of autonomous development." The Treaty of Sèvres forces the Sultan's government to renounce all claims to non–Turkish territory and establishes British and French mandates in the Arab Middle East. The treaty also envisages local autonomy in predominantly Kurdish areas and the possible creation of an independent Kurdish state.

1922 A split between the Sultan's government and the Turkish nationalists led by Mustapha Kemal leads to the abolition of the Sultanate and a revision of the Treaty of Sèvres which has not yet been ratified by the Turks. Fearing that they are to be robbed of independence or autonomy, the Kurds under Sheikh Mahmud launch an open revolt.

1923 The conflict over Turkey's post–war borders is finally terminated with the signing of the Treaty of Lausanne, although the status of the oil–rich territory around Mosul is still to be determined. This agreement effectively replaces the former Treaty of Sèvres, but no mention is made of an independent Kurdistan.

The semi–nomadic Kurdish people now find themselves distributed among several countries.

1924 The League of Nations fixes a provisional line (Brussels Line) assigning Mosul to Iraq. The two–year Kurdish revolt led by Sheikh Mahmud is finally suppressed.

1925 The suppression of religion by the government of the newly–created Turkish republic leads to an uprising amongst the predominantly Sunni Muslim Kurds. The revolt is quickly crushed and the leaders executed.

1926 Despite the signing of a Soviet–backed Persian–Turkish–Afghan treaty of mutual security, there is friction between Iraq, Persia and Turkey over the activities of the Kurdish population in the frontier regions

1929 A further Kurdish revolt against Turkish reforms takes place during June–July in the region of Mount Ararat.

1930 In September, Sheikh Mahmud leads a major new Kurdish uprising that strains relations between Iraq and Persia.

1932 The independence of Iraq leads to yet another insurrection by the Kurds whose army is driven across the border into Turkey by British and Iraqi forces.

1934 An oil pipeline from Mosul to Tripoli is opened.

1935 A second oil pipeline from Mosul to the Palestinian port of Haifa is opened.

1937 General Bakr Sidqi is assassinated by a Kurd. Leader of Iraq since a military coup in October 1936, Sidqi was a prime mover in the cause of Pan–Arabism.

1941 In August, British and Russian troops enter Iran, topple Rez Shah and establish a regime that will co-operate with them. The British–Soviet occupation leads to a loosening of central government control in a country that has long been opposed to Kurdish autonomy.

1945 Kurdish nationalist hopes in Iran are realized with the creation of the Kurdish Republic of Mahabad in December.

1946 When Soviet troops withdraw from northern Iran in April–May, the Iranian army moves in to regain control. The short–lived republic collapses, its leaders are executed and the newly–formed Kurdish Democratic Party is banned.

1947 The followers of the Iraqi Kurdish leader Mustapha Barzani are forced to retreat in Soviet Azerbaijan by a combined Iraqi–British military force.

1961 Iranian and Iraqi Kurds join forces in a revolt against the government of Iraq.

1963 Following a February coup d'état in Iraq the new National Revolutionary Council announces that it will honour "the rights of the Kurds", but when promises of autonomy remain unfulfilled hostilities break out between Iraqi troops and Kurdish forces.

1964 After nine months of fighting a ceasefire is announced on 10 February by President Arif of Iraq and the Kurdish leader, Mustapha Barzani. A government statement recognizes "the national rights of the Kurds within one Iraqi national union," but this does not prevent Kurdish leaders meeting in Vienna in November from announcing the formation of a parliament in exile.

1965 The Kurds renew their revolt against the Iraqi government. In the fighting that ensues an estimated 40 000 troops are sent to northern Iraq. Government forces are accused of using napalm and gas against the Kurds.

1966 In mid–January a major offensive is launched against the Kurds, but in June a ceasefire is agreed when the Iraqi government promises some form of local autonomy and recognition of the Kurdish language. The Kurds do not surrender their arms and the situation remains tense.

1968 The right–wing Baathist Party sets up a Revolutionary Command Council that recognizes the rights of the Kurds within the framework of national unity. The new leader of Iraq, General Ahmad Hassan al–Bakr, adopts a policy of "divide and rule" by taking sides with Talabani's Patriotic Union of Kurdistan against Mustapha Barzani's Kurdish Democratic Party.

1969 Forces loyal to Barzani attack the Talabani stronghold at Sulaymaniyah. Later in the year two new administrative regions are created in northern Iraq in an attempt to give some form of autonomy to the local Kurdish majority.

1970 The Revolutionary Command Council in Iraq opens up a four–year dialogue with the Kurds on the subject of local autonomy following secret negotiations with Kurdish leaders in Beirut. A 15–point peace agreement signed on 11 March confers nominal autonomy in the Kurdish areas of northern Iraq. Five Kurdish government ministers are appointed and a statement is made suggesting that the constitution be amended to recognize the existence of both Iraqi and Kurdish nationalities.

1972 Relations between the Iraqi government and the Kurds deteriorate over the implementation of the 1970 agreement. Iraq signs a Treaty of Friendship with the Soviet Union, a measure that signals Moscow's support for the Iraqi government's moves against Kurdish separatists.

1973 Barzani appeals to the USA, Israel and Iran for help.

1974 On 11 March the government of Iraq grants autonomy to the Kurds, but the conditions fall far short of demands made by the Kurdish Democratic Party under Mustapha Barzani. Fighting breaks out again as the five Kurdish Ministers are replaced by Kurds known to be sympathetic to the Baghdad government. By August full–scale conflict between Iranian-backed Kurdish guerrillas and Iraqi troops has resumed and 130 000 Kurds are forced to take refuge across the border in Iran. A Kurdish Legislative Council is set up in Arbil by the Iraqi government but this and other concessions are rejected by the Kurds.

1975 The Kurdish revolt collapses when Iran and Iraq resolve their border dispute and mutually agree to end "infiltrations of a subversive character." Barazani, who cannot continue the fight without Iranian aid, flees to Teheran and in March a ceasefire is arranged. A series of amnesties encourages Kurdish refugees to return from Iran. In an attempt to clear the frontier area with Iran, many Kurds are forcibly resettled in less sensitive areas of Iraq.

1976 A new political organization, the National Union of Kurdistan (later the Patriotic Union of Kurdistan), is established in Damascus and Kurdish guerrilla forces begin to regroup in northern Iraq. Renewed fighting by units under Jalal Talabani is, however, contained by the Iraqi government which has embarked on a programme of reconstruction in Kurdish areas.

1977 In July over 40 000 Kurds who had been forcibly resettled in other parts of the country are allowed to return to northern Iraq.

1978 A rapprochement between the Baathist régimes in Baghdad and Damascus in September starves Talabani's Patriotic Union of Kurdistan of Syrian support and PUK military operations in Iraq come to an end.

1979 With the end of the Shah's regime in Iran, Kurdish nationalists press the leaders of the new Islamic republic for autonomy. In August Ayatollah Khomeini responds by banning all Kurdish political parties and ordering a military offensive against the rebels in Kurdistan.

1980 In September the invasion of Iran by Iraq and the military take-over in Turkey add new dimensions to the Kurdish problem. While the Gulf War leads to an abatement of fighting within Iranian Kurdistan, the new regime in Turkey sets out to restore law and order by banning all political activity and arresting large numbers of terrorists including left–wing Kurdish separatists.

1983 Iranian troops restore government control in the Kurdish strongholds of Sardasht and Mahabad where 59 civilians are executed in June. Meanwhile, in Iraq KDP guerrillas backed by Iranians and Iraqi Shi'ite dissidents recapture the mountain stronghold of Hajj Omran, six kilometres from the Turkish frontier. In the following months Iranian forces make further incursions into Iraq to join forces with Kurdish rebels.

1984 There is an upsurge in Kurdish separatist activity in Turkey, with frequent clashes between government troops and rebels of the radical Kurdistan Workers' Party. Martial law is maintained in Turkey's five south-eastern provinces and in October Iraq and Turkey agree to allow each others' troops to cross the frontier in search of guerrilla fighters. In the same month Turkish forces cross the border into Iraq in pursuit of Kurdish rebels.

1985 While Kurdish separatists continue to clash with Turkish, Iraqi and Iranian security forces, the governments of Turkey and Iran now agree to co-operate over the policing of their frontier.

1986 In March Turkey reaches a border security agreement with Syria that further limits the Kurdish guerrillas who are now fighting on four fronts. A total of 271 Kurdish activists are sentenced in mass trials that take place in Diyarbakir, Erzerum and SE Turkey.

1987 In April Kurdish rebels, well–supplied with Soviet weapons, effectively establish a second front against the Iraqi government which is engaged in a major conflict with Iran to the east. Several villages in the province of Sulaymaniyah are captured, power stations are badly damaged and the road link between Kirkuk and Turkey is cut.

Faced with an increasing number of attacks on civilian and military targets in the south eastern provinces of Turkey, the Turkish government declares all–out war on Kurdish insurgents. Armed "village guards" are paid to protect their communities from attack by Kurdistan Workers' Party guerrilla fighters.

1988 In March Iranian Revolutionary Guards and Kurdish rebels capture the towns of Khormal and Halabja in the north–eastern province of Sulaymaniyah. Fearing that the Dokan Dam on Lake Darbandikhan will be

destroyed, the Iraqi government quickly retaliates by bombing the town of Halabja with chemical weapons. The deaths of 5000 people cause an international outcry. Four months later, following a ceasefire between Iran and Iraq, Iranian troops withdraw from positions in the Kurdish areas of N Iraq. In September–October the Iraqi government turns its attention to the suppression of Kurdish insurgency. In fear of their lives over 100 000 Kurds flee across the frontier into Turkey as 60 000 Iraqi troops move into the Kurdish areas of northern Iraq. An estimated 61 000 refugees return to Iraq following an amnesty only to be faced with a resettlement programme that involves the evacuation of over 200 villages and the relocation of large numbers of Kurds in Arab areas of SW Iraq.

In Turkey, Kurdish insurgency during four years of open conflict is estimated to have cost 3000 lives. The presence of over 38 000 Kurdish refugees from Iraq adds to the problem which is partially resolved by the illegal transport of 20 000 Kurds across the border into Iran. Many of these Kurds are then provided with arms and returned to Iraqi where they rejoin the struggle for independence.

1989 International criticism is directed at the Iraqi government and its policy of depopulating Kurdish areas, but in June force is used once more to deport a further 100 000 Kurds from the towns and villages of northern Iraq. The government claims that civilians have to be moved in order to create a defensive "security zone" along Iraq's northern frontier.

In July the Iranian Kurdish leader, Abdul Rahman Qasemlu, is killed in Vienna while engaged in secret negotiations for Kurdish autonomy with representatives of the Iranian government. A weekend international conference in Paris, that he was to have chaired in October, brings together leaders of all the main Kurdish separatist movements for the first time in 60 years. Although the conference is restricted to issues of cultural identity and human rights, Kurdish delegates express concern at the lack of international action to protect the rights of Kurds and fears that a peace settlement between Iran and Iraq will lead to a concerted effort to strangle Kurdish resistance.

In response to the human rights violations that have received international attention, Jalal Talabani, leader of the Patriotic Union of Kurdistan, announces the beginning of a Kurdish campaign of guerrilla warfare aimed at cities throughout Iraq.

1990 In SE Turkey, where more than 2100 people have been killed in escalating violence since 1984, sympathy for the PKK grows. In April, President Ozal threatens to impose special powers over the 17 Kurdish–speaking provinces as the Turkish army scores a series of successes against rebel guerrillas.

■ Who's who

Barzani, Idris Son of the Iraqi Kurdish leader, Mustafa Barzani. In 1979 he became co-leader of the Iraqi Kurdish Democratic Party with his brother Masoud. Idris Barzani was killed during an Iraqi air raid in January 1987.

Barzani, Masoud Son of Mustafa Barzani and co-leader of the Iraqi Kurdish Democratic Party with his brother Idris from 1979 until 1987. In January of that year he became sole leader of this faction of Iraqi Kurds following the death of his brother.

Barzani, Mustafa Former leader of Iraq's largest Kurdish separatist movement, the Kurdish Democratic Party. Despite frequent feuds with Jalal Talabani's Patriotic Union of Kurdistan, Barzani dominated the Kurdish struggle for autonomy in Iraq until his death in 1979. Despite collaborating with Iranians against the Iraqi government in 1965–66, Iran regarded Barzani as little more than an agent of Iraqi and Soviet interests.

Hasan al–Bakr, Ahmad A former Prime Minister of Iraq who re-emerged as President following a military coup in 1968. In the early 1970s he tried to reach a peaceful settlement with the Kurds by establishing a Kurdish Autonomous Region in N Iraq, but his plans were eventually rejected by Mustapha Barzani, leader of the Kurdish Democratic Party. Bakr resigned in July 1979 when he was succeeded by the hard-line General Saddam Hussein.

Hussein, General Saddam President of Iraq and Chairman of the Revolutionary Command Council since 1979. His use of chemical weapons against the Kurds and his policy of depopulating Kurdish areas in N Iraq has focused international attention on the Kurdish problem.

Husseini, Sheik Izzedin A Sunni Muslim religious leader who attracted a strong following in 1979–80 when he spoke out in favour of Kurdish autonomy. He was forced to flee from the Iranian town of Mahabad but by 1983 was in command of a radical Kurdish nationalist group calling itself the National Organization. In the spring of 1984 he sent envoys to a number of Western countries in order to focus international attention on the plight of the Kurds.

Mohammed, Ghazi Leader of the Iranian Kurdish Democratic Party which he founded in 1945, and president of the Kurdish Republic of Mahabad set up by the Soviet Union in 1945. When the Soviets withdrew from Iran in 1946 Ghazi Mohammed was executed and the Kurdish Democratic Party was outlawed.

Mohtadi, Abdullah Leader of the Marxist Komalah movement, the second largest Kurdish nationalist group in Iran.

Ocalan, "Apo" Abdullah Founder and leader of the Turkish Kurdistan Workers' Party which was outlawed in 1980. Ocalan's Kurdish guerrillas operate largely from bases in Iraq.

Ozal, Turgut Born in the Turkish province of Malatya in 1923, Ozal worked as an under secretary at the State Planning Department and as a representative of the World Bank before his appointment as Prime Minister of Turkey in 1983. After three years of oppressive military rule (1980–83), the election of a civilian government under Ozal marked the beginning of violence amongst left-wing Kurdish separatists. Despite a reduction in human rights violations, attempts to suppress the Kurdish revolt in the east have not helped Ozal's prospects of bringing Turkey into the European Community.

Qasemlu, Abdel Rahman   Leader of the Iranian Kurdish Democratic Party and a major figure in the Kurdish autonomy movement which he led for ten years until his assassination at a conference in Vienna in July 1989. For 20 years Qasemlu lived in exile in Paris where

he was a lecturer in economics at the Sorbonne University. In 1978 he returned to Iran to lead the Iranian Kurdish separatist movement. While Iranians joined forces with Kurdish rebels to form a second front against the Iraqis during the Gulf War, Qasemlu led an estimated 11 000 Iranian Kurds in the fight against the Islamic government of Iran.

Talabani, Jalal al Din   Socialist leader of the Patriotic Union of Kurdistan, the second most powerful Kurdish nationalist group in Iraq. Often at odds with the rival Kurdish Democratic Party led by the Barzanis, Talabani received strong backing from Syria between 1975 and 1978.

■ Key places

Arbil also **Erbil** or **Irbil**   A Kurdish market town and capital of a province of the same name in N Iraq. Situated between the Great and Little Zab rivers, Arbil occupies the site of ancient Arbela which has been inhabited since Assyrian times. Alexander the Great defeated the Persian forces of Darius III here in 331 BC. Following four years of negotiations on Kurdish autonomy, a Kurdish Legislative Council was convened in Arbil in October 1974. Population (1985) 334 000. The province of Arbil, with a population (1985) of 742 700 and an area of 14471km², is one of three provinces that form a Kurdish Autonomous Region in N Iraq.

Diyarbakir   An agricultural and textile centre in Turkish Kurdistan once famous for its gold and silver crafts. Situated on the Tigris, the city was the scene of mass trials of Kurdish separatists in 1986. Population (1985) 305 300.

Dohuk or **Dahuk**   The northernmost of the three provinces of N Iraq that constitute a Kurdish Autonomous Region; population (1985) 330 400; area 6120km². The chief town, also named Dohuk, has a population of 19 700.

Hajj Omran   An Iraqi mountain stronghold six kilometres from the Iranian frontier, held by Kurdish rebels until 1975 but later captured by

Iraqi forces. The site was retaken by an alliance of Kurdish, Iranian and Iraqi dissident Shi'ite troops in July 1983.

Halabja or **Alabja**   A Kurdish town in the province of Sulaymaniyah, NE Iraq, situated close to the Iran border, 56km south-east of the town of Sulaymaniyah. In August 1988 an estimated 5000 Kurds died when Iraqi planes dropped poison gas on the town.

Kirkuk   A Kurdish market town and capital of a province of the same name in N Iraq. Situated 145km south-east of Mosul, Kirkuk developed rapidly after World War I as a centre of the oil industry. A pipeline links Kirkuk with Haifa and Tripoli on the Mediterranean coast. Population (1985) 208 000.

Mahabad   A Kurdish town in the Iranian province of W Azerbaijan, situated 30km south of Lake Orumiyeh (Rezaiyah) and 60km E of the Iraq frontier; population (1983) 63 000. Russian troops occupied Mahabad in 1941 and a Soviet–backed Kurdish Republic of Mahabad was established four years later in December 1945. When Soviet forces withdrew and Iran re-occupied the area in 1946 the short-lived Kurdish republic collapsed and its leader, Ghazi Mohamed, was executed. Mahabad again became a centre of Kurdish dissent in the early 1980s when the religious leader and founder of the National Organization, Sheikh Izzedin Husseini, stirred up opposition to the anti–Kurdish policies of Ayatollah Khomeini. In 1983 Husseini was forced to flee from Mahabad when Iranian government troops regained control of the area for the first time since the 1979 revolution.

Mosul   Situated on the River Tigris, 350km north-west of Baghdad, Mosul is the largest city in Kurdistan and the third largest city in Iraq. Ancient Niniveh stood on the opposite side of the river. Mosul lies not only at the centre of Iraq's northern oilfields but also at a strategic position on the route from the Persian Gulf to Turkey. Always at the centre of territorial disputes, Mosul was finally handed over to Iraq in 1925. Population (1985) 571 000.

Qala Diza   A town in the province of Sulaymaniyah, NE Iraq, situated 16 km from the Iranian frontier; population 100 000. In June 1989 the Iraqi government ordered the deportation of 50 000 Kurds from Qala Diza and the nearby Twoesuran camp, while allegedly encouraging the settlement of Arab Iraqis, Yemenis and Egyptians.

Sulaymaniyah or **Suleimaniya**   One of three northern provinces of Iraq forming a Kurdish Autonomous Region ; population (1985) 906 000; area 15756km². The chief town, Sulaymaniyah, lies 256km north-east of Baghdad.

Tigris   A river rising in the mountains of Turkish Kurdistan near Mt Elazig. Flowing SSE past Diyarkabir it continues into Iraq, passing through Mosul and Baghdad before joining the Euphrates at Al–Qurna where it becomes the Shatt al–Arab. The total length of the Tigris is 1 888km.

Van, Lake   A salt lake with no outlet in E Turkey. The ancient city of Van, which lies at the heart of Turkish Kurdistan, fell to the Seljuk Turks in 1071 and was later ruled by the Ottoman Turks from 1543 until 1922.

Zagros Mountains   A mountain range extending in a great arc c.1700km from Azerbaijan in NW Iran to Baluchistan in the SE. Iran's main oilfields are located in the western foothills of the Zagros range. It was in the Zagros Mountains that the Kurds first settled.

■ Key words

Algiers Agreement   An agreement resolving the border dispute between Iran and Iraq, concluded at an OPEC meeting in Algiers on 6 March 1975. The peace between Iran and Iraq led to the withdrawal of Iranian support for the Kurds and the collapse of the 1974–75 Kurdish revolt.

Arabization   The deportation of Kurds or the introduction of Arab settlers into Kurdish areas is viewed by Kurds as part of a process of "Arabization" adopted by central governments in an attempt to dilute or stamp out Kurdish nationalism.

Brussels Line   A line drawn by the Council of the League of Nations assigning the oil–rich territory of Mosul to Iraq in 1924–25.

Jiraz al Rasd   A secret branch of Iraqi intelligence responsible for carrying out operations against the Kurds.

Komalah (Revolutionary Organization of the Workers of Kurdistan)   A small Marxist group of Iranian Kurdish nationalists, occasionally at odds with the Kurdish Democratic Party.

Kurds   Numbering about 20 million, the Kurds have existed as a tribal people with their own cultural tradition and language for at least 3000 years. Ethnically and linguistically related to the Iranians, they were originally nomadic herdsmen, but today the majority are either seminomadic or sedentary. Despite a strong desire for independence a number of factors, such as differing dialects and tribal divisions, have always prevented the Kurds from uniting under one ruler. Kurdistan was conquered by the Arabs and converted to Islam in the 7th century. Except for a few in Iran, the majority of Kurds throughout Iraq, Iran, Turkey, Syria and the Soviet Union are Sunni Muslim.

Kurdish Democratic Party (KDP)   The dominant Kurdish nationalist group in Iran. Founded in 1945 by Ghazi Mohamed, it commands the powerful 12000–strong Pesh Merga guerrilla force. Supported by Iraq the moderately left-wing KDP seeks Kurdish autonomy within a democratic Iranian state.

Kurdish Democratic Party of Turkey (KDPT)   A Kurdish nationalist group created in 1965 and closely allied to the Iraqi KDP.

Kurdish Democratic People's Party (KDPP)   A Libyan–backed Iraqi Kurdish nationalist group founded in 1981 by Muhamad Mahmud Abd al–Rahman.

Kurdish Socialist Party of Turkey (KSPT)   A Marxist Kurdish nationalist movement founded in 1974 by members of the former Turkish Workers' Party. Many of its members have either been imprisoned or forced into exile since 1980.

Kurdistan Workers' Party (PKK) or Apocus   The most active of the radical Kurdish nationalist groups in Turkey. Founded by "Apo" Abdullah Ocalan of the Turkish Revolutionary Youth in 1974 it moved its base from Ankara to Kurdistan in 1979. Following the military take-over in 1980 the PKK was banned and Ocalan moved his base to Syria.

Lausanne, Treaty of   A treaty signed by the Allied powers and Turkey on 24 July 1923 by which Turkey gave up its claims to non–Turkish territories. Although Turkey accepted treaties to protect the rights of minorities, no mention was made of Kurdish autonomy or independence. The resulting boundaries fixed by this treaty left the Kurds distributed among several countries and with little prospect of gaining the independence envisaged in the earlier, but unratified, Treaty of Sèvres.

Milli Istchbarat Teskilati (MIT)   The Turkish Security Police whose powers were reduced in 1988 in an attempt to clean up Turkey's human rights image with respect to the treatment of political prisoners and Kurdish nationalists.

mohafaza   A first order administrative region or province in Iraq.

Mountain Turks   A term used by Turkish officials to describe the Kurdish minority who are not recognized as a separate nationality in Turkey.

Naqshbandiyya   A Kurdish religious brotherhood which, with the Qadiryya order, became influential in the early 19th century.

National Front of Kurdistan (NDF)   A tactical alliance formed in 1987 by two rival Kurdish nationalist groups in Iraq, the Kurdish Democratic Party and the Patriotic Union of Kurdistan. With a combined fighting force of 30 000 combatants, the guerrilla alliance was able to take effective control over large areas of north and north-east Iraq in 1988.

National Organization   A radical Kurdish separatist group founded in 1983 by the Iranian religious leader, Sheikh Izzedin Husseini. Allied to the Iranian Komalah nationalist movement, this group favours a form of autonomy that leaves foreign affairs, defence and economic planning to the central government.

National Union of Kurdistan   A Kurdish political organization set up in Damascus in 1975 following the withdrawal of Iranian support for the Kurds and the collapse of the 1974–75 Kurdish revolt against the Iraqi government. This movement declared itself separate from Barzani's Kurdish Democratic Party. Under the leadership of Jalal Talabani, it later came to be known as the Patriotic Union of Kurdistan.

Operation Sun   The codename given to an offensive launched by Turkish troops against Kurdish Nationalists in 1984. By agreement with the Iraqi government Turkish soldiers pursued rebel Kurds across the frontier into Iraq.

Patriotic Union of Kurdistan (PUK)   With a regular fighting force of 4000, the PUK is the second largest Kurdish nationalist guerrilla group in Iraq. Operating mainly in the province of Sulaymaniyah, its membership covers a wide political spectrum from conservative to Marxist. Between 1975 and 1983 this group, originally known as the National Union of Kurdistan, had a base in Damascus. Led by Jalal Talabani, the PUK has often been at odds with the Kurdish Democratic Party.

Pesh Mergas ("those who face death")   A Kurdish name for their resistance fighters. Pesh Merga is also the name particularly applied to the guerrilla wing of the Iranian Kurdish Democratic Party. This group has an estimated fighting force of 12 000 combatants.

Qadiriyya   A Kurdish religious brotherhood which became influential after the eclipse of the emirs in the early 19th century. Combining religious and secular duties, the sheiks of this order achieved great power.

Qiadeh Movaqat (Provisional Command) or **Kurdish Democratic Party (KDP)**   A left–wing Iraqi Kurdish nationalist group founded by Mulla Mustapha Barzani. With an estimated fighting force of 10 000, this group is most active in the extreme north and north-east of Iraq. Although this is the dominant Kurdish guerrilla movement in Iraq, it mainly operates from bases within Iran. Favouring autonomy

within a democratic coalition government, the Provisional Command broadcasts to its supporters through the *Voice of Iraqi Kurdistan* radio.

Sèvres, Treaty of   A treaty signed in 1920 by the Sultan of Turkey and the Allied powers that effectively carved up the former Ottoman Empire in the aftermath of World War I. In addition to creating the Arab states of Hejaz, Iraq and Syria, the agreement envisaged a form of local autonomy for the Kurds, but with the overthrow of the Sultanate by Turkish nationalists in 1922 the treaty was never ratified by the Turkish National Assembly. The subsequent Treaty of Lausanne made no reference to the possibility of creating an independent Kurdistan.

Socialist Party of Kurdistan (Pasok)   An Iraqi Kurdish nationalist group formed in 1981 when the two–year–old United Socialist Party of Kurdistan broke up. Backed by Syria and closely linked with the Iraqi Communist Party, this group favours the creation of a separate Kurdish state.

Yperite   A form of mustard gas first used in combat during World War I. This chemical was produced in Iraq and used against both Iranians and Kurds who joined forces against Iraq at the height of the Gulf War.

■ Further reading

Edgar O'Ballance, *The Kurdish Revolt, 1961–70*, Faber, London, 1973

E. Ghareeb, *The Kurdish Question in Iraq*, Syracuse University Press, Syracuse, 1981

Chris Hellier, Pawns of the Middle East Mosaic, *Geographical Magazine*, 61(8), 1989

Sheri Laizer, *Into Kurdistan – System Under Fire*, Zed Books, London, 1990

Minority Rights Group, Report No. 23, *The Kurds*, London, 1989

III Asia/Far East

1
Afghanistan

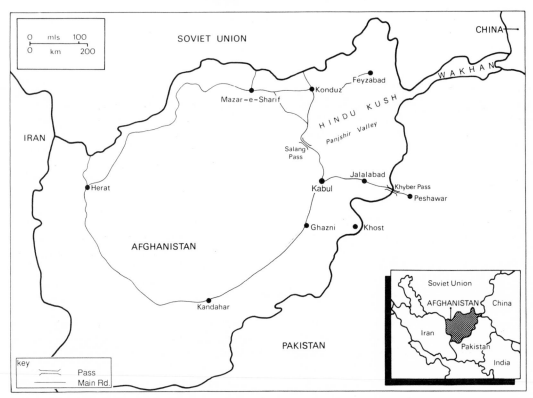

■ Profile

Official name: The Republic of Afghanistan
- **Area:** 652 225 km²
- **Population:** 14.4 million
- **Ethnic groups:** Pashtu 50%, Tadzhik 25%, Uzbek 9%, Hazara 3%
- **Official languages:** Pashtu and Dari (Persian)
- **Religion:** Muslim 99% (Sunni 87%, Shia 12%)
- **Life expectancy:** 42 years
- **Infant mortality rate:** 205 per 1000
- **Currency:** afghani of 100 puls
- **Administrative Divisions:** 29 provinces (*valayat*)
- **Timezone:** GMT +4 hours
- **Capital:** Kabul
- **Chief towns:** Kabul (1 179 000), Kandahar (203 000), Herat (160 000), Mazar-e-Sharif (118 000)

■ Introduction

The inhospitable mountainous terrain of Afghanistan has long been a focus of conflict involving competing external powers. Between 1839 and 1919 Britain fought three wars to bring the unruly tribesmen on the Indian north-west frontier within its sphere of influence. The main British aim was to counter the perceived threat to India posed by Russian expansion southwards. For nearly four decades after 1880 Britain effectively controlled Afghan affairs, but after World War I the third Afghan war resulted in Afghanistan achieving independence within boundaries agreed by an earlier Russo–British demarcation. In the inter-war period the Afghan monarchy enjoyed some room for manoeuvre between the fledgling Soviet state (with which it signed a treaty of friendship in 1919) and a British Raj whose days were numbered. Following the British withdrawal from India, however, Afghanistan came under the shadow of its giant neighbour to the north.

In the post-1945 global competition between the superpowers, Afghanistan's geographical proximity to the Soviet Union ensured that Soviet interest in its internal affairs was as keen as that of the United States in, for example, those of Mexico. For Moscow the pro-US stance of neighbouring Iran (until 1979) and Pakistan, combined with the latter's anti-Indian alignment with China, made the extension of Soviet influence in Afghanistan an important objective. In 1973 the 200-year-old Afghan monarchy was overthrown by Mohammed Daoud, who proclaimed a republic and steered the country towards closer relations with Moscow. He also revived Afghanistan's aim of creating an autonomous "Pashtunistan" state or province uniting ethnic Pashtuns (Pathans) on both sides of the international Afghan–Pakistani frontier. As Kabul had declined to recognize this border since the creation of Pakistan in 1947, its Pashtunistan policy was seen as a Soviet-backed strategy to gain access to the sea at Pakistan's territorial expense.

Apparently content with President Daoud's pro-Soviet leanings, Moscow ordered the competing factions of the (communist) People's Democratic Party of Afghanistan (PDPA) to support his regime. This directive was initially followed by most of the Parcham faction, but Daoud's vigorous repression of communist opposition assisted the emergence in mid-1977 of a reunited PDPA under the leadership of the Khalq faction. In April 1978 Daoud was overthrown and killed by pro-PDPA army officers, who installed a Revolutionary Council headed by Mohammed Taraki, a Khalqi. The Soviet Union disclaimed any direct responsibility for this "Saur" revolution, but quickly recognized the new regime, with which it signed a 20-year friendship treaty in December 1978. It also backed Taraki in his efforts to curb the revolutionary zeal of his colleagues, whose agrarian reform and other radical policies were alienating large sections of the traditionalist Muslim population.

For Moscow the moment of truth came in September 1979 when, on returning from a visit to the Soviet Union, Taraki was deposed and killed by a hardline Khalqi faction led by Hafizullah Amin. As was to be revealed later, the outrage in Moscow over Amin's action was intense. For a while the Soviet authorities had no option but to support the new regime; but the Soviet military personnel who now began arriving in Afghanistan to assist in operations against anti-government rebels also had another purpose. In December 1979 Amin became the third Afghan leader to be deposed and killed within 18 months, this being accomplished with the involvement of Soviet troops stationed in Kabul. The new Soviet-installed leader was Babrak Karmal, leader of the Parcham PDPA faction, on whose invitation there was a rapid build-up of the Soviet military presence in Afghanistan. The Soviet purpose was to assist the Afghan army in combating an insurgency by what became known as the *mujahedin* guerrilla movement, the dominant Sunni Muslim wing of which was based in Pakistan and the smaller Shia wing in Iran.

Soviet motives for the Afghanistan intervention had several strands. For the rigidly orthodox Brezhnev government, it was at one level a question of adherence to the Brezhnev Doctrine of "proletarian internationalism" first enunciated to justify the Soviet-led invasion of Czechoslovakia in 1968. This decreed that fraternal communist regimes were to be maintained in power by force if necessary, especially where, as in Afghanistan, anti-government groups were being financed and armed by "Western imperialism". Also critical were perceived Soviet strategic interests in a region adjoining its borders where instability had been sharply increased by the advent earlier in 1979 of a fundamentalist Iranian regime proclaiming hostility to Western imperialism and Soviet communism in equal measure. With a large and restive Muslim population in its own southern republics, Moscow had an obvious interest in preventing the spread of Islamic fundamentalism into Afghanistan, many of whose *mujahedin* groups were of that orientation. As for the powerful Soviet military establishment, it saw the Afghanistan adventure as an opportunity to give Soviet troops their first extensive combat experience since World War II and to test new weaponry in war conditions.

On the international plane, the Soviet intervention greatly exacerbated already deteriorating East-West relations. The hopes for détente raised by the signature of the SALT-2 treaty in June 1979 had been largely dissipated by NATO's decision in December to deploy a new generation of intermediate-range nuclear missiles in Europe. The hostile Soviet reaction to that initiative was matched by Western condemnation of the Afghanistan action, which precipitated diplomatic, economic and cultural sanctions against the USSR, including the deferment of US ratification of SALT-2. It also lost Moscow many friends in the non-aligned Third World, especially among Islamic countries, and was condemned by most communist parties outside the Soviet bloc. However, such broad international censure failed to budge either the Brezhnev regime or its two short-lived successors, despite repeated UN and other peace initiatives. Not until Mikhail Gorbachev came to power in 1985 did a serious reassessment of Soviet policy begin.

Afghanistan was frequently described as "the Soviet Union's Vietnam". Just as US military might had in the end failed to prevent a communist victory in Indo-China, so the vast panoply of Soviet power proved incapable of quelling the *mujahedin* in Afghanistan. In that sense, the conflict provided further proof that determined guerrilla forces, provided they are well-armed and have secure bases, can exact an attritional cost from far superior regular troops which ultimately becomes unacceptable. Although some 115 000 Soviet soldiers were deployed in Afghanistan, they were never able to establish control outside the larger towns. Operating from bases across the Pakistani and Iranian borders, the *mujahedin* employed the classic guerrilla tactics of harassment, attacking convoys on the long Soviet supply routes and avoiding pitched battles. Their supply of US-inspired finance and modern weaponry, including ground-to-air missiles, was plentiful. They could also draw on an inexhaustible supply of manpower among the millions of Afghani refugees. Soviet air strikes against guerrilla bases in Pakistan barely dented *mujahedin* capability, their main effect being to strengthen Pakistan's anti-Soviet stance.

Gorbachev's economic and political reform priorities and the concomitant need to rein back the East-West arms race had obvious implications for Soviet policy towards Afghanistan. The first clear sign of a new approach, in May 1986, was the replacement of Karmal as regime leader by Major-Gen. Najibullah (also of the Parcham faction) and the launching of a Soviet-backed "national reconciliation" programme. This involved not only the offer of a ceasefire and an amnesty to the *mujahedin* but also the adoption of a new constitution under which the PDPA ceased, theoretically, to have a monopoly of power. Although the *mujahedin* groups rejected such overtures, the process of international negotiation gathered pace. The culmination was the signature in Geneva in April 1988 of a series of accords between Afghanistan and Pakistan and of a US-Soviet agreement on "interrelationships" under which "foreign" (i.e. Soviet) troops were to be withdrawn from Afghanistan by 15 February 1989. This undertaking was carried out by the Soviet side, despite the failure of Moscow's diplomatic efforts to secure a prior acommodation between the *mujahedin* and the Kabul regime.

Many experts predicted that the Najibullah regime would not survive the Soviet withdrawal, given the declared intention of the *mujahedin* to pursue the war to complete victory. In anticipation of the speedy overthrow of the regime, an interim government-in-exile was set up by the Pakistan-based *mujahedin* groups in late February 1989, despite their fierce internal divisions as between fundamentalists and moderates. However, Afghan government forces, well-equipped with Soviet arms, proved to be unexpectedly resilient. *Mujahedin* assaults on the key city of Jalalabad were repulsed with heavy losses for the anti-government side, and from March 1989

Soviet arms supplies were resumed to Kabul. Protracted guerrilla conflict accordingly seemed the likely prospect for Afghanistan, given that the US government, in the words of President Bush, was committed to backing the *mujahedin* for "as long as the resistance struggle for self-determination continues". At the end of 1989 the Najibullah regime remained firmly in power in Kabul, the *mujahedin* were more divided than ever and the Jalalabad garrison continued to repel attempts to take the city.

■ Chronology of events

1839–42   The first Afghan war. British attempts to prevent Russian advances in Central Asia result in a fierce Afghan resistance to foreign rule.

1878–80   The second Afghan war. Amir Shir Ali receives a Russian envoy in Kabul but refuses to accept a British mission. The ensuing conflict brings the pro-British Amir Abdur Rahman to the Afghan throne. Britain virtually controls Afghan foreign affairs.

1885–96   The boundaries of modern Afghanistan are established by Britain and Russia. Between 1885 and 1888 the Afghan–Russian frontier is demarcated, and in 1893 the border between Afghanistan and India's North–West Frontier province (the Durand Line) is agreed.

1907   An Anglo–Russian agreement guarantees the independence of Afghanistan under British influence.

1919   Abdur Rahman's successor, Habibullah, is assassinated by an anti-British movement. His son launches the third Afghan war and wrests control of foreign policy from a war-weary Britain. With the Treaty of Rawalpindi, signed on 8 August, 1919, Britain formally gives up its rights in Afghanistan. August 19 is celebrated as Independence Day.

1950   Pashtun demands for self-determination result in conflict along the disputed Durand

Line which separates Afghanistan and Pakistan.

1961   Afghanistan severs diplomatic relations with Pakistan.

1963   Sardar Mohammad Daoud, pro-Russian cousin of King Zahir Shah, is dismissed as Prime Minister of Afghanistan in March. During ten years in office, his attempts to set up a Pashtun state on the eastern border had created tension with neighbouring Pakistan.

1965   The People's Democratic Party of Afghanistan is founded by Mohammed Taraki.

1973   In July Daoud stages a military coup, seizes power and abolishes the monarchy. A republic is proclaimed with Daoud as its first President.

1974   Conflict between Afghanistan and Pakistan over the Pashtun issue is renewed.

1978   After five years of instability, Daoud is assassinated in April during a bloody coup. The PDPA comes to power and the Democratic Republic of Afghanistan is established under the leadership of Nur Mohammad Taraki, a moderate communist.

In December Moscow signs a 20–year Treaty of Friendship, Good Neighbourliness, and Co-operation with Afghanistan, but the new Marxist-style government, with its unpopular land reforms and its policy of de-Islamicising the country, meets strong opposition. Soviet military assistance is extended in the face of increased conflict between government troops and Muslim rebels along the Pakistan frontier.

1979 A hardline communist, Hafizullah Amin, is appointed Prime Minister by Taraki in March. The split between the Khalqi and Parchami factions of the PDPA widens as Parchami followers are purged and imprisoned. Fighting increases in eastern provinces and in Herat the Army stages a revolt after troops are ordered to crush a local uprising.

In September Hafizullah Amin ousts Taraki who is killed in a palace shoot-out. Widespread insurgency and the near collapse of the Afghan Army makes the survival of the regime more and more dependent on Soviet military assistance.

Between 24 and 27 December the Soviet Union launches an airborne invasion of Kabul. Amin is killed and Babrak Karmal, leader of the Parchamis, is brought back from exile and installed as Head of State. Karmal requests that Soviet military assistance be maintained.

On 30 December the Soviet Union acknowledges, sending a "limited military contingent" to repel outside agression (referring to US and Pakistani aid to resistance fighters). Soviet troops are to be withdrawn when no longer needed.

1980 Soviet troops are increased to a total of 85000 and martial law is declared in Kabul. The UN General Assembly calls for the immediate withdrawal of Soviet forces, a demand that is repeated each year, but the UN Security Council is unable to take action because of the veto power exercised by the Soviet Union. The USA leads a boycott of the Moscow Olympic Games. In response to growing international pressure Babrak Karmal and Soviet leader, Brezhnev express a willingness to promote negotiations between Afghanistan and Pakistan, but Pakistan refuses to hold direct talks with Kabul.

1981 The European Council proposes a

two-stage international conference designed to assure Afghanistan's future as an independent and non-aligned state. The proposal receives no support from the Soviet Union, but Karmal agrees to UN–mediated talks with Pakistan and Iran. The UN Secretary General appoints a "personal representative", Javier Pérez de Cuellar. He engages in shuttle diplomacy between Afghanistan and Pakistan, both of whom agree to an agenda for future talks.

1982 Diego Cordovez succeeds Javier Pérez de Cuellar as the UN Secretary General's "personal representative" and manages to establish the basis for "indirect" talks between Afghanistan and Pakistan. Foreign ministers take part in the first round of "indirect" talks in Geneva.

1983 A second and third round of "indirect" talks in Geneva during April and August help to identify elements for a future settlement, but the timing of Soviet troop withdrawal remains unresolved. Meanwhile, heavy fighting continues in Afghanistan, particularly in and around the southern city of Kandahar.

1984 Soviet and Afghan regime forces launch a major offensive against Islamic resistance fighters in the Panjshir Mountains. and the number of Soviet troops in Afghanistan rises to about 115 000. By now three million Afghan refugees have fled to Pakistan and one million to Iran. Diplomatic momentum is maintained by Diego Cordovez who visits Kabul, Islamabad, Moscow and Tehran. A fourth round of talks takes place in Geneva in August. These are dubbed "proximity" talks since both Afghan and Pakistani delegations were in the same building at the same time. The Karmal regime refuses, however, to talk with representatives of the resistance groups.

1985 Although the USA and the Soviet Union agree to act as guarantors for the UN peace plan, further "proximity" talks fail to make progress because of the Afghan regime's insistence on direct talks with Pakistan as a prerequisite to the withdrawal of Soviet troops. International criticism of Afghanistan's human rights record results in the staging of a Loya Jirga or Grand Council of tribal elders, many of whom turn out to be regime functionaries. The seven main groups of the Islamic resistance join together under the name *mujahedin*. Heavy fighting is concentrated around the frontier garrison towns of Khost and Barikot where Afghan and Soviet forces are attempting to cut *mujahedin* supply routes from Pakistan.

1986   In May Babrak Karmal is replaced as the regime leader by security chief, Major–General Mohammed Najibullah. The US steps up its supplies of missiles to the *mujahedin*, a move which denies the Afghan regime its former control of the skies. Prior to another round of "proximity" talks and the US–Soviet summit in Reykjavik, Gorbachev announces the withdrawal of six Soviet regiments. Earlier, at his party congress, he had described Afghanistan as a "bleeding wound", indicating that a settlement might soon be reached to enable troop withdrawal to begin. Despite this indication of a turning point in Soviet policy, new weapon systems are deployed and major offensives are launched against resistance fighters. The UN estimates the total number of refugees to be about four and a half million – the largest number recorded from any country in the world.

1987   Najibullah's Soviet–backed attempts to promote "national reconciliation" by announcing a ceasefire, an amnesty, and the possibility of a coalition government fail and *mujahedin* resistance escalates. A new constitution and the appointment of Najibullah as State President confirms the regime's determination to hold onto power. The Revolutionary Council gives its approval to the formation of political parties.

1988   The Peshawar-based *mujahedin* alliance leaders present plans for a transitional government. Convinced that a military solution in Afghanistan is impossible, Gorbachev announces that Soviet troops will start to withdraw in May. After a final round of UN–mediated talks in Geneva, accords are signed on 14 April by Afghanistan and Pakistan and by the USA and the Soviet Union acting as their guarantors. The four main instruments of accord are (1) an agreement between Afghanistan and Pakistan not to interfere in each others affairs; (2) an agreement between these two countries on the voluntary return of refugees; (3) a declaration of international guarantees by the USA and the Soviet Union; and (4) a schedule for the withdrawal of Soviet troops. The gradual Soviet withdrawal during the summer and autumn of 1988 is marked by an upsurge in *mujahedin* attacks on Soviet and Afghan positions and a halt to the pullout of troops is only averted by US calls on resistance fighters to refrain from attacking Soviet troops.

1989   After nine years in Afghanistan at a cost of some 15 000 lives, the departure of 115 000 Soviet troops is completed by 15 February. Fighting continues and a state of emergency is declared on 19 February. The rebel Interim Islamic Government under the leadership of President-elect Seghbatullah Mujjaddedi, holds its first Cabinet meeting on Afghan soil in March. Despite the defection of soldiers from the Afghan army, the regime, using weaponry left by the Soviets, puts up a stubborn resistance against the badly organized *mujahedin* alliance forces whose position is weakened by internal disagreements.

1990   Fighting between *mujahedin* rebels and government forces continues but despite an attempted coup in March, Najibullah maintains his hold on the major cities of Afghanistan.

■ Who's who

Amin, Hafizullah   Hardline communist of the Khalqi faction of the PDPA, appointed Deputy Prime Minister after the coup in 1978 and then Prime Minister in March 1979. Six months later, in September 1979, he ousted his colleague, President Mohammed Taraki. After only a short period as Head of State, Amin was killed during the Soviet invasion of December 1979 when he was replaced by the Soviet-backed Parchami leader, Babrak Karmal.

Cordovez, Diego Ecuadorian-born "personal representative" of the UN Secretary–General appointed to the Afghanistan problem in 1982. For over 6 years he tirelessly engaged in shuttle diplomacy in an attempt to maintain the momentum of the peace talks in Geneva.

Daoud, Sardar Mohammed Appointed governor of Kandahar province in 1932, Daoud became leader of the armed forces in 1937, Prime Minister of Afghanistan, 1953–63, and Head of State, 1973–78. Although a relative of King Zahir Shah, Daoud overthrew the monarchy and after a near bloodless coup, staged in July 1973 when the King was out of the country, he declared a republic with himself as Head of State. Political instability resulted in his eventual assassination in April 1978 when a Democratic Republic was established under Mohammed Taraki.

Dost, Shah Mohammed Appointed Afghan Ambassador to the UN in December 1986. Formerly he held a cabinet position as Foreign Minister in both the Taraki and Karmal governments.

Ermacora, Dr Felix The UN's Special Rapporteur on Human Rights in Afghanistan who was allowed to visit Afghanistan before submitting his third report on that country to the Committee for Social, Humanitarian and Cultural Questions in 1987. Dr. Ermacora also reported on the plight of Afghan refugees in Pakistan.

Gailani, Pir Sayyed Ahmed An hereditary Sufi saint, Gailani is a westernized Pashtun with a strong following amongst the traditionalist National Islamic Front which he leads.

Ghulabzoi, Lt.–Gen. Sayed Mohammed Afghan Minister of Internal Affairs and leader of the Khalqi faction of the PDPA. One of the few members of the Khalqi faction to retain a cabinet post in the Parchami-dominated Karmal regime after having served under Mohammed Taraki.

Gromov, Lt.–Gen. Boris Commander of the Soviet forces in Afghanistan and the last Soviet soldier to leave Afghanistan on 15 February 1989.

Haq, Abdul A leading figure in the Khales faction of the Hezb-i-Islami resistance movement. Responsible for organizing attacks on Kabul and other important economic targets.

Hekmatyar, Gulbuddin Anti-Western leader of the predominantly Pashtun faction of the Sunni Muslim Hezb-i-Islami, Hekmatyar was elected chairman of the Peshawar-based *mujahedin* resistance movement in March 1988. He was wounded in a bomb attack on his Peshawar headquarters in September 1987.

Karmal, Babrak A law graduate of the University of Kabul, Karmal became leader of the Parchami faction of the PDPA. After the April 1978 coup that ousted President Daoud he was appointed Vice-Chairman of the Revolutionary Council and Deputy Prime Minister in the first government of the Taraki regime. After falling out with Prime Minister Amin he was removed from the cabinet and sent to effective exile in Prague as Afghan ambassador to Czechoslovakia. Following the Soviet invasion of December 1979 and the removal of Amin, Karmal was brought back to Afghanistan by the Soviets and installed as General Secretary of the PDPA and President of the Afghan Revolutionary Council. Failing to reach a satisfactory political or military settlement, he maintained his position as leader until 1986 when he was pressurized to resign, allegedly on health grounds. He was finally exiled to a *dacha* on the Black Sea.

Keshtmand, Soltan Ali The only Shia Muslim in the Afghan leadership, Keshtmand served as Deputy Prime Minister under Babrak Karmal. In 1986, after Karmal's effective replacement by Najibullah, he was appointed Prime Minister, a post he held until May 1988. When Mohammed Hassan Sharq, his successor, resigned in February 1989 Keshtmand accepted the post of chairman of the newly created Executive Committee of the Council of Ministers.

Khales, Mohammed Yunis Fundamentalist leader of a branch of the Sunni resistance group, Hezb-i-Islami. A spokesman for the Peshawar-based rebel alliance and *mujahedin* chairman, October 1987 – March 1988. With Professor Abdul Sayef he resigned from the resistance alliance in protest at a decision to send a *mujahedin* delegation to the Geneva talks.

Khalili, Karim Leader of the "Tehran Eight" Shia fundamentalist *mujahedin* groups based in Iran.

Khan, Ismael A leader of the Jamiat-i-Islami resistance movement, operating in the Herat province of W Afghanistan.

Masood, Ahmed Shah ("'the Lion of Panjshir") Northern field commander of the Jamiat-i-Islami resistance group in the Panjshir Mounatins of NE Afghanistan.

Mohammadi, Maulavi Mohammed Nabi Moderate leader of the Islamic Unity resistance movement, Mohammadi was nominated as Minister of Defence in the *mujahedin* transitional government in 1989.

Mujjaddedi, Professor Seghbatullah A monarchist Imam favouring the re-establishment of the pre-1973 Pashtun order. After the 1979 Soviet invasion he led the moderate, pro-Western Sunni Muslim National Liberation Front from a base in Peshawar. On 23 February, 1989, he was elected President of a transitional government at a meeting of Afghan rebels.

Najibullah, Sayid Mohammed A doctor by training, Mohammed Najibullah became a member of the PDPA when it was established in 1965. Opposition to the governments of King Zahir Shah and his successor President Daoud resulted in periods of imprisonment, but following the 1978 "Saur" revolution he became a member of the Revolutionary Council. His opposition to the Khalqis prompted his expulsion from the PDPA in September 1978 and he spent the next 12 months in exile as ambassador to Iran. Shortly before the Soviet invasion of December 1979, which he helped plan, he returned to Afghanistan. Serving in

the Parchami-dominated government of Babrak Karmal as head of KHAD – the security police – he succeeded in gaining support in the Pashtun tribal belt along the Pakistan frontier. Popularly known as Comrade Najib, Major–General Mohammed Najibullah replaced Babrak Karmal as the Soviet-backed leader of Afghanistan in 1986 at the age of 39. In order to broaden the regime's popular support he initiated a programme of "national reconciliation", emphasizing his Pashtun origins as the son of an Ahmadzai tribal chief from Paktia province.

Rabbani, Barhannudin A former Professor of Islamic Law turned leader of the fundamentalist Jamiat-i-Islami resistance movement.

Sayyef, Professor Abdur Rasul A Wahhabi Muslim leader of the Ittehad-i-Islami resistance movement strongly supported by Saudi Arabia. Nominated Prime Minister of the *mujahedin* transitional government in 1989.

Shah, Ahmed Deputy leader of the fundamentalist Ittehad-i-Islami resistance movement. In 1988 the *mujahedin* nominated Ahmed Shah to be head of state and government in a transitional government. His nomination was not a popular choice amongst Afghans and in 1989 he was replaced as leader by the more moderate Seghbatullah Mujjaddedi. An Ahmadzai Pashtun, Shah trained as an engineer in the USA before teaching at the King Faisal University in Saudi Arabia.

Shah, King Zahir The last King of Afghanistan, Zahir Shah came to the throne in 1933 at the age of 19 following the assassination of his father, Nadir Shah. In July 1973, while out of the country, the King was ousted from power in a coup staged by his cousin Sardar Mohammed Daoud. Thereafter, Zahir Shah lived in exile in Rome. The return of King Zahir to Afghanistan was suggested by former US Secretary of State, Henry Kissinger.

Sharq, Dr Mohammed Hassan Succeeded Soltan Ali Keshtmand as non-PDPA Prime Minister of Afghanistan in May 1988, but resigned following the declaration of a state of emergency on 19 February 1989. Formerly a

Deputy Chairman of the Council of Ministers and Minister of the newly created Ministry of Returnees' Affairs.

Tanai, Shahnawaz   A leading Afghan general who defected from the government forces to become a rebel leader in March 1990 when he joined forces with Hekmatyar's fundamentalist Hezb-i-Islami faction with the aim of intensifying the war against the Najibullah regime.

Taraki, Mohammed   A writer and journalist, Taraki was sent to the Afghanistan Embassy in Washington as a press attaché in 1953. In the following year he was dismissed after voicing opposition to the appointment of Daoud as Prime Minister. In 1978, as leader of the Khalq faction of the PDPA he staged a coup which overthrew the Daoud regime. As Soviet-backed Head of State his Marxist-style reforms and purging of Parchamis generated considerable opposition. A year later he was killed in a coup led by his Prime Minister, Hafizullah Amin.

Wakil, Abdul   Replaced Shah Mohammed Dost as Foreign Minister of Afghanistan in December 1986. A former Finance Minister, Wakil was also appointed a full member of the Politburo and head of the Kabul party organization.

■ Key places

Amudar'ya or **Oxus**   The largest river in central Asia, formed by the junction of the Pyandzh and Vakhsh rivers which rise in the Pamir Mountains. Flowing west past the city of Termez it follows the boundary between Afghanistan and the Soviet republics of Tadzhikistan and Uzbekistan for about 320km before turning north–west through Turkmenistanand back through Uzbekistan. After a total distance of 1415km it discharges into the Aral'skoye More (Aral Sea) where it forms a wide delta. During the 1980s river ports on the Afghanistan side of the frontier were developed with Russian aid at Hayratan (Kheyratan), Shir Khan and Tor Ghundi.

Bamian   The capital of a province of the same name in N central Afghanistan. Situated in a valley between the Hindu Kush and the Paropamisan Mountains, it was once reckoned to be the only pass across the Himalayan chain practicable for artillery. The Nil Kowtal Pass, linking the Bamian valley to the westward route to Turkestan, rises to 3538m west of the town. A prominent centre of Buddhism in the 7th century AD, it later became a Muslim fortress town. Remains of carved Buddhas and the ruins of the city of Ghulghuleh, destroyed by Ghengiz Khan c.1221, are to be found nearby. In 1984 the town had an estimated population of 8000.

Barikot   A garrison town on the Konar river in Konar province, E Afghanistan, close to the frontier with Pakistan and about 150km north–east of Jalalabad. In February 1985 it was reported that 300 Afghan regime and Soviet soldiers had been killed in an attempt to relieve the garrison whose chief function had been to disrupt the flow of supplies from Pakistan to resistance fighters in Nuristan and Panjshir. After a major operation involving thousands of Soviet troops with air support the besieged Afghan forces were relieved in June 1985. The town, however, remained under siege.

Durand Line   The frontier between Afghanistan and the North–West Frontier province of Pakistan, agreed in 1893 and delimited in 1894–96. This much-disputed border line cuts through the Pashtun ethnic region. The Pashtunistan issue has been the source of conflict between Afghanistan and Pakistan since 1947, particularly in 1950, 1961 and 1974. The Durand Line is named after the diplomat, Sir Henry Durand.

Friendship Bridge   A Soviet-built road and railway bridge across the Amudar'ya river linking the border town of Hayratan (Kheyratan) in the northern Afghan province of Balkh with the town of Termez in Soviet Uzbekistan. The bridge was built after the signing of the Afghan-Soviet Treaty of Friendship in 1978.

Ghazni An historic walled city and capital of a province of the same name in E Afghanistan. Situated about 120km south–west of Kabul on the River Ghazni, it is an important market town for grain, fruit, sheep, wool, camel hair and locally-made Afghan coats.

Helmand The longest river in Afghanistan. Rising in the Baba Range of the Hindu Kush, W of Kabul, it flows south–west for 1 125km before emptying its water into the marshland surrounding Lake Saberi on the Iran–Afghanistan frontier.

Herat The largest city in W Afghanistan and capital of a province of the same name, Herat lies at the crossroads of ancient trade routes from Persia to India and from Central Asia to China. To the north lie the Paropamisus Mountains and to the south the Harirud river flows westwards until it crosses the Iran-Afghanistan frontier 120km west of the city. Herat's most important landmark is the 12th-century Great Mosque of Jama Masjid. With an estimated population of 160 000 (mostly Sunni Muslims) in 1984, the city is noted for its textile and carpet weaving industries and for its trade in fruit which is grown in the fertile river valley nearby. In 1979 disturbances in and around Herat resulted in the closure of the border by Iran in an attempt to stem the flow of refugees out of Afghanistan.

Hindu Kush A southwesterly extension of the Himalayas, the Hindu Kush mountain range extends some 800 km WSW from the Pamirs of the North–West Frontier province of Pakistan to the Afghan province of Bamian. Rising to 7 690m at Tirich Mir, the Hindu Kush is crossed by several high altitude passes of which the most important is the Salang Pass – a strategic point on the routeway that links Kabul with the Soviet Union to the north.

Jalalabad or **Jelalabad** The capital of Nangarhar province, E Afghanistan. Situated 146km east of Kabul and 130km west of Peshawar in Pakistan, Jalalabad had an estimated population of 61 000 in 1984. An influx

of refugees during the mid-1980s swelled the population to over one million, but thousands fled from the city after it came under attack and was cut off by *mujahedin* forces in 1989. Between 1977 and 1985 an olive processing and canning plant was developed with Soviet aid.

Kabul The capital of Afghanistan since 1773, Kabul lies in the valley of the Kabul river, a western tributary of the Indus. The city is linked by road to Peshawar in the east via the Khyber Pass and to the Soviet Union in the north via the Salang Road over the Hindu Kush. Chief landmarks of the old city (Shahri Kuhna) include the Royal Palace, the Independence Column and the mausoleums of Abdur Rahman and Timur Shah. Most foreign embassies are located to the north of the river in the Shahri Naw and Akbar Xan Mena districts while the university, established in 1931, lies to the west in the Kartayi Char district and government buildings lie to the east in the Micro-Rayon district. Soviet aid in the 1980s was used to rebuild Kabul airport (1981–84) and to develop vehicle manufacturing and servicing plants. As a result of heavy fighting in the countryside after 1978, villagers migrated into the city in large numbers. The total population of the city soon increased more than threefold from a figure of 318 000 in 1971 to an estimated 1 180 000 in 1984. After the departure of Soviet troops in 1989, the city came under virtual siege from *mujahedin* forces. Food supplies are maintained by farming on the outskirts of Kabul and by imports flown in from the Soviet Union.

Kandahar or **Qandahar** The capital city of a province of the same name in S Afghanistan, Kandahar developed at a focal point on the ancient trade route through Persia to India and was capital of Afghanistan 1748–73. With an estimated population of 203 000 in 1984, Kandahar has been traditionally a centre for trade in wool, textiles, sheep, grain, tobacco and fruit. The city was partly controlled by resistance fighters and was the scene of heavy fighting throughout the 1980s. After the departure of Soviet forces, who maintained an airforce base in Kandahar, the city came under virtual seige from surrounding *mujahedin* forces. An important centre of the dominant Pushtun ethnic group, it has been considered by some observers as a potential alternative capital for an Islamic state run by the fundamentalist resistance parties.

Khost or **Khowst**   A city in Paktia province about 120km WSW of Ghazni. Heavily garrisoned since 1981, it is of strategic importance to the Afghan government as a forward position in the fight to disrupt the flow of rebel supplies across the Pakistan–Afghanistan border into Paktia province. By 1985 almost all civilians had abandoned the town to Afghan government forces and the KHAD. In that year the city came under more or less continuous siege from *mujahedin* forces backed by Pakistani artillery. In December 1987 Khost was the scene of a key battle in the Afghan war when the *mujahedin* launched a major but unsuccessful offensive to capture the city.

Konduz or **Kunduz**   The chief town of a province of the same name on the north side of the Hindu Kush, N Afghanistan. Adjoining the Soviet–Afghan frontier and on a major supply route from the Soviet Union to Kabul, Konduz was an important target for *mujahedin* guerrillas between 1979 and 1989. In 1984 the province had an estimated population of 606 000 and the city of Konduz a population of 60 000. Thereafter, heavy fighting and a scorched earth policy adopted by Soviet and Afghan regime forces resulted in large scale desertion of villages and the abandonment of once fertile farm land.

Khyber Pass   A mountain pass on the Afghanistan–Pakistan frontier at an altitude of 1080m at the east end of the Safed Range. The Khyber Pass forms part of the main routeway from Peshawar to Kabul via Jalalabad. Many of the 3 million refugees who fled from Afghanistan after 1979 followed this route into Pakistan.

Mazar-e-Sharif   The largest city in N Afghanistan. A major industrial centre and capital of Balkh province. The estimated population in 1984 was 118 000. In the 1980s a thermal power station, an agro-chemical laboratory, a nitrogen fertilizer plant and trucking services were developed with Soviet aid.

Paghman   A former health resort in Parawan province; situated in the E foothills of the Paghman Range, 20km west of Kabul. By 1987 the town had been virtually destroyed by continuous heavy fighting.

Paktia   A province in E Afghanistan on the frontier with Pakistan. The province has an area of 9 581km^2 and had an estimated population of 525 000 in 1984 before food shortages and the worst of the fighting drove many people from the land. Gardez is the capital, the garrison town of Khost being the only other significant urban centre. The mountains of Paktia, and in particular *mujahedin* bases at places such as Zhawar, are at the end of a major supply route from Pakistan to which the province is linked by the Batat Pass.

Panjshir Valley   The valley of the River Panjshir which flows down from the Panjshir Range and then south–west for about 100km before turning sharply south–east near Charikar. Within 80km of Kabul, the Panjshir has been a principal centre of *mujahedin* resistance since 1979. In 1984 Soviet forces began a major offensive to gain control of this area. High altitude bombing preceded the advance of ground forces, but with the onset of winter Soviet and Afghan army units had to withdraw to lower and safer positions. The Panjshir has remained a focal point of *mujahedin* resistance.

Peshawar   With a population of just over half a million, the Pashtun city of Peshawar is the capital of the North–West Frontier province of Pakistan. Situated 172km west of Rawalpindi and 277km east of Kabul, Peshawar has been used since 1979 as a base by leaders of the Islamic resistance groups opposed to the Soviet-backed Afghan regime.

Puli–Khumri or **Pol-e Khomri**   An industrial centre in Baghlan province, N Afghanistan; situated on the Puli–Khumri river and the main highway between Kabul and the Soviet frontier. In the 1980s food industries, oil storage facilities, trucking services and a hydro-electric power plant were developed with Soviet aid.

Salang Pass A high-altitude section of the main road that crosses a major break in the Hindu Kush mountain range, linking Kabul and S Afghanistan with the Soviet frontier to the north. The Salang Pass and tunnel, which lie about 100km north of Kabul, were built by the Soviets in 1964. An important supply route between the Soviet Union and Kabul, the Salang Road is a major *mujahedin* resistance target.

Samarkhel A military base 20km from the city of Jalalabad. Captured by the *mujahedin* at the beginning of their offensive against that city in March 1989, it was the most significant target to be taken by the rebels in the immediate aftermath of the Soviet pull-out. Samarkhel was recaptured by government troops in July 1989.

Shindand or **Sabzawar** An old fortified town in Farah province, W Afghanistan. To the north–east of the town lies western Afghanistan's principal airforce base. The arrest, in 1985, of 15 Afghan pilots in connection with the destruction on the ground of 20 aircraft led to the defection to Pakistan of two air crews with modern Soviet Mi-25 helicopters.

Wakhan Salient A narrow corridor of wild and mountainous land in NE Afghanistan that once formed a political buffer between Russian and British spheres of influence. Demarcated by the Anglo–Russian Pamir Commission in 1895–96, the Wakhan Salient forms a "panhandle" over 300 km in length. It is bounded to the north by the Soviet Union, to the east by China and to the south by Pakistan. Between 1980 and 1989 the Russians effectively annexed this remote area of the Hindu Kush in order to prevent arms supplies reaching rebel guerrillas from Pakistan amd China.

Waziristan A mountainous region of North-West Frontier Province, Pakistan, on the frontier with Afghanistan. The region is inhabited by Wazirs, a Pashtun tribe.

Zhawar An important mountain base of the *mujahedin* in Paktia province, E Afghanistan. Situated close to the Afghanistan–Pakistan frontier near the town of Khost, it is at the end of a major supply route across the Salanaki hills from Miram Shah in Pakistan's North Waziristan Tribal Agency. During the spring of 1986 it was captured for a short time by Soviet and Afghan regime forces.

■ Key words

Afghan interim government An Islamic government in exile, formed by the Peshawar-based Mujahedin resistance in 1989 and backed by the USA and Pakistan.

Bakhtar The official Afghan news agency.

Basic Principles The underlying concepts of the Afghan constitution ratified by the Soviet–backed Revolutionary Council in 1980. Islam as the religion of the majority of the Afghan people was recognized, as was the right to practise any other religion, provided there was no conflict with state laws.

Democratic Youth Organization A non-party regime front organization.

Durrani A subdivision of the Pashtun ethnic group from south and west Afghanistan. All of the country's rulers until the coup of 1978 were from the Durrani tribe.

dushman The Soviet term for an Afghan resistance fighter.

Geneva Accords An agreement signed by Afghanistan and Pakistan on 14 April 1988 after a final round of UN–mediated talks in Geneva. The USA and the Soviet Union added their signatures as guarantors to the agreement which established the principle of non-interference between the two countries prior to the Soviet withdrawal of troops.

Harakat-i-Inqilab-i-Islami or **Movement for the Islamic Revolution (Islamic Unity)** A moderate member of the *mujahedin* alliance. Based in Peshawar, this Sunni Muslim group is mainly active in the south and west of Afghanistan and around Kabul.

Harakat-i-Islami A moderate, nationalist Shia Muslim minority resistance group operating in the Hazara ethnic region of central Afghanistan.

Hazara The third largest ethnic group in Afghanistan, occupying the centre of the country, east of Bamian. Numbering nearly one million, they are believed to be descended from the Mongol hordes of Ghengiz Khan.

Hezb-i-Islami or **Islamic Party** Led by Gulbuddin Hekmatyar, this fundamentalist Sunni Muslim group has a base in Peshawar, but is mostly active in east and north–east Afghanistan where it operates as one of the seven members of the *mujahedin* alliance. An offshoot of this group, led by Mohammed Yunis Khales, is active in the south–east of the country.

High Council of Ulema A group of Muslim clergy which, with the Ministry of Islamic Affairs, oversees all religious activities and property. Although the clergy has been allowed to retain some of its land, most religious property is now administered by the state, as are the mosque endowment funds.

Interservices Intelligence (ISI) Pakistan's military intelligence agency. The main channel for arms, money and military advisers supplied to the *mujahedin* by the USA, China and Saudi Arabia.

Ittehad-i-Islami A Saudi-backed coalition of four small fundamentalist Sunni Muslim groups forming one of the seven parties of the Afghan *mujahedin* resistance movement.

Jabhyar-i-Milli-Niyat or **National Islamic Front** A moderate Sunni Muslim group forming one of the seven parties of the *mujahedin* alliance. Led by Professor Seghbatullah Mujjaddedi, it is active mostly in north and

east Afghanistan. In 1979 it was known as the Afghan National Liberation Front.

Jamiat-i-Islami A fundamentalist Sunni Muslim member of the *mujahedin* alliance. Led by Professor Burhanuddin Rabbani, its supporters are mostly Tajiks and Uzbeks of N Afghanistan. In July 1989 seven commanders and 23 rebel fighters were massacred in the Farkhar valley by members of the rival Hezb-i-Islami resistance group.

jirga A tribal council. A Loya Jirga, or Grand National Assembly of 1796 tribal leaders, was convened in 1985 in response to criticism of the regime voiced by the UN Human Rights Commission. The reinstatement of the traditional jirga system down to village level was designed not only to approve a new constitution but also to attract popular support for the Soviet–backed regime by giving the people some semblance of involvement in local and national government. The legislative National Assembly comprises the Wolesi Jirga, or Council of Representatives, and the Sena or Meshrano Jirga, or Council of Elders. Elections to local councils, or jirgas, began in August 1985, a month after the passing of the Law on Local Organs of State Power and Administration. Limited powers have been devolved to local executive committees which can include non-elected members, notably mullas who are recommended by the Ministry of Islamic Affairs and tribesmen who are recommended by the Ministry of Tribal Affairs.

Khalq or **People's Party** A faction of the PDPA comprising mostly Pashtu-speaking people of rural origin from E Afghanistan. More radical and nationalist than the opposing Parchami faction, the Khalquis predominate in the armed forces.

KHAD The former Afghan State Information Service upgraded in January 1986 to become the Ministry of State Security. It is responsible to the Council of Ministers. President Najibullah was head of KHAD prior to the demise of Babrak Karmal in 1986.

Mahaz-i-Milli-yi-Islami or **National Islamic Front** A moderate Sunni Muslim member of the seven-party *mujahedin* alliance based in Peshawar. Led by Pir Sayed Ahmed Gailani, it is active mostly in the Pashtun province of Kandahar.

mujahedin or fully **Ittehad-i-Mujahedin** ("holy warriors")   A strongly Islamic resistance movement formed in 1985 as the result of an alliance among seven separate moderate and fundamentalist Sunni Muslim groups. The leading fundamentalist groups include the Hekmatyar and Kahles factions of the Hezb-i-Islami, the coalition Ittehad-i-Islami and the Jamiat-i-Islami. Moderate members of the alliance include the Harakat-i-Inqilab-i-Islami, the Jabhyar-i-Milli-Niyat and the Mahaz-i-Milli-yi-Islami. Based in, and supplied from Peshawar in Pakistan, the *mujahedin* alliance is led by an elected long-term president or "Rais". In January 1988 *mujahedin* leaders announced plans to form a transitional government which they claimed should be a signatory to the Geneva accords.

Muslim International Brigade   A brigade of fundamentalist Muslim volunteers from Saudi Arabia, Morocco, Kuwait, Pakistan and Egypt fighting alongside the *mujahedin* resistance movement in Afghanistan. Many of the volunteers joined the international brigade in 1987 in order to gain experience for future revolution in their own countries.

National Front formerly **National Fatherland Front (NFF)**   A popular front organization formed in December 1980 in order to widen the regime's popular base by bringing together various non-party groups such as the Democratic Youth of Afghanistan.

Operation Salaam   A $1.3 billion UN programme for the settlement of Afghan refugees after the Soviet withdrawal in 1989. Headed by Prince Sadruddin Aga Khan, the programme aimed to repatriate an estimated two million refugees living in camps at Mashhad, Birjand and Zahedan in E Iran and a total of 3.72 million registered refugees located near Peshawar and Quetta in NW Pakistan.

Parcham or **Flag Party**   A pro-Soviet, Marxist faction of the PDPA which has been in power since 1979. The Parchamis are identified with the Dari language used by the urban and administrative elite. They have support in the police, press and university. In 1976–77 the Parchamis united with their rivals in the Khalq faction in order to overthrow President Daoud.

Pashtun or **Pathan**   The largest tribal group within Afghanistan, occupying most of the south and east of the country. Prior to 1979, they constituted about half of the country's population of 15 million, but since then an estimated three million have moved into neighbouring Pakistan where they have kinship with the tribesmen of the North–West Frontier Province. President Daoud was the last Afghan ruler from the historically dominant Durrani tribe of the Pashtun ethnic group. The two subsequent Marxist leaders of Afghanistan, Taraki and Amin, were members of the rival Ghilzai Pashtun clan from SE Afghanistan. The language of the Pashtuns is Pashtu, and their code of conduct is known as Pashtunwali.

People's Democratic Party of Afghanistan (PDPA) or **Jamiyat-e Demokrati Khalq-e Afghanistan**   Between 1979 and 1987, the sole legal political party in Afghanistan. Founded in 1965 by Nur Mohammed Taraki, the PDPA is divided into Pashtu-speaking (Khalq) and Dari-speaking (Parcham) factions. In 1973 the Parcham faction, led by Babrak Karmal, withdrew from the PDPA following the Khalqi defiance of a Soviet directive to support the Daoud regime. The two factions were reunited in 1977 but by 1985 most of the Khalq leaders had been ousted from government posts. Under the 1987 constitution the PDPA ceased theoretically to be the sole ruling party, although it continued to dominate the National Front.

People's Islamic Party of Afghanistan   An Islamic political party set up after the government approved the formation of political parties in 1987.

Peasant's Justice Party of Afghanistan   A political party created following the government's approval of the formation of political parties in 1987.

Peshawar Seven   A name given to the seven resistance groups comprising the Sunni Muslim, *mujahedin* alliance based in Peshawar, Pakistan.

proximity talks   A series of peace talks held in Geneva, the first taking place in August 1984. Previous communications between the respective foreign ministries of Afghanistan and Pakistan had been "indirect" negotiations channelled through the UN Secretary–General's Personal Representative. The August 1984 talks were the first to take place with both delegations in close "proximity" to each other, i.e., in the same building.

Raabt-i Alam-i Islami   An extremist anti-Soviet Afghan resistance group set up in Islamabad in January 1988 with a view to attacking Soviet targets worldwide.

Revolutionary Council   Legislature and final court of appeal in Afghanistan. The President of the Council acts as Head of State. Ministers appointed by the Central Committee of the PDPA are approved by the 57–member Revolutionary Council. In March 1990 fundamentalist factions of the *mujahedin* under Gulbuddin Hekmatyar formed their own "Revolutionary Council" in the fight against the Najibullah regime.

Sarandoy   The Afghan police force. Numbering about 30 000, it is controlled by the Ministry of the Interior which, since 1984, has also organized civil defence groups known as "Guardians" or "Defenders of the Revolution".

Saur revolution   The "April" revolution that overthrew Mohammad Daoud on 27–28 April 1978.

Sazmani Naser   A Shia Muslim minority resistance group formed in 1972 by students opposed to the Shora-i-Itifaq Islami. This pro-Iranian faction operates in the western Hazara ethnic region.

Sepah-e-Pasdaran   A Shia Muslim minority resistance group formed in 1981 under the supervision of the Iranian Revolutionary Guard. This group is active in the western Hazara ethnic region.

Sholaye-Jaweid   A small pro-Beijing faction of the Afghan PDPA.

Shora-i-Itifaq Islami   A nationalist Shia minority resistance group operating in the Hazara ethnic region of central Afghanistan.

Shura   The parliament of Afghanistan prior to the 1973 coup. In February 1988 the *mujahedin* alliance leaders held what was called a "shura" in Rawalpindi at which they elected a transitional government-in-exile.

Supreme Extraordinary Commission for National Reconciliation   A commission set up in January 1987 as part of the Afghan regime's peace programme for Afghanistan. In order to appease Islamic interests, the main tasks of the commission were to elect "people's" judges, to send volunteers to serve in the army and to solve disputes involving property, land and water reform.

Teheran Eight   A name given to the eight factions of Shia Muslim resistance fighters based in Iran and led by Karim Khalili.

Teiman-Atahad-Islami ("those who have sworn to fight for Islam")   A Peshawar-based alliance of rebel groups which united in August 1979 in opposition to the government. The alliance included the Afghan National Liberation Front, the Khales faction of Hezb-i-Islami, the Jamiat-i-Islami and the Islamic Revolution Movement.

United Nations Good Offices Mission in Afghanistan (UNGOMA)   A team of political, legal and military advisers from 10 countries sent by the UN to monitor the Soviet withdrawal from Afghanistan in 1988–89. The observers were led by Major–General Rauli Helminen of Finland.

■ Further reading

Richard Evans, Afghanistan: Another Lebanon?, *Geographical Magazine*, 60:4, pp.2–10, 1988

A.S. Ghaus *The Fall of Afghanistan: An Insider's Account*, Pergamon-Brassey's, London and Washington, 1988

E.R. Giradet, *Afghanistan: The Soviet War*, Croom Helm, London, 1985

Mike Martin, *Afghanistan: Inside a Rebel Stronghold; Journeys with the Mujahedin*, Sterling, New York, 1984

O. Roy, *Islam and Resistance in Afghanistan*, Cambridge University Press, Cambridge, 1986

Amin Saikal and William Maley, *The Soviet Withdrawal from Afghanistan*, Cambridge University Press, Cambridge, 1989

2
Kashmir

SOVIET UNION

AFGHANISTAN

CHINA

Khunerjab Pass

KASHMIR

Afg.

Pks

China

India

Gilgit

K2

Siachen glacier

Karakoram Pass

Aksai Chin

Shyok

NJ9842

Indus

Line of Control

Khardungla Pass

Muzaffarabad

Srinagar

Leh

Jammu-Kashmir

PAKISTAN

Jammu

INDIA

| 0 | mls | 100 |
| 0 | kms | 200 |

■ Profile

- **Total area:** 222 236km²
- **Area occupied by India:** 100 569km²
- **Area occupied by Pakistan:** 78 932km²
- **Area occupied by China:** 42 732km²
- **Population of the state of Jammu–Kashmir occupied by India:** 5 981 600
- **Population of Azad Kashmir and Northern Areas occupied by Pakistan:** 2 800 000
- **Official language (Jammu–Kashmir):** Urdu
- **Commonly spoken languages:** Kashmiri, Hindi, Ladakhi, Punjabi, Balti and Dogri
- **Religions (Jammu–Kashmir):** Muslim 64%, Hindu 32%, Sikh, Buddhist, Christian and Jain 4%

■ Introduction

Predominantly Muslim since the late 14th century, Kashmir became part of the Mogul Empire in 1586 and later passed under Sikh rule. On the defeat of the Sikhs by the British in the 1840s, Kashmir was awarded to a Hindu military adventurer called Gulab Singh, who had become Rajah of Jammu in 1820 and had conquered Ladakh on the Chinese frontier in 1834. For the next 100 years the Hindu Maharajahs of Jammu and Kashmir ruled autocratically over their mainly Muslim subjects as autonomous princelings recognizing British paramountcy. Under the British Raj, Kashmir gained world renown for its scenic beauty and rich natural endowments. In the maelstrom of the British withdrawal and partition of India in 1947 Kashmir was expected to join Muslim Pakistan, but Maharajah Sir Hari Singh had other ideas. He first opted for independence, then joined the Indian Union when Pashtun irregulars, supported later by the Pakistani army, sought to integrate Kashmir into the new Muslim state of Pakistan. The resultant Indo–Pakistani war ended in late 1948 in stalemate and a UN-sponsored ceasefire on a line which left India in control of the populous southern and eastern parts of Kashmir, while Pakistan held the north and west (part of which was designated Azad Kashmir). The lines of confrontation were thus drawn and changed little over the next four decades.

For Pakistan the emotional and political significance of the Kashmir dispute was bound up with the desire of the new state to encompass all predominantly Muslim areas of the old Raj. In India, where the Hindu leadership had initially rejected the concept of partition, Kashmir was viewed as a test for the secular identity of the post-colonial Union, which even after partition included many millions of Muslims (as well as other minorities). That India consistently rejected a plebiscite in Kashmir to determine the wishes of its population was cited by Pakistan as evidence of the weakness of the Indian case. India maintained that such a vote would not be valid in the presence of Pakistani forces. It later pointed out that elections in Kashmir had produced majorities for Muslim parties favouring the retention of Indian status.

Apart from the political factors, strategic imperatives impelled both India and Pakistan to regard Kashmir as crucial to their national security. The area formed a substantial part of their common border and each side feared attack by the other. That the main actual or potential *casus belli* was the status of Kashmir itself only added to the area's importance. For Pakistan, economic factors provided an additional strategic dimension in that Kashmir's three main rivers (the Indus, Jhelum and Chenab) all flow into Pakistan and are a major irrigation source for that country. For India, strategic calculations were also heavily influenced by the "China factor", arising from Beijing's claim to the Aksai Chin and other

Himalayan territory inside what India regarded as the historic borders of Kashmir. Against this background, Pakistan's alignment with communist China (and with the United States) was countered by India's gravitation towards increasingly close relations with the Soviet Union.

India's fear of a Sino–Pakistani axis was accentuated by its experience in the 1962 Sino–Indian war, in which Chinese forces consolidated their hold on the Aksai Chin. A year later Indian concern deepened when Pakistan and China signed an agreement demarcating the border between Pakistani Kashmir and China's Xinjiang province. Claiming that Pakistan had ceded territory belonging to India (i.e., to Kashmir), the Indian government denounced the agreement and thereafter initiated moves for the closer integration of Indian Kashmir into the Union. This provoked armed incursions across the Kashmir ceasefire line by Azad Kashmiri irregulars, which in turn led to the 1965 Indo-Pakistani war. The outcome was the Moscow-mediated Tashkent Declaration of January 1966 under which the two sides returned close to the 1949 ceasefire line in Kashmir. It was evident, however, that India had gained the advantage over Pakistan in the fighting, in which the threat of direct Chinese intervention did not materialize.

Indian military superiority in the subcontinent was confirmed in the 1971 Indo–Pakistani war, during which Indian forces "liberated" East Pakistan (Bangladesh) from West Pakistan. Prior to the hostilities India had signed a 20-year friendship treaty with the Soviet Union, whereas Pakistan's military regime had been subjected to a US arms embargo since 1965. On the Kashmir front, limited fighting produced minor changes in the lines of control, which were confirmed by the Simla Agreement of July 1972. Over the next decade, the two sides did not openly challenge the status quo, although the activities of Pakistani-backed Muslim insurgents in Indian Kashmir were a constant source of friction (as was Pakistan's clandestine support for Sikh separatism in the Punjab – *see section 3.3*). To this extent, India and Pakistan continued to regard one another as the principal potential enemy, with the added ingredient of the popular Hindu perception of Pakistan as part of a great Islamic alliance seeking to restore the Mogul Empire. India's detonation of a nuclear device in 1974 further emphasized its military superiority, while later reports that Pakistan was also developing a nuclear capability raised the stakes of any future conflict to unthinkable levels.

Shared subcontinental disquiet over the Soviet invasion of Afghanistan in late 1979 resulted in improved Indo–Pakistani relations in the early 1980s. But military tension and armed clashes developed from 1984 over control of the undemarcated Siachen Glacier region of northern Kashmir. There was also a resurgence of Muslim/Hindu strife in Indian Kashmir and more strident Islamic fundamentalism in Pakistan itself. This time the two governments sought to manage and defuse the crisis, especially after Pakistan returned to civilian rule in 1988 under Benazir Bhutto, who struck up a good working relationship with the Indian Prime Minister, Rajiv Gandhi, within the framework of the new South Asian Association for Regional Co-operation. However, only five months after the two sides had agreed in June 1989 to work constructively for a settlement of the Siachen dispute, Gandhi found himself ejected from office by the Indian electorate. This created new uncertainties for Indo-Pakistani in general and for the Kashmir dispute in particular, not least because the new Indian government depended on the parliamentary support of militant Hindu elements opposed to any concessions to the "Muslim enemy" in the north. Within Indian Kashmir, moreover, unplacated and increasingly militant pro-Pakistan Muslim activists posed a major obstacle to any resolution of this longstanding dispute. By early 1990 the situation had deteriorated to such an extent that the two sides were again squaring up for full-scale war.

■ Chronology of events

1846   The Hindu Jammu dynasty of Gulab Singh is established in Kashmir by the British , after three centuries of Mogul rule.

1906   Formation of the All–India Muslim League which aims to represent Muslim interests in Indian affairs.

1940   Mohammed Ali Jinnah, leader of the Muslim League, publicly endorses the idea of establishing Parkstan as a separate Muslim state.

1947   The Congress Party and the Muslim League fail to agree on the terms for a draft constitution for an independent India and in June the British Government declares its intention to grant dominion status to two separate countries - India and Pakistan. The Muslim-majority districts of British India, Bengal and the Punjab are to be partitioned and the remaining princely states are to be offered the chance to accede to either India or Pakistan. Independence within the Commonwealth is granted to both countries in August. Despite the fact that Kashmir has a Muslim majority, the Maharajah of Jammu and Kashmir cannot decide whether to reach an agreement with India or Pakistan. Kashmir is eventually impelled to accede to India in October when Pashtun tribesmen from Pakistan invade the state in support of their Muslim allies. Indian forces take control of eastern portions of Kashmir, including Srinagar, while the northern and western parts of the state are occupied by Pakistan.

1948   In January India takes the Kashmir dispute to the United Nations, but in the meantime offers the possibility of a referendum on self-determination once the threat of invasion by Pakistan has been removed. The Kashmiri nationalist, Sheik Mohammed Abdullah, becomes Prime Minister of Kashmir.

1949   A ceasefire between India and Pakistan takes effect in January and the subsequent Karachi Agreement establishes a line of control between the two countries. The line

of demarcation, however, stops short of the Karakoram Mountains where no fighting had taken place. India maintains control over the territory in the densely-populated Vale of Kashmir which lies to the south of the ceasefire line while Pakistan establishes its authority over the territory to the north and west of the ceasefire line.

1953 Hindus demand the secession of Jammu from the Muslim majority in Kashmir and Sheik Abdullah uses the agitation as an excuse to throw doubt on India's intention to hold a referendum. Having split not only the Kashmiri government but also the National Conference party that he founded, Abdullah is forced to resign and is imprisoned for maladministration and for plotting the secession of Kashmir.

1954   The Kashmir Constituent Assembly confirms the Act of Accession to India which Prime Minister Bakshi Ghulam Mohammed describes as "irrevocable."

1960   Under the terms of the Indus Water Treaty, India and Pakistan agree a plan for the equitable distribution of waters from the Kashmir system.

1962   On 3 May, Pakistan and China sign an agreement demarcating the frontier between Pakistani Kashmir and China's Xinjiang province. Pakistan also abandons its claim to more than 33 650km^2 of territory previously shown as part of Kashmir on Pakistani maps. This action prompts India to contest that any such common boundary between Pakistan and China exists. In July fighting breaks out between Indian and Chinese troops in the Aksai Chin region of the Karakoram Mountains.

1964   India's attempts to draw Kashmir more closely into the Union lead to an increasing number of incidents along the ceasefire line where casualties total 315 Pakistanis and 109 Indians.

1965   Attempts are made to integrate Kashmir more fully into India, and in May fighting breaks out between Pakistan and India in the mountainous Kargil area north–east of Srinagar. The Chief Minister of Kashmir, Sheikh Abdullah, is arrested in New Delhi after holding secret talks with the Prime Minister of China in Algiers. Abdullah had publicly advocated the use of force if necessary to secure the independence of Kashmir and was suspected of soliciting Chinese support in exchange for recognition of their claim over Ladakh.

1966 A ceasefire is followed by the signing of the Tashkent Declaration in January and troops are withdrawn from the line of control. Further talks on the Kashmir problem held in Rawalpindi founder when India refuses to recognise Kashmir as a disputed territory.

1971 West Pakistan's attempts to control Bengali dissidents in East Pakistan erupt into open conflict. Meanwhile India signs a 20-year treaty of friendship with the Soviet Union in August. Four months later India invades Pakistan in a brief war that ensures the independence of East Pakistan as Bangladesh. Hostilities in the east and on the Kashmir front come to an end after a ceasefire on 17 December.

1972 A new line of control between Pakistan and India in Kashmir is delineated by the Simla Agreement.

1975 The nationalist politician, Sheikh Mohammed Abdullah, is returned as Chief Minister of Kashmir.

1984 One hundred troops of the Indian High Altitude Warfare School, who had been sent in small units to the Siachen Glacier since the late 1970s, occupy strategic positions on the edge of the glacier, deep inside territory claimed by Pakistan to be on their side of the line of control. Pakistan had previously encouraged mountaineering expeditions into this area which on some modern maps was shown to be part of Pakistan. On 17 April a Pakistan army helicopter is shot down and in June Pakistan makes an abortive attempt to dislodge the Indian troops. India and Pakistan establish permanent high altitude bases in the Karakoram Range.

1985 In June and September Pakistan makes two more unsuccessful attempts to remove Indian troops from the Siachen Glacier.

1986 Tension between Pakistan and India mounts as military exercises take place on either side of the line of control in the Ravi–Chenab corridor. Because of its inability to control Hindu–Muslim violence, the government of Jammu and Kashmir is dismissed and the state is put under President's rule.

1987 Meeting in February, President Zia of Pakistan and Prime Minister Rajiv Gandhi of India agree to negotiate peacefully the sovereignty of the Siachen Glacier region and to give no support to separatist movements in either country. Elections are subsequently held in Jammu and Kashmir and a coalition government is formed under the leadership of Dr. Farooq Abdullah. In defeat, leaders of the newly-formed pro-Pakistan Muslim United Front accuse Abdullah of vote-rigging and are forced underground where they form militant resistance groups. In September there are further heavy casualties during fighting between Pakistan and Indian forces around the Siachen Glacier.

1988 Muslim opposition to New Delhi increases in Kashmir as further demands for a referendum on self-determination are ignored. Guerrilla leaders call for a boycott on future polls and threaten violence. Despite this, relations between India and Pakistan begin to improve after a meeting between Prime Ministers Benazir Bhutto and Rajiv Gandhi in December, when both are founder members of the South Asian Association for Regional Co-operation.

1989 In June Pakistan and India hold talks at which they discuss the setting up of a demilitarised zone as a prerequisite to defining a precise line of control in the Karakoram Range. Meanwhile, Muslim extremists seeking to take Kashmir out of India step up their acts of terrorism. In September a leading pro-India National Congress party official is killed and Srinagar is crippled by a series of one-day strikes.

1990   Between January and May escalating violence and unrest on both sides of the Line of Control leads to increased animosity and the threat of war between India and Pakistan. In January the Chief Minister of Jammu Kashmir resigns and direct rule is imposed from New Delhi. A month later, on 23 February, over half a million Muslims demonstrate on the streets of Srinagar demanding the independence of Kashmir which is in a virtual state of siege.

■ Who's who

Abdullah, Dr. Farooq   Son of the former Chief Minister of Kashmir, Sheikh Abdullah, and leader of the Kashmir National Conference Party. In March 1987 he was elected to the post of Chief Minister of Jammu and Kashmir at the head of a National Conference–Congress (I) coalition government. His conciliatory policy towards New Delhi brought few tangible rewards to Kashmir and accusations of vote-rigging in the 1987 election only served to increase his unpopularity. His resignation in January 1990 amidst increasing separatist unrest led to a further period of direct rule being imposed from New Delhi.

Abdullah, Sheikh Mohammed   Born in 1905, Sheikh Abdullah became synonymous with Muslim nationalism in Kashmir where he founded the National Conference Party and suffered imprisonment for his opposition to the Hindu maharajah. Known as the "Lion of Kashmir", he acted as Chief Minister of Jammu and Kashmir for a period of six years following the partition of India in 1947. Attempts to manipulate the secession of Kashmir from India led to his resignation in 1953 and further imprisonment for a term of 11 years. Leading the Plebescite Front, which he founded in 1968, he regained power in 1975 as Chief Minister of Jammu and Kashmir, a position he held until his death in 1982.

Farooq, Mirwaiz Mohammed   The most senior Muslim cleric in the city of Srinagar.

Gujral, Indar   Foreign Minister of India and former ambassador in Moscow, responsible for drawing his country back from the brink of war during the Kashmir insurrection of 1990.

Jagmohan, J.   Appointed Governor of Jammu and Kashmir in January 1990 following the resignation of Chief Minister Farooq Abdullah and the imposition of direct rule from Delhi.

Khan, Abdul Qayyum   President of the Pakistani-controlled Azad Kashmir where he is leader of the ruling Muslim Conference Party.

Khan, Ammanullah   Leader of the secessionist Jammu Kashmir Liberation Front rebels. The Indian government applied for his extradition from the USA where he was allegedly directing the activities of "terrorist elements" in Kashmir.

Khan, Sahinzada Yakub   Foreign Minister of Pakistan responsible for negotiating with his Indian counterpart in an attempt to prevent another military confrontation between India and Pakistan in the wake of escalating violence in Kashmir.

Nanda, Lieut.–General B.C.   Commander of India's northern army forces operating in the region of the Siachen Glacier.

Sheikh, Abdul Jabar   A Former Kashmir state minister assassinated by Muslim secessionists in April 1990 at the height of renewed unrest.

Singh, Yuvraj Karan   The last Maharajah of Jammu and Kashmir. He took over as regent three years after his father had signed the Instrument of Accession that attached the state to the newly independent but partitioned India. On the ending of hereditary rule in 1952 he was elected head of state.

■ Key places

Aksai Chin Territory forming a plateau in the Himalayas where it is of strategic importance as a link between the Chinese provinces of Tibet and Xinjiang (Sinkiang). Extending over an area of some 36000km², Aksai Chin has been occupied by China since 1950 but is claimed by India as part of Kashmir. The territorial dispute between the two countries erupted into armed conflict for a period of four months in 1962.

Azad Kashmir ("Free Kashmir") A narrow strip of Kashmir occupied by Pakistan and lying to the west of Indian-held Jammu and Kashmir state. While the Northern Areas territory of Baltistan and Gilgit are ruled directly from Islamabad, this part of Pakistani Kashmir has its own 42-member Legislative Assembly based in the city of Muzaffarabad. The name Azad Kashmir is often applied to the whole of Pakistani–held Kashmir.

Baltistan or **Little Tibet** Territory in the Karakoram Range of NE Kashmir, situated in west Ladakh, south of Mt K2. The area is occupied by Baltis who are Muslims of Tibetan origin. The chief settlement is Skardu, but the location of greatest significance to Pakistanis is Ghyari, the site of a simple stone mosque said to have been set up by Sayyid Ali Hamadani, a Persian who brought Shia Islam to Baltistan in the 14th century. Ghyari is also an important Pakistan army base.

Baltoro Glacier A large glacier just south of Mt K2 in the Karakoram Range at a height of about 5300m. In 1984 the Pakistani army established a high-altitude outpost here as a counter to the presence of Indian troops on the Siachen Glacier 11km to the south–east.

Gilgit A district in N Kashmir bounded on the south by the river Indus and north by the Wakhan Salient of Afghanistan. In 1947 the area was transferred to Kashmir but the populace, which is over 87% Muslim, opted in favour of alliance with Pakistan. The ancient Buddhist centre of Gilgit, 210km NNW of Srinagar, is the only town of importance and a setting off point for mountaineering expeditions into the Karakoram Range.

Indus Rising in the Himalayan Kailas Range of Tibet, the great Indus river first flows north–west, cutting its way through the Ladakh Range into Jammu and Kashmir. Crossing the India–Pakistan line of control east of Kargil, it skirts the northern edge of the Punjab Himalayas of Baltistan before turning south onto the Punjab plain where it continues on its way to the Indian Ocean south-east of Karachi. Its total length from source to sea is just over 3000km.

Jammu Winter capital of the state of Jammu and Kashmir; population(1981) 206100. Jammu is linked by road to Srinagar 150km to the north through the Banihal Pass and Jawahar Tunnel which cross the Pir Panjal Range.

K2 Rising to 8611m in the Karakoram Range, K2 is the second highest mountain in the world. In 1888 the peak was alternatively named Mt Godwin Austen after the English soldier and surveyor, Lt.–Col. Henry Godwin–Austen (1834–1923). K2 was the survey sign used by the Survey of India at this location. The summit was first reached in 1954 by an Italian expedition.

Karakoram Range A Himalayan mountain range on the frontier between Kashmir and China. Rising to its highest point at Mt K2, it is crossed at an altitude of 5575m by the Karakoram Pass which lies on a historic caravan route linking India with the Chinese province of Xinjiang (Sinkiang).

Kargil A mountain town in central Kashmir on the Suru river, 130km north–east of Srinagar. Situated close to the line of control it was the scene of heavy fighting between India and Pakistan in 1948 and 1945.

Khardungla Pass Reckoned to be the highest road in the world at an altitude of 5662m, the Khardungla Pass is an important link in the Indian supply route from the town of Leh to the Siachen Glacier via Pratapur and the Nubra river valley.

Khunerjab Pass   A high-altitude pass on the Karakoram highway linking China and Pakistan. The pass was opened in 1982.

Ladakh   A high-altitude region of E Kashmir, geographically forming the western-most limit of Tibet to which it was attached politically until the mid-19th century when it was annexed to Kashmir by Gulab Singh. The whole region is divided into Ladakh proper in the east and Baltistan in the west. While Islam is the dominant religion in Baltistan, Buddhism is common in the east. The chief town is Leh.

Leh   The capital of Ladakh region, E Kashmir; situated to the east of the Indus river, 240km east of Srinagar. This is the nearest hospital and supply base to the Indian army outposts in the Karakoram Range.

Muzaffarabad   Chief administrative centre of Pakistani-held Azad Kashmir; situated at the meeting of the Jhelum and Neelum rivers.

Northern Areas   That part of Kashmir held by Pakistan under direct rule from Islamabad. Lying to the north of Pakistani-held Azad Kashmir and the Indian state of Jammu and Kashmir, the Northern Areas includes the districts of Diamir, Gilgit and Baltistan.

Nubra   A river rising at the south end of the Siachen Glacier. It flows about 80km before reaching the Shyok river, a tributary of the Indus. The Nubra river valley is a major supply route from Leh and Pratapur to the Indian army outposts in the Siachen Glacier area.

Pir Panjal Range   A southern range of the Punjab Himalayas extending south–east from the Jhelum river to form the western border of the Vale of Kashmir in SW Kashmir.

Pratapur   A town in Ladakh; situated on the Shyok river, north of Leh on the Indian supply route to the Siachen Glacier. The base of the 102nd Brigade of the Indian army.

Ravi–Chenab corridor   A strip of land between the Ravi and Chenab rivers on the frontier between Pakistan and Jammu and Kashmir in India.

Saltoro Range   A range of the Karakoram mountains forming a frontline to the west of the Siachen Glacier in the high-altitude conflict between Indian and Pakistani armed forces.

Shyok   A river in the Ladakh region. From its source as the Chip Chap river it flows south–east, separating the Chinese occupied Aksai Chin territory from the main range of the Karakoram which it skirts in a great bend before changing direction to flow north–west past Pratapur and Ghyari before meeting the Indus 25km SE of Skardu.

Siachen Glacier   With a length of 120km, the Siachen Glacier is one of the world's longest mountain glaciers. Situated at an altitude of about 5300m in the Karakoram Range south–east of Mt K2, its southern end is the source of the Nubra river. In 1984 the Indian army established a presence here which precipitated a high-altitude armed conflict between India and Pakistan.

Srinagar   Textile manufacturing city and summer capital of the state of Jammu and Kashmir, situated on the Jhelum river, north–west of the Pir Panjal Range; population(1981) 586 000.

■ Key words

Congress Party   The largely Hindu National Congress Party which ruled India from independence until 1989, except for a brief period in 1977–79. In the 1920s Mahatma Gandhi transformed the party into a mass movement opposing British colonial rule by means of nonviolent resistance and nonco-operation, but his attempts to reconcile Muslim and Hindu interests could not prevent partition.

Jammu and Kashmir Liberation Front A Kashmir separatist movement. Its military wing, the Kashmir Liberation Army, was responsible for the kidnapping and subsequent murder of the Indian Assistant High Commissioner in the UK in February 1984 following demands for the release of Liberation Front president, Magbool Boot, who had been sentenced to death for the murder of a policeman.

Jammu and Kashmir National Conference (JKNC) A socialist party advocating autonomy for Kashmir within the Indian Union, the JKNC ruled the state of Jammu and Kashmir from 1947 until 1965. For over a decade it allied itself to the Congress Party, but in 1975 its independence was renewed under Sheikh Mohammed Abdullah. Two years later the JKNC won a majority in the State Assembly.

Karachi Agreement An agreement reached between India and Pakistan following a ceasefire in January 1949. This agreement established the line of control between the two countries in Jammu and Kashmir state.

line of control A temporary ceasefire line delimiting the frontier negotiated between two countries. The India–Pakistan line of control in the state of Jammu and Kashmir was established by the Karachi Agreement after conflict between the two countries during 1947–49. At this stage the line extended vaguely northwards into the heights of the Karakoram mountains from the last demarcated point just north of the Shyok river at map coordinate NJ 39842. The line of control was later modified by the Tashkent Declaration and the Simla Agreement following further conflict in 1965 and 1971, but the line remained undemarcated in the glacier region where no fighting had taken place. Similar lines of control separate both India and Pakistan from Kashmir territory occupied by China.

Muslim League In 1906 a number of prominent Muslim leaders formed themselves into the All-India Muslim League in order to represent the interests of Muslims more effectively. Although their aim, like that of the Hindu Indian National Congress, was to achieve self-government for India, they failed to agree with the Congress Party on a formula for the protection of Muslim economic and religious rights.

Operation Meghdoot ("Cloud Messenger") The codename given to the rapid deployment of Indian troops at key positions on the western edge of the Siachen Glacier in April 1984 in an attempt to pre-empt an alleged planned Pakistani move into the undemarcated Karakoram Mountains.

Pakistan Resolution The idea of establishing Pakistan as a separate Muslim state which was advocated in the 1930s and eventually publicly endorsed at Lahore in March 1940 by Mohammed Ali Jinnah, leader of the All–India Muslim League.

partition The separation of Muslim Pakistan from Hindu India following the end of British colonial rule in the Indian subcontinent in 1947. In the 1930s the idea of establishing a separate Muslim state had been advocated by the Muslim League.

Simla Agreement An agreement by which India and Pakistan established a new line of control in Jammu and Kashmir state. Signed in July 1972, it came into force on 17 December of that year.

Tashkent Declaration A Soviet–mediated ceasefire agreement between India and Pakistan signed in January 1966 after a period of armed conflict between the two countries in the previous year.

United Front A pro-Pakistan Muslim political party formed in Kashmir in the 1980s in opposition to Dr. Farooq Abdullah's National Conference Party. The supposed wave of support for this party was not reflected in the 1987 election, a fact that led to accusations of vote rigging. Muslim leaders subsequently went underground and formed themselves into militant resistance organizations allied to mujahedin groups in Afghanistan, Iran and Lebanon.

■ Further reading

P.N.K. Bamzai, *A History of Kashmir*, Delhi, 1962

S.M. Burke, *Pakistan's Foreign Policy*, Oxford University Press, Oxford, 1973

S. Gupta, *Kashmir: A Study in India–Pakistan Relations*, London, 1967

A. Hyman, et al, *Pakistan: Zia and After*, London, 1989

K. Siddiqui, *Conflict, Crisis and War in Pakistan*, Macmillan, London, 1972

3
Sikh Nationalism

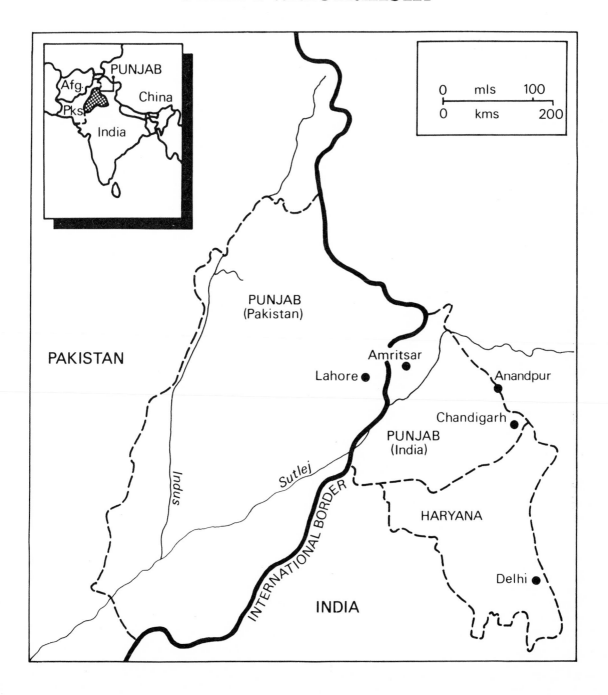

■ Profile

Punjab (India)

Area: 50 362km²
- **Population:** 16 670 000
- **Capital:** Chandigarh
- **Official language:** Punjabi
- **Total Sikh population of India:** 13 100 000

Punjab (Pakistan)

- **Area:** 205 334km²
- **Population:** 47 292 000
- **Capital:** Lahore
- **Languages:** Punjabi, Urdu and English are the most common languages
- **Sikhs living outside Asia:** USA 250 000 (80 000 in New York); UK 400 000

■ Introduction

In the mosaic of India's ethnic and religious diversity the Sikhs have always stood out for several reasons, including the distinctive appearance of their menfolk. Founded as a monotheistic sect in the 15th century by Guru Nanak, Sikhism fashioned elements of meditative Hinduism and Islamic mysticism into a new religion, which drew many adherents from the Hindu community and some from the Muslims. Opposed to the Hindu caste system, the Sikhs evolved their own language, holy scriptures and rituals, as well as a distinct system of social mores which emphasized the virtues of active communalism as the framework for personal achievement. The early Sikh gurus stressed the importance of communal tolerance and taught that all religions shared a fundamental common identity.

From c.1700 Sikhism assumed a militaristic dimension, as the Sikhs engaged in successful wars against the Muslim Mogul Empire which had ruled northern India for several centuries. In was then that the five "signs" of the Sikh warrior brotherhood – who all took the name Singh after their founder – became obligatory, namely uncut hair and beard, turban, ceremonial dagger, arm bracelet and undershorts. Usually making common cause with Hindus against Muslim despotism, the Sikhs had by the mid-18th century established a substantial empire in the Punjab and adjoining areas. From the early 19th century, however, the Sikhs came into conflict with encroaching British power and were decisively defeated by the British in the 1840s. Their territories were promptly annexed to the Raj.

Notwithstanding this experience, Punjabi Sikhs became a mainstay of British rule in India. Recruited into the Indian Army in large numbers, they remained fiercely loyal to the British in times of Hindu or Muslim revolt, notably during the Indian Mutiny (or Sepoy Rebellion) of 1857–58. Sikhs thus became willing accessories to the classic British colonial ploy of "divide and rule", with consequential damage to their historically tolerant relations with Hindus. After World War I the Sikh political movement, Akali Dal, joined in the growing general agitation for an end to British rule. But its associated demand for the creation of an independent Sikh state (Khalistan) again set it at odds with a Hindu leadership which wanted a united independent India. In the event, the Sikhs' long service to the Raj went unrewarded by the British, who saw the creation of a separate state for the much larger Muslim community as a more urgent requirement.

The British withdrawal and partition of the Raj in 1947 found Sikhs caught up in the intercommunal strife which disfigured the birth of independent India and Pakistan. The division of the Sikh-populated Punjab between the two new countries caused a great migration of peoples in which many Sikhs in the western (i.e. Pakistani) Punjab opted to move to the Indian sector, along with millions of Hindus. Although Sikh/Hindu clashes occurred, both communities regarded Muslims as the principal enemy, and both not only sustained atrocities from the adherents of Islam but also returned them in kind. There was thus some identity of interest between Sikhs and Hindus in the new Indian Union, given that both communities shared a negative perception of Muslim Pakistan. An axiom of India's Congress government was that only a universal commitment to secularism could preserve the Union. With so many minorities existing within the new state, recognition of any one separatist claim was seen as likely to stimulate others. In the case of the Sikhs, the government was unyielding in its opposition to separate statehood, but also sought to accommodate legitimate Sikh aspirations and to restrain Hindu extremism. This strategy had the support of moderate Sikh leaders, who concentrated on obtaining concessions rather than on challenging the status quo. The most important was the division of the Indian Punjab in 1966 into Hindu-majority Haryana and Sikh-dominated Punjab. However, militant Sikh aspirations to national recognition remained strong.

India's support for Bengali separatism in East Pakistan led to the creation of independent Bangladesh in 1971 and had a knock-on effect in the Indian Punjab. Despite the history of Sikh/Muslim conflict, Sikh separatism thereby acquired an unacknowledged ally in Pakistan, which had its own unresolved disputes with India, notably over Kashmir (*see section 3.2*). Nevertheless, not until a decade later did the first major Sikh terrorist action occur, namely the hijacking of an Indian airliner in September 1981. Thereafter, and despite the election of a Sikh as President of India in 1982, Sikh militants seized the initiative in the Punjab. When in 1984 pro-Khalistan extremists occupied the Golden Temple in the Sikh holy city of Amritsar, and were forcibly expelled by Indian troops, it was clear that the Indian Union faced a major crisis. The reprisal assassination of Indian Prime Minister Indira Gandhi later that year, by Sikh members of her bodyguard, only served to accentuate the crisis and provoked the bloodiest intercommunal violence since 1947.

Shifting from the previous rigid Congress commitment to centralism, the new Indian Prime Minister, Rajiv Gandhi, reached an agreement with the moderate Sikh leadership in July 1985 conceding some of their demands for greater autonomy. But militant Sikhs were not satisfied, and terrorist actions escalated in the succeeding years. An aggravating factor was the easy availability to Sikh groups of sophisticated weaponry intended for Afghani *mujahedin* guerrillas based in Pakistan. Further concessions by the government failed to stem the violence, in which indiscriminate killings of Hindus by Sikhs set off reprisal actions by Hindus. With the Punjab under direct rule from New Delhi, the crisis became more intractable in May 1988 when Indian troops were again sent in to remove Sikh militants from the Golden Temple. After the death toll arising from the agitation had risen to over 3000 in 1988 alone, Gandhi again tried to initiate a political solution in March 1989. The violence continued, however, and in November 1989 Gandhi and his Congress party were defeated in general elections.

Bequeathed India's most serious crisis since independence, the new government of V.P. Singh moved quickly to defuse the situation by lifting the emergency laws still in force in the Punjab. There seems, however, no easy route to a lasting reconciliation of militant Sikh nationalism. The fact that the new government depended for its parliamentary majority on the support of the Hindu revivalist Bharatiya Janata Party (BJP) was seen by some observers as likely to make it more receptive to communal demands of all types. Others feared that the militant communal aspirations of the BJP could increase Hindu/Sikh antagonisms and thus place an even bigger question-mark over the future of the Indian Union.

■ Chronology of events

1469   Birth of Guru Nanak, founder and first spiritual leader of the Sikhs.

1574   Amritsar, holy city of the Sikhs is founded.

1699   Gobind Singh, last Guru, forms the five-member brotherhood of Khalsa, establishing the Sikhs' militaristic tradition.

1767   Ranjit Singh establishes Lahore as the capital of the united Sikh Empire.

1809   Britain signs a treaty with the Sikh rulers of the Punjab in order to maintain a link with British interests west of the Indus as well as creating a buffer zone against a Russian advance from the north.

1845   Conflict between Sikh and British interests leads to the Sikh Wars.

1849   The Sikhs loose their independence when the Punjab is annexed to British India but quickly become staunch supporters of the Raj.

1857   Sikh troops support British soldiers in suppressing the Indian Mutiny.

1919   After the killing of over 400 civilians, some of them Sikhs, at Amritsar, the Sikhs join the crusade to end British colonial rule in India.

1947   Sikh autonomy is frustrated with the partition of India and the division of the Punjab between India and Pakistan.

1956   The Indian state of Punjab is created when East Punjab is enlarged by the addition of Patiala and East Punjab States Union.

1966   The Punjab Reorganization Act divides the Indian Punjab State into two separate states, Punjab and Haryana. Both states share a joint capital at Chandigarh.

1981   In the first major Sikh terrorist action, young militants hijack an Indian airliner on a flight to Lahore (Pakistan) in September.

1982   Despite the election of Zail Singh as the first Sikh president of India Sikhs continue to demand greater religious tolerance, settlement of land and water rights and a separate capital city for the Punjab. Extremist groups within the Sikh community begin to make strong demands for an independent Khalistan.

1983   In October direct rule by the Indian government is imposed in the Punjab in an attempt to stem the rising tide of conflict between Sikh and Hindu.

1984   On 31 May Sikh extremists threaten to cut off supplies of grain, water and power to other areas of India and a group of pro-Khalistan terrorists led by Jarnail Singh Bhindranwale takes over the Golden Temple in Amritsar which is used as an arsenal. The government imposes a curfew in the Punjab and on 6 June sends in troops to dislodge the terrorists. In a 36-hour clash Bhindranwale and 600 of his followers are killed. This move prompts mutiny amongst over 2500 Sikh soldiers in the Indian army. In October the Prime Minister of India, Indhira Gandhi, is assassinated by militant Sikh members of her personal bodyguard and in the communal bloodshed that ensues over 4000 Sikhs are killed and 10 000 flee from Delhi to the Punjab.

1985   Peace talks between the Indian government and Harchand Singh Longowal, the moderate leader of the Sikh Akali Dal party, demonstrate Prime Minister Rajiv Gandhi's more flexible approach to the problem of Sikh nationalism. After agreeing that his party would take part in elections, Longowal is killed by radical Sikhs who still demand an independent Sikh state.

1986   Conflict between Sikh and Hindu escalates as violence takes the lives of 650 people. Many Sikhs in Haryana state cross the border into the Punjab. Sikh extremists break away from the more moderate elements of the Akali Dal. In an attempt to remain conciliatory, Rajiv Gandhi allows the election of a Punjabi state government to take place and in May appoints Sikhs to two senior positions in the Union Cabinet.

1987   Radical Sikh factions come together in February to form the Unified Akali Dal. The death toll in 1987 reaches nearly 1250 and in May the conflict spreads into Haryana where 72 Hindus in two buses are killed by Sikh terrorists. Direct rule from Delhi is imposed once more.

1988   Sikh extremists massacre a further 34 Hindus in NE Punjab on 4 March, the same day that some of the "Jodhpur detainees" are released. A month later India indirectly accuses Pakistan of giving support to Sikh separatists in the Punjab. In May Sikh militants again occupy the Golden Temple, and are expelled by the Indian Army who launch an attack codenamed "Operation Black Thunder". By the end of the year the death toll reaches over 3000.

1989   In March Rajiv Gandhi announces a series of initiatives aimed at restoring the political process in the Punjab, but in June intercommunal violence flares up again following a bomb attack in New Delhi's main station and the killing of 25 Hindus at a rally in the town of Moga.

■ Who's who

Bhindranwale, Jarmail Singh   Leader of the extremist, pro-Khalistan separatist Sikh movement known as the Bhindranwale Tiger Force of Khalistan. He and many of his followers were killed by Indian army forces in June 1984 after they had established a terrorist stronghold inside the Golden Temple in Amritsar.

Gandhi, Indira   (1917–84)   Daughter of Jawaharlal Nehru and Prime Minister of India 1966–77 and 1980–84. Her attempts to crush Sikh extremism reached a climax with the storming of the Golden Temple in Amritsar in June 1984, an action that led to her assassination at the hands of a Sikh bodyguard in October of the same year.

Gandhi, Rajiv   (b. 1944) Prime Minister of India, elected with a large majority after the assassination of his mother, Indira Gandhi, by Sikh extremists in 1984. Following allegations of corruption, he was eventually defeated at the polls in 1989.

Gobind Singh   The tenth Guru leader of the Sikhs. In 1699 he founded the brotherhood of the Khalsa or "Pure Ones" who inherited the spiritual and military leadership of the Sikhs when Gobind Rai was assassinated in 1708.

Longowal, Harchand Singh   Moderate president of the main Sikh political party, the Shiromani Akali Dal, Longowal was killed by Sikh extremists in August 1985 shortly after agreeing with the Indian government, to participate in state elections in the Punjab following two years of Presidents Rule.

Nanak, Guru (1469–1539) Born near Lahore, Nanak claimed to have had a vision that prompted him to teach a new religion that reconciled Hinduism and Islam. He attracted disciples or Sikhs for whom he was a spiritual leader.

Ranjit Singh   Khalsa leader who took advantage of the break up of the old Mogul empire to unite the various Sikh factions and declare himself Maharajah of the Punjab. Although he signed a treaty with the British in 1809, the empire that he created was destroyed after his death in 1839 when it came into collision with expanding British interests.

Rode, Jasbir Singh   One of the 366 Sikh "Jodhpur detainees",   released from detention in March 1988 and installed as supreme priest at the Golden Temple.

Sayeed, Muft Mohammed India's first Muslim Home affairs Minister. Appointed in 1990 by the new Prime Minister, V.P. Singh, to negotiate with Sikh militants.

Zail Singh The first Sikh to hold the office of president in India, a position to which he was elected by the Indian parliament in 1982.

■ Key places

Amritsar Holy city of the Sikhs in N Punjab state, India; population(1981) 589 000. Founded in 1577 next to the sacred tank or "pool of immortality", by Ram Das, fourth Guru of the Sikh religion. The holy temple housing the sacred Sikh scriptures was destroyed in 1761, but was rebuilt three years later. The building came to be known as the Golden Temple in 1802 when it was roofed over with gilded copper plates. A centre of the Sikh Empire until the Sikh wars of 1845–46, Amritsar is now a focal point of Sikh nationalism. Guru Nanak University was founded in 1969 to commemorate the 500th anniversary of the birth of the first Guru of the Sikhs.

Anandpur A town in north central Punjab, Pakistan; situated in the valley of the Sutlej river. The tenth Guru, Gobind Singh, established the Khalsa brotherhood here, but the town is also revered by the Sikhs as the place where the head of the martyred ninth Guru was cremated.

Chandigarh A Union Territory and joint capital city of the Indian states of Punjab and Haryana since the creation of Haryana under the Punjab Reorganization Act in November 1966. Situated on the edge of the Siwalik Hills in the SW foothills of the Himalayas, 250km north of Delhi, the city takes its name from the nearby temple of Chandi, goddess of power; population(1981) 450 000; area 114km². Laid out in a grid pattern of self-contained neighbourhood units in the 1950s by the French architect Le Corbusier, the city has a university (1947) and a rose garden, claimed to be the largest in Asia. Eventually Chandigarh is to become the capital of the Punjab alone.

Haryana A state of India created in November 1966 under the Punjab Reorganization Act which separated the Hindi-speaking south-east from the rest of Punjab state; population(1981)

12 851 000; area 44 222km². Punjab and Haryana states share a joint capital at Chandigarh. This flat and arid region produces sugar, oilseed and cotton with the help of water supplied by the Sutlej–Beas irrigation scheme. Rail routes crossing the state converge on Delhi, a large and important market for local produce lying on the SE frontier. Conflict between Sikh and Hindu in the Punjab spread over the border into Haryana in July 1987 when members of the Sikh extremist Khalistan Commando Force killed 72 bus passengers from that state.

Hemkund Lake A Sikh holy place near the Valley of Flowers, in the Himalayan foothills of Uttar Pradesh state. Surrounded by seven snow-capped mountains, this is the place Sikhs believe that the Guru Govind Singh meditated in a previous life.

Lahore Since 1947, a city in the Punjab province of Pakistan; situated on a fertile plain between the Ravi and Sutlej rivers, just west of the India–Pakistan frontier. With a population of just under three million, Lahore is the second largest city in Pakistan. An important centre of the great Mogul Empire, it became the seat of Ranjit Singh's Sikh Empire in 1767, and capital of British controlled Punjab in 1846.

Moga A Hindu town in Punjab state, India, situated 150km west of Chandigarh. The scene of serious intercommunal unrest which flared up in June 1989.

Nankana Sahib A town in E central Punjab, Pakistan. The birthplace of Guru Nanak in 1469. Formerly known as Talwandi, it has a population in excess of 13 000.

Patna The winter capital of Bihar state in northern India; situated on the Ganges. The birthplace of the tenth Guru, Gobind Singh.

Punjab   A region of the NW Indian sub-continent lying between the Indus and Yamuna rivers. The Punjab derives its name from the Sanskrit for the "five rivers" that water the fertile alluvial plain, namely, the Ravi, Chenab, Sutlej, Jhelum and Beas. Politically, a former north–western province of British India with its capital at Lahore, the Punjab was partitioned in 1947 between Pakistan and India as West and East Punjab. Indian East Punjab changed its name to Punjab and in 1956 it merged with the enclave of Patiala and East Punjab States Union. Ten years later, under the Punjab Reorganization Act of 1966, the Punjab of India was reconstituted as a Punjabi-speaking state. At the same time, the Hindi-speaking south–eastern region was partitioned to form a new state called Haryana. Pakistani West Punjab lost its provincial status in 1955 but was reconstituted in 1970 when the province of Punjab was established.

Sutlej   Largest of the "five rivers" of the Punjab, it rises in the Himalayas and follows a course of 1370km down onto the Punjab plain where it meets the Chenab east of Alipur. The Sutlej acted as a frontier between Sikh and British spheres of influence until the destruction of the Sikh Empire during the Sikh Wars of 1845–46.

■ Key words

Adi Granth or **First Book**   The sacred scriptures of the Sikhs. A volume of the teachings of Guru Nanak, founder of Sikhism, and his followers, compiled in the 17th century and housed in the Golden Temple in Amritsar.

Amrit Ceremony   An occasion when people join the Khalsa brotherhood and become full members of the Sikh religion. Amrit is a mixture of sugar and water stirred with a two-edged Khanda sword while reciting prayers.

Bhindranwale Tiger Force of Khalistan   The pro-Khalistan followers of the   extremist Sikh leader Jarmail Singh Bhindranwale, responsible for establishing a stronghold in the Golden Temple in 1984. In the battle to dislodge the terrorists Bhindranwale and hundreds of his supporters were killed by the Indian army. In 1987 the group joined with 15 other extremist organisations to form the Council of Khalistan.

Dharm–Yadha   The name given by the Akali Dal to the "holy struggle" for an autonomous Sikh state.

gurdwara ("Guru's door")   A Sikh place of worship.

Guru   A Sikh religious teacher.

Guru Granth Sahib ("large book")   The Sikh holy book containing the teachings of the Gurus. Sahib is a word that shows respect.

Jodhpur detainees   The name given to 366 Sikh extremists arrested after the 1984 storming of the Golden Temple and jailed in the high security prison at Jodhpur in Rajasthan. The last 188 of the so-called "Jodhpur detainees" were released in June 1989 as part of a set of initiatives announced by Rajiv Gandhi in an attempt to defuse the ethnic unrest in the Punjab.

Kaur   The female equivalent of Singh, meaning princess.

Khalistan ("land of the pure")   An independent Sikh nation advocated by Sikh extremists including members of the militant Khalistan Liberation Force and the Khalistan Commando Force.

Khalsa   A brotherhood of five "Pure Ones" established in 1699 by Gobind Rai, last of the Guru leaders of the Sikhs. When Gobind Singh was assassinated in 1708 the military and spiritual leadership of the Sikhs was taken up by the brotherhood of the Khalsa, each bearing the surname Singh, meaning "lion". The Babba Khalsa is an extremist Sikh guerrilla group.

Misra Commission A commission set up in July 1985 by the Indian government to investigate the massacre of Sikhs after the assassination of Indira Gandhi in the previous year. The subsequent Jain–Banerjee Commission attempted to identify guilty parties but was blocked by the Delhi High Court.

nishan sahib The yellow flag of the Sikhs.

Operation Black Thunder The codename given to the Indian army siege of the Golden Temple in Amritsar in May 1988.

President's Rule Direct rule over an Indian state by the central government. In October 1983 and again in May 1987 violence between Sikhs and Hindus led to the removal of the Punjabi government and the imposition of President's Rule.

Radcliffe Award Under the Indian Independence Act of 1947 the Indo-Pakistan frontier in the Punjab was determined by the Radcliffe Award which created the division between East and West Punjab.

Rashtriya Swayansewak Sangh A right-wing Hindu revivalist group that has organised opposition to the Sikhs in the Punjab. On a number of occasions since 1986 they have come under attack by Sikh terrorists.

Sarbat Khalsa A general assembly of baptised Sikhs.

Shiromani Akali Dal A Sikh political party founded in 1920 with the aim of establishing autonomy for all states. With a membership of over one million people in the Indian state of Punjab, it dominated the political scene after 1969. In January 1986 Sikh violence escalated when extremist sections of the party broke away from the moderate core of the Shiromani Akali Dal. These and other militant factions reunited in 1987 under the name Unified Akali Dal.

Shiv Sena or **Army of Shiva** A militant Hindu group formed in 1986 with the aim of organising resistance against Sikh terrorism.

Sikh (Hindu "disciple") The follower of a monotheistic religion embracing elements of the Hindu and Muslim faiths, founded by Guru Nanak (1469–1539). True Sikhs traditionally wear the "five ks": the Kesh, uncut hair; the Kach, short trousers; the Kara, an iron bangle; the Kirpan, a two-edged sword; and the Khanga, a comb. Out of a total of some 20 million Sikhs (2.5 per cent of the population) over eight million are to be found in the Punjab state, NW India. Their attempts to obtain more regional autonomy following partition in 1947 and demands by some extremists to form an independent state of Khalistan have fuelled conflict between Sikh and Hindu. For many years Sikhs have played an important role in the security forces and in 1982 the first Sikh president was elected by the Indian parliament.

Sikh Temple Management Committee or **Shiromani Gurdwana Prabandhak Committee** A committee of Sikhs responsible for looking after Sikhdom's holiest shrine, the Golden Temple in Amritsar.

■ Further reading

A.S. Ahmed, *Religion and Politics in Muslim Society: Order and Conflict in Pakistan*, Cambridge University Press, Cambridge, 1973

D.H. Butani, *The Third Sikh War?: Towards or away from Khalistan?*, Promilla, New Delhi, 1986

R.A. Kapur, *Sikh Separatism: The Politics of Faith*, Allen and Unwin, London, 1986

Z. Khalizad, *The Security of Southwest Asia*, Gower, London, 1984

Minority Rights Group, Report No. 65, *The Sikhs*, London, 1986

K. Siddiqui, *Conflict, Crisis and War in Pakistan*, London, 1972

Khushwant Singh, *A History of the Sikhs*, (2 vols.) Oxford University Press, Oxford, 1964–67

4
Sri Lanka

■ Profile

Official name: The Democratic Socialist Republic of Sri Lanka

Area: 65 610km²
- **Population:** 16 600 000
- **Ethnic groups:** Sinhalese 74%, Tamil 18%, Moor 7%, Burgher, Malay and Veddha 1%
- **Religion:** Buddhist 69%, Hindu 15%, Muslim 8%, Christian 8%
- **Languages:** Sinhala (official); Sinhala and Tamil are national languages
- **Life expectancy:** 70 years
- **Infant mortality rate:** 36 per 1000
- **Currency:** Sri Lankan rupee of 100 cents
- **Administrative divisions:** 8 provinces divided into 25 districts
- **Timezone:** GMT +5
- **Capital:** Colombo
- **Chief cities:** Colombo (588 000), Dehiwala–Lavinia (181 000), Moratuwa (137 000), Jaffna (200 000), Kandy (98 000), Kotte (102 000)

■ Introduction

The tragedy of Sri Lanka's ethnic strife has some striking parallels with the troubles of Northern Ireland (*see section 5.6*). Just as Northern Ireland is endowed with great temperate-zone natural beauty and fertility, so Sri Lanka is a tropical paradise capable of supporting all its people in plenty. Just as the physical differences between Protestants and Catholics in Ulster go unnoticed by the outsider, so the Sinhalese and Tamils of Sri Lanka seem to the uninitiated to be divided by little more than shades of brown. However, just as a person in Northern Ireland is defined first and foremost by religious/ethnic affiliation, so in Sri Lanka the Sinhalese/Tamil divide dominates most aspects of political and social life. In both countries conflict between the two communities appears to be endemic, with grievous economic consequences. Another similarity is that both problems are, at least in part, legacies of British colonial rule, although with deeper historical roots in Sri Lanka's case.

Dating from the 6th century BC, the settlement of Sri Lanka by Aryan Sinhalese from northern India is bound up in tradition with their selection by Buddha to perpetuate his holy message. When the first Dravidian Tamil migrants arrived from southern India is unclear; certainly by AD 1000 invading Tamils had established a vibrant Hindu kingdom at the territorial expense of the Buddhist Sinhalese. After taking control in the early 16th century, the Portuguese dealt with the Tamil and Sinhalese kingdoms separately, as did the succeeding Dutch from the mid-17th century. Roman Catholicism made some headway among the Sinhalese under the Portuguese, as had Islam among Tamils much earlier. Established in 1796, British rule led speedily to the island's administrative union as the Crown Colony of Ceylon. It also resulted in the importation of large numbers of Tamils from India to toil in British-owned plantations, to the extent that "Indian" Tamils came to outnumber the long-established "Ceylon" Tamils. Like other minorities under colonial rule, the Tamils were readier than the majority Sinhalese to adapt to British requirements, so that they acquired a disproportionately large share of civil service and professional jobs. Tamils played their part in the independence movement, but, once it was achieved in 1948, they were exposed to unleashed Sinhalese nationalism and Buddhist fervour.

The post-independence government of the United National Party (UNP) endeavoured to reconcile ethnic differences, being itself drawn from the Western-educated elite with a strong Catholic component. But the inability of most Indian Tamils to meet slanted requirements for citizenship and voting rights presaged future troubles. When the left-wing Sri Lanka Freedom Party (SLFP) came to power in 1956, its espousal of grass-roots Sinhalese/Buddhist aspirations, notably the elevation of Sinhala as the country's official language in place of English, provoked the first serious sectarian violence. Recognition of Tamil as a minority language in 1957 eased tensions, but the SLFP government's rejection of Tamil demands for autonomy within a federal structure left the basic problem unresolved. Increasingly concerned about the situation, the Indian government, in 1964, secured a Ceylonese commitment to grant citizenship to some Indian Tamils on the basis that the majority would be repatriated to India. This pact was never properly implemented, however, and served to arouse Sinhalese fears of Indian interference in Sri Lanka's affairs. A crucial factor was Sinhalese concern about the potential threat posed by the 50 million Tamils in the southern Indian state of Tamil Nadu.

By now more attuned to Sinhalese nationalism, the UNP returned to power in 1965, but only on the strength of support from Tamil deputies. When limited concessions to Tamil demands were tabled, Sinhalese mobs took to the streets and the government retreated. The emergence of the extremist Sinhalese Janatha Vimukti Peramuna (JVP) increased tensions, which were ratcheted up several notches by the SLFP's return to power in 1970. Commanding the necessary two-thirds parliamentary majority, the SLFP government introduced a new constitution renaming the country Sri Lanka, giving Buddhism special status and institutionalizing Sinhala as the official language. The Tamil minority was largely ignored. The effect was to weaken Tamil moderates and to strengthen Tamil secessionists seeking an independent state in the northern and eastern provinces where Tamils constitute the majority. Amid a rapid

escalation in violence, efforts by another UNP government from 1977 to meet moderate Tamil demands came too late to halt the polarization. This in turn led to the suspension of the electoral process pending the defeat of what by the early 1980s was a full-scale insurgency headed by the separatist Tamil Tigers, combined with a murderous terrorist campaign by Sinhalese extremists of the JVP.

As the human and economic costs of the conflict mounted, the UNP government turned increasingly to India for a solution. The Delhi government supported recognition of Tamil rights but had no interest in Tamil independence, not least because of the possible consequences in its own Tamil-populated south (where Sri Lanka's Tamil separatists had their bases and received much unofficial Indian support). India therefore used its influence in Moscow to ensure that the Tamil guerrillas did not receive Soviet-bloc backing, while also leaning on the Colombo government to ensure that reports, current in 1982, of Sri Lanka's readiness to enter a military pact with the USA remained mere reports. At the same time, however, Indian peace initiatives in the mid-1980s failed to bridge the gulf between Sri Lanka's firm rejection of any form of federalism and the Tamil extremists' demand for an independent state. By 1987 the civil strife had reached such a pitch that Sri Lanka had little option but to call in Indian troops to impose a settlement based on limited autonomy for the Tamil provinces.

The arrival of the Indian Peace-Keeping Force (IPKF) in Sri Lanka in August 1987 highlighted India's new role as military policeman for the smaller members of the seven-nation South Asian Association for Regional Co-operation (SAARC). A year later Indian troops went into another SAARC member, the Maldives, to put down a rebellion in which Sri Lankan Tamils were involved. In Sri Lanka itself, the IPKF found that its allotted task was easier stated than achieved. The Tamil Tigers and other militant Tamil groups vowed to fight on, while the JVP demanded vengeance for an alleged sell-out of Sinhalese interests. Although a start was made on implementing the Tamil autonomy plan, unabated violence cast a shadow over general elections in February 1989 (the first for 12 years), from which the

UNP emerged narrowly victorious. By then the government had become impatient at India's failure, despite the IPKF's advance into Tamil strongholds, to deliver a political settlement. The turning-point came in April 1989 when the Tamil Tigers decided that half a loaf was better than none and offered to make peace with the government on the basis of the autonomy offer. A ceasefire followed, as the UNP government, under pressure from militant Sinhalese, engaged in acrimonious dispute with India on the date of the IPKF's withdrawal. India prevaricated because it wanted Tamil autonomy to be fully in place, preferably with pro-India Tamils in power. In the event, Indian forces withdrew by the end of March 1990 with neither of these objectives achieved.

The Indian withdrawal left the Tamil Tigers, newly legitimized as a political party, in control of the Tamil provinces of Sri Lanka, but in uneasy coexistence with the Colombo government and under challenge from other Tamil groups opposed to any settlement short of acceptance of an independent Tamil state. The scenario for conflict therefore remained. Militant Sinhalese/Buddhist opinion, of which the government would have to take account if it wished to survive, showed no sign of accepting the political division of Sri Lanka. Tamil militants remained committed to some form of national recognition sooner rather than later.

■ Chronology of events

c. BC 500–600   The Sinhalese migrate from India to the dry, northern region of the island of Sri Lanka where they develop a culture that is based on a highly sophisticated system of irrigation. A capital is established at Anuradhapura.

c. BC 240   Buddhism reaches Sri Lanka and is adopted by the Sinhalese.

c. AD 1000   Successive invasions by Hindu Tamils from southern India force the Sinhalese to abandon their capital at Anuradhapura and move to Polonnaruwa in the south–east.

c.1215   A Tamil kingdom based in Jaffna is established.

c.1300   The Sinhalese are forced to abandon Polonnaruwa and flee into the central highlands and to the south–west corner of the island.

1505   The Portuguese settle on the coastal areas of Sri Lanka and introduce Christianity.

1658   The Portuguese are expelled by the Dutch who introduce their legal system to the island.

1796   The Dutch are forced out by the British who administer the settlements from Madras.

1802   Although the whole island has yet to be conquered, the Tamils in the north cease to be ruled as a separate entity and Sri Lanka, then known as Ceylon, becomes a British Crown Colony.

1815   The Kandyan Kingdom in the central highlands is overcome and the whole island is united under one administration. A plantation economy based on tea, coconuts and rubber is established by the British.

1915   A freedom movement known as the Ceylon National Congress is formed. It includes both Sinhalese and Tamils.

1920–30   Debate over a new constitution raises tension between the Tamils, who want ethnic representation, and the numerically superior Sinhalese, who advocate a political system of majority rule based on "one man, one vote".

1931   The British introduce limited self-government based on individual voting rights rather than ethnic representation. The first elections are boycotted by Tamils in the northern and eastern provinces where they form a majority of the population.

1936   In the absence of political parties the legislative council continues to be dominated by the Sinhalese following the second election.

1944 As World War II draws to a close the British prepare to grant independence to Ceylon. Lord Soulbury begins to draft a constitution for a multi-racial democracy.

1947 The British parliament passes legislation to enable Ceylon to gain full independence and elections are held to choose a government. Although dominated by the Sinhalese, the United National Party (UNP) sweeps into power with broad multi-ethnic support.

1948 Ceylon becomes an independent state within the Commonwealth on 4 February, but over one million Tamils of Indian origin fail to be recognized as citizens.

1951 S.W.R.D. Bandaranaike leaves the ruling United National Party to form the Sinhalese–Buddhist Sri Lanka Freedom Party (SLFP).

1956 Sinhalese nationalism reaches a peak during the celebrations to mark the 2500th anniversary of Buddha's *nirvana*. A report on the state of Buddhism produced by the All-Ceylon Buddhist Congress highlights the suppression of Buddhism by the English-educated Christian élite. In elections, the SLFP gain power under the leadership of Solomon Bandaranaike who immediately replaces English by Sinhalese as the official language of the country. This "Sinhala-Only" enactment causes ethnic unrest between Tamil and Sinhalese communities.

Tensions are somewhat eased by the Bandaranaike–Chelvanayakan agreement under which a Tamil civil disobedience campaign is called off in return for official recognition of Tamil as "the language of a national minority" in Ceylon.

1958 In an attempt to recapture the Sinhalese vote the UNP drops its multi-ethnic stance and adopts a "Sinhala-Only" policy. Tamils and Muslims now fear that they will be treated as second-class citizens under a government dominated by either of the two main political parties and Tamil leaders call for the setting-up of an autonomous Tamil state within a federal union of Ceylon. Violent ethnic clashes break out on the east coast and spread throughout the island. Over 10 000 Tamils are shipped from Colombo to the relative safety of Jaffna in the north and 12 000 move into refugee camps.

1959 Prime Minister S.W.R.D. Bandaranaike is assassinated by a Buddhist monk opposed to any reforms that would accommodate the Tamils.

1960 Sirimavo Bandaranaike succeeds her husband as Prime Minister following an election in which the leaders of the Tamil Federal Party call for the creation of a federal state with an autonomous Tamil homeland called Eelam.

1964 Mrs Bandaranaike reaches an agreement with the Indian Prime Minister over the status of an estimated 1 123 000 Tamils of Indian origin who had been virtually "stateless" since the independence of Ceylon in 1948. Ceylon and India agree to divide the Indian Tamils and give citizenship in a 4:7 proportion, with those not qualifying being "repatriated" to India over a 15–year period. The process is to begin in 1968.

Committed to a non-aligned foreign policy, Mrs Bandaranaike bars all foreign naval vessels from the eastern port of Trincomalee.

1965 The SLFP in alliance with the communist Lanka Sama Samaj Party (LSSP) are defeated in elections which return the UNP under Dudley Senanayke to power in a hung parliament. S.V.Chelvanayakam, leader of the Tamil Federal Party which now holds the balance of power, strikes a deal with Prime Minister Senanayke who agrees to limit Sinhalese colonization and restore the use of the Tamil language in the courts and local authorities of the northern and eastern provinces.

1966 When the government tries to implement the Tamil concessions agreed in the previous year, the Sinhalese stage massive demonstrations and a state of emergency is declared. The threat of large-scale civil unrest led by the radical left-wing Sinhalese youth movement, the Janatha Vimukti Peramuna (JVP), forces the government to back away from honouring the Chelvanayakam–Senanayke pact.

1968   The 1964 agreement with India on citizenship for the Tamils of Indian origin is put into effect when the two countries invite applications for citizenship. Over 700 000 Indian Tamils decide to opt for Ceylonese citizenship but the Ceyon government will only agree to accept 225 000 of them. The remainder continue to be regarded as aliens. The situation is complicated by the return to Ceylon of many of those who opted for Indian citizenship. Most of these people find themselves lodged in refugee camps in the eastern provinces.

1970   In May Sirimavo Bandaranaike returns to power at the head of a United Front coalition of left–wing parties that include the Communist Party of Ceylon and the LSSP. With a two–thirds majority in Parliament, the government is able to begin drafting a new constitution.

The Tamils demand that the Tamil language be recognized as an official language and oppose the move towards making Buddhism the sole state religion.

1971   The ultra-left JVP youth movement is banned after an abortive attempt to overthrow the government in April.

1972   Despite opposition from the UNP and the Tamil political parties a new constitution is approved and Ceylon is declared a republic to be known as Sri Lanka. Demands for Tamil autonomy are ignored and Sinhalese is institutionalized as the official language. Although Buddhism is not declared a state religion it is given special status under the new constitution. Opposed to these blatant expressions of Sinhalese–Buddhist nationalism, the Tamil political parties unite to form the Tamil United Front. Student radicals dissatisfied with the non-violent campaign of the TUF found the militant Liberation Tigers of Tamil Eelam (LTTE) to fight for an independent Tamil state.

1973   The formation of a unitary state in the previous year leads to the setting up of a Tamil Action Committee which drafts a constitution for a separate Tamil state, adopts a new flag and plans to boycott all official celebrations on Republic Day.

1974   Disturbances take place in the northern town of Jaffna during the World Congress of Tamil Scholars and a campaign of civil disobedience is only called off when the government releases several young Tamil leaders in December.

1975   Ethnic unrest among the Tamils results in the death of the Mayor of Jaffna. New emergency regulations are introduced making it illegal to question the constitution.

1976   The Tamil United Front changes its name to the Tamil United Liberation Front (TULF) and when its leaders make further separatist demands they are arrested.

1977   Mrs Bandaranaike's United Front is heavily defeated in elections by the United National Party under the leadership of the 72-year-old Junius V. Jayawardene. Soon after taking office he lifts the ban on the use of Trincomalee harbour by foreign vessels imposed by Mrs Bandaranaike in 1964.

1978   The constitution is amended in order to create a strong executive presidency and on 4 February Prime Minister Jayawardene is elected the country's first President. On 7 September the new constitution comes into effect and the country's official name changes to the Democratic Socialist Republic of Sri Lanka. Sinhalese is retained as the official language but Tamil is recognized as a national tongue.

1979   Civil unrest in the northern provinces brings the police and Tamils into direct conflict with each other and in July a state of emergency is declared in Jaffna.   In the same month an *Act to Control Terrorism* is passed by Parliament. Tamil MPs operating a political boycott only return to Parliament when a presidential committee is set up in August to look at the decentralization of power.

1980   Parliament strips Mrs Bandaranaike of all her civic rights for a period of seven years owing to her abuse of power while in office.

1981   President Jayawardene seeks to accommodate Tamil demands by introducing an all-island system of district development councils enjoying considerable autonomy. This fails to satisfy militant Tamils who begin to set up their headquarters in Madras, capital of the Indian state of Tamil Nadu.

Civil unrest spreads throughout Sri Lanka and when a four-month state of emergency is declared TULF politicians withdraw from Parliament once again in protest.

1982   In the face of growing ethnic unrest the government sets up a joint military–police anti-terrorism unit and declares a further state of emergency following riots between Sinhalese and Muslims. President Jayawardene is re-elected through a referendum rather than by an election.

1983   Intercommunal violence escalates rapidly as separatist movements take up arms against the Sinhalese–dominated Sri Lankan government. The funerals of 13 Sinhalese soldiers killed by Tamils in July leads to widespread rioting in Colombo and the retaliatory murder of 54 Tamil inmates of Welikada jail. As a result of the unrest that follows, an estimated 125 000 Tamils flee to India. The government closes the international airport, imposes a curfew in Colombo and orders press censorship.

In August the growing tension between Sri Lanka and India reaches a climax when the state government of Tamil Nadu in India organizes a protest strike in support of the Tamils of Sri Lanka. Although Mrs Gandhi meets President Jayawardene she is unwilling to help resolve the situation and denies any knowledge of Tamil separatists being trained and supplied in Tamil Nadu. Jayawardene's attempts to set up "harmony talks" fail when the TULF leaders refuse to co-operate.

1984   In January President Jayawardene convenes an "All-Party Conference" to work out a solution to the communal strife, but after a year of debate talks break down.

In a year that sees the February bombing of Gurunagam military camp, the death of 50 people during riots in Jaffna and the destruction of a large part of the business quarter of Mannar, a total of 2500 are killed in ethnic conflict.

1985   Tension between Sri Lanka and India is further heightened in January when Sri Lankan naval vessels open fire on Indian fishing boats suspected of ferrying aid to Tamil insurgents. India retaliates by seizing a Sri Lankan boat.

On 5 February President Jayawardene announces a plan to settle 200 000 Sinhalese in the northern and eastern Tamil provinces.

Intercommunal violence is further complicated by Tamil–Muslim riots in the eastern provinces and in the town of Mannar. Four Tamil groups join forces in April to form the Eelam National Liberation Front but by the end of the year a further 50 000 Tamils have fled to southern India. When over 100 people are killed in the holy city of Anuradhpura, both the government and Tamil leaders agree to a ceasefire and direct negotiations. The ceasefire takes effect in June and all sides meet for the first time in Thimpu, capital of Bhutan. Talks finally break down when Sri Lankan armed forces fail to prevent the death of 200 Tamils in the northern district of Vavuniya on 16 August. When the militant Tamils show no sign of accommodation, the TULF leaders attempt to revive negotiations by presenting their own proposals for a federal state. The Sinhalese-dominated government, however, will not agree to federalism or even the merging of the two Tamil provinces.

1986   The year opens with a government offensive against Tamil militants in the northern and eastern provinces where one-kilometre-radius security zones are designated round each of the sixty-odd Sri Lankan military camps. While Tamil guerrillas try to contain the government forces within these camps, the military responds by destroying villages and by launching aerial attacks on civilian targets in Jaffna city.

President Jayawardene blames India for the conflict and urges Rajiv Gandhi to intervene in the search for a solution. The Indian Prime Minister presses the TULF and the militant Tamil groups to resume negotiations with the Colombo government, but when talks eventually take place militant leaders refuse to accept Jayawardene's proposals which include the setting-up of provincial councils. While attempts to find a political solution fail yet again Sri Lankan troops are unable to make any headway in the face of stiff opposition from Tamil guerrillas.

By now the LTTE Tamil guerrillas virtually control the five districts of the northern province. Attempts to extend control over the districts of the eastern province are hindered by conflict with the EPRLF Tamil guerrillas during November–December.

Mrs Bandaranaike, whose rights are restored, returns to Parliament.

In November, the Sri Lankan Parliament passes an act granting citizenship to 233 000 stateless Indian Tamils.

A confidential World Bank Report points out the economic cost to Sri Lanka of escalating defence spending which has risen from 3.5 per cent of the total budget in 1983 to 15 per cent in 1986. Within the space of a year the budget deficit rises a further eight billion rupees to a record 29.8 billion rupees.

1987   When LTTE Tamil guerrillas decide to take over the administration of the Jaffna peninsula on I January, the government imposes an economic blockade of the area and launches a military offensive. After heavy fighting the Sri Lankan armed forces regain control of four of the five districts of the northern province, pushing the guerrillas back into the Jaffna peninsula. Velupillai Prabhakaran returns from three years in India to reassert his control over the LTTE.

The Sri Lankan forces refrain from launching a final assault on Jaffna and when India resumes its mediation efforts in March a unilateral ceasefire is announced by the government to coincide with Sinhalese and Tamil festivals in April. The massacre of 127 Sinhalese on Good Friday and the death of 150 people following a car bomb explosion in Colombo brings the ceasefire to an abrupt end. On 25 May Sri Lankan forces renew their offensive against Jaffna ("Operation Liberation"), but fearing that a virtual civilian genocide would bring India into the conflict, they do not press home their attack.

In July Jayawardene and Gandhi hastily put together an India–Sri Lanka agreement that provides for a limited devolution of power to the Tamil provinces. The deal is rejected by the LTTE leaders but India agrees to ensure Tamil consensus in favour of it and to overcome any military opposition. In return, India's strategic interests are to be secured by the reimposition of the bar on foreign naval vessels using Tricomalee harbour. Despite strong Sinhalese opposition led by the JVP movement and Buddhist clerics, the agreement is signed on 29 July while an uneasy curfew reigns over Colombo.

In August an Indian Peace-Keeping Force (IPKF) arrives in northern Sri Lanka. While it succeeds in disengaging Sri Lankan and Tamil forces it is unable to disarm militant Tamil groups or prevent clashes between LTTE and EPRLF units in the eastern province. The LTTE is offered seven places in the twelve-member Interim Administrative Council proposed for the unified Tamil province, but when ethnic violence between Sinhalese and Tamils breaks out again the civil war resumes with increased ferocity. The IPKF contingent is increased by 15 000 and as the year draws to a close it is clear that Indian troops are now fighting Sri Lanka's war.

1988   Elections to new provincial councils begin in April amidst a background of political boycotts and continued violence. In May the IPKF launches an offensive codenamed "Operation Checkmate" in an attempt to restore order in the northern and eastern provinces where elections are unable to take place. India increases the strength of the IPKE to 70 000 and successfully contains Tamil militancy which briefly extends as far as the Maldives where an attempted coup is quickly put down.

In September the northern and eastern Tamil provinces are temporarily merged into a single North–Eastern Province and two months later the EPRLF leader, Annamalai Varatharaja Perumal, is appointed Chief Minister of the new administration.

In Presidential elections, held on 19 December,

the UNP Prime Minister Premadasa is returned as the country's new President.

1989 In elections to Sri Lanka's Parliament, held in an atmosphere of JVP and LTTE terrorism, the UNP is returned with a reduced majority. A month later the IPKF resumes its offensive against the LTTE.

In April the LTTE, in a dramatic turn-around, decides to negotiate with the Colombo government in an attempt to bring an end a conflict that has cost the lives of 12 000 people in six years. As talks proceed President Premadasa calls on India to withdraw its peace-keeping force by the end of July. Gandhi refuses to withdraw Indian troops until a Tamil regional authority is in place.

In September the LTTE signs a ceasefire agreement with India and Rajiv Gandhi agrees to make "all efforts" to pull out the remaining 50 000 Indian troops from Sri Lanka. With the prospect of an IPKF withdrawal leading to an LTTE take-over in the Tamil provinces, the moderate Tamil ENDLF begins to establish a Tamil National Army (TNA).

Late in the year the extremist JVP movement suffers a setback when security forces capture and kill its top leaders.

1990 After a 2-year operation in Sri Lanka that has cost the lives of 6000 civilians, 1555 Indian soldiers and 800 Tamil Tigers, Indian troops are withdrawn through the port of Trincomalee. Fearing they will be liquidated, thousands of EPRLF supporters flee to India, leaving the North–Eastern Province in the hands of the LTTE. All hopes of peace disappear as fighting between Tamil Tigers and Sinhalese government troops escalates.

■ Who's who

Bandaranaike, Solomon W.D. The Oxford-educated son of an Anglican Christian, who quit the United National Party in 1951 to become a Buddhist and to form the Sri Lanka Freedom Party. In 1956 his party swept to power, but three years later he was assassinated by a Buddhist monk whose action reflected Sinhalese disenchantment with his concessions to the Tamil community.

Bandaranaike, Sirimavo The wife of SLFP founder and leader S.W.D. Bandaranaike. Following the assassination of her husband in 1959 she succeeded to the leadership of the SLFP and became the world's first female Prime Minister at the head of an SLFP–LSSP coalition which lasted from 1960 until 1965. She returned to power at the head of the United Front in 1970 but was defeated seven years later in 1977 by J.R. Jayawardene's United National Party. In 1980 a presidential commission deprived her of her civic rights on the basis of alleged abuses of privilege that occurred during her years in office.

Chelvanayakam, S.J.V. Leading Sri Lankan politician who broke away from the moderate Tamil Congress in 1949 to form his own Federal Party. In the hope of securing Tamil parity with the majority Sinhalese, Chelvanayakam entered into two successive pacts with the ruling SLFP and UNP leaders in 1957 and 1960.

Dharmapala, Anagarkia An early 20th century Buddhist teacher who revived ancient Buddhist myths and legends in an attempt to establish the fact that the Sinhalese were the original inhabitants of Sri Lanka.

Elara or **Eelala** According to Tamil legend, the last Tamil king of Anuradhapura which became the seat of a Sinhala dynasty in 101 BC.

Jayawardene, Junius R. Elected leader of the United National party in 1973, Jayawardene came to power as Prime Minister after Mrs Bandaranaike's defeat in the 1977 election. Seeking to establish a strong executive presidency, he amended the constitution in

1978 and again in 1982 to allow himself a period of nearly eleven years in office as President of Sri Lanka.

Kalkat, A.S.   Military commander of the Indian Peace–Keeping Force   sent to Sri Lanka to disarm Tamil militants and help maintain order within the Tamil community between 1987 and 1990.

Krishna Kumar, Sadasivam (alias **Kittu**)   Chief LTTE representative in Madras, responsible for engaging in talks with the Indian government during 1987–88. Arrested in September 1988, he was returned to Sri Lanka a month later after threatening to fast to death.

Maheswaran, Uma   A former Secretary–General of the LTTE who broke away in 1982 to form the PLOTE which became the second largest of the Tamil guerrilla groups.

Perumal, Annamalai Varatharaja   Leader of the Eelam People's Revolutionary Liberation Front EPLF, appointed Chief Minister of the new provincial administration of the Tamil North-Eastern Province on 28 November 1988.

Prabakharan, Vellupillai   Leader of the militant Liberation Tigers of Tamil Eelam (LTTE) which he founded at the age of 18 in 1972. Based in Madras for much of the 1980s, he returned to the Jaffna peninsula in January 1987.

Premadasa, Ranasinghe   Prime Minister of Sri Lanka during the presidency of Junius Jayawardene, Premadasa was himself elected to the post of President in December 1988. A strong opponent of the India–Sri Lanka Agreement of 1987, he succeeded in negotiating the withdrawal of Indian troops from Sri Lanka within a year of taking over the presidency.

Ramachandran, M.G.   Chief Minister of the Indian State of Tamil Nadu whose sympathy for the Tamil cause in Sri Lanka resulted in widespread support for militant Tamil groups. In December 1987, shortly after his attempt to organize a ceasefire in Sri Lanka was vetoed by Rajiv Gandhi, he died in Madras.

Senanayke, Don Stephen   A Cambridge-educated politician who founded the right-of-centre United National Party (UN) in 1946. In 1947 he was elected Ceylon's first post-independence Prime Minister.

Senivaratne, Lieut.-General Nalin   First Sri Lankan Army Commander of the new Tamil North-Eastern Province appointed on 30 November 1988.

Silva, Dr Colvin R. de   Prominent academic and political theoritician of the Trotskyite Lanka Sama Samaj Party (LSSP) who died in February 1989 at the age of 82. A student at the London School of Economics, he returned to Sri Lanka in 1935 to take part in the formation of his country's first socialist party. In 1970 de Silva was Minister of Plantation Industries and Constitutional Affairs in Mrs Bandaranaike's coalition government. He was also a leading author of the 1972 constitution that established Sri Lanka as a republic.

Thero, Buddharakkita   A Buddhist monk responsible for encouraging a Buddhist revival amongst the Sinhalese in the early 1950s. In 1951 he founded the Sri Lankan Freedom Party along with S.W.D. Bandaranaike. Although he did not hold a position in the SLFP government when it came to power, he remained a powerful political influence. In 1959 Thero was among those charged in connection with Bandaranaike's assassination.

Thero, Somarama   A Buddhist monk responsible for the shooting of Prime Minister S.W.D. Bandaranaike at his residence in Colombo in 1959.

Vijaya   Mythological grandson of a union between a north Indian king and a lioness, whose banishment for misconduct led to the founding of the Sinhala race which is alleged to have arrived in Sri Lanka about 500 BC. The Sinhalese claim that their name is derived from the legend of the lioness. (*Sinha* in Sanskrit means a lion.)

Wijesekera, Mahinda   Leading member of the radical Janatha Vimukti Peramuna (JVP) movement.

Wijeveera, Rohana   Leader of the ultra-left
Janatha Vimukti Peramuna (JVP) Sinhala
youth group.

■ Key places

Adam's Bridge   A chain of small islets
stretching a distance of nearly 50km from
Mannar on the north-west coast of Sri Lanka
towards SE India. The legendary Rama, hero
of the *Ramayana*, is supposed to have built the
island causeway to allow his army a passage
from India to Sri Lanka in order to rescue his
wife Sita.

Adam's Peak   A sacred mountain rising
to a height of 2243m in Ratnapura district,
south–east of Colombo. A hollow in the shape of
a footprint has turned the summit into a site of
pilgrimage for Hindus, Buddhists, Muslims and
Christian who all hold different beliefs as to its
origin.

Anuradhapura   Ancient capital of the
Sinhalese kings of Sri Lanka from its foundation
in the 5th centuryBC until abandoned in the 11th
century AD. Now the capital of a district of the
same name and of the North Central Province
of Sri Lanka, situated just over 200km north of
Colombo; population (1981) 36 000. The city is
sacred to Buddhists as the site of the conversion
to Buddhism of the Sinhalese ruler Mahinda in
the 3rd century BC.

Ceylon   Under British rule Sri Lanka was
known as Ceylon, the corruption of a native
word that had taken the form Ceilao under the
Portuguese and Ceylan under the Dutch. In
1972 the island's name was officially changed
to Sri Lanka, a return to the original Sinhalese
name, Lanka, to which was added the word Sri,
which means "auspicious" or "resplendent".

Colombo   The largest city and capital
of Sri Lanka, situated on the west coast of
the island to the south of the River Kelani;
population (1981) 588 000. Greater Colombo
has a population of about one million. Settled
by the Portuguese in 1517, Colombo became

the country's principal seaport in 1875.
Government buildings have been located in the
outer suburb of Jayawardenapura since 1983.

Eelam   The homeland of the Tamils of Sri
Lanka, Eelam derives its name from Elara, the
last Tamil king of Anuradhapura, who was
defeated by the Sinhalese prince Dutthagamani
in 101BC. Although Tamil history refers to the
whole of Sri Lanka as Eelam, the demand for
secession first publicly voiced by the TULF
in 1976, only envisaged the breakaway of the
northern and eastern provinces to form a
separate Tamil state to be called Eelam.

Elephant Pass   A narrow strip of land linking
the Jaffna peninsula with the rest of the
mainland of northern Sri Lanka.

Galoya   A predominantly Sinhalese
settlement established after the completion of
a government–sponsored irrigation scheme in
the Tamil district of Ampurai, SE Sri Lanka.

Jaffna   A district at the northern tip of Sri
Lanka forming a peninsula linked to the rest of
the island by a narrow strip of land known as
Elephant Pass; population 830 000. The district
capital is Jaffna which lies at the western end
of the Jaffna lagoon; population 200 000. Noted
for its Dutch colonial fort and its many Hindu
temples, Jaffna city is a stronghold of Tamil
secessionist guerrillas and was a virtual no–go
area for Sri Lankan forces for a time during the
mid-1980s.

Kandy   Known as "the city of the five hills",
the Buddhist holy city of Kandy is situated
116km south–west of Colombo in the mountains
of Sri Lanka's Central Province; population
(1981) 98 000. Every year in August there is
a ten-day festival during which a tooth of the
Buddha is paraded through the streets in a

torchlight procession of elephants. In 1941 Kandy became the wartime headquarters of the South–East Asia Command under Lord Louis Mountbatten. UNP leader J.R. Jayawardene led a Buddhist march to Kandy in 1957 to invoke the blessing of the gods for his campaign against the so-called Bandaranaike–Chelvanayakam agreement that offered concessions to the Tamil community.

Kantale   A Sinhalese settlement established in the Tamil district of Trincomalee following the completion of a government–sponsored irrigation scheme in the 1980s. Tamils regard the Sinhalese occupation of this territory as an invasion of their homeland.

Mahaweli   The principal river of Sri Lanka. Rising in the mountains of the Central Province, it flows 330km northwards to meet the Bay of Bengal south of Trincomalee. The giant Mahaweli irrigation scheme's Victoria Dam was completed in 1984 and ceremonially opened a year later by British Prime Minister Margaret Thatcher.

Mannar   The capital of Mannar district in the former Northern Province, situated on an island off the north-west coast of Sri Lanka; population (1981) 14 000. In 1984 a large part of the business sector of the town was destroyed during a military operation against Tamil separatists.

Padaviya   A controversial Sinhalese settlement laid down by the government on irrigated land at the northern tip of Anuradhapura district, on the frontier with the predominantly Tamil district of Trincomalee.

Palaly   A military camp and airbase at the far north of the Jaffna peninsula.

Palk Strait   A 64km–wide channel to the north of Adam's Bridge, separating NE Sri Lanka from S India. The Sri Lankan navy patrols the Palk Strait in an attempt to stem the supply of arms from southern India to Tamil insurgents on the Jaffna peninsula.

Polonnaruwa   The capital of Polonnaruwa district in the North Central Province of Sri Lanka, situated on the shore of Lake Parakrama Samudra; population (1981) 11 600. When the Sinhalese abandoned Anuradhapura during the 11th century in the face of Tamil expansion, they moved their capital southwards to Polonnaruwa.

Serendib or **Serendip**   The name given to the island of Sri Lanka by early Muslim traders. In 1754 Horace Walpole coined the word ''serendipity'' to describe the gift of making fortunate discoveries by accident, as in the traditional Sri Lankan fairy-tale *The Three Princes of Serendip*.

Tamil Nadu   A state in southern India with a predominantly Tamil population; area 130 358km^2; population (1981) 48 400 000. In 1981 Tamil Nadu began to provide a sanctuary for militant Tamil groups whose leaders established their headquarters in the state capital, Madras.

Thimphu   Capital city of the Himalayan kingdom of Bhutan. The first talks between representatives of the Sri Lankan government and Tamil secessionist groups were held here in July–August 1985.

Trincomalee   Described by Lord Nelson in 1770 as the ''finest harbour in the world'', Trincomalee is the principal seaport of Sri Lanka and the administrative centre of the new North–Eastern Province; population (1981) 44 300. Situated on the E coast, it lies 257km north-east of Colombo near the mouth of the Mahaweli River. In World War II it became the chief British naval base in South East Asia after the fall of Singapore. The strategic importance of the harbour was later recognized by Mrs Bandaranaike who continued her late husband's policy of non-alignment by banning its use by foreign naval vessels. In 1977 the ban was lifted by President Jayawardene, but in 1987 its closure to naval vessels of a third party was reimposed as a precondition for India's participation in the India–Sri Lanka Agreement.

■ Key words

Burghers   Descendants of the Dutch settlers who ousted the Portuguese from Ceylon in 1640 and who ruled until the British arrived in 1795. Following the rise of Sinhalese nationalism in the 1950s over 40 000 Burghers emigrated to Australia.

Ceylon Citizenship Act   An Act passed in 1948 by the UNP government of newly-independent Ceylon granting citizenship to those who could prove that they had three generations of paternal ancestry on the island. The Act effectively disenfranchised the Indian Tamils who were largely unable to establish their claims to citizenship.

Ceylon Moors   Numbering just over one million, the Moors are descendents of Arabs who settled on the island from around the 8th century.

Ceylon Tamils   About two-thirds of the Tamils of Sri Lanka are "Ceylon Tamils" who have lived on the island for many generations. Mostly to be found in the north and north–east, they have full citizenship and voting rights. According to the 1981 census there were 1 872 000 Ceylon Tamils.

Ceylon Workers' Congress   An organization representing the Indian Tamils brought to Sri Lanka in the 19th century to work on estate plantations.

Deshapremi Janatha Viyaparaya (DJV)   The militant wing of the extremist JVP movement.

Eelam National Democratic Liberation Front (ENDLF)   An alliance between the EPRLF and PLOTE moderate Tamil secessionist groups which joined forces in May 1987 with a view to establishing a Tamil National Army that might prevent extremist Tamils taking over following the departure of the IPKF. When Indian troops did eventually leave Sri Lanka in 1990, a large number of ENDLF members fled to India, fearing annihilation at the hands of the Tamil Tigers.

Eelam National Liberation Front (ENLF)   An umbrella organization formed by four Tamil groups (LTTE, EROS, EPRLF and TELO) in 1985.

Eelam People's Revolutionary Liberation Front (EPRLF)   A moderate left-wing Tamil group committed to regional autonomy but opposed to the more militant LTTE. The EPRLF emerged as the result of a split that took place in the ranks of EROS in 1981. In 1987 it united with PLOTE to form the ENDLF.

Eelam Revolutionary Organization of Students (EROS)   A Marxist–Leninist student Tamil group founded by E. Ratnasabapathy in London in 1975. Initially trained by Yasser Arafat's Palestine Liberation Organization, it concentrated its militant activities in the Eastern Province of Sri Lanka. In 1988 it formed the EDF political party in order to take part in elections to the Sri Lankan Parliament.

Eelam Shipping Service   A nickname for the boats that travel back and forwards across the Palk Strait, linking Tamil guerrillas on the Jaffna peninsula with their headquarters in Tamil Nadu.

Eelavar Democratic Front (EDF)   A political party formed by the militant Tamil EROS group in December 1988. Participating in the first elections to be held in the new North Eastern Province in February 1989, EDF–sponsored MPs became the third largest grouping in the Sri Lankan Parliament.

Federal Party   A Tamil political party formed in 1949 when S.J.V. Chelvanayakam decided to break away from the moderate Tamil Congress. The party formed a pact with the UNP when it returned to power in 1965, but few of the Tamil concessions agreed between Chelvanayakam and Senanayke were honoured. In 1972 the Federal Party joined with other political groups to form the Tamil United Front (TUF).

India Doctrine   Sometimes called India's Monroe Doctrine, the India Doctrine was developed by the Indian government as a diplomatic and strategic initiative designed to keep foreign powers out of South East Asia.

Indian Peace–Keeping Force (IPKF) An Indian military peace–keeping mission sent to Sri Lanka in August 1987 at the request of President Jayawardene after the signing of the India–Sri Lanka Agreement. The purpose of the Indian presence was to disarm Tamil insurgency groups and ensure Tamil support for the setting-up of a new North–Eastern Province. After 2 years the IPKF was finally withdrawn from Sri Lanka in March 1990. In that period 1555 Indian soldiers were killed and 2987 wounded in battles with the Tamil Tigers.

India–Sri Lanka Agreement to Establish Peace and Normalcy in Sri Lanka An agreement signed by President Jayawardene of Sri Lanka and Prime Minister Rajiv Gandhi of India on 29 July 1988 in Colombo. Although rejected by the main Tamil guerrilla groups, the agreement provided for the disengagement of Sri Lankan forces and Tamil insurgents as a prelude to the creation of a new Tamil province in NE Sri Lanka. In return for India's participation in maintaining the peace, disarming Tamil rebels and ensuring Tamil support for the deal, Sri Lanka agreed to abide by the Indian Doctrine and reimpose the ban on foreign naval vessels using the port of Trincomalee.

Indian Tamils Nearly one-third of the Tamils of Sri Lanka are "Indian Tamils" whose forebears were brought from India in the late 19th century to work on the tea and rubber plantations of central Ceylon. A large number of Indian Tamils became "stateless" in 1948 when they were denied citizenship in both Sri Lanka and India. Agreements in 1964 and 1986 provided for the repatriation of some to India and the granting of Sri Lankan citizenship to others. The total number of Indian Tamils fell from 1.2 million in 1971 to 825 000 in 1981 as a result of emigration.

Janata Vimukti Peramuna (JVP) or People's Liberation Front A militant left–wing Sinhalese movement founded in 1965 by a group of disaffected radical youth who sought a "Maoist" solution to the country's economic and political problems. In 1971 the JVP was banned after it attempted to

overthrow the United Front government of Mrs. Bandaranaike. In 1983 the movement was again made illegal as a result of its growing terrorist activities. Following the India–Sri Lanka Agreement of 1987, which it denounced as a Sinhalese sell-out, the JVP exploited fears that India might attempt to annexe the island. Since then it has waged a terrorist campaign which has taken on the guise of a crusade for Sinhalese national liberation. Between 1987 and 1990 JVP terrorism led to the deaths of some 17 000 people in southern Sri Lanka, but in 1989 the movement suffered a severe set back when most of its top leaders were killed by security forces in an operation that cost over 6000 lives.

Lanka Sama Samaja Party (LSSP) Founded in the mid-1930s, the Trotskyite LSSP was the country's first socialist political party. In 1970 it formed an alliance with the SLFP in a coalition government led by Mrs Bandaranaike.

Liberation Tigers of Tamil Eelam (LTTE) The largest of the militant secessionist Tamil groups. Commonly referred to as the Tamil Tigers, it has been fighting to establish a separate state for the Tamil minority of Sri Lanka since 1972 when a change in the constitution led a younger generation to abandon the non-violent campaign for regional autonomy. With the departure of the IPKF in 1990 the LTTE remained in virtual control of the North–Eastern Province.

Mahajana Eksath Peramuna A coalition of the SLFP and the Viplavakari Lanka Samaj Party which came to power under Solomon Bandaranaike in 1956.

nirvana The Buddhist belief in a final release from the cycle of reincarnation which is attained by the extinction of all earthly desires. Sri Lankan Buddhists believe that the arrival of the Sinhalese race from northern India on the island of Sri Lanka coincided with the Gautama Buddha's *nirvana*, an event that they claim predates the arrival of the Dravidian settlers of southern Indian whose descendants are the Tamils.

Operation Checkmate The codename for a major offensive against Tamil militants carried out in May 1988 by the Indian Peace–Keeping Force.

Operation Liberation   The codename given to a major offensive launched by Sri Lankan armed forces against Tamil secessionist guerrillas in the Jaffna peninsula following the breakdown of a ceasefire in April 1987.

Operation Pawan   A codename for the Indian Army offensive against the city of Jaffna in October 1987.

People's Liberation Organization of Tamil Eelam (PLOTE)   A moderate Tamil secessionist group which broke away from the Tamil Tigers in 1982, declaring its opposition to hit-and-run guerrilla tactics that risk the lives of civilians. In May 1987 PLOTE joined with the EPRLF to form the Eelam National Democratic Liberation Front (ENDLF).

Proteg (Protection of Tamils of Eelam from Genocide)   A civil rights group based in Madras, India. The group includes lawyers, economists and other professionals committed to the establishment of a separate Tamil state.

Research and Intelligence Wing (RAW)   India's foreign intelligence agency, allegedly responsible for training members of at least five Sri Lankan Tamil separatist groups at the Indian army's Dehra Dun base in the foothills of the Himalayas.

Sinhala or **Sinhalese**   The language of the Buddhist Sinhalese ("People of the Lion") spoken by over 70 per cent of the total population of the island. The controversial "Sinhala Only" policy which brought Bandaranaike's SLFP to power in 1956 made Sinhala the sole official language of Sri Lanka.

Sri Lanka Freedom Party (SLFP)   A left-of-centre political party founded in 1951 by Solomon Bandaranaike. Adopting a Sinhalese–Buddhist nationalist stance, the SLFP first came to power in 1956 advocating a "Sinhala Only" policy.

swabasha ("own language")   A term initially applied to the replacement of English by the predominant Sinhala tongue after independence in 1948. When English was phased out as an official language in the 1950s,

parity between the Sinhala and Tamil languages became a strong political issue.

Tamil Congress   An organization founded in 1944 to represent the Ceylon Tamils. In 1949 a breakaway section led by S.J.V. Chelvanayakam formed the Federal Party.

Tamil National Army (TNA)   A militia force set up by the Eelam National Democratic Liberation and armed by Indian troops prior to the departure of the IPKF in 1990. Fearing that they would be liquidated by the Tamil Tigers, many of the TNA conscripts subsequently fled to India.

Tamil New Tigers   A militant Tamil group founded in 1972 by the 18-year-old Velupillai Prabhakaran who galvanized the radical youth of the Northern Province in support of the Tamil cause. Opposed to the moderate, non-violent stance of the TUF the organization changed its name four years later to the Liberation Tigers of Tamil Eelam (LTTE), commonly referred to as the Tamil Tigers.

Tamil United Front (TUF)   An alliance of moderate Tamil groups that took place in 1972 when the Federal Party, Tamil Congress and Ceylon Workers' Congress joined forces to form a united Tamil political front in the Sri Lankan Parliament. In May 1976 the party changed its name to the Tamil United Liberation Front (TULF) and publicly advocated the creation of a separate Tamil state of Eelam.

United Front   A left-of-centre political alliance of the SLFP, the LSSP and the Communist Party which united to form a coalition government under the leadership of Mrs Bandaranaike (1970–77).

United National Party (UNP) A right-of-centre political party founded in 1946 by Don Stephen Senanayke who became Ceylon's first Prime Minister following the departure of the British in 1948.

Veddhas   An aboriginal group representing the remnants of an early hunting and fishing culture on Sri Lanka. Living in the tropical rain forest, only about 100 have survived to the present day.

■ Further reading

K.M. de Silva, *A History of Sri Lanka*, Oxford University Press, New Delhi, 1981

Shantha K. Hennayake and James S. Duncan, A Disputed Homeland: Sri Lanka's civil war, *Focus*, 37:1, 1987, pp. 21–27

Lucy M. Jacob, Constitutional Development and the Tamil Minority in Sri Lanka, *South Asian Studies*, 13:2, 1979, pp.66–79

C. Manogaran, *Ethnic Conflict and Reconciliation in Sri Lanka*, University of Hawaii Press, Hawaii, 1987

Minority Rights Group, Report No. 25, *The Tamils of Sri Lanka*, London, 1988

Satchi Ponnambalam, *Sri Lanka: National Conflict and the Tamil Liberation Struggle*, Tamil Information Centre, Thornton Heath, 1983

Mohan Ram, *Sri Lanka: The Fractured Island*, Penguin, London, 1989

S.J. Tambiah, *Sri Lanka: Ethnic Fratricide and the Dismantling of Democracy*, University of Chicago Press, Chicago, 1986

5
Cambodia

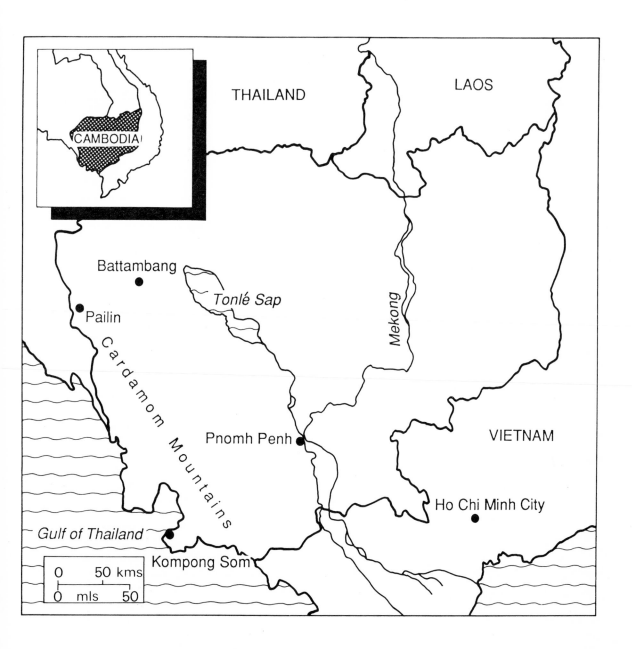

■ Profile

Official name: People's Republic of Kampuchea

- **Area:** 181 040km²
- **Population:** 8 350 000 (1976); 6 250 000 (1986)
- **Ethnic groups:** Khmer 93%, Vietnamese 4%, Chinese 3%
- **Official language:** Khmer
- **Religion:** Therevada Buddhism 95%
- **Life expectancy:** 43 years
- **Infant mortality rate:** 263 per 1000 (1975–80); 157 per 1000 (1982)
- **Currency:** new riel of 100 sen (since 1985)
- **Administrative divisions:** 18 provinces (*khet*)
- **Timezone:** GMT +7
- **Capital:** Phnom Penh
- **Chief cities:** Kompong Cham, Battambang, Phnom Penh

■ Introduction

The international complexities of the conflict in Cambodia are highlighted by the fact that most UN members do not recognize its government. Instead, they continue to recognize a government-in-exile whose strongest component, the Khmers Rouges, were deposed from power in 1979 in favour of the present regime. Vietnamese troops brought about that coup and maintained the new regime thereafter, with backing from the Soviet Union. The alternative government, usually headed by Prince Norodom Sihanouk, has the support of China, traditional foe of Vietnam, and most Western countries, although in the latter case with enduring distaste for the Khmers Rouges' bloody excesses when they were in power. One irony is that the alternative governments are both communist-dominated, whereas on the few occasions that the Cambodian people have been consulted they have voted heavily against communism.

Descended from the Indian-founded state of Funan and its 6th-century successor, Chenla, the Khmer kingdom reached its zenith in the 11th-century Angkor Empire, which extended over much of Indo-China. In decline from the 13th century, Buddhist Cambodia later became sandwiched between the rising power of Thailand to the north-west and the Vietnamese to the east. By the early 19th century both neighbours claimed suzerainty over Cambodia, whose absolute ruler accepted French protection in 1863. This led inevitably to full colonial rule as part of the French Indo-China Union (with Vietnam and Laos), a status which the Cambodian elite embraced with enthusiasm. On the defeat of France in Europe in 1940, the Japanese extracted military and economic concessions from the French authorities but left the colonial administration in place until the last months of World War II. Then the Japanese took over and offered subordinate independence to the three Indo-China colonies, Cambodia's being declared by the youthful King Sihanouk in March 1945. Japan's surrender in August 1945 led to the reinstatement of French rule, but the wartime spectacle of once-mighty Europeans kow-towing to oriental Japanese had left its impression on Indo-Chinese nationalists aspiring to independence.

Granted autonomy within the French Union in 1946, Cambodia entered an unsettled period in which a weak government faced a pro-independence insurgency by Cambodian communists aligned with the Viet Minh forces fighting the French in Vietnam. King Sihanouk managed the situation with great skill, eventually placing himself at the head of the "legitimate" movement for independence. When this was granted by France in 1953, Sihanouk could justly claim it as his achievement. Unlike their comrades in Vietnam and Laos, Cambodia's communists did not get a look-in at the 1954 Geneva conference which confirmed the end of French rule in Indo-China. Flushed with this success, Sihanouk abdicated in 1955 to escape constitutional restraints on his political activity and triumphed electorally by combining Buddhist rectitude with socialism. Over the next 15 years, he steered a wily course of international non-alignment and regional neutrality. Close relations with China served to deny dissident communists support from that quarter and underpinned Sihanouk's policy of non-involvement in the Vietnam war. Internally, his overt anti-US stance and appointment of Marxist intellectuals to government posts pleased the left while leaving effective military and economic power in the hands of the right, which pleased the United States. But even Sihanouk's juggling skills could not cope with the escalation of the Vietnam war in the late 1960s and the growing use of Cambodian territory by forces opposed to the US-backed regime in South Vietnam.

Sihanouk claimed that the right-wing coup which deposed him in 1970 was engineered by Washington to ensure co-operation in the bombing and pursuit of Vietnamese guerrillas taking refuge in Cambodia. Whatever the truth of the episode, the new regime quickly displayed its pro-US colours by acceding to a full-scale US/South Vietnamese invasion of Cambodia. This failed in its objectives but unleashed what Sihanouk had averted, namely massive communist insurrection backed by both China and North Vietnam. After the United States admitted defeat in Vietnam in 1973, a communist victory in Cambodia followed in 1975. Disguised at first by the reinstatement of Sihanouk as head of state, from 1976 the new regime became a dictatorship of the Beijing-backed Khmers

Rouges. Unspeakable atrocities on the Cambodian people occurred over the next three years, but the inevitable riposte from unified and pro-Soviet Vietnam was not long in coming. By early 1979 invading Vietnamese troops, supposedly backing anti-regime forces, had installed a pro-Vietnam communist regime. Later that year, moreover, Vietnam fought off a Chinese punitive assault on it own territory. Now it was again China's turn to foment insurgency in Cambodia, which it did by backing a coalition "government-in-exile" headed by its old friend, Prince Sihanouk. The amalgam included Sihanoukists and remnants of the 1970–75 right-wing regime, but was dominated militarily by the Khmers Rouges.

East-West rivalries, a Sino-US axis on Cambodia and Sihanouk's image-building efforts ensured that his coalition retained majority support in the international community. The Vietnam-backed regime nevertheless remained in control in Phnom Penh and Vietnamese troops, well-versed in jungle warfare, kept the resistance forces at bay. The latter were in any case severely restricted by having to operate mainly from bases on the Thai border, with long supply lines to China. Thailand's role as host to the rebels raised the spectre of open conflict with Vietnam, although an alternative scenario was that Vietnam would succeed in detaching Thailand from its pro-US alignment on the basis of an agreement to back one another's historic claims on Cambodian territory. Interminable negotiations during the 1980s sought to reconcile the various sides of the conflict and to secure broad agreement on a neutral Cambodia, a transitional government and UN-supervised elections. In the late 1980s US–Soviet détente, the end of the Cold War in Europe and improved Sino–Soviet relations created a more hopeful climate for a settlement, especially when at Moscow's prompting Vietnam announced the withdrawal of its troops during 1989. But resistance claims that Vietnam remained in effective military control of Cambodia indicated that basic differences were still far from resolved.

■ Chronology of events

1858   A joint French and Spanish expedition attempts to open up Indo-China which is dominated by the isolationist Emperor of Annam. Saigon is occupied.

1859   King Norodom succeeds his father as ruler of Cambodia and continues to ask for French protection against Vietnam and Siam.

1862   Under the Treaty of Saigon, France acquires sovereignty over the three eastern provinces of Cochin China and forces the Emperor of Annam to open the ports of Tourane, Balat and Kuang-An to French trade.

1863   Cambodia comes under the protection of France.

1867   France persuades Siam to drop its claim over all of Cambodia except Battambang and Siem Riep provinces.

1884   In June France extends its military control over Cambodia which effectively becomes a French colony.

1887   Cambodia, Annam, Cochin China and Tonkin are united under French rule as the *Union Indo-Chinoise*.

1907   The provinces of Battambang and Siem Riep are returned to Cambodia following a Franco–Siamese treaty.

1941   The French install a great grandson of King Norodom, Norodom Sihanouk, as king of Cambodia. In the same year, the Japanese occupy strategic locations in Cambodia and extract economic concessions from the French authorities.

1945   After allowing Vichy France to administer Cambodia, the Japanese dissolve the French colonial administration. On 12 March King Sihanouk declares independence, but in October the anti-colonial government under Son Ngoc Thanh is deposed by Allied troops. Son Ngoc is exiled to France but his supporters remain in Cambodia where they form the Khmer Issarak independence movement.

1946   France recognizes Cambodia as an autonomous kingdom within the French Union.

1947   In the run-up to National Assembly elections the Democratic and Liberal parties emerge as the two main political parties. The Democratic Party wins a decisive majority and drafts its own constitution.

1948   The ruling Democratic Party opposes a draft treaty establishing Cambodia as an associated state within the French Union.

1949   The National Assembly is dissolved and King Sihanouk ratifies a treaty that gives Cambodia limited independence. The Khmer Issarak, which will have nothing less than outright independence, joins the Viet Minh in its armed struggle against the French.

1951   The Democratic Party, committed to full and immediate independence, is elected once again and the political struggle between king and parliament intensifies.

1952   Son Ngoc Thanh returns to Cambodia and, amidst antigovernment demonstrations by Communists and nationalists, King Sihanouk dissolves the Democratic government.

1953   Having declared martial law and dissolved the National Assembly, King Sihanouk leaves the country for self-imposed exile, declaring he will not return until full independence is granted to Cambodia. On 9 November France finally grants independence to Cambodia.

1954   At a conference held in Geneva there is agreement on the cessation of hostilities in Cambodia and the withdrawal of foreign armed forces; King Sihanouk's government achieves international recognition and Vietnam is divided along the 17th parallel. Only Vietnam and the United States decline to sign the final agreement. While agreeing to the neutrality of the three Indo-Chinese states, Cambodia reserves the right to call for outside military assistance should the Viet Minh of North Vietnam or anyone else threaten its territory.

1955 Sihanouk, who has returned to Cambodia, attempts to strenghten his position by trying to amend the constitution. This attempt fails and he abdicates the throne in favour of his father, Norodom Suramarit, in order to form his own political party (People's Socialist Community) and contest the National Assembly elections. Winning the election, Prince Sihanouk becomes Prime Minister. In declaring that Cambodia will adopt a neutral, non-aligned foreign policy he refuses to join the Southeast Asia Treaty Organization (SEATO).

1956 Opposed to Cambodia's neutral stance and close economic relations with Communist countries, South Vietnam and Thailand impose an economic blockade.

1958 Units of the South Vietnamese army invade Cambodia and with US backing both Thailand and South Vietnam give support to the antimonarchist Khmer Serai resistance led by Son Ngoc Thanh.

1960 King Suramarit dies, but Prince Sihanouk does not resume the throne. Instead, he resigns the post of Prime Minister to become head of state.

1962 Prince Sihanouk calls for another Geneva conference to guarantee the territorial integrity of Cambodia.

1965 Cambodia breaks off diplomatic relations with the United States following further border violations by South Vietnamese troops pursuing communist insurgents.

1966 In National Assembly elections Sihanouk is defeated by the right-wing opposition under General Lon Nol.

1967 A Communist uprising takes place in Battambang province and in August Lon Nol is forced to resign in the face of growing Khmer Rouge insurgency. Prince Sihanouk forms a provisional government.

1968 Sihanouk appoints Penn Nouth to the post of Prime Minister. Left-wing insurgency grows and the conservative opposition encourages anti-Vietnamese sentiment. Following a special mission to Phnom Penh, the United States is allowed to pursue North Vietnamese forces from bases in Cambodia.

1969 The government of Penn Nouth falls and Lon Nol returns to the Premier's office. Cambodia restores diplomatic relations with the United States, balanced, at Sihanouk's insistence, by recognition of the provisional Communist government of South Vietnam.

1970 Reputedly with US support, Lon Nol ousts Prince Sihanouk who leaves Cambodia and forms a government-in-exile in Beijing. In October the monarchy is banned and the country's name is changed to the Khmer Republic.

As North Vietnamese Army and Viet Cong forces move deeper into Cambodia, the Phnom Penh government joins with the United States and South Vietnam in operations against the Communists.

1971 The United States escalates its bombing in Cambodia as thousands of refugees flee into cities from rural areas now held by the Khmers Rouges.

1972 A new constitution is adopted and in the republic's first presidential election Lon Nol is returned with 55 per cent of the vote. Elections to the new parliament are boycotted by opposition parties and the pro-government, right-wing Socio–Republican party wins all seats by default.

1973 The United States withdraws from Vietnam and ends its bombing raids over Cambodia. By the end of the year the Khmers Rouges are in control of 60 per cent of the country.

1974 Fearing the withdrawal of US support, the Cambodian government offers to open talks with the Khmers Rouges and Prince Sihanouk. Talks are rejected as the Communists increase their grip on the greater part of rural Cambodia.

1975   On New Year's Day the Khmers Rouges launch a major and devastating offensive that lasts 117 days. Phnom Penh eventually falls on 17 April. Lon Nol flees to Indonesia and Prince Sihanouk is reinstated as head of state with Penn Nouth restored to the premiership. The seizure of the US container ship *Mayaguez* by the Cambodians prompts a rescue bid involving a US Marine attack on Tang Island.

1976   A new constitution in January establishes Cambodia as a Communist People's Republic under the name Democratic Kampuchea. Effective power rests with a Paris–educated leadership that includes Pol Pot, Ieng Sary and Khieu Samphan. In April Sihanouk and his government resigns. Pol Pot takes over as Prime Minister and a reign of terror lasting nearly four years begins. The new regime introduces sweeping reforms which include the evacuation of Phnom Penh and the resettlement of its population in the countryside. Vietnamese residents of Cambodia are again brutally oppressed.

1977   While close ties are maintained with China, relations with Vietnam and Thailand worsen. Armed clashes take place on the border between Cambodia and Vietnam.

1978   When Vietnamese troops enter Cambodia the Pol Pot government breaks off diplomatic relations with Vietnam and appeals for help to the United Nations. A number of Khmer Communists fail in their attempt to overthrow Pol Pot and escape to Vietnam where they form the Kampuchean United Front for National Salvation (KUFNS) under Heng Samrin, a former Khmers Rouges divisional commander. On Christmas Day Vietnamese forces launch a full-scale invasion of Cambodia.

1979   Vietnamese troops capture Phnom Penh and oust the Pol Pot regime which has been responsible for an estimated 2 million deaths since 1976. Prince Sihanouk who has been under house arrest since 1976 is released

by the Khmers Rouges. He goes to the United Nations and denounces the Vietnamese invasion. On 10 January Heng Samrin is installed as head of state of the People's Republic of Kampuchea. He immediately concludes a 25–year treaty of friendship legitimizing the presence of over 200 000 Vietnamese troops in Cambodia.

A number of non-Communist groups join forces under former prime mimister Son Sann to form the Khmer People's National Liberation Front (KPNLF).

1981   Prince Sihanouk forms his own liberation movement, the National United Front for an Independent, Neutral, Peaceful and Co-operative Cambodia (FUNCINPEC).

1982   The three main anti-Vietnamese Cambodiam resistance groups form an alliance. Under the leadership of Prince Sihanouk, the alliance establishes an alternative Coalition Government of Democratic Kampuchea (CGDK) based in Kuala Lumpur.

Vietnamese forces and the 30 000–strong Cambodian regular army launch a major dry season offensive against the main Khmers Rouges base at Phnom Melai, but fail to capture it.

1983   An estimated 80 000 refugees cross the border into Thailand when government forces begin to attack civilian camps near the Thai frontier.

1984   The Heng Samrin regime launches an offensive against resistance bases but suffers heavy losses during the seige of Amphil in early April.

1985   Vietnamese and Cambodian troops launch an early dry season attack on the bases of all three resistance movements which are driven out of the country and into Thailand along with an estimated 230 000 civilians.

Pol Pot announces that he is to hand over the leadership of the Khmers Rouges to his Defence Minister, Son Sen.

Hun Sen becomes Prime Minister of the People's Republic of Kampuchea and initiates a programme of reforms.

1986   The Vietnamese attempt to consolidate their gains by sealing off the entire length of the Thailand–Cambodia border with minefields, trenches and wire fences.

The exiled coalition government devises an eight-point peace plan introducing the idea of a four-party coalition government, but there are no safeguards against Khmers Rouges military dominance.

1987   International pressure prompts Heng Samrin to call for national reconciliation and talks with resistance groups. He refuses to negotiate with the Khmers Rouges leaders but indicates that Prince Sihanouk would hold a "high position" in any future coalition government. Sihanouk meets the PRK Prime Minister, Hun Sen, in Paris but is unable to reach an agreement on the issue of a transitional government and the timing of elections.

1988   In May the Vietnamese government announces that 50 000 troops will be withdrawn from Cambodia by the end of the year. Prince Sihanouk resigns as leader of the resistance coalition in mid-July and on 25–28 July leaders of the PRK meet with CGDK representatives at an ASEAN-sponsored informal meeting held in Jakarta, Indonesia. Both sides present peace plans and a degree of common understanding is reached. All parties agree to the formation of a senior-level working group in October. A

month later Cambodia is the main topic under discussion at a Sino–Soviet summit in Beijing.

Peace plans suffer a setback when representatives of the Khmer Rouge fail to turn up at the October working group meeting.

1989   In February Prince Sihanouk resumes the presidency of the tripartite CGDK resistance alliance and a week later a second round of informal talks take place in Jakarta. In February Vietnam announces that all troops will be withdrawn by 27 September whether a peaceful solution to the conflict has been negotiated or not. Since 1978 over 25 000 Vietnamese soldiers have died in Cambodia.

In August, after months of intense diplomatic activity all sides are brought together at an international conference which is held in Paris under the chairmanship of France and Indonesia. After a month talks break down over, amongst other issues, the inclusion of the Khmers Rouges in any future coalition government. Military activity increases and by the end of the year the Khmers Rouges have cut off government supply routes to north-west Cambodia.

The Khmers Rouges begin a repatriation scheme designed to lodge Cambodian civilians from the refugee camps in so-called "liberation zones".

1990   As the civil war escalates Australia presents a peace plan that involves the temporary partition of the country in the run-up to UN-supervised elections.

■ Who's who

Altas, Ali   The Foreign Minister of Indonesia responsible for co-chairing the Paris conference on Cambodia in August 1989 and for continued efforts to bring all sides together to resolve the Cambodian conflict.

Nol, General Lon   Right–wing Prime Minister of Cambodia 1966–67 and then again from 1969 until elected President of the Khmer Republic

in 1972. Faced with growing insurgency he was eventually forced to flee to Indonesia when the Supreme Committee of the Khmer Republic surrendered to Pol Pot's Khmers Rouges in 1975.

Nouth, Samdech Penn   A Sihanouk adviser who held the post of Prime Minister for a year from January 1968 until August 1969 when he was replaced by Lon Nol. In 1970 he became Prime Minister of Sihanouk's Government of National Unity in exile in Beijing. Penn Nouth returned to power in Cambodia for a year following the surrender of the Khmer Republic to the Khmers Rouges in 1975. When Sihanouk resigned as head of state in April 1976 Pol Pot took over the premier's post.

Pot, Pol (also known as Pol Porth, Tol Sant or Saloth Sar)   Born in May 1928, he worked on rubber plantations before joining Ho Chi Minh's anti-French resistance in the 1940s. A committed member of the Indo-China Communist Party until 1946 and the Praechon Party in Cambodia thereafter, he joined with Khieu Samphan and Ieng Sary in 1967 to lead the Khmers Rouges against the Lon Nol regime. As Prime Minister of Democratic Kampuchea between 1976 and 1979 Pol Pot's name has come to be associated with a reign of terror that led to the death of over two million people. In 1979, although still in effective control of the Khmer Rouge, he was replaced as premier by Khieu Samphan. Claiming to have retired in 1985 the leadership of the Khmer Rouge passed to Son Sen and Ieng Sary. Pol Pot resigned his sole remaining official post in June 1989.

Samphan, Khieu   Paris–educated leader of the Communist Party of Kampuchea and co-leader, with Pol Pot and Ieng Sary, of the armed opposition to Lon Nol's right-wing government of the Khmer Republic. When Prince Sihanouk resigned as head of state in 1976, Khieu Samphan became President of the new Democratic Kampuchea with Pol Pot as his Prime Minister. Three years later, following the 1979 fall of Phnom Penh and removal of Pol Pot, he assumed the triple offices of President, Prime Minister and Commander in Chief in areas near the Thai border still controlled by the Khmers Rouges. In 1982 he participated with other resistance leaders in the formation of the CGDK government in opposition to the Vietnamese-backed Heng Samrin regime, taking on the role of Vice-President for Foreign Affairs.

Samrin, Heng   Born in 1934, Heng Samrin rose through the ranks of the Cambodian army to become Commanding Officer of the 4th Infantry Division in 1976. Two years later he led an abortive attempt to oust Pol Pot and was forced to flee to Hanoi where he was placed at the head of the Kampuchean United Front for National Salvation (KUFNS). Following the Vietnamese invasion of Cambodia and the removal of the Pol Pot regime in 1979 he was installed as President of the new People's Republic of Kampuchea.

Sann, Son   A former Prime Minister of Cambodia and leader of the Khmer Serai who gathered noncommunist support in an attempt to lead the political struggle against the Heng Samrin regime. In 1979 he formed the KPNLF and in 1982 he joined with other resistance movements to become Prime Minister of the Coalition Government of Democratic Kampuchea (CGDK).

Sary, Ieng   A founding leader of the Khmers Rouges with Pol Pot and Khieu Samphan. Commanding the military wing of the Khmers Rouges resistance throughout the 1980s, he was eventually wounded during a raid by government troops.

Satsukhan, General Sak   Military commander of the KPNLF. He is reported to have been a signatory to a document in August 1989 supporting a move to   repatriate refugees from the Site Two camp. He is also alleged to have used orphaned children from the camps to carry supplies through mine fields.

Sen, Hun   Prime Minister of the People's Republic of Kampuchea since 1985 and chief government negotiator in talks with the resistance coalition since 1988. He is the principal driving force behind socio-economic reforms that include the introduction of private medicine and schooling as well as hereditary land tenure for peasants.

Sihanouk, Prince Samdech Preah Norodom   Born in October 1922, Prince Sihanouk was educated in Saigon, Paris and at the military training school at Saumur. Elevated to the throne above his obvious successor in 1941, he abdicated in favour of his father in 1955 in order to form his own political party and contest the National Assembly elections. Between

October 1955 and April 1960 he was Prime Minister of Cambodia five times. When his father died in 1960, Prince Sihanouk declined to resume the throne and was instead elected head of state, a position he held until forced into exile by General Lon Nol in 1970. From a base in Beijing he led a Royal Government of National Unity, but in April 1975 he returned once more as head of state. A year later, in April 1976, he was replaced by the Khmers Rouges leader Khieu Samphan and put under virtual house arrest. Released in 1979 he formed his own political movement, (FUNCINPEC), and military resistance, (ANS). As leader of the CGDK resistance alliance he engaged in an endless series of negotiations aimed at the restoration of Cambodian independence as a neutral democratic state. He twice resigned as leader of the CGDK (1988 and 1990).

Sovan, Pen   A soldier and politician born in 1930. He rose through the military ranks to become deputy to a Divisional Commander in 1970 and eventually Commander in Chief of the Cambodian armed forces following the installation of the Heng Samrin regime in 1979. In 1981 he was elected Vice-President of the People's Republic of Kampuchea and for a period of eight months he was Secretary–General of the People's Revolutionary Party.

Suramarit, King Norodom   Father of Prince Norodom Sihanouk appointed king of Cambodia following the abdication of his son in 1955. When King Suramarit died in 1960 his son did not resume the throne.

Thanh, Son Ngoc   Leader of the first anti-colonial government in Cambodia formed in March 1945 following the declaration of independence by King Sihanouk. Ousted by allied troops in October 1945, Thanh was arrested and sent into exile in France. In 1952 he posed a threat to the monarchy when he returned to Cambodia as leader of the Khmer Issarak independence fighters. Continuing his antimonarchist struggle throughout the 1950s and 1960s, Son Ngoc Thanh supported the eventual overthrow of Sihanouk by Lon Nol in 1970 and for a period of eight months from March to October 1972 acted as head of state of the Khmer Republic.

Van Linh, Nguyen   A municipal communist leader in Ho Chi Minh City (Saigon) after Hanoi's victory over US–backed South Vietnam in 1975, Nguyen Van Linh succeeded Truong Chinh as Secretary–General of the Vietnamese Communist Party in 1986. Under his leadership Vietnam was able to withdraw its troops from Cambodia during 1988–89.

■ Key places

Amphil   A settlement in Battambang province, NW Cambodia, situated close to the frontier with Thailand. In April 1984 a large-scale offensive launched by the People's Army of Vietnam against the main KPNLF base here resulted in heavy casualties and the eventual withdrawal of Vietnamese troops.

Angor   The capital city of the former Angkor Empire that flourished in SE Asia between the 9th and 13th centuries. Situated to the north of Tonlé Sap, near Siem Riep the magnificent remains of Angkor reflect the change from Hinduism to Buddhism in the 12th century. Abandoned in the 15th century, the forest-clad ruins of this great city were rediscovered by French archaeologists four hundred years later.

Battambang   A province of W Cambodia, situated between the NW corner of Tonlé Sap and the Thai frontier. Watered by the Sangker River, it is the principal rice-growing region of Cambodia and consequently of vital strategical importance. Route 5, the principal supply line to Phnom Penh from Battambang (280km) has been a major target for attack by Khmers Rouges rebels who operate from bases along the Thai–Cambodia border. The provincial capital, Battambang, is Cambodia's second largest city.

Bogor   A hill resort and university city situated 58km south of Jakarta on the Indonesian island of Java; population (1980) 247 400. Founded in 1745, its palace was the former residence of the Dutch governor of the East Indies. Noted for its botanical gardens, Bogor was the idyllic scene of the first so-called Jakarta Informal Meeting (JIM) held during 25–28 July 1988.

Cardamom Mountains or **Banthat** (Thai)   A range of mountains in SW Cambodia, stretching over 160km from the province of Kampot on the Gulf of Thailand to southern Battambang on the Thai–Cambodia frontier. The highest point is Phnom Aural which rises to 1813m south of Pailin. The Cardamom Mountains give their name to a type of semi-precious stone.

Dangrek Range or **Dong Rak** (Thai)   Rising to heights in excess of 3000m to the west of the Mekong River, the Dangrek Range extends over 300km from N Cambodia into Thailand.

Hanoi   Capital of Vietnam and former capital of French Indo-China (1887-1955). Situated on the Red River, it has a population of 2.5 million.

Ho Chi Minh City   With a population of four million, it is the largest city in Vietnam. Formerly known as Saigon, its name was changed following the defeat of the US-backed government of South Vietnam by the North Vietnamese under the leadership of Ho Chi Minh. In January 1990 Cambodian leaders Hun Sen and Heng Samrin fled to Ho Chi Minh City following a series of grenade attacks on Phnom Penh by Khmers Rouges guerrillas.

Kompong Som   The principal deepwater port and commercial centre of Cambodia, situated on the Gulf of Thailand at the western tip of Kampot province, SW Cambodia. The city was known as Sihanoukville until the overthrow of the monarchy and the removal of Prince Sihanouk from his position as head of state in 1970.

Kampuchea   The Khmer name for Cambodia.

Khao I Dang   One of nine Cambodian resettlement centres set up after the fall of the Pol Pot regime to handle refugees flooding across the border from Cambodia into Thailand. The camp, which has a population of some 24 000 refugees, lies 185km E of Bangkok on the Cambodia–Thailand frontier.

Mekong River   With a length of about 4160km, the Mekong is one of the chief rivers of SE Asia. Rising in E Tibet, it flows through Yunnan province in S China before following the Burma–Laos and Burma–Thailand frontiers. Continuing south into Cambodia, it empties into the South China Sea in a wide, fertile   delta.

Pailin   A ruby-mining town in Battambang province, W Cambodia, situated within 10km of the Thai frontier. Abandoned by Vietnamese troops in 1988, the town was captured by the Khmers Rouges after heavy fighting in October 1989 and held for a month before being recaptured by government troops.

Phnom Penh   The capital city of Cambodia and centre of administration of the People's Republic of Kampuchea, situated at the confluence of the Tonlé Sap and Mekong rivers. Since the early 1970s the population of the city has changed dramatically, rising from an estimated 470 000 in 1970 to 2.5 million in 1975 as refugees fled from the countryside in the wake of Khmers Rouges resistance to the Lon Nol regime. With the fall of Phnom Penh to the Khmers Rouges in January 1975 the city was almost deserted following the introduction of a policy of rural repatriation designed to avert widespread famine. The Vietnamese invasion of 1978-79 once more forced people off the land and back into Phnom Penh which in 1983 had an estimated population of 500 000.

Sihanoukville   Former name of Kompong Som until 1970.

Site Two   Known to its 140 000 residents as "Bamboo City", Site Two is the largest of the Cambodian refugee camps on the Thai border. It was set up in 1985.

Taluan   With a population of 55 000, Taluan is the largest of four official Khmers Rouges civilian refugee camps receiving international aid in E Thailand. In 1989 4000 refugees were taken from the camp and repatriated in Cambodia in a Khmers Rouges plan to establish civilian bases or "liberated zones" inside Cambodia.

Tonlé Sap ("Great Lake")   A freshwater lake in central Cambodia, linked to the Mekong River by the 115km Tonlé Sap River. During the dry season the lake has an area of 2850km². In the wet season (June–November) the area of the lake is tripled and the water level rises over nine metres as it receives flood water from the Mekong. The lake is a major source of fish.

■ Key words

Armée Nationale Sihanoukiste (ANS)   The military wing of Prince Sihanouk's National United Front for an Independent, Neutral, Peaceful and Co-operative Cambodia (FUNCINPEC).

Chams   Descendants of the old kingdom of Champa who were converted to Islam by the Malays and subsequently assimilated into a Cham–Malay community. They number about 100 000 in Cambodia.

Coalition Government of Democratic Kampuchea (CGDK)   An alternative Cambodian government-in-exile set up in Kuala Lumpur in June 1982 in opposition to the Vietnamese-backed People's Republic of Kampuchea. The CGDK includes the three main groups opposed to the Samrin regime, namely: the Party of Democratic Kampuchea (Khmer Rouge), the Armée Nationale Sihanoukiste (ANS) and the Khmer People's National Liberation Front (KPNLF). This government is recognized by the UN.

cocktail party   A name given to the informal meeting of representatives of the Heng Samrin regime and the resistance coalition held in Jakarta, Indonesia, in July 1988.

Communist Party of Kampuchea (CPK)   A small pro-China resistance group formerly identified with Pol Pot's Khmers Rouges faction of the larger Communist Party of Kampuchea that had been formed in 1951 as the Kampuchean People's Revolutionary Party but renamed in 1960. Until 1977 it was also known as the Kampuchean Revolutionary   Organization of Angka.

Democratic Kampuchea (DK)   Established under a new constitution in January 1976, Pol Pot's Democratic Kampuchea replaced the former Khmer Republic. In 1979 Democratic Kampuchea was in turn replaced by the People's Republic of Kampuchea under the Vietnamese-backed Heng Samrin regime.

Geneva Agreements   A series of agreements negotiated in Geneva in 1954, bringing to an end hostilities in Indo–China. The agreement relating to the cessation of fighting in Cambodia, which was announced on 20 July, 1954, provided for a ceasefire, withdrawal of all foreign armed forces and military personnel, and the establishment of an International Control Commission.

International Control Commission   An international commission including representatives from Canada, India and Poland, set up in July 1954 to supervise the ceasefire and withdrawal of foreign troops following the independence of Cambodia.

Jakarta Informal Meeting (JIM)   An informal meeting hosted by Indonesia in July 1988, that brought together leaders of the three resistance movements and the PRK government for the first time since the Vietnamese invasion of 1979. After four days of talks the participants agreed to set up a "working group" and reconvene a second round of JIM talks in February 1989. Peace plans suffered a setback when the Khmers Rouges failed to take part in the later talks.

Kampuchean United Front for National Salvation (KUFNS)   A Cambodian administration set up in Vietnam during the weeks prior to the Vietnamese invasion of Cambodia in December 1978. Led by Heng Samrin, it was largely composed of Khmer communists who had remained in Vietnam after 1975 and Khmer Rouge officials who had fled Cambodia after a failed coup attempt against Pol Pot in 1978. In January 1979 Vietnam installed Heng Samrin and the KUFNS leadership as rulers of the new People's Republic of Kampuchea. In 1981, at its third congress, the Front changed its name to the Kampuchean United Front for National Salvation and Defence (KUFNCD).

Kampuchean People's Revolutionary Party (KPRP)   The sole legal political party in Cambodia following the establishment of Heng Samrin's People's Republic of Kampuchea (PRK) in 1979. The party was founded in 1951 when the Indo-Chinese Communist Party led by Ho Chi Minh was divided into separate entities for Vietnam, Laos and Cambodia. At its 1960 Congress, when it changed its name to the Communist Party of Kampuchea, the party divided into two factions, one supporting Vietnam, and the other China. The pro-Vietnamese faction went into exile in 1974, but returned in 1979 after the installation of the Heng Samrin regime. A "Reorganization Congress" gave the party its present name in order to distinguish it from the Chinese-backed Khmers Rouges.

Khmer Issarak ("free Khmer")   An independence movement formed by the supporters of Son Ngoc Thanh whose anti-colonial government was deposed by allied troops in October 1945. Undermining the position of King Sihanouk, the Khmer Issarak fought alongside the Viet Minh against the French in the early 1950s. This group later came to be known as the Khmer Serai.

Khmer Kandal ("centre Khmer")   Khmer people of the ricelands of west and central Cambodia.

Khmer Krom ("lower Khmer")   Khmer people of Vietnam's Mekong Delta.

Khmer Loeu ("upper Khmer")   The indigenous hill people of NE Cambodia where they form the majority of the population in the provinces of Rotanokiri and Mondol Kiri. Belonging to several ethnolinguistic groups, they are divided into two broad racial types (Negroid and Indonesian) and over a dozen groups. The Khmer Loeus number about 50 000.

Khmer People's National Liberation Armed Forces   The military wing of the political KPNLF formed in 1979-80 by a number of groups who had fought against the Khmers Rouges after 1975.

Khmer People's National Liberation Front (KPNLF)   A noncommunist political resistance movement formed in 1979 under the leadership of former Prime Minister Son Sann.

Khmer Republic   Following the abolition of the Cambodian monarchy in October 1970, the National Assembly established the Khmer Republic. In 1976 the Khmer Republic became Democratic Kampuchea.

Khmers Rouges or **Party of Democratic Kampuchea** ("red Khmers")   A left–wing political resistance movement formed in 1967 in opposition to the right–wing government of General Lon Nol. Named the Khmers Rouges by Prince Sihanouk, this group was held responsible for a 1967 peasant uprising in Battambang province. Initially fighting in small units against the Cambodian army the Khmers Rouges was in control of 60 per cent of the country by 1973. On 17 April 1975 the government of the Khmer Republic was finally overthrown by the Khmers Rouges under Pol Pot who began to restructure the country in a regime of terror that lasted nearly four years. Following the Vietnamese invasion of Cambodia in 1978 the Khmers Rouges lost control of the country and were driven out of Phnom Penh. Supporters of the Khmers Rouges regrouped in the mountains of western Cambodia from where they continued to launch attacks on the armed forces of the Vietnamese-backed People's Republic of Kampuchea.

Killing Fields   A name given to the genocide of the Khmers Rouges during the four-year reign of terror under Pol Pot in the 1970s.

National United Front for an Independent, Neutral, Peaceful and Co-operative Cambodia (FUNCINPEC)   A noncommunist party established in 1981 by former head of state Prince Norodom Sihanouk. Its military wing is the Armée Nationale Sihanoukienne (ANS).

People's Army of Vietnam (PAVN)   The regular army of Vietnam whose troops invaded Cambodia in 1978 and remained in support of the Heng Samrin regime until 1989. While in Cambodia PAVN forces, totalling an estimated maximum of 200 000 in number, provided military support and training to the People's Republic of Kampuchea Armed Forces (PRKAF).

People's Republic of Kampuchea (PRK)   In January 1979 the Democratic Kampuchea of the Pol Pot regime was replaced by the People's Republic of Kampuchea under the leadership of Heng Samrin who was installed as head of state by the Vietnamese.

People's Republic of Kampuchea Armed Forces (PRKAF).   The regular army of the Heng Samrin regime, numbering about 40 000 men.

People's Socialist Community (Sangkum Reastr Niyum)   A political party formed in March 1955 by Prince Sihanouk who abdicated the throne in order to contest National Assembly elections.

Pracheachon or **People's Party**   A procommunist political party in opposition to Prince Sihanouk's Sangkum party in the 1950s.

Royal Government of the National Union of Kampuchea (RGNU)   An alternative Cambodian government-in-exile formed in Beijing by Prince Sihanouk who left the country in 1970. In October of that year the Cambodian monarchy was abolished and the Khmer Republic established.

United Nations Border Relief Operation (UNBRO)   A UN programme set up in 1982 to provide relief to the Cambodian refugees living in camps along the Thailand–Cambodia frontier.

Vietnamization   In 1982 Heng Samrin issued directives making it easier for Vietnamese people to settle in Cambodia and obtain occupations and land. Two years later tax concessions favouring the Vietnamese forced many Khmer and Chinese merchants out of business. Claims by the government that only 56 000 Vietnamese had settled in Cambodia during the period 1979–85 were disputed by resistance parties which alleged that a figure nearer 700 000 was more realistic in what amounted to a calculated policy of "Vietnamization". Most of the settlers from Vietnam are traders, fishermen or farmers.

■ Further reading

D.A. Ablin and M. Hood (eds.), *The Cambodian Agony*, Shape, London, 1987

David P. Chandler, *A History of Cambodia*, Bowker, Epping, 1983

Stanley Karnow, *Vietnam: A History*, Viking Press, New York, 1983

K. Kiljunin (ed.), *Kampuchea: Decade of the Genocide*, Zed, London 1984

Michael Vickery, *Cambodia 1975–1982*, South End Press, Boston, 1984

Michael Vickery, *Kampuchea: Politics, Economics and Society*, Pinter, London, 1986

6
Korea

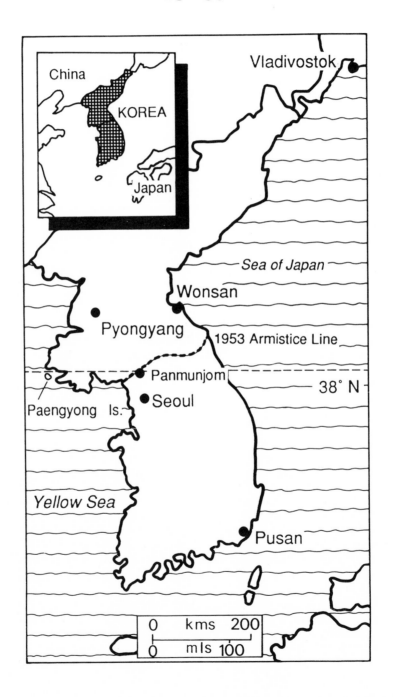

China

KOREA

Japan

Vladivostok

Sea of Japan

Wonsan

Pyongyang

1953 Armistice Line

Panmunjom

Seoul

38° N

Paengyong Is.

Yellow Sea

Pusan

| 0 | kms | 200 |
| 0 | mls | 100 |

■ Profile

North Korea

Official name: Democratic People's Republic of Korea

- **Area:** 122 370km²
- **Population:** 21 984,000
- **Life expectancy:** 65 years
- **Infant mortality rate:** 32 per 1000
- **Per capita income (US$):** 1123 (1986)
- **GNP growth rate:** 2% (1986)
- **Capital:** Pyongyang (1 500 000)

South Korea

Official name: Republic of Korea

- **Area:** 99 143km²
- **Population:** 42 773,000
- **Life expectancy:** 67 years
- **Infant mortality rate:** 29 per 1000
- **Per capita income (US$):** 2296 (1986)
- **GNP growth rate:** 12.2% (1987)
- **Capital:** Seoul (9 646 000)

■ Introduction

Of the three countries partitioned into pro-Soviet and pro-Western states after World War II, Vietnam was reunified in 1973 and Germany took the same path in 1990. This left Korea as the only surviving anachronism of the Cold War era, divided as it remained between communist North Korea and capitalist South Korea. The precise line of division resulted from the costly Korean War of 1950–53 and has endured despite periodic efforts to find a reunification formula. Although an armed truce has been maintained in relative stability since 1953, mutual hostility has hardly abated and the two Korean states have grown far apart economically as well as politically. Given the maintenance of huge armies by both sides, combined in South Korea's case with a large US military presence, divided Korea therefore remains a major source of regional tension as well as a potential threat to world peace.

Korean history over 4500 years has been shaped by external powers, firstly by China, later by the Japanese and Russians, and recently by the Americans. The ancient Choson civilization came under Chinese domination until the "Three Kingdoms" of Korea emerged in the 4th century AD. Of these, Shilla conquered Paekche and Koguryo in the 7th century to form the first all-Korea kingdom but in 935 succumbed to secessionist Koryo, from which the name Korea is derived. Mongol suzerainty from 1259 gave way in 1392 to the Korean Yi dynasty, which revived the name Choson and ruled for over 500 years from Seoul. It survived the first Japanese invasion of Korea in the 1590s, at the cost of becoming a vassal state of Manchu China. But it could not withstand the new imperialist aggression of Japan in the late 19th century. China's defeat in the 1894–95 Sino-Japanese war gave Korea nominal independence. Japan's 1904–05 victory over Russia resulted in Korea becoming a Japanese protectorate and being annexed in 1910. Meanwhile, the Catholic Church had converted many Koreans from Buddhism, although without denting the elite's Confucianism.

Japanese rule brought industrialization but its brutalities stimulated Korean nationalism both in conservative circles and in a growing communist movement, promoted respectively by Nationalist China and, mainly, the Soviet Union. In both countries the desire to settle scores with Japan was strong, irrespective of changes of regime. In 1943 the World War II Allies decided that Korea should become independent. But as one incentive to Soviet participation in the anticipated costly invasion of Japan, it was agreed that in the interim Korea would be divided into Soviet and US zones on the 38th parallel. Apparently, it was not appreciated at the time that this line would separate most Korean industry in the north from the bulk of population and agriculture in the south. The US atomic bomb rendered invasion of Japan unnecessary, but shortly before the Japanese surrender in August 1945 a Soviet army moved into northern Korea, to be faced a month later by US troops in the south. The inevitable consequence, as the Cold War set in, was the creation in 1948 of two states, one communist-ruled and the other US-backed, each claiming jurisdiction over the whole of Korea.

Less predictable was North Korea's invasion of South Korea in June 1950 and its rapid penetration down the peninsula. The Soviet Union's absence from the UN Security Council at the crucial time enabled the United States to make resistance to the North a UN cause. When China intervened in late 1950, however, the war became essentially a Sino-US conflict. The UN/US forces, commanded by the dynamic General MacArthur and with air and naval superiority, had by then reversed the initial North Korean thrust and overrun most of the North. Reunification on Western terms had seemed a real possibility, but so too had a US advance on China's new communist regime. The Chinese onslaught changed all that by forcing a rapid UN/US retreat back into the South. MacArthur then had his famous row with President Truman over whether China should be bombed, perhaps with atomic weapons, but Truman ruled that the war must

be confined to Korea. By mid-1951 the front had stabilized on roughly the pre-war line, but attritional conflict continued for another two years as truce talks became bogged down in a dispute over the fate of North Korean and Chinese prisoners-of-war. Not until Stalin had died in February 1953, and newly-elected President Eisenhower had hinted at US use of atomic weapons, did the North negotiate seriously. An armistice signed at Panmunjom in July 1953 established a ceasefire line, adjacent to the 38th parallel, which became the *de facto* border between North and South. The fiercest criticism of the agreement came from the South Korean regime, on the grounds that it legitimized the division of Korea.

Both Korean states made a surprisingly rapid recovery from the devastation of war. In the North, communist leader Kim Il Sung instituted Soviet-style central planning, with Soviet and Chinese aid, and for a time appeared to be getting results. Chinese troops withdrew in 1958, after which North Korea set a course independent of the two communist giants, based on the concept of *juche* (self-reliance). Kim used Stalinist techniques to consolidate his grip on power, developing a cult of personality and dynastic rule which put even Stalin's record in the shade. Political stability was more elusive in the South, which by 1988 was on its Sixth Republic since the war and had experienced long periods of military rule. Some democratic trappings were usually preserved, but student and other dissidents encountered ruthless repression, enabling the North to depict the South as groaning under the yoke of capitalist exploiters. The truth was that with Japanese and US support the South achieved a remarkable economic take-off in the 1960s, becoming a major manufacturing and exporting power, second only to Japan in the Pacific Basin. This new prosperity spread to South Korean workers, who became much better-off than their counterparts in the North. By the late 1980s, moreover, a more stable democratic system seemed to be operating in South Korea.

Since 1953 both Korean states have regularly called for the reunification of Korea, but have stipulated terms unacceptable to the other side. The Sino–US rapprochement of the early 1970s led to direct talks between the two sides from

1973, but little progress was made. There was no question of the US government allowing Korea to follow Vietnam in reuniting under communist leadership. Although the 1953 ceasefire was never seriously in jeopardy, regular incidents on the armistice line and elsewhere kept tensions high, as did North Korea's state-sponsored terrorism against South Korean targets. The United States maintained its powerful military presence in South Korea. When President Carter proposed the withdrawal of ground troops in 1979, US intelligence suddenly discovered that the North's strength was much greater than previously thought, and the proposal was shelved. In the 1980s new reunification scenarios from each side gave the impression of movement, but the acrimony surrounding the holding of the 1988 Olympic Games in Seoul showed that the deadlock remained as intractable as ever.

As the 1990s opened, the end of the Cold War in Europe and Soviet acquiescence in Germany's reunification raised new hopes of a knock-on effect in Korea. Yet US-Soviet détente and better Sino-Soviet relations could not of themselves deliver a settlement in Korea, especially after the 1989 events in Tiananmen Square had shown that for all its economic liberalism China remained wedded to communist orthodoxy. In any case, great power diktat was unlikely to cut much ice with the Kim II Sung regime, whose intransigence seemed to increase as the evidence mounted that reunification would only make sense if the South Korean economic and political system were extended to the North. The succession to the aged Kim therefore assumed critical importance. Optimists anticipated that a new regime would see the writing on the wall and move to accept reunification on Western terms. Pessimists feared that Kim's son and designated successor, Kim Jong Il, would prove to be a chip off the old block if he gained power.

■ Chronology of events

668 The Shilla emerge as the dominant power on the Korean peninsula and for the first time the "Three Kingdoms" unite to form a single state and a common opposition to Chinese domination.

735 After decades of war with the Shilla, China finally recognizes the Shilla claim to all land south of the Tumen River.

935 The secessionist Koguryo state conquers the Shilla Empire and establishes the Kingdom of Koryo, from which the name Korea is derived.

1259 After a series of invasions the Koryo state is dominated by the Mongols.

1392 The collapse of the Mongol Empire leaves a political vacuum in Koryo. General Yi Song Gye steps in to take advantage of the situation and stages a coup. Founding a new dynasty, Yi establishes a capital at Seoul and renames the state the Kingdom of Choson ("morning calm").

1592–99 The Japanese invade Korea and sack Seoul, transporting thousands of Koreans to Japan as virtual slaves, before intervention by the Chinese forces them to withdraw.

1627 Choson is forced to become a vassal state of Manchu China.

1876 Japan forces Korea to enter into a trade agreement and to allow Japanese bases to be established on the Korean peninsula.

1882–84 The government of China, which has tried to counter the growing Japanese influence in Korea, sends in troops to quell anti-Chinese riots.

1894–95 The conflict between Chinese and Japanese interests in Korea leads to the Sino–Japanese war and the humiliating defeat of China. When a peace treaty is signed, Russia, France and Germany prevent Japan from annexing Korea, which becomes a nominally–independent Japanese protectorate.

1904–05   The defeat of Russia in the Russo-Japanese war confirms Japan's military superiority in the Far East and its domination of Korea.

1910   After a series of assassinations, Japan formally annexes Korea on 22 August. The monarchy is abolished and Korean nationalism is suppressed.

1919   A nationalist uprising organized by the March 1st movement is brutally put down with the loss of 6000 Korean lives. Having proclaimed a "Declaration of Independence", a government-in-exile is formed in China under the presidency of Dr Syngman Rhee. Guerrilla action against the Japanese is organized by the March 1st movement and by two communist factions, one based in Shanghai and the other in the Soviet union.

1931   Japan uses Korea as an important base from which to invade Manchuria and the Japanese administration becomes increasingly repressive.

1941   Following the outbreak of war with the USA, Japan conscripts Koreans into the army and transports over 1 000 000 people to Japan where they are used as forced labour.

1943   Chiang Kai-Shek, Winston Churchill and Franklin Roosevelt meet in Cairo and agree that Korean independence should be granted "at the earliest possible moment".

1945   At the April Yalta conference the United States and Soviet Union agree to establish a temporary joint trusteeship over the Korean peninsula. The Soviet Union enters the Pacific War on 8 August and by the time Japan surrenders on 15 August, Soviet troops have reached Manchuria and the Korean peninsula. The US military administration decrees that a line demarcating Soviet–occupied territory in the north from US–occupied territory in the south should be drawn along the 38th parallel. This decision effectively divides Korea in half separating the industrial north from the agricultural south.

Before US forces begin to arrive on 8 September, the Japanese governor-general transfers power to the left–wing nationalist Yo Un Hyong who establishes a Committee for the Preparation of Korean Independence (CPKI). A national assembly is quickly set up and two days before the US military arrives, a People's Republic of Korea, claiming jurisdiction over the whole country, is established.

People's Committees, largely composed of noncommunist and communist nationalists, are formed at all levels throughout the country, but while the Russians in the north support and co-operate with this new political order, the US administration in the south is less sympathetic. Believing the People's Committees to be little more than communist fronts, the Americans maintain the Japanese-style administration and create a Representative Democratic Council (RDC). This organization includes the right–wing nationalist leader Syngman Rhee who is in favour of setting up a separate, noncommunist south Korean state.

In December a conference of Foreign Ministers from the USA, UK and Russia is held in Moscow. All parties agree that Korea should be administered through a joint commission of US and Soviet commands as an interim measure leading towards the formation of a provisional government for the whole peninsula.

1946   The plan proposed at the Moscow conference does not come to fruition. In the south, the People's Committees are virtually eliminated and in October elections confirm the dominant position of the political right–wing. In the north, a radical land reform programme is initiated following the creation of   a Soviet–backed provisional government named the North Korean Interim People's Committee (NKIPC). In July left–wing groups north of the 38th parallel are further united by the formation of the North Korean Worker's Party.

1947   The USA, which has "little strategic interest" in Korea, fails to establish a regime that carries any popular support and calls on the UN to intervene. On 14 November the UN Temporary Commission on Korea

(UNTCOK) is set up for the purpose of guaranteeing the future of a reunified Korea.

1948 Despite Soviet opposition, UNTCOK decides to go ahead with a US plan to hold elections in May. UNTCOK officials, however, are denied access north of the 38th parallel and elections are held only in the South. Amidst charges of corruption and malpractice the right–wing sweeps to power and forms an administration under the leadership of Syngman Rhee who claims that the newly–elected government has sovereignty over the whole of Korea. On 12 July the national assembly approves a constitution establishing the Republic of Korea and three days later Rhee is elected President. In series of uprisings that follow, at least 30 000 people are killed.

In August elections to a new 575–member Supreme People's Assembly take place in the North. The Korean Workers' Party wins a clear majority and a month later the Democratic People's Republic of Korea is proclaimed. Led by Kim Il Sung, the new state in the north also claims sovereignty over the whole peninsula. In December Soviet forces are withdrawn from the North but the UN declares that the Republic of Korea is the only lawful government in Korea.

1949 Although the opposition to the Syngman Rhee regime has developed into a guerrilla struggle, the USA decides to withdraw its armed forces.

1950 On 25 June, following a series of border incidents, 60 000 Soviet-equipped North Korean troops invade South Korea and within days Seoul is captured. The UN Security Council (under boycott by the Soviet Union) quickly condemns the invasion and calls for the immediate withdrawal of North Korean forces to positions north of the 38th parallel. When this does not happen, a second resolution is passed two days later calling on member states to provide military assistance to South Korea. On 7 July General Douglas MacArthur is appointed commander of a joint UN military force that includes contingents from 16 UN countries.

By late July the North Koreans have reached as far as the south eastern tip of the Korean peninsula. Their advance on Pusan is halted by the arrival of UN troops and by the complete air superiority of the US Airforce. A UN counter-offensive, involving an amphibious landing at Inchon near Seoul in September, successfully cuts off the over-extended North Korean supply lines and by early October all territory south of the 38th parallel is liberated.

MacArthur sees an opportunity to reunite the two Koreas and, despite warnings from the People's Republic of China, drives the UN forces north of the 38th parallel towards the North Korean capital. On 19 October Pyongyang is captured and by 1 November UN troops have reached the banks of the Yalu River on the North Korean frontier with China. When a final offensive begins on 24 November, the UN forces are completely surprised when 150 000 Chinese "people's volunteers" launch an attack across the border. The Chinese push southwards, rapidly driving the UN forces back across the 38th parallel.

1951 On 4 January Seoul falls for the second time as the war develops into a Sino–US conflict. By mid-January, however, the Chinese advance is halted and in mid-March UN forces recapture Seoul. A stalemate is reached as the frontline settles in the region of the 38th parallel. MacArthur is relieved of his command in April and peace talks begin three months later in July.

1952 Peace negotiations make slow progress and falter on the question of prisoner of war repatriation.

1953 With the death of Stalin and the inauguration of Dwight D. Eisenhower to the US presidency, there is a new commitment to ending the military stalemate and resolving the Korean conflict. On 27 July an armistice agreement is eventually signed at Panmunjon on the 38th parallel and a joint commission is established to supervise a 4km–wide demilitarized zone along the 250km front between North and South Korea.

During three years of warfare total UN casualties are estimated at 160 000 killed, wounded, captured or missing. South Korean losses total an estimated 1 313 000, while North

Korean and Chinese casualties amount to 520 000 and 900 000 respectively. In addition to military losses over 1 000 000 civilians are reckoned to have been killed in North Korea as a result of the extensive US bombing of cities.

1954   Representatives of the 19 nations involved in the Korean War meet in Geneva in April but fail to make progress towards the signing of a peace treaty. Both North and South Korea outline reunification plans which are totally incompatible.

1955   In August South Korea demands the withdrawal of the multinational commission supervising the armistice, alleging that North Korea is building up its military strength and that Polish and Czechoslovakian members are obstructing the work of the commission. Switzerland and Sweden also propose that the commission be abandoned as unworkable.

1956   North Korea proposes a reunification plan that involves the establishment by peaceful means of a Korean federation. In South Korea a more aggressive stance is adopted by the 81-year-old Syngman Rhee who advocates the "March to the North" as a vote-winning slogan.

The multinational team abandons its supervision of the armistice in June.

1960   A popular uprising forces Syngman Rhee to resign the presidency of South Korea and the uncompromising "March to the North" plan is abandoned in favour of peaceful progress towards reunification.

1961   In May a military coup in South Korea brings to power Major–General Park Chung Hee. Ties with the USA are strengthened and all attempts to negotiate with the communist government of North Korea are suppressed.

Apprehensive of Park's anticommunist stance, North Korea adopts a more militant approach to reunification that involves encouraging revolution in South Korea rather than direct military confrontation. Kim Il Sung enhances North Korea's military security by signing treaties of Friendship and Mutual Co-operation with both China and the Soviet Union in July.

1963   A civilian government returns to South Korea and in an attempt to secure economic and technical assistance, relations with Japan are normalized.

1964   South Korea agrees to send troops to fight in Vietnam in return for economic and technical aid from the USA.

1965   The economic development of South Korea is further strengthened with the signing of a normalization treaty with Japan which becomes the country's second largest source of foreign capital. North Korea attempts to destabilize the position in the south by launching guerrilla attacks and by infiltrating espionage agents across the border.

1967   Within the space of a year the number of border incidents rises from 50 to 566. As a result of this, the US and South Koreans construct a barbed wire barrier along the entire length of the Demilitarized Zone in order to prevent the infiltration of North Korean guerrillas.

1968   North Korean guerrilla activities in the south reach a peak. Incidents include an attempt to assassinate President Park Chung Hee and the capture of the US intelligence ship *Pueblo*.

1971   North Korea begins to abandon its guerrilla activities and on 12 April Foreign Minister Ho Dam proposes an eight-point plan for unification. This formula is rejected by South Korea which offers a less ambitious three-stage proposal. The first-ever bilateral dialogue between North and South Korea begins in August when the North Korean Red Cross and South Korean Red Cross meet in Panmunjom to discuss the problem of families divided as a result of the partition of Korea.

1972   The visit of US President Nixon to China provides a further impetus towards rapprochement between North and South and on 4 July both sides issue a communiqué agreeing that a peaceful reunification should be reached as soon as possible. In order to facilitate any future agreements a South–North Co-ordinating Committee (SNCC) is formed.

1973 North Korea claims five small islands off the NW coast of the Korean peninsula and initial contacts developed through the Red Cross in the previous year break down in August.

1974 A proposal by President Park to form a non-agression pact is rejected by the North Korean government which will only agree to negotiate a peace agreement with the USA alone.

1975–76 Repeated attempts to reopen the dialogue between North and South fail since the USA refuses to negotiate without the participation of South Korea.

1977 President Carter announces the proposed withdrawal of all US ground forces from Korea over a period of four to five years. North Korea unilaterally extends its maritime jurisdiction 80km into the Yellow sea and 320km into the Sea of Japan.

1978 Some 3400 US troops are withdrawn from South Korea.

1979 New intelligence estimates of North Korean military strength force President Carter to postpone further troop withdrawals. He visits Seoul and proposes tripartite talks and the admission of both North and South Korea to the UN. The assassination of President Park in October prompts the North Koreans to put forward proposals for high level talks between North and South.

1980 On 12 January the North Korean government recognizes the government of South Korea for the first time and attempts are made to revive talks. However, the situation suddenly deteriorates following a series of incidents involving the infiltration of North Korean agents into the South and the sinking of naval vessels. Talks are broken off and President Kim Il Sung, who is anxious to replace the 1953 armistice with a peace treaty, declares that there is "a constant danger of war breaking out at any moment".

1981 In January the newly elected President of South Korea, Chun Doo Hwan, offers to meet Kim Il Sung and reaffirms his government's intention to reunify the country into an independent and democratic state.

1982 President Chun puts forward a set of proposals for reunification and advocates the setting up of a joint Consultative Conference for National Reunification. The proposals are again rejected by North Korea.

1983 Six leading South Korean politicians, including four members of the cabinet, are killed in a bomb blast while visiting Rangoon, Burma. North Korean responsibility for this action leads to increased tension along the Demilitarized Zone.

1984 In January North Korea attempts to improve its international image by proposing a tripartite conference involving North Korea, South Korea and the USA. Although the proposal now involves South Korea in discussions it is rejected by the USA on the grounds that China should also be included in talks. A softening of attitudes leads to some cross-border economic co-operation and the resumption of economic and Red Cross talks.

1985 Although interparliamentary talks make little headway, Red Cross negotiations result in the reunion of families who are allowed to return to their respective countries.

1986 When South Korea refuses to cancel its annual military exercises with the USA, North Korea calls off all bilateral talks. North–South dialogue reaches an impasse and tension between the two countries is heightened by arguments over the possible co-hosting of the 1988 summer Olympics.

1987 In an attempt to discourage countries from participating in the 1988 Olympics a South Korean airliner is destroyed by North Korean agents killing 115 passengers and crew.

1988 North Korea fails in its attempt to co-host the Olympics and representatives from 161 countries arrive in Seoul to compete in the games.

In April, South Korea's incoming President, Roh Tae Woo, declares his willingness to open up a constructive dialogue and to "respond to talks of any kind" in an attempt to reduce the tension that has built up in recent years between North and South. This initiative results in a series of interparliamentary meetings at Panmunjom between August and December, convened in an attempt to bring together the two national assemblies.

1989 North Korea refuses to attend further meetings in Panmunjom until the joint US–South Korean military Team Spirit exercises end. Other bilateral negotiations make little progress. These include the Red Cross talks and meetings of representatives of the two National Olympic Committees who have come together to discuss a joint team for the 1990 Asian Games in Beijing.

1990 In January Kim Il Sung proposes top-level talks to discuss the dismantling of barriers in the Demilitarized Zone. President Roh reciprocates by offering to reduce the annual Team Spirit military exercises, but within weeks both Red Cross negotiations and Asian Games talks reach a deadlock.

In South Korea there is a major political realignment in January when the ruling Democratic Justice Party is joined by the Reunification Democratic Party and the New Democratic Republican Party to form a grand conservative alliance which is named the Democratic Liberal Party.

■ Who's who

Choi Kyu Hah Prime Minister of South Korea who held the presidency for a year following the assassination of Park Chung Hee in 1979.

Chun Doo Hwan An army major–general who was named president following the resignation of Choi Kyu Hah in 1980 and who retired from the military to stand for election as President in 1981. His seven–year term of office was marked by a succession of student demonstrations and a series of incidents that heightened tension between North and South Korea.

Kim Dae Jong Leader of the South Korean opposition Party of Peace and Democracy. Arrested in 1979 and sentenced to death, he was eventually released from prison in July 1988.

Kim Il Sung President of North Korea and Secretary–General of the Korean Workers' Party since the creation of the Democratic People's Republic of Korea in 1948. Born in 1912, he fought against the Japanese in Manchuria in the 1930s and with the Soviet Army in the Far East during World War II. Surrounded by a personality cult, Kim Il Sung has wielded dictatorial power as the "Great Leader" in North Korea. For nearly half a century he has ruled the country through an elaborate party

structure and a hierarchy of civilian and military bureaucracies.

Kim Jong Il The son of North Korean President Kim Il Sung and a leading member of the Korean Worker's Party (KWP) Politburo. After working as his father's private secretary he was appointed to the KWP Secretariat and made head of the propaganda department in 1973. In 1977 he was seriously injured in a car accident that was thought to be an assassination attempt, but at the Sixth Congress of the KWP in October 1980 his position as successor to his father was confirmed. Since then a personality cult has developed around Kim Jong Il, the "Dear Leader".

Kim Jong Pil Leader of the opposition New Democratic Republican Party which joined the South Korean ruling Democratic Justice Party to form a grand conservative alliance in January 1990.

Kim Young Sam Leader of the Reunification Democratic Party which formed a conservative alliance with the New Democratic Republican Party and the ruling Democratic Justice Party in January 1990.

MacArthur, General Douglas   A hero of the US Pacific War against Japan, General MacArthur was selected by the USA to command the UN joint forces sent to Korea in 1950 following the North Korean invasion of South Korea. Having pushed the North Koreans back across the 38th parallel MacArthur's decision to continue northwards and reunify Korea met with considerable opposition and resulted in China's involvement in the conflict. While MacArthur favoured using the atomic bomb against China, President Truman preferred to confine the war to the Korean peninsula. MacArthur's subsequent attempt to sway US public opinion to his point of view resulted in his replacement by General Clarke in April 1951.

Park Chung Hee   A major–general and deputy commander of the South Korean Second Army who ousted the civilian government of President Yun during a military coup that took place on 16 May 1961. Pledging to reconstruct the economy, strengthen ties with the USA, fight communism and reunify Korea, Park's military regime governed with authoritarian ruthlessness for nearly two years until the restoration of civilian rule in March 1963. Retiring from the army, Park Chung Hee was elected President of the Third Republic, a position he held until his assassination in October 1979. During his presidency South Korea experienced great economic growth and rapid industrial modernization.

Rhee, Syngman   A leading political figure in Korea between 1919 and 1960. Born into a minor branch of the Korean Royal family in 1875, Syngman Rhee was elected president of the Korean government-in-exile in China following the nationalist uprisings and "Declaration of Independence" of 1919. After seven years imprisonment he fled to the USA where he raised financial and political support for the cause of Korean independence. In 1945 he joined the newly-created government of the People's Republic of Korea, formed in the aftermath of Japanese occupation. As a member of the centre-right Representative Democratic Council he opposed communism and advocated the establishment of a separate, non-communist, South Korean state. Despite widespread opposition to his administration, Rhee was able to maintain control of the Republic of Korea after its creation in 1948. By strengthening the power of the presidency and by aligning himself with the USA he was able to cling to power until, overwhelmed by public opposition and unrest, he was forced to resign in April 1960. A month later he left the country to live in exile in Hawaii.

Roh Tae Woo   Elected President of South Korea in 1988, Roh Tae Woo united moderate opposition groups to form a grand conservative alliance party in 1990. Despite an improved human rights record his government has been criticized for its suppression of trade unions and its treatment of opponents of its position on North Korea.

Yun Po Sun   President of South Korea during the Second Republic of 1960–61.

■ Key places

Chongsan   A village in Kangso county, North Korea, which was visited by Kim Il Sung in February 1960, and which gave its name to the *Chongsan-ni* method of improving agricultural production by increased communication between leaders and peasants and by profit–sharing at the work–team level.

Choson ("morning calm")   The name of the united Korean kingdom ruled by the Yi Dynasty from 1392 until 1910.

Han River   A river that rises in central South Korea and flows 467km north–west through Seoul to meet the Yellow Sea north of Inchon.

Hermit Kingdom   A nickname applied to Korea during the 19th century when the Yi

Dynasty rulers adopted a closed-door policy in order to protect themselves from foreign interference in the face of a long history of attack from China, Japan and Mongolia.

Inchon   South Korea's principal port on the Yellow Sea, 40km west of Seoul; population (1985) 1 387 500. It was through Inchon that most western foreigners first came to Korea in the 1880s and it was near here that the Japanese navy engaged and defeated the Russian navy in 1904. In September 1950 General MacArthur launched a UN counter–offensive against the North Koreans by making a surprise landing at Inchon and cutting off their lines of supply.

Korea   The Western name for the Korean peninsula which had been conquered in AD 935 by the Koguryo who renamed it the Kingdom of Koryo.

Kumgangsan   The site of a proposed hydro-electric dam on a northern tributary of the Han River about 10km north of the Demilitarized Zone. Work on this project commenced in 1986, causing a further source of tension between North and South. In November 1986, the South Korean Defence Minister threatened to take "self-defence measures" unless work ceased immediately, claiming that, if released, the water stored by the dam would submerge most of central Korea.

Paengyong Island   A flat, fertile island in the Yellow Sea just off the north-west coast of the Korean peninsula; area 29 km². The five small islands of Paengyong, Daechong, Sochong, Yonpyong and U have been under the military control of the UN Command since the armistice agreement of 1953, but in December 1973 they were claimed by North Korea. Four years later, on 1 August 1977, the North Korean Military Command announced that the country's military boundary extended 80km from the coast of North Korea into the Yellow Sea. Neither claims have been recognized internationally.

Panmunjom   The historic truce village where the armistice ending the Korean War was signed by representatives of the United Nations, North Korea and China on 27 July, 1953.

Situated on the Demilitarized Zone, 56 km north of Seoul.

Pusan   The second largest city and principal port of South Korea, situated at the south-eastern tip of the Korean peninsula; population (1985) 3 516 800. The Japanese had a concession here in the 19th century and during the Korean War it was the only major city not to fall to the North Koreans in 1950.

Pyongyang   The oldest city on the Korean peninsula and capital of North Korea since 1948, situated on the Taedong River. Almost completely destroyed by US bombing during the Korean War, the city now has a population of 2 639 400. It is the centre of administration of the government of the Democratic People's Republic of Korea.

Rangoon   The Chief port and capital of Burma. Once known as Dagon, it was renamed Rangoon ("end of conflict") in 1755. Since 1989 it has been called Yangon in Burmese. Population (1983) 2 458 700. In October 1983, a terrorist attack killed six of South Korea's leading politicians while on a visit to Rangoon. As a result of this incident the Burmese government broke off diplomatic relations with North Korea and arrested two North Korean army officers believed to have been sent to kill South Korean President Chun Doo Hwan.

Seoul   Capital of South Korea, situated on the Han River 120km from its entrance into the Yellow Sea; population (1985) 9 646 000. Founded in the 14th century as the capital of the Yi Dynasty, it was known as Hanyang until the late 19th century. During the Korean War the city was captured twice by the North Koreans in 1950. Seoul in 1988 was the venue for the summer Olympic Games which were attended by 161 national teams.

Tumen River   A river that flows 520km NE from the Changbai Mountains of NE China to the Sea of Japan. For part of its course it follows the frontier between North Korea and the Chinese province of Jilin.

Wonsan   Seaport and capital of Kangwon province, SE Korea, situated on the Sea of

Japan; population (1984) 350 000. In January 1968 four North Korean patrol boats captured and brought into the port the US intelligence ship *Pueblo* which had allegedly strayed into North Korean waters.

Yalu River   A river flowing a distance of 790km south–west from the Changbai Mountains of NE China to the Korea Bay, an inlet of the Yellow Sea. On its way it follows the greater part of the frontier between North Korea and the Chinese provinces of Jilin and Liaoning. The Japanese-built Sui-Ho hydro-electric scheme on the Yalu river was used by both China and Korea. In 1950 the approach of UN forces towards the Yalu River prompted the entry of China into the Korean War.

■ Key words

armistice   On 27 July 1953 three years of hostilities were brought to an end when representatives of the North Korean Army, the UN Command and China signed an armistice at Panmunjom. A Demilitarized Zone straddling a 250km–long Military Demarcation Line was established and a joint commission was set up to supervise the implementation of the terms of the armistice. In addition, the armistice called for an international conference to reach a lasting peace agreement that would resolve the problem of Korea's division.

Central People's Committee   The 25–man top policy–making body in North Korea.

Chollima ("flying horses")   The North Korean version of the Chinese Great Leap Forward which was introduced in 1956 as a means of achieving rapid modernization through a technical revolution in which workers were exhorted to strive for ever greater production in the name of socialism.

Committee for the Preparation of Korean Independence (CPKI)   Before the arrival of US troops in September 1945 the Japanese governor-general handed over power to the left-wing nationalist Yo Un Hyong who established the CPKI as a first step towards the creation of a national assembly and the establishment of the People's Republic of Korea.

Demilitarized Zone   A 4km–wide no-man's-land stretching the full length of a Military Demarcation Line established at the end of the Korean War. This 250km–long zone, which straddles the 38th parallel from coast to coast, acts as a *de facto* frontier between North and South Korea. As a result of the demarcation of the armistice line on 27 July 1953, North Korea gained some 2000km^2 of territory on the western front, south of the 38th parallel, while South Korea acquired nearly 6000km^2 of land in the central and eastern sectors of the front to the north. Following a dramatic increase in the number of cross-border incidents the US and South Korean forces built a barbed wire fence along the entire length of the Demilitarized Zone in the autumn of 1967.

Democratic Liberal Party   A South Korean conservative political alliance formed in January 1990 when the ruling Democratic Justice Party under President Roh united with the Reunification Democratic Party and the New Democratic Republican Party.

Geneva Conference   A conference convened in April 1954 for the purpose of discussing the Korean conflict. Attended by 19 nations, the conference failed to make any progress towards the signing of a peace treaty.

Hangul   The alphabet adopted by the Koreans in the 15th century and still widely used in North Korea.

juche   The North Korean concept of economic "self-reliance" introduced by Kim Il Sung in 1955.

Military Armistice Commission   A ten–member commission set up in July 1953 with power to supervise the implementation of the terms of the armistice.

Neutral Nations Supervisory Commission (NNSC)   A twenty–member commission comprising representatives from Switzerland, Poland, Sweden and Czechoslovakia, set up in 1953 to supervise the armistice. This group proved unworkable and was eventually disbanded in June 1956.

North Korean Workers' Party   The ruling communist party of North Korea founded in July 1946 by Kim Il Sung who united all of the left–wing parties in the North.

Party of Peace and Democracy (PPD)   Led by Kim Dae Jung, the PPD is the principal opposition party in South Korea.

People's Committees   Self-appointed councils which sprang up at village, urban and provincial levels throughout Korea following the establishment of the People's Republic of Korea in the immediate aftermath of World War II. Largely composed of Korean nationalists, the People's Committees were supported by the Soviet Union in the North but viewed with suspicion by the US–backed administration that developed under Syngman Rhee in the South.

Red Cross Talks   Bilateral talks between North and South Korea held through their respective Red Cross societies. Such talks were first held in August 1971 with the aim of reuniting families separated by the partition of Korea after the war.

Team Spirit exercises   Annual military exercises carried out jointly by the US and South Korean armed forces. The South Korean government's decision not to cancel these exercises resulted in the breakdown of bilateral talks between North and South in January 1986.

UN Command (UNC)   A 16-nation joint military force established by the United Nations following the North Korean invasion of South Korea on 25 June 1950.

UN Temporary Commission on Korea (UNTCOK)   A commission established by the UN on 14 November 1947 for the purpose of supervising elections throughout Korea and establishing a single government. Viewed with suspicion by the North Koreans and the Soviet Union, UNTCOK officials were barred from supervising the political process north of the 38th parallel when they arrived in May 1948.

Yalta Conference   A conference convened in April 1945 at which the Soviet Union and the USA agreed to establish a temporary joint trusteeship over Korea.

■ Further reading

Brian Bridges, *Korea and the West*, Routledge and Kegan Paul, London, 1986

Y.W. Kihl, *Politics and Policies in Divided Korea*, Westview Press, Boulder, 1984

Young Jeh Kim, *Towards a Unified Korea: History and Alternatives*, Seoul, 1987

D.S. Lewis (ed.), *Korea: Enduring Division*, Keesing's Special Report, Longman, Harlow, 1988

Peter Lowe, *The Origins of the Korean War*, Longman, Harlow, 1986

M.P. Srivastava, *The Korean conflict: Search for Unification*, New Delhi, 1982

7
East Timor

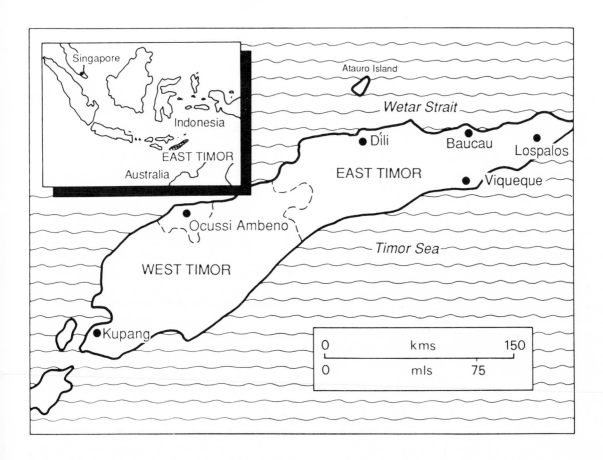

■ Profile

- **Area:** 14 874km²
- **Total area of Timor island:** 33 900km²
- **Population (1970):** 610 500
- **Population (1980):** 555 000
- **Capital:** Díli
- **Main exports:** Sandalwood, coffee, copra, tobacco
- **Ethnic groups:** Malay, Papuan and Chinese
- **Religions:** Muslim 60%, Christian 40%

■ Introduction

Third World states created from European colonial empires have sometimes proved to be as keen on territorial aggrandizement as their former masters once were, and similarly willing to ride rough-shod over the right to self-determination. Usually the governments concerned have had what they regard as overriding justification for such claims, be it ethnic ties, historic political connexions or simply the perceived shortcomings of colonial boundary-drawing. But in some instances disregard of the principle of self-determination has left a sour taste in the mouth of international opinion. A case in point is the post-independence expansion, and would-be expansion, of Indonesia, which has absorbed nearby territories and coveted others despite clear evidence that their peoples wished otherwise. Among these actions, the seizure of East Timor in 1975–76 remains the most controversial internationally and the most disputed locally.

Under the persuasive propagation of the powerful Sultanate of Malacca to the west, Islam made its mark on the Antoni people of western Timor well before the arrival of the Portuguese in 1520. With the Portuguese came the Roman Catholic Church, which in Timor had its customary success in converting backward people to its version of the Christian faith. Catholicism became particularly strong among the Belu people of eastern and southern Timor, so that when the Dutch captured the western half of the island in the early 17th century a partial Muslim/Christian divide already existed. Over the next 250 years East Timor continued under Portuguese rule and languished economically, apart from the profitable sandalwood trade to China, while West Timor made some progress within the trading framework of the Dutch Empire.

When the Dutch East Indies achieved independence as Indonesia in 1949, West Timor became part of the new, predominantly Muslim, state. But East Timor remained subject to the Portuguese, whose attachment to empire long outlasted that of the other European colonial powers. Under the long Salazar dictatorship, all the Portuguese

overseas territories came to be regarded as part of metropolitan Portugal, a stance backed by force, particularly in Africa (*see sections 1.4, 1.5*). Nothing much changed under the successor Caetano regime, although disquiet built up within the armed forces about the prosecution of unwinnable colonial wars. When Caetano was deposed in the 1974 revolution, a central purpose of the new military rulers was to terminate the wars in Africa and to grant independence to the territories involved. There was, however, no such commitment to East Timor, because a speedy withdrawal was seen as likely to lead to an Indonesian takeover rather than to self-determination.

As for Muslim Indonesia, its military rulers had long since set themselves the task of absorbing the remaining colonial outposts in the East Indies. Christian Ambon and the South Moluccas had quickly been integrated into Indonesia, which in 1963 had asserted its claim to Dutch New Guinea (Irian Jaya) by force of arms. Confirmed in possession of Irian Jaya by the United Nations in 1963, Indonesia had then laid claim to the British-ruled parts of Borneo, but had failed to prevent Sabah and Sarawak from joining the Malaysian Federation, or Brunei from opting for separate independence. Undeterred, it turned its sights on East Timor, and seized its opportunity in the confused situation created by the 1974 revolution in Lisbon. An inestimable advantage for the Jakarta regime in its pursuit of territorial expansion was that the United States – the major military power in the region – saw a strong Indonesia as a bulwark against communism. The same was true of Australia, the only other regional power with the capacity to oppose Indonesian aims.

Indeed, it was the then Labour government of Australia that helped to bring on the 1975 crisis by signalling to Indonesia in September 1974 that annexation of East Timor was preferable to separate independence. For both governments (and for the United States) a crucial factor was that East Timor's independence movement, Fretilin, contained a strong communist element and had external communist backing. As for the third option, namely continued Portuguese status, the probability that a majority of the East Timorese people would have preferred this (if they had been consulted) did not deter Indonesia, although it presented difficulties to the new government in Lisbon. Conscious of its military weakness, Portugal vacillated between upholding the principle of self-determination in East Timor and finding a plausible means of making a speedy exit from the territory.

When the pro-Indonesian parties of East Timor attempted a coup in mid-1985, the Portuguese government condemned their action but began to evacuate its personnel as civil war developed between these parties and Fretilin. Portugal was equally condemnatory of Fretilin's unilateral declaration of independence in November 1975, but by then its authority in East Timor was a dead letter and the United Nations could do little to help. In consequence, the way was open for Indonesia to send in troops in December 1975, officially to assist the East Timorese people in their "liberation struggle". This meant enabling the pro-Indonesian parties to set up a government, combined with ruthless suppression of Fretilin resistance. Despite international censure, Indonesia then moved speedily to formal annexation of East Timor in August 1976.

Having gained possession of East Timor, the Indonesians sat back and waited for international recognition to follow. It proved to be slow in coming, although a steady trickle included the important, and entirely expected, formal acceptance of Indonesian sovereignty by Australia in January 1978. Thereafter, a majority of UN members, including Portugal itself, the United States and Britain, continued to regard Indonesia's action as illegal, although nothing was done in the UN or anywhere else to implement calls for East Timor to be given the right of self-determination under UN auspices. Indonesia has therefore remained in possession of East Timor, which it renamed Loro Sae.

Internally, on the other hand, a regrouped and revitalized Fretilin launched a new guerrilla campaign in the early 1980s, aiming to force an Indonesian withdrawal and achieve self-determination for East Timor. Its increasing successes caused serious embarrassment to the Indonesian authorities, not least because Fretilin had extensive support among the East Timor people. Indonesia responded in the classic colonialist vein by instituting massive population resettlement combined with an enhanced military presence and repression of the local populace. The stage was therefore set for a protracted internal guerrilla war, with the twist that the "government" side regarded itself as being in the vanguard of non-alignment and anti-colonialism.

■ Chronology of events

1520 In their penetration of the islands of the East Indies, the Portuguese establish themselves on Timor.

1618 Despite the arrival of the Portuguese in the previous century, the Dutch establish a dominant role as rulers of the islands of present-day Indonesia including the western half of the island of Timor. The eastern half of the island, with its rich reserves of sandalwood, stays in Portuguese hands.

1859 The Dutch and Portuguese settle on a frontier between East and West Timor.

1904 The 1859 frontier agreement is confirmed with the signing of a treaty by Portugal and the Netherlands.

1914 The 1904 frontier treaty dividing the island of Timor finally comes into effect.

1926 Formerly governed from Portuguese Macao, East Timor becomes an independent colony of Portugal with an administrative capital at Díli.

1949 West Timor, with its largely Moslem population, joins with other parts of the former

Dutch East Indies to become the Republic of Indonesia, but East Timor, strongly influenced by the Roman Catholic Church, remains a Portuguese colony.

1974   In April the government of Marcelo Caetano in Portugal is overthrown during a military coup, an event that will eventually lead to the decolonization of Portuguese overseas territories. At a meeting in Java, President Suharto of Indonesia and Prime Minister Gough Whitlam of Australia discuss the situation in East Timor and are reported to agree that, while neither side will interfere, annexation by Indonesia would be in the best interests of the territory. A month later, on a visit to Jakarta, the Portuguese Minister for Inter-Territorial Co-ordination, Dr Antnio de Almeida Santos, suggests that, although he does not consider East Timor capable of surviving as an independent state, a referendum should be held to determine the way in which decolonization should proceed.

1975   The proposed referendum does not take place, but in June the Portuguese government holds a conference in the colony of Macao to discuss the future status of the territory. Representatives of the two main political parties of East Timor, the UDT and Apodeti, are present. An agreement is reached extending Portuguese authority until October 1978 and affirming the right of the Timorese people to determine their own future. A constitutional law is published a month later, providing for elections to a Timorese People's Assembly scheduled for October 1976.

Under attack from the left–wing Fretilin liberation movement, the UDT stages a coup on 11 August and demands immediate independence from Portugal as well as the arrest of all Fretilin supporters. By 21 August the Portuguese authorities have lost control of the territory which is now gripped by full-scale civil war between the forces of Fretilin and those of the UDT, fighting as an anti-communist movement with the support of Apodeti and the two smaller groups, the Kota and Trabalhista parties. Large numbers of Portuguese nationals are evacuated to Australia and on 17 August the governor and his administration finally leave

East Timor for the safety of the island of Atauro which lies 25 km north of Díli.

By 8 September Fretilin claims to have gained complete control of the territory and offers peace talks. Meanwhile Indonesia threatens to retaliate with force if Fretilin military action brings the civil war any closer to the Indonesian frontier. In addition, it refuses to accept any attempt by Portugal to hand over power to a Fretilin government, declaring a right to intervene in Portuguese Timor if the war endangers Indonesian territory.

A memorandum of understanding signed by the Foreign Ministers of Portugal and Indonesia in Rome on 3 November confirms that Portugal is still the legitimate authority in East Timor with responsibility for decolonization. The Fretilin transitional administration does not recognise the results of the Rome meeting and claims that an Indonesian invasion is imminent.

On 28 November the Fretilin government announces the independence of the territory as the Democratic Republic of East Timor. On the following day Francisco Xavier do Amaral is sworn in as president and two days later a government is formed with Nicolau dos Reis Lobato as Prime Minister. The pro-Indonesian parties within East Timor claim that the declaration of independence by Fretilin   has "removed the last remains of Portuguese sovereignty in Timor", thus legitimizing union with Indonesia. Rejecting both the Fretilin and pro-Indonesian stances, the Portuguese government formally requests help from the United Nations in order to find a solution to the East Timor conflict.

On 7 December 1000 paratroopers, described by the Indonesian government as "volunteers", enter East Timor and capture Díli with the backing of a naval bombardment. Portugal immediately breaks off diplomatic relations with Indonesia and reaffirms its intention of administering a peaceful decolonization process. On 13 December the Portuguese exclave of Ocussi Ambeno on the north coast of West Timor is annexed by Indonesia and by 28 December all Portuguese links with the former colony come to an end when the

Portuguese governor and his staff are forced to leave the island of Atauro which is occupied by pro-Indonesian resistance forces. The UN General Assembly passes a resolution condemning Indonesia's military intervention and the Security Council calls on Indonesia to withdraw its troops from East Timor. Both actions are ignored by Indonesia. By the end of December it is alleged that over 60 000 people have died in the civil war which continues with each side claiming control of the greater part of the territory.

1976   On 21 March the Indonesian Foreign Ministry announces that the provisional government in East Timor is to form a parliament that will sanction the integration of the territory into Indonesia. Two months later on 31 May the newly-formed People's Representative Council approves the merger. Of the 25 countries invited to send observers to the Council Sessions, only representatives from India, Iran, Malaysia, New Zealand, Nigeria, Saudi Arabia and Thailand turn up. On 7 June the Council's petition to become part of Indonesia is presented to President Suharto of Indonesia and on 24 June the former Portuguese colony is transferred to an Indonesian fact-finding mission. The United Nations declines to send an observer on the basis that the election of the People's Representative Council had not been supervised by the UN and on 29 June the Indonesian government announces its acceptance of the merger proposal. On 17 July a bill legalizing the annexation of East Timor is passed by the Indonesian Parliament and a month later East Timor is declared Indonesia's 27th province with the name Loro Sae. Meanwhile, the war with Fretilin guerrillas continues.

1977   An unofficial report published in February by James Dunn, former Australian Consul in East Timor, claims that after the 1975 invasion Indonesian troops massacred 100 000 Timorese including nearly half of the territory's Chinese population. In June a further report, compiled by two Australian Foreign Ministry officials, states that the Australian government accepts the annexation of East Timor by Indonesia as an "irreversible fact". During an amnesty ordered in August by President Suharto it is claimed that 60 000 Fretilin rebels surrender. Among them is the former President of the Democratic Republic of East Timor, Francisco Xavier do Amaral, who has been sacked by his Fretilin comrades.

1978   In January the Australian government recognizes the annexation of East Timor by Indonesia but is critical of the way in which it was achieved.

1979   Despite assurances made by President Castro of Cuba to President Suharto of Indonesia in April, the sixth conference of heads of state and government of the Non-Aligned Movement (NAM) held in Havana in September adopts a resolution reaffirming the right of self-determination for the people of East Timor. In the same month Portugal demonstrates its continued interest in the East Timor problem when the Portuguese Prime Minister meets representatives of the newly-formed National Movement for the Liberation of and Independence of Timor–Díli. In the five–year period to the end of 1979 it is officially estimated that 60 000 people have died in the conflict and that 25 000 people have moved to West Timor and a further 5000 to Australia.

1980   The Portuguese government continues to claim sovereignty over East Timor and, in an attempt to keep alive the possibility of self-determination under a Christian regime, it announces that it will seek direct talks with Indonesian officials to discuss independence for the territory. Indonesia refuses to discuss the independence of East Timor with Portugal.

1981   The People's Representative Council of East Timor writes to President Suharto in June offering "undying gratitude" but objecting to the conduct of Indonesian troops who are accused of acts of murder and violence.

1982   The conduct of Indonesian forces is again brought to light in a statement by the Catholic Institute for International Relations in London which points out that Indonesian troops are still engaged in large-scale operations at the eastern end of the island.

1983   In July representatives of the governments of Indonesia and Portugal meet to discuss the East Timor conflict.

1984   The Bishop of Timor, Monsignor Carlos Ximenes Belo, is held for four days after accusing Jakarta of human rights violations. Pope John Paul II later rebukes the Indonesian government for obstructing relief efforts. International pressure is maintained when the US Secretary of State George Schultz expresses concern about the situation during a visit to Jakarta.

1985   A report published in June by Amnesty International claims that since the 1975 invasion over 500 000 people have been killed or "resettled" in East Timor.

1986   Reports reaching friends of the East Timorese in Lisbon suggeste that ill-equipped but well organized Fretilin guerrillas are still active in ten military zones in the east and central highlands, an area amounting to nearly half of East Timor. This is contrary to the claim from Jakarta that resistance activities present no problem to peaceful administration of the territory.

1988 Fresh supplies of explosives reach the Fretilin guerrillas and raiding parties mount a series of attacks that include the blowing up of an army supply dump at Lospalos. Explosions in widely separate locations indicate that Fretilin is able to operate with impunity throughout the territory and that Indonesian forces have failed in their attempt to push the rebels towards the Eastern tip of the island.

■ Who's who

Almeida Santos, Dr Antonio de   As Minister for Inter-Territorial Co-ordination following the Portuguese revolution of April 1974, Almeida Santos was responsible for initiating the process of decolonization in East Timor. Although he doubted whether the territory could survive as an independent state, he suggested that a constituent assembly should be elected in Portuguese Timor as a prerequisite to holding a referendum on self-determination in 1975.

Amaral, Francisco Xavier do   President of the anti-Indonesian Fretilin revolutionary movement who was sworn in as the first President of the Democratic Republic of East Timor on 29 November 1975, a week before the invasion of the former Portuguese territory by Indonesian troops. In September 1977 Amaral, who had been removed from his position as leader of Fretilin, surrendered to the Indonesian authorities during an amnesty and was appointed Deputy Governor of the province.

Belo, Carlos Jimenez   Acting Bishop of East Timor who was held for four days in 1984 for accusing Jakarta of human rights violations.

Dunn, James   A former Australian consul in East Timor and head of the foreign affairs division of the Australian Parliament's research service. He was responsible for publishing an unofficial report on 21 February 1977 in which it was estimated that up to 100 000 Timorese people had been massacred by Indonesian troops following the invasion of East Timor in 1975.

Lopes da Cruz, Francisco Xavier   President of the Democratic Union of Timor (UDT) party which staged the August 1975 coup that sparked off the civil war and brought to an end the Portuguese administration of East Timor. He later returned to power as the Vice-Chairman of the Provisional Government that replaced the Fretilin regime in December 1975. Following the merger of the territory with Indonesia, Lopes da Cruz was appointed Deputy Governor of Indonesia's 27th province.

Malik, Dr Adam   Indonesian Foreign Minister who declared in September 1975 that his country had the right to intervene in East Timor if the civil war endangered Indonesian territory. Despite signing a memorandum of understanding in Rome that recognized Portuguese responsibility for the peaceful decolonization of East Timor, he later justified Indonesia's military intervention by claiming that Portugal had lost control of the situation and was therefore unable to implement the Rome Memorandum.

Reis Araujo, Arnaldo dos Leading member of the pro-Indonesian Timorese Democratic Union Party (Apodeti) who was appointed Chief Executive of the provisional government that replaced the Fretilin regime following the invasion of East Timor by Indonesian forces in December 1975. In August 1976, when the territory was officially proclaimed Indonesia's 27th province, Reis Araujo was appointed its first Governor.

Reis Lobato, Nicolau dos Prime Minister of the government of the Democratic Republic of East Timor established by the Fretilin movement in December 1975 six days before the Indonesian invasion of the territory. Reis Lobato replaced Amaral as the President of Fretilin

in September 1977, but was killed in action 16 months later in January 1979.

Sha Na Na, José Gusmão Leader, since 1982, of the Revolutionary Council of National Resistance, a reorganized command structure of the Fretilin guerrilla forces fighting for the independence of East Timor.

Suharto, General A former military commander whose rise to prominence followed the crushing of an attempted Communist coup in 1965. Exposing mismanagement and corruption by government officials, Suharto wrested power from the hands of President Achmad Sukarno and took effective control of Indonesia in 1967. A year later he was elected to the post of President. Although he was able to move away from the radical ideology of his predecessor, take his country into ASEAN and end confrontation with Malaysia, his presidency has been marred by the annexation of East Timor and the subsequent allegations of human rights violations by Indonesian armed forces there.

■ Key places

Atauro Also known as **Pulo Cambing** and **Kambang**, the island of Atuaro lies in the Ombai Strait 25km north of Dili, capital of East Timor. A former dependency of Portugal. On the outbreak of civil war in August 1975, the governor of East Timor and his staff were evacuated to the island where they remained for four months prior to the occupation of Atauro by pro-Indonesian forces.

Baucau Formerly known by its Portuguese name, Vila Salazar, the seaport of Baucau lies on the north coast of East Timor, 96km east of Díli. A trade centre for agricultural and forest produce, the town is a base for Indonesian troops who have attempted to drive Fretilin guerrillas towards the eastern peninsula by developing a military cordon from Baucau to the south coast.

Díli Capital and chief commercial port of East Timor on the north coast of the island of Timor.

With a population (1980) of 60 000, the port trades in rice, coffee, cotton and sandalwood. Following the outbreak of civil war in August 1975, Díli became the focal point of attempts to seize control of the territory.

Kupang Capital of the Indonesian province of Nusa Tenggara Timur. Situated on the south-west coast of the island of Timor, it was formerly a Dutch trading post and port of call for British and American whaling ships. Captain Bligh ended his epic voyage here after experiencing a mutiny on his ship *The Bounty* and Somerset Maugham used the tropical setting of Kupang in his novels and short stories. Population (1980) 52 700. The port is used as a naval base by Indonesia.

Lesser Sunda Islands The Sunda islands, which occupy the west part of the Malay archipelago between the South China Sea and the Indian Ocean, are divided into the Greater

Sundas, which include the larger islands of Borneo, Java and Sumatra, and the Lesser Sundas to the east of Java from Bali to the island of Timor.

Loro Sae or **Timor Timur**   Known locally as "Tim Tim", Loro Sae is the name given by the Indonesian government to the former Portuguese colony of East Timor following its incorporation into Indonesia as the country's 27th province in August 1976.

Lospalos   A town in the Lautem district of East Timor, situated near the eastern tip of the island of Timor, 150km east of DIíli. A trading centre for copra, tobacco and timber, and an Indonesian military base. In 1988, during a resurgence of Fretilin guerrilla activity, an Indonesian army supply dump in Lospalos was destroyed by a raiding party.

Macao   An overseas province of Portugal at the mouth of the Pearl River, SE China. Population (1981) 262 000. Portuguese East Timor was administered from Macao until 1926.

Nusa Tenggara Timur or **East Nusa Tenggara**   A province of Indonesia in the Lesser Sundas comprising the islands of Sumba and Flores as well as the western part of the island of Timor. The majority of the population of 2 737 000 earn a living from agriculture, forestry and fishing. The provincial. capital is Kupang in West Timor; area 47 876km^2.

Ocussi Ambeno   Until the civil war of 1975 a Portuguese exclave of East Timor on the north coast of Indonesian West Timor. Sandalwood, rice and copra were the chief products traded by the Portuguese through the port of Pantemacassar which lies 150km WSW of Díli. Also known simply as Oe-Cusse, Oekusi or Ambeno.

Ombai Strait or **Selat Ombai** also **Matu Strait**   A stretch of water 30–80km wide, separating the island of Timor from the island of Alor to the north.

Viqueque   A trading centre near the south coast of East Timor, situated in an area that produces rice, cotton, copra, palm oil and timber. The town is also a base for Indonesian troops at the southern end of the military cordon that extends from the north coast at Baucau in an attempt to isolate Fretilin guerrillas in the eastern peninsula of East Timor.

West Timor   A name generally applied to that part of the island of Timor formerly held by the Dutch but included as part of the independent republic of Indonesia in 1949. Area 19 026km^2. Now part of the province of the Indonesian Nusa Tenggara Timor. The chief town is Kupang which is also provincial capital.

Wetar Strait or **Selat Wetar**   A stretch of water separating the island of Timor from the island of Wetar to the north.

■ Key words

Democratic Union of Timor (Unio Democratica de Timor – UDT)   One of the three principal political parties formed in East Timor after the Portuguese revolution of 1974. Advocating continued, though looser, ties with Portugal, the UDT took power by force in August 1975. This action led to the subsequent outbreak of full-scale civil war. In 1979 the UDT joined with Fretilin and other anti-Indonesian Timorese resistance forces to form the National Movement for the Liberation of and Independence of Timor Díli.

Fretilin (Frente Revolucionara de Timor-Leste Independente)   The principal anti-Indonesian movement to emerge in East Timor after the Portuguese revolution of April 1974. Advocating immediate independence, it opposed the power take-over staged by the UDT party in August 1975. During the civil war that followed, Fretilin gained control of the greater part of East Timor, declaring the territory independent as the Democratic Republic of East Timor with the party leader, Francisco Xavier do Amaral, as President.

Ousted during the Indonesian annexation of the territory in December 1975, Fretilin forces retreated into the eastern and central highlands from where they organized a guerrilla campaign against Indonesian troops. Although many of their leaders surrendered or were captured, Fretilin was able to regroup under new leadership in 1982. Fielding at most 3000 armed men, Fretilin continued to harass the 15 000–strong Indonesian military force which was attempting to contain them at the eastern tip of the island. In 1979 Fretilin joined with other Timorese resistance groups to form the National Movement for the Liberation of and Independence of Timor–Díli.

Kota   A minority political party in East Timor which lent its support to the UDT in opposing the anti-Indonesian Fretilin movement at the outbreak of the civil war in August 1975.

National Movement for the Liberation of and Independence of Timor–Díli   A union of anti-Indonesian Timorese resistance forces formed in 1979 with the aim of uniting their efforts to achieve independence for East Timor under a Christian regime.

Operasi Keamanan ("operation security") The codename given to the military operation mounted against the forces of Fretilin by Indonesian paratroopers during the annexation of East Timor in December 1975.

People's Revolutionary Council   The 28–member government of East Timor established in the wake of the annexation of the island by Indonesian forces and dominated by members of the Apodeti party. In May 1976 the Council approved the merger with Indonesia and presented a petition to Jakarta with a view to formalizing the arrangement to become Indonesia's 27th province.

Revolutionary Council of National Resistance   A reorganized command structure within the anti-Indonesian Fretilin resistance movement set up in 1982 to revitalize the guerrilla campaign against Indonesian troops in East Timor.

Rome Memorandum   A memorandum of understanding signed by the Foreign Ministers of Portugal and Indonesia in Rome on 3 November 1975 in which they agreed that Portugal represented the legitimate authority responsible for the decolonization of East Timor. Rejected out of hand by Fretilin, the Rome understanding was soon ignored by the Indonesian government which forcibly annexed East Timor a month later, claiming that Portugal had lost control of the situation to such an extent that the Rome memorandum could not be implemented.

Timorese Democratic People's Union (Apodeti)   One of the principal pro-Indonesian political parties formed in East Timor after the Portuguese revolution of April 1974. Apodeti advocated the merger of the territory with Indonesia as an autonomous province. In 1976 the party leader, Arnaldo dos Reis Araujo, became the first Governor of the province after annexation by Indonesia.

Timorese Social Democratic Association (ASDT)   A nationalist political party formed in East Timor after the Portuguese revolution of April 1974. Advocating full independence for the territory over a possible five–year transition period the ASDT did not support the idea of an immediate referendum on self-determination on the grounds that 90 per cent of the population was uneducated and therefore open to manipulation. Within months this party was superceded by the anti-Indonesian Fretilin revolutionary movement.

Trabalhista   A small socialist political group in East Timor which lent its support to the UDT at the outset of the civil war in August 1975.

■ Further reading

Noam Chomsky, *East Timor and the Western Democracies*, Bertrand Russell Foundation, Nottingham, 1979

Harold Crouch, *The Army and Politics in Indonesia*, Norton, New York, 1978

R.C. Deiongh, *Indonesia: Yesterday and Today*, Sydney, 1973

A. Kohen, *An Act of Genocide: Indonesia's Invasion of East Timor*, Tapol, London, 1979

Wilfred T. Neil, *Twentieth–Century Indonesia*, Columbia University Press, London and New York, 1973

Peter Polomka, *Indonesia Since Sukarno*, Penguin Books, London, 1971

IV Americas

1
Nicaragua

■ Profile

Official name: Republic of Nicaragua

- **Area:** 127 849km²
- **Population (1987 est.):** 3 500 000
- **Ethnic groups:** Mestizo 69%, European 14%, African 8%, Zambo 5%, Amerindian 4%
- **Official language:** Spanish; English and Indian languages are spoken in the east
- **Religion:** Roman Catholic 90%
- **Life expectancy (1985):** 59 years
- **Infant mortality rate (1985):** 69 per 1000
- **Currency:** new córdoba of 100 centavos (since 1988)
- **Administrative divisions:** six regions and three special zones (since 1981)
- **Timezone:** GMT −6
- **Capital:** Managua
- **Chief towns:** Managua (682 000), Léon (101 000), Granada (88 600)

■ Introduction

Nicaragua emerged from three centuries of Spanish colonial rule in 1821 with an uncertain political identity and indistinct borders. Shortlived membership of the United Provinces of Central America (1823–38) gave way to internal strife between Liberals and Conservatives based respectively in the cities of Léon and Granada. Not until 1852 did the two sides patch up a compromise establishing Managua as the capital, although without resolving their ideological differences. The latter led to the first direct US military intervention in Nicaragua, by the adventurer William Walker. His brief hold on power (1856–57) was ended by other Central American states backed by Britain, then the dominant military and trading power in the Caribbean. But British strategic designs on Nicaragua as the then-favoured site of an Atlantic-Pacific canal were quickly thwarted by a US government determined to apply the 1823 Monroe Doctrine to further its own regional interests. Under the 1860 Treaty of Managua Britain relinquished its protectorate over the Mosquito Coast (on the Nicaraguan and Honduran Atlantic seaboard), the southern section of which was incorporated into Nicaragua in 1894. By 1906, when Britain finally renounced all claims to the Mosquito Coast, the United States was the dominant regional power, already with a role in Nicaragua.

As the 20th century opened, US policy towards Latin America combined a self-appointed "civilizing" mission with, at least in some quarters, a conviction that what European colonialists were then doing in Africa and Asia the United States could do in its own hemisphere. Under President Theodore Roosevelt's 1904 corollary to the Monroe Doctrine, the United States assumed the right to intervene in countries displaying any "loosening of the ties of civilized society". His successor, William Taft, went further in 1912 by looking forward to the day when "the whole hemisphere will be ours in fact as by virtue of superiority of race it already is ours morally". Such dreams of empire receded after World War I, although in 1927 the US State Department noted candidly that "Central America has always understood that governments which we recognize and support stay in power, while those we do not ... fall". These sentiments were not universally shared in the region, whose 20th-century history has largely turned on resistance to US political and economic domination, known to its opponents in Nicaragua and elsewhere as "Yankee imperialism".

In Nicaragua the US-orchestrated deposition of the Liberal President Zelaya in 1910 led to his successor-but-one, Adolfo Díaz, placing Nicaragua under the protection of the United States in 1911 in return for financial support. When this arrangement encountered internal resistance, Washington responded in an already familiar manner by sending in the US Marines, for what proved to be an almost continuous occupation of over two decades. During this period Nicaraguan presidential elections were "supervised" to ensure the return of pro-US candidates, the economy came under wholesale US domination and the US military trained a Nicaraguan National Guard to deal with internal opposition. The inevitable legacy, when US forces finally withdrew in 1933, was a burgeoning insurgent movement, to some extent inspired by Bolshevist ideas but essentially nationalist in its basic aim of ending Nicaragua's client relationship with the United States. Led by Augusto César Sandino, the rebels scored some notable successes against the departing US troops, who received an early lesson in the difficulty of defeating determined guerrillas enjoying popular support. Sandino's murder by the National Guard in February 1934 only served to elevate him to the status of folk hero among those opposed to the right-wing authoritarian regime established by the Somoza clan in 1936.

In the post-1945 global competition between the superpowers, the United States was initially confident of keeping communism at bay in its "own backyard". If this basic aim meant bolstering right-wing dictatorships, that was to be preferred to allowing the Soviet Union to gain a foothold in the Americas through the agency of local left-wing movements. In Nicaragua the Somoza regime continued to enjoy US backing even after the 1959 Cuban revolution had demonstrated the dangers of this strategy. It is true that the shock of Cuba inspired new US efforts, notably through President Kennedy's Alliance for Progress, to cultivate non-communist popular movements in Latin America, and that this policy switch had some successes. But in countries such as Nicaragua, deep-rooted anti-Americanism ensured that politicians who responded to US overtures were regarded as paid lackeys of the CIA (which they often were). When the lid finally blew off

the Nicaraguan cauldron in 1978–79 and the Somoza regime was swept away, all currents of the victorious Sandinista National Liberation Front (FSLN) – social democrats and Catholics as well as Marxists – were united in viewing the United States as the main external enemy.

Faced with what it saw as a "second Cuba", the United States opted for the same confrontation tactics which had been tried, without success, against the Castro regime. As they once had in Indo-China, US strategists feared a "domino effect" by which the Nicaraguan revolution would cause other Central American regimes to fall. Accordingly, a diplomatic and economic boycott was imposed on the Sandinista regime, and the latter's opponents, the Contras, were given US arms and funds to launch a guerrilla struggle from bases in neighbouring Honduras. Whereas the United States had never been able to create an effective opposition inside island Cuba, the Contras wrought havoc on Nicaragua's infrastructure, although without posing a serious threat to the new regime. The Sandinistas responded by forming a revolutionary axis with Cuba, by accepting large quantities of Soviet aid and weaponry and by channelling support to the guerrillas seeking to topple the pro-US government of nearby El Salvador (*see section 4.2*).

Contra attacks and US sanctions were cited by the FSLN as the prime causes of Nicaragua's deepening post-1979 economic crisis. At least part of the blame lay in the regime's pursuit of Marxist policies such as nationalization and central planning. The overall effect was that efforts to reverse the social neglect of the Somoza decades were undermined. In Washington congressional opposition to the Contra connexion failed to deflect the White House from its conviction that Nicaragua had fallen under the sway of Cuban-backed communists who must be deposed. Under the Reagan presidency the administration's increasingly folorn hope that this would be achieved by the less-than-dedicated Contras led it into the quagmire of the Iran-Contra scandal of the late 1980s. Meanwhile, all manner of international and regional peace initiatives failed to resolve the Nicaraguan and broader Central Amercian conflicts. Although the US government held intermittent talks with the

Managua regime (and the latter did likewise with the Contras), a series of much-trumpeted regional peace agreements proved to be false dawns.

During the 1980s the Managua regime had come under increasing pressure, especially from its sympathizers among West European socialists, to demonstrate its right to rule by holding democratic elections with full opposition participation. When these eventually took place in February 1990, the FSLN suffered an unexpected and decisive defeat at the hands of a broad opposition coalition. Having backed the winning side, a delighted White House declared its readiness to normalize relations with Nicaragua under its new government. Coming as it did amid accelerating East-West détente, the FMLN's defeat was seen as potentially unblocking the path to a general settlement of the Central American imbroglio. Much depended on how the Sandinistas conducted themselves in opposition and on how the Salvadorian and other insurgent groups responded to events in Managua. Also crucial was whether the Cuban regime would continue to support such groups.

■ Chronology of events

1821   Nicaragua joins other provinces of Central America in declaring independence from Spanish colonial rule.

1823   Nicaragua unites with Guatemala, San Salvador, Honduras and Costa Rica to form the United Provinces of Central America. Britain extends its interest southwards from Belize when it establishes a protectorate over the Mosquito Indians. Opposed to European interference in this region, the US President, James Monroe, establishes the principle that the Americas should not be considered as subjects for colonization by any European power. This principle comes to be known as the Monroe Doctrine.

1824   Britain establishes a protectorate over the Mosquito Coast on the Atlantic seaboard of Nicaragua and Honduras.

1838   The union of Central American provinces created in 1823 is dissolved and Nicaragua becomes a separate state.

1850   The United States and Britain sign the Clayton–Bulwer treaty agreeing that neither will have exclusive control of the currently-favoured route for a transisthmian canal through southern Nicaragua.

1855–57   Supported by a private army, the US adventurer William Walker takes control of Nicaragua for a short period in an unsuccessful attempt to set up a proslavery colony.

1860   Under the Treaty of Managua, Great Britain recognizes the sovereignty of Honduras and Nicaragua over the Mosquito Coast.

1893   The Liberal President José Santos Zelaya comes to power and attempts to reunite the former Central American provinces.

1901   The Clayton–Bulwer treaty is abrogated by the second Hay-Pauncefort treaty, leaving the United States free to develop the Nicaraguan canal route unilaterally.

1907   Zelaya attacks Honduras and prepares to invade El Salvador, but all-out war in the region is averted through the mediation of the USA and Mexico who organize a conference of Central American states.

1909   A US-backed Conservative revolt forces Zelaya out of office.

1911   On 6 June Nicaragua signs the Knox–Castillo   treaty with the United States in order to secure a loan. When the US Senate refuses to ratify the treaty, the loan is restricted.

1912   The outbreak of civil war in July prompts the United States to send in troops to support both the Conservative government and US interest in building a canal across the country.

1916 On 5 August the USA concludes the Bryan–Chamorro treaty with the government of Nicaragua, establishing the right to construct a canal across Nicaragua and to set up naval bases on each coast at the Bay of Fonseca and on the Corn Islands. El Salvador and Costa Rica immediately oppose the treaty, claiming an infringement of their sovereignty.

1917 The Central American court of justice declares the Bryan–Chamorro treaty a violation of the treaties signed after the 1907 peace conference.

1917–24 An American financial commission helps stabilize the economy of Nicaragua.

1925 After Carlos Solórzano (Conservative) is elected President and includes Liberals in his administration, US forces are withdrawn. A revolt led by former President Emiliano Chamorro in October forces out all Liberal members of the government including Vice-President Juan Sacasa.

1926 Emiliano Chamorro deposes Solórzano; the USA will not recognize his government, but when a Liberal revolt is launched in May by Lieutenant Augustino Sandino, the US government hastily sends back armed forces to Nicaragua. The USA supports the installation of a Conservative President in November. A month later former Vice-President Juan Sacasa returns from exile to form an alternative Liberal government which is backed by Mexico.

1927–28 The United States brings the two factions together and persuades the Liberal opposition to disarm by promising to supervise elections which take place on 4 November 1928. Lieutenant Sandino, who had continued the fight against US military presence in Nicaragua, is forced into exile.

1931 Sandino returns to Nicaragua and organizes a peasant army.

1933 Unable to dislodge Sandino and his supporters, US troops withdraw in the face of heavy international criticism. A treaty is signed giving concessions to the peasants and a voice in government to Sandino.

1934 Sandino is murdered by members of the National Guard which is headed by Anastasio Somoza.

1936 President Juan Sacasa is deposed by Anastasio Somoza who makes himself virtual dictator of Nicaragua and establishes the Somoza dynasty.

1956 President Somoza is assassinated and control passes to his elder son Luis Somoza.

1961 The Sandinista National Liberation Front (FSLN) is organized as a guerrilla opposition to the Somozas.

1967 General Anastasio Somoza, brother of Luis Somoza, is elected President of Nicaragua.

1970 The Bryan–Chamorro treaty giving the USA rights to a canal through Nicaragua and a 99-year option on two naval bases is terminated.

1972 On 23 December an earthquake devastates the centre of Managua, killing 15000 people. Millions of dollars of relief aid are appropriated by Somoza who declares himself Chairman of a National Reconstruction Commission.

1974 In the run-up to the presidential election FSLN guerrillas clash with government troops and a state of emergency is declared. At Christmas several members of the government are held hostage by the rebels who launch a new campaign against Somoza.

1976 In November the FSLN suffers a setback when three of its leaders are killed during a series of military manoeuvres in the guerrilla-dominated Nueva Segovia area.

1977 Although the martial law declared in 1974 is lifted, opposition to Somoza is repressed with increasing harshness by the National Guard. An increasing regime of torture and murder forces church and business groups to set up organized resistance.

1978 The murder of Pedro Joaquin Chamorro, editor of the opposition newspaper *La Prensa*, leads to a massive popular uprising in which the FSLN takes the dominating role as the country's only organized military rebel force.

1979 After several weeks of heavy fighting during which an estimated 50 000 are killed, the USA withdraws its support for Somoza who is forced to leave the country on 17 July. Two days later a provisional five-member "junta of national reconstruction" is set up by the FSLN which assumes power in Managua. With the help of international aid, the junta and 18-member government begin to rebuild a devastated country. The new government takes over the land and businesses formerly held by Somoza. Banks and insurance companies are nationalized.

1980 A state of emergency imposed in July of the previous year is lifted at the end of April. In that month a leading member of the junta, Dr Moises Hassan Morales, visits the Soviet Union where a trade and co-operation agreement is signed. With the aid of nearly 1200 Cuban teachers, the government begins a large scale literacy campaign. Violeta Chamorro quits the ruling junta.

1981 The United States causes indignation in Nicaragua when it accuses the Sandinistas of giving support to the FMLN guerrillas in El Salvador. The Reagan administration suspends US aid to Nicaragua and Congress approves $19 million in covert aid to the Somoçista or "Contra" rebels. Faced with military opposition from supporters of former President Somoza operating on the Honduras frontier, Nicaragua begins to build up its defence militia.

1982 The Sandinista government suspects that rebel activity is being co-ordinated from the United States and extends the state of emergency when 100 people are killed during guerrilla raids. Press freedom and other rights are suspended in Nicaragua.

1983 The Nicaraguan army, which numbers 60 000 regulars and 120 000 reservists, restricts Contra activity to the mountains, forests and coastal swamps along the borders with Honduras and Costa Rica. In an attempt to deprive the Contra rebels of support in the north, the Sandinista government begins to eject Miskito Indians from their villages. This action brings criticism from the church in Nicaragua and from the Pope in Rome. The US steps up its support for the Contras with a show of force in the form of military manoeuvres off the coast. Worried by the deteriorating situation in Central America, the Foreign Ministers of Colombia, Mexico, Panama and Venezuela meet on the Panamanian island of Contadora to consider the worsening situation. The "Contadora Group", as it comes to be known, produces a 21-point plan which receives wide international support as the only means of reaching a comprehensive peace settlement in the region.

1984 In a series of sudden attacks, the US-backed Contras cripple oil and port facilities at Puerto Sandino, Corinto, Montelimar and El Bluff. While President Reagan accuses Nicaragua of "exporting revolution", the US Senate votes to cut off aid to the Contras (Boland Amendment). In August the Nicaraguan government brings to an end the emergency measures imposed in 1982 and in November Daniel Ortega is returned as president.

1985 In February both President Reagan and Secretary of State George Schultz state publicly that they seek the removal of the Sandinista government in Nicaragua and when Ortega visits the Soviet Union in April, Reagan calls for an economic embargo of Nicaragua. Two months later the US Senate approves $38 million over two years in nonmilitary aid to the Contras.

1986 In May the presidents of the five Central American states meet in the Guatemalan town of Esquipulas where they endorse the Contadora process. A month later immediate peace hopes are dashed when Nicaragua files suits against Costa Rica and Honduras in the International Court of Justice, accusing them of "co-operating with rebel groups". Despite a lull in guerrilla activity, civil liberties are restricted in Nicaragua. Across the border in Honduras the Contras build up their strength in readiness for an offensive to be launched in the spring of the following year. In November the Nicaraguan National Constituent Assembly approves a new constitution (effective from January 1989) providing for democratic presidential and legislative elections according to a system of proportional representation.

In November, US Attorney General Edwin Meese discloses the diversion of Iran arms-sales profits to the Contras (Iran-Contra Affair).

1987   The scale of civilian casualties in the guerrilla offensive alienates international support for the Contras who are ordered to leave their bases in Honduras by President José Ascona del Hoyo.   In August Central American presidents meet in Guatemala City where they agree on a "procedure for the establishment of a firm and lasting peace in Central America" based on proposals put forward by President Arias of Costa Rica. Four days later, President Ortega invites opposition parties and the Catholic Church to join a Commission for National Reconciliation. A month later, a ceasefire agreement is reached with the Miskito Indians on the east coast. Restrictions imposed on the Catholic radio station and the newspaper *La Prensa* are lifted and, in November, Ortega agrees to hold indirect talks with the Contras in an attempt to negotiate a ceasefire.

1988   An inflation rate approaching 3000 per cent forces President Ortega to devalue the currency. Blaming the desperate state of the Nicaraguan economy on US sanctions and the Contra insurgency, he launches a major offensive against key rebel bases in Honduras. The US administration promptly orders an army division into Honduras on 18 March, in a move that President Reagan hopes will force the Nicaraguans to pull back. Rebel leaders agree to a ceasefire with the government as part of the Arias peace plan.

1989   At a meeting of Central American Presidents in the Honduran town of Tela in August, an agreement is reached to adopt a plan that will lead to the demobilization of the Contras over a period of 90 days. In November, however, the Arias peace plan receives a set-back when the Sandinista government calls off its ceasefire. and launches another offensive against the Contra rebels. President Menem of Argentina flies to Nicaragua in an attempt to revive the demobilization plan but UN/OAS-sponsored talks between the government and Contra leaders come to nothing.

1990   In presidential and legislative elections the Sandinistas are defeated by a 14-party coalition (UNO) led by Violeta Chamorro. This electoral victory prompts the US government to withdraw its economic blockade of Nicaragua. Under UN supervision, over 8 000 contra guerrillas gather in ceasefire zones where they have agreed to lay down their arms but, despite an apparent end to hostilities, a hard core of contras refuses to accept reconciliation.

■ Who's who

Arias Sanchez, Oscar   President of Costa Rica whose plan for peace in Central America formed the basis of the 1987 Guatemala Agreement and earned him the Nobel Peace Prize.

Bermúdez, Enrique   A former Somoza officer who became field commander of the largest of the Contra rebel groups, the Nicaraguan Democratic Force, operating from bases in northern Nicaragua and Honduras. In 1988 the hardline Bermúdez survived a contra mutiny after the signing of a truce between rebel leaders and the Sandinista government.

Calero, Adolfo   Civilian leader of the Nicaraguan Democratic Force (FDN) since 1983 and former member (until 1987) of the three-member directorate of the United Nicaraguan Opposition. A Conservative, the US-educated Calero has fallen out with his Contra colleagues Arturo Cruz and Alfonso Robelo, but has continued in his attempts to bring the Contras into the Central American peace negotiating process. In April 1988 he made an unsuccessful attempt to oust Enrique Bermúdez from his position as FDN field commander.

César Aguirre, Alfredo   Political leader of a more moderate faction of the Contra rebel force operating in the south. Opposed to the hardline Nicaraguan Democratic Forces operating in the north, César was Secretary of the provisional government formed after the fall of the Somoza regime in July 1979.

Chamorro Coronel, Edgar   High ranking Contra leader who returned to Nicaragua during an amnesty in October 1988. He was a member of the Contra directorate 1982–84.

Chamorro Rapaccioli, Fernando   Field commander of a coalition of Costa Rican-based Contra rebel groups, the Nicaraguan Democratic Union and the Nicaraguan Revolutionary Armed Forces (FARN). Known as "El Negro", he succeeded Eden Pastora in 1984 as leader of the larger Democratic Revolutionary Alliance (ARDE), but in 1988 he returned to Nicaragua to campaign as a conservative politician.

Chamorro Cardenal, Pedro Joaquin   Editor and publisher of the newspaper *La Prensa* who led the opposition against the Somoza regime in the 1970s. His assassination in January 1978 provoked the civil uprising that eventually led to the downfall of Somoza.

Chamorro, Violeta Barrios de   Widow of Pedro Joaquin Chamorro Cardenal, she was a member of the first Sandinista government, but later joined the opposition. In February 1990 elections she was the successful presidential candidate of the National Opposition Union (UNO), decisively defeating President Ortega.

Cruz, Arturo   Along with Alfonso Robelo and Adolfo Calero, Cruz was one of the three leaders of the Contra political wing known as the United Nicaraguan Opposition. In 1987 he resigned from the opposition directorate after falling out with his colleagues.

Galeano, Israel   A contra rebel military chief known as "Franklyn".

Hasenfus, Eugene   Pilot of a US supply aircraft shot down over Nicaragua in 1986. Hasenfus was tried by a court in Nicaragua but was later pardoned by President Ortega and returned to the USA.

Huembes, Carlos   Leader of an anti-Sandinista group known as the Democratic Coordinator.

North, Lieut.–Colonel Oliver L.   A US marine officer, born in Texas in 1943, who became Deputy Director for Political and Military Affairs on the National Security Council in 1981. Five years later he was dismissed because of his involvement with secret operations to aid Contra rebels in Nicaragua with funds diverted from the illegal sale of arms to Iran. North retired from the military in 1988 and was tried and found guilty on three charges relating to the "Irangate" affair in February 1989.

Obando y Bravo, Cardinal Miguel   Outspoken Archbishop of Managua opposed to the restrictions on civil liberties imposed by the Sandinista government in the 1980s. In 1987 he was asked by President Ortega to head the new National Reconciliation Commission.

Ortega Saavedra, Daniel   A prominent member of the five-man junta that took power and formed a Sandinista provisional government in the aftermath of the revolution that forced Somoza into exile in 1979. Born in the mining town of La Libertad in 1946, Ortega was arrested for the first time at the age of 15 years. By 1967 he was head of the Sandinista urban resistance. Ortega was returned as president in the 1984 national elections but was decisively defeated in 1990 by opposition leader Violeta Chamorro, a former member of the Sandinista government.

Ortega Saavedra, Humberto   Brother of Daniel Ortega and member of the three-man army directorate appointed in July 1979. He later became Defence minister in the Sandinista government.

Pastora Gomez, Eden   Also known as "Commander Zero", Pastora was the leader of the largest of the more liberal Costa Rican-based Contra rebel groups, the Democratic Revolutionary Alliance (ARDE). Refusing to join forces with the more hardline Nicaraguan Democratic Force (FDN) in the north, Pastora was seriously wounded in a bomb attack during a press conference in May 1984. Later in that year he was replaced by Fernando Chamorro Rapaccioli, leader of the smaller Nicaraguan Democratic Union and Nicaraguan Armed Forces. In 1988 Pastora returned to Nicaragua to take part in the political process.

Rivera, Brooklyn   Leader of the Miskito Indian rebels and an ally of the Nicaraguan Democratic Force (FDN).

Robelo Callejas, Alfonso   A member of the five-man ruling Sandinista junta formed after the overthrow of Somoza in July 1979. He later opposed the Sandinista government and joined the directorate of the moderate Costa Rican-based Nicaraguan Resistance. In February 1988 he resigned his position on the directorate when President Arias ordered all Contra rebels to leave Costa Rican territory.

Sandino, Augusto César   A military commander who started a popular revolt in May 1926 following the expulsion of Liberals from the government. Despite the signing of an armistice in September of that year he continued to lead guerrilla attacks against the US troops that had been hastily landed in Nicaragua. In 1933 the USA withdrew its armed forces and concessions were made to the peasants who had supported Sandino. A year later Sandino was killed by members of the National Guard then headed by Anastasio Somoza.

Somoza Debyle, Anastasio   The Younger son of Anastasio Somoza Garcia, elected to the presidency of Nicaragua in 1967 following the death of his brother Luis. During his repressive regime Somoza acquired a monopoly of wealth for his family, but in July 1979 his government was overthrown by leftist Sandinista rebels. Forced into exile, he fled to Paraguay where he was shot a year later.

Somoza Debyle, Luis   The Elder son of Anastasio Somoza Garcia whom he succeded as President of Nicaragua in 1956.

Somoza García, Anastasio   Commander of the National Guard who, in 1934, ordered the assassination of General Sandino and ousted the Liberal president Juan Sacasa. Under his virtual dictatorship Communists and radicals were victimized. In September 1956 he died of gunshot wounds and was succeeded by his son Luis.

Zelaya, José Santos   Liberal president of Nicaragua elected in 1893 but forced out of office in 1909 following a US-backed Conservative revolt. His attempts to form a Central American confederation brought him into conflict with Honduras, El Salvador and Guatemala.

■ Key places

Bluefields   Capital of Zelaya Sur Special Zone on the east coast of Nicaragua, the port of Bluefields lies on an inlet of the Caribbean Sea opposite the island of Venado. With its outer port at El Bluff, it is one of three major port facilities on the east coast. Population 18 000.

Chinandega   Chief town and commercial centre of a coastal region in NW Nicaragua. Population 68 000.

Coco River   Once known as the Segovia, the Coco River rises in Choluteca department,

SW Honduras and flows 720km along the Nicaragua-Honduras frontier before emptying into the Caribbean near Cape Gracias a Dios. Miskito Indians living near the river were moved from the region in order to deprive the Contra rebels of support in N Nicaragua.

Corinto Formerly called Punta Icacos, Corinto is the largest of Nicaragua's three main Pacific ports. In 1984 it was one of a number of strategic targets attacked by Contra rebels in an attempt to damage oil imports and cripple the economy of Nicaragua. Population 24 000.

Corn Islands or **Islas del Maiz** A tiny group of islands off the east coast of Nicaragua, situated in the Caribbean nearly 80km east of Bluefields. When the USA signed the Bryan–Chamorro treaty in 1914 it gained an option on a canal route through Nicaragua as well as a 99-year option on naval bases at either end. The Corn Islands were selected as a marine base in 1916 but were returned to Nicaragua in 1971 following the abrogation of the treaty in the previous year.

El Almendero A rural municipality of 14 000 farmers which was designated as one of seven UN-supervised ceasefire zones where contra rebels could lay down their arms following an accord signed in April 1990. An area of 5 810 hectares was allocated for the resettlement of former rebels and their families.

El Bluff An important Caribbean port on the east coast of Nicaragua. El Bluff is situated on a peninsula not far from the town of Bluefields. In 1984 it was one of a number of important strategic targets attacked by Contra guerrillas.

Esquipulas A town in Chiquimula department, SE Guatemala. Once a religious shrine to the Mayan god of war, the town became the seat of the ''Black Christ'', a symbol of peace to all Central Americans. For this reason it was chosen as the meeting place, in May 1986, of five Central American presidents who came together to endorse the Contadora peace process.

Fonseca, Bay of An inlet of the Pacific Ocean in the far north-west corner of Nicaragua. In

1914 the Bryan–Chamorro treaty gave the USA a permanent option on a canal route through the country and a 99-year option on a naval base in the Bay of Fonseca. Between 1916 and 1933 US marines were based here; but the treaty was terminated in 1970.

Granada The third largest city in Nicaragua after Managua and León, situated on the W shore of Lake Nicaragua. Founded in 1524, it became a Conservative stronghold in the years following independence from Spanish colonial rule. Polulation 88 600.

León A regional capital of NW Nicaragua situated 20 km from the Pacific coast. The original city, which was destroyed by an earthquake in 1609, was founded some distance away in 1524 by León Viejo. Capital of Nicaragua until 1858, León was a Liberal stronghold in the years following independence from Spanish colonial rule. Population 101 000.

Managua Capital of Nicaragua since 1858, Managua has twice been destroyed by an earthquake this century (1931 and 1972). The city is situated on the south shore of Lake Managua which, with an area of 1000km^2, is the second largest lake in Nicaragua. Population 682 000.

Mosquito Coast A 65-km-wide strip of swamp, lagoon and tropical forest that stretches along the Caribbean coast of E Honduras and Nicaragua. Largely undeveloped, this territory is occupied by Miskito Indians, Zambos and Garifunas, many of whom speak English. Between 1824 and 1860 the British maintained a protectorate over the Mosquito Coast where a succession of Mosquito kings ruled over the Indian population.

Nicaragua, Lake The largest lake in Nicaragua and in Central America, separated from the Pacific Ocean by a 15-km-wide isthmus. The lake, which is connected to the Caribbean by the San Juan river, has an area of 8026km^2. US interest in Nicaragua during the second half of the 19th century and early years of the 20th century was based on the belief that a canal could be built linking the Pacific with the Caribbean via Lake Nicaragua.

Nueva Segovia   A former department of N Nicaragua located on the frontier with Honduras. Drained by tributaries of the Coco River, the mountains of the Jalapa and Dipilto cordilleras have provided shelter for Sandinista guerrillas in the 1970s and Contra rebels in the 1980s. The chief town is Ocotal.

Puerto Cabezas   One of Nicaragua's three main ports on the Caribbean east coast, situated to the north of the Huahua Hiver, 175km north of Bluefields.

Puerto Sandino   Known as Puerto Somoza until 1979, Puerto Sandino is one of three major ports on the Pacific west coast of Nicaragua. The oil facilities here were attacked by US-backed Contra rebels in 1984 during a campaign to undermine the economy of Nicaragua.

San Juan del Sur   The southernmost of Nicaragua's three main ports on the Pacific west coast.

Yamales   The principal Nicaraguan contra base in Honduras between 1982 and 1990.

Zelaya   A former department of E Nicaragua divided in 1982 into two "Special Zones" - Zelaya Sur, with its capital at Bluefields, and Zelaya Norte, with its capital at Rosita. The region takes its name from the former Liberal president of Nicaragua ousted during a US-backed Conservative revolt in 1909. The population of 325 000 includes a large number of Miskito Indians, Zambos and Garifunas.

■ Key words

Arias Plan   A Central American peace plan proposed by President Arias of Costa Rica and incorporated into the Guatemala Agreement which was signed by the presidents of five Central American countries who met in Guatemala City in August 1987. The plan called for an immediate ceasefire in all Central American conflicts, cessation of aid to all guerrilla groups, a general amnesty and negotiations between all interested parties. After securing initial observance, the plan broke down in 1988.

Atlantic Coast Autonomy Act   An Act passed by the Sandinista government following international condemnation of its treatment of Miskito Indians in the fight against Contra rebels. An estimated 10 000 Miskito refugees returned to Nicaragua from Honduras during 1986–87.

Barricada   The official newspaper of the Sandanista government of Nicaragua.

Boland Amendment   An amendment passed by the US Congress in 1984 prohibiting further US military aid to the Contra rebels who had received US support since 1981.

Caraballeda Message   A message for "peace, security and democracy" announced in January 1986 by the foreign ministers of the Contadora countries, who met in the Venezuelan town of Caraballeda in an attempt to give a new impetus to the peace process in Central America.

Central American Defence Council (CONDECA)   A Central American defence alliance abandoned in 1979. CONDECA manoeuvres in the Sandinista-held Nueva Segovia region of northern Nicaragua were allegedly supported by the presence of over 1000 US troops in November 1976.

Contadora Group   A name given to the group of countries, namely Panama, Mexico, Venezuela and Colombia, whose foreign ministers first met in January 1983 on the Panamanian island of Contadora to discuss ways of creating peace in Central America. Although the "Contadora process" reached an impasse in 1986 and again in 1989, it helped reduce tension in the region by bringing together the presidents of the five Central American countries.

Contras The US-backed right–wing opponents of the Sandinista government in Nicaragua. With an estimated fighting force of 15 000, the contras operated in several distinct groups, the largest of which was the Nicaraguan Democratic Force (NDF). Headed by Enrique Bermúdez, the NDF attacked government targets from bases on both sides of the Nicaragua-Honduras frontier. In the south, the Sandinistas were opposed by the 3000-strong Democratic Revolutionary Alliance (ARDE). The Contra rebel force was disbanded in 1990.

Democratic Conservative Party (Partido Conservador Demócrata de Nicaragua - PCDN) The main right-wing political party in Nicaragua headed by Clemente Guido. The Conservatives, with a strong political base in Granada, are descended from the wealthy, aristocratic landowning and merchant families of the 19th century.

Democratic Coordinating Committee (CDN) A former coalition of 14 anti-Sandinista political, business and labour groups with broadly the same goals as the Contra rebels, but in general support of the proposed Central American peace plan.

Democratic Revolutionary Alliance (Alianza Democrática Revolucionaria - ARDE) A Costa Rican-based rebel Contra group opposed to the hardline approach of the northern Nicaraguan Democratic Force.

Government of National Reconstruction (GRN) A coalition government formed in July 1979 following the collapse of the Somoza regime. Dominated by Sandinistas, it was organized into a five-member Junta and an 18-member Council of Ministers.

Guatemala Agreement An agreement based on the Arias peace plan, signed by the presidents of five Central American countries who met in Guatemala City in August 1987.

Hurricane Joan A hurricane that devastated Nicaragua in October 1988, destroying 80% of all palm oil and coffee trees, 40% of banana plantations, 75% of the domestic fishing fleet and the entire rice crop.

Independent Liberal Party (Partido Liberal Independtiente - PLI) The second largest opposition political party in Nicaragua. The Liberals are descended from small landholders and artesans who were influenced by English notions of free trade and were keen to replace colonial stagnation with a more broadly based export economy. The Liberals have a strong political base in the city of León.

Iran-Contra Affair In November 1986, US Attorney General Edwin Meese disclosed that profits from the secret sale of arms to Iran had been diverted to the Contra rebels in Nicaragua. Oliver North, who admitted in 1987 that $14 million in private funding was solicited for the Contras, was later tried and convicted on three charges relating to this affair.

Kisán or **Nicaraguan Indigenous Communities Union** A multi-ethnic organization of local Indian groups who joined together in support of the Contra rebels in 1985. By 1987 internal disagreements within the group resulted in a large number of Miskito Indians choosing to accept a government amnesty.

La Prensa A former opposition newspaper. The murder in 1978 of its publisher and editor, Pedro Joaquín Chamorro Cardenal, helped spark off the revolution that toppled the Somoza regime a year later. During the 1982–86 state of emergency publication of the paper was banned.

literacy campaign An educational programme established in March 1980 with the aid of 1200 Cuban teachers. It was claimed that within the space of three years (1980–83) illiteracy dropped from 60 per cent to 12 per cent.

Misatán An organization claiming to represent over 200 000 Miskito Indians, formed in July 1984 when delegates from 63 settlements met in Puerto Cabezas. The organization replaced the smaller Misurasatas guerrilla movement led by Brooklyn River.

Miskitos A Central American Indian group living on the Mosquito coast of E Nicaragua and Honduras.

Misurasatas   A small guerrilla movement fighting in support of the rights of Miskito Indians and led by Brooklyn Rivera.

national dialogue   A national debate involving the Catholic Church, government and opposition parties initiated in October 1984 just prior to the November election that returned President Ortega to power. In this way the Sandinista government hoped to reassure voters that all parties could participate in discussing the post-election political process.

National Opposition Union (Union Nacional de la Oposición - UNO)   A broad-based anti-Sandinista coalition whose presidential candidate, Violeta Barrios de Chamorro, defeated President Ortega in the February 1990 elections.

National Reconciliation Commission   On 11 August 1987 the Nicaraguan government invited opposition parties and the Catholic Church to join a National Reconciliation Commission. Cardinal Miguel Obando y Bravo was named as President of the Commission.

Nicaraguan Democratic Forces (Fuerzas Democráticas Nicaraguense - FDN)   A faction of the rebel Contra movement operating from bases on both sides of the Nicaragua-Honduras border. The largest of the Contra groups opposing the Sandinista government.

Operation Danto   The name given to a Sandinista government offensive launched on 6 March 1988 against Contra guerrillas operating from bases within Honduras. This incursion into Honduran territory provoked the landing of US troops 12 days later (Operation Golden Pheasant).

Operation Golden Pheasant   The codename for the landing of the US 82nd airborne division in Honduras on 18 March 1988 following the Sandinista incursion into Honduran territory in pursuit of Contra rebels.

Operation Martyrs of Quilali   A three-day period during the process of monetary reform in February 1988 when people could exchange old Córdobas for new Córdobas.

Panama Message   A 12-point statement making general recommendations for establishing peace in Central America that formed part of the draft Contadora Act devised by foreign ministers of Contadora and Central American countries who met in Panama City in June 1986.

Sandinist National Liberation Front (Frente Sandinista de Liberación Nacional - FSLN)   A guerrilla organization founded in 1961 in opposition to the Somoza regime. Initially drawing support from the rural peasantry of N Nicaragua, the Sandinistas established a popular resistance in the urban ''barrios'' during the 1970s prior to the outbreak of full scale civil war in 1978–79. In the Council of State, set up in 1980 a year after the revolution, 31 of the 47 seats were allocated to Sandinistas.

Sandinista People's Army (Ejercito Popular Sandinista - EPS)   The armed forces of Nicaragua formed by decree on 22 August 1979, a month after the revolution that toppled the Somoza regime. In 1985 the army had a total manpower of 60 000 regulars and 120 000 reservists.

Somoçistas   Supporters of the deposed President of Nicaragua, Anastasio Somoza.

Strategy for Reconstruction   A national economic strategy that concentrated on major projects designed to improve the country's agro-export base following the 1979 revolution. In the face of world recession, US sanctions and a costly civil war, this policy was abandoned in 1983 in favour of a ''strategy for survival''.

Strategy for Survival   A shift in the emphasis of national economic strategy that took place in 1983 as a result of a deterioration in export income brought about by world recession and the guerrilla activities of the US-backed Contras. The ''strategy for survival'' replaced the earlier ''strategy for reconstruction''.

Subtiava-86   The name given to the large scale military exercises of mid-December 1986 which were designed to test the readiness of the armed forces and reservists in the event of a US-backed invasion of Nicaragua.

Tasbi Pri   ("free land") The name given to settlements set up by the government in N Zelaya region in 1982 at a time when many Indians thought to be supporting Contra rebels were forced to leave their homes near the Coco River.

Tela Declaration   An agreement reached by the presidents of five Central American countries who met in the Honduran town of Tela in August 1987. Amongst a number of issues, the presidents formulated a plan for the demobilization of the Contra guerrilla force.

Terceristas or **Insurrectionaries**   Led by Daniel Ortega, the Terceristas was one of the three factions of the FSLN which joined forces in January 1979 to form a united Sandinista opposition to the Somoza government.

Unified Indigenous Armed Forces of the Atlantic Coast   A union of Misurasta and Kisán Indian guerrillas which joined forces in March 1987.

■ Further reading

Shirley Christian, *Nicaragua: Revolution in the Family*, Random House, New York, 1985

Janel M. Curry–Roper, Nicaragua: Land of Conflict, *Focus*, 38(3), 1988, pp.18–24

Richard Evans, Central America's Slide to Ruin, *The Geographical Magazine*, 59(12), 1987, pp. 582–91

R.L. Harris and C. Vilas (eds.), *Nicaragua: A Revolution Under Seige*, Zed Books, London, 1985

Doreen Massey, *Nicaragua*, Open University Press, Milton Keynes and Philadelphia, 1987

William I. Robinson and Kent Norsworthy, *David and Goliath: Washington's War Against Nicaragua*, Zed Books, London, 1987

R.J. Spalding, *The Political Economics of Revolutionary Nicaragua*, Allen and Unwin, London, 1987

H. Weber, *Nicaragua: The Sandinista Revolution*, NLB, London, 1981

2
El Salvador

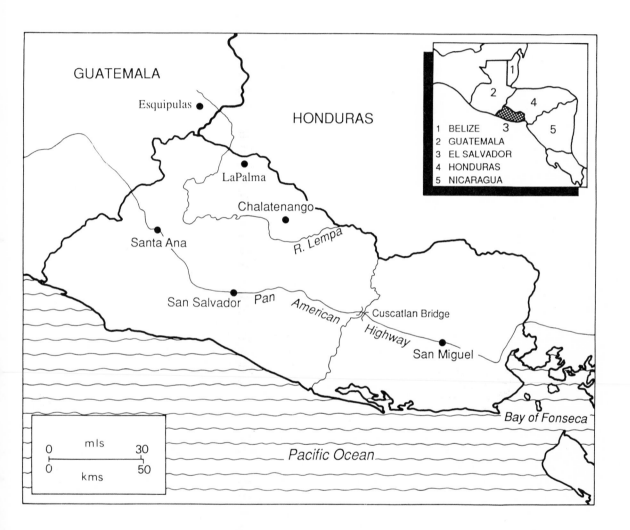

GUATEMALA

Esquipulas ●

HONDURAS

LaPalma ●

Chalatenango ●

Santa Ana ●

R. Lempa

San Salvador ● Pan American Highway

Cuscatlan Bridge

San Miguel ●

Bay of Fonseca

1 BELIZE
2 GUATEMALA
3 EL SALVADOR
4 HONDURAS
5 NICARAGUA

mls
0   30
0   50
kms

Pacific Ocean

■ Profile

Official name: Republic of El Salvador

- **Area:** 21 073km²
- **Population (1988):** 5 388 600
- **Ethnic groups:** Mestizo 89%, Indian 10%, European 1%
- **Official language:** Spanish; Nahua is spoken by some Indians
- **Religion:** Roman Catholic 80%
- **Life expectancy (1987):** 60 years
- **Infant mortality rate (1984):** 41 per 1000
- **Currency:** El Salvador colón of 100 centavos
- **Timezone:** GMT −6
- **Administrative divisions:** 14 departments
- **Capital:** San Salvador
- **Chief towns:** San Salvador (452 600), Santa Ana (135 186), San Miguel (86 700)

■ Introduction

Two years after throwing off Spanish colonial rule in 1821, El Salvador joined its neighbours in the United Provinces of Central America, of which San Salvador provided the capital from 1834. Although the federation collapsed in 1838, El Salvador retained a particular interest in regional unity, perhaps because of its status as the smallest Central American state. Its politics in the 19th century revolved around endless struggle between Liberals and Conservatives, combined with increasing interest in its internal affairs on the part of the United States. By the early 20th century dispossession of the country's large Indian population of their communal lands, to facilitate profitable coffee and sugar-cane production for export, had concentrated wealth and political power in El Salvador's famous "14 families". Their hegemony ensured stability, but at the expense of respect for elected governments, which were mostly ciphers of the 14 families. Moreover, grossly inequitable land distribution – the most glaring in Central America – became the focus of simmering social tensions centred in the Indian population.

Hopes of reform, raised by the presidential election victory of Arturo Araujo (Labour Party) in 1931, were quickly dashed by a military coup led by General Maximiliano Hernández Martínez. Peasant leader Farabundo Martí and the Salvadorian Communists responded by launching a general revolt, which was suppressed with great bloodshed in *La Matanza* ("the massacre") of 1932. The regime's execution of Martí provided the revolutionaries with a martyr of timeless appeal, as more recent events have demonstrated. The eccentric Martínez proceeded to establish a semi-fascist system glorifying El Salvador's traditional, i.e. semi-feudal, way of life. His resignation in 1944 opened the way for "modernizers" within the military to come to power in 1948, but efforts to promote industry and commerce went hand in hand with continued repression.

During the 1950s El Salvador's rigorous anti-communism and deference to US strategic and economic interests gave Washington little cause for concern in its Cold War competition with the Soviet Union. The seismic impact of the 1959 Cuban revolution transformed this comfortable state of affairs almost overnight. Now the Salvadorian left-wing opposition had supporters not only in distant Moscow but also across the Caribbean Sea in Havana, where the new regime quickly set about "exporting" the revolution. To meet the new situation the United States opted in El Salvador for a "civilian-military" junta which would keep communism at bay by introducing some reforms. A regime of this type came to power in 1961 under Colonel Julio Adalberto Rivera, a keen supporter of President Kennedy's Alliance for Progress. It continued under Colonel Fidel Sánchez Hernández, who benefited from a surge of nationalism during the 1969 "football war" with Honduras. But the government's repressive face remained ever-present, notably in its promotion of anti-communist vigilante actions in rural areas thought to have left-wing sympathies.

Criticism of the army-dominated regime intensified in the early 1970s, as opposition groups, from Christian Democrats to Communists, formed a popular front for the 1972 elections on a platform of economic reform, land redistribution and social justice. Amid evidence of electoral fraud the military right emerged victorious from that contest and proceeded to suppress another popular uprising. During the 1970s US-backed military juntas continued in power, from 1977 under General Carlos Umberto Romero, who maintained that the choice before El Salvador was "democracy or communism" and halted a land redistribution programme initiated by his predecessor at Washington's urging. In 1979, however, the region's second post-war political earthquake, the Sandinista revolution in Nicaragua, had an immediate effect in El Salvador. Romero was forced to flee to Guatemala and replaced by a broad-based junta, including Christian Democrats, moderate left and Communists, committed to wide-ranging reform and to the promotion of friendly relations with Nicaragua and Cuba.

With the alarm bells ringing in Washington, the new junta quickly found itself caught between pressure for speedy social change and determined opposition from the conservative establishment and its supporters in the military. By early 1980 the junta had disintegrated, as its left-wing components withdrew in protest against the failure to introduce reforms or to curb the activities of right-wing "death squads". A key event was the assassination in March 1980 of Archbishop Oscar Romero, whose outspoken support for "liberation theology" had influenced many progressive Christian

Democrats to join the opposition. By mid-1980 the Salvadorian left had formed the Democratic Revolutionary Front (FDR), which then established an alliance with the Farabundo Martí National Liberation Front (FMLN), newly created as the opposition's military wing with Cuban and Nicaraguan support. Early in 1981 the FMLN launched an offensive against the ruling junta, by now headed by conservative Christian Democrat José Napoléon Duarte, who enjoyed both military and US backing.

Committed to vigorous anti-communism in Central America and elsewhere, the post-1981 Reagan administration had little option but to maintain US military and financial support for the Duarte government. It nevertheless entered periodic reservations about the extremist inclinations of the Salvadorian military. Under US pressure Duarte sought to curb the excesses of the "death squads" and also to introduce progressive social and economic measures, although with little effect in either area. The junta's attempts to establish its democratic legitimacy were also frustrated by the FDR's refusal to participate in elections while right-wing intimidation continued and until a negotiated agreement had been reached on the country's constitutional future. On the ground, the escalating civil war took a huge toll in lives and destruction. It followed the familiar pattern of guerrilla assaults on key targets and inconclusive government counter-attacks, with the FMLN claiming to have "liberated" a third of the country by the late 1980s. While not intervening directly, the United States kept a watchful eye on the conflict and regularly held military manoeuvres just across the border with neighbouring Honduras.

During the 1980s unceasing international and regional peace initiatives sought to find a solution to the El Salvador and other Central American conflicts. Arising out of the regional Contadora process, the 1987 Arias plan appeared initially to have unlocked the door to peace, on the basis of an immediate ceasefire in all conflicts and an agreed timetable for the cessation of aid to all guerrilla groups, a general amnesty and negotiations between the interested parties. However, the plan soon became stalled in the inevitable disputes over detailed implementation. Direct talks with the FDR initiated by both Duarte and his successor,

Alfredo Cristiani of the right-wing Arena party, likewise failed to halt the fighting.

A persistent complication in these various negotiations was the strife in Nicaragua, where US-backed Contra insurgents were seeking to overthrow, or at least destabilize, the FMLN's Sandinista backers. It therefore appeared to many observers that the election defeat of the Sandinistas in February 1990 created better prospects for regional peace than for many years past. Under this scenario,

a US government flushed with success in Nicaragua (and Panama) would nudge the Salvadorian regime into an accommodation with the FDR/FMLN, which would itself sense the direction of the Central American wind and accept a compromise deal. There were many possible pitfalls to such an outcome, most notably Cuba's declared determination to maintain its support for revolutionary struggle in the region (*see section 4.1*).

■ Chronology of events

1821   The Central American provinces of Guatemala, San Salvador, Honduras, Costa Rica, Nicaragua and Chiapas declare their independence from Spanish colonial rule.

1822   Opposed to incorporation in the Mexican empire, a congress in San Salvador proposes a union with the USA.

1823   Guatemala, San Salvador, Nicaragua, Honduras and Costa Rica join to form the United Provinces of Central America with its capital in Guatemala City.

1839–40   The United Provinces dissolves into its component states.

1871-82   Aided by the abolition of Indian rights to communal land and the establishment of a rural police force, the most productive coffee and sugar-cane lands fall into the hands of El Salvador's "14 families", which dominate political, economic and military affairs.

1907   President Zelaya of Nicaragua attempts to re-establish a Central American confederation by force. He invades Honduras and openly aids a revolution in El Salvador.

1931   General Maximiliano Hernàndez Martínez overthrows Arturo Araujo, the popularly elected President of El Salvador, and establishes a dictatorship. Throughout the 1930s communism and other radical movements are suppressed.

1932   A peasant rebellion led by the popular hero Farabundi Martí is crushed by Hernàndez whose troops kill nearly 30 000 people in what becomes known as *La Mantanza* ("the massacre"). Martí himself is executed by firing squad.

1944   After 12 years of semi-fascism, Hernàndez resigns and hopes rise for a modernization of the country's social and economic structures.

1948   "Modernisers" within the military come to power on a US-backed programme of promoting trade and industry, combined with firm anticommunism.

1961   In the shadow of the 1959 Cuban revolution, a US-backed "civilian–military" junta assumes power under Colonel Julio Adalberto Rivera who is committed to limited social reforms. The creation of the rural vigilante National Democratic Organization (Orden) demonstrates his regime's determination to stamp out left-wing activities among the peasantry.

1969   An undeclared four-day war between El Salvador and Honduras is precipitated by the defeat of Honduras in a football match and the presence of 300 000 migrant Salvadorean workers in Honduras.

1972   The centre-left National Opposition Union appears to win elections, prompting a military coup that forces the moderate leaders,

Guillermo Manuel Ungo and José Napoleón Duarte, into exile for seven years.

1977 A right-wing military leader, General Carlos Humberto Romero, stages a coup and puts an end to a land reform programme that had been backed by the USA. Agrarian reform is strongly opposed by the wealthiest 10 per cent of El Salvador's landowners who own almost 80 per cent of the country's arable land. Human rights violations under Romero force the USA temporarily to withdraw aid to El Salvador.

1979 Worried by the fall of the Somoza dictatorship in neighbouring Nicaragua, the military leaders of El Salvador take a heavy hand with political demonstrations. In May 20 people are killed by troops following a peaceful demonstration outside the cathedral in San Salvador. Although elections are promised for 1980, a group of liberal military officers led by Colonel Jaime Abdul Gutiérrez and Colonel Arnaldo Majano succeed in overthrowing General Romero in October. This does not prevent an outburst of terrorist activity during which insurgents seize over 300 hostages including three cabinet ministers.

1980 The new six-member civilian-military junta looks close to collapse when the three civilian members resign on 2 January. A pact is made with the moderate Christian Democrats and in March José Napoleón Duarte joins the junta. Attempts at liberal reform are frustrated by the activities of right-wing death squads who terrorize the population by kidnapping or killing anyone suspected of left-wing sympathies. On 18 March 48 people are killed following a peaceful demonstration and at the funeral of one of the demonstrators the outspoken Archbishop of El Salvador, Oscar Romero, is shot dead. Although the election of President Reagan had resulted in an increase in military aid to El Salvador, the USA threatens to withdraw support when three North American nuns and a Catholic lay worker are found dead in a shallow grave. In November the junta leader, Colonel Majano, is replaced by Duarte. Earlier in the year, the resignation from the government of the social democratic politician Guillermo Manuel Ungo prompt the

unification of the major left-wing guerrilla forces into a more coherent insurgency movement.

1981 While death squads continue to murder an average of 2000 people each month, the civilian-military junta under Duarte fails to gain control of large areas of the countryside now held by insurgents. A January "final offensive" by FMLN guerrillas makes little headway but a campaign during July-August succeeds in disrupting communications and consolidating their hold in the departments of Chalatenango, Morazán and Usulután. Attempts by Mexico and Venezuela to initiate peace talks come to nothing when the Front rejects the offer of a mediated settlement. By the end of the year the escalating conflict has displaced 300 000 people and caused 220 000 to leave the country. Within the space of 12 months 13 353 people have died and at least 2000 have disappeared without trace. When President Duarte visits Washington in September he is told that future US aid is dependent on a reduction in human rights violations.

1982 The FMLN brings the conflict to the outskirts of San Salvador when it cuts off power supplies in January. The country's human rights record is again called into question in the USA when four Dutch journalists reporting the conflict are killed near El Paraiso in March. Two months later five members of the National Guard are sent for trial charged with the murder of Catholic nuns in December 1980. Elections to the 60-member Constituent Assembly take place in March. The Christian Democratic Party with 40.7% of the vote gains the highest number of seats, but the right-wing Arena and Party of National Conciliation unite to form a 33-seat coalition that brings the 38 year old former Chief of Intelligence, Robert D'Aubuisson to the the presidency. Within days pressure from the USA results in the formation of a more broadly-based coalition incorporating the Christian Democrats. Alvaro Magaña is elected as a compromise president in place of D'Aubuisson. Right-wing activities, however, prevent any progress on land reform as death squad killings escalate to a total of 1200 per week by December. At the end of another bloody year official figures record the murder of 5399 people.

1983 President Reagan's growing offensive against communism in North America's "back yard" leads to an increase in US military aid to the Salvadorean government in order to combat an alleged Soviet, Cuban and Nicaraguan presence in the country. This aid is used to launch a June counter-insurgency offensive. Pope John Paul II visits El Salvador in March but his appeal for peace falls on deaf ears. A week later Roman Catholic Bishops anger the right-wing when they state their opposition to increased military aid from the USA.

1984 In March presidential elections are won by Duarte who makes a daring attempt to open up peace talks when he meets leaders of the Democratic Revolutionary Front at Las Palmas, deep in the heart of guerrilla territory.

1985 Peace talks collapse and a new military offensive against guerrillas in Chalatenango provokes the FMLN to retaliate with attacks aimed at disrupting the March municipal and National Assembly elections. Despite public unrest the elections take place and Duarte's Christian Democratic Party wins 34 of the 60 Legislative Assembly seats and two-thirds of the municipal elections. With the economy under seige Duarte attempts to introduce a war tax and controls on imported goods, but he is frustrated by a series of strikes and by strong opposition from the business community. In September the President is forced to release 34 captured guerrillas in exchange for the return of his daughter who had been kidnapped by insurgents.

1986 Government troops dislodge FMLN guerrillas from the Guazapa volcano region and launch attacks on guerrilla strongholds in Chalatenango and Morazán. The cost of these military operations is high and the government cannot afford to carry out social reforms or even help the victims of a major earthquake that kills 1500 people and displaces 300 000.

1987 Now operating in smaller groups, FMLN guerrillas carry out successful attacks on military bases at El Paraiso and San Francisco in March. Duarte reopens peace talks with the FMLN-FDR in a move that allows over 4000 refugees to return from Honduras, but negotiations break down when Herbert Ernesto Anaya, president of the Salvadorean Civil Rights Commission is killed.

1988 Duarte, now suffering from terminal liver cancer, remains in office, but power effectively lies in the hands of the armed forces which oppose the US strategy of low-intensity conflict. The appointment of a "La Tandaro" Chief of Staff, Colonel René Emilio Ponce, consolidates support for the right amongst military leaders in the run-up to Assembly and municipal elections in March. The Arena party wins a decisive majority in these elections and immediately pushes through an Act that abolishes the state coffee-marketing monopoly, INCAFE. Its powers are transferred to a growers association - the Salvador Coffee Council.

1989 In presidential elections the right-wing Arena party led by 41 year old Alfredo Christiani Burkard sweeps to power with 53.8% of the vote. Despite opposition from within both the Arena party and the army, Cristiani is committed to a negotiated settlement to the civil war.

The presidents of five Central American countries meet in the Honduran town of Tela in August and agree that the best way forward is to negotiate with the FMLN. A month later Cristiani opens up a dialogue with FMLN-FDR representatives in Mexico. The violence, however, continues unabated throughout the year with the rebels taking the upper hand in bringing the conflict to the heart of the country's urban centres. In April the Attorney General, Roberto Garcia Alvarado, is murdered and on 11 November, FMLN guerrillas launch a surprise offensive aimed at the cities of San Salvador, Santa Ana, San Miguel, San Francisco, Chalatenango and Usulután. Heavy fighting in San Salvador forces the government to declare a state of seige and a curfew in the capital on 12 November. Three days later the FMLN declares the establishment of (a "liberated zone" covering an area of 6000km² in eight of the 14 departments. In the space of a week 2000 people are killed. Amongst these is the British journalist David Blundy. On 16 November six Jesuit priests of the University of Central America are murdered by right-wing death squads. The Attorney General warns the Church that further deaths are inevitable if Archbishop Rivera Y Damas and his auxiliary bishops continue to voice left-wing sympathies.

1990 Prospects for peace are raised when the FMLN's principal backer, the Nicaraguan Sandinista government, is defeated in presidential and legislature elections.

■ Who's who

Alvarado, Roberto Garcia Salvadorean Attorney General killed by guerrillas in San Salvador on 14 April 1989. Alvarado was replaced by the Arena hardliner Mauricio Colorado.

Blundy, David British journalist killed during a week of violence in San Salvador while covering the conflict for the *Sunday Correspondent* in November 1989.

Castañeda, Eduardo Sanchez Leader of the Armed forces of National Resistance. Also known as Ferman Cienfuegos.

Cristiani, Alfredo A wealthy coffee producer, Alfredo Cristiani Burkard was elected to the presidency at the age of 41 in 1989. As leader of the right-wing Arena party his image is less tarnished by associations with death squads than that of the former party leader Roberto D'Aubuisson. Although committed to a negotiated settlement, Cristiani has made little progress in pursuing peace talks in the face of opposition from within the Arena party and the army.

D'Aubuisson, Roberto A former Chief of Intelligence and ultra right-wing leader of the Arena party in the early 1980s, D'Aubuisson's name came to be associated with the activities of death squads. Elected president in 1982 at the age of 38, he was forced out of office after a week in favour of a compromise president at the head of a more broadly based coalition that included the Christian Democrats. Described by a former US Ambassador as a "psychopathic killer", D'Aubuisson still remains in effective control of the Arena party.

Duarte, José Napoleón Former President of El Salvador and leader of the Christian Democratic Party. Duarte led a centre-left coalition with Guillermo Manuel Ungo which was widely believed to have won the 1972 elections, but was forced to leave the country for seven years following a military takeover in the same year. Returning to El Salvador in 1979, he joined the fragile civilian–military junta a year later. In November 1980 he replaced Colonel Arnoldo Majano in the presidency which he held until 1982. In 1984 he was returned to office for a further five years after which he retired as a result of ill health. Throughout the 1980s Duarte enjoyed the support of the Reagan administration but was unable to resolve the country's economic problems or bring to an end the civil war.

Fronius, Staff Sergeant Gregory A US military adviser killed along with the commanding officer and 42 soldiers of an army base at El Paraiso during an FMLN guerrilla attack in March 1987.

González, Leonel Leader of the 3000-strong Popular Liberation Forces.

Gutiérrez, Colonel Jaime Abdul Commandant of the army cadet school, Gutiérrez joined forces with Colonel Arnoldo Majano to stage a coup that ousted President Romero in October 1979.

Handal, Shafik Jorge Leader of the Salvadorean Communist Party and its military wing, the Armed Forces of Liberation.

Majano, Colonel Arnoldo   As commander of the military arsenal, Majano was co-leader of the military coup that toppled President Romero in October 1979. A year later he was replaced as leader of the military-civilian junta by José Napoleón Duarte.

Martí, Farabundo   A peasant hero who led a revolt against the government of General Maximiliano Hernàndez in 1932. The FMLN guerrilla organization has adopted his name.

Magaña, Alvaro   A 56 year old economist and lawyer appointed to the presidency of El Salvador at the head of a broadly based coalition government in April 1982.

Monterosa, Colonel Domingo   A popular army officer whose death in a helicopter crash contributed to the demoralization of the armed forces in the struggle against terrorism in the early 1980s.

Ochoa, Colonel Sigfredo   Vice-president of the right-wing Arena party, Ochoa was a tough and effective army combat commander responsible for establishing "free-fire" zones in guerrilla-held territory in 1986.

Oquelí, Héctor   Deputy leader of the National Revolutionary Movement and co-leader, along with Zamora and Ungo, of the rebel Democratic Revolutionary Front killed in January 1990 at the age of 44 while on a visit to Guatemala. Formerly secretary of the Law Faculty of the National University in San Salvador and later an officer of the London-based Socialist International, Oquelí travelled the world to mobilize international opposition to successive US-backed governments in El Salvador.

Ponce, Colonel René Emilio   Leader of the influential 1966 Military School graduating class, known as "La Tandaro", Ponce was the US choice for the position of Army Chief of Staff in the final months of Duarte's presidency prior to the 1988 Assemby and municipal elections.

Rivera y Damas, Arturo   Archbishop of El Salvador in succession to Oscar Romero who was murdered in 1980.

Roca, Roberto   Leader of the small Central American Workers' Revolutionary Party.

Romero, General Carlos Umberto   A right-wing army commander who came to power following the military coup of 1977. He ended the US-backed land reform programme of the previous government and gained a reputation for human rights violation that forced the USA temporarily to   withdraw aid to El Salvador. In 1979 the general was ousted by another coup that led to the formation of a military-civilian junta.

Romero, Oscar Arnolfo   An outspoken advocate of the poor, Archbishop Oscar Romero was killed by a death squad in March 1980 at the age of 63. Ordained in 1942, Romero became a bishop in 1970 and an archbishop in 1977.

Ungo, Guillermo Manuel   A Social Democratic politician who led a liberal coalition with José Duarte following elections in 1972. His subsequent resignation from the joint military-civilian government in 1980 provided a major impetus for the unification of left-wing guerrilla forces into the Democratic Revolutionary Front-Farabundo Martí Front for Nátional Liberation (FDR–FMLN). A leader of the left-wing National Revolutionary Movement, Ungo stood as a Democratic Revolutionary Front candidate in the 1989 presidential elections, but when D'Aubuisson's Arena party swept to power he fled the country for fear of his life.

Villalobos, Joaquin   At the head of the 4000-strong People's Revolutionary Army, Villalobos became the most prominent FMLN guerrilla leader in 1983.

Zamora, Reubén   A Christian Democrat minister during the short-lived reformist government of 1980, Reubèn Zamora Rivas was forced to spend seven years in exile before returning to El Salvador in 1987, at the age of 45, to resume his leadership of the Popular Social Christian Movement and vice-presidency of the Democratic Revolutionary Front.

■ Key places

Chalatenango   One of the 14 departments of El Salvador, Chalatenango is situated on the country's northern frontier with Honduras. Bounded to the west and south by the Lempa River, this remote and mountainous tropical region is a major haven for guerrilla fighters. Area 2 507km². Population (1981) 23 5700.

Contadora   An island in the Gulf of Panama where the foreign ministers of Colombia, Mexico, Panama, Venezuela and Colombia met in January 1983 in an attempt to find a solution to the socio-political problems of Central America. This group came to be known as the Contadora Group.

Cuscatlán Bridge   Crossing the Lempa River on the frontier of San Vicente department, the Cuscatlàn Bridge is the largest and most heavily defended bridge in El Salvador. The destruction of the bridge effectively cuts off communication between east and west along the Pan-American Highway. A surprise attack by FMLN guerrillas destroyed this strategic target on New Year's Day 1984.

El Paraíso   A town in Chalatenango department, 30km north of San Salvador. While reporting the conflict, four Dutch journalists were killed near here in 1982. A major assault on the resident army base in March 1987 resulted in the deaths of the local commanding officer, a US adviser and 42 soldiers.

Guazapa   A guerrilla stronghold in an area dominated by the 1438 metre-high Guazapa volcano, Cuscatlán department, central El Salvador. Government forces dislodged FMLN guerrillas from this area during a major offensive in 1986.

La Palma   A town in the department of Chalatenango close to the Honduras border and 80km north of San Salvador. On 15 October 1983 President Duarte travelled to La Palma to meet guerrilla leaders in a daring but unsuccessful   attempt to bring the country's civil war to an end. Population 3000.

Lempa   One of the principal rivers of Central America. Rising near Esquipulas in Guatemala, it flows southwards through Honduras into El Salvador where it winds its way through the mountains in a southerly and an easterly direction before falling into the Pacific Ocean just west of the Bahia de Jiquilisco. The river is a major source of hydro-electric power. Its total length is about 320km.

Morazán   A department formerly known as Gotera in east El Salvador on the frontier with Honduras; area 1364km²; population (1981) 215 000. In 1986 a major offensive was launched against FMLN guerrillas occupying the territory to the north of the Torola river, but in the following year terrorists were able to counter-attack, hitting the army base at the departmental capital, San Francisco.

San Miguel   Capital of a department of the same name in east El Salvador, 142km ESE of San Salvador. Situated at the foot of the San Miguel and Chinameca volcanoes, San Miguel developed as a gold and silver mining centre. Population (1984) 86 700.

San Salvador   Capital of El Salvador, situated at an altitude of 680m in an intermontane basin. The city was founded in 1525 but was severely damaged by an earthquake in 1854. In 1986 1 500 people were killed and 300 000 made homeless when an earthquake hit the city and surrounding area again. Population (1984) 452 600.

Santa Ana   The second largest city in El Salvador and capital of a department of the same name. Situated on the Pan American Highway 35km from the Guatemalan frontier, Santa Ana is a commercial centre for coffee and sugar-cane which is grown in the surrounding area. Population (1984) 135 000.

Santa Ana   Rising to a height of 2381m in W El Salvador, Santa Ana is the highest volcano in the country. Izalco volcano to the south was created in 1770 following an eruption from the side of the Santa Ana volcano.

Sumpul A river rising near the town of Nueva Ocotepeque in Honduras. It flows 58km south-east along the border with El Salvador before meeting the Lempa River 27km east of Chalatenango. In May 1980 an estimated 600 refugees were killed by Salvadorean and Honduran soldiers while trying to escape across the river into Honduras.

Torola A river rising in the Salvadorean province of Cabañas about 50km north-east of San Salvador. Flowing generally east and south-east, it follows the Honduras frontier for much of its course. Along with the Cordillera Cacaguateque, it effectively cuts off the guerrilla-held northern part of Morazán department before turning north into Honduras.

Zona Rosa The fashionable residential district of El Salvador's capital, San Salvador.

■ Key words

Arena Party See Nationalist Republican Alliance.

Arias Plan A peace plan for the Central American region proposed in 1986 by President Oscar Arias of Costa Rica who was eventually awarded the Nobel Peace Prize. Adopted by the five presidents of Central America meeting in Guatemala in August 1987, the Arias plan called for an immediate ceasefire in all Central American conflicts, cessation of aid to all guerrilla groups, a general amnesty and negotiations between all interested parties.

argolleras A faction of the Christian Democratic Party led by Adolfo Rey whose election as a presidential candidate in the run up to the 1989 elections was overturned by the US-backed *institutionalistas*.

Armed Forces of National Resistance (FARN) A 1500-strong FMLN guerrilla wing of the Salvadorean Communist Party headed by Shafik Jorge Handal.

Central American Workers' Revolutionary Party (PRTC) A small 300-member leftist FMLN guerrilla group led by Roberto Roca.

Christian Democratic Party (Partido Demócrata Cristiano - PDC) The principal opposition party in El Salvador. Adopting a more moderate approach to resolving the country's problems the Christian Democrats, under the leadership of José Napóleon Duarte, joined the fragile civilian-military junta in 1980. In 1982 US pressure prompted the formation of a coalition government including the Christian Democrats. Two years later the party won a decisive victory in elections following three years of civil war in which over 30 000 had been killed. Unable to bring the civil war to an end, the Christian Democratic Party was eventually defeated in the elections of 1988–89 when the the right-wing Arena Party swept to power.

death squads Owing their origin to the military-controlled vigilante groups of the 1960s and 1970s, the death squads of the early 1980s were responsible for the large scale repression of left-wing opposition to D'Aubuisson's right-wing Arena party. In December 1982 it was reckoned that death squad killings were being carried out at a rate of 1200 per week.

Democratic Convergence A political union of the Social Democratic Party with Zamora's Popular Social Christian Movement and Ungo's National Revolutionary Movement. Formed in November 1987, the union sought to achieve a negotiated settlement to the conflict.

Democratic Revolutionary Front (FDR) An Alliance of left-wing political parties and revolutionary groups formed in 1980 and led by Reubén Zamora, Guillermo Manuel Ungo and Hector Oqueli.

Farabundo Marti National Liberation Front (Frente Farabundo Martí de Liberacion Nacional - FMLN) An amalgamation of leftist guerrilla groups which joined forces in 1980 in the fight against the government of El Salvador. The group is named after Farabundo Martí, peasant revolutionary hero of the 1930s.

free-fire zones   Areas of the country in which everyone is considered to be a terrorist and in which security forces destroy all buildings, crops and animals. Free-fire zones were first conceived by Colonel Sigifredo Ochoa who designated twelve such areas in the province of Chaltenango in 1986.

Gerardo Barrios Civil Front   A guerrilla group, describing itself as "an essentially democratic force", that emerged in 1989. This group claimed reponsibility for the April 1989 murder of the Attorney General, Roberto Garcia Alvarado and the attempted assassination of Vice-president Francisco Merino.

INCAFE   The government coffee marketing monopoly abolished by the ruling Arena party in 1988 in favour of a growers organization called the Salvador Coffee Council.

institutionalistas   A faction of the Christian Democratic Party led by Fidel Chavéz Mena whose candidacy for the post of president was supported by the USA in the run up to the 1989 elections.

land of the tiller programme   A government land reform programme aimed at enabling 20 000 peasants to buy plots of up to seven hectares, initiated but not followed through in 1982.

mano blanco   The mano blanco or "white hand" is the sign of the right-wing death squads that operate in El Salvador.

National Democratic Organization (Orden)   Formed in 1961 as a rural vigilante organization under military control, Orden achieved notoriety for its repression of alleged communists and was the forerunner of the later right-wing "death squads".

National Revolutionary Movement   A left-wing political opposition group headed by Guillermo Manuel Ungo and, until his death in 1990, Hector Oqueli.

Nationalist Democratic Union   The political wing of the Armed Forces of Liberation.

Operation Phoenix   A US-backed counter-insurgency operation carried out in early 1986 in an attempt to deprive guerrillas of support by removing civilians from the Guazapa volcano region.

Party of National Conciliation (Partido de Conciliacion Nacional - PCN)   A military-backed political party that formed the core of the 1979-82 civilian-military junta. Led by Rafael Moran, the party succeeded in winning 4.1% of the vote in the 1989 presidential election.

patriotic civil defence   A paramilitary group formed in 1989 by 74 businessmen in order to combat the increasing number of attacks by guerrilla "urban commandos". Sponsored by the hardline commander of the Army First Brigade, the group has been criticized by the Catholic Church which likens it to the death squads of the early 1980s.

People's Patriotic Movement   (Movimiento Patriotico del Pueblo - MPP)   A left-wing guerrilla movement formed in April 1988 with the aim of establishing a democratic government free of US intervention.

People's Revolutionary Army (ERP)   A 4000-strong leftist FMLN guerrilla group led by Joaquin Villalobos. Its political wing is the February 28 Popular League.

Popular Liberation Forces (FPL)   A 3000-strong leftist FMLN guerrilla group led by Leonel González. Its political wing is the Popular Revolutionary Bloc.

Popular Liberation Movement   The political wing of the Central American Workers' Revolutionary Party.

Popular Revolutionary Bloc   The political arm of the Popular Liberation Forces.

Popular Social Christian Movement   A left-wing political group founded by

Reubén Zamora, leader of the Democratic Revolutionary Front.

Republican Nationalist Alliance (Alianza Republicana Nacionalista - Arena)   Right-wing political party whose leader, Alfredo Cristiani, was elected to the presidency in 1989. In the early 1980s the party was led by the ultra right-wing former intelligence chief, Roberto D'Aubuisson, whose name came to be associated with death squads and whose presidential candidacy was blocked by the USA in 1982 and again in 1989.

Socorro Juridico   A Roman Catholic organization providing legal aid in El Salvador.

Tandaro   A nickname given to a group of ruthless, right-wing army officers who graduated from the Military Academy in 1966.

Tela declaration   An agreement reached in August 1989 by the presidents of five Central American countries who met in the town of Tela in N Honduras to discuss a Central American Peace Plan. In addition to discussing the demobilization of the Contra rebels in Nicaragua they suggested that the best way to find a solution to the civil war in El Salvador was to negotiate a settlement with the FMLN.

Tutela Legal   The human rights office of the Roman Catholic Church in El Salvador.

Unified Popular Action Front   The political wing of the Armed forces of National Resistance.

Unified Revolutionary Directorate (URD)   A 15-member war council of guerrilla leaders.

■ Further reading

R. Armstrong and J. Shenk, *El Salvador: The Face of Revolution*, Pluto, London, 1982

James Dunkerley, *The Long War: Dictatorship and revolution in El Salvador*, Junction, London, 1982

Joe Fish and Cristina Sganga, *El Salvador: Testament of Terror*, Zed, London, 1987

T.S. Montgomery, *Revolution in El Salvador: Origins and Evolution*, Westview Press, Boulder, 1982

Richard Ware, *The Crisis in El Salvador*, House of Commons Library, London, 1981

Alastair White, *El Salvador*, Ernest Benn Ltd, London and Tonbridge, 1973

3
Colombia

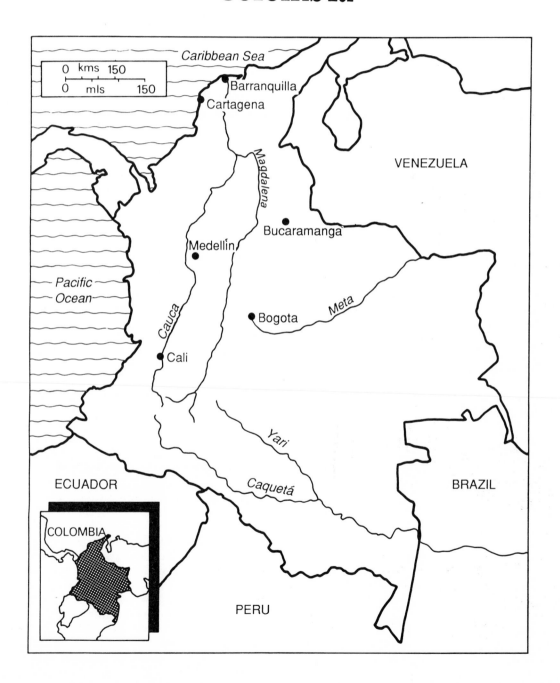

Caribbean Sea

Barranquilla
Cartagena

Magdalena

VENEZUELA

Bucaramanga

Medellín

Pacific
Ocean

Cauca

Bogota

Meta

Cali

Yari

Caquetá

ECUADOR

BRAZIL

COLOMBIA

PERU

0 kms 150
0 mls 150

■ Profile

Official name: Republic of Colombia

- **Area:** 1 138 910km²
- **Population (1988):** 31 300 000
- **Ethnic groups:** Mestizo 50%, Mulatto 23%, European 20%, African 5%, Amerindian 1%
- **Official language:** Spanish
- **Religion:** Roman Catholic 97%
- **Life expectancy:** 67 years
- **Infant mortality rate (1985):** 56 per 1000
- **Currency:** Colombian peso of 100 centavos
- **Administrative divisions:** 23 departments, 5 commissariats, 4 intendencies and 1 special district
- **Timezone:** GMT −5
- **Capital:** Bogotá
- **Chief cities:** Bogotá (3 983 000), Medellín (1 468 000), Cali (1 350 000), Barranquilla (900 000)

■ Introduction

Colombia underwent a number of boundary changes after declaring independence from Spain in 1819. These culminated in the US-induced secession of Panama in 1903, when the country's present-day borders were established apart from some remaining issues with Nicaragua and Venezuela. From about 1840 internal politics revolved around frequently bloody competition between Liberals and Conservatives. This established a tradition of political violence which remains pervasive to this day. Various country-wide and provincial conflicts included the great Liberal–Conservative civil war of 1899–1902 in which some 100 000 Cololmbians perished. Similar political struggles in the 20th century were to prove even more costly. But none of these earlier conflicts posed such a threat to state authority and regional security as did the rise of the Colombian drug-trafficking cartels in the 1980s.

Colombia's territorial dispute with Nicaragua concerns the sovereignty of the Caribbean archipelago of San Andrés, Providencia and other cays. Although they are located within Nicaragua's 200-mile maritime limit, Colombia has held them since the 19th century. This derives from the fact that until 1903 Colombia encompassed present-day Panama, which is nearer to the cays than either of the other two protagonists (and which itself has a dormant claim to them). A 1928 treaty confirmed Colombian sovereignty over the islands, but in 1980 the new Sandinista government of Nicaragua declared this instrument null and void. The central claim of the Sandinistas (and other Nicaraguans) was that earlier treaties had been imposed by US pressure. Colombia totally rejected the Nicaraguan claim and declared itself ready to oppose it in the International Court of Justice.

Venezuela's claim against Colombia is rather more complex. The inevitably vague colonial land boundaries between the two countries were not finally determined until 1922, through the mediation of the Swiss government. But this adjudication left vague seaward boundaries in the Gulf of Venezuela. In recent years Colombia has challenged Venezuelan sovereignty over certain islands in the Gulf, seeking to establish rights in areas thought to contain oil. A draft delimitation treaty was drawn up in 1980 but encountered strong opposition in both countries and was never signed. In 1987 there were reports of Colombian land and seaward incursions into territory held by Venezuela, although both sides expressed their desire for a peaceful resolution of the dispute. In 1989 Spanish mediation was invoked to find a settlement.

Internally, Colombia entered the post-1945 era with its deep-rooted economic and social problems creating an ideal scenario for political violence and instability. Despite substantial (mainly US) investment, the economy remained over-dependent on coffee production for export. Peasant farmers laboured under an archaic land tenure system, and a small financial oligarchy clung tenaciously to its wealth and power. The assassination of a progressive President, Jorge Gaitán, in 1948 precipitated another wave of civil conflict, which was arrested only by periods of military dictatorship in 1953–57 and 1962–63. Yet Colombians retained their traditional aversion to military rule. Since 1962 the Liberals and Conservatives have effectively shared power, or exercised it in turn, with the former edging ahead as the natural majority party in the 1980s. The trouble has been that the left-wing guerrilla movements which emerged in the wake of the 1959 Cuban revolution have regarded civilian governments as being as oppressive as those of the uniformed variety. Numerous peace initiatives in the 1980s brought only temporary or partial respites in the guerrilla war.

The darker dimension of Colombia's internal strife – the country's role as the world centre of the illegal drugs industry – became a major problem from the late 1970s. The remote rural uplands in the north were ideal for growing coca, from which cocaine is derived. For poverty-stricken peasants coca leaves were a readily marketable cash crop when prices for coffee and other commodities were slumping. To organize the production and distribution of cocaine, powerful criminal networks sprang up, notably the infamous Medellín cartel in Colombia's second-largest city. They amassed colossal wealth from the drugs trade, principally by supplying the US market, and

came to represent a major challenge to law and order throughout the region. Not only did they establish a network of collaborators in high places throughout the Caribbean, they also either bribed Colombian law enforcement officials or assassinated them. Evidence emerged, moreover, of links between the drugs cartels and the financing and arming of the various Colombian guerrilla movements.

The inexorable rise of the Colombian cartels caused particular concern in the United States, where drug trafficking and its attendant social ills became the most pressing domestic issue by the late 1980s. Concentrated among blacks and Hispanics, drug addiction or abuse fed brutality and lawlessless on inner-city streets, as rival gangs fought to control the lucrative distribution trade. Drugs were also seen as a prime cause of the relative failure of blacks, especially, to improve their economic and social lot. The US government therefore took the lead in international and regional initiatives to combat drug trafficking in the countries of supply. Top of the list was Colombia, to which some 100 US military advisers were sent in September 1989.

The governments of the region declared their willingness to co-operate in such efforts, but some criticisms were voiced that the United States was seeking to export the blame for its own domestic problems. Without the huge US domestic demand for drugs, the argument ran, there would be no supply. There was also considerable scepticism about the likely effectiveness of US-sponsored anti-drugs programmes in supplying countries. Faced with the intractabilities of the problem, some influential voices, including *The Economist* of London, advanced the view that legalization of hard drugs was the only realistic way of breaking criminal control of the trade. No Western government was expected to accept this advice in the foreseeable future.

■ Chronology of events

1819 The Republic of Great Colombia, consisting of present-day Venezuela, Panama, Colombia and Ecuador, declares its independence from Spanish colonial rule. The liberator Simón Bolívar is elected first President of the republic and Francisco de Paula Santander Vice-President.

1830 Venezuela and Ecuador withdraw from the republic.

1846 The United States concludes a treaty with the Bogotá government acquiring the right of transit across the Isthmus of Panama.

1886 Following a revolution in the previous year the states of the former confederation of Colombia are united to form the Republic of Colombia.

1899–1902 Bitter class rivalry between Liberal and Conservative factions reaches a peak in the "War of a Thousand Days". Victory eventually goes to the Conservatives who favour a strong centralized government and a limited franchise, but the civil war has cost 10 000 lives.

1903 Backed by the United States Panama declares its independence.

1909 Colombia recognises the independence of Panama and terminates the 1846 treaty with the USA.

1914 Introduced into Colombia in the 1850s, coffee is now the country's most important export.

1930 The election of the moderate Liberal Enrique Olaya to the presidency brings to an end 46 years of Conservative rule. The Liberals embark on a programme of social reform that includes the disestablishment of the Catholic Church. Their programme of reform is frustrated by world economic depression and a fall in coffee prices.

1948 The assassination of the popular left-wing Liberal Jorge Gaitán, champion of the underprivileged classes, sparks off a major revolt that leads to the loss of 1400 lives.

1949 Following a violent election campaign in which 1000 are killed, the Conservatives regain power. The sustained civil unrest and escalating terrorism that claims the lives of up to 20 000 people during the next two decades comes to be known as *La Violencia* ("the violence").

1953–57 The military dictator, General Gustavo Rojas Pinilla, enjoys wide support, partly as a result of his success in reducing *La Violencia*. When he fails to restore democratic government he is overthrown by the military and both major political parties.

1957 Liberal and Conservative leaders issue the "Declaration of Sitges" in which the formation of a National Front coalition government is proposed.

1958 Colombian voters approve a constitutional amendment that brings in a National Front government led by Liberal and Conservative presidents who alternate every four years.

1961 Despite opposition from major landowners, the government sets up the Colombian Institute for Agrarian Reform (INCORA) in an attempt to redistribute land amongst smallholders and to improve the standard of living of peasant farmers.

1962–63 General Gustavo Rojas Pinilla briefly returns to power once again.

1965–66 The newly-formed pro-Cuban Army of National Liberation (ELN), the Maoist People's Liberation Army (EPL) and the pro-Soviet wing of the Colombian Communist Party (FARC) all join forces in waging a guerrilla war against the government.

1968 After a decade of social reform, the coalition government brings to an end 20 years of civil unrest. Guerrilla insurgency in rural

Colombia, however, remains to be overcome. The National Association of Peasant Land Users, formed by Dr Carlos Lleras Restrepo, united 1 500 000 peasants to form the largest mass organization in Latin America. Designed to speed up the process of land reform, the movement quickly begins to fragment into radical revolutionary groups which engage in land seizure and guerrilla activities.

1974 Elections in April mark a return to the traditional two-party competition for the presidency. By the end of the year a state of economic emergency is declared.

1975 Strikes, rioting and the seizure of land by peasants forces President Alfonso Lopéz Michelson to declare a state of emergency. At the end of June 5000 people are arrested within the space of 48 hours.

1976 The pro-Cuban M–19 guerrilla group takes up arms against the Colombian government, first as a popular nationalist organization and then as a left-wing Marxist movement.

1979 Cuba agrees to provide the Colombian drug mafia with landing facilities for drugs in transit from Colombia to Florida in exchange for the delivery of arms and ammunition to the pro-Castro M–19 guerrillas. In the same year Colombia signs an extradition treaty with the United States.

1979–83 In the face of world recession, falling prices for export goods and high interest rates the economy of Colombia takes a down turn. In the space of four years the gross domestic product drops from 6.1 per cent to 1 per cent and unemployment rises from 7 per cent to 13.5 per cent.

1980 The news is dominated by the two-month seige of the embassy of the Dominican Republic in Bogotá where 16 M–19 guerrillas hold 45 diplomatic hostages. Meanwhile, drug trafficking is now the number-one source of income in Colombia, which has become the Latin American centre for refining and exporting cocaine.

1982 A new guerrilla group calling itself the Workers' Self-Defence (ADO) joins the

guerrilla war. In May the Conservative Belisario Betancur is elected to the presidency.

1984 Colombian drug traffickers, who monopolize the world trade in narcotics, now supply 75–85 per cent of the cocaine and 60 per cent of the marijuana entering the United States. In March, a raid by Colombian narcotics squads on a major drug operation provokes the assassination, a month later, of the Minister of Justice. Announcing a state of emergency on 1 May, President Betancur declares war on the cocaine barons by sanctioning the extradition of drug traffickers to the USA and beginning a programme of aerial spraying to destroy coca crops. In the hope of establishing peace with militant rebel groups, Betancur initiates a series of ceasefires on 28 May.

1985 The ceasefire agreements of the previous year come to an end when first the M–19 guerrillas and then the People's Liberation Army resume fighting. In November 115 people, including 11 Supreme Court Justices, die when M–19 guerrillas attack the Supreme Court in Bogotá.

1986 Although the government is able to extend its truce with the Marxist Columbian Revolutionary Armed Forces and the Patriotic Union (FARC–UP), the armed conflict with M–19, the People's Liberation Army and other small guerrilla groups continues. The Betancur administration is replaced by a Liberal government led by Virgilio Barco. He promises peace but is faced with a rising tide of narcoterrorist violence which includes a series of assassinations of left-wing Patriotic Union leaders.

In April the government co-operates with 21 other Latin American countries in setting up an Inter-American Drug Control Commission to fight drug trafficking and drug abuse. A few days later Colombia signs the Rodrigo Lara Bonilla accord with other Andean Pact countries who have decided to organize joint anti-narcotics operations.

1987 The Medellín drug cartel attempts to undermine the government using terrorist tactics that include the killing of the Attorney

General, Carlos Mauro Hoyos Jiminez, and the kidnapping of Andres Pastrana, the Social Conservative candidate in the campaign for mayor of Bogotá. At the same time, a feud develops between the Cali and Medellín drug cartels for control of the New York cocaine market. In 1987 alone, an estimated 11 000 people meet their death, mostly at the hands of right-wing paramilitary death squads or *sicarios*. In the United States, Carlos Lehder Rivas is sentenced to life imprisonment on drugs charges following his extradition from Colombia in February.

1988 In the first few months of the year guerrilla attacks on key installations intensify, particularly in the Barrancabermeja oilfield region. Right-wing death squads launch a campaign of violence, slaughtering residents of villages known to sympathize with left-wing causes. Six of the leading guerrilla groups unite under an umbrella organization known as the Simón Bolívar Guerrilla Co-ordinating Board, but in September a peace plan put forward by President Barco prompts the M–19 guerrillas to offer a ceasefire.

1989 Although at least 1500 people are killed by paramilitary death squads in the first three months of the year, the government reaches a ceasefire agreement with the M–19 guerrillas on 17 March. Later in the year, the war against the drug cartels escalates when the deaths of a Superior Court Magistrate, the Police Chief of Medellín and the Liberal Presidential candidate all take place within the space of three days. The government reacts immediately by striking out against the leaders of the drug cartels. In an operation involving 20 000 police and soldiers, property is confiscated and 11 000 people are arrested. Amongst these is the top financial adviser to the Medellín cartel, the 31 year old Eduardo Martinez Romero. His extradition to the United States to face drug charges in Atlanta prompts a violent backlash from the drug barons who declare "total and absolute war" on the government. The leaders of the Medellín and Cali cartels, who have been fighting each other for control of the North American cocaine markets, are now forced to move their headquarters to Brazil.

The strong measures taken by President Barco to fight the campaign of terror waged by the drug barons is backed by President Bush who, in September, announces a $2000 million special Andean aid programme under which the United States will help South American anti-narcotics squads stem the flow of drugs coming out of Peru, Bolivia and Colombia. Some 100 US military advisers are sent to Colombia to train local forces in the use of US military equipment.

1990 On 15 February the presidents of Colombia, Bolivia, Peru and the United States hold a one-day summit in the Colombian port of Cartagena and decide to set up an "anti-drugs cartel" to fight the narcotics industry.

In March the M–19 guerrillas sign a peace treaty and field candidates for the first time in congressional, provincial and local elections after fighting for nearly 15 years.

■ Who's who

Barco Vargas, Virgilio Liberal President of Colombia since 1986 and first leader of a single-party government after a generation of coalition rule by Liberals and Conservatives. His plans for agrarian, urban, tax and civil service reforms have been frustrated by the fragmentation of his party and the escalation of drug-related violence. Faced with no realistic political solution to the problem of drug trafficking he opted to use force against the powerful Colombian cocaine barons following the deaths of three prominent figures at the hands of terrorists in August 1989.

Botero Moreno, Hernán The first Colombian drug dealer to be extradited to the United States following the US–Colombian extradition treaty of 1979. Botero Moreno's extradition in 1984 resulted in the formation of an "extraditable" guerrilla group named the Hernán Botero Moreno Command.

Calvo Ocampo, Jaime de Jesús   Known as Comandante Ernesto Rojas, Calvo Ocampo was leader of the EPL guerrilla group and Chief of Staff of the Guerrilla Co-ordinating Board until his murder on 16 February 1987.

Duarte Acero, José Ivan   One of the 12 most wanted drug barons in Colombia, Duarte faces indictment in Miami for the attempted murder of two drug enforcement agents.

Escobar Gaviria, Pablo   Billionaire leader of the Medellín drug cartel which dominates the world cocaine trade. Known as "El Napoles", he is under indictment in Los Angeles, Atlanta and Miami. Escobar, who has a fortune totalling an estimated $2 billion, built up a powerful drug operation in the 1970s using extortion and violence to gain access to the US drug market. In order to gain popular support as well as a market for *bazuko*, the "poor man's cocaine", he built a huge housing estate around Medellín for the impoverished people of the shanty towns.

Galán, Luis Carlos   The 46 year old Liberal Party leader and presidential candidate shot dead by terrorists at a political rally outside Bogotá on 18 August 1989. The murder of the Medellín police chief and a court magistrate in the same week led to all out conflict between the government and the Colombian drug dealers.

Gaviria Rivero, Gustavo de Jesús   Cousin and right-hand man of drug leader Pablo Escobar.

Gomez Padilla, Miguel Antonio   National Police Director leading the fight against the powerful drug barons of Colombia. Faced with daily bombings and murders his declared intention to "wipe these gangsters off the face of this earth" was admission that force rather than politics was the only way to tackle the drug cartels.

Lara Bonilla, Rodrigo   Colombian Justice Minister murdered by drug traffickers in 1984. He gave his name to the 1986 Rodrigo Lara Bonilla accord by which Andean Pact countries agreed to join forces in the fight against drug trafficking and drug abuse.

Lehder Rivas, Carlos   Prominent Colombian drug trafficker who was extradited to the United States in February 1987 to face drug charges in Florida.

Martínez Romero, Eduardo   A leading financial expert employed by the Medellín drug cartel until his arrest in August 1989. Wanted in the USA in connection with the laundering of $1.2 billion-worth of drug proceeds through fictitious jewellery and gold-trading businesses, he was deported in September 1989 to face charges in Atlanta. His extradition provoked another round of retaliatory bombings and terrorist attacks throughout Colombia.

Marulanda, Manuel   Leader of the Colombian Revolutionary Armed Forces (FARC), the most powerful of the rural guerrilla groups.

Moncada, Geraldo   Under indictment in Atlanta, Moncada is one of the 12 most wanted men in Colombia where he has laundered money for the powerful Escobar and Ochoa families.

Ochoa Vásquez, Fabio   Known as "Fabito", Fabio Ochoa is the youngest member of the Ochoa family to hold a senior position in the family drug business.

Ochoa Vásquez, Jorge Luis   Powerful Chief executive officer of the Medellín drug cartel, Ochoa is under indictment in Miami. Arrested in November 1987 for illegally importing Spanish fighting bulls, Ochoa managed to secure his release from prison a month later. Faced with the prospect of rearrest and extradition to the USA, he fled the country.

Ochoa Vásquez, Juan David   Elder brother of the drug baron Jorge Ochoa.

Orejuela Caballero, Jaime Raúl   One of the leading "dirty dozen" drug barons of Medellín. Under indictment in New York since 1985 for drug dealing.

Pizzaro Leongomez, Carlos   Leader of the M–19 guerrilla movement involved in direct talks with the Colombian government that led to a ceasefire in 1989 and the signing of a peace agreement in March 1990.

Quintero, Colonel Vallemar Franklin   Police chief of Colombia's drug capital, Medellín, shot by terrorists on 17 August 1989. The killing of a Bogotá court magistrate on the previous day and the murder of the Liberal Party presidential candidate 24 hours later sparked off an open "war" between the government and the powerful drug dealers of Colombia.

Rodriguez Gacha, José Gonzalo   Known as "El Mexicano", Gacha has been described as one of "the most vicious" of the Medellín drug dealers. He was shot dead by police in December 1989.

Rodriguez Orejuela, Gilberto José   Head of the drug dealing cartel in the Colombian city of Cali. His gang controls the supply of drugs to New York, but attempts by Escobar to take over this market have led to a fierce war between the Cali and Medellín drug cartels. Under indictment in New York, New Orleans, Los Angeles and Miami, Rodriguez is the owner of the Drogas Rebaja chain of drug stores. He was also the owner of a Medellín football team and the First Interamericas Bank in Panama.

Rodriguez Orejuela, Miguel Angel   Elder brother of Gilberto Rodriguez and owner of big businesses in Medellín. He faces indictment in New Orleans for drug trafficking.

Santacruz Londoño, José   A leading member of the Cali drug cartel in partnership with Miguel and Gilberto Rodriguez.

Valencia, Carlos   Superior Court Magistrate in Bogotá. Murdered by terrorists on 16 August 1989 at the age of 39. His death along with that of liberal politician Luis Carlos Galán and Medellín police chief Vallemar Franklin Quintero prompted the President of Colombia to "declare war" on the drug barons of Colombia.

■ Key places

Barrancabermeja   A port and petroleum centre on the east bank of the Magdalena River, situated 80km west of Bucaramanga in the NE Colombian department of Santander. A major outlet for the nearby De Mares oilfields which are linked by pipeline to the Caribbean coast at Cartagena. The oil installations in this area have come under heavy attack by guerrillas.

Barranquilla   Colombia's leading industrial port on the Caribbean Sea, linked to the interior by the Magdalena River. Population (1985) 899 800. The first air terminal in Latin America was opened here in 1919.

Bucaramanga   Known as the "garden city" of Colombia, Bucaramanga lies at the heart of a cotton, coffee and tobacco growing region and is the capital of the north-eastern province of Santander.

Bogotá   Largest city and capital of Colombia, situated at an altitude of 2650m in the Andes of central Colombia. Population (1985) 3 983 000. Founded by the Spanish in 1538, the city's two main attractions are the fabulous collection of Pre-Columbian treasures in the Gold Museum and the Quinta de Bolívar, home of the liberator, Simón Bolívar.

Cali   Third largest city in Colombia, Cali is situated in the Valle de Cauca at the centre of a wealthy sugar-producing region. Well known for its bull fighting, the city is the base of a drug cartel which controls the New York cocaine market.

Cartagena or fully **Cartagena de los Indes**   Seaport capital of the department of Bolívar on the Caribbean N coast of Colombia. Sacked by Sir Francis Drake in 1586, the city was originally founded in 1533 as an outlet for

Spanish gold. Today, in addition to oil-refining and the manufacture of chemicals and plastics, the city has a thriving tourist industry that is based on the Boca Grande, a sand spit that stretches out into the sea from the old fortified city. On 15 February 1990 President Bush of the United States came to Cartagena to meet the presidents of Colombia, Bolivia and Peru. This one-day summit resulted in a decision by these countries to form a so-called "anti-drugs cartel" to combat the flow of narcotics from South to North America.

Los Monjes   An island group in the Caribbean Sea lying to the north-east of the Goajíra Peninsula, N Colombia. Included within that part of the Gulf of Venezuela whose sovereignty is disputed by Colombia and Venezuela, a dispute that arose in the 1920s following the discovery of oil in the Gulf.

Magdalena River   The principal river of Colombia, rising in the central Andes in the southern department of Cauca, it flows 1610km north to meet the Caribbean near the port of Barranquilla. Navigable for most of its course, the upper river valley runs parallel to the upper reaches of its tributary, the Cauca River. This is the most fertile agricultural region of the country.

Medellín   The second largest city in Colombia, Medellín is the industrial and commercial centre of the department of Antioquia. It is also the headquarters of a drug cartel that, under the leadership of Pablo Escobar, controls the greater part of the world cocaine market. In the 1980s terrorism and drug-related violence gave Medellín the doubtful reputation of having the highest murder rate of any city in the world.

Meta   A thinly-populated department in the *llanos* or eastern plains of Colombia. Population (1985) 412 000. Drained by the Meta River, this infertile region was chosen in the 1960s and early 1970s as the unlikely location for peasant colonization by the agrarian reform agency INCORA.

Nevado del Ruiz   A volcano rising to 5 399m in the Andean mountains of central Colombia near Manizales. The volcano erupted in November 1985 and in the resulting mudslide and flooding there was heavy loss of life.

San Andrés–Providencia   An intendency of Colombia in the Caribbean Sea, consisting of two small islands and their associated reefs 180km E of Nicaragua and 480km north of Colombia. The islands are a duty free zone and San Andrés is an international airline stopover. Administered by Colombia following the 1928 Bárcenas Menese–Esguerra treaty between Colombia and Nicaragua, the islands were later claimed by the Sandinista government of Nicaragua in 1980.

Yarí River   A river that rises in the Cordillera Oriental of S Colombia and flows about 480km south-east through tropical forest before meeting the Caqetá River. In March 1984 Colombian anti-narcotics squads raided a major drug operation and seized over one billion dollars' worth of cocaine at a location known as Tranquilandia ("land of tranquility") on the Yarí River, 650km south of Bogatá.

■ Key words

acullicadores   A Spanish name for those Amerindians in the South American Andes who chew coca leaves as a stimulant, as a pain killer or to relieve hunger.

Army of National Liberation   (Ejército de Liberación Nacional - ELN)   A pro-Cuban guerrilla movement founded in 1965. The ELN operates mostly in NE Colombia.

bazuko   A coca paste combined with tobacco to produce a drug known as the "poor man's cocaine" which is sold to an estimated one million drug addicts in Colombia.

coca   A light-weight but high-value plant (*Erythroxylum coca*), harvested two or three times a year over a wide altitudinal range in the South American Andes. For centuries coca leaves have been chewed, brewed into a *mate* or applied as a poultice to alleviate *soroche* (altitude sickness), stomach disorders, headaches and the stresses of hard physical labour. Legal uses of coca also include the manufacture of extracts for flavouring. Its value on the international drug market as a source of the drug cocaine increased during the 1970s and South American peasant farmers, particularly in Peru, Bolivia and Colombia, abandoned traditional subsistence and export crops in favour of growing coca. Although Colombia grows less coca than Peru or Bolivia, it has become a world centre for refining and exporting cocaine.

cocal   A coca plantation.

Colombia–212 connection   The scale of Colombia's link with the New York cocaine market was indicated by a 1989 survey which showed that Colombia was the 8th most popular destination for telephone calls from New York – area code 212.

Colombian Institute for Agrarian Reform (Instituto Nacional Colombiano para la Reforma Agraria - INCORA)   An organization set up in 1961 with the aim of redistributing land amongst smallholders and improving the standard of living peasant farmers. In the face of landlord opposition, INCORA advocated the colonization of the infertile eastern plains of Meta rather than the expropriation of the larger latifundia of the highlands. As a result of ineffective policies of this kind, the institute was largely overtaken in 1968 by the more radical National Association of Peasant Land Users founded by Dr Carlos Lleras Restrepo.

Colombian Revolutionary Armed Forces (Fuerzas Armadas Revolucionarias Colombianes–FARC)   The military wing of the pro-Soviet Colombian Communist Party led by Manuel Marulanda. The most powerful of the rural guerrilla groups, FARC operates mostly to the south-west of Bogotá in the departments of Huila, Tolima, Quindio and Valle.

Communal Insurgency   A small guerrilla group formed in 1987, the Communal Insurgency claimed responsibility for a bomb explosion outside the Defence Ministry in Bogotá on 19 October 1987.

crack   When cocaine powder is heated it turns into a crystalline solid that is said to be more addictive when inhaled.

Death to Kidnappers Group   One of a number of right-wing paramilitary groups.

extraditables (Los Extraditables)   A name applied to those cocaine dealers who fear extradition to the United States where they have been indicted for drugs offences. Washington has supplied the Colombian government with the names of at least 120 such "extraditables".

Guerrilla Co-ordinating Board (Co-ordinadora Nacional Guerrillera – CNG)   A guerrilla umbrella organization set up in 1985.

Inter-American Drug Control Commission   An anti-narcotics agency set up in 1986 following an agreement signed on 25 April of that year in Río de Janeiro by the 22 countries of the Organization of American States.

latifundia   A large landholding in South America, characterized by underutilization and low levels of production. Agrarian land reform in this region has attempted to increase the productivity of the latifundia by redistributing it amongst peasant farmers. The owner of a latifundia is a *latifundista*.

minifundia   Small parcels of land cultivated by peasant farmers in South America.

M–19 (Movimiento 19 de Abril)   A guerrilla group formed in April 1976 following a split in the National Popular Alliance (ANAPO). The group takes its name from the day, on 19 April 1970, when the populist leader of ANAPO, General Gustavo Rojas Pinilla, failed in his attempt to regain the presidency that he held between 1953 and 1957. Originally a right-wing movement, M–19 changed its stance to become a Marxist organization in the late 1970s. In

March 1990 the group finally signed a peace agreement with the government.

money laundering The process of passing money derived from the sale of drugs through a series of businesses or financial institutions so as to make it difficult to trace.

narcotraficante A Spanish word for a dealer in drugs.

National Association of Peasant Land Users (Asociación Nacional de Usuarias Campesinas – ANUC) A radical peasant movement founded by Dr Carlos Lleras Restrepo in 1968 with the aim of speeding up the process of land reform in a country where it was recorded that 67.5% of the land was owned by 4.3% of the people. With 1 500 000 members, this organization became the largest mass movement in Latin America, but faced with right-wing leadership it soon disintegrated into radical and revolutionary groups.

National Popular Alliance (ANAPO) A popular nationalist opposition political party which gained 19% of the vote in the 1972 local elections. Two years earlier the party leader, General Gustavo Rojas Pinilla, failed to regain the presidency which he held between 1953 and 1957. The date of his defeat in the April 1970 presidential election is commemorated in the name of the M–19 guerrilla group.

operación limpieza ("operation clean-up") A so-called clean-up campaign, funded by right-wing landowners and drug barons, carried out on the streets of Cali and Medellín by urban vigilante groups who murder prostitutes, homosexuals, drug addicts and beggars. With the virtual collapse of the judicial system in the late 1980s, an estimated 99% of these crimes have passed unpunished.

Operation Hat Trick Codename for an antidrug manoeuvre launched by the US Navy off the coast of Colombia in 1984. Sea checkpoints were set up, but the operation was

eventually cut short because the results did not seem to justify the costs.

Operation Red Dance A right-wing campaign of murder and terrorist violence directed at members of the left-wing Patriotic Union in 1986.

Patriotic Union The political wing of the pro-Cuban FARC guerrilla group. Subjected to an onslaught of violence from right-wing paramilitary death squads between 1986 and 1988 (Operation Red Dance), the Patriotic Union was forced to withdraw from the Congress.

Popular Liberation Army (Ejército Popular de Liberación - EPL) A Maoist guerrilla group formed in the 1960s.

Rodrigo Lara Bonilla accord An accord signed by member states of the Andean pact who agreed in April 1986 to join forces in the fight against the narcotics industry. The accord takes its name from the Colombian Justice Minister who was killed by drug dealers in 1984.

sicarios The name given to the death squad hit-men hired by cocaine dealers.

Simón Bolívar Guerrilla Co-ordinating Board (Co-ordinadora Guerrillera Simon Bolívar – CGSB) A guerrilla umbrella organization formed in October 1987. With an estimated manpower of 30 000, it comprises M-19, the Workers' Revolutionary Party, the Quintin Lame Commandos, EPL, ELN and FARC.

Statute for the Defence of Democracy A government declaration of January 1988 defying attempts by the drug barons to intimidate the judiciary and undermine democracy by the use of violence.

Violencia, La The name given to the 20-year period of civil unrest and terrorism between 1948 and 1968 during which up to 200 000 Colombians lost their lives.

■ Further reading

Paul Eddy, Hugo Sabogal and Sara Walden, *The Cocaine Wars*, Century, London, 1988

J. Hartlyn, *The Politics of Coalition Rule in Columbia*, Cambridge University Press, Cambridge, 1988

T. Hudson, South American High: A Geography of Cocaine, *Focus*, 1985, pp.22–29

Harvey F. Kline, *Colombia: Portrait of Unity and Diversity*, Westview Press, Boulder, 1983

Paul Oquist, *Violence, Conflict and Politics in Colombia*, University of California Press, Berkeley, 1978

Jenny Pearce, *Colombia: Inside the Labyrinth*, Latin America Bureau, 1990

World Bank, *Colombia: Economic Development and Policy under Changing Conditions*, Washington, 1984

4
Peru

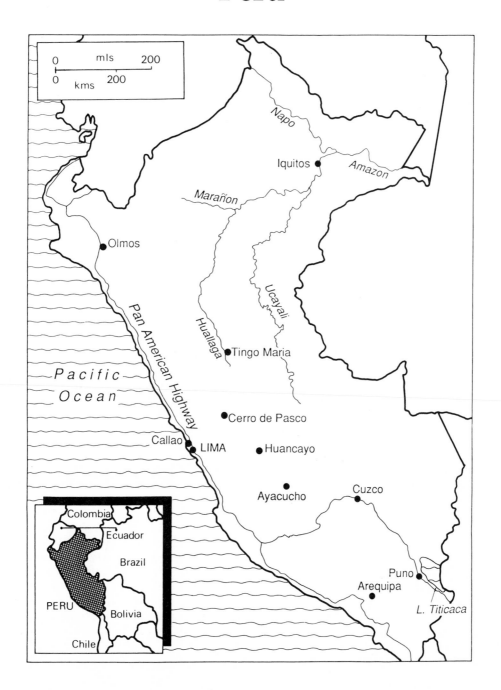

■ Profile

Official name: Republic of Peru

- **Area:**   1 285 000km²
- **Population (1988):**   21 300 000
- **Ethnic groups:** Quechua 47%, Aymará 5%, Mestizo 32%, European 12%
- **Official languages:**   Spanish and Quechua
- **Religion:**   Roman Catholic 92%
- **Life expectancy:**   58 years
- **Infant mortality rate:**   85 per 1000
- **Currency:**   inti of 1000 soles (since 1985)
- **Timezone:**   GMT −5
- **Administrative divisions:**   Prior to 1986 there were 24 departments and one constitutional province (Callao); thereafter the country was reorganized into 12 new regions
- **Capital:**   Lima
- **Chief cities (population 1988 est):**   Arequipa (591 700), Trujillo (491 100), municipality of Lima (417 900), Chiclayo (394 800), Callao (318 300), Cuzco (255 300)

■ Introduction

Independent since the 1820s, Peru has had its share of European-style territorial conflicts. To the north, Ecuador has pursued, periodically, its claim to a large swathe of Peruvian-controlled territory in the Amazon basin. In the 20th century two brief wars have been fought over this remote area. To the south, Peru's loss of its southern coastal province to Chile over a century ago continues to generate rancour. Neighbouring Bolivia, landlocked in the same struggle, feels even more aggrieved. Internally, the past decade has witnessed a murderous insurgency by the Maoist *Sendero Luminoso* (SL) guerrilla movement, whose support principally lies in Peru's majority but disadvantaged Indian population. The conflict has reduced Peru to a state of virtual civil war, with adverse consequences for regional stability and the democratic process.

Peru's dispute with Ecuador arose from the latter's long quest to gain access to the headwaters of the Amazon and thus to the Atlantic. Defeated by Ecuador in a war of 1828–29, Peru gained its revenge in 1941. Under the 1942 Rio Protocol the whole of the disputed territory went to Peru and the present international border was established. Now

it was Ecuador's turn to nurture thoughts of revenge, although not until 1960 did it repudiate the 1942 settlement. In 1981 the two sides engaged in another bout of hostilities, in which encroaching Ecuadorian forces were expelled by the Peruvians. Since then, Peru has maintained that no territorial dispute exists with Ecuador. But the latter's official maps continue to show a large section of what is now northern Peru as part of Ecuador.

Resistance to handing over any territory to Ecuador arises in part from Peru's own experience of contraction in the Pacific War of 1879–81. Joining in what ought to have been a private argument between Chile and Bolivia, Peru shared in the decisive defeat of the latter. Both countries ceded extensive coastal regions to Chile, whose frontier was moved 1000 kilometres northwards, while Bolivia became one of only two landlocked states in South America. Peru won back some of its lost territory under the 1929 Treaty of Ancôn, which also stipulated that Chile could not cede any former Peruvian territory to a third country without Peru's consent. Peru has accordingly taken a close interest in Bolivia's ongoing campaign to regain access to the sea, particularly where proposals to achieve this envisage the transfer of former Peruvian territory. The issue caused renewed strains between the three countries in the late 1980s, although Bolivia's main grievance was with Chile rather than with Peru.

Peru's recent political history has centred on deep tensions between the military, as representing an entrenched propertied class, and the populist American Popular Revolutionary Alliance (APRA). Founded in the 1920s and banned for most of the period up to 1956, APRA articulated the grievances of the Indian population and other disadvantaged groups. In the 1962 presidential elections the Aprista leader, Víctor Raúl Haya de la Torre, narrowly headed the poll, whereupon the armed forces seized power. New elections in 1963 were won by Fernando Belaúnde Terry of the centre-right Popular Action (AP) party. But he was overthrown in 1968 by another coup, which brought to power leftist officers led by General Juan Velasco Alvarado. The latter's radical reform programme was in turn cut short in 1975 by traditionalist officers under General Francisco Morales Bermúdez.

Through all these changes the Apristas remained the strongest party in Congress and in the country, where they enjoyed an extensive trade union base. But the party's evolution to a more moderate stance in the 1970s made room for the emergence of new peasant-based revolutionary movements on the left. Of these, the SL posed the biggest threat when, in 1980, it launched an armed struggle from its strongholds in the poverty-stricken Ayacucho region in south-eastern Peru. Descended by way of numerous splits from the Peruvian Socialist (later Communist) Party, the SL described

itself as "a new type of Marxist-Leninist-Maoist party" and committed itself to "total war" to bring about the overthrow of the government and the existing social order. Another guerrilla group which achieved prominence from the mid-1980s was the Tupac Amaru Revolutionary Movement (MRTA), named after an 18th-century indigenous rebel leader and reputed to have links with radical army officers. Between them, these and other groups stretched Peru's internal security system to the limits and beyond.

Hopes that the Aprista victory in the 1985 presidential and congressional elections would bring an end to the civil conflict were quickly disappointed. Indeed, the SL and the MRTA stepped up their military campaigns in the late 1980s, as the government of President Alan García grappled with a deteriorating economic situation and made little progress with its promised social reform programme. Such was the criticism, even among Apristas, of the government's orthodox austerity policies that García broke with the party in December 1988 by resigning the leadership. He nevertheless continued as President, amid steadily escalating violence and with no political solution in sight. By the end of the decade, moreover, the activities of Peruvian drug traffickers, in association with the powerful cartels of neighbouring Colombia (*see section 4.2*), presented an added challenge to government authority. In the 1990 presidential elections in Peru the surprise victor was Alberto Keinya Fujimori (a Peruvian of Japanese extraction), who attracted extensive Indian and left-wing support for his reformist "Change 90" Movement.

■ Chronology of events

1821   With a population of 1.3 million, the former Vice-Royalty of Peru declares its independence from Spain in July although the struggle for freedom from colonial rule goes on until December 1824.

1919–30   Under the leadership of Augusto Leguía the government of Peru undertakes a programme of socio-economic reforms and secures large loans from the USA. Corruption is widespread and Leguía is eventually forced to resign in the face of economic depression and growing unrest.

1930 The American Popular Revolutionary Alliance (APRA) party is founded.

1932–33 A war between Peru and Colombia over the disputed territory of Leticia is narrowly averted after mediation by the League of Nations.

1933–39 The government of Oscar Benavides is opposed by the radical new APRA party.

1941–42 A territorial dispute regarding access to the Amazon results in open conflict between Peru and Ecuador. Hostilities are brought to an end with the signing of the internationally agreed Protocol of Rio de Janeiro, under which the whole of the disputed area (325 000km²) was allocated to Peru (Loreto department).

1960 The Ecuadorean government stakes a claim to the disputed Amazonian territory by unilaterally declaring the 1942 Protocol of Rio de Janeiro null and void.

1962 A military junta overthrows President Manuel Prado Ugarteche, bars the congress from convening and suspends constitutional guarantees. The United States breaks off diplomatic relations and stops all military and economic aid for a month.

1963 After a year of military rule Fernando Belaúnde Terry is elected President of Peru.

1964 Within a year of taking office the government of President Fernando Belaúnde Terry pushes through an Agrarian Reform Law that provides for the redistribution of church and state land amongst Indian communities and landless tenant farmers.

1967 A deepening economic crisis forces the government to devalue the currency by 50 per cent.

1968 On 3 October Belaúnde is overthrown by a military junta and General Juan Velasco Alvarado is installed as President of a so-called "Revolutionary Government" that aims to

resolve the country's economic problems before embarking on constitutional reform. A programme of nationalization and continued land reform is promised while trade links are developed with Soviet and Eastern bloc countries.

1975 President Velasco is ousted in a coup and replaced by the right-wing military leader General Francisco Morales Bermúdez.

1979 In August six peasants are killed during a clash with police on a co-operative farm in NE Peru. A new constitution, to be adopted after elections in 1980, is drafted.

1980 Following elections on 18 May, Belaúnde is returned to the presidency at the head of a civilian government dominated by the centrist Popular Action Party (AP). Although inflation stands at 55 per cent the economy is boosted by good fish catches and high world prices. The Maoist *Sendero Luminoso* (SL) movement emerges in the central Andean department of Ayacucho and adopts guerrilla tactics in order to force the government to carry out out extensive social reforms.

1981 The year opens with a general strike and the arrest in Ayacucho of 130 peasants accused of supporting SL guerrillas. Inflation climbs to 81.6 per cent in May as Belaúnde attempts to introduce a free market economy while maintaining a vast programme of public sector spending designed to alleviate hunger and unemployment. In an attempt to control spiralling prices and wages the government adopts a policy of *concertación* or collective bargaining with management and labour.

The unresolved dispute over territory in the Amazon basin flares up again with Peru and Ecuador engaging in five days of armed conflict.

1982 The action of SL guerrillas in freeing over 250 prisoners from a jail in Ayacucho leads to the imposition of a state of emergency in the departments of Ayacucho and Apurimac and the stepping-up of anti-terrorist operations by police in the Central Andean mountains of

Peru. Later in the year the state of emergency is extended to the city of Lima and its port of Callao.

1983   A counter-insurgency drive by security forces achieves some success but does not prevent terrorists from cutting power supplies and blacking out the city of Ayacucho. Nine journalists are killed at Uchuraccay near Ayacucho while covering the conflict. SL guerrillas begin to extend their attacks to targets in Lima.

1984   Economic recession coupled with the high cost of counter-insurgency measures combine to create an inflation rate that reaches 120 per cent and causes the resignation of the Finance Minister. The SL campaign of violence intensifies and in the second half of the year guerrillas extend their influence northwards into the coca-growing jungle region of the Upper Huallaga river valley in NE Peru, where they form a tactical alliance with drugs traffickers. Attacks on local mayors and peasant farmers reduce the effectiveness of anti-narcotics operations which are designed to encourage farmers to grow rice and cacao rather than coca. Security forces move into the Andean mountains to join with local police in the fight against terrorism. Between July and September an estimated 1500 people are killed during counter-insurgency operations in the central Andean provinces.

In Ayacucho, which is at the centre of an 11-province emergency zone, the city council attempts to hold a peace rally in early February but police and security forces seal off the main square. The regional military commander, Brigadier Adrián Huanán Centeno, criticizes the government for failing to tackle poverty in the area and is dismissed. While SL attacks on political, economic and strategic targets in and around Lima increase between July 1984 and July 1985, the government is faced with the added problem of a terrorist campaign launched in Lima by the Tupac Amarú Revolutionary Movement which declares its oppposition to human rights violations allegedly carried out by counter-insurgency forces.

1985   The year begins with a series of attacks by SL guerrillas who bomb the Army Club in Lima, paralyse the copper mines of Cerro Pasco and black out the city of Lima during a visit to Peru by Pope John Paul II. A new group of terrorists calling themselves Popular Revolutionary Commandos denounce the unjust social order in Peru and launch their own campaign of violence. Despite increased civil and economic disorder, congressional and presidential elections take place in April. The centre-left American Popular Revolutionary Alliance (APRA) party, led by the 36 year olf Alan García, defeats its principal oposition rival, the United Left (IU), which is led by Alfonso Barrantes Lingán.

García, who is the first civilian to succeed another as President of Peru in over 70 years, immediately offers an amnesty to SL guerrillas, but in August over 1400 people are detained during a renewed counter-insurgency campaign. Tupac Amarú guerrillas agree to a ceasefire for a year in order to allow García a chance to introduce a programme of poverty relief. An Amnesty International report attributes the killings uncovered in mass graves to an elite marine unit based in Huanta, N of Ayacucho. In September President García sets up a six-member Peace Commission to draft a policy that will lead to a peace formula and ensure the defence of human rights.

1986   The state of emergency in seven Andean departments is repeated for 60-day periods and is extended to Lima following guerrilla attacks on banks and offices of the ruling APRA party. In May terrorists kill Admiral Carlos Poncé de Léon Canessa and on 18 June a guerrilla-inspired mutiny takes place in the three prisons of Lurigancho, El Frontón and Santa Barbára. Security forces using tanks and heavy weapons quash the riots but kill 250 inmates in the process. Although the SL guerrillas immediately respond by attacking a tourist train en route from Cuzco to the Inca ruins of Machu Picchu, the loss of key leaders results in a reduced number of terrorist   attacks during the second half of the year.

Tupac Amarú guerrillas who had given García a year's grace resume their violent opposition to the government in August. Their attacks are aimed principally at US targets which include the US embassy in Lima and the offices of Citibank in San Isidro. In response to pressure from the USA, the government launches the "Condor 6" operation against Andean drug traders in August. The following month an estimated one million peasants form themselves into vigilante groups to protect their villages against acts of terrorism that have included the murder of mayors in Huancavelica and Auycayacu and government officials in Careccampa. In an attempt to support the peasants in their opposition to the SL movement, the government adopts a policy of decentralization. Twelve new regions with elected assemblies are created, the legal status of peasant militia groups is acknowledged and a new peasant loan scheme is set up.

In October all political parties unite to sign an accord confirming the commitment to combat all forms of terrorism. The Peace Commission set up in 1985 proves ineffective and by the end of January all six members have resigned after complaining of a "lack of political influence". García sets up a second Peace Commission but this also collapses when its three members resign following the suppression of the prison riots in June. Despite this setback, President García initiates a "moralization" campaign designed to clean up and streamline the police force. Over half of the leading police generals and 1800 policemen of all ranks are dismissed. Meanwhile, with the economy on the verge of collapse, the Peruvian government is declared "ineligible" for further loans.

1987   While the SL movement resumes its attacks on targets in Lima and Callao, the Tupac Amarú guerrillas step up their campaign against US targets which include the offices of IBM, USAID, Eastern Airlines and the US–Peruvian Cultural Institute. After the assassination of two high ranking officers in April the Army High Command declares all-out war on the SL movement, but García decides to reduce military representation at cabinet level by amalgamating the Ministries of War, Navy and Air Force under one Defence Ministry. This move forces the dismissal of the Air Force commander and precipitates

a mutiny by soldiers guarding the airfields at La Joya and Las Palmas. García attempts to tackle the economic crisis by renegotiating the $1000 million debt to the Soviet Union and by adopting expansionist measures.

1988   In July the leader of the SL movement, Abel Guzmán, breaks a ten year silence by making a press statement in which he announces a new stage in the struggle which is to be directed at cities. A state of emergency still exists in six departments and in Lima. On the eve of President García's anniversary speech in July, guerrillas black out Lima and nearly 300km of the coastline. In November the SL backs strikes which paralyse Ayacucho and power supplies are disrupted throughout the country.

In June inflation reaches a staggering 400 per cent and by the end of the year four Finance Ministers, unable to resolve the economic crisis, have resigned in quick succession. President García is adamant in his refusal to deal with foreign lending agencies and reiterates his option of "debt or democracy" as he introduces an austerity package in September. Facing growing criticism within his own ranks, García resigns the APRA party leadership in December and is no longer regarded as representing that party.

1989   The SL concentrates its terrorist activities in the central Andes once more. A renewed campaign of violence in May causes a major three-day "armed strike" in the departments of Junin, Pasco and Huancano, and leads to the death of a British tourist, the assassination of a parliamentary deputy and the killing of 73 people on a single day (17 May). Unable to stem the tide of violence, the Prime Minister, Armado Villanueva del Campo, resigns and is replaced by the veteran politician Luis Alberto Sanchez.

In September US President Bush announces a $2000 million special Andean aid programme designed to help stem the flow of drugs from South America. Coca leaf production in Peru reaches a total of 110 000 metric tons in 1989 compared with 70 000 tons in Bolivia and 20 000 tons in Colombia.

1990 The leaders of Peru, Colombia and Bolivia meet with President Bush in Cartagena, Colombia, to discuss a strategy in the war against the drug barons of South America.

In June Alberto Fujimori, leader of the Change 90 Movement, defeats Mario Vargas Llosa in presidential elections.

■ Who's who

Abram, Lieut.–General Luis Former Air Force Commanding Officer who objected to the amalgamation of his Air Force Ministry into the new Ministry of Defence in April 1987. His enforced retiral by President García precipitated mutinies at the La Joya and Las Palmas airfields. Abram, who was replaced by Lieut.–General Pablo Varela, was eventually charged with sedition.

Alberto, Luis A veteran politician, Luis Alberto Sanchez was appointed Prime Minister at the age of 88 following the resignation of Armado Villanueva del Campo in 1987.

Alva, Luis Prime Minister of Peru under García until his resignation in 1987 following the President's adoption of expansionist measures to solve the economic crisis. He was replaced by Guillermo Larco Cox, a member of the so-called "bold" group.

Barrantes, Alfonso Leader of the United Left (IU) left-wing opposition party until his resignation in May 1987. At the age of 56 Barrantes stood as a candidate in the presidential elections of 1985 but was defeated by Alan García. In 1983 he was elected Mayor of Lima at a time when SL guerrillas were beginning to direct terrorist attacks on targets in the capital city.

Bartley, Edward A British tourist killed on 25 May 1989 by SL guerrillas in the town of Olleros in the province of Ancash.

Belaúnde Terry, Fernando President of Peru from 1963 until ousted by a military coup in 1968, Fernando Belaúnde Terry was re-elected President following the restoration of civilian rule in 1980. In 1985 he was the first civilian president to hand over power peacefully to another civilian president in over 70 years.

Bellido, Claudio Third in command of the SL guerrilla movement, Claudio Bellido Huaytalla was killed near Ayacucho along with 39 other terrorists in October 1986.

Blanco, Hugo A former Trotskyist and congressional deputy, Blanco is the secretary of the Peruvian Peasants' Confederation. In February 1989 he was arrested after leading an 8000-strong demonstration of peasant farmers in the jungle town of Pucallpa in E Peru.

Cantoral, Saul Miner's union leader who organized two successful strikes in 1988 but was murdered in February 1989 while on the point of calling a third. Although his death was attributed to the SL movement, he had been threatened repeatedly by the right-wing Commandos Rodrigo Framco death squad.

Díaz, Emilio Antonio Second in command of the Shining Path guerrilla movement, Emilio Antonio Díaz Martínez was killed during the prison riots of 1986.

Franco, Rodrigo A leading member of the ruling Aprista party killed during a wave of violence in 1987. Shortly after his death a right-wing counter-insurgency group, the Commandos Rodrigo Franco, adopted his name.

Fujimori, Alberto The son of Japanese immigrants and leader of the Change 90 Movement who defeated Maria Vargas Llosa to become President of Peru in June 1990.

García, Alan Leader of the APRA party, García was elected President of Peru in April 1985 at the age of 36. His immediate offer of an amnesty to guerrillas and his attempts to clean up a corrupt police force did little to stem the tide of violence. The excesses of the security forces in quashing the prison riots of June 1986 and an inability to control an economy in crisis by adopting expansionist measures left his party short of credibility in the run up to the 1990 elections. In December 1989 García resigned as leader of the APRA party in the face of growing opposition.

Guzmán, Abimael   A former Professor of Law and founder of the Maoist *Sendero Luminoso* (SL) guerrilla movement. Seldom appearing in public, the 53-year-old Guzmán made a statement to the press in July 1988 announcing that his organization would be directing its terrorist activities at targets in the cities of Peru.

Huamán Centeno, Brigadier Adrian
Appointed regional commander of the security forces in the central Andes in January 1984, Brigadier Adrian Huamán Centeno adopted a less hardline approach in the pursuit of terrorists. His criticism of the government for failing to tackle rural poverty resulted in his dismissal in August of the same year. He was replaced by the US-trained counter-insurgency specialist Colonel Wilfredo Mori Ozo.

Mariategui, Juan (José) Carlos   Founder of the Peruvian Socialist (later Communist) Party in 1928, he was the author of the pamphlet *The Shining Path of Juan Carlos Mariategui,* from which the *Sendero Luminoso* movement later took its name. Born in 1894, Mariategui advocated the restoration of the peasant

communes which had flourished under the Inca Empire. He died in 1930.

Morales, General Francisco   Leader of the ruling military junta between 1975 and 1980 when he handed over power to a civilian president.

Morote, Osman   Deputy leader and military comander of the SL guerrilla movement, arrested in June 1988.

Polay, Victor   Known as Commandante Rolando, Victor Polay is a former APRA party member now leading the Revolutionary Tupac Amarú Movement.

Raúl Haya de la Torre, Victor   Founder of the Aprista party, Victor Raúl Haya de la Torre was the leading political figure in Peru from the 1930s until his death, at the age of 84, in 1979.

Vargas Llosa, Mario   One of the best known novelists in Latin America, Mario Vargas Llosa spent 20 years in London as a writer. In 1989, at the age of 52, he joined the political rostrum as a liberal candidate in an unsuccessful bid for the presidency, launching his new *Libertad* ("Freedom") organization at a rally in Lima, attracting over 100 000 people. As a student he was a supporter of Fidel Castro and active member of a Communist cell.

■ Key places

Arequipa   The capital of a department of the same name that stretches from the high Andes to the Pacific coast of S Peru. Situated at the foot of the conical El Misti volcano (5843m), Arequipa is the principal commercial city of southern Peru. Population (1988) 591 700.

Ayacucho   The capital of a mountainous department of the same name in the Andean Cordillera Oriental. The last great battle in the War of Independence against Spain was fought near here on 9 December 1824. The *Sendero*

Luminoso (SL) guerrilla movement first emerged in this region of Peru in 1980. Population (1988) 94 200.

Callao   Peru's principal seaport, situated on the Pacific coast to the west of Lima. Handling over 75 per cent of the country's exports, Callao first experienced terrorist violence at the hands of the SL guerrillas in 1982. The Santa Barbára prison was the scene of a riot brutally put down in June 1986. Population (1988) 318 300.

Cerro de Pasco   A copper mining centre and capital of the Andean department of Pasco, 176km north-east of Lima. At 4259m it is one of the highest cities in the world. The mines are connected by rail to smelters in the town of La Oroya. Population (1988) 72 000.

Cuzco   Ancient capital of the Inca empire and chief town of a department of the same name in the Andean Cordillera Oriental at an altitude of 3500m on the Pan–American Highway. Its colonial buildings and markets are a major tourist attraction en route to the ruined Inca city of Machu Picchu. Population (1988) 255 300.

Huallaga River   A river flowing through tropical rainforest in the north-eastern departments of Huanuco and San Martin. Rising to the south of the Andean mining town of Cerro de Pasco, it flows 1120km north to meet the Marañon at the head of the Amazon basin. The remote upper part of this river valley is a notorious coca-growing area and major source of the drug cocaine. A tactical alliance with drug traffickers in this region in the second half of 1984 provided the SL movement with a useful source of income despite the anti-narcotics operations of a 400-strong contingent of marines based in the town of Tingo Maria at the southern end of the valley.

Huancavelic   A mining town and capital of a mountainous department of the same name in the central Andean Cordillera Oriental at an altitude of 3680m. The assassination of the mayor of Huancavelica in 1986 was one of a number of murders that drove villages and towns to organize *rondas* or vigilante groups to protect people from terrorist violence. Population (1988) 24 700.

Huancayo   A market town and capital of Junin department in the central Andes at an altitude of 3271m. Population (1988) 199 200.

La Brea   Along with Pariñas, La Brea forms part of the greater Negritos oilfield in the coastal department of Piura in NW Peru. The oil refining centre of Talara lies 16km WNW. An agreement to allow the International Petroleum Company to exploit this area was one of the factors that precipitated the military coup which toppled President Fernando Belaundé Terry in 1968.

Lima   Founded as the "city of the kings" by Pizarro in 1535, Lima was the chief city of South America until the end of Spanish colonial rule in the 1820s. Situated on the Rimac river, it is the modern capital of the Republic of Peru. Population (1988) 417 900 (municipality); Lima/Callao metropolitan area 4 605 000.

Machu Picchu   Ruined Inca city set high in the Andes, 120km north of Cuzco to which it is linked by rail. The site was rediscovered by Hiram Bingham in 1911. Following the prison riots of June 1986 a tourist train was attacked by SL guerrillas who killed seven and wounded 28 passengers.

Olleros   A town in the department of Ancash. Edward Bartley, a British tourist was murdered here by SL guerrillas on 25 May 1989.

Olmos   A small town on the Pan–American Highway, at the eastern edge of the Sechura desert in Lambayeque department, NW Peru. The Soviet-backed Olmos irrigation project was initiated by the military junta prior to the elections of 1980 that returned Peru to civilian rule. As far back as 1926 attempts were made to water the desert soil and increase cotton and sugar cane production by damming the Chancay river. The planners of the grandiose Olmos project initially proposed the diversion of the eastward-flowing Chotano river onto 110 000 hectares of the plain but also suggested the transport of water from the Amazon basin by way of a tunnel through the Andes.

Pariñas   Along with La Brea, Pariñas forms part of the greater Negritos oilfield in the department of Piura in the far north-west of Peru. Pariñas Point is the most westerly point of the South American Continent.

Puno   Capital of a province of the same name on the north-west shore of Lake Titicaca, S Peru, at an altitude of 3855m. Linked by rail to Cuzco (386km).

Tingo Maria   A former rubber and lumbering centre in the tropical department of Huanuco, at the confluence of the Huallaga and Monzón rivers. A contingent of 400 marines was based here in 1984 in order to combat the joint activities of SL guerrillas and drugs traffickers.

Titicaca   The largest lake in South America and, at 3812 m, the highest lake in the world. Of its 8289km² area, 4996km² lies within Peru. The remainder is in Bolivia.

■ Key words

Amazon Co-operation Treaty   An international agreement signed in 1978 by those countries with an interest in the development of the Amazon Basin.

American Popular Revolutionary Alliance (Alianza Popular Revolucionaria Americana – APRA).   A centre-left political party founded by Victor Raúl Haya de la Torre in 1930 and strongly opposed to the government of Oscar Benavides. The party came to power following the 1985 elections that brought Alan García to the Presidency.

Andean Pact   An alliance of five South American countries established in 1969 in response to dissatisfaction with their position in the Latin American Free Trade Association. The original signatories were the Andean states of Bolivia, Chile, Colombia, Ecuador and Peru. Chile left the pact in 1976 and Venezuela joined in 1973. The pact aims to promote economic development in the Andean region by supporting less-favoured areas and by facilitating trade between member countries. In 1981 the Peru–Ecuador territorial dispute threatened the survival of the Andean Pact.

Aprodeh   A Peruvian human rights organization.

"bold" group   Those politicians and economists committed to expansionist measures as a means of lifting Peru out of its economic crisis. Guillermo Larco Cox, who replaced Luis Alva Castro as Prime Minister in 1987, was a member of this group.

British solution   An approach to solving the conflict in Peru that involves the military recruiting the help of the peasant population in exchange for defending them against terrorism.

Commandos Rodrigo Franco   A counter-terrorist death squad formed after the murder in 1987 of Rodrigo Franco, a leading member of the ruling APRA party. Its targets include people and organizations linked with the SL guerrillas.

concertación   A policy of collective bargaining with management and labour adopted by the Belaúnde government in 1982 in an attempt to control spiralling prices and wages.

Democratic Convergence (Convergencia Democratica)   A political alliance of the Christian Democratic Party and the right-wing Popular Christian Party formed in 1984.

desaparecidos   (Spanish "the disappeared") The name given to those people who have disappeared without trace since 1980 in Peru's "Shining Path" war. Between 1980 and 1988 an estimated 8 000 Peruvians, mostly peasants, were taken by government security forces in an attempt to root out supporters of the *Sendero Luminoso* guerrillas.

French solution   An approach to solving the conflict in Peru that essentially depends on meeting terror with terror. This is the method adopted by the Commandos Rodrigo Franco counter-insurgency group.

"moralization" campaign   A campaign against widespread corruption amongst police officers launched by President García in the spring of 1986. Over half of the country's police generals and nearly 1800 officers of all ranks were dismissed in an attempt to clean up and streamline the police force.

Partido Unido Mariateguista (PUM)   A Peruvian left-wing opposition party founded in 1928 by Juan Carlos Mariategui.

Peace Commission A six-member commission set up by President García on 14 September 1985 to draft a policy for bringing an end to terrorism and human rights violations. By the end of January 1986 all six members had resigned, complaining of a "lack of political influence". A second commission also collapsed six months later when its three members resigned in the wake of the brutal suppression of prison rights.

Peruvian Peasants' Confederation (CCP) A union representing the collective interests of peasant farmers in the struggle against poverty, terrorism and human rights violations.

Popular Action Party (Acción popular - AP) The ruling political party under the civilian Presidency of Fernando Belaúnde Terry between 1980 and 1985.

Popular Revolutionary Commandos (Commandos Revolucionarios del Pueblo) A left-wing terrorist group that emerged in July 1985. Seizing a radio station in Lima, leaders of this group denounced what they described as the "unjust social order in Peru".

Protocol of Rio de Janeiro An international agreement bringing to an end nearly seven months of hostilities between Peru and Ecuador in 1941–42. Under this protocol, disputed territory in the Amazon basin was allocated to Peru. In 1960 the government of Ecuador declared the protocol null and void, opening up its territorial claim once again to what was by then Peru's main inland oil-producing region.

Puma Special Forces Group A government military force based in the southern city of Arequipa from where it pursues *Sendero Luminoso* rebels operating on the frontier with Bolivia and Chile.

rondas Organized civilian defence forces set up by peasant farmers in 1986 to protect villages from the Sendero Luminoso guerrillas. Although lightly armed they oppose the "popular committees" which the Maoist rebels try to establish in villages.

Sendero Luminoso (SL) ("Shining Path") A left-wing Maoist guerrilla movement operating against the government of Peru since 1980. The group, which was founded in the Andean town of Ayacucho by Professor Abimael Guzmán, operates mostly in the southern and eastern provinces, close to the frontiers with Chile and Bolivia, but its influence has spread northwards to the coca-growing area of the Upper Huallaga river valley where a tactical alliance with drug traffickers has provided a useful source of funds.

Shining Green Path A terrorist group formed in 1986 by police officers dismissed during the "moralization" campaign.

Sinchis Police counter-insurgency forces.

Tupac Amarú Revolutionary Movement (Movimiento Revolucionario Tupac Amarú) A Marxist urban terrorist movement operating throughout South America and named after Tupac Amarú, the assumed name of the Peruvian Indian leader, Jose Gabriel Condorcanqui, who was executed following his revolt against the Spanish in 1780. This group was especially active in Uruguay during the 1960s when it was responsible for bank robberies, kidnappings and bomb attacks on government buildings. Adopting an anti-imperialist stance, its motto is "For the cause of the poor, with the masses and arms in hand". In Peru members of the Tupac Amarú Movement or Tupamaros became active in September 1984. They concentrated their attacks on US property and personnel in Lima, using weapons largely purchased with profits derived from the international trade in drugs.

Unidad Tactica Anti-Terrorista A hardline intelligence organization co-operating with police corps in the fight against SL guerrillas.

United Left (Izquierda Unida - IU) The main opposition political party in the 1980s, the IU was led by Alfonso Barrantes Lingán until his resignation in May 1987.

■ Further reading

James Anderson, *Sendero Luminoso; A New Revolutionary Model?*, London Institute for the Study of Terrorism, London, 1987

A. Figueroa, *Capitalist Development and the Peasant Economy of Peru*, Cambridge University Press, Cambridge, 1984

Maria Esther Gilio, *The Tupumaros*, Secker and Warburg, London, 1972

Isabel Hilton, Shining Path of Insurgency, *Geographical Magazine*, 61(8), 1989, pp.22–26

C. McClintock and A.F. Lowenthal (eds.), *The Peruvian Experiment Reconsidered*, Princeton University Press, Princeton, New Jersey, 1983

Lewis Taylor, *Maoism in the Andes: Sendero Luminoso and the Contemporary Guerrilla Movement in Peru*, Liverpool Centre for Latin American Studies, Liverpool, 1983

5
Falklands/Malvinas

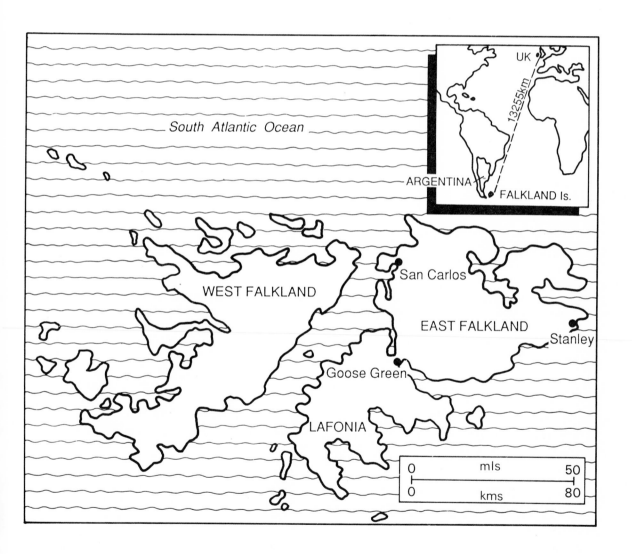

South Atlantic Ocean

UK

13255km

ARGENTINA

FALKLAND Is.

San Carlos

WEST FALKLAND

EAST FALKLAND

Stanley

Goose Green

LAFONIA

| 0 | mls | 50 |
| 0 | kms | 80 |

■ Profile

Spanish name: Islas Malvinas

- **Status:** British Crown Colony
- **Area:** East Falkland and adjacent islands 6760km²; West Falkland and adjacent Islands 5413km²
- **Population (1988):** 1821
- **Armed forces (1989):** 1600 British troops
- **Ethnic groups:** British
- **Official language:** English
- **Religion:** Christian 93%
- **Currency:** Falkland Islands pound of 100 pence
- **Timezone:** GMT −4
- **Capital:** Stanley, on East Falkland
- **Airports:** Stanley and Mount Pleasant
- **Livestock (1988):** 705 000 sheep, 6000 cattle, 1800 horses

■ Introduction

The Falkland Islands are a classic case of what has been called "the confetti of empire". Distant outposts of imperial domains which once straddled the globe, they were left in a South Atlantic limbo by Britain's retreat from empire after World War II. As with other dots on the map where the Union Jack continued to fly, there was no easy way for Britain to divest itself of responsibility. The islanders opted to remain under British rule and rejected the only viable alternative, namely incorporation into Argentina, long a claimant to Las Islas Malvinas. Almost all the Falklanders are of British stock (unlike some other residual colonial subjects), a factor of great importance in the court of British public opinion. Even so, Britain might well have been prepared to cede sovereignty had not the Argentinians taken the law into their own hands in 1982 by invading the islands and obliging Britain to repossess them by force, at huge material and considerable human cost.

Like most such disputes, the Falklands/ Malvinas issue involves conflicting versions of historical events and their significance. Broadly speaking, Argentina's claim lays stress on the islands' proximity to its own coast in comparison with far-distant Britain and on its possession of them in the years immediately preceding the formal establishment of British sovereignty in 1833. Argentina also contends that Britain's acquisition of the islands was a "colonial" act which has been perpetuated in defiance of UN enjoinders about decolonization. Britain bases its claim on early settlement (pre-dating the brief Argentinian rule) and on "open, continuous, effective and peaceful possession, occupation and administration of the islands since 1833". It also points out tirelessly that the vast majority of the islands' population favour British rule and that British sovereignty therefore accords with UN enjoinders about the right to self-determination.

In the court of international opinion Argentina has obtained most mileage out of the colonialism charge. This appeals to the large majority of UN member states which are themselves ex-colonies of European powers and can attribute their present economic and social ills to that historical factor. In Argentina's case, the fact that it was once the world's fifth-richest nation (in 1900) and now qualifies as a developing country adds to its sense of grievance. Britain has riposted that the "colonization" of the Falklands was part of the same process which led to the European settlement of Argentina, and was less cruel. Whereas the forbears of present-day Argentinians displaced an indigenous population, the Falklands were empty when Europeans arrived. Such observations struck a chord in other Latin American states resentful of the "European" Argentinians' traditional assumption of superiority over their more racially-mixed neighbours. Nevertheless, they joined with the rest of the Third World (and the Soviet bloc) in endorsing Argentina's claim that the Falklands required decolonization rather than self-determination. As for the "kith and kin" argument, its international appeal has inevitably been confined to a few countries also of British stock.

The stark geographical fact is that the Falklands are only 480 kilometres from Argentina and more than 13 000 kilometres from Britain. For the Argentinians, this distance factor alone justifies its contention that Britain has no rights in the Falklands, or anywhere else in the South Atlantic. To their longstanding claim to the Falklands, they added one to British South Georgia in 1927, while in 1948 they also claimed the British South Sandwich Islands. For good measure, Argentina's territorial claim in Antarctica overlaps with Britain's, and both overlap with Chile's. The Antarctic dispute is currently frozen until 1991 (along with all other such claims), but it indicates that more is at stake in the Falklands and points south than competition for ownership of inhospitable rocks and frozen wastes. The region is not only rich in fish and krill stocks but also believed to contain huge reserves of minerals and hydrocarbons. When technology permits exploitation of these riches, states possessing sovereignty there will expect to divide the spoils.

Such factors help to elucidate the UK–Argentinian negotiations entered into from 1966 at the UN's request. Britain was seeking some sort of regional co-operation agreement guaranteeing British and Falklander rights, perhaps under a "lease-back" or a condominium. In return, it would have pressed the Falklanders to accept a transfer of sovereignty. But the Argentinians insisted that the sovereignty question must come first, and in the 1970s began sporadic harassment against alleged British moves to change the economic status quo. The situation darkened when a military junta came to power in Buenos Aires in December 1981. The new regime was keen to demonstrate greater virility on the Falklands than its predecessors. It also received the wrong signal from Britain's declared intention to withdraw the remaining Royal Navy ship from the South Atlantic. After staging a surrogate occupation of South Georgia in March 1982, the following month Argentina invaded the Falklands, announcing that they had been recovered "for the nation".

Britain's response was to send a military task force to the South Atlantic to recapture the islands. After a sharp conflict, this was accomplished by mid-June 1982. Heroic deeds by the Argentinian air force could not compensate for the low morale of the occupying troops. US intelligence and material support was also crucial to the British victory. On the diplomatic front, Britain obtained backing from its fellow European Community members, although grudgingly in some cases. Italy had to take account of the Italian ancestry of many Argentinians, and Ireland had its own grievances against Britain (*see section 5.6*). The war showed that possession of nuclear weapons did not prevent aggression by a non-nuclear state, although a British nuclear-armed submarine was present in the South Atlantic and it remains an open question what might have happened if the Argentinians had gained the upper hand. Much controversy surrounded the single most costly engagement of the war, namely the sinking by a British submarine of the Argentinian battle-cruiser *General Belgrano* on 2 May 1982, outside the British-imposed exclusion zone. Seen by some as intended to thwart unwanted Peruvian/UN mediation, the sinking later became something of a *cause célèbre* in Britain. Nevertheless, the Conservative government of Margaret Thatcher rode to victory in the 1983 UK election on the back of its Falklands triumph. Argentina's military junta quickly fell.

As far as Britain was concerned, the 1982 war removed the sovereignty of the Falklands from the agenda. Committing itself to defending the islands against any further Argentinian assault, Britain established a strong garrison and built a new airstrip capable of receiving reinforcements from long distance. It also gave a categoric assurance that the status of the Falklands would not be changed without the consent of their inhabitants. Although UK-Argentinian trade relations were normalized in 1985, various attempts to achieve an accommodation on the substantive issue foundered. The UK government maintained that the sovereignty of the Falklands was non-negotiable, while Argentina continued to insist that any negotiations must address that issue. A partial breakthrough early in 1990, when the two sides agreed to resume full diplomatic relations on the basis of an end to hostilities, left the basic dispute unresolved.

■ Chronology of events

1592 According to unauthenticated records, the uninhabited Falkland Islands are first sighted on 14 August by the British navigator Captain John Davis of the *Desire*.

1594 In the second unauthenticated sighting, Sir Richard Hawkins names the island group "Hawkin's Maidenland."

1600 The first conclusively authenticated sighting of the Falklands is made by the Dutch navigator Sebald van Weert.

1690 Captain John Strong of the *Welfare* makes the first recorded landing on the Falkland Islands which are named after Viscount Falkland, Treasurer of the Navy.

1748–49 The British Admiralty abandons plans to send an expedition to survey the islands following objections made by the Spanish court.

1764 The French explorer, Captain Louis-Antoine de Bougainville, lands on East Falkland which he claims in the name of Louis XV of France. A settlement, Port Louis, is established by the French who name the islands "Les Malouines" after their home town of St Malo.

1765 Unaware that the French have settled on East Falkland, a British survey team under Commodore Byron lands on West Falkland, establishes a settlement and claims the islands in the name of George III.

1766 A second expedition led by Captain McBride arrives at Port Egmont, augmenting the British settlement there to about 100 people.

McBride discovers the French settlement of Port Louis and warns the French to leave.

1767 The French sell their settlement to Spain for a sum totalling the equivalent of about 24000. Port Louis is renamed Puerto de la Soledad and placed under the jurisdiction of the Captain-General of Buenos Aires. Britain refuses to accept the Spanish claim to sovereignty.

1769 Captain Hunt commanding a British frigate at Port Egmont warns the Spanish to leave following an incident involving a Spanish ship.

1770 A Spanish expeditionary force of five ships and 1400 soldiers is sent from Buenos Aires and the British are forced to leave the islands and return to Britain. This action brings Spain and Britain to the brink of war.

1771 An Exchange of Declarations between the governments of Britain and Spain on 22 January results in both sides accepting a return to the status quo ante. On 15 September Port Egmont is restored to Britain.

1774 For economic reasons Britain withdraws its garrison at Port Egmont, but before leaving the islands the commanding officer leaves a British flag flying and a plaque declaring that the Falkland Islands are the "sole right and property" of George III.

1775 Captain Cook lands on South Georgia and takes possession in the name of King George III.

1790 At the Anglo-Spanish Convention of Nootka Sound (St Lawrence Convention) Spain concedes to Britain the right to navigate and fish in the South Pacific and South Atlantic and to trade and settle in unoccupied regions. Britain agrees not to sail or fish within ten maritime leagues of any Spanish territory.

1795   The Convention of 1790 is terminated when Spain declares war on Great Britain.

1811   For economic reasons Spain abandons the Falkland Islands.

1816   The government of Buenos Aires declares its independence from Spanish colonial rule and a lengthy struggle begins within the provinces of Argentina as centralist and federalist groups argue over the future structure of the nation.

1819   Captain W. Smith discovers and takes possession of the South Shetland Islands on behalf of Great Britain.

1820   An American, Daniel Jewett, lands in the Falklands and claims possession in the name of the government of Buenos Aires. He returns to Buenos Aires after a few days.

1821   Captain G. Powell discovers the South Orkney Islands which he claims on behalf of Great Britain.

1823   The government in Buenos Aires appoints a governor to the Falkland Islands. In the same year the USA recognizes the existence of the United Provinces of La Plata which includes Buenos Aires.

1824   Great Britain recognizes the United Provinces of La Plata and sends a consul-general to Buenos Aires.

1825   Britain and the government of Buenos Aires sign a Treaty of Amity, Trade and Navigation, but no mention is made of the Falkland Islands,

1826   Backed by the Buenos Aires government, a French-born adventurer Louis Vernet establishes a new settlement at Puerto de la Soledad.

1829   In June, the United Provinces issues a decree claiming sovereignty over "the Islands of the Malvinas and those adjacent to Cape Horn in the Atlantic Ocean", and Vernet is appointed Political and Military Governor. The British government immediately sends a letter of protest to Buenos Aires stating that the withdrawal from the islands in 1774 did not invalidate Britain's title.

1831   The US Secretary of State in Washington supports Britain's claim to the Falkland Islands and in February lodges a protest against Argentine attempts to establish title to the islands. In retaliation Vernet captures three American sealing ships, *Harriet*, *Breakwater* and *Superior* operating in Falkland Islands waters, during July and August. This prompts the US government to dispatch the sloop *Lexington* to the Falklands in December. The Americans disperse the colonists and destroy the fort at Puerto de la Soledad.

1832   The US Chargé d'Affaires and the Buenos Aires Foreign Minister engage in a heated argument over the incidents of the previous year; no settlement is reached and the United States breaks off diplomatic relations with Argentina. When the Buenos Aires government appoints Juan Mestivier as interim Civil and Military Governor of the Falkland Islands the British government repeats its protest at infringement of British sovereignty. The warship *HMS Clio* is sent to the Falklands where its commander, Captain Onslow, occupies Port Egmont on West Falkland and puts up a signal post dated 23 December 1832, clearly stating British possession of the Island group. On East Falkland Mestivier arrives on the schooner *Sarandi* but is murdered soon after during a mutiny by soldiers who have been left on the island.

John Biscoe takes British possession of the Antarctic Peninsula discovered 12 years earlier by Edward Bransfield.

1833   Captain Onslow sails from West Falkland to take possession of the settlement on East Falkland. José Pinedo and the members of his garrison are easily persuaded to leave without force. The Argentine government protests at

British repossession of the Falkland Islands but, in July, Britain's Chargé d'Affaires in Buenos Aires delivers a strongly worded note to the Foreign Minister stating that the British government had only exercised its "full and undoubted right" in reclaiming the Falklands as a Crown Colony.

1841   The British government appoints a civil Lieutenant-Governor to take over from the naval officer in charge of the islands.

1844   The United States restores diplomatic relations with Argentina after a period of 12 years, while in the Falklands the administrative seat is moved from Port Louis to Port William which is renamed Stanley.

1846   The southern half of East Falkland is sold to Samuel Lafone, a cattle farmer from Montevideo.

1849   A garrison of 25 Royal Marines replaces the small contingent of sappers.

1851   Lafone sells his property in the Falklands to the newly established Falkland Islands Company which acts as shipping agent and general merchant in Stanley.

1860–80   Sheep-farming, first attempted by the Whitington brothers on East Falkland, gradually replaces cattle farming as the main enterprise on the Falkland Islands.

1885   Having received a grant-in-aid from the British government since 1841, the Falklands become self-supporting for the first time.

1904   South Georgia begins to develop as a whaling centre. Shore stations established here operate until 1965.

1908   Britain establishes sovereignty over South Georgia and the South Sandwich Islands in Letters Patent issued by the Crown.

1912   Wireless communication with the outside world is established.

1914   On 8 December the Falkland Islands are the scene of Sturdee's celebrated naval victory over Graf von Spee. The battle is commemorated by a memorial at Stanley and 8 December is adopted as the colony's national day.

1927   Argentina makes a formal claim to the island of South Georgia.

1943–44   The first British Antarctic Survey research stations are established at Deception Island and Port Lockroy in an exercise codenamed "Operation Tabarin".

1947   In December an Argentine naval expedition lands on the South Shetlands and South Orkneys and bases are established in British Antarctica. The British government submits a claim of sovereignty over these dependencies to the International Court of Justice, but both Argentina and Chile assert their "undisputed rights" to the "South American Antarctic."

1948   Argentina makes a formal claim to the South Sandwich Islands.

1956   The International Court of Justice will not hear Britain's resubmission of her claims over the Antarctic dependencies since neither Argentina nor Chile will recognise the jurisdiction of the court.

1962   The British Antarctic Territory comprising the Antarctic Peninsula, the South Shetland and South Orkney Islands, Shag Rocks and Clerke Rocks, is established by the British government on 3 March.

1966   The United Nations instigates talks to resolve the dispute between Britain and Argentina over the Falkland Islands and its dependencies.

1969   The British Antarctic Survey establishes a research station on South Georgia at King Edward Point.

1972   A weekly air link is established between the Falklands and the Argentine port of Comodoro Rivadavia.

1976 Argentina establishes an unauthorized "scientific station" on South Thule in the South Sandwich Islands.

1979 Britain restores diplomatic relations with Argentina and talks over the Falklands resume.

1980 Nicolas Ridley, British Minister of State at the Foreign and Commonwealth Office, visits the Falklands in December and offers the island's Legislative Council three options for the future. These include (i) a 25-year freeze on the dispute, (ii) the surrender of sovereignty to Argentina with the islands being leased back to Britain, and (iii) a joint UK-Argentine administration.

1981 In January the islanders opt for a freeze on the dispute but Argentina rejects this solution, stating that future talks must presuppose Argentine sovereignty over the islands.

1982 In February the dispute is discussed at a further round of talks which take place in New York. When no solution is found the Argentine Foreign Ministry threatens to "put an end" to negotiations and "seek other means" to resolve the dispute. Three weeks later on 19 March 60 Argentines, claiming to be scrap metal merchants, land at Leith Harbour on South Georgia and hoist the Argentine flag. The British government is pressurized in the House of Commons not to withdraw from service the ice patrol ship *HMS Endurance*.

On 2 April Argentine troops land on East Falkland and overwhelm the 70-strong contingent of Royal Marines. The British governor is deported to Uruguay and replaced by an Argentine military governor. In Buenos Aires the military junta led by General Galtieri announces that the Falklands have been recovered "for the nation". In Great Britain the Foreign Secretary and two ministers resign.

In defiance of a UN Security Council Resolution Argentina consolidates its hold on the Falkland Islands. Meanwhile Britain rapidly assembles a large military task force which arrives in the South Atlantic at the end of April. In an attempt to reach a negotiated

settlement, the US Secretary of State, Alexander Haig, engages in intense diplomatic exchanges between the two sides.

When the Argentine junta refuses to withdraw from the islands, British troops recapture South Georgia on 25 April. With Argentina and Great Britain now "technically at war" both sides engage in naval and military combat for just over seven weeks. On 2 May a British submarine torpedoes and sinks the battle-cruiser *General Belgrano*. In response, Argentina uses Exocet missiles against the Royal Navy, sinking the destroyer *HMS Sheffield*. Argentine forces eventually surrender to the British on 14 June, but the struggle to regain control of the islands costs the lives of 254 British troops and 750 Argentines. The financial cost of the war to Britain is estimated to be in the region of £700 million.

On 25 June Rex Hunt returns to the Falklands as the Civil Commissioner in a joint civilian-military Rehabilitation Committee. In May Lord Shackleton is invited to update his 1976 economic survey of the islands and in July a Commission chaired by Lord Franks begins to investigate "the way in which the responsibilities of government in relation to the Falkland Islands and the Dependencies were discharged in the period leading up to the Argentine invasion".

On 22 July the 200-mile Total Exclusion Zone around the Falklands is replaced by a Protection Zone of 150 miles and in September both sides agree to lift the financial restrictions imposed during the conflict. Attempts by the European Community to normalize economic and commercial ties with Argentina are frustrated by Argentina's insistence that the British government should first enter into discussions on the issue of sovereignty over the Falkland Islands.

The British government promises in December to provide £31 million for the economic development of the islands over a period of six years and announces the setting up of the Falkland Islands Development Agency.

1983 In January the Franks Commission finds no fault with government action but criticizes the intelligence services in the weeks prior to the Argentine invasion. In June the House of Commons Defence Committee publishes *The Future Defence of the Falkland Islands* in which the government is urged to promote capital spending projects including the building of a strategic airport at Mount Pleasant. Following elections on 30 October, civilian democracy is restored in Argentina under President Raúl Alfonsín. A series of confidential exchanges between the Argentine and British governments seeks to establish a way of restoring bilateral relations.

1984   Representatives of the British and Argentine governments meet in Berne on 18–19 July but when the issue of sovereignty is raised the talks end in deadlock.

1985   The British government tries in March to reopen talks with Argentina but receives no response. In May the airport at Mount Pleasant is completed and Britain is accused by Argentina of destabilizing the region by establishing a strategic base. On 8 July Britain attempts to encourage the normalization of relations with Argentina by unilaterally lifting the ban on Argentine imports imposed during the 1982 conflict.

Under a new constitution that comes into effect on 3 October, South Georgia and the South Sandwich Islands cease to be dependencies of the Falkland Islands. The constitution also reasserts the right of the Falkland Islanders to self-determination.

Concern about over-fishing in the region is expressed at a fisheries conference organized in April by the UN Food and Agriculture Organization's (FAO) Committee of Fisheries. In November the FAO launches a major fisheries study.

1986   Argentina effectively undermines the possibility of a multilateral fisheries conservation agreement by signing bilateral fishing agreements with the Soviet Union and Bulgaria over waters claimed as part of the Argentine Exclusive Economic Zone. Argentine attempts to impose sovereignty over Falklands waters results in an incident

involving a Taiwanese fishing boat. On 29 October the British Foreign Secretary announces Britain's intention to declare a Falkland Islands' entitlement to a fishery limit up to a maximum of 200 nautical miles from the Falklands, subject to the need for a maritime boundary with Argentina.

1987   On 1 February the British government establishes a Falkland Islands Interim Conservation and Management Zone around the islands in a radius extending to 150 nautical miles. The object of this is to conserve fish stocks and in doing so, help diversify the economy of the Falkland Islands. A revenue from fishing licences of 13.7 million in 1987 dramatically increases the prosperity of the islands and brings emigration to a halt.

1988   Exercise "Fire Focus" in March demonstrates that, with the opening of Mount Pleasant Airport, Britain is capable of rapidly reinforcing its military garrison in the Falklands. The UN General Assembly adopts a resolution in November encouraging both sides to resolve the dispute by entering into negotiations that cover "all aspects" of the future of the islands. A month later, the British Prime Minister reaffirms the islanders' rights and states that sovereignty is not for negotiation.

1989   A new supply ship, the Bahamanian-registered *Indiana I*, is refused docking facilities in Uruguay and Brazil when it attempts to start up a ferry service linking the islands with mainland South America. Later in the year, the newly elected president of Argentina, Carlos Menem, agrees to leave the question of sovereignty to one side in an attempt to allow progess on other issues of common interest. Following three days of talks held in Madrid, a formal end to hostilities is declared in October despite the fact that the issue of sovereignty remains unresolved. Elections in the Falklands, however, are a clear indication that the islanders do not wish to develop close links with Argentina.

1990   On 15 February a decision is made to restore full diplomatic relations between Argentina and the UK.

■ Who's who

Alfonsín, Raúl   President of Argentina 1983-89, Alfonsin viewed British military presence in the Falklands as "illegal" and a source of instability in the region. During his period of presidency all talks between Britain and Argentina foundered on the question of sovereignty. Beset by economic crises in Argentina, Alfonsin's Radical Civic Union Party was eventually defeated at the polls by the right-wing Peronists under Carlos Menem.

Carrington, Lord   Conservative Foreign Secretary who resigned along with two other ministers on 5 April 1982 following the Argentine invasion of the Falklands three days earlier. He was replaced by Francis Pym, former Leader of the House of Commons.

Franks, Lord Oliver Shewell   An Oxford academic and former British Ambassador to the United States (1948–52) who chaired the committee of enquiry into the events leading up to the Argentine invasion of the Falklands in 1982.

Fullerton, W.H.   Colonial Governor of the Falkland Islands and Commissioner of South Georgia and the Sandwich Islands, appointed in 1985 by the British government.

Galtieri, Lieut.-General Leopoldo Fortunato
From 1979 until 1982 Galtieri was leader of the three-man military junta that ruled Argentina from 1976 until the election of a civilian president, Raúl Alfonsín, in 1983. The strong-arm measures adopted by the military in an attempt to crush terrorism resulted in extensive human rights violations and the eventual trial of Galtieri in 1983. Although acquitted, he was brought to trial again in 1986 and sentenced to 12 years imprisonment for his part in leading Argentina into the Falklands war. Galtieri and others were pardoned in October 1989 by the new Peronist President, Carlos Menem.

García, Major-General Osvaldo Jorge   First Argentine commander of the Falklands garrison following the invasion of 2 April 1982,
García was replaced four days later by General Benjamin Menéndez.

Haig, Alexander   US Secretary of State dispatched by President Reagan on 6 April 1982 on a mission to London and Buenos Aires in an attempt to find a peaceful solution to the Falklands conflict following the Argentine invasion of the islands four days earlier.

Hunt, Sir Rex   Governor of the Falkland Islands at the time of the Argentine invasion in April 1982. Forced to leave the colony on 5 April he returned on 25 June as civilian commissioner in the joint civil-military Rehabilitation Committee set up in the aftermath of the war. Knighted in 1982, Sir Rex Hunt was replaced in 1985 when a new governor was appointed.

Lombardo, Vice-Admiral Juan José   Argentine naval commander based at Puerto Belgrano and charged with the "defence of the national sovereignty" in the "South Atlantic theatre of operations" during the 1982 conflict.

Luce, Richard   British Minister of State at the Foreign Office who resigned along with Lord Carrington and the Lord Privy Seal following the Argentine invasion of the Falkland Islands in April 1982.

Méndez, Dr Nicanor Costa   Argentine Foreign Minister during the Falklands war of 1982.

Menem, Carlos Saúl   Born in 1943, Menem trained as a lawyer before entering local politics to become Governor of La Rioja province. In 1989, as leader of the Peronists, he was elected president of Argentina. Menem has taken a less dogmatic stance on the issue of sovereignty over the Falklands in an attempt to advance discussions with the British government in other areas.

Menéndez, General Mario Benjamin
Commander of the Falklands garrison and Military Governor of the Falkland Islands following the Argentine invasion of April 1982.

Nott, Sir John British Defence Secretary during the 1982 Falklands war.

Shackleton, Lord Edward Arthur Alexander Born in 1911, Lord Shackleton is the son of the polar explorer, Sir Ernest Shackleton, who was buried on South Georgia. A former expedition organizer, BBC producer and Leader of the Opposition in the House of Lords (1970–74), he carried out an economic survey of the Falkland Islands in 1976. In the aftermath of the Falklands war in 1982 he was asked by the British government to update his survey and make recommendations for the future development of the islands.

Tickell, Sir Crispin British representative at the United Nations whose Madrid talks with the Argentine special envoy, Lucio García del Solar, brought the Falklands conflict to a formal end in October 1989.

Woodward, Rear-Admiral John (Sandy) Operational Commander of the British task force sent to the South Atlantic in April 1982 to recapture the Falkland Islands.

■ Key places

Antarctica A continental landmass extending to 13 900 000 and its associated ice sheet lying to the south of 60° S. Territorial claims to this area, which contains reserves of oil, gas, coal and other minerals as well as substantial fish resources, were frozen under a treaty signed by 12 countries in 1959 and ratified in 1961. Seven of the original signatories to the Treaty of Antarctica have claims to territory in Antarctica, namely, Argentina, Australia, Chile, France, New Zealand, Norway and the United Kingdom.

Ascension A small volcanic island in the South Atlantic 3300 nautical miles north of the Falklands. Ascension is a British possession with an airbase leased by the United States. During the 1982 Falklands war Ascension was used by the British as an operational base from which to launch bomber attacks on the Falkland Islands. It subsequently became an important staging post in the air link between the Falklands and the UK. The 88-km² island was discovered by the Portuguese on Ascension Day 1501 but remained uninhabited until 1815 when it was settled by a garrison of British soldiers.

Camp The name given by Falkland Islanders to the countryside outside Stanley.

Clerke Rocks A group of uninhabited islets lying to the SE of South Georgia.

Comodoro Rivadavia Naval port and largest settlement on the Patagonian coast of Chubut region, SE Argentina. The city, which developed after the discovery of oil in 1907, has a population of 97 000. In 1972 a weekly air service to the Falkland Islands was inaugurated.

Bluff Cove A settlement on East Falkland lying 24km south-west of Stanley. A second bridgehead was established here, and at Fitzroy, on 6–8 June 1982 in the final push by British forces to regain control of the Falkland Islands.

Goose Green A settlement with an airfield on the land bridge between East Falkland and Lafonia. With a population of 100, Goose Green is the largest rural settlement on the Falklands outside Stanley. It was captured along with Darwin on 28 May 1982 during the final push by British troops to retake the Falkland Islands. In the offensive over 1400 Argentine prisoners were taken and 250 soldiers killed. British casualties totalled 17.

Grytviken The chief settlement of South Georgia. Established as a whaling station in 1904 by C. A. Larsen, founder of the Compania Argentina de Pesca. Abandoned in 1966, there has been a military garrison at Grytviken since the Falkland war of 1982.

Lafonia A land mass to the south of East Falkland to which it is linked via a narrow land bridge that separates the Choiseul Sound from the Grantham Sound. Darwin, Goose Green and Walker Creek are the principal settlements. The territory is named after Samuel Lafone who farmed here between 1846 and 1851.

Mount Pleasant   The site of a second airport for the Falklands, completed in 1986 and situated on East Falkland 40km south-west of Stanley.

Mount Tumbledown   The last area of high ground on East Falkland to be taken by British troops prior to the recapture of Stanley which lies immediately to the NE.

Mount Usborne   The highest peak in the Falklands, rising to a height of 705m on East Falkland, 65km west of Stanley.

Pebble Island   A small islet off the north-west tip of West Falkland. On 13–14 May 1982 48 Special Air Service Commandos landed here and destroyed Argentine military aircraft.

Puerto Belgrano   A naval port on the east coast of Argentina, situated to the south-east of Bahía Blanca. This was the naval command base of the Argentine South Atlantic theatre of operations during the Falklands conflict in 1982.

Puerto Madryn   A port and resort town on the Patagonian coast of SE Argentina. Situated 56km north of Rawson, the capital of Chubut region, Puerto Madryn was founded by Welsh settlers in 1865. On 14 July 1982 593 Argentine prisoners were returned to Puerto Madryn by the British following the Argentine surrender.

San Carlos   A settlement on East Falkland at the head of the San Carlos Water, 80km west of Stanley. On 21 May 5000 British troops landed here, establishing a first bridgehead in the final push to regain control of the Falkland Islands.

Shag Rocks   A group of small islets lying to the west of South Georgia.

South Georgia   A mountainous, barren island with an area of 3754km², situated in the South Atlantic, 1200km east of the Falkland Islands.

Formerly a dependency of the Falkland Islands, South Georgia, since 1985, has been a British Crown Colony administered with the South Sandwich Islands by a commissioner resident in the Falkland Islands. Although Captain Cook was probably the first to set foot on the island, it was not taken into formal possession by Great Britain until 1908. Throughout the 19th century the island was visited by seal hunters but in 1904 it became a centre for whalers who built seven stations including the island's main settlement at Grytviken. In 1966 the whaling stations were abandoned, but three years later the British Antarctic Survey set up research stations at King Edward Point. Argentina, which had laid claim to the island in 1927, landed forces on South Georgia on 3 April 1982 but the island was retaken by British troops three weeks later on 25 April. After the 1982 Falklands war a British military contingent was garrisoned at Grytviken and a new British Antarctic Survey research station was established on Bird Island. The explorer Sir Ernest Shackleton is buried on South Georgia.

South Orkney Islands   A group of barren unihabited islands in the S Atlantic lying to the north-east of the Antarctic Peninsula; area 620km². Currently forming part of the British Antarctic Territory (since March 1962), but claimed by Argentina. When Argentina landed so-called scientific expeditions on the islands in 1947, Britain proposed the submission of contending claims to the International Court of Justice.

South Sandwich Islands   A group of barren, uninhabited volcanic islets situated 480 km south-east of South Georgia with which it is administered from the Falkland Islands as a British Crown Colony. The islands were formally declared to be part of the Falkland Island Dependencies in July 1908 but were claimed by Argentina in 1948.

South Shetland Islands   A group of uninhabited islands in the South Atlantic lying to the north-west of the Antarctic peninsula. Discovered in 1819 by the British navigator, William Smith. Part of the British Antarctic Territory since March 1962, but claimed by Argentina and Chile.

Southern Thule   An island of the South Sandwich group where a small party of Argentinians were stationed in December 1976 without British authority. On 20 June 1982 the UK government announced that, on the previous day, the Argentinians based on the island had surrendered.

Stanley   Port and chief settlement of the Falkland Islands, situated on the east coast of East Falkland on an inlet of the South Atlantic. Originally named Port William, Stanley replaced Port Louis as the capital of the Falklands in 1843. Following the Argentine invasion of April 1982 Stanley had its name changed at least four times. On 6 April it was renamed Puerto Rivero, but during the subsequent six weeks leading up to its recapture by the British it became Puerto de la Isla Soledad, Puerto de las Islas Malvinas and finally Puerto Argentino. The settlement has a population totalling about 1000.

■ Key words

Argentine Exclusive Economic Zone   An exclusive fishing zone extending 200 nautical miles from the coast of Argentine territory to include the waters around the Falkland Islands. In 1986 Argentina signed bilateral agreements with the Soviet Union and Bulgaria in order that fishermen from these countries could fish under licence in South Atlantic waters. In the same year the enforcement of this exclusion zone led to an incident involving a Taiwanese fishing boat.

British Nationality (Falkland Islands) Amendment Act   An Act of the British Parliament which came into effect on 1 January 1983, giving British citizenship to those islanders not already covered by the 1981 Act.

Falkland Islands Development Corporation   An organization set up in June 1984 by the British government following recommendations made by the Shackelton Report in December 1982. The aim of the agency is to promote the economic development of the Falkland Islands.

Falkland Islands Interim Conservation and Management Zone   An exclusive fishing zone operating within a radius of 150 nautical miles of the Falkland Islands. Established on 1 February 1987, this conservation and management zone is designed to help regulate and conserve fishing stocks and in so doing, help strengthen the economy of the islands. In its first two years of operation the Falkland Islands derived an income of 13.7 million and 16 million from fishing licences.

Fire Focus   The codename given to the Falkland Islands Reinforcement Exercise of March 1988, a military exercise designed to test Britain's capability to reinforce the garrison in the Falklands following the completion of the new airport at Mount Pleasant.

General Belgrano   An Argentine battle-cruiser considered a "major threat" to shipping and consequently torpedoed by a British submarine on 2 May 1982 while some 30 miles outside the Total Exclusion Zone. An estimated 370 lives were lost. Two days later, Argentina responded with its first Exocet missile attack on a Royal Navy destroyer, *HMS Sheffield*.

Haig Mission   A US peace initiative involving the US Secretary of State, Alexander Haig, who made a series of visits to London and Buenos Aires in an attempt to find a solution to the Falklands conflict following the Argentine invasion of April 1982.

Madrid, Declaration of   A joint statement issued on 13 June 1984 by the governments of Spain and Argentina supporting their respective claims to Gibraltar and the Falkland Islands.

Peruvian Peace Plan   An unsuccessful attempt by the Peruvian government to help find a solution to the crisis in 1982.

South Atlantic Theatre of Operations   A special naval command created by the Argentine government in 1982 with the task of defending the national sovereignty in waters up to 200 nautical miles from the coast of Argentine territory which included the Falkland Islands as well as the island of South Georgia and the South Sandwich Islands. Based in the naval port of Puerto Belgrano, the "theatre of operations" was directed by Vice-Admiral Juan Losé Lombardo.

South Atlantic Zone of Peace   A war-free zone proposed for the South Atlantic following the Falklands conflict of 1982.

Task Force   The name given to the British military expedition sent to the South Atlantic to engage Argentine forces and recapture the Falkland Islands. Under the command of Rear-Admiral John Woodward, a rapidly-assembled fleet of 70 ships carrying 5000–6000 troops set off from Plymouth and Gibraltar on 5–6 April 1982 to sail the 8000 miles to the Falklands. The fleet arrived in the South Atlantic three weeks later and successfully landed British forces on the islands.

Total Exclusion Zone   A 200-nautical mile British Maritime Exclusion Zone was established by the British government around the Falklands on 12 April 1982, ten days after the Argentine invasion of the islands. The Defence Secretary announced that Argentine warships entering the zone could expect to come under attack. On 30 April the British Maritime Exclusion Zone became a "Total Exclusion Zone" within which all Argentine ships, naval or merchant, were liable to come under attack. Seven days later the Total Exclusion Zone was extended to within 12 nautical miles of the South American coast in an attempt to prevent Argentine shipping from setting out for the Falklands. The exclusion zone was lifted on 22 July 1982, a month after the recapture of the islands.

Voluntary Restraint Arrangements   Faced with the possibility of a rapid increase in Far Eastern fishing fleets entering Falkland waters in search of squid and other fish, the British government tried to negotiate Voluntary Restraint Arrangements in December 1985. When it became clear that a multilateral fisheries management agreement could not be reached for the 1987 season the British government established the Falkland Islands Interim Conservation and Management Zone on 1 February 1987. Since that date international fishing in Falklands waters has been regulated by licence.

■ Further reading

Peter Calvert, *The Falklands Crisis: The Rights and the Wrongs*, Pinter, London, 1982

Falkland Islands Review [Franks Report] Cmnd. 8787, HMSO, London, 1983

Lawrence Freedman, *Britain and the Falklands War*, Institute of Contemporary British History, Basil Blackwell, Oxford and New York, 1988

Lawrence Freedman and Virginia Gamba–Stonehouse, *Signals of War: The Falklands Conflict of 1982*, Faber, London, 1990

Julius Goebel, *The Struggle for the Falklands Islands*, Yale University Press, New York and London, 1982

Max Hastings and Simon Jenkins, *The Battle for the Falklands*, Michael Joseph, London, 1983

C.C. Joyner, 1988 Antarctic Minerals Convention, *Marine Policy Reports*, 1(1), 1989, pp.669–85

L.A. Kimball, The Antarctic Treaty System, *Oceanus*, 31(2), 1988, pp.14–19

E. Shackleton, *Falkland Islands Economic Study 1982*, HMSO, London, 1982

V Europe

1
Baltic Republics

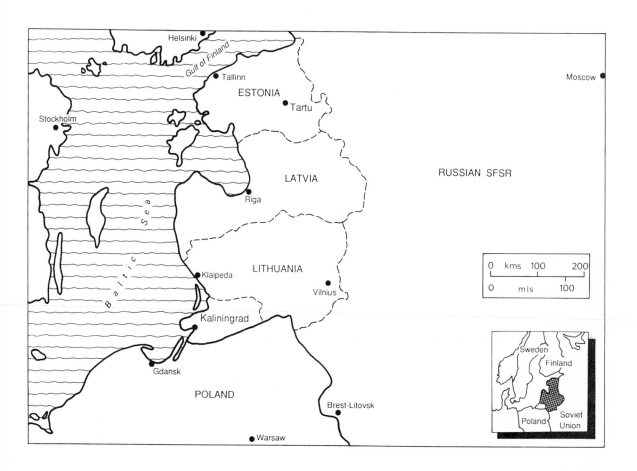

■ Profile

Estonia
- **Area:** 45 100 km²
- **Population:** 1 556 000
- **Ethnic groups:** Estonians 64.7%, Russians 27.9%, Ukrainians 2.5%, Belorussians 1.6%
- **Capital:** Tallinn

Latvia
- **Area:** 63 700 km²
- **Population:** 2 647 000
- **Ethnic groups:** Latvian 53.7%, Russian 32.8%
- **Capital:** Riga

Lithuania
- **Area:** 65 200 km²
- **Population:** 3 641 000
- **Ethnic groups:** Lithuanian 80%, Russians 8.6%, Poles 7.7%
- **Capital:** Vilnius

■ Introduction

The Soviet Union's annexation of Lithuania, Latvia and Estonia in 1940, by virtue of the infamous Nazi–Soviet non-aggression pact of 1939, has never been fully recognized in the West. Reasserted at the end of World War II, Soviet rule became less of an issue over the succeeding 40 years. As Moscow pointed out, the annexations had restored the Russian sovereignty exercised before the Baltic states became independent in 1918. But the Baltic peoples themselves not only remembered that they had had a long history before passing into the Russian Empire in the 18th century but also cherished their brief inter-war independence. This became glaringly apparent in the late 1980s, as gradual democratization unleashed a torrent of long-suppressed national feeling.

Polish, German and Scandinavian influences were dominant in the early history of Lithuania, Latvia and Estonia respectively. Only Lithuania experienced early statehood, being unified in the 13th century. Allied with Poland, Vytautas the Great of Lithuania crushed the Teutonic Knights at Tannenberg in 1410, after which the Lithuanian-Polish royal union

became Europe's largest state, stretching from the Baltic to the Black Sea. Meanwhile, the Teutonic Knights from Germany had acquired Estonia from the Danes in 1346 to add to their 12th-century conquest of Latvia. On the demise of the Teutonic Knights in 1560, Estonia came under Swedish rule while Poland/Lithuania acquired Latvia. But this was the high point of the pre-Russian Baltic empires. Sweden's defeat in the Great Northern War (1700–21) obliged it to cede Estonia to Peter the Great's emerging Russia. In the late 18th-century partitions of Poland, Latvia and Lithuania were likewise absorbed by the Russian Empire, except for German-populated Memel (modern Klaipeda) on Lithuania's Baltic coast, which went to Prussia.

The Lithuanians led a 19th-century national revival in the Russian Baltic provinces, although Latvia in particular remained under the heel of ethnic-German "Baltic barons" serving the Tsar. In World War I Germany's military victories over Tsarist Russia were combined with promotion of Baltic secession. When the new Bolshevik regime in Moscow sued for peace, the 1918

Brest-Litovsk treaty enabled all three provinces to assert independence. For a while it looked as though Russian rule would be replaced by imperial German hegemony, especially over Latvia. But Germany's eventual defeat led to the consolidation of republican governments in the Baltic states, which all obtained international recognition and admission to the League of Nations. Lithuania's independence was complicated by the re-emergence of Poland, which became embroiled in war with the Bolsheviks and took consolation for its defeat by seizing Vilnius, historic capital of Lithuania. That the League awarded Memel to Lithuania in 1923 was little compensation in light of the later revival of German dreams of eastern empire.

The three Baltic republics made some economic progress in the inter-war years, although political stability was elusive. Estonia had 18 governments between 1920 and 1934. Lithuania succumbed to authoritarian rule in 1926, followed by Estonia and Latvia in 1934, when recession began to bite. The growth of Moscow-backed communist opposition groups ensued. But the semi-fascist regimes which they opposed were by no means puppets of Berlin: the devil of Germany's quest for *Lebensraum* was as threatening as the deep red sea of Bolshevism. After Hitler had "liberated" Memel, the 1939 Molotov–Ribbentrop Pact provided secretly for the division of Eastern Europe between the German and Soviet giants. By mid-1940 the Baltic states had become republics of the Soviet Union (and Lithuania had regained Vilnius). Hitler's onslaught on the Soviet Union followed in mid-1941, resulting in the Baltic states becoming parts of Germany's *Ostland*. That they gave some support to the Nazi cause sealed their fate in Stalin's eyes. After the Red Army had reimposed Soviet rule in 1944, demands by the Western powers that the Baltic states should be restored to their pre-war independence fell on deaf ears in Moscow.

In the post-war era the three republics had great strategic value for Moscow because they provided southern Baltic naval and air bases for the Soviet military. Moreover, as well as restoring Memel/Klaipeda to Lithuania, Stalin had also annexed northern East Prussia, with its major port of Kaliningrad (once Königsberg), which was co-terminous with the Soviet Union proper only through Lithuania. Moscow therefore set about integrating the Baltic republics fully into the Soviet system. The exodus of most ethnic Germans made room for Russian settlers, who came to form sizeable minorities in Latvia and Estonia. The full panoply of Communist Party control was installed, and the republics' economies were brought under Moscow-directed central planning. Nevertheless, the three republics retained their sense of national separateness, and they fared better economically than the rest of the Soviet Union, thanks in part to their historic Scandinavian links. Nor were aspirations to freedom ever far below the surface. Suppressed for a generation, they burst into full bloom in the era of *glasnost* and *perestroika* initiated by Mikhail Gorbachev in 1985.

The new wind of democracy swept nationalist movements to power in all three Baltic republics, where measures to re-establish national identity and to escape from the diktat of Moscow followed in rapid profusion. The opening of the Berlin Wall and the death of communism in Eastern Europe accelerated the pace of events in the Baltic states, whose declaration that the 1940 annexations had been illegal was endorsed by the Soviet parliament. Seizing the moment, Lithuania declared full independence in March 1990, thereby overstepping Moscow's mark. Although prepared to concede the right of secession, the Gorbachev government insisted that a legal procedure must be followed and that Soviet interests and rights must be respected in the security and economic spheres. A crucial political factor was that the central government faced national agitation in other republics, notably in Armenia and Azerbaijan (*see section 5.2*), which would be greatly encouraged by unilateral Baltic secessions. The result was a major crisis, involving economic blockade and military confrontation, which became sharper when the Latvian and Estonian parliaments also voted for independence in May 1990. Some saw Moscow's response as reminiscent of earlier Soviet actions in Eastern Europe, while others hoped that the crisis could be resolved by negotiation. The latter hope was widely shared in the West, where sympathy for the Baltic states was balanced by concern that

Gorbachev should survive politically. After the miraculous transformation of the East European scene in 1989, any reversion to Cold War politics was seen as a nightmare scenario to be avoided at all costs.

■ Chronology of events

1158   Latvia is conquered by the Teutonic Knights.

1219   Estonia is conquered by the Danes.

c.1240–63   United by the threat of the Teutonic Knights, Lithuania is the first of the Baltic regions to achieve statehood when Pope Innocent IV grants a crown to Mindovg, a Lithuanian chieftain.

1346   The Danes sell Estonia to the Teutonic Knights.

1386   Poland and Lithuania are united by a royal marriage that ultimately leads to the creation of a kingdom stretching from the Baltic to the Black Sea.

1410   A combined Polish–Lithuanian army under Vytautas the Great of Lithuania defeats the Teutonic Knights.

1560   Following the final dissolution of the Teutonic Knights, Latvia is acquired by Poland–Lithuania and northern Estonia passes to Sweden.

1629   After an eight–year war with Poland, Sweden adds southern Estonia to its possessions.

1721   At the conclusion of the Great Northern War between Sweden and Russia, Estonia is ceded to Russia under the terms of the Treaty of Nystadt.

1772   Following a civil war, Poland loses one–third of its territory to Russia, Prussia and Austria.

1793 In the second partition of Poland between Russia, Austria and Prussia, the greater part of Lithuania is absorbed by Russia.

1795   Under a third partition of Poland, Russia absorbs Latvia and what is left of Lithuania. Thereafter Estonia, Latvia and Lithuania (except for the German–populated Memel region, which goes to Prussia) are part of the Russian Empire.

1917   Taking advantage of the Russian revolution, Lithuania and Latvia establish national councils and demand independence from Russia. Estonia follows the lead taken by its neighbours and proclaims its independence in November, but finds itself under German occupation when the Soviet government tries to recapture the territory.

1918   While the Central Powers negotiate peace with the new Soviet government, Latvia, Lithuania and Estonia all seize the chance to make formal declarations of independence. Despite a Bolshevik invasion of Lithuania in February, a peace treaty is eventually signed in March at Brest–Litovsk. Under the terms of this agreement Russia is obliged to abandon a number of territories including the Baltic states.

When German power collapses after the November armistice, the Bolsheviks again invade the Baltic States in an attempt to regain control.

1919   At the insistence of the Allied Powers German troops are obliged to withdraw from the Baltic states under the terms of the Treaty of Versailles.

1920   When the Bolsheviks are finally driven out of the Baltic states, the Soviet government is obliged to sign a series of treaties recognizing the sovereignty of Latvia, Lithuania and Estonia as independent states.

1921   The three Baltic states are admitted as members of the League of Nations in September.

1923 Estonia signs defence treaties with Lithuania and Latvia, a move that paves the way for the eventual setting up of the Baltic Pact.

1926 The government of Lithuania, which signs a treaty of friendship with the Soviet Union, is toppled in December during a right-wing coup led by Antanas Smetona.

1932 Latvia concludes a non-agression pact with the Soviet Union.

1934 In March and May respectively the governments of Estonia and Latvia are replaced by semi-fascist dictatorships. Later in the year the right–wing governments of Estonia, Latvia and Lithuania enter into an entente (Baltic Pact) that is designed to provide a common front in defence of independence.

1939 Despite signing non-aggression pacts with Latvia and Estonia and guaranteeing Lithuania's independence, Germany proceeds to sign a non-aggression pact with the Soviet Union on 23 August (Molotov–Ribbentrop Pact). A secret protocol signed a month later on 28 September effectively transfers the Baltic states to the Soviet sphere of influence.

1940 The Baltic states are forced to establish governments acceptable to the Soviet Union when ultimatums alleging hostile activities are sent from Moscow with German connivance on 15 and 16 June. A month later, after Estonia, Latvia and Lithuania have declared themselves soviet socialist republics, the new People's Diets in each republic apply for admission to the Soviet Union. Their applications are immediately accepted by the Supreme Soviet of the USSR and all three states are finally absorbed into the Soviet Union during the first week in August.

1944–51 During the process of enforced collectivization of agriculture, some 600 000 Baltic nationals (nearly 10 per cent of the population) are deported to Siberia.

1978 The republics of the USSR adopt new constitutions which include an article stating that "Each republic shall retain the right freely to secede from the Soviet Union".

1985 After 45 years of hardline communist rule the rise to power of Mikhail Gorbachev marks the beginning of an era of reforms that reawaken nationalist sentiments in the Baltic republics.

1987 Demonstrations take place in all three Baltic republics on 23 August to mark the anniversary of the Nazi–Soviet pact of 1939. Despite attempts by the government to prevent subsequent demonstrations on the anniversary of Latvia's first independent government in November, over 2000 turn out in Riga.

In September, a group of communist party social scientists propose that Estonia become a special economic zone with wide scope for private enterprise and overseas trade.

1988 At a rally in Vilnius to mark the 70th anniversary of Lithuania's independence, participants are attacked by soldiers and police. A month later in Latvia and Estonia the authorities are unable to prevent demonstrations marking the anniversary of the deportation of thousands of Latvians and Estonians to the labour camps of Siberia in 1949.

In November the Supreme Soviet of Estonia forces Russians to acknowledge Estonian as the main language of the republic.

1989 In March, in the Soviet Union's first genuine multi-candidate elections since 1917, the President of Lithuania and the Prime Ministers of Latvia and Lithuania lose their seats in the Congress of People's Deputies. Following their election successes the Popular Fronts of Estonia, Latvia and Lithuania join forces to form a Baltic Council. The first Assembly of Popular Fronts, meeting in Tallinn in May, presses for economic autonomy from Moscow but stops short of demanding outright independence.

As communist governments fall throughout Eastern Europe the leaders of the Baltic states grow more confident and begin to talk of independence. Estonia is the first to oppose Moscow when it refuses to adopt several Soviet laws, including a 9 April decree on anti-state activity. When Estonia introduces a controversial law curtailing the right of non-Estonians to stand for, and vote in, elections, Russian workers organize strikes and demonstrations.

In July the Soviet parliament agrees to allow wider economic freedom in the Baltic republics and in August the Soviet authorities admit for the first time that the secret Nazi–Soviet agreement of 1939 did exist. On 23 August the 50th anniversary of the Molotov–Ribbentrop pact receives worldwide attention when the Baltic Council organizes a mass rally of one million people who form a 600km human chain linking all the Baltic capital cities.

The issue of secession approaches a crisis point in December when the Communist Party of Lithuania declares itself independent of the Communist Party of the Soviet Union.

1990   The Latvian and Estonian Communist Parties follow Lithuania's lead and declare themselves independent of the CPSU in January. In the following month the Lithuanian Restructuring Movement (*Sajudis*) secures 97 out of the 141 parliamentary seats in the Soviet Union's first multi-party elections and 58 year old Vytautas Landsbergis is selected the republic's first non-communist leader in over half a century. On 11 March Lithuania unilaterally declares its independence and drops the words "Soviet Socialist" from the republic's name. Claiming that independence can only be achieved "within the framework of the constitution", the Soviet government then proceeds to introduce sanctions in the form of an economic blockade. Nearly two months later, on 4 May, Latvia follows the lead taken by Lithuania when it declares independence.

■ Who's who

Astrauskas, Vytautas   President of Lithuania for two years until replaced by Lithuanian Communist Party leader Algirdas Brazauskas in January 1990. Astrauskas was one of a number of leading communists who lost his seat on the Congress of People's Deputies following elections in 1989.

Brazauskas, Algirdas   First Secretary of the Communist Party of Lithuania which made an historic break with the Communist Party of the Soviet Union in December 1989. In January 1990 he was elected President of Lithuania following the resignation of Vytautas Astrauskas. A month later he opposed Vytautas Landsbergis in the February 1990 parliamentary elections but failed to retain the presidency after advocating a more cautious approach towards independence from Moscow.

Chebrikov, Viktor   A Soviet politburo member and former KGB chief who suggested to the Communist Party Central Committee that, in the face of a rising tide of nationalism, each of the Soviet Union's 15 republics should be considered like real sovereign states.

Gorbunov, Anatoly   President of Latvia at the time of that republic's unilateral declaration of independence in May 1990.

Ivans, Dainis   Leader of the Latvian Popular Front appointed Deputy President of Latvia's Supreme Council at the time of Latvia's declaration of independence in May 1990.

Landsbergis, Professor Vytautas   A musicologist and leader of the Lithuanian Restructuring Movement (*Sajudis*) who was elected first non-Communist President of Lithuania following elections in February 1990.

Prunskiene, Kazimira   The first non-communist Prime Minister of Lithuania, appointed after the decisive victory by the Lithuanian Restructuring Movement (*Sajudis*) in the February 1990 elections to the Supreme Soviet in Vilnius. When the Soviet Union imposed sanctions on Lithuania following its unilateral declaration of independence, Prime Minister Prunskiene headed an anti-blockade commission in a bid to establish trade links with other countries and regions.

Rubiks, Alfred   Hardline leader of the dominant pro-Soviet faction of the Latvian Communist Party.

Sakalauskas, Vytautas   Lithuanian Prime Minister who lost his position on the Congress of People's Deputies during the Soviet Union's first multi-candidate elections in 1989. A year later he was replaced as Prime Minister of Lithuania following the victory of the Lithuanian Restructuring Movement at the polls.

Vaivods, Cardinal Julian   A Latvian cardinal arrested in 1958 and imprisoned for two years for having written a number of religious books with "anti-Soviet content". On 12 June 1989 the Latvian Supreme Court rehabilitated Cardinal Vaivods.

■ Key places

Brest–Litovsk   A river port in Belorussia, situated at the junction of the Bug and Mukhavets rivers, close to the Polish frontier. Brest–Litovsk was the scene of peace negotiations between Russia and the Central Powers held during February–March 1918. On 3 March the Russians signed the Treaty of Brest–Litovsk abandoning several territories including the Baltic states.

Klaipeda   An ice-free port on the Baltic and Lithuania's only outlet to the sea; population (1985) 195 000. Founded in 1252 by the Teutonic Knights, it became an important commercial centre of the Hanseatic League. Formerly known as Memel, the city remained in Prussian hands until World War I when it was occupied by Russia. Administered by the French between 1919 and 1923, the Memel territory extending to 2656km^2 was then awarded to Lithuania by the League of Nations as compensation for the loss of Vilnius to Poland. In March 1939 Germany annexed the territory but in January 1945 it was recaptured by Soviet troops and reunited with Lithuania. Klaipeda is an important fishery base and industrial centre but its harbour is not deep enough to provide an anchorage for larger vessels.

Kohtla Járve   An Estonian industrial city on the Gulf of Finland 120km east of Tallinn; population (1985) 77 000. A major centre for engineering and the production of gas from shale.

Mazeikiai or **Mozheiki** (Russian)   An industrial city in NW Lithuania, close to the Latvian frontier. Known as Muravyeno until 1920, the city is the site of Lithuania's only oil refinery.

Riga   The Capital of Latvia and principal seaport of the Baltic republics, situated near the mouth of the Daugava or South Dvina River where it flows into an inlet of the Baltic Sea; population (1985) 883 000. The city, which was founded in 1201 as a German crusading and missionary centre, later became a major commercial outlet for flax, hemp, timber and grain.

Tallinn   Known as Revel until 1917, Tallinn is the capital of Estonia and a seaport on the Gulf of Finland; population (1985) 464 000.

Tartu or **Yurev** (Russian), also **Dorpat** (German)   The second largest city in Estonia, situated on the Ema River, 160km south–east of Tallinn; population (1985) 111 000. Successively under Russian, Polish and Swedish rule, the city was an important commercial centre of the Hanseatic League. Peace treaties between the USSR and Estonia and the USSR and Finland were signed here in 1920.

Vilnius or **Vilna**   The capital city of Lithuania, situated on the Vilnya River near the south-east frontier with Belorussia; population (1985) 544 000. Between 1920 and 1939 the city was held by the Poles who named it Wilno.

■ Key words

Baltic Council A nationalist organization embracing the Estonian and Latvian Popular Fronts and the Lithuanian Restructuring Movement (*Sajudis*). On 23 August the Baltic Council organized a 600km human chain linking the capital cities of the Baltic republics to commemorate the 50th anniversary of the signing of the 1939 Nazi–Soviet non-aggression pact.

Baltic Pact An entente signed by the three Baltic states in September 1934 for the purpose of providing mutual assistance in defence of independence and in foreign affairs.

Brest–Litovsk A treaty of March 1918 under which the Soviet government was obliged by the Central Powers to recognize the independence of the three Baltic States.

Curzon Line The boundary between Poland and Lithuania as defined by the Allied Powers in December 1919. The city of Vilnius was awarded to Lithuania under this arrangement.

Estonian Popular Front The leading Estonian nationalist movement.

glasnost A policy of open accountability in government introduced by Mikhail Gorbachev following his election to the Soviet leadership in 1985.

Intermovement An organization with a predominantly Russian membership opposed to nationalism in the Baltic states. In March 1989 Intermovement organized a mass demonstration of 40 000 people in Tallinn in protest against the new Estonian language law.

Latvian Popular Front A Latvian nationalist movement seeking greater autonomy for Latvia.

Lithuanian Restructuring Movement (Sajudis) A Lithuanian nationalist movement which came to prominence in 1989 when it won 36 of the 42 contested seats in the Congress of People's Deputies. Although originally a party of reform in support of perestroika, Sajudis ("movement") later came to be associated with the drive towards independence from the Soviet Union. In February 1990 Sajudis won a decisive victory over the Communist Party in elections to the Supreme Soviet in Vilnius.

Midnight Party A nickname for Lithuanian Communists who chose to remain within the Communist Party of the Soviet Union.

Molotov–Ribbentrop Pact A non-aggression pact signed by the foreign ministers of Germany and the USSR on 23 August 1939. Secret protocols attached to the pact and to a Nazi friendship treaty signed a month later on 28 September divided Eastern Europe into Soviet and German spheres of influence, providing a pretext for the Soviet annexation of the Baltic states in 1940.

Moscow, Treaty of A treaty signed in July 1920 bringing to an end hostilities between Russia and Lithuania. At war with Poland, the Bolsheviks recognized the sovereignty of Lithuania and its possession of Vilnius.

perestroika A process of socio-economic restructuring and reform initiated by Mikhail Gorbachev after he came to power in the Soviet Union in 1985.

Riga, Treaty of An agreement signed in August 1921 under which the Soviet government renounced all rights to Latvian territory.

Tartu, Treaty of A treaty signed in February 1920 under which the Soviet government renounced all rights to Estonian territory.

■ Further reading

A. Bilmanis, *A History of Latvia*, Princeton University Press, Princeton, New Jersey, 1951

Andres Kung, *A Dream of Freedom: Four Decades of National Survival Versus Russian Imperialism in Estonia, Latvia and Lithuania*, Boreas, Cardiff, 1980

R.J. Misiunas and R. Taagepera, *The Baltic States: Years of Dependence 1940–1989*, Hurst, London, 1983

T.U. Raun, *Estonia and the Estonians*, Hoover Institute Press, Stanford University, California, 1987

S. Vardys and R.J. Misiunas (eds.), *The Baltic States in Peace and War, 1917–45*, Pennsylvania State University Press, Pennsylvania, 1978

2
Armenia/Azerbaijan

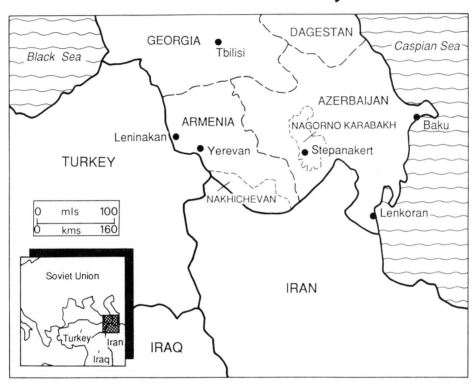

■ Profile

Armenia

- **Status:** Union republic of the USSR
- **Area:** 29 800km²
- **Population:** 3 412 000
- **Ethnic groups:** Armenians 89.7%, Azerbaijanis 5.3%, Russians 2.3%, Kurds 1.7%
- **Capital:** Yerevan

Azerbaijan

- **Status:** Union republic of the USSR
- **Area:** 86 600km²
- **Population:** 6 811 000
- **Ethnic groups:** Azerbaijanis 78.1%, Armenians 7.9%, Russians 7.9%, Daghestanis 3.4%
- **Capital:** Baku

Introduction

The outbreak of virtual civil war between the Soviet republics of Armenia and Azerbaijan in the late 1980s provided a vivid demonstration of how long-suppressed national aspirations and antagonisms are liable to reassert themselves when constraints are relaxed. In both republics Mikhail Gorbachev's new *glasnost* freedoms not only revealed general dissatisfaction with communist rule but also enabled the Christian Armenians and the Muslim Azeris to rediscover publicly their ancestral fear and hatred of one another. Among the Azeris the relaxation of Moscow's iron grip also accentuated a turning southward to the Muslim world and to their ethnic kin in northern Iran. Among Armenians it revived hopes of genuine nationhood, after centuries of subjection to alien rule, chronic persecution and global dispersal.

It is a matter of special pride to Armenians that in 301 the ancient Armenian kingdom was the first state to adopt Christianity as its official religion. That the Armenian Catholic Church was independent of Rome and Constantinople reflected the kingdom's long autonomy within the Roman Empire. This ended when Armenia was partitioned between the Eastern (Byzantine) and Persian empires in 387, after which many Armenians in the latter were massacred by their new Zoroastrian rulers. Having regained autonomy in the 9th century, the Byzantine part of Armenia, like the Empire itself, came under pressure from the Seljuk Turks in the 11th but survived as two separate kingdoms. Twice devastated by Mongol hordes in the 13th and 14th centuries, Greater Armenia succumbed in the 15th to the Ottoman Turks, who had already overrun Little Armenia. By the late 16th century the Turks had extended their eastern frontiers at Persia's expense to encompass all of ancient Armenia. Later, Turks and Persians fiercely contested control of the lands west of the Caspian Sea where Muslim Azeri tribes predominated. In the 18th century, however, Turkish/Persian rivalries were overtaken by the rapid expansion southwards of imperial Russia.

By 1828 Russia had acquired by war or treaty most of modern Soviet Transcaucasia, including present-day Soviet Armenia and Azerbaijan. But much conflict was to come over national borders, not least because the bulk of the Armenian people remained under despotic Turkish rule. That Christian Armenians had taken advantage of Muslim torpor to prosper as merchants was an old source of Turkish grievance. When awakened Armenian nationalism gave an extra dimension to the religious divide, the position of Armenians became precarious. Armenian hopes of independence were dashed at the 1878 Congress of Berlin, which awarded another piece of Turkish Armenia to Russia. Thereafter the accelerating break-up of the empire in the west strengthened Turkey's resolve, as represented by the nationalism of "Young Turks" in the officer class, to defend its Asia Minor heartland at all costs. When Armenian nationalists took to armed struggle in the 1890s, they provoked Turks into the first Armenian massacre of modern times. The great powers responded with only moral disapproval, mainly because Russia had no wish to encourage nationalism among its own Armenian subjects. Instead, Russia concentrated on quelling early clashes between its Azeri and Armenian subjects and planning expansion southwards into Azeri-populated northern Persia.

Turkey's alliance with the Central powers in World War I brought more misery for its Armenians, who were seen as a fifth column ready to assist Russian designs on Constantinople in return for statehood. The resultant Turkish final solution involved mass deportation and slaughter of Armenians in 1915. In 1917 prospects brightened when Russia's new Bolshevik regime withdrew from the war and accepted German terms which included withdrawal from Transcaucasia. Russian Armenia became a German-controlled republic and Armenians co-operated in putting down a revolt by Azeris. The Central powers' defeat in 1918 gave even more hope to Armenians, who declared an independent Greater Armenia uniting the Turkish and ex-Russian regions and secured Western recognition in 1920. However, the revitalized Turkey of Kemal Atatürk, in alliance with the Soviet Bolsheviks, speedily crushed the new state. As with previous

Turkish massacres, the numbers killed are still disputed. Suffice it to say that the 1920 campaign completed the virtual elimination of Armenians from Turkey. Those who escaped the killing took refuge across the Soviet border (restored to the pre-1878 line) or were dispersed in exile around the world. Meanwhile, Azeri hopes of independence had also been thwarted. By 1922 Bolshevik rule had been consolidated throughout the region, within the modern Soviet borders with Turkey and Persia/Iran.

Soviet rule in Armenia and Azerbaijan had to contend with two main problems. Firstly, the Soviet–Persian border divided the Azeri people, who still aspired to unity and independence. The division therefore posed a threat to Soviet Azerbaijan, where the Baku oilfields became vital for the Soviet Union's programme of rapid industrialization. Secondly, it was impossible to draw boundaries for the new Armenian and Azerbaijan Soviet Socialist Republics in which all of the historic lands of the two peoples could be made co-terminous. The solution adopted, after much dispute, was to make the Armenian-populated enclave of Nagorno-Karabakh, situated in Azerbaijani territory, an autonomous region of Azerbaijan, while Azeri-populated Nakhichevan, on the Soviet borders with Persia and Turkey, became an autonomous republic attached to Soviet Azerbaijan, from which it was separated by Armenian territory. At the same time, many Armenians continued to live in Azerbaijan, as did Azeris in Armenia. The scenario for conflict was therefore in place, although for 60 years the rigidities of communist rule kept the lid on local tensions.

Soviet sensitivities remained high on the Persian border issue, particularly in times of crisis. Soviet forces occupied northern Persia (and Britain the south) during World War II and withdrew in 1946 only after Western pressure had been exerted. Disappointed in its aim of recovering the area of former Turkish Armenia restored to Turkey in 1921, Moscow gave some backing to Azeri separatists in Iran (as Persia had become) against the pro-Western regime of the Shah. But this was a dangerous game in view of the impact which revived Azeri nationalism might one day have in Soviet Azerbaijan. In Soviet Armenia, the national question was largely defused in the post-war era by effective local autonomy (albeit communist-controlled) and by full recognition of Armenian language and culture. Nevertheless, the emergence in the 1970s of militant nationalist groups among Armenians in exile, notably in Lebanon, showed that the Armenian question had not been solved to universal satisfaction. Although such groups concentrated their terrorism on Turkey as the alleged perpetrator of genocide against the Armenian people, their programme for a restored Armenia within its ancient borders could not fail to strike a chord among Soviet Armenians.

The event which finally shattered Soviet complacency that the regional status quo was immutable was the 1979 Islamic revolution in Iran. It was all the more destabilizing for having been a long time in coming. Suddenly Moscow faced the grim prospect of Iranian-style fundamentalism infecting its own Muslim southern republics, with Azerbaijan especially vulnerable because of its cross-border links. That the new regime in Teheran was even more hostile to Azeri separatism than its predecessor served only to strengthen these links. To compound its new problems, the Soviet Union's invasion of Afghanistan in late 1979 (*see section 3.1*) was seen in much of the Islamic world as a continuation of pre-1917 Russian encroachment on the Muslim south. Against this background, a post-1979 upsurge of nationalism among Soviet Azerbaijan's Muslims revived old fears in Soviet Armenia, focusing on the highly sensitive issue of Nagorno-Karabakh. When the post-1985 Gorbachev reforms removed the chains on freedom of expression, a massive popular movement developed for the transfer of the enclave from Azerbaijan to Soviet Armenia.

Categorically rejected by Azerbaijan, the Armenian demand inexorably led to full-scale confrontation between the two republics in 1988, amid escalating inter-ethnic atrocities where Armenians and Azeris were in close proximity. Forced to intervene directly, the Moscow government found itself powerless to impose a settlement, not least because of the collapse of communist authority in each republic. As the conflict worsened early in 1990, talk of outright secession mounted in Azerbaijan, while the new nationalist leaders of Armenia unilaterally declared Nagorno-Karabakh to be part of the Armenian Republic.

As elsewhere in the Soviet Union (*see section 5.1*), uncorking the bottle of democracy had unleashed a heady mixture of nationalism and separatism which threatened the very survival of the Soviet Union as a multinational empire, with unforeseeable regional and international consequences.

■ Chronology of events

AD 301   King Tiridates III is converted to Christianity by St Gregory the Illuminator and Armenia becomes the first kingdom to adopt Christianity as a state religion.

AD 387   Armenia is partitioned between Zoroastrian Persia and Christian Byzantium. Many Christians are massacred by the Persians.

AD 886   Armenia achieves autonomy for the first time in 900 years.

AD 912   King Sembat "the martyr" of Armenia is captured and beheaded by Youssouf the Turkish governor of Azerbaijan. This incident is a setback to Byzantium's efforts to establish its eastern frontier.

1080   Prince Reuben establishes the independent Armenian state of Cilicia (Little Armenia) in southern Turkey.

1375   The Armenian kingdom of Cilicia is captured by the Turks.

1405   The Ottoman Turks begin to invade Armenia.

1552   Under Ivan the Terrible, Russia begins its conquest of Muslim lands by capturing Kazan.

1590   After a 13–year war, the Turks, who now hold all of Armenia,   capture Georgia and Azerbaijan from the Persians. In succeeding centuries Persia, Turkey and later Russia struggle for control of the Transcaucasus.

1603   Abbas I, shah of Persia, regains control of Azerbaijan.

1813   Part of Persian Azerbaijan north of the Araks River is ceded to Russia under the Treaty of Gulistan.

1828   Under the terms of the Treaty of Turkamanchai, Russia completes its expansion into the Turkish and Persian Khanates of the Transcaucasus with the acquistion of part of Armenia and Nakhichevan.

1877–78   The Russo–Turkish war gives rise to Armenian aspirations of an independent "Greater Armenia", but at the end of the day the Congress of Berlin awards the regions of Kars, Ardahan and Batum to Russia.

1894–96   Following armed attacks by Armenian nationalists, the Turkish oppression of the Armenians begins and the first in a series of alleged massacres takes place. The great powers decline to intervene directly.

1905   During the first Russian revolution Armenians and Azeris clash in the streets of Baku.

1907   When Persia is partitioned into British and Russian spheres of influence, Persian Azerbaijan effectively comes under Russian control.

1915   The Turks accuse the Armenians of coming to the aid of the Russians during World War I and over 1 750 000 Armenians are forced at gunpoint to move into the deserts of Syria and Mesopotamia. In the process, some 600 000 Armenians are allegedly massacred.

1918   In March Russian communists join forces with Armenians to suppress a Muslim revolt. When the Turkish army occupies Baku in September, Azeris massacre thousands of Armenians in an act of revenge for the so-called "March days".

The Treaty of Brest–Litovsk in March establishes Russian Armenia as an independent republic under German control. Opposed to the Bolsheviks, the Caucasian states of Georgia, Armenia and Azerbaijan (with part of Persia's Azerbaijan province) declare their independence during April–May.

1919 The British forces occupying Transcaucasia depart in August following bitter clashes over the Armenian enclave of Nagorno–Karabakh. The British military administration awards the enclave to the Azeris.

1920 The Treaty of Brest–Litovsk is superseded by the Treaty of Sèvres which establishes an independent Greater Armenia over both Russian and Turkish Armenia. The short-lived independence quickly comes to an end when Bolsheviks ally with Turkish Nationalists and recapture the Caucasus. Now in the hands of the communists, Russian Azerbaijan and Armenia are proclaimed Soviet Socialist Republics in April and November respectively. The communist leader of Azerbaijan agrees to hand Nagorno–Karabakh to the Armenians as a gesture of fraternal solidarity.

The Azeris in NW Iran stage an abortive uprising.

1921 Soviet governments are set up in Georgia, Armenia and Azerbaijan and under the terms of a Russo–Turkish treaty Kars and Ardahan are returned to Turkey in a process that lays down the present frontier between the two countries.

1922–36 Azerbaijan and Armenia join the Soviet Union as constituent administrative divisions within the Transcaucasian Soviet Federal Socialist Republic.

1923 After three years of confusion Stalin, then Lenin's Commissar for Nationalities, awards the predominantly Armenian enclave of Nagorno–Karabakh to Azerbaijan with the status of an Autonomous Region.

1924 In February Nakhichevan is established as an Autonomous Republic attached to Azerbaijan.

1928 The Iranian province of Azerbaijan is divided into the two provinces of East and West Azerbaijan.

1936 Russian Azerbaijan and Armenia become separate constituent republics of the Soviet Union under the new "democratic" constitution.

1941 Soviet troops occupy Iranian Azerbaijan.

1946 Soviet troops withdraw from Iranian Azerbaijan in May after an autonomous local government is established, but in November the independence of Azerbaijan is abruptly terminated when Iranian troops reoccupy the region and suppress the autonomous movement.

1969 The Abkhazians, who number just over 250 000, are the first Soviet Muslims to demonstrate against so-called Moscow–inspired repression. Ethnic unrest between Christian Georgians and Muslim Abkhazians in the Black Sea coastal resort of Sukhumi is brutally crushed by Soviet troops.

1975 The emigration of Armenians to the West is opposed by Armenian terrorist organizations who bomb the headquarters of the World Council of Churches in Beirut. The attack illustrates the emergence of several Armenian terrorist groups based in Lebanon and elsewhere, committed mainly to action against Turkish targets.

1979 The Islamic revolution in Iran heightens differences between the Azeri minority and the Iranian central government. The fear of nationalist fragmentation prompts the Khomeini regime to ban the use of the Azeri Turkish language in education and the media.

1980 Azeris in the Iranian city of Tabriz renew their demands for regional autonomy and take up arms in support of their spiritual leader Kazem Shariat–Madari.

1985 President Gorbachev sacks Geydar Aliev, the hardline Azeri political leader of the Transcaucasus. Armenians take advantage of the new era of *glasnost* and begin publicly to demand the incorporation of Nagorno–Karabakh into their republic.

1986 Over 100 000 Armenians sign a petition to President Gorbachev on the Nagorno–Karabakh question. There is minimal official response.

1988 On 12,18 and 20 February thousands of Armenians turn out in Yerevan to demand the return of Nagorno–Karabakh and the closure of a chemical plant near the town. Although the demonstrations in Yerevan are halted when Gorbachev agrees to take personal control of the issue, ethnic riots break out between Azeris and Armenians in the Azeri city of Sumgait. A curfew is imposed and by 4 March 32 people are reported to have been killed. As the situation deteriorates, over 5000 Soviet troops are sent to the region to contain the ethnic unrest between Christian Armenians and Muslim Azeris.

By the end of the year 158 000 Armenians have fled from Azerbaijan and 140 000 Azeris have left Armenia.

In December 49 senior Armenian Communist Party officials are removed. In the same month, 250 000 die when a massive earthquake hits Armenia.

1989 In January Nagorno–Karabakh is placed under direct rule from Moscow as attempts are made to find a solution to the problem. Meanwhile, a wave of strikes

and demonstrations begin to take place in Azerbaijan where the unofficial Popular Front organizes public protests demanding that Azerbaijan be given greater autonomy and that Nagorno–Karabakh be kept within their republic.

On 23 October the nationalist Azerbaijani Popular Front is legalized by the Supreme Soviet of Azerbaijan. In the republic of Armenia the Armenian Pan–National Movement is given similar recognition.

Moscow ends direct rule of Nagorno–Karabakh on 28 November and on 1 December Armenia declares the region part of a "unified Armenian Republic". When the Armenian Supreme Soviet votes not to ban the Communist Party a few days later, thousands of people come out onto the streets to demonstrate.

By the end of the year Nagorno–Karabakh is virtually isolated by an Azeri rail and road blockade. Armenian nationalists form themselves into armed militia groups.

1990 Clashes between Azeris and Armenians escalate, and in January the Azeri enclave of Nakhichevan unilaterally declares independence. In an attempt to bring an end to the violent clashes between Azeris and Armenians, the Baltic Council offers to mediate and arranges talks between representatives of the Armenian Pan–National Movement and the Azerbaijani Popular Front.

■ Who's who

Abdul Hamid II Sultan of the Ottoman Empire from 1876 until deposed in 1909. During his reign Armenians were subjected to a series of repressive measures and alleged massacres.

Aliev, Geydar Hardline communist political boss in the Transcaucasus whose dismissal by President Gorbachev in 1985 paved the way for ethnic conflict between Azeris and Armenians.

Arutyunyan, Suren First Secretary of the Armenian Communist Party.

Arutyunyan, Usik Armenian Interior Minister reprimanded by the Supreme Soviet in 1988 for his failure in dealing with the ethnic unrest in Armenia.

Gorgesyan, Movses A leader of the unofficial Armenian Independence Movement, killed in a clash with Azeris in January 1990 near the border with Nakhichevan.

Kasparov, Garry International chess

champion, born in Baku of part Armenian parentage.

Kevorkov, Boris   First Secretary of the Communist Party in Nagorno–Karabakh from 1973 until his dismissal in 1988. Opposed to reunification with Armenia, he was replaced by Genrykh Pogosyan, an advocate of union.

Mamedov, Ekhsidar   A nationalist leader of the Azerbaijani Popular Front which has organized strikes and demonstrations demanding greater autonomy for Azerbaijan and assurances that Nagorno–Karabakh will not be separated from the republic. In January 1990 Mamedov was arrested while on a mission to Moscow.

Mutalibov, Ayaz   An engineer in an electrical appliance factory who worked his way through the party apparatus to become Prime Minister of Azerbaijan in February 1989.

Shariat–Madari, Ayatollah Kazem   Spiritual leader of the Shia Muslim Azeris of Iran.

Supported by the minority Muslim People's Republican party, Shariat–Madari found himself opposed to the views of Ayatollah Khomeini after the 1979 Islamic Revolution. When his home in Qom was attacked by Revolutionary Guards in 1980 a wave of riots took place in the city of Tabriz where Azeri demonstrators renewed their demands for regional autonomy.

Vazgen I   The respected Supreme Patriarch of the Armenian Church who asked President Gorbachev in February 1988 to personally intercede in favour of the Armenians of Nagorno–Karabakh.

Vezirov, Abdul Rakhman   First Secretary of the Azerbaijan Communist Party from May 1988 until January 1990 when he was dismissed for losing control of the situation in Azerbaijan.

Volsky, Arkady   A Soviet official appointed by the Communist Party central committee to administer Nagorno–Karabakh during the period of direct rule from Moscow in 1989.

■ Key places

Araks or **Aras** (Turkish)   A river that rises in the mountains of Turkish Armenia and flows 900km eastwards to the Caspian Sea. For part of its course it follows the frontier between Iran and the Soviet republics of Armenia and Azerbaijan. That part of Persian Azerbaijan north of the Araks was ceded to Russia in 1813 and 1828. In 1989–90 hundreds of Soviet Azeris attempted to forge a link with their allies in Iran when they started to build a bridge across the Araks River 10km west of the Iranian town of Poldasht.

Artsakh   The Armenian name for Nagorno–Karabakh.

Azerbaijan, East   A province of NW Iran created in 1928 when the former province of Azerbaijan was divided in two; area 67 102km²; population (1982) 3 198 000. Its capital is Tabriz.

Azerbaijan, West   A province of NW Iran; area 38 850km²; population (1982) 1 408 000. Its capital is Orumiyeh.

Baku   Seaport capital of the Soviet republic of Azerbaijan, situated on the Apsheron peninsula on the W coast of the Caspian Sea; population (1987) 1 741 000. A centre of Russia's oil refining and petrochemical industries, Baku is connected by oil pipeline to Batum on the Black Sea. When oil was discovered in the 1920s, the Baku region quickly prospered as the world's first major exporter of petroleum.

Caucasus or **Kavkaz**   A mountain range separating Europe from Asia and rising to a height of 5642m at Mt Elbrus which is the highest peak in Europe. The Greater Caucasus (Bolshoy Kavkaz) stretches from Sochi on the Black Sea to Baku on the Caspian Sea. To the south, the Lesser Caucasus (Malyy Kavkaz) extends from the SE corner of the Black Sea through Soviet Armenia to the northern frontier of Iran.

Cilicia or **Little Armenia** A region of southern Turkey that became an independent Armenian state in 1080. The Armenians maintained their independence against the Turks until overrun by the Mamelukes in 1375. A mountain pass known as the Cilician Gates crosses the Taurus Mountains, linking Cilicia with Cappadocia.

Echmiadzin A monastery near Yerevan in Soviet Armenia. The seat of the principal See of the Armenian Apostolic Church.

Gandzha or **Kirovabad** The second largest city of the Azerbaijan republic, situated on the Gandzha River, 176km south-east of Tiflis. Once the capital of the Gandzha Khanate, it was incorporated into Russia in 1804 and named Elizavetpol. In 1920 its name was changed to Gandzha and in 1935 it was renamed Kirovabad. In December 1989 its name reverted to Gandzha.

Khutor An Armenian shanty town on the northern edge of the city of Baku. Most of its Armenian residents fled from the city in the face of Azeri pogroms during 1989–90.

Leninakan Known as Aleksandropol until 1924, Leninakan developed from a Turkish fortress town into an industrial city with a population of 218 000. The city is situated 10km from the Turkish frontier in the Soviet republic of Armenia. In 1926 Leninakan was destroyed by a major earthquake. In December 1988 the city was once more devastated by an earthquake that cost the lives of some 25 000 people.

Lenkoran A seaport in SE Azerbaijan, situated on the south-west coast of the Caspian Sea, close to the frontier with Iran; In January 1990 radical members of the nationalist Azerbaijani Popular Front took control of the city.

Nagorno–Karabakh or **Artsakh** (Armenian) A mountainous autonomous region within the Soviet Socialist Republic of Azerbaijan, situated in the southern foothills of the Caucasus mountains, midway between the Black Sea

and the Caspian Sea. Formerly a khanate, it became an autonomous region of the Soviet Union in 1923; area 4 400km^2; population (1987) 180 000. Its capital is Stepanakert. Although it lies within the predominantly Muslim republic of Azerbaijan, the region has a largely Armenian population estimated at just over 75 per cent of the total. Since 1985 the Armenians have publicly demanded the incorporation of Nagorno–Karabakh into their republic. The resulting ethnic conflict forced the Soviet government to bring the region under direct rule from Moscow in 1989.

Nakhichevan An autonomous Soviet socialist republic of the USSR on the frontier with Turkey and Iran (with which it shares a 140–km border); area 5 500km^2; population (1987) 278 000. Its capital is Nakhichevan. The region was annexed from Persia by Russia under the 1828 Treaty of Turkamanchai. Although it has formed part of the Soviet Socialist Republic of Azerbaijan since 1923, it is physically separated from that republic by a 50–km–wide strip of Armenia. In 1924 it was given its present autonomous status. About 85 per cent of the population are devoutly Muslim Azeris whose expression of kinship with Iranian Azeris has led to conflict with Armenians and attempts to build bridges across the Araks River into Iran. In January 1990 Nakhichevan was the first territory unilaterally to declare its independence from the Soviet Union since the Bolshevik Revolution of 1917.

Shusha A town in Nagorno–Karabakh, just to the south of Stepanakert. A stronghold of the Azeri minority in that region, the town was sacked in 1905. In 1988 the town was again the scene of conflict between resident Azeris and Armenians.

Stepanakert Capital city of the Autonomous Region of Nagorno–Karabakh; population (1985) 33 000. Originally known as Khankendy, the city was renamed in the 1930s after Stepan Shaumyan, a Baku revolutionary.

Sumgait An industrial city with steel, iron and aluminium works in the Soviet republic of Azerbaijan, situated on the west coast of the Caspian Sea, 45km north-west of Baku;

population (1987) 234 000. The scene of ethnic riots in February 1988 between the Azeri majority and Armenian minority.

Transcaucasia or **Russia–beyond–the–Caucasus**   A division of the Russian Empire constituted in 1846. Between 1922 and 1936 the republics of Armenia and Azerbaijan formed constituent parts of the larger Transcaucasian Soviet Federal Socialist Republic. Lying to the south of the Caucasus mountains, the Transcaucasus is a term now generally applied to the geographical region encompassing the Soviet republics of Armenia and Azerbaijan.

Yerevan or **Erivan**   Capital city of the Soviet republic of Armenia, situated on the Razdan River, 15km from the Turkish frontier. At the centre of a vodka and wine producing region, Yerevan was severely damaged by an earthquake in December 1988.

■ Key words

Armenian Apostolic Church   The national church of Armenia. Led by a Supreme Patriarch, the independent Armenian Apostolic Church has been a potent force in shaping the national and political culture of the Armenians since their conversion to Christianity at the begining of the 4th century AD. Although theologically the Armenian Church is one, administratively it is fragmented. The See of Echmiadzin, which is based in Soviet Armenia, encompasses the Armenian diaspora in Russia, Europe, Australia, South America and parts of North America. The See of Cilicia–Antelias, based in Beirut, controls Armenian religious institutions in Lebanon, Syria, Iraq, Iran, Venezuela and parts of North America. The Patriarchs of Jerusalem and Constantinople (Istanbul) administer separately their own small spheres of influence.

Armenian Pan–National Movement   An international political movement representing Armenians throughout the world. Officially recognized by the Supreme Soviet of the Armenian Republic, it held its first congress in Yerevan during November 1989.

Armenian Popular Movement for Lebanon   The political front for the ASALA amongst the Armenians in Lebanon.

Armenian Revolutionary Army   An Armenian terrorist organization responsible for periodic acts of political violence which have included a suicide commando raid on the Turkish embassy in Lisbon in 1983.

Armenian Secret Army for the Liberation of Armenia (ASALA)   A small Armenian terrorist group which began a campaign of political violence in 1975 with the bombing of the Beirut headquarters of the World Council of Churches.

Armenians   People of the Thraco–Phrygian ethnolinguistic group whose traditional homeland was centred on the Anatolian plains of northern Turkey, but whose culture today thrives further east in the Soviet Transcaucasus. Adhering to a form of Orthodox Christianity, the Armenian diaspora has spread throughout the world from Australia to Venezuela.

Azerbaijan Popular Movement   A political front organization representing the Azeri people. Officially recognized by the Supreme Soviet of the Republic of Azerbaijan in October 1989, the movement advocates political and economic autonomy for Azerbaijan as well as control over Nagorno–Karabakh. During 1989 the movement organized demonstrations and a general strike in Baku in protest against Armenian demands for a "unified Armenian Republic" including Nagorno–Karabakh. In February 1990 representatives of the Azerbaijan Popular Movement and the Armenian Pan–National Movement meet in the Baltic city of Riga to discuss the ethnic conflict in the Transcaucasus.

Azeris   The native Muslim inhabitants of Azerbaijan, occupying a region encompassing NW Iran and the adjacent border area within the Soviet Union. With a population variously estimated between five and ten million, the Azeris are the largest ethnic minority in Iran. Unlike the Kurdish and Baluchi minorities, the Azeri Turks or Azerbaijanis adhere to the Shia Muslim sect.

Brest-Litovsk, Treaty of   A treaty of 1918 by which Soviet Armenia was made an independent republic under German auspices.

Catholicos The head of the Armenian Apostolic Church.

Federation of Armenian Revolutionaries (ARF)   An Istanbul–based Armenian political organization founded in 1890 and responsible for periodic acts of political terrorism.

Gulistan, Treaty of   A treaty of 1813 under which the Russians gained control of part of Persian Azerbaijan north of the Araks River.

Interior Ministry (MVD)   Charged with maintaining order within the Soviet Union, the MVD deploys about 340 000 troops backed by tanks throughout the country. Over 5000 MVD personnel are committed to the task of keeping hostile partisan groups from killing each other in the republics of Armenia and Azerbaijan.

Karabakh Committee   An unofficial Armenian organization in Yerevan supporting the union of Nagorno–Karabakh with Armenia. The eleven leaders of this group responsible for promoting strikes and demonstrations were arrested during December 1988–January 1989.

millett   A community of Armenians, defined by their adherence to the Armenian Apostolic faith.

Pamyat ("Memory") **Society**   An unofficial Russian nationalist organization established in the early 1980s by people wanting to prevent the destruction of Russia's cultural and historical heritage.

pogrom   Originally used to describe the organized massacre of Jews in Russia during 1905–06, the term has more recently been applied to the Azeri repression of the ethnic Armenian minorities in the cities of Azerbaijan.

self–defence units   Armed civilian militia units sent into Azerbaijan in 1990 to protect Armenian communities,

Sèvres, Treaty of   A treaty of 1920 under which Turkish and Russian Armenia were joined to create an independent Greater Armenia. The treaty superceded the 1918 Brest–Litovsk arrangement, but with the recapture of Soviet Armenia by the Bolsheviks it was never fully implemented.

Social–Democratic Hunchag Party   An Armenian underground political organization founded in 1887. With a leadership based in Istanbul, this group has been responsible for periodic political violence.

soviet ("council")   A governing council of the Soviet Union or any of its constituent republics. In Nagorno–Karabakh the powers of the regional soviet were suspended between January and November 1989 when direct rule from Moscow was imposed.

Turkamanchai, Treaty of   A treaty of 1828 under which the Azeri region of Nakhichevan was annexed by Russia.

■ Further reading

D.M. Lang, *The Armenians, a People in Exile*, Unwin, London, 1981

Minority Rights Group, Report No. 32, *The Armenians*, London, 1987

J. Missakian, *A Searchlight on the Armenian Question, 1878–1950*, Boston, 1950

H. Myklebost, Armenia and the Armenians, *Norsk Geografisk Tidsskrift*, 43(3), 1989, pp. 135–54

Ronald G. Suny, *Transcaucasia: Nationalism and Social Change, Essays on the History of Armenia, Azerbaijan and Georgia*, Ann Arbor University, Michigan, 1983

Amir Taheri, *Crescent in a Red Sky: The Future of Islam in the Soviet Union*, Hutchinson, London, 1989

C. Walker, *Armenia: The Survival of a Nation*, Croom Helm, London, 1980

3
Romania

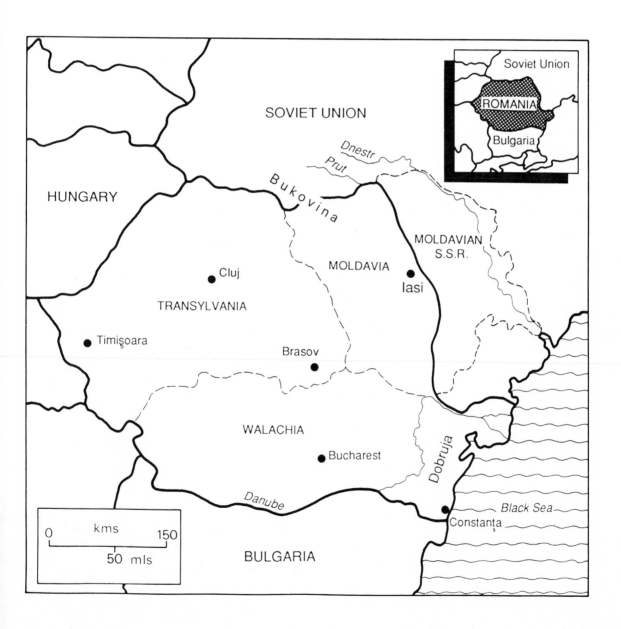

■ Profile

- **Area:**   237 500km²
- **Population (1988):**   23 041 000
- **Ethnic groups:**   Romanian 89.1%, Hungarian 7.8%, German 1.5%, Russian, Ukrainian, Serb, Croat, Gypsy, Turk 1.6%
- **Religion:**   Romanian Orthodox 80%, Roman Catholic 6%
- **Languages:**   Romanian, Hungarian, German
- **Life expectancy:**   72 years
- **Infant mortality rate:**   24 per 1000
- **Administrative divisions:**   40 counties (*judet*) and one municipality (*municipiu*)
- **Currency:**   leu of 100 bani
- **Timezone:**   GMT +2
- **Capital:**   Bucharest
- **Chief cities:**   Bucharest (2 272 500), Brasov (346 600), Constanța (323 200), Timisoara (319 000)

■ Introduction

Soviet hegemony over Eastern Europe after World War II served to call a halt to the bitter territorial and national conflicts which had repeatedly rent the region asunder over centuries. Yet just as Soviet-backed communist regimes could never completely extinguish the flame of democracy, so antagonisms from a previous era never died. Prime cases in point are Romania's two major territorial/national issues. One involves Romania's sovereignty over Transylvania and its treatment of the region's large ethnic Hungarian minority. The other concerns the status of the ethnic Romanian majority of Bessarabia, now part of Soviet Moldavia. When the post-war order began to crumble in Eastern Europe in the late 1980s, both questions returned to the international spotlight.

The Transylvania dispute involves radically different versions of history. Romanians claim descent from the Dacians of the Roman Empire (and thus insist on "Romania" rather than "Rumania"), contending that Dacian Romans preserved their language and culture in Transylvanian strongholds after the legions had been forced to retreat south of the Danube by the barbarian invasions of the 3rd century AD. According to this version, the sub-Danubian Dacians, who joined the Eastern Roman (Byzantine) Empire and embraced the Greek Orthodox faith, later moved back across the Danube into what became Moldavia and Walachia to form the Romanian nation with their Transylvanian cousins. The Hungarian version is that only Slavonic tribes were in possession when King Stephen conquered Transylvania in 1003 and initiated Magyar (*Szekler*) and Saxon German colonization. Romanians, say Hungarians, did not begin to cross the Carpathians into Transylvania until the 13th century, when they arrived as nomads with the permission of Magyar rulers who later exercised suzerainty over Moldavia and Walachia. Romanians retort that both principalities enjoyed long periods of effective independence in the 13th to 15th centuries and that Transylvania formed part of these historic Romanian lands.

Whatever the historical truth, Transylvania in the Middle Ages was not only physically separated from the lands south and east of the Carpathians but also ethnically and culturally distinct, albeit very mixed. Its Magyar rulers and German settlers looked to the Catholic west, while Moldavia and Walachia had a vibrant Byzantine inheritance. The era of Ottoman rule accentuated the differences. By the early 16th century the Hungarian dominions had all fallen to the Turks, but Transylvania retained exceptional autonomy and thus ensured the continuity of the Hungarian state. This role continued when, at the end of the 17th century, Transylvania and Hungary passed to Austrian Hapsburg rule, whereas Moldavia and Walachia continued under Ottoman suzerainty. When they finally achieved full independence as Romania in 1878, Transylvania had already been incorporated into the Hungarian part of the Austro–Hungarian Empire, although Romanians clearly formed a majority in the province. Also excluded from Romania was Moldavia east of the River Pruj, i.e., Bessarabia. For a century or more, Russia had combined its role as "protector" of its Moldavian and Walachian co-religionists with territorial designs on the decaying Ottoman Empire. The detaching of Bessarabia from Moldavia had been one of its aims, first achieved in 1812 and confirmed in 1878 by the Congress of Berlin.

The result was that Romanian irredentism, in both west and east, governed the new state's foreign policy. Its chance came in World War I, in which it opted for the winning Anglo-French side and Russia was weakened by defeat and revolution. Despite a calamitous military effort, Romania's reward was a doubling of its territory, its three main prizes being Transylvania and Bukovina from the dismantled Austro–Hungarian Empire and Bessarabia from Russia. In the inter-war period Romania was courted for its oil and grain wealth and sought to play the powers off against one another. But "Greater Romania" was not to survive World War II. Following the conclusion of the 1939 Nazi–Soviet non-aggression pact, Romania was forced to cede a third of its territory in 1940, including Bessarabia and Northern Bukovina to the Soviet Union and Northern Transylvania to Hungary. The Soviet *démarche* brought to power a pro-Axis Romanian regime, which in 1941 joined the German-led invasion of Russia in quest of its eastern lands. But this time Romania had backed the wrong horse, although a late

change of sides in 1944, as the Red Army approached, retrieved something from the disaster. Under its 1947 peace treaty Romania recovered Northern Transylvania, whereas Soviet rule was confirmed in Bessarabia and Northern Bukovina.

The post-war establishment of communist rule in the Soviet sphere appeared to end centuries of territorial dispute in Eastern Europe. The latest Soviet-imposed changes were accepted as final by the regimes concerned, which all formally renounced territorial claims. In Transylvania an exodus of ethnic Germans strengthened the majority status of Romanians over ethnic Hungarians, even in the northern region held by Hungary during the war. Most of Bessarabia was incorporated into the Moldavian Soviet Socialist Republic, in which the Russification process first launched in the 19th century was intensified. Yet even the weight of communist ascendancy could not obliterate old aspirations and antagonisms. Russification was resisted by the Romanian majority in Soviet Moldavia, where nationalism remained a powerful force. As the Ceausescu regime distanced itself politically from Moscow, such sentiments found a growing semi-official irredentist response in Romania itself. Moreover, Hungarian–Romanian relations deterioated over the alleged mistreatment of Hungarians in Transylvania, who formed Europe's largest ethnic minority group.

The collapse of communism in Eastern Europe in 1989 and the resurgence of national unrest in the Soviet Union accelerated the reappearance of old national and territorial issues throughout the region. Those affecting Romania were among the most sensitive for regional stability. Although ethnic Hungarians played an important role in the overthrow of the Ceausescu regime, open conflict with Romanians soon followed, to the alarm of the new pluralist government in Hungary. In Soviet Moldavia, moreover, the Romanian revolution strengthened popular hopes of a change in the status quo.

■ Chronology of events

10th century Magyar settlers begin to move into Transylvania.

1003 King Stephen of Hungary conquers the province of Transylvania

12th century German settlers begin to arrive in Transylvania.

1365 Moldavia gains its independence from Hungary.

1369 Walachia obtains independence from Hungary.

1387–97 Moldavia, Walachia and Bessarabia come under Polish–Lithuanian rule.

1389 Walachia comes under Ottoman rule.

1504 Moldavia becomes a vassal state of the Ottoman Empire.

1526 King Louis of Hungary is defeated by the Turks at the Battle of Mohacs. Transylvania becomes a vassal state of the Ottoman Empire.

1699 The Austrians defeat the Turks and receive all of Hungary and the province of Transylvania under the terms of the Treaty of Karlowitz. Moldavia and Walachia remain under Turkish rule.

1777 The Austrians receive the province of Bukovina from the Turks.

1812 Under the Treaty of Bucharest Bessarabia is detached from the Turkish–ruled principality of Moldavia and ceded to Russia.

1829 Following a year–long war between Russia and Turkey the principalities of Moldavia and Walachia come under Russian influence.

1853 In July Russian troops occupy the Danube principalities. Three months later Turkey declares war on Russia.

1856 Under the Treaty of Paris which ends the Crimean War a strip of southern Bessarabia is returned to Moldavia. Moldavia and Walachia are placed under an international guarantee.

1859 The semi-independent state of Romania, still under nominal Turkish suzerainty, is created by the union of the former principalities of Moldavia and Walachia.

1867 Transylvania is incorporated into the Hungarian part of the newly- created Austro–Hungarian Empire.

1878 The full independence of Romania is recognized under the Treaty of Berlin but the the whole of Bessarabia is declared Russian territory.

1881 Prince Charles is declared king of a united Romania.

1883 Fearing Russian interference, the Romanian king establishes a secret alliance with Austria.

1913 In the second Balkan War Romania helps to defeat Bulgaria and obtains Southern Dobruja under the Treaty of Bucharest.

1916 Despite the 1883 alliance and attempts to remain neutral at the outset of World War I, Romania declares war on Austria–Hungary on 27 August. A day later the Romanian army invades Transylvania, but within weeks the Romanians suffer a humiliating defeat at the hands of Austro–German forces.

1917 Anti-Bolsheviks in Bessarabia set up a Council with a view to bringing about union with Romania.

1918 In May Romania signs a disadvantageous peace treaty with the Central Powers, but two days before the November Armistice re-enters the war on the side of the Allies and invades Transylvania once again. When hostilities end, Romania maintains its hold over the whole of Transylvania, Bukovina and Bessarabia. The

Soviet Union, however, does not recognize the Treaty of St Germain which formalizes the Romanian annexation of Bessarabia.

1924   The Soviet Union reasserts it right to Bessarabia by setting aside a narrow strip of Ukrainian territory to the east of the Dnestr for the establishment of an "Autonomous Moldavian Soviet Socialist Republic".

1933   In July Romania and the Soviet Union sign a non–aggression pact under which Romanian possession of Bessarabia is recognized.

1939   Nazi Germany and the Soviet Union sign a non-aggression pact with secret provisions for the division of Eastern Europe into "spheres of influence".

1940   In June Romania is forced to cede Bessarabia and Northern Bukovina to the Soviet Union, causing Romania to align with the Axis powers. Two months later, after the return of Southern Dobruja to Bulgaria, Romania transfers the northern two-thirds of Transylvania to Hungary under the German-arbitrated "Vienna Award". King Carol abdicates in favour of his son Michael in September.

1941   Romania enters World War II in June and, in return for supporting the German invasion of the Soviet Union, regains control over Bessarabia, Northern Bukovina and Southern Dobruja.

1944   With Romanian forces suffering heavy losses in fighting against the Red Army, King Michael dismisses the cabinet and accepts the terms of an armistice. Romania's surrender leads to the Russian occupation of Bucharest in August.

1945   A pro–communist National Democratic Front government is formed under the left–wing leadership of Petru Groza.

1947   Hungary and Romania sign peace treaties with the Allies in Paris. Under the terms of these agreements, Bessarabia and Northern Bukovina are returned to the Soviet Union and Southern Dobruja to Bulgaria, but Northern Transylvania is restored to Romania.

Under pressure from the communists, King Michael abdicates on 30 December.

1948   Following an election in which the People's Democratic Front receive 91 per cent of the votes, a Soviet–style constitution is adopted. The new Socialist Republic of Romania is a virtual satellite of the Soviet Union.

1958   On 26 July the government announces the withdrawal of Soviet occupation forces from Romania. Thereafter, measures are introduced suppressing the national identity of the Hungarian minority in Transylvania.

1963   Gheorghiu–Dej, premier of Romania since 1955, asserts Romania's independence from the Soviet Union.

1965   Following the death of Gheorghiu–Dej, Nicolae Ceausescu is elected Communist Party chief.

1967   Ceausescu is elected President of Romania.

1968   The Soviet invasion of Czechoslovakia prompts Ceausescu to step up his attempts to "improve the position of the Transylvanian Hungarians and Germans and cement national unity".

1977   Carol Kiraly, a party official of Hungarian extraction, alleges government repression of the Hungarians in Romania, but the government–sponsored Hungarian and German national councils do not support his contention that ethnic minorities are subject to discrimination.

1978   Three prominent members of the Hungarian community including Deputy Premier Janos Fazekas, send separate appeals to government leaders protesting against discriminatory policies towards minority groups. Although the Hungarian government makes no official comment on the ethnic minority issue, the newspapers of Hungary and Romania focus on the problem.

During April new constitutions extending the rights of national minorities are promulgated in each of the union republics of the Soviet Union. In the Moldavian SSR the new constitution provides for the publication of laws, decrees and other notices in both the Russian and Moldavian languages.

1982 Relations between Hungary and Romania are strained when allegations are made in Hungary of official Romanian discrimination against the Transylvania Hungarians.

1983 In March the Foreign Ministers of Hungary and Romania agree that the ethnic minority problem must be solved by diplomatic means, but the Hungarian press criticizes what it views as distinctly nationalist celebrations to mark the 65th anniversary of Transylvania's union with Romania.

1984 In September a delegation of Romanian officials visiting Hungary is presented with a 12–page document outlining ways in which the position of the Hungarians in Transylvania could be improved. Later in the same month, the parliamentary assembly of the Council of Europe calls on the Romanian government to respect the rights of ethnic minorities. Despite this criticism, Romanian officials refuse to admit that there is any discrimination against the Transylvanian Hungarians.

In December the polemics that have developed between newspapers and journals in Romania and Hungary reach a climax when the Romanian news agency strongly criticizes a Hungarian journal for publishing articles that support Hungary's claim to the Hungarian–inhabited areas of Northern Transylvania. The ruling Hungarian Socialist Workers' Party for the first time raises the issue of Hungarian minorities abroad when it publishes a document in which it is stated that "citizens of Hungarian nationality in neighbouring countries should be permitted to develop fully their national culture and to use their mother tongue".

1985 A memorandum protesting at discrimination against ethnic minorities is compiled by Transylvanian Hungarians

and presented to the European Cultural Forum meeting in Budapest during October–November.

1986 Hungary joins Canada in sponsoring a resolution on the protection of national minorities submitted to a meeting of the Conference on Security and Co-operation in Europe (CSCE) which is held in Vienna during November.

1987 In February a three–volume history of Transylvania published by the Hungarian Academy of Science is publicly condemned by President Ceausescu. A month later, in a television interview, the Hungarian Secretary of State for Foreign Affairs draws attention to the plight of ethnic Hungarian minorities abroad although he does not specifically mention Romania.

In June senior officials from Romania and Hungary meet in Budapest in an attempt to defuse the tension over Northern Transylvania. The talks, which fail to ease the situation, are not helped when the Romanian government orders the closure of the Hungarian consulate in Cluj because of "unacceptable" behaviour by the consul.

Ceausescu faces growing discontent as a result of political repression and domestic austerity measures. In November food shortages trigger riots in the Transylvanian city of Brasov, but the unrest is quickly stiffled by the Securitate police.

1988 At the beginning of the year President Ceausescu initiates his grand rural "systematization plan" by which an estimated 8000 of Romania's 13 000 villages are to be demolished and replaced by 550 large-scale agro–industrial centres. This programme, which envisages the destruction of nearly half the Hungarian villages of Transylvania, receives widespread international condemnation. By the end of the year over 12 000 ethnic Hungarians have fled from Romania into Hungary.

1989 The Ceausescu regime, which is widely condemned for economic mismanagement, corruption and brutal repression, comes under growing pressure when an open letter criticizing government policy is published in March. Signed by six former communist party officials, the letter accuses Ceausescu of "discrediting socialism".

After three days of bitter debate, the parliament of the Soviet republic of Moldavia passes a controversial law making Moldavian the state language of the republic.

On 16 December a deportation order is served on the Protestant pastor, Fr Lazlo Tokes, who has attacked the Romanian government for its treatment of the Hungarian minority. This action results in a wave of civil unrest that culminates on 21–25 December in a bloody revolution which sees the overthrow of Ceausescu's communist regime. Both Nicolae Ceausescu and his wife Elena are captured and executed on 25 December after a brief trial held before a military tribunal.

1990 The National Salvation Front (NSF), which had taken control of the country after the revolution, struggles to maintain unity under growing criticism that its leading members are too closely associated with the former Ceausescu regime. Ethnic Hungarians begin to demand cultural and political rights as well as an end to Romanian immigration into Transylvania, but Romanian nationalists, particularly the extremist Vatra Romanesca, oppose the Hungarian demands which they interpret as nascent separatism. Violence explodes on the streets of Tirgu Mures when four leaders of the Hungarian Democratic Union are savagely attacked during the run–up to elections in May. In the ethnic unrest that follows three people die and scores are wounded. The overwhelming election victory of Ion Iliescu and his National Salvation Front only serves to heighten the traditional divisions in society.

■ Who's who

Bitaly, Odon Leader of the Hungarian Democratic Union, an ethnic Hungarian minority party based in Tirgu Mures.

Bobu, Emil A leading member of the Romanian Communist Party who headed a delegation to Budapest in June 1987 in an attempt to defuse the tension that had arisen between Hungary and Romania over the situation in Northern Transylvania.

Bodyul, Ivan The First Secretary of the Communist Party in the Soviet republic of Moldavia. Opposed to Romanian nationalism, Bodyul denounced those who endorsed the Romanian claim to Bessarabia.

Brucan, Professor Silviu A leading executive member of the National Salvation Front provisional government created after the fall of the Ceausescu regime on 25 December 1989.

Ceausescu, Elena The wife of President Nicolae Ceausescu. Elena Ceausescu held leading government appointments including the posts of First Deputy Premier and Chairman of the Science and Technology Council. Arrested on 22 December 1989, she was tried and then executed along with her husband.

Ceausescu, Nicolae President of Romania 1967–1989. Born of peasant stock in Scorniscesti in 1918, Ceausescu served his apprenticeship in the Communist Party through the Party's youth organization which he joined in 1933. In 1945 he became secretary of the Bucharest branch of the party and in 1950 he was appointed Deputy Minister of the Armed Forces. Joining the Central Committee in 1952, he eventually succeeded Gheorghiu–Dej as national First Secretary in 1965. Following his election to the state presidency in 1967 Ceausescu pursued a policy of Romanian nationalism and began to develop a strong personality cult that was backed by a powerful and repressive security apparatus. While initially maintaining friendly links with the West, he later became increasingly isolated following condemnation of human rights violations in Romania. His attempts to pay off Romania's foreign debt resulted in severe domestic austerity, a situation that ultimately led to his downfall in the revolution of December 1989. Captured near the city of Tirgoviste, Elena and Nicolae Ceausescu were brought back to Bucharest where they faced a military tribunal before being executed on 25 December.

Coposa, Corneliu   Leader of the National Peasant's Party whose opposition to the participation of the National Salvation Front provisional government in elections led to a massive demonstration in Bucharest on 29 January 1990. Born in 1916, Coposa supports the introduction of a free market economy.

Cornea, Doina   A former teacher of French at the University of Cluj where she became an outspoken dissident and critic of President Ceausescu in 1983. Under virtual house arrest, she was eventually imprisoned after distributing political pamphlets. Following the December 1989 revolution she opposed the decision of the National Salvation Front to turn itself into a political party.

Fazekas, Janos   A prominent representative of the ethnic Hungarian community and Deputy Premier of Romania. One of three leading members of the Romanian Communist Party who protested against the government's handling of the ethnic minority problem in April 1978.

Grossu, Semyon   Communist Party apparatchik put in charge of the Soviet Republic of Moldavia by President Brezhnev. His administration, which was marked by corruption, was eventually brought to an end in November 1989 after Moldavian nationalists disrupted the annual Revolution Day celebrations in Kishinev.

Hohenzollern, Michael   Ex–king of Romania. King Michael first came to the throne in 1927 at the age of six following the death of his grandfather and the abdication of his father. In 1930 his father King Carol II returned to take the throne, but abdicated again in 1940

after pursuing a disastrous foreign policy that led to the loss of Transylvania, Bessarabia and Southern Dobruja. King Michael held the throne until December 1947 when he was forced under communist pressure to abdicate and leave Romania.

Iliescu, Ion   A former Communist Party leader who held senior posts in regional administration before falling out with Ceausescu in the early 1980s. Iliescu, who had studied at Moscow university with Gorbachev, was named as President of the National Salvation Front government which took control of Romania on 25 December 1989.

Kiraly, Carol   A former high–ranking Romanian Communist Party official of Hungarian extraction who made allegations of discrimination against the Hungarian minority in an open letter sent to the party leadership in December 1977. Kiraly later became a Deputy President in the stop–gap National Salvation Front government that took power after the overthrow of the Ceausescu regime.

Lache, Stefan   Romanian historian and co-author with Gheorghe Tsutsiu of *Romania and the Paris Peace Conference of 1946*, a controversial book published in 1979 in which the Soviet Union was criticized for the way it had annexed Bessarabia and Northern Bukovina in 1946.

Mazilu, Dumitri   An international lawyer and former Romanian representative at the United Nations who had often criticized the human rights record of the Ceausescu regime. He was appointed Vice-President of the National Salvation Front government which took control of the country on 25 December 1989, but a month later, on 26 January, he resigned following a power struggle within the interim administration.

Milea, General Vasile   Romanian Defence Minister denounced on 22 December 1989 as a "traitor" by President Ceausescu who reported that he had committed "suicide". It later transpired that Milea had been shot by a presidential bodyguard after refusing to order troops to open fire on civilians who had gathered in Bucharest to demonstrate against the regime.

Ratiu, Ion Head of the British–based World Union of Free Romanians who attempted to become the presidential candidate of the National Peasant's Party in 1990.

Roman, Peter A former administrator at the Bucharest Polytechnic who was appointed Prime Minister of the interim National Salvation Front government when it took control of Romania on 25 December 1989.

Suto, Andreas A well-known ethnic Hungarian writer and poet who protested against government repression of ethnic minorities in April 1978. In April 1990 Suto lost an eye during the civil unrest that broke out between Romanians and Hungarians in Tirgu Mures.

Szürös, Matyas Secretary of the Hungarian Socialist Workers' Party who in June 1987 represented Hungary in talks with Romanian officials designed to defuse the tension between Romania and Hungary as a result of the situation in Northern Transylvania.

Takacs, Professor Lajos A former chancellor of the University of Cluj in Transylvania who protested against the government policy of discrimination against ethnic minorities in April 1978.

Tamás, Gáspár Miklós An ethnic Hungarian intellectual who in 1984 tried to draw the attention of the Western media to the repression of the Hungarian minority in Romania. Expelled from Romania, Tamás lived in exile in Budapest where he continued his outspoken campaign on behalf of the Transylvanian Hungarians.

Tokes, Fr Laszlo A Protestant pastor from Timisoara who suffered official harassment when he protested against government repression of ethnic Hungarians. When he was served with a deportation order on 16 December 1989 hundreds of people surrounded his house in an effort to prevent the police putting the order into effect. This incident sparked off a wave of unrest that finally led to the bloody revolution that toppled the Ceausescu regime.

Tsutsiu, Gheorghe Romanian historian and co-author with Stefan Lache of the controversial *Romania and the Paris Peace Conference of 1946*.

■ Key places

Bessarabia A strip of territory lying between the Dnestr and Prut rivers and bounded to the south and south–east by the Danube and the Black Sea; area 36 900km². Once an eastern division of the ancient Roman province of Dacia, it later came under Turkish rule as an eastern part of the autonomous principality of Moldavia. In 1812 Bessarabia was ceded to Russia under the terms of the Treaty of Bucharest and a process of Russification began, largely through the resettlement of Bulgarians, Germans, Cossacks and gypsies. Under the Treaty of Paris which ended the Crimean War in 1856, a southern strip of Bessarabia was returned to Moldavia, but in 1878 when the independence of Romania was finally recognized, the whole of Bessarabia was declared Russian territory once again.

In December 1918 Bessarabia was annexed by Romania and held until June 1940 when King Carol was forced to hand the territory back to the Soviet Union. Between 1941 and 1944 Romania held Bessarabia once more when it joined forces with Germany against the Soviet Union. Thereafter, most of Bessarabia was joined with the former Autonomous Moldavian SSR to become the Moldavian SSR, but a strip of land extending to 5000km² along the Black Sea coast was incorporated into the Ukraine.

Brasov Known as Kronstadt until 1918 and as Stalin between 1950 and 1960, Brasov is the leading city of Transylvania and the second largest city in Romania; population (1985) 346 600. The city is situated in the

Transylvanian Alps, 150km NNE of Bucharest. In November 1987 Brasov was the focal point of demonstrations that reflected a growing disenchantment with President Ceausescu's policies of political repression and economic austerity.

Bucharest or **Bucureşti** (Romanian)   The capital city of Romania, situated on a tributary of the Danube; population (1985) 1 975 800. An important commercial centre on the historic trade route to Constantinople (Istanbul), Bucharest became capital of Walachia in 1698 and capital of the independent state of Romania in 1861. Between 1948 and 1956 Bucharest was the headquarters of the Cominform international communist organization. Under the rule of Nicolae Ceausescu much of central Bucharest was demolished and replaced by modern boulevards and apartment blocks. The December 1989 revolution brought to an end most of Ceausescu's grandiose construction projects, the largest of which was the building of the vast "House of the Republic" which was to have been a presidential palace.

Bukovina   A territory of some 76 220km² which formed a province of Moldavia until 1777 when the Turks handed it over to the Austrians. After 1786 it came to be known as the circle of Chernowitz and in 1849 it was re-constituted as a duchy of Austria. In November 1919, following the break–up of the Austro–Hungarian Empire, Bukovina was annexed by Romania, but in 1940 the northern half of the region was ceded to the Soviet Union and absorbed into the Ukrainian SSR. The painted monasteries of Bukovina are an important element of European architecture.

Carpathian Mountains   A mountain system extending through the Ukraine and into Romania from the Czechoslovakian–Polish frontier. In Romania the Carpathians form a natural crescent–shaped boundary separating Transylvania from the rest of the country. The 1400km–long mountain system also forms the principal boundary between the watersheds of the Baltic and the Black Sea. Negoiul, rising to 2548m, is the highest peak in Romania. The southern arm of the Carpathians is often referred to as the Transylvanian Alps while the eastern mountains are known as the Romanian Carpathians.

Cluj–Napoca or **Kolozsvar** (Hungarian)   Formerly known as Klausenberg, the university city of Cluj–Napoca, is the cultural centre of Transylvania; population (1985) 310 000. The city, which has the largest Hungarian community in Romania, is situated on the Somes River, in the eastern foothills of the Apuseni mountains.

Constanţa or **Constanza**   Romania's principal port on the Black Sea. With a population (1985) of 323 200, it is the third largest city in Romania. Founded in the 7th century BC, the city became a Greek colony and the home of the exiled Roman poet Ovid. In the 4th century AD it was named after the Emperor Constantine I. There are some 40 000 Muslims living in Constanţa.

Danube   Known to the Romanians as the Dunarea, the Danube follows the greater part of the southern boundary of Romania with Bulgaria. At Silistra it turns northwards across the plains of SE Romania and at Galati it turns sharply eastwards before flowing into the Black Sea just south of the Soviet frontier. There are two joint Romanian–Yugoslavian hydro–electric schemes on the Danube at the Iron Gates.

Dnestr or **Dneister**   Rising in the Carpathian Mountains, the Dnestr River flows for a distance of 1400km through the Ukraine and Soviet Moldavia before discharging into the Black Sea south–west of Odessa. For much of its course the Dnestr used to form the eastern frontier of Bessarabia.

Dobruja   A strip of land lying between the Danube and the Black Sea held entirely by Bulgaria. Under the terms of the 1878 Treaty of Berlin, Northern Dobruja was ceded to Romania, giving it direct access to the Black Sea. Southern Dobruja, which was obtained by Romania in 1913, was retained until after World War I. In August 1940 Southern Dobruja was given back to Bulgaria, which retained it after a period of Romanian occupation during World War II.

Iaşi or **Jassy**   A city in NE Romania; population (1985) 314 100. Between 1565 and 1859 Iaşi was the capital of the principality of Moldavia. Prior to the December 1989 revolution the city was run by the local branch of the Romanian Communist Party under the leadership of Maria Ghitulica, a niece of former President Ceausescu.

Jiu River   A river that rises in the Carpathian Mountains north-west of Tirgu Jiu. It flows east then south–east to meet the Danube 50km south of Craiova. Strikes among miners in the Jiu valley were harshly suppressed in 1977 and again in 1981 when shortages of food stuffs and energy reached crisis points.

Kishinev or **Chisinau** (Romanian)   Capital of the Moldavian SSR, situated on the Byk River; population (1983) 580 000.

Moldavia   A former Danubian principality under Turkish rule which united with Walachia in 1859 to form the independent state of Romania. Its capital was Iasi (Jassy) and its chief port on the Danube Galtz (Galaţi).

Moldavian Soviet Socialist Republic   A republic of the Soviet Union formed by the union of part of the former Moldavian Autonomous Soviet Socialist Republic (created in 1924) and areas of Bessarabia ceded by Romania to the Soviet Union in 1940; area 33 700km². Of a population (1987) of 4 185 000, 64% are Moldavians, 14.2% Ukrainians, 12.8% Russians, 3.5% Turkish–speaking Gagauzi and 2% Jews. Its capital is Kishinev. Mostly lying between the Prut and Dnestr rivers, the republic is a major producer of agricultural crops including maize, wheat, tobacco and grapes. Although Moldavian links with Romania have been suppressed since the Soviet annexation of Bessarabia, Moldavian nationalists of the Popular Front successfully pushed through legislation in 1989 establishing Moldavian as the official language. As a result of this, the largely urban Ukrainians and Russians living in Moldavia organized strikes and rail blockades in protest at the new language laws which they felt left them second–class citizens.

Prut or **Prutul**   Rising in the eastern foothills of the Carpathians, the River Prut flows 850km south–eastwards along the Romanian frontier until it meets the Danube at Reni.

Timisoara   A Transylvanian city in W Romania; population (1985) 319000. The persecution of a local Protestant Pastor, Laszlo Tokes, sparked off the revolution that led to the overthrow of the Ceausescu regime in December 1989.

Tirgu Mures   A Transylvanian city situated on the Mures River, in the western foothills of the Romanian Carpathians; population (1985) 157400. In the spring of 1990 the city was the scene of bitter civil unrest following a violent attack on four leading ethnic Hungarians.

Transdnistria   A province established by the Romanians in 1941 over land captured from the Soviet Union. Lying between the Bug and Dnestr rivers, this territory was retaken by the Russians and reincorporated into the Ukraine in 1944.

Transylvania   A natural plateau of some 62000km² situated to the north–east of the Carpathian Mountains which form a crescent that separates it from the rest of Romania. The chief cities are Brasov, Cluj–Napoca, Timisoara and Oradea. Settled by the Hungarian Magyars nearly 1000 years ago, Transylvania was eventually incorporated into the Austro–Hungarian empire in 1867. With the break–up of the Austro–Hungarian empire after World War I, Transylvania was ceded to Romania, but in 1940 Northern Transylvania was transferred to Hungary. At the end of the second world war this territory was restored to Romania under the terms of the 1947 Paris peace treaties. Since then the treatment of the ethnic Hungarian minority, which is the largest ethnic minority group in Europe, has been a source of conflict.

Walachia or **Wallachia**   A former autonomous principality under Turkish rule which united with Moldavia to form the independent state of Romania in 1859. Situated between the Transylvanian Alps and the Danube, the area of the former principality was about 69900km². Its capital, Bucharest, became the state capital of Romania in 1861.

■ Key words

Council of Romanian Working People of Magyar Nationality   A government–sponsored organization representing the ethnic Hungarian minority in Romania.

Hungarian Democratic Union   A political party formed after the 1989 revolution to represent the Hungarian minority in Transylvania. Violent physical assault on its leaders by right–wing Romanian nationalists in March 1990 led to an outbreak of ethnic unrest in the city of Tirgu Mures which is the party's headquarters.

National Peasant Party (NPP)   One of nearly 20 opposition parties formed after the fall of Ceausescu and the restoration of democracy in Romania. Professing moral values derived from the pre-war Christian peasantry of Romania, the NPP was revived after nearly 43 years of communist single–party rule in Romania.

National Salvation Front (NSF)   A revolutionary organization formed during the uprising that overthrew the Ceausescu regime in December 1989. With its headquarters in the Bucharest television station, it formed itself into a provisional government with an initial 11–strong executive bureau. During the final week of 1989 the NSF issued a number of decrees, the foremost of which were the abolition of the leading role of the Romanian Communist Party and the termination of Ceausescu's systematization plan. On 23 January 1990 the NSF decided to turn itself into a political party and contest forthcoming elections.

Operation Romanian Villages   A campaign initiated by a group of Belgians in February 1989 in an attempt to raise international opposition to President Ceausescu's rural systematization plan. The adoption of Romanian villages by villages all over western Europe was announced in the Romanian language over Radio Free Europe.

Romanian Communist Party (RCP)   Known as the Romanian Workers' Party from 1948 until the rise to power of Nicolae Ceausescu in 1965, the RCP was the sole legal party in Romania until the revolution of December 1989.

Securitate   A powerful internal security police force used by President Ceausescu to enforce his authority throughout Romania. During the December 1989 revolution the Securitate remained loyal to Ceausescu until his execution. On 1 January 1990 the Securitate was finally abolished by a decree of the National Salvation Front.

Systematization plan   A rural resettlement programme under which President Ceausescu proposed the demolition of about 8000 of Romania's 13 000 villages and the creation of some 550 large–scale agro–industrial centres by the year 2000. The plan, which involved the destruction of at least half of the ethnic Hungarian villages of Transylvania, envisaged the reclamation of 348 000 hectares of land for use by collective farms. Initiated in 1988, the systematization plan was cut short by the downfall of Ceausescu in December 1989. At the end of the day only 10 villages were completely destroyed.

Szeklers   The original Hungarian Magyar–speaking settlers who began to move into Transylvania in the 10th century.

Vatra Romanesca ("Romanian Hearth")   An extreme right–wing Romanian nationalist organization with headquarters in Tirgu Mures. Claiming to have a membership of three million, it is alleged to include large numbers of former Securitate officials.

Vienna Award   An arrangement by which Northern Transylvania was transferred from Romania to Hungary in August 1940. In the previous two months, Bessarabia and Northern Bukovina had been ceded to the Soviet Union and Southern Dobruja returned to Bulgaria.

■ Further reading

F. Cadzow, Andrew Ludanyi and Louis J. Elteto (eds.), *Transylvania: The Roots of Ethnic Conflict*, Kent State University Press, Kent, Ohio, 1983

R.R. King, *History of the Romanian Communist Party*, Hoover Institution Press, Stanford, 1980

Maria Manoliu-Manea, *The Tragic Plight of a Border Area: Bessarabia and Bucovina*, Humboldt State University, Los Angeles, 1983

Minority Rights Group, Report No. 37, *The Hungarians of Romania*, London, 1978

D.N. Nelson, *Romania in the 1980s*, Westview Press, Boulder, 1981

M. Shafir, *Romania: Politics, Economics and Society*, Pinter, London, 1985

D. Turnock, *The Romanian Economy in the Twentieth Century*, Croom Helm, London, 1986

4
Kosovo

■ Profile

- **Status:** an autonomous province of Yugoslavia in Serbia
- **Area:** 10 887km²
- **Population (1981):** 1 584 400
- **Population density (1981):** 145.5 per sq. km
- **Ethnic groups (1981):** Albanians 77.4%, Serbs 13.2%
- **Currency:** Yugoslav dinar
- **Timezone:** GMT +1
- **Provincial capital:** Pristina
- **Chief towns:** Pristina (216 000), Prizren (134 500), Urosevac (113 700), Pec (111 000), Titova Mitrovica (105 300)

■ Introduction

By an irony of history, it was at Kosovo that the armies of medieval Serbia, including Albanians, succumbed to the might of the Turks in 1389, after which most of present-day Yugoslavia came under Ottoman rule. The Slavic Serbs had penetrated the Balkans 700 years earlier and in the 12th century had carved out their own state from the crumbling Byzantine Empire. By the mid-14th century the Serbian kingdom of Stephen Dushan had extended over much of the peninsula, including Albania, and had created a flourishing Orthodox Christian culture which was to sustain the Serbs through five centuries of Muslim rule. Descended from the ancient Illyrians, the Albanians also produced an early national hero, Scanderbeg, who in the mid-15th century organized protracted resistance to the Turks until his death in 1468. Under Turkish rule, the Serbs and other Balkan Slavs mostly retained their Christian faith, whereas most Albanians converted to Islam.

Albania enjoyed autonomy under native chieftains from 1798, but the Serbs were the first to throw off the Turkish yoke. Supported by Russia, Serbia won autonomy in 1817 and independence in 1878, together with Montenegro. Albania followed, gaining independence under a German prince in 1913, when Serbia obtained northern Macedonia and the historic Serbian province of Kosovo, despite Albania's protests that the latter contained an Albanian majority. Sparked off by a Serb, World War I found Serbia fighting bravely on the winning side, whereas pro-German Albania fell into internal chaos. The Serbs obtained their reward in the post-war settlement, becoming dominant in an amalgamation of Serbia (including Kosovo) and Montenegro with the Slav areas of Austria–Hungary. Renamed Yugoslavia in 1929, the new kingdom became immersed in disputes between its many nationalities, while Albania came under the domination of fascist Italy. In World War II both countries were occupied by the Axis powers, under whom Kosovo was detached from Yugoslavia and administered as part of Italian-run Albania. There was widespread Albanian collaboration with the occupiers.

Both Yugoslavia and Albania were liberated by Tito's communist partisans in 1944, whereupon Kosovo reverted to Yugoslav rule. The advent of communist regimes in Belgrade and Tirana eased border tensions for a few years, as economic and political co-operation became the order of the day. But the Kosovo issue had not gone away, and Albania's leaders maintained a healthy suspicion that the real aim of their Yugoslav comrades was absorption of Albania. When Yugoslavia broke with Moscow in 1948, territorial and national antagonisms with Albania quickly resurfaced, bringing the two countries to the brink of war in the early 1950s. Relations did not improve when, after 1956, Albania declined to toe Moscow's anti-Stalinist line and aligned itself with Maoist China. Within Yugoslavia, the Tito regime sought to defuse the Kosovo problem by recognizing Albanians as a distinct national group and granting official status to their language, notably in education. But this only increased the Kosovo Albanians' dissatisfaction with their political subordination to Serbs, which was ruthlessly maintained by Serbian control of the state security apparatus.

The 1963 constitution raised Kosovo to the status of one of two autonomous provinces within the Serbian republic, itself one of Yugoslavia's six constituent republics. Like most compromises, this one failed to satisfy either side. The Kosovo Albanians insisted on full republic status. The Serbians were determined to retain control of a province which had been at the heart of medieval Serbia and contained their most sacred monuments. The fall in 1966 of the hardline Serbian Vice-President of Yugoslavia, Aleksander Rankovic, led to a relaxation of Serbian domination of Kosovo's party and state apparatus. However, the onset of violence in Kosovo from 1968 caused further polarization. Yet another federal constitution in 1974 gave Kosovo some of the rights of a republic, but Albanian nationalists were not appeased. When some began to call openly for union with Albania, Serbian fears that republic status would inevitably lead to secession were confirmed. Also affected was neighbouring Macedonia: if Albanian-populated western Macedonia were to join a secessionist Kosovo what was left would be more exposed to Bulgarian and Greek irredentism.

The main problem for the Serbs was that demographic trends were inexorably against them in Kosovo. The Albanians had a very high natural birth rate and Serbs were leaving in increasing numbers. Officially forming just under 80 per cent of Kosovo's population in the late 1980s, Albanians probably had a 90 per cent majority by then (and even dominated some southern areas of Serbia proper). Also important were economic factors, in that Kosovo remained backward, with high unemployment, despite its natural wealth. Only full control of its own affairs could bring improvements, claimed the Albanian nationalists, who stepped up their agitation after Tito's death in 1980. Disturbances in Kosovo in 1981 developed into a full-scale uprising, to which the authorities responded with vigorous security measures and by purging nationalist Albanians from leadership bodies. Significantly, the 1981 violence resulted in Yugoslavia switching from coded references to external "Stalinist" interference to directly accusing the Tirana regime of stirring the Kosovo pot by supporting secessionist elements.

Following Enver Hoxha's death in 1985, the new Albanian regime became less belligerent towards Belgrade over the Kosovo issue. But internal developments in Yugoslavia in the late 1980s added new dimensions to the problem. A rediscovered taste for democracy heralded the end of one-party rule, but at the cost of unleashing militant nationalism. In Serbia's case, moreover, democratization took a back seat to nationalist aims. A mass movement developed in favour of bringing Kosovo back under the full control of the Serbian republic, with plans being mooted for resettlement of the province by Serbs to restore the ethnic balance. The result was further serious violence in Kosovo from 1988 and a deepening of the racial divide, to which, as the 1990s opened, no solution was in sight. As in other countries of Eastern Europe, the lifting of rigid communist hegemony was exposing some of the darker conflicts of previous eras.

■ Chronology of events

AD 650   The Slavs complete their occupation of the Balkans.

1340   Stephen Dushan, greatest of the Serbian rulers of the Middle Ages, conquers the Albanian coast during a period of Serbian expansion in the Balkans.

1389 Serbian expansion is brought to an end on 15 June when a coalition of Serbs, Albanians, Bosnians and Wallachians are defeated at the Battle of Kosovo by the Turks under Murad I. Serbia becomes a vassal state of the Ottoman Empire.

1443–68 The Albanian chieftain Scanderbeg leads a successful revolt against Turkish rule, but the Albanians succumb after his death in 1468.

1817 Serbia achieves autonomy within the Turkish Empire.

1876 Serbia makes an unsuccessful attempt to break free from Ottoman rule.

1877 Russia declares war on Turkey.

1878 Russia concludes an armistice with Turkey in January, and in March the two countries sign a treaty that gives independence to Serbia and Montenegro.

1912 Serbia, Montenegro, Bulgaria and Greece declare war on Turkey in an attempt to force the Turks to grant regional autonomy to Macedonia. Albania declares its independence from Turkey.

1913 The Treaty of London ends the First Balkan War, confirming Albania's independence and granting additional territory to Serbia, including the Albanian–majority province of Kosovo. In September Serbia invades Albania in response to Albanian raids into Kosovo. A month later, under pressure from Austria, Serbian troops are withdrawn.

1914 World attention focuses on the Balkans when Austrian Archduke Ferdinand is assassinated in Sarajevo by a Bosnian revolutionary operating on behalf of a Serbian society known as *The Black Hand*. This incident sparks off World War I.

1918 On 1 December the Yugoslavs unite under the Serbian royal house to form the Kingdom of Serbs, Croats and Slovenes.

1921 In April the adoption of a new constitution establishes a centralized administration dominated by Serbs and Slovenes. This leads to nationalistic conflict between Serbs and Croats. In the political struggle that follows, the Croats press for a federal structure that will allow a certain amount of regional and ethnic autonomy.

1928 Ethnic unrest breaks out when the Croatian leader, Stepan Radic, is shot by a Serb in Parliament.

1929 The country's name is changed to Yugoslavia.

1939 Italian forces occupy Albania, which is annexed to the Italian Crown.

1941 The armed forces of Germany, Bulgaria, Italy and Hungary invade Yugoslavia in April. In response, Yugoslav communists establish a resistance (the Partisans) and in November help to set up a communist party in Albania. The region of Kosovo–Metohija (Kosmet), formerly party of Serbia, is integrated with Albania under Italian administration.

1944 Albania and Yugoslavia are liberated from German/Italian occupation by Partisan forces under the leadership of Marshal Tito. The communist regimes that subsequently take power in both countries develop close economic and political ties with each other. The Kosovo–Metohija region is returned to Serbia.

1946 In January a Soviet-style constitution is adopted by Yugoslavia which becomes a "people's republic" under Tito.

1948 Stalin orders the expulsion of Yugoslavia from the international communist organization Cominform and imposes an economic blockade. Albanian communist leaders take advantage of the Moscow–Belgrade rift and terminate the former close relationship with Yugoslavia.

1950 The Yugoslavian legation in Tirana is closed following a series of incidents on the Albanian frontier with Macedonia and Kosovo–Metohija.

1953 Relations between Albania and Yugoslavia are normalized and the border between the two countries is marked with demarcation posts.

1958 Relations between Albania and Yugoslavia deteriorate when an Albanian attempting to escape from a Yugoslavian detention camp is shot. The Albanian press uses this incident as an excuse to highlight Serbian suppression of ethnic Albanians in Kosovo. In addition, allegations are made that up to 36 000 Albanians were massacred by partisans in Yugoslavia after liberation in 1944. Yugoslavia responds by staging a series of trials of alleged Albanian spies.

1961 Yugoslavia circulates a White Paper to members of the United Nations in which it is claimed that between 1948 and 1960 there were 649 incidents involving 12 deaths on the border between Albania and Yugoslavia. It was also claimed that in the same period 657 armed spies were sent into Yugoslavia. Of these, 115 had been caught and convicted.

1963 Under a new constitution the Kosovo–Metohija region is elevated to the status of an autonomous province within Serbia.

1965 The government of Yugoslavia decentralizes the economic decision-making process by devolving considerable economic and political authority to the six republics.

1966 The strongly pro-Serbian Vice-President of the Republic, Alexander Rankovic, is forced to resign following allegations that he has used the state security police in order to promote violent repression of Albanians in Kosovo–Metohija.

1968 Kosovo–Metohija (Kosmet) region changes its name to Kosovo. In November ethnic unrest boils over in Kosovo when students at the University of Pristina take part in a series of violent demonstrations demanding the designation of Kosovo as an autonomous Yugoslavian republic largely governed by Albanians.

1971 Albania resumes full diplomatic relations with Yugoslavia where a collective presidency is introduced as a means of minimizing possible disputes between republics on President Tito's death or retirement.

1973 A general re-awakening of nationalism throughout the provinces of Yugoslavia leads to the imposition of increased penalties for crimes related to the promotion of nationalism or separatism. The Serbian Minister of the Interior, Vojin Lukic, is imprisoned for his pan-Serbian nationalist stance and for describing the Albanians of Kosovo as "an unsafe element". In the same year a major purge involving 2000 dismissals takes place within the Serbian League of Communists.

1974 A new constitution is introduced in February (the third since 1945) establishing assemblies with a considerable degree of autonomy in each of the republics and autonomous provinces. Kosovo is allowed 20 delegates in the Federal Chamber and equal status in the collective presidency which is reduced from 23 to nine members.

In September attention focuses on the trial of 27 persons in Kosovo and five in neighbouring Montenegro, accused of "conspiring against the people and the state" in what President Tito described as an attempt to form a new Stalinist-type political party.

In Pristina, over 100 demonstrators protesting against the persecution of Albanians in Yugoslavia are arrested in December and charged with promoting the concept of a "Greater Albania".

1978 The close association between Albania and China that began in 1961 comes to an end in July when the Tirana government openly opposes Chinese support for the Pol Pot regime in Cambodia. Economic contacts begin to develop between Albania and Yugoslavia despite the continued presence of a distinct anti-Yugoslavian propaganda campaign in Albania.

1979 Following nationalist demonstrations in Kosovo during December, 50 Yugoslavian Albanians are arrested. Some are charged with "crimes against the state".

1980 Following the death of Marshall Tito in May, the post of President is abolished in Yugoslavia. The country continues to be ruled by an eight–member collective presidency representing all the republics and provinces.

In June, eight of the 50 Yugoslavian Albanians arrested in December 1979 are sentenced to prison terms of up to eight years. Albania denies any involvement with the incidents that gave rise to the arrests.

The Albanian Minister of Commerce tours the Yugoslavian republics and on 14 July the two countries sign a five–year trade agreement.

1981 A census indicates that while the population of Yugoslavia as a whole has grown by 9.3 per cent since 1971, the country's Albanian population has increased by about 30 per cent.

On 11–12 March student protests over conditions at Pristina University develop into full–scale demonstrations in support of republic status for Kosovo. Over 500 people are arrested and a state of emergency is declared on 3 April as the province is sealed off from the outside world. In the months that follow, the provincial government and League of Communists in Kosovo are purged of ethnic Albanians and the Yugoslavian authorities introduce a series of measures against dissident groups. As a result of ethnic unrest in Kosovo, Serbians begin to emigrate at a rate estimated at around 10 000 per year.

On 25 May (Yugoslavia's "Youth Day") two small bombs explode outside the Yugoslavian Embassy in Tirana. Although the Albanian government denies any responsibility, Yugoslavia now openly accuses the Albanians of encouraging nationalist unrest in Kosovo.

1985 In April Enver Hoxha the hardline leader of Albania dies. He is replaced by Ramiz Alia as First Secretary of the Central Committee of the

Albanina Party of Labour, the position Hoxha had held since 1944.

Although the expulsion of alleged Albanian separatists from prominent positions in Kosovo continues, 2000 Serbs sign a petition in October demanding greater protection against what they claim is a rising tide of attacks by ethnic Albanians.

1986 Yugoslavian police claim to have foiled a possible insurrection when they uncover arms and ammunition in the hands of a 150–member separatist group.

Despite ethnic tensions in Kosovo, a second five–year trade agreement between Albania and Yugoslavia is agreed. In August a new railway line is opened linking Titograd in the Yugoslavian republic of Montenegro with Scutari in northern Albania.

1987 Fadil Hoxha, a prominent Albanian politician, is expelled from the League of Communists and Ivan Stambolic, President of Serbia, is forced out of office for not taking a strong enough line over ethnic unrest in Kosovo. Slobodan Milosevic shoots to prominence and begins to mobilize massive popular support for constitutional changes that will bring the autonomous provinces of Kosovo and Vojvodina more directly under the control of Serbia. Ethnic unrest in Kosovo results in the imposition of martial law in October.

1988 Constitutional changes approved by the Federal Assembly in December 1987 and seeking to strengthen federal powers, meet stiff opposition when they are passed to the republics for ratification. During the summer, the Socialist Alliance organizes a series of demonstrations at which Serbs protest against harrassment of the Serbo–Croat–speaking minority in Kosovo and demand the unification of the Serbian republic. These demonstrations culminate in September when huge rallies are held in the cities of Nis and Novi Sad.

The first major ethnic Albanian protest since 1981 is prompted by the resignation of leading Albanian members of the Kosovo provincial administration. Between 17 and 21

November Kosovar Albanians hold a series of demonstrations in defence of the 1974 constitution and the continued autonomy of Kosovo's leadership. The largest of these rallies is led by miners from the Stri Trg mines near Pristina.

1989   The dismissal of the popular ethnic Albanian, Azem Vlasi, from the League of Communists and a decision of the Serbian Republican Assembly to extend its control over Kosovo, lead to a protest strike by miners in the town of Trepca on 4 February. On 20 February the strike spreads to other mining towns in Kosovo and about 7000 students from Pristina occupy a sports stadium. When a general strike develops, 10 000 troops and 100 tanks are sent to the province. The capitulation of the Kosovo leadership to the strikers prompts a Serbian backlash which culminates in a demonstration outside the Federal Assembly buildings attended by some 700 000 people.

In March the 186–member Kosovo provincial assembly endorses the measures extending Serbian control over the internal affairs of Kosovo and Vojvodina. This action leads to a wave of riots despite a ban on public protests. The situation continues to deteriorate when leading Albanian politicians including the popular Azem Vlasi are arrested on the grounds that an insurrection is underway. By the end of the month civil unrest has cost the lives of 24 people.

In June over 500 000 Serbs celebrate the 600th anniversary of the Battle of Kosovo Field.

1990   During the last week of January civil disorder breaks out again on a large scale in Kosovo as Albanians take to the streets following a mass poisoning scare and Serbia's imposition of more curbs on the autonomy of Kosovo.

In July the Kosovo parliament is suspended when delegates proclaim independence from Serbia.

■ Who's who

Alia, Ramiz   Leader of Albania since the death of Enver Hoxha in April 1985. While remaining loyal to Hoxha's fiercely nationalist ideals and maintaining a tightly centralized party control over the domestic economy, Alia has attempted to introduce modest reforms and develop closer economic ties with Yugoslavia.

Bakali, Mahmut   Albanian leader of the League of Communists in Kosovo until removed from office during the purges that followed the ethnic Albanian disturbances of 1981. In April 1983 he was finally expelled from the League of Communists.

Hoxha, Enver   Leader of Albania for over 40 years from the end of German occupation in 1944 until his death in April 1985 at the age of 77. He was one of the founders of the Albanian Communist Party in 1941 and was its Secretary–General from 1954 until 1985. Hoxha maintained an independent foreign policy that virtually isolated Albania from the outside world. At the same time he held a firm grip on the domestic economy through the hierarchy of a highly centralized party structure. Until his death, Hoxha complained about the persecution of Albanians in Yugoslavia and on occasions demanded the overthrow of the Yugoslavian government.

Hoxha, Fadil   Prominent Albanian nationalist politician and leader of the League of Communists in Kosovo until 1986 when he was replaced by Azem Vlasi. A year later, at the age of 77, he was expelled from the League of Communists after making a careless remark about Serbian women.

Kuchi, Jetulah   Ethnic Albanian Chief of Police in Podujevo, killed during riots in the town at the end of March 1989.

Milosevic, Slobodan Serbian Communist Party chief who rose to prominence in 1987 when he became President of the Serbian Republic. Taking advantage of the anger and frustration surrounding the harrassment of the Serbian minority in Kosovo, he mobilized popular support to back his efforts to gain more direct control over the autonomous province. A staunch communist, Milosevic has opposed the reforms that have brought multi-party politics to Yugoslavia.

Morina, Rahman An ethnic Albanian appointed President of the Kosovo League of Communists presidium in January 1989 following the resignation of Kacusa Jasari. Within a month he was himself forced to resign by striking Trepca miners who opposed his pro–Serbian stance. His removal prompted a Serbian backlash and the arrest of popular Albanian politician Azem Vlasi.

Nimani, Dzavid Former Albanian President of Kosovo, removed from office along with Prime Minister Bari Oruci and Communist Party leader Mahmut Bakali during the purges that followed the 1981 ethnic riots.

Oruci, Bari Albanian Prime Minister of Kosovo province removed from office in the purges that followed the 1981 disturbances.

Rankovic, Aleksander Vice–President of Yugoslavia, forced out of office in 1966 as a result of his strongly pan–Serbian stance and his suppression of Kosovar Albanians through the UDBA (State Security Administration) which he controlled formerly. Rankovic, who was also an organizational secretary of the League of Communists of Yugoslavia, died in 1983.

Suvar, Dr Stipe Leader of the Yugoslav Communist Party and Croatia's representative in the collective state presidency since 1989. His support of Kosovo and criticism of Serbian nationalist protests has heightened ethnic tensions and led to direct confrontation with the Serbian leader, Slobodan Milosevic.

Tito, Josip Broz The communist President of Yugoslavia from 1953 until his death in May 1980. Tito, a Croat from Slovenia, led the partisan movement against the German occupation of Yugoslavia during World War II. After the war he forced the abdication of King Peter II and took control of the country. Breaking with Stalin in 1948, he adopted a non–aligned foreign policy and turned the country into a liberal communist nation which he ruled with a combination of charisma and ruthlessness. By granting a degree of autonomy, not only to the six republics but also to the provinces of Kosovo and Vojvodina, he was able to unite the country under a single–party federal system that minimized ethnic conflict.

Vlasi, Azem A prominent ethnic Albanian politician selected for high office by Tito. In 1986 he replaced Fadil Hoxha as Chairman of the League of Communists in Kosovo, but in November 1988 he was forced to resign from office by pro-Milosevic supporters. His eventual dismissal from the central committee of the League of Communists at the beginning of February 1989 provoked a protest strike by Trepca miners and immediate calls for the dismissal of the pro-Serbian League of Communists leader, Rahman Morina. Vlasi's subsequent arrest and trial on charges of "counter-revolutionary" activities sparked off a further round of strikes and civil unrest throughout Kosovo in March 1989.

■ Key places

Belgrade or **Beograd** ("white mountain") Capital of Yugoslavia and of the republic of Serbia, situated at the confluence of the Danube and Sava rivers; population (1981) 1 407 000. The ethnic problems of Kosovo reached the streets of Belgrade in February–March 1989 when massive pro-Serbian demonstrations took place in the city following the resignation of the leaders of Kosovo.

Bosnia and Herzegovina A constituent republic of central Yugoslavia; area 51129km²; population (1981) 4 124 200. Its capital is Sarajevo. The predominant ethnic groups are Muslims (39%), Serbs (32%) and Croats (18%).

Croatia or **Hrvatska** One of the most prosperous of the six republics of Yugoslavia, lying to the north and west of Bosnia and Herzegovina; area 56538km²; population (1981) 4 601 500. Its capital is Zagreb. The Croats who migrated to this region were dominated by the Hungarians from the 11th century until the break-up of the Austro–Hungarian empire after the First World War.

During the Second World War Croatia briefly functioned as a fascist state before being reincorporated into Yugoslavia in 1946. While republics like Serbia remain firmly under Communist Party control, Croatia has been in the forefront of reforms leading towards democratic multi-party elections. Ethnic tensions in Yugoslavia are heightened by the extreme right-wing HDZ party which favours the creation of a Great Croatian State that will incorporate part of Bosnia and Herzegovina.

Goles A magnesite mine near Pristina, capital of Kosovo province. The Goles mine was the scene of a strike in March 1989 when miners came out in protest at the arrest of the Albanian politician Azem Vlasi and Serbia's imposition of more direct control over Kosovo. Saboteurs damaged the mine and 25 workers were sentenced to 60 days in jail for refusing to enter the pit.

Gracanica A small town situated about 10km south of Pristina. Prince Lazar, Serbian hero of the Battle of Kosovo in 1389, is buried in the 14th century Gracanica monastery.

Kosovo–Metohija (Kosmet) The official name of Kosovo region until the designation Metohija was dropped in 1968.

Kosovo Polje ("field") A wide plain to the west of Pristina, capital of Kosovo. On 15 June 1389, an important date in Balkan history, the Serbian hero Prince Lazar led a united army of Serbs, Bosnians, Wallachians and Albanians in an attempt to block the advance of the Turks under Murad I. The Turks won a decisive victory and Lazar was captured and killed. Thereafter. Serbia remained a vassal state of the Ottoman Empire until 1878. In June 1989 over 500 000 Serbs made the pilgrimage to the site of the Battle of Kosovo Field where Christian Serbs had been defeated by Muslim Turks. The occasion was used by Serbian President, Slobodan Milosevic, to reinforce Serbian nationalism.

Macedonia or **Makedonija** Lying to the south of Serbia and Kosovo, Macedonia is one of the six constituent republics of Yugoslavia; area 25 713km²; population (1981) 1 909 000. Its capital is Skopje. Nearly 20 per cent of the population are ethnic Albanians, a fact that has prompted Macedonia's support of Serbia in its attempt to gain more direct control over the province of Kosovo. There is, however, some resentment at the Serbian Church's adherence to the name "South Serbia" when describing Macedonia, a style that dates from the interwar years when Macedonia formed part of Serbia.

Montenegro ("black mountain") or **Crna Gora** One of the six republics of Yugoslavia, situated to the west of Kosovo and to the north-west of Albania; area 13 812km²; population (1981) 584 300. Its capital is Titograd. Nearly 6.5 per cent of the population are ethnic Albanians.

Pec A town in the province of Kosovo, situated close to the Albanian frontier, 72km west of Pristina; population (1981) 111 000. Once at the heart of the Serbian state, the walled Kremlin of churches known as the "Pec Patriarchate" remains the spiritual seat of the Serbian Church.

Pristina Capital of the autonomous province of Kosovo and a former capital of Serbia, situated on the eastern edge of the Kosovo Polje ("field") valley; population (1981) 216 000. The 1981 ethnic unrest, which saw the death of nine people and the arrest of 500, was centred on the University of Pristina.

Podujevo Situated 25km north of Pristina in the province of Kosovo, Podujevo was the scene of violent anti-Serbian riots in March 1989 that resulted in the death of the local

Chief of Police. A year later, in February 1990, in a further wave of ethnic unrest over 5000 demonstrators clashed with police. Population (1981) 75 500.

Sarajevo   Capital of the Yugoslavian republic of Bosnia and Herzegovina; population (1981) 448 500. On 28 June 1914, the Archduke Ferdinand was assassinated here by Gavrilo Princip, an event that sparked off the First World War.

Serbia or **Srbija**   The largest of the six constituent republics of Yugoslavia, bounded to the east by Romania and Bulgaria; area 88 361km²; population (1981) 9 313 700. Its capital is Belgrade (Beograd), which is also the Yugoslavian state capital. The republic incorporates the autonomous provinces of Kosovo and Vojvodina, both of which were forced to surrender much of their autonomy to Serbia in March 1989. Under the leadership of Slobodan Milosevic, the Serbian Communist Party has resisted attempts to decentralize power or adopt the democratic reforms that have taken place in other Yugoslavian republics.

Shkoder or **Scutari**   A market town in NW Albania linked by rail with Titograd in Yugoslavia since August 1986 when a freight line was opened between the two countries.

Slovenia   The northernmost and wealthiest of the six constituent republics of Yugoslavia; area 20 251km²; population (1981) 1 892 000. Its capital is Ljubljana. Settled by Slovenes in the 6th century, Slovenia was eventually incorporated into the Austro–Hungarian empire. In Slovenia, where the Communist Party ruled for nearly 45 years, a multi-party system now operates. The leaders of Slovenia have been in the forefront of attempts to introduce political reforms leading to further decentralization of power and the reconstitution of Yugoslavia as a loose "confederation". This stance, coupled with support for the ethnic Albanians of Kosovo, has brought them into direct conflict with Milosevic's Serbian Communist Party which is opposed to any form of pluralism.

Tirana or **Tiranë**   Founded by the Turks in the 17th century, Tirana has been capital of Albania since 1920. The city is situated in the north-western foothills of the Pindus mountains, 40 km east of the Adriatic port of Durrës.

Titograd   Formerly known as Podgorica, Titograd was renamed after Josip Tito, President of Yugoslavia. Situated to the north of Lake Scutari, Titograd is the capital of the republic of Montenegro.

Titova Mitrovica   A mining town in Kosovo province, situated 35km north-west of Pristina; population (1981) 105 300. In 1989 a hunger strike by miners at the nearby Trepca lead and zinc mines led to a general strike and an outbreak of ethnic unrest between Kosovo's Albanians and Serbians.

Trepca   The site of lead and zinc mines near the town of Titova Mitrovica in NW Kosovo. An eight-day strike by miners in February 1989 forced the resignation of the pro-Serbian leaders of Kosovo and sparked off a series of strikes, demonstrations and ethnic riots throughout Serbia.

Urosevac   The third largest town in the province of Kosovo, situated 32km south of the capital, Pristina; population (1981) 113 700. The town was the scene of some of the worst riots during the ethnic unrest of February–March 1989.

Vojvodina   Like Kosovo, Vojvodina is an autonomous province within the republic of Serbia; area 21 506km²; population (1981)2 035 000. Its capital is Novi Sad. In 1989 Serbia passed legislation that gave it more direct control over the province which has a Hungarian population of 385 300.

Yugoslavia   A socialist federal republic in SE Europe, Yugoslavia gained its independence under the Serbian monarchy in 1918 and changed its name to Yugoslavia in 1929. Its capital is Belgrade (Beograd); area 25 5804km²; population (1985) 23 137 000. Ethnic groups include Serbs (36.2%), Croats (19.7%), Bosnian Muslims (8.9%), Slovenes (7.7%), Macedonians (5.9%), Yugoslavs (5.4%), Montenegrins (2,5%), Hungarians (1.9%), Gypsies, Turks, Slovaks, Romanians, Ukrainians (2%).

■ Key words

Albanian Party of Labour The sole political party in Albania, founded in 1941 with the aid of Yugoslavian communists. It had close ties with the League of Communists of Yugoslavia until the rift between Stalin and Tito in 1948.

autonomous provinces The constitution of April 1963 set up the two provinces of Vojvodina (with an ethnic Hungarian minority) and Kosovo (with an ethnic Albanian majority). Both provinces lie within the republic of Serbia which succeeded in gaining more direct control over them in March 1989.

Chamber of Republics and Autonomous Provinces A chamber of the Yugoslav Federal Assembly composed of 12 delegates from each of the republican assemblies and eight from each of the provincial assemblies.

collective state presidency In order to minimize argument amongst the republics of Yugoslavia, Tito introduced a collective presidency consisting of representatives from each of the republics and provinces. After his death in 1980 the post of President was abolished and each republic took it in turn to provide a President of the collective presidency for a one–year term.

Cominform A Moscow–led international communist organization which maintained an economic blockade of Yugoslavia for five years after Yugoslavia's expulsion from its ranks in 1948. Ethnic Albanians arrested following civil disorders in the 1970s and 1980s were often described as "pro-Cominform emigrés" engaged in hostile activities against the state.

Democratic Forum A political party leading the ethnic Albanian opposition to the suppression of Kosovo's autonomy.

Federal Assembly The federal legislature of Yugoslavia which has two chambers: the Federal Chamber and the Chamber of Republics and Autonomous Provinces. The Assembly's executive and administrative arm is the Federal Executive Council.

Federal Chamber A chamber of the Yugoslav Assembly which consists of 30 delegates elected from communities, trade unions, factories and other socio-Apolitical organizations from each of the six republics. Twenty delegates are elected on the same basis from each of the two autonomous provinces.

Initiative for a Democratic Yugoslavia A Yugoslav opposition party founded by Slovene, Croat and Serb intellectuals. Claiming to be the first nationwide alternative to the League of Communists it held its inaugural meeting in Zagreb on 11 January 1990.

League of Communists of Yugoslavia (LCY) The sole political party in Yugoslavia for nearly 45 years following the end of the Second World War. With a membership in 1982 of about two million people (9% of the population), the party operates in each of the republics and provinces through a system of "delegate democracy" which allows representation from a wide range of socio–political organizations. Although the monopoly of power held by the communists came to an end in 1990, Serbia has remained resolutely loyal to the idea of the one–party state.

opstina A Serbo–Croat word for a commune. Yugoslavia is divided into 527 administrative divisions or *opstina*.

self–management Since the war, the economy of Yugoslavia has been based on a socio–economic theory of organization known as "workers self–management". The system is based on the principle that factories, resources and institutions belong not to the state but to society as a whole. Under self–management, responsibility for investment, prices, wage levels and other decisions lies with individual firms which are run by self–management councils.

Serbo–Croat Two variants of the Slavic tongue which are regarded as a single language and which serve as a *lingua franca* throughout Yugoslavia.

Socialist Alliance of the Working People   A front organization for the League of Communists of Yugoslavia responsible for arranging pro-Serbian rallies in Belgrade and other major cities in 1988.

State Security Administration (UDBA)   The Yugoslavian security police which, under Aleksander Rankovic, was accused of the violent repression of Albanians in Yugoslavia during the 1960s.

Youth Day   Originally celebrated as the birthday of President Tito until his death in 1980. Thereafter, this holiday on 25 May came to be known as Youth Day.

Yugoslavs ("south Slavs")   A general term describing the people of Yugoslavia but more particularly those who speak Serbo–Croat, Slovene or Macedonian. The term is also applied to those who do not profess any ethnic group within Yugoslavia, as in 1981 when 1 219 405 people declared themselves "Yugoslavs" rather than Serbs, Croatians, etc. in the population census.

■ Further reading

S.L. Burg, *Conflict and Cohesion in Socialist Yugoslavia: Political Decision–making since 1966*, Princeton University Press, 1983

A.N. Dragwich and Slavko Todorovich, *The Saga of Kososvo: Focus on Serbian–Albania Relations*, Boulder East European Monographs, New York, 1984

H. Lydall, *Yugoslavia in Crisis*, Oxford University Press, Oxford, 1989

B. McFarlane, *Yugoslavia: Politics, Economics and Society*, Pinter, London, 1988

Minority Rights Group, Report No. 82, *Minorities in the Balkans*, London, 1989

S.K. Pavlowitch, *The Impossible Survivor: Yugoslavia and its Problems, 1918–88*, Hurst, London, 1988

5
Cyprus

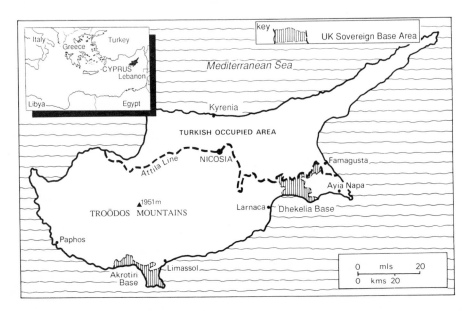

■ Profile

- **Population (1987):** 680 400
- **Area:** 9 251km²
- **Ethnic groups:** Greek Cypriot 80%, Turkish Cypriot 18%
- **Languages:** Greek and Turkish
- **Religion:** Orthodox Christian 80%, Muslim 18%
- **Life expectancy:** 72 years
- **Infant mortality rate:** 11 per 1000
- **Currency:** Cyprus pound of 100 cents
- **Timezone:** GMT +2
- **Capital:** Nicosia
- **Chief towns:** Nicosia (161 100), Limassol (118 200), Larnaca (52 800), Paphos (22 600)

The Turkish Republic of North Cyprus

- **Population:** 162 700 (24% of the total population of Cyprus)
- **Area:** 3 355km² (37% of the island)
- **Capital:** Nicosia
- **Chief towns:** Famagusta (19 400), Morphou (10 200), Kyrenia (6 900)
- **Currency:** Turkish lire

■ Introduction

The centuries-long confrontation between Christianity and Islam in Europe was largely resolved in favour of the former by the early 20th century. By then the Muslim Ottoman Empire retained only a tiny portion of its once vast dominions in south-eastern Europe. However, retreating Ottoman power left behind substantial communities of Muslim Turks in many regions restored to Christian rule, with inevitable results in the form of ethnic and religious antagonisms. A prime case in point is Cyprus, whose Turkish population in the north of the island today maintains Europe's only Muslim "state". This is unrecognized internationally except by Turkey, its military begettor and protector, and is regarded as illegal by the government of the Greek Cypriot majority.

Cyprus came under Ottoman sway relatively late. Once part of the Byzantine Empire, the island was ruled by French feudal lords from c.1200 to 1489, when the Venetians took over. Not until 1571 did Cyprus finally fall to the Ottomans, just as Christian Europe was registering its first decisive victory over the Turks at Lepanto. Over the next three centuries Muslim Turks came to form about a fifth of the island's population. When Britain established a protectorate over Cyprus in 1878, intercommunal tensions were already apparent. Part of a strategy to contain Russian expansion towards Constantinople/Istanbul and to safeguard lines of imperial communication, the British presence had the effect of insulating the Cypriot population from the struggles between Greek and Turk elsewhere in the eastern Mediterranean before and after World War I. But awakening Greek nationalism in Cyprus and the aspiration of Greece itself to unify all Greeks already provided the seeds of future conflict over the status of the island's Turkish minority.

Formally annexed by Britain in 1914 when Turkey allied itself with the Central powers in World War I, Cyprus was offered to Greece in 1915 as a carrot to persuade it to declare war on the Anglo-French side. The offer was declined, however, and was not repeated when Greece eventually entered the war in 1917. Thus the

"greater Greece" granted to Athens under the 1921 Treaty of Sèvres did not include Cyprus. In any case, Greece unwisely tried on its own to impose the Sèvres terms on the rejuvenated Turkish Republic of Kemal Atatürk and suffered ignominious defeat for its pains. Under the 1923 Treaty of Lausanne, "greater Greece" aspirations were effectively abandoned and both Greece and Turkey formally recognized British sovereignty over Cyprus, which became a Crown Colony in 1925.

In the 1930s Greek Cypriot agitation for self-government and/or union with Greece (*Enosis*) caused mounting problems for the British authorities. Such sentiments were strengthened by World War II, during which Cyprus remained in British hands and both Greece (from 1940) and Turkey (from February 1945) took the side of the Allies. After 1945 Britain continued to reject the *Enosis* option for Cyprus, which acquired enhanced strategic importance following the withdrawal of British troops from the Suez Canal in 1954–56. The idea of institutional links between Cyprus and Athens also aroused strong opposition from Turkey, which from 1952, together with Greece, became allied with Britain within NATO. The inevitable consequence was the growth of a powerful anti-British movement among Greek Cypriots headed by Archbishop Makarios, accompanied by growing violence by the pro-*Enosis* EOKA organization led by General George Grivas.

Faced with a deteriorating security situation, Britain in 1959 secured the agreement of Greece and Turkey for an independent Republic of Cyprus in which power-sharing would operate between the two communities (and Britain would retain its military bases as sovereign territory). But hardly had independence been celebrated (August 1960), with Makarios becoming President, than inter-communal conflict rendered power-sharing a dead letter. By late 1963 Turkish Cypriots were boycotting the Cypriot government and parliament and from early 1964 a UN force had to be deployed to keep the two communities apart. Violence nevertheless continued and brought Greece and Turkey to the brink of war in 1967, when the advent of a right-wing military regime in Greece did nothing to ease tensions. By 1968 the Turks were running an "autonomous" administration in northern Cyprus, to the fury of militant Greek Cypriots, who condemned Makarios for failing to act against it.

Matters came to a head in mid-1974 when, with the backing of the Athens military regime, Greek-born officers of the Cypriot National Guard deposed Makarios and installed a former EOKA leader as President. Turkey's response to what it saw as a prelude to forcible *Enosis* was immediate: its forces speedily occupied the northern part of Cyprus. The Nicosia coup collapsed within a week, together with the military regime in Athens, but too late to prevent the effective partition of Cyprus along a ceasefire line (the Attila Line) which ran through Nicosia and left the northern two-fifths of the island under Turkish military control. In that area a "Turkish Federated State", declared in 1975, was succeeded in 1983 by the "Turkish Republic of Northern Cyprus". The flight of Greek Cypriots from the north and some movement in the other direction by Turks consolidated the island's division.

Deep mutual suspicion between Greece and Turkey over respective intentions in Cyprus was compounded by an unresolved dispute over the delimitation of the Aegean Sea continental shelf. For Turkey, Greek claims embodied an historic aim to make the Aegean a "Greek lake" up to the coast of Turkish Asia Minor. Its resistance to such claims on strategic grounds also explained its determination, further south, to maintain Turkish Cypriot control of northern Cyprus. For Greece, the presence to the east of a potentially hostile neighbour, more than five times bigger than itself in area and population, was a

constant source of insecurity, compounded by memories of its humiliation at Turkish hands in 1921–22. Not surprisingly, such antagonisms between two of its members caused serious problems for NATO, which was accused by Greece of failing to act against Turkey's aggression in Cyprus and generally of favouring Ankara because of Turkey's strategic importance on the Alliance's southern front with the Soviet Union.

The 1981 military coup in Ankara further exacerbated tensions with Greece over Cyprus and related issues, leading to another military confrontation in 1986–87. However, Turkey's gradual return to civilian rule in the mid-1980s assisted a partial rapprochement with Greece, leading to the January 1988 Davos Agreement between the two Prime Ministers and, later that year, to the first official visit to Athens by a Turkish Prime Minister since 1952. This in turn produced a more conciliatory approach in Cyprus itself, a mood sustained at a meeting in Geneva in August 1988 between the new Greek Cypriot President and his Turkish Cypriot counterpart. However, their pledge on that occasion to complete UN-sponsored negotiations on a settlement by mid-1989 was not in the event honoured, because of the perennial difficulty of reconciling the Greek Cypriot insistence that Cyprus should remain a unitary state with the Turkish Cypriot demand for national recognition. Nor was there any change in the Ankara government's longstanding rejection of Greece's proposal that Cyprus be demilitarized and that the Aegean dispute be submitted to the International Court of Justice. Never far beneath the surface in Cyprus, intercommunal violence again broke out in Nicosia in July 1989, causing a suspension of the creaking negotiating process.

■ Chronology of events

1571 Cyprus is captured by the Ottoman Turks who govern the various ethnic groups through their religious leaders. This system reinforces the position of the Orthodox Church and the cohesion of the Greek community which has lived on the island for centuries.

Over the next 300 years Turks from Asia Minor settle throughout the island.

1878 An Anglo–Turkish agreement at the Congress of Berlin places Cyprus under the control of Great Britain. For a rent of £93 000 per year the British use the island as a base from which to check Russian expansion in the Near East.

1914 At the outbreak of World War I Cyprus is annexed by Britain when Turkey aligns herself with Germany.

1915 The British offer the island of Cyprus to Greece in return for Greek support in the fight against Germany and her allies. The offer is rejected.

1920 Under the Treaty of Sèvres Greece is awarded former Ottoman territories including most of Thrace west of Constantinople (Istanbul), the Dodecanese (except Rhodes), the Aegean islands of Imbroz and Tenedos and the Anatolian port of Smyrna (Izmir).

1921 Greece goes to war with Turkey in order to secure the territories it had been awarded by the Treaty of Sèvres.

1922 Greece receives no support from the rest of Europe and is driven out of Anatolia by the Turks.

1923 Under the conditions of the Treaty of Lausanne Turkey relinquishes all rights to Cyprus. Greece reluctantly recognizes Turkish authority over the territories that gave rise to the disastrous 1921–22 conflict while the Dodecanese are ceded to Italy.

1925 Cyprus is declared a British Crown Colony.

1931 A rising tide of opposition to British rule by Greek Cypriots pressing either for self-government or for union with Greece (*Enosis*) culminates in a series of riots in which Government House is burned down. A state of emergency is declared.

1950 Makarios III is elected Archbishop and Primate of the Orthodox Church of Cyprus. He organises a plebiscite that indicates a majority of Greek Cypriots are in favour of Enosis.

1954 Greece appeals to the United Nations for the application of the principle of self-determination in Cyprus. Turkish Cypriots oppose union with Greece and state their preference for the partition of the island.

Aided by Greece, anti-British supporters of Enosis begin a campaign of terrorism and intercommunal violence. In November a state of emergency is declared and British troops totalling 10 000 are reinforced. Britain invites both Turkey and Greece to a conference on the future of Cyprus.

1956 The Governor of Cyprus discusses plans for the future independence of the island with Archbishop Makarios. Talks break down in March and Makarios is deported to the Seychelles because of alleged "seditious activities" and his involvement with EOKA terrorists. The Radcliffe Report puts forward proposals for internal self-government.

1957 Released from imprisonment in the Seychelles but exiled from Cyprus, Makarios flies to Athens. Little progress is made during the continuing talks on self-government since Greek Cypriots claiming majority rule object to the demands for special protection made by the Turkish Cypriot community.

1958 Anti-British and intercommunal violence increases as Britain introduces a greater degree of self-government under the Macmillan Plan which suggests a system of condominium over Cyprus by Britain, Greece and Turkey. In April the first UN Conference on the Law of the Sea provides both Greece and Turkey with a basis for reasserting claims over Aegean waters that were a source of dispute between then two countries in 1921–22.

1959 At a meeting in Zurich in February the Prime Ministers of Greece and Turkey reach a compromise on the future independence of Cyprus and at a conference in London Greek, Turkish, Cypriot and British representatives reach an agreement that leads to the drafting of a new power-sharing constitution. A treaty of Alliance allows Greece and Turkey to maintain limited military contingents on the island and a Treaty of Guarantee allows Greece, Turkey and Britain to intervene if the arrangements agreed in London are endangered. Britain is to maintain its two military bases at Akrotiri and Dhekelia.

1960 On 16 August Cyprus gains its independence with Archbishop Makarios as its first President.

1963 The implementation of the constitution causes serious disagreement between Greek and Turkish Cypriots and intercommunal violence breaks out in December.

1964 Violence escalates and the Cyprus government asks the United Nations to send a peace-keeping force to the island. By May over 7000 UN troops have arrived in Cyprus and a UN mediator has been appointed to open talks with Nicosia, Athens and Ankara. The Turkish Cypriot Vice-President advocates partition and is supported by the Turkish government, which threatens invasion. The US President, Lyndon B. Johnson, warns the Turkish Prime Minister against such action.

1967 Intercommunal violence in Cyprus leads to a major confrontation between Greece and Turkey when the Greek Cypriot National Guard attacks two Turkish Cypriot villages. Turkey moves troops towards its frontier with Greece and into ports facing Cyprus. The situation is eventually defused following mediation by US presidential emissary Cyrus Vance. General Grivas, commander of the Greek Cypriot National Guard, resigns and leaves the island, but this does nothing to reassure the Turkish community, which forms a Provisional Cypriot Turkish Administration.

1968 The Turkish Cypriot Community forms a separate Turkish Cypriot Autonomous Administration in the north of Cyprus.

1971 With the support of the Greek military dictatorship, General Grivas returns secretly to Cyprus where he campaigns for union with Greece and forms a new guerrilla force known as EOKA–B.

1973 During presidential elections Archbishop Makarios, who favours an independent Cyprus, challenges an EOKA–B

candidate to stand but is returned unopposed. In November tension between Greece and Turkey is heightened when the Turkish *Official Gazette* publishes a map claiming half the continental shelf of the Aegean and the Turkish government grants the state-owned Turkish Petroleum Corporation the right to start exploring for oil in disputed Aegean waters.

1974 The Turkish government offers to discuss the question of territorial jurisdiction in Aegean waters with Greece, but when Greece fails to respond, Turkey begins seismic exploration for oil during April–May. This prompts Greece to come to the negotiating table but only on the basis of the 1958 Geneva Conference on the Law of the Sea. Turkey rejects this as a basis for discussion.

On 15 July elements of the Cypriot National Guard and EOKA–B collaborate with Greek army officers in the overthrow of President Makarios and his government. Fearing Greek-imposed Enosis, Turkish Cypriot leaders immediately call on Britain and Turkey to enforce Cypriot independence. Britain refuses to intervene but Turkey acts unilaterally on 20 July when it lands 30 000–40 000 troops on the island. Turkish forces quickly advance along a narrow 25km corridor linking the port of Kyrenia with Nicosia. The resignation of the Greek military government on 23 July is quickly followed by the collapse of the short-lived regime of Nicos Sampson and the return to power of the recently ousted Cypriot government. A ceasefire allows talks to take place in Geneva between Britain, Greece and Turkey but these soon break down when Turkey insists on the creation of a federated state of Cyprus with 34 per cent of the island under the control of Turkish Cypriots. Fighting is renewed and Turkish forces occupy the whole of the island north of the so-called Attila Line. In December Archbishop Makarios returns to Cyprus and resumes the Presidency.

In view of the dispute over territorial jurisdiction in the Aegean and the Turkish invasion of Cyprus, Greece begins to build up its military presence in the eastern Dodecanese islands. Turkey responds by concentrating a new Fourth Army division on the Aegean coast.

1975 UN–sponsored intercommunal talks take place in Vienna. The Greek Cypriot negotiator, Glafcos Clerides, proposes a multi-regional federation with strong central government while the Turkish negotiator, Rauf Denktash, advocates a bi-zonal federation. They cannot agree and Denktash declares a Turkish Federated State of Cyprus on behalf of 120 000 Turkish Cypriots occupying the northern 37 per cent of the island. Intercommunal negotiations make little headway although agreements are reached to allow 20 000 Turkish Cypriots to be transported north into Turkish-occupied Cyprus and nearly 200 000 Greek Cypriots to move south of the Attila Line.

In January Greece suggests to Turkey that the Aegean territorial dispute should be placed before the International Court of Justice. Turkey will only agree to a Court ruling on matters that cannot be decided by bilateral negotiations.

1976 Rauf Denktash is elected President of the new Turkish Federated State of Cyprus and in the south elections are won by the Democratic Front under the leadership of Spyros Kyprianou, a supporter of Makarios.

Bilateral discussions between Greece and Turkey begin in New York in an attempt to resolve the Aegean dispute following a confrontation between Greek and Turkish vessels near the island of Lesbos in July. In November, at a meeting in Berne, the two sides agree not to explore for oil in each other's territorial waters while the continental shelf issue remains unresolved.

1977 Talks in March between Makarios and Denktash result in a stalemate and in August the death of Makarios brings Kyprianou to the Presidency. He reaches an agreement with Denktash to resume talks, giving priority to the Greek Cypriot resettlement of the Varosha resort area south of Famagusta.

1979 Intercommunal talks resume.

1983 After years of intercommunal talks and UN initiatives there is no progress towards reuniting the Turkish and Greece sectors of the island. In November the Turkish Cypriot community declares itself the independent Turkish Republic of Northern Cyprus, an action that is almost universally condemned by the rest of the world which has grown weary of the conflict.

1985 Despite near agreement between Kyprianou and Denktash UN–sponsored talks collapse on a procedural issue.

1986 A new Soviet plan for a settlement is rejected by the Turkish Cypriots and another UN draft agreement to form a federal state comes to nothing. In July the Turkish Prime Minister sparks off Greek Cypriot riots in the south when he visits northern Cyprus.

Tension in the Aegean is heightened in July when the Greek government protests that Greece's coastal limits have been violated by the Turkish scientific research vessel *Piri Reis*. In a further incident in September it is alleged that Turkish warships opened fire close to a Greek patrol boat.

1987 After 24 years in Cyprus as part of the UN– peace-keeping force and with no sign of a solution to the conflict, Sweden decides to pull its troops out.

Further incidents relating to oil exploration activities in the disputed waters of the Aegean come to a head in March when Greek and Turkish troops are allegedly reported to be on full alert. The prime ministers of both countries eventually agree not to conduct explorations in disputed waters and discuss the possibility of taking the problem to the International Court of Justice.

1988 After 11 years in power Spyros Kyprianou is replaced as President by George Vassiliou. Promising to disband all Greek Cypriot military forces, Vassiliou calls on the Turkish Prime Minister to pull out the 29 000 turkish troops occupying northern Cyprus. Rauf Denktash objects to this direct approach to Ankara but, prompted by a new rapprochement between Greece and Turkey, intercommunal talks open up again in September.

1989   Denktash rejects Vassiliou's proposal for the demilitarization of Cyprus. The arrest of over 100 Greek Cypriots demonstrating in north Cyprus on the 15th anniversary of the Turkish invasion results in the adjournment of yet another round of UN–backed talks and the postponement of a scheduled summit meeting in New York in September.

1990   In February–March the UN Secretary–General, Javier Pérez de Cuellar presides over another round of talks between Greek Cypriot President George Vassiliou and Turkish Cypriot leader, Rauf Denktash.

■ Who's who

Clerides, Glafcos   Former Speaker of the House of Representatives and leader of the Unified Party which won 15 seats in the elections of 1970 to become the largest party. During the run-up to the 1976 elections he formed the conservative Democratic Rally in response to the setting-up of the left-of-centre Democratic Front by Spyros Kyprianou. During the 1960s Clerides engaged in intercommunal talks with the Turkish Cypriot leader Rauf Denktash.

Denktash, Rauf   Turkish Cypriot leader and President of the Turkish Republic of Northern Cyprus which was declared by him in 1983 following the breakdown of talks to resolve the Cyprus conflict. Born in Ayios Epiphanios, Denktash became internationally known as a negotiator in successive intercommunal talks between Greek and Turkish Cypriots. In 1968 he was appointed Vice-President of the breakaway autonomous administration set up in the north by   leaders of the Turkish community. As leader of the National Solidarity Party he was elected President of the self-declared Turkish Federated State of Cyprus in 1976.

Grivas, General George Theodorou (1898–1974)   Leader of the anti-British EOKA terrorist movement in Cyprus. During World War II Grivas commanded a Greek army division and an underground organization in German-occupied Greece. After the war he headed a nationalist campaign against the Communists but in 1954 he returned to Cyprus to promote Enosis by organizing guerrilla activities against the British administration.

Calling himself "Dighenis" after a legendary Greek hero, Grivas soon had a price of 10 000 on his head. His secret diaries, which linked Archbishop Makarios with EOKA, were discovered in 1956. After the Cyprus settlement of 1959 had assured independence, Grivas went to Greece where he was promoted to the rank of General in the Greek army. In 1964 he returned to Cyprus as commander of the Cypriot National Guard, but in 1967 he was recalled to Athens following the Greek military coup. In 1971 he secretly made his way back to Cyprus to direct the EOKA–B terrorist campaign for union with Greece.

Konuk, Nejat   Prime minister of the Turkish Cypriot Federated State 1976–78 and first leader of the government of the newly-proclaimed Turkish Republic of North Cyprus in 1983.

Kütchük, Dr. Fazil   A Turkish Cypriot leader who took part in pre-Independence negotiations with Greece, Turkey, Britain and Greek Cypriots. He initially suggested a bicameral legislature for a self-governing Cyprus within the British Commonwealth but later took the Turkish viewpoint that partition was the only viable solution to the problem. In 1960 he became Vice-president of the newly independent Cyprus, but in 1968 he abandoned that post to lead the Turkish Cypriot Autonomous Administration in the north.

Kyprianou, Spyros   Second President of Cyprus from the death of Archbishop Makarios in 1977 until his defeat in the Presidential elections of 1988 when he was succeeded by George Vassiliou. Born in Limassol in

1932, Kyprianou became a Foreign Minister and Speaker of the House of Representatives in the government of newly independent Cyprus. In 1976 he formed the new left-of-centre Democratic Front Party.

Makarios III (1913–1977)   Archbishop and Primate of the Orthodox Church of Cyprus from 1950 until his death in 1977 and President of Cyprus 1959–1977. Born in the village of Ano Panciyia near Paphos in 1913, his proper name was Mikhail Christodoulou Mouskos. In the 1950s he was a strong supporter of the Enosis movement but latterly he advocated an independent Cyprus. Exiled to the Seychelles in 1956 for his association with EOKA terrorism, Makarios returned to Cyprus to become first President of the independent Republic of Cyprus. In 1974 Makarios fled to England following a Greek-backed coup but he returned to the island in December of the same year to resume the presidency until his death just over two years later.

Papadopoulos, Tassos   An independent Cypriot politician who held a ministerial appointment under Makarios and acted as intercommunal negotiator under President Kyprianou.

Papaioannou, Ezikias   Secretary–General of the Communist AKEL party since 1945.

Sampson, Nicos   A former EOKA gunman appointed to the Presidency of Cyprus after the coup that temporarily dislodged Archbishop Makarios and his government on 15 July 1974. Backed by the National Guard under the leadership of Greek army officers, the Sampson regime lasted for just over a week until the fall of the Greek military government on 22 July. Nicos Sampson was eventually arrested in March 1976 and sentenced to 20 years imprisonment.

Vassiliou, George   Hungarian-educated millionaire, elected President of Cyprus in 1988. Although an independent politician he was supported in his bid for the presidency by the minority Communist, Socialist and Liberal parties. His solution to the Cyprus conflict has been based on the withdrawal of all troops from the island.

■ Key places

Aegean Sea   An arm of the Mediterranean Sea lying between Greece and Turkey and extending as far south as the islands of Crete and Rhodes. All the islands of the Aegean, except the Turkish islands of Imroz and Bozcaada (Tenedos), are administered by Greece. Since the Treaty of Svres awarded former Ottoman territory to Greece in 1920, the Aegean waters have been a source of dispute between Greece and Turkey. In a brief war with Turkey during 1921–22, Greece failed to secure the territories awarded to it but subsequently claimed the greater part of the Aegean seabed up to and beyond the Greek islands that lie close to the Turkish coast. The Turks, on the other hand, claim sovereignty of the entire eastern Aegean continental shelf. Since the first UN Conference on the Law of the Sea in 1958, and with a growing interest in oil exploration, both sides have repeatedly pressed their claims to sovereignty in Aegean waters and have come close to open conflict.

Akrotiri   A village close to the south coast of Cyprus with a population of about 700 inhabitants; situated 10km south–west of the port of Limassol on a peninsula that separates Episkopi Bay from Akrotiri Bay to the east. The peninsula is part of the Akrotiri Sovereign Base Area, the western of two military bases held by the British after the independence of Cyprus in 1960. The Salt Lake to the north of Akrotiri village is noted for its migrant birds.

Dhekelia   The eastern of the two British sovereign base areas of Cyprus; situated between Larnaca and Famagusta. The combined area of Akrotiri and Dhekelia bases is 256km^2.

Dodecanese or Southern Sporades   A group of 12 Greek islands in the SE Aegean Sea off the south–west coast of Turkey. All except Rhodes were held by Italy between 1912 and 1943. In 1974 Greece built up its military presence in the islands following incidents in disputed waters and the Turkish invasion of Cyprus.

Famagusta   Built in the 3rd century BC by Ptolemy II, the seaport of Famagusta on the E coast of Cyprus was fortified by the Venetians whose governor island lived in the city. Once the island's chief port, international trade came to a halt in October 1974 three months after the Turkish invasion of Cyprus. The cessation of trade and tourism and the movement of Greek Cypriots to the south has resulted in a fall in population from a total of 39000 in 1973 to a figure of just over 19000 in 1985.

Imroz or **Imbros** also **Gökçeada**   A Turkish island claimed by Greece in the NE Aegean Sea near the entrance to the Dardanelles; area 285km²; Occupied by Greece in 1912–14 and then by the British during the Gallipoli campaign, it was awarded, along with Bozcaada (Tenedos) and the Dodecanese, to Greece in 1920 but was given back to the Turks in 1923 after the war between Greece and Turkey.

Izmir   Formerly known as Smyrna, the Anatolian port of Izmir is a capital of a province of the same name lying on an inlet of the Aegean Sea. Population(1985) 1 490 000. In July 1974 the city became headquarters for the new Turkish Fourth Army Division known as the "Aegean Army". This Division was built up on the Aegean coast in response to Greek military development on the Dodecanese islands following the Turkish invasion of Cyprus and incidents in disputed waters.

Kyrenia   Seaport capital of Kyrenia district; situated on the north coast of the island in the Turkish Republic of North Cyprus; population (1973) 3900; population (1985) 6900. In July 1974 Turkish forces landed here before making for Nicosia which lies 25km to the south.

Larnaca   Originally known as Kition, Larnaca was founded in the 13th century BC by the

Mycenaeans who developed the port as a major centre of the copper trade. Capital of a district of the same name, the town is situated at the western end of Larnaca Bay on the south coast of Cyprus. The birthplace of Zeno the Stoic (335–263 BC) and Apollonius, the Alexandrian physician (c.50 BC).   An influx of Greek Cypriot refugees from Turkish-occupied northern Cyprus and the opening of the international airport stimulated an increase in the population from a figure of 19 600 in 1973 to an estimated total of 52 800 in 1987. Since 1975 Larnaca International Airport has been one of the main points of entry and exit by air for the Greek community in the south.

Limassol   Lying between the ancient Greek city sites of Curium and Amathus, Limassol is the seaport capital of a district of the same name. Situated on Akrotiri Bay, which lies on the south coast of Cyprus, the city is close to many fine beaches. An influx of Greek Cypriot refugees following the Turkish invasion of 1974 caused the population of the island's second largest city to rise from a figure of 79 600 in 1973 to an estimated total of 118 200 in 1987. The production of wine and spirits is a major industry.

Nicosia   Built on the site of the ancient city of Ledra, Nicosia has been Capital of Cyprus since the 7th century AD. Situated on the Pedias river at the centre of the Mesaoria plain it has a population (1987) of 164500. Following the Turkish invasion of 1974, the city was bisected by the "Green Line" which separates the Greek and Turkish Cypriot communities. The former international airport has been closed to civil aviation since 1974 but is used by the UN peace-keeping force which maintains a "no-man's-land" between north and south.

Paphos   Resort and seaport capital of Paphos district on the west coast of Cyprus, comprising the twin towns of Nea Paphos and Ktima. Once a small fishing port, Paphos expanded from a population of 9000 in 1973 to an estimated 22 800 in 1987. There is an international airport.

Troödos Mountains   The highest mountain range in Cyprus, lying to the south of the Attila

Line and rising to 1951m at Mt Olympus on the summit of which there is a radar station and observation post. At 1725m the winter and summer resort of Troödos is the highest continually inhabited settlement on the island.

Tymbou   A village 12km south–east of Nicosia in the Turkish Republic of North Cyprus. The airfield nearby became the major point of entry and exit by air for Turkish Cypriots when the two communities could not agree on the joint administration of Nicosia International Airport in 1975.

Varosha   A southern suburb of the port of Famagusta with some of the finest beaches on the island of Cyprus. Largely inhabited by Greek Cypriots, Varosha was a popular tourist resort until the Turkish invasion of 1974 made it inaccessible; its status has been a particular bone of contention in the intercommunal negotiations.

■ Key words

Aegean Army   The name given to the Turkish Fourth Army Division assembled on the Aegean coast of Turkey in July 1975 during the crisis that followed the invasion of Cyprus and incidents in Aegean waters claimed by both Greece and Turkey. The division was based in the Anatolian port of Izmir.

Alliance, Treaty of   An agreement, initialled in London in February 1959 and later signed by Greece, Turkey and Cyprus in 1960, allowing Greece and Turkey to maintain respectively contingents of 950 and 650 troops on Cyprus. The treaty was unilaterally terminated by Cyprus in 1964 when the Turkish government refused to remove troops from the road between Kyrenia and Nicosia in north Cyprus.

Attila Line   The frontier or "no-man's-land" dividing the Turkish Cypriot community of north Cyprus from the Greek Cypriots in the south. Stretching from Morphou Bay in the west to Famagusta in the east and cutting through the city of Nicosia, the line separates the Republic of Cyprus from effective control of 28 per cent of the island's population and 37 per cent of its land. The Atilla Line was established by Turkish troops who invaded the island in July 1974 and likened their action to that of Attila the Hun.

Communal Liberation Party or **Socialist Salvation Party (Toplumcu Kurtulus Partisi – TKP)**   One of the three main political parties in the Turkish Republic of Northern Cyprus.

Founded in 1976, it entered into a coalition with the National Unity Party in 1985.

Democratic Front   A centre-right political party formed by Spyros Kyprianou during the 1976 election campaign. Supporting Archbishop Makarios, the Democratic Front swept to victory, winning 21 out of the 35 Greek Cypriot seats in the government controlled area.

Democratic National Party   An extreme right-wing political party founded in 1968 under the leadership of Renos Christodoulides.

Democratic Rally   A conservative political party formed by Glafcos Clerides during the run-up to the 1976 elections. Although the party polled 28 per cent of the vote, it failed to gain a single seat in the government controlled area.

Enosis   A Greek word meaning "one" and signifying the Greek Cypriot aim of achieving union with Greece.

Green Line   The boundary or "no-man's-land" separating the Turkish and Greek Cypriot sectors of the city of Nicosia since the Turkish invasion of July 1974. Also known as the Attila Line.

Guarantee, Treaty of   An agreement initialled in London in February 1959 by Greece, Turkey, Cyprus and Britain allowing Greece, Turkey or Britain to intervene in Cyprus if the conditions specified in the London agreement were thought to be endangered.

intercommunal talks The name given to periodic discussions and negotiations between representatives of the Greek and Turkish Cypriot communities attempting to resolve the Cyprus conflict.

London agreement An agreement reached at a meeting in London in February 1959 that formed the basis for drafting the 1960 constitution for independent Cyprus.

Macmillan Plan A seven-year plan leading to the independence of Cyprus put forward by the British Prime Minister Harold Macmillan in June 1958. The scheme, which came into operation in October of that year, proposed a large degree of self-government in association with a Governor's Council that included members of the mainland Greek and Turkish governments as well as Greek and Turkish Cypriots. An escalation of EOKA violence in 1958–59 resulted in a more rapid transition to independence following agreements reached in Zurich and London.

National Organization of Cypriot Fighters (Ethniki Organosis Kypriakon Agonos – EOKA) A pro-Enosis militant movement led by George Grivas who united the more extreme advocates of Enosis in a campaign of insurgency directed against the British Administration in Cyprus between 1954 and the independence of the island in 1960. In 1971 he returned to Cyprus to form a new guerrilla group known as EOKA-B. On this occasion he directed terrorist activities against Archbishop Makarios who no longer advocated Enosis but favoured an independent Cyprus.

National Unity Party The largest of the political parties of the Turkish Republic of Northern Cyprus, founded by Rauf Denktash in 1975.

New Dawn Party (Yeni Dogus) A minority political party of the Turkish Republic of Northern Cyprus representing settlers from mainland Turkey. Founded in 1984, largely from the membership of the Turkish Nationalist Party.

Progressive Party of the Working People (Anorthotikon Komma Ergazomenou Laou – AKEL) The legal wing of the Communist Party of Cyprus which was formed in 1926 but banned by the British in 1933. Founded in 1941, AKEL claims a membership of about 14 000.

Radcliffe Report A report published in December 1956 and prepared by Lord Radcliffe, Commissioner for Constitutional Reform. He proposed that defence, foreign affairs and internal security should be controlled by the Governor of Cyprus, while domestic affairs should be in the hands of a Cabinet of Cypriot Ministers responsible to an elected legislature. His proposals included safeguards for Turkish Cypriots which were opposed by the Greek government.

taksim A Turkish word used to describe the partition of the island of Cyprus proposed by the Turkish government. In 1958, following the outbreak of Turkish Cypriot riots in Nicosia and Lanarca, 200 000 Turks demonstrated in Istanbul for taksim, a word that now forms the name of a square in that city.

TMT A Turkish Cypriot resistance movement formed in 1957 in response to EOKA attacks on the Turkish Cypriot community.

Turkish Petroleum Corporation (TPAO) A state-owned Turkish company given the sole rights to prospect for oil in the Eastern Aegean by the Turkish government in November 1973. Foreign companies were only allowed to search for oil in disputed waters after a new regulation was passed in January 1980.

Turkish Republican Party (Cumhuruyetçi Türk Partisi – CTP) One of the three main political parties in the Turkish Republic of Northern Cyprus. Founded in 1970.

United Democratic Union of Greece (Eniea Demokratiki Enosi Kyprou – EDEK) The socialist political party of the Republic of Cyprus, founded in 1969.

United Nations peace-keeping force in Cyprus (UNFICYP) A multinational contingent of about 7000 soldiers sent to the island in 1964 to keep the peace between the Greek and Turkish communities. Over 20 years later 2500 UN troops were still based on the island.

Zürich agreement   In February 1959 a meeting in Zürich between the prime ministers of Greece and Turkey concluded with a compromise agreement that outlined the fundamental structure of an independent Cyprus.

■ Further reading

J. Alford (ed.), *Greece and Turkey*, Gower Press, London, 1984

Michael A. Attilides, *Cyprus: Nationalism and International Politics*, Q Press, Edinburgh, 1979

Andrew Borowiec, *The Mediterranean Feud*, Praeger, New York, 1983

Nancy Crawshaw, *The Cyprus Revolt: An Account of the Struggle for Union with Greece*, George Allen and Unwin, London, 1978

Necati Ertekun, *The Cyprus Dispute and the Birth of the Turkish Republic of Northern Cyprus*, K. Rustem and Brother, London, 1984

C. Foley, *Legacy of Strife: Cyprus from Rebellion to Civil War*, Penguin, New York, 1964

Sir George F. Hill, *A History of Cyprus*, (4 vols.), Cambridge University Press, Cambridge, 1940–52

Christopher Hitchens, *Cyprus*, Quartet Books, London, 1984

N. Kliot, Co-operation and Conflict in Maritime Issues in the Mediterranean Basin, *GeoJournal*, 18(3), 1989, pp.263–72

P.G. Polyviou, *Cyprus: Conflict and Negotiation, 1960–1980*, Duckworth, London, 1980

6
Northern Ireland

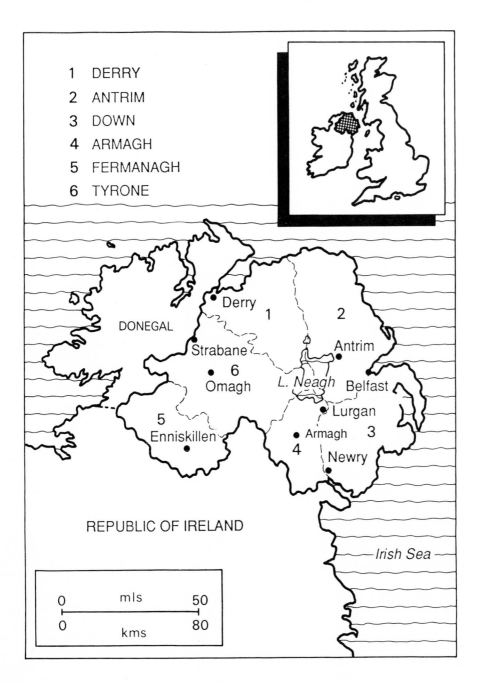

1 DERRY
2 ANTRIM
3 DOWN
4 ARMAGH
5 FERMANAGH
6 TYRONE

Derry

DONEGAL

Strabane

6
Omagh

L. Neagh

Antrim

Belfast

Lurgan

5
Enniskillen

4
Armagh

3

Newry

REPUBLIC OF IRELAND

Irish Sea

0   mls   50
0   kms   80

■ Profile

Area: 14 120km²
Population (1981): 1 556 000
Religion: Roman Catholic 28%, Presbyterian 23%, Church of Ireland 19%, Methodist 4%
Administrative divisions: six counties and 26 local government areas
Capital: Belfast
Chief towns: Belfast (303 800), Derry (62 700), Lisburn (40 400), Ballymena (28 200)

■ Introduction

Partitions of countries usually create as many problems as they solve. The division of Ireland in 1922, into an independent Catholic state in the south and a Protestant-majority province of the United Kingdom in the north, proved to be no exception. On the one hand, it created a territorial dispute between Britain and what became the Irish Republic over the latter's aspiration to an all-Ireland state. On the other, it ensured a conflict of national loyalties between the sizeable Catholic minority in Northern Ireland and a Protestant majority determined to remain British and to preserve its political and economic ascendancy. Even so, only a generation ago most Britons would have found it inconceivable that bloody civil strife could occur anywhere in the United Kingdom: such things, it was believed, only happened in benighted foreign lands. By the early 1970s, however, they were witnessing killings and destruction in Northern Ireland on a huge scale, as simmering national and religious antagonisms came to the boil.

That the Irish did not follow Wales and Scotland in coming to terms with the English within a united kingdom was mainly because of religious differences, accentuated by the physical gulf of the Irish Sea and the special brutalities of English rule. Ireland had undergone English conquest long before the Reformation; but when England embraced Protestantism in the 16th century the Catholic Irish were regarded as little better than heathens. Under the Tudors Irish support for England's Catholic enemies abroad increased

English determination to impose Protestantism. When this was resisted, the Stuarts gave confiscated Irish land to Scottish Presbyterians, who began the Protestant "plantation" of Ulster. Dispossession of Catholics in favour of Protestants continued after Cromwell's ruthless suppression of another Irish rebellion. In 1690 the celebrated victory of William of Orange at the Battle of the Boyne confirmed Catholic Ireland's subjection to a Protestant ascendancy under which the native Irish had no political rights and their language and culture barely survived. The inevitable legacy was one of deep anti-British feeling among Catholics, but with the complication that a substantial Protestant community in the north also regarded Ireland as its homeland.

The American and French revolutions inspired new rebellion in Ireland in the late 18th century. Britain responded with the 1800 Act of Union, giving the Irish representation at Westminster of the kind that the Welsh and Scots had long enjoyed. Emancipation of Catholics soon followed. But special Irish grievances ensured that the path of political integration would not be followed. The great famine of the 1840s highlighted the iniquities of land ownership in Ireland and strengthened Irish nationalism. Protestants were to the fore in this movement, although rapid industrialization in the north was accentuating its separateness from the backward south. Irish efforts focused on obtaining home rule under the Crown. By 1886 this had been conceded by enlightened British opinion but was blocked by pro-unionists until 1914, and then shelved because of the outbreak of war. Thus was the last chance of preserving the unity of the British Isles lost. Northern Protestants vowed to oppose all-Ireland home rule by force, while Irish militants opted for full independence and showed in the abortive Easter Rising of 1916 that they too were prepared to use force to achieve it.

Irish nationalists contend that Irish unity could have been preserved on the basis of the majority vote in the 1918 elections, in which the pro-independence Sinn Féin won three-quarters of the Irish seats. However, Britain had incurred a special debt to Ulster Protestants for their sacrifices in World War I, and boundary redrawing was in vogue in Europe. Faced with polarization in Ireland, Britain opted for partition, disguised at first as the granting of separate home rule to the six Protestant-majority counties of Ulster's nine. A "free state" within the Commonwealth was then offered to the nationalists on condition that the six counties could choose to remain British. When this treaty was reluctantly accepted, the six counties did so choose. The self- governing Irish state born in 1922 therefore consisted of only 26 of Ireland's 32 counties, to the chagrin of many nationalists. The anti-treaty Irish Republican Army (IRA) lost the resultant Irish civil war but anti-partition nationalists won political power in 1927 as Fianna Fáil, which has dominated Irish politics ever since. Although the use of force to end partition was publicly abandoned, a new constitution in 1937 described the national territory as "the whole island of Ireland", a provision which remains in force. When the newly-declared Irish Republic left the Commonwealth in 1949, Britain responded with legislation guaranteeing Northern Ireland's status as part of the United Kingdom and thus refuting the Irish constitution's aspiration.

Having been a minority within a Catholic majority, Northern Ireland's Protestants became from 1922 a majority facing a Catholic minority of suspect loyalty. Organized in the Unionist Party and the Orange Order, the Protestants institutionalized political and economic discrimination against Catholics, backed by their control of the security forces. So blatant had the abuses become by the 1960s that London, under pressure from Dublin,

was forced to demand reforms. This did not prevent the emergence of a mass movement for Catholic civil rights, whose campaigns led to a rapid escalation of intercommunal violence in which Catholics were exposed to the Protestant security apparatus. Britain's fateful response in 1969 was to send in troops, who were at first welcomed by Catholics but came to be seen as an occupying force backing Protestant rule. A "provisional" wing of the IRA assumed the leadership of Catholic resistance to "British occupation", as the toll of death and destruction mounted. Protestant paramilitary groups matched their Catholic counterparts in carrying out sectarian attacks. The IRA and other republican movements later spread their campaign to Britain and to other countries where British military and official targets were available.

On the political front, the British government showed its disenchantment with the Unionists' record by imposing direct rule in Northern Ireland. But efforts to establish Protestant/Catholic power-sharing in the province repeatedly collapsed in the face of opposition from both sides of the religious divide. The IRA and its supporters wanted a British commitment to withdraw from Ireland. Protestant loyalists resolutely resisted any steps which appeared to undermine majority rule or UK status. Nor were loyalists impressed by the Republic's (mostly unsuccessful) attempts to amend its constitution to make it more palatable to Northern Protestants. Britain nevertheless pursued co-operation with Dublin on the Northern Ireland problem and in 1985 signed the Anglo-Irish Agreement. This gave Dublin a consultative role in the North's affairs, in return for the Republic's formal acceptance, for the first time, that reunification was possible only with the consent of a Northern majority. But the agreement's clear signal that Irish reunification was the long-term solution so outraged Northern Protestants that little progress could be made within its framework. Moreover, serious strains developed between Dublin and London over their respective judicial procedures for suspected terrorists, summed up by the charge that British courts imprisoned the innocent while Irish courts released the guilty.

As the 1990s opened, the Northern Ireland conflict appeared to be one of the world's deep-seated clashes of national loyalties for which there was no obvious solution. Unilateral British withdrawal, favoured by many in Britain and elsewhere, was seen as likely to provoke full-scale civil war between Protestants and Catholics. While reunification remained the Republic's long-term aim, sovereignty over almost a million rebellious and well-armed Protestants, who would probably declare unilateral independence, had little attractions. The idea of replacing British troops with a UN or European peace-keeping force has also been floated, but would not of itself resolve the deadlock. Nor was there any prospect,

dreamt of by some, of Irish unity on the basis of all-Ireland dominion status under the Crown. Despite previous failures, some form of power-sharing in Northern Ireland, under British sovereignty but with a role for Dublin, therefore seemed to be the only way forward. Sooner or later, proponents of this scenario contended, British and Irish membership of a European Community committed to political union would diminish the significance of the Irish border and create a wider sense of security and belonging. The more sceptical could not see this happy state coming to pass in the foreseeable future.

■ Chronology of events

1170–72   Henry II of England conquers Ireland and forces the native Irish to accept large numbers of Anglo–Norman settlers. The independent Irish Church is united with the Church of Rome.

1366   The English, who regard the Irish with mistrust, forbid intermarriage between Irish and English under the Statutes of Kilkenny.

1494   Henry VII sends Sir Edward Poyning to Ireland to ensure that no Irish parliament enacts legislation without the prior consent of King and Council in England.

1558–1603   Under Elizabeth I of England Roman Catholics in Ireland are persecuted during the Reformation. Two insurrections in 1579–83 (the Geraldine rebellion) and 1595 (the O'Neill rebellion) are crushed by the English.

1607   James I initiates the "Plantation of Ulster" with English and Scottish Protestant colonists. This process creates divisions between Catholic and Protestant within Ulster and between Ulster and the rest of Ireland.

1641   The Catholic Irish rise up and massacre an estimated 30 000 Protestant Planters in Ulster.

1649   Cromwell brutally suppresses the Irish rebellion, massacring the garrisons at Drogheda

and Wexford. In the succeeding years Catholic landholders are disposessed in favour of Protestants.

1660   Following the restoration of Charles II the Catholic religion in Ireland is tolerated.

1690   The Catholic Irish support the deposed James II in his struggle to regain the throne from William of Orange, but both James and the Catholics are defeated at the Battle of the Boyne on 1 July.

1692   An exclusively Protestant legislature is established in Dublin.

1695   The British parliament approves Irish pacification terms that include religious liberty and amnesties, but the Irish parliament refuses to confirm them. Instead, a series of anti-Catholic legislation is passed.

1703   After nearly 100 years in Ireland the Protestant "planters" own an estimated 86 per cent of the land in Ulster.

1739–41   Nearly one–third of the population of Ireland dies during years of famine.

1782   Ireland is granted an independent parliament.

1791 A revolutionary organization known as the United Irishmen is formed by Wolfe Tone in an attempt to unite Catholic and Protestant for the common purpose of securing the complete separation of Ireland from Britain.

1793 Under the Catholic Relief Act parliamentary franchise is extended to Catholics on equal terms with Protestants.

1795 The Orange Order is founded as an Episcopalian peasant self defence organization.

1798 An insurrection mounted by the United Irishmen fails.

1801 By an Act of Union passed in the previous year, the legislatures of Ireland and Great Britain are united under the name of the United Kingdom. The Irish are represented in the British parliament by 28 peers and four bishops in the House of Lords and by 100 members in the House of Commons. At the same time, the churches of the two countries are united into one Protestant Episcopal church.

1803 A rebellion against the Act of Union led by Robert Emmet is quickly suppressed.

1829 The Roman Catholic Emancipation Act enables Catholics to sit in the House of Commons.

1834 The Orange Order accepts Presbyterians into its membership.

1835 The first serious Catholic–Protestant intercommunal riots of the 19th century take place in Belfast.

1840 The radical Young Ireland Party is formed under the leadership of William Smith O'Brien. Seeking the repeal of the Act of Union, this group rejects the peaceful methods advocated by the Irish nationalist leader Danniel O'Connell.

1844 On 13 February Lord John Russell opens a nine–day debate in the House of Commons on the "Irish Question". Although his motion that "Ireland is occupied not governed" is defeated,

Ireland is recognized as a special area requiring special treatment for the first time.

1845–46 As a result of the Great Potato Famine nearly one million people die out of a total population of eight million. A further 1 250 000 people are forced to emigrate, 250 000 of them to Britain.

1848 The Young Irelanders lead an unsuccessful rebellion against the Union.

1850 A Tenants–Right League is formed for the purpose of fighting injustices within the Irish land tenure system. The movement campaigns for the "three F's" – fair rent, fixity of tenure and free sale.

1858 A revolutionary nationalist organization known as the Irish Republican Brotherhood is founded in the USA by James Stephens. Its members are called Fenians after an ancient Irish race.

1867 The Fenians, who carry their "war of independence" to the streets of England, stage an unsuccessful revolt.

1868 Elected Prime Minister for the first time, Gladstone declares: "My mission is to pacify Ireland". He attempts to solve the Irish Question by tackling land tenure and the role of the established Church.

1869 An Act is passed disestablishing the Irish (Episcopal Church). Church property and revenue are purchased by landowners.

1870 The Irish Land Act, the first in a series of Irish agrarian laws, fails to bring unrest to an end.

1871 Isaac Butt founds the parliamentary Home Rule Party in an attempt to establish by peaceful means a separate legislature for Ireland.

1879 Constitutional and revolutionary movements join forces to form the Land League which is set up under the ex-Fenian Michael Davitt at Irishtown, County Mayo in April. The League is successful in its attempts to introduce reforms to the system of land tenure in Ireland.

1881 A second Land Act establishes land courts for the purpose of fixing "fair" rents and mediating between landlord and tenant.

1882 Following the murder in Dublin's Phoenix Park of Sir Frederick Cavendish, the new Secretary of State for Ireland, and his permanent undersecretary, Thomas Burke, the government pushes through the Prevention of Crimes Bill which suspends trial by jury and allows police unlimited power to search and arrest suspected terrorists. Irish extremists react by launching a bombing campaign in England.

1886 The first Home Rule Bill is defeated following bitter Conservative opposition.

1893 A second Home Rule Bill is passed by the House of Commons but is defeated in the Lords.

1898 The Ulster Unionist Party is established with the support of the British Conservative Party as the main voice of Protestant Unionists.

1905 In the North Sir Edward Carson sets up a provisional government known as the Ulster Unionist Council, while in the South nationalists unite under Arthur Griffith to form the Sinn Féin political party.

1912 In September the Ulster Covenant is signed in Belfast by an estimated 471 414 people who pledge opposition to home rule. An Ulster Volunteer Force is set up to act as a Protestant defence miltia and is armed with rifles and ammunition smuggled into the country.

1913 For the third time a Home Rule Bill is presented to parliament, but before it is rejected for the second time by the House of Lords 5 000 Ulstermen gather at Craigavon to voice their opposition to home rule and threaten resistance by force of arms if necessary. A paramilitary Nationalist Volunteer Force is established in the South.

1914 The Home Rule Bill is finally passed, but the outbreak of World War I delays its implementation.

1916 On 24 April a rebellion breaks out in Dublin, but within a week the so-called Easter Rising is contained.

1917 Following an amnesty, the Sinn Féin leader Eamon de Valera is released. At a Sinn Féin convention held in Dublin in October a constitution for the Irish Republic is adopted and de Valera is elected President.

1918 In elections to the UK House of Commons Sinn Féin candidates win, but do not take up, 72 of the 105 Irish seats.

1919 The Sinn Féin members elected to the British parliament in the previous year organize their own parliament and declare Irish independence. When the Sinn Féin movement led by Michael Collins is eventually suppressed in November a guerrilla war breaks out. The country's constabulary is backed up by a British security force which comes to be known as the Black and Tans.

1920 At the end of a year of bitter conflict the British parliament passes an act which effectively enables the Protestant Unionists in the north to retain control of six counties of the Irish province of Ulster. At the same time, a Council of Ireland is created as a means of encouraging co-operation between the two parts of Ireland.

1921 In the north, Unionists accept the partition of Ireland and elect a Northern Ireland parliament in May. In the south the Sinn Féin declares itself to be the National Parliament (Dáil Eireann) and ignores the 1920 Act after winning 124 out of 128 seats.

On 6 December an Anglo–Irish treaty is signed establishing an Irish Free State, but Northern Ireland is allowed to retain the right to opt out, which it duly does.

1922 On 6 December the Irish Free State is officially proclaimed and a constitution is adopted by the Dáil, but civil war escalates between pro- and anti-treaty factions of Sinn Féin.

1923 The civil war ends with the pro-treaty side victorious, although militant elements continue to oppose partition within the Irish Republican Army (IRA).

1925 The boundary between the Irish Free State and Northern Ireland is established.

1926 The Council of Ireland, set up in 1920, is formally dissolved.

1927 The assassination of Kevin O'Higgins, a prominent government figure, discredits the tactics of the Republicans and when de Valera decides to rejoin the democratic political process the IRA cause collapses.

1931 A new public safety law in the Irish Free State bans the IRA.

1937 In December a new constitution ignoring the British Crown comes into effect in the South where the fully independent state of Eire is established. Articles 2 and 3 of the constitution define "the national territory" as "the whole island of Ireland", but state that "pending reintegration of the national territory" the constitution only applies in the 26 counties.

1938 All hope of a merger between Northern Ireland and the Irish Free State is abandoned when Unionists win an overwhelming victory in elections in the North.

1939 The IRA launches a bombing campaign in England.

1949 The constitutional links between Eire and the UK are severed when the Republic of Ireland Act 1948 comes into effect on Easter Sunday. The constitutional position of Northern Ireland, which remains an integral part of the United Kingdom, is guaranteed by the British government under the Ireland Act 1949.

1956 The IRA re-emerges in the North with a bombing campaign designed to force the British out of Northern Ireland, but the Protestant two–thirds of Ulster's 1.5 million people rejects

union with the Irish Republic's 3.2 million Catholics, preferring home rule from Belfast.

1962 The IRA abandons its bombing campaign on the mainland of Britain.

1964 A Campaign for Social Justice in Northern Ireland is formed in Dungannon by Catholics seeking reform of institutionalized discrimination against Catholics.

1966 Attempts to improve the position of Ulster Catholics are opposed by the Rev. Ian Paisley whose supporters in the Free Presbyterian Church stage a riot in Belfast.

1967 Following the success of the civil rights campaign in America, a broadly-based Northern Ireland Civil Rights Association is formed as a means of co-ordinating non-violent protest against inequality.

1968 Paisley and his Protestant extremists again voice strong opposition to the Belfast government's moderate reform programme.

1969 Intercommunal violence breaks out in Londonderry and Belfast in April and at the request of the Northern Ireland government the British send troops to the province. After further violence in August the governments in London and Belfast issue a joint declaration affirming the committment to equality and the protection of the people of Northern Ireland from sectarian violence (Downing Street Declaration).

1970 When violence escalates the British take over responsibility for security which had been in the hands of local Protestant militias. Feuding within the IRA leads to a split into provisional and official factions.

1972 When British soldiers shoot 13 demonstrators at a rally in Londonderry on 30 January ("Bloody Sunday"), violence spirals out of control. Two months later the Unionist government in Belfast resigns and direct rule is imposed from London. The British government appoints a Secretary of State for Northern Ireland. In this year alone, 485 people are killed and 4866 are injured as a result of intercommunal unrest and terrorist acts of violence.

1973 In March a referendum on the status of the province is boycotted by the Catholic community. The British government thereupon proceeds to set up a Northern Ireland Assembly, to be elected by proportional representation, and an Executive based on power–sharing by Catholics and Protestants. Fearing that jurors will be subject to intimidation, the government also sets up Diplock Courts without juries to try suspected terrorists. In December, an Anglo–Irish agreement is reached at Sunningdale in Berkshire where power–sharing is endorsed and a Council of Ireland is proposed.

1974 The search for a political solution to the Northern Ireland conflict suffers a setback with the suspension of the National Assembly in January after a split in the Unionist Party. In May Unionists endorse a general strike that effectively wrecks the Sunningdale power-sharing agreement, and direct rule from London is reimposed.

Following a series of IRA explosions and killings at Balcombe Street, Birmingham, Guildford and Woolwich, the British government extends Police powers of arrest and detention under the Prevention of Terrorism Act.

1975 Following talks with the British Government (Feakle Talks) the IRA announces a ceasefire that lasts from February until terminated by Protestant sectarian killings and the collapse of a convention exploring a new constitutional settlement. A women's peace movement organized by Mairead Corrigan and Betty Williams gains widespread support but fails to make any lasting impact.

1979 During a campaign of political assassinations Airey Neave and Lord Mountbatten are killed by terrorists.

1980–81 Media attention focuses on the "dirty protests" and hunger strikes staged by IRA terrorists in the prisons of Northern Ireland. Ten Hunger strikers die.

1982 Britain proposes a 78–member Assembly for Northern Ireland, but when elections are held the Catholic parties refuse to take their seats.

1983 In May the Social Democratic and Labour Party (SDLP) meets with the three main Irish Catholic parties in a New Ireland Forum. The British government rejects the options of a united Ireland, joint authority or confederation proposed by this constitutional forum.

1984 Mrs Thatcher and her cabinet narrowly escape death when an IRA bomb goes off in a Brighton hotel during the annual Conservative Party conference.

1985 The British government finally recognizes Dublin's legitimate interest in the North by entering into an Anglo–Irish Agreement in November. While reaffirming Northern Ireland's position in the United Kingdom, London seeks to allow Dublin a consultative role in Northern Ireland affairs in an attempt to combat terrorism.

1986 The Northern Ireland Assembly set up in 1982 is dissolved as a result of a series of boycotts in protest at the Anglo–Irish Agreement.

An investigation into the "shoot to kill" policy of the RUC in Armagh receives public attention when John Stalker is replaced as leader of the inquiry.

1987 In May it is announced that, in the face of a rising level of IRA recruitment, the RUC is to be enlarged by some 500 new officers. It is also reported that the Special Air Service Regiment (SAS) are to be given a greater role in security operations.

1988 Three IRA terrorists are killed by British security forces in Gibraltar on 6 March. In the subsequent *Death on the Rock* inquiry the media focuses on the possibility that there was a predetermined plan to kill the IRA members.

In October the Home Secretary announces an immediate ban on the broadcasting of interviews with representatives of 11 terrorist organizations in Northern Ireland. A day later the Secretary of State for Northern Ireland announces that the right of suspected terrorists to remain silent during police investigations or in court is to be curtailed.

Official British statistics for the period 1971–88 record a total of 2 573 killings during the troubles in Northern Ireland. Of these 1831 were civilians (including suspected members of paramilitary organizations), 588 were army or UDR personnel and 254 were members of the RUC or RUC Reserve. In the same period acts of violence resulted in injuries to 20 631 civilians, 3 816 army and UDR personnel and

4 810 RUC members or reservists. The statistics also detail 30 570 shooting incidents, 8 640 bomb blasts (involving an estimated 293 40 lb of explosives) and 13 817 armed robberies. In all a total of 13 992 people were charged with terrorist offences during that 18–year period.

1989   In October the "Guildford Four" are released after 14 years in prison following a decision of the Court of Appeal.

1990   A British–Irish consultative body, first mooted in 1980, meets for the first time in February, but Unionists refuse to take part until the 1985 Anglo–Irish Agreement is suspended.

■ Who's who

Adams, Gerry   Sinn Féin president, elected to Westminster in June 1983 as MP for West Belfast, a seat formerly held by Gerry Fitt of the SDLP.

Black, Christopher   A notorious IRA "supergrass" whose arrest in November 1981 led to the conviction of 35 other terrorists as a result of his evidence. The "supergrass" system that subsequently developed was responsible for the conviction of 590 terrorists in the space of two years.

Craig, William   Former Northern Ireland Minister of Home Affairs who founded the Vanguard Unionist Party in 1973.

Daly, Miriam   A Belfast activist and leader of the Irish Republican Socialist Party.

Ewart–Biggs, Christopher   British ambassador to Ireland, murdered by the IRA in Dublin in July 1976.

Faulkner, Brian   The last Prime Minister of Northern Ireland prior to the suspension of the Belfast government and the imposition of direct rule from London in 1972.

Fitt, Lord Gerry   A Republican Labour MP elected to Westminster for West Belfast in

March 1966 and later elected leader of the Catholic Social Democratic and Labour Party (SDLP). Opposed to the British Labour Party's offer of more power to the Unionists through proportional representation, Gerry Fitt abstained in the crucial vote of no-confidence that brought down the Callaghan government by a margin of one vote in 1979. After his defeat in the June 1983 election he was elevated to the House of Lords.

Hermon, Sir John   Chief Constable of the RUC in Northern Ireland since January 1980.

Hume, John   Leader of the Catholic SDLP since 1980. In the 1960s Hume was a co-leader of the civil rights movement with the protestant Ivan Cooper.

Lowry, Lord   Lord Chief Justice of Northern Ireland 1971–1988.

McAliskey, Bernadette (née Devlin)   A leading member of the civil rights movement in the 1960s, Bernadette McAliskey was a co-founder in 1974 of the Irish Republican Socialists, a party she abandoned a year later because of its "militarism".

Mallon, Seamus   Deputy leader of the Catholic SDLP and MP for Newry and Armagh.

Molyneux, James   Leader of the Unionist Party since 1979.

Mountbatten, Lord Louis   A leading member of the Royal family killed on 27 August, 1979 ("Bloody Monday"), while yachting at Mullaghmore, County Sligo.

Neave, Airey   A former intelligence officer and leading Conservative Party politician killed by an INLA bomb outside the House of Commons in 1979. Prior to his death Neave had advocated the strengthening of the SAS and the UDR, the introduction of hanging and the re-introduction of internment. With the return to power of the Conservatives it was suspected that he might succeed Roy Mason as Secretary of State of Northern Ireland.

O'Hare, Desmond (Dessie)   A leading member of the INLA wanted on both sides of the border. Known as "the border fox" he was eventually arrested and sentenced to 40 year imprisonment by the Special Criminal Court in Dublin in April 1988.

Paisley, Rev. Ian Kyle   A fundamentalist Free Presbyterian minister and leader of the Democratic Unionists, a breakaway faction of the "Official" Unionist Party.

Robinson, Peter   Deputy Leader of Ian Paisley's Democratic Unionist Party. Robinson was arrested by the Gardai of the Irish Republic in August 1986 following incidents in the town of Clontibret in County Monagahan.

Sands, Robert (Bobby)   An IRA prisoner in the Maze prison in Belfast who was elected MP for Fermanagh–South Tyrone in April 1981 while staging a hunger strike in support of demands for political status for Republican prisoners.

After his death a few weeks later, Owen Carron of the Sinn Féin was elected to represent his constituency.

Stalker, John   Deputy Chief Constable of Greater Manchester who was appointed in 1984 to head an eight-man team of detectives to investigate the alleged "shoot to kill" policy of the RUC. Having submitted an interim report recommending the prosecution of seven senior RUC officers Stalker was replaced in June 1986 by Colin Sampson, Chief Constable of West Yorkshire. Suspended from duty for an alleged serious breach of the disciplinary code, he was later restored to duty following an official inquiry into his conduct. In March 1987 Stalker resigned from the force, later suggesting that his removal from the investigation had been politically motivated.

Twomey, Seamus   IRA chief of staff arrested in 1977 after four years on the run following a daring escape from Mountjoy prison in 1973. A report found on him when he was recaptured revealed the new IRA cell system.

Tyrie, Andy   A leading member of the Ulster Defence Association (UDA) responsible for shifting emphasis from terrorism to political activity.

UK Secretaries of State for Northern Ireland
1972–73 William Whitelaw (Cons.), 1973–74 Francis Pym (Cons.), 1974–76 Merlyn Rees (Lab.), 1976–79 Roy Mason (Lab.), 1979–81 Humphrey Atkins (Cons.), 1981–84 James Prior (Cons.), 1984–85 Douglas Hurd (Cons.), 1985–89 Tom King (Cons.), 1989– Peter Brooke (Cons.),

■ Key places

Andersonstown   A south–western suburb of Belfast. The Lenadoon housing estate in Andersonstown was the scene of bitter conflict between Protestants and Catholics in July 1975, a feud that brought to an end a brief IRA ceasefire.

Antrim   One of the six counties of Northern Ireland lying to the east of the River Bann and to the north of County Down; area 2 831km²; population (1981) 642 300. Its capital is Belfast.

Armagh   Lying between Lough Neagh and the frontier with the Irish Republic, Armagh is the smallest of the six counties of Northern Ireland; area 1 254km²; population (1981) 118 800. Its capital is the historic town of Armagh, the former seat of the Kings of Ulster.

Bann   A river flowing north–eastwards from the Mourne Mountains of County Down to Lough Neagh and on to the Atlantic Ocean west of Portstewart. The Bann is often considered the boundary line separating the predominantly Protestant east from the rest of Northern Ireland.

Belfast   The capital city of Northern Ireland, situated at the mouth of the Lagan River where it flows into Belfast Lough; population (1981) 359 000. Chartered in 1613, the city became the capital of the six counties in 1920. The former Parliament Buildings at Stormont (completed in 1932) lie to the east of the city.

Bogside   A predominantly Catholic area of Derry which was the focal point of intercommunal violence in the aftermath of the traditional Apprentice Boys of Derry march in August 1969.

Boyne   A river that rises in the Bog of Allen, County Kildare, and flows 112km eastwards to meet the Irish Sea beyond Drogheda. Five kilometres west of Drogheda an obelisk marks the site of the famous Battle of the Boyne in which the army of William of Orange defeated the Catholic Jacobites under James II on 1 July 1690.

Crossmaglen   A market town near the border between Armagh and Monaghan in the Irish Republic. With a predominantly Catholic population, the town has been the focal point of a number of incidents involving IRA terrorism.

Crumlin Road   The site of a maximun security terrorist prison on the NW outskirts of Belfast.

Derry or **Londonderry**   One of the six counties of Northern Ireland; area 2 067km²; population (1981) 186 700. Its capital is Derry (Londonderry). The original Celtic city of Derry was rebuilt by Protestant settlers and proclaimed part of the Corporation of the City of London by King James VI in 1613. Renamed Londonderry, the city was officially restored to its original Irish name in 1984. On 12 August 1969 the traditional march of the Protestant Apprentice Boys of Derry ended in a violent seige of the Catholic Bogside area. This incident led to a sharp increase in intercommunal violence in Northern Ireland. Three years later on 30 January 1972 ("Bloody Sunday"), Derry was again the focus of world media attention when 13 demonstrators were shot during a civil rights march through the city.

Down   One of the six counties of Northern Ireland, situated to the south of Belfast; area 2 448km²; population (1981) 339 200. Its capital is the pilgrimage town of Downpatrick where St Patrick is said to have landed in AD 432.

Fermanagh   With a population (1981) of 51000 and an area of 1676km², Fermanagh is the least densely populated of the six counties of Northern Ireland. Its capital is Enniskillen.

Hillsborough Castle   Situated on the outskirts of Belfast, Hillsborough Castle was the former seat of the Governors of Northern Ireland. In November 1985 the Anglo–Irish Agreement was unveiled here.

Irish Republic   An independent republic (since 1949) occupying four–fifths of the island of Ireland; area 68900km²; population (1986) 3 537 000. Its capital is Dublin.

Larne   A seaport in County Antrim with ferry links to Cairnryan and Stranraer in Scotland. Situated 30km north of Belfast, Larne is also an important centre of the textile and engineering industries.

Long Kesh   A notorious internment camp near Lisburn, nicknamed "The Maze". Characterized by its H– block buildings, Long Kesh was the scene of riots in October 1974 and of the much publicized "dirty protests" and hunger strikes of 1980–81.

Lower Falls   A largely Catholic area of Belfast which includes the Divis Flats.

Magilligan   A prison camp in Derry.

Mountjoy   A prison on the North Circular Road, Belfast.

Shankill Road   An area of west Belfast noted as the centre of Protestant paramilitary groups including the UDA and the UVF.

Tyrone   The largest of the six counties of Northern Ireland; area 3 136km²; population (1981) 143 900. Its capital is Omagh.

Ulster   The northernmost of the ancient provinces of Ireland comprising the six counties of present-day Northern Ireland and the three counties of Cavan, Monaghan and Donegal (which form a province of the Irish Republic). The name Ulster is often solely applied to Northern Ireland.

■ Key words

Alliance Party   A non-sectarian political party founded in Northern Ireland in 1970.

Ancient Order of Hibernians   A Catholic counterpart to the Orange Order formed in 1938 in support of a united Ireland and loyalty to the Pope.

Anglo–Irish Agreement   An agreement signed on 15 November 1985 by the Prime Ministers of the United Kingdom and the Irish Republic who met at Hillsborough Castle near Belfast. The agreement aimed to improve co-operation in combating terrorism by allowing Dublin a consultative role in Northern Ireland affairs. At the same time it reaffirmed the majority's right to decide on the constitutional future of Northern Ireland.

Anglo–Irish Agreement of 1938   An arrangement made by Neville Chamberlain and Eamon de Valera by which Britain ceded the Irish "treaty ports" whose use had been retained under the 1921 Anglo–Irish Treaty. This agreement ensured the neutrality of the Irish Republic during World War II.

Anglo–Irish Treaty of 1921   A treaty establishing the Irish Free State as a dominion of the British Empire and creating a Boundary Commission to delineate the border of Northern Ireland. Although the treaty included Northern Ireland, the six counties were given the power to opt out of the Free State, which they promptly did.

Birmingham Six   The name given to the six Irishmen arrested and convicted for their alleged role in the Birmingham bombings of 1974 in which 21 people died and 168 were injured.

Bloody Sunday   The name given to Sunday 30 January, 1972, on which 13 people were shot dead by British paratroopers during an illegal Civil Rights procession through Derry.

British–Irish Parliamentary Body   A joint Anglo–Irish parliamentary consultative body consisting of 25 members from each of the United Kingdom and Irish parliaments. The body, which held its first meeting in London in February 1990, was boycotted by the Unionists in Northern Ireland.

B–Special Corps   A Protestant militia established in 1919 by Lord Brookeborough from members of the pre-First World War Ulster Volunteer Force and former members of the British army. Originally set up to patrol the border of Fermanagh County, B–Special Corps eventually spread to all of the six counties of Northern Ireland. Their role in the violent unrest of 1969 enraged public opinion and led to the setting up of a committee of inquiry into the activities of the police and the B–Specials. On the advice of the commission, which was chaired by Sir John Hunt, security was taken out of the hands of militias and made the direct responsibility of the General Officer Commanding Northern Ireland. In April 1970 the B–Specials were disbanded and a new corps, the Ulster Defence Regiment, set up in its place.

Campaign for Social Justice   A Catholic organization founded in Dungannon in 1964 as a means of organizing non-violent protest against inequality, principally in the area of housing allocation.

Democratic Unionist Party   One of the rival groupings within the Unionist Party in Northern Ireland, led by the fundamentalist Free Presbyterian the Rev. Ian Paisley.

Diplock Courts   A court system established in 1973 enabling terrorist cases to be heard without a jury because of fear of intimidation. Diplock Courts were introduced by the government following recommendations made by Lord Diplock in a report on the administration of law in Northern Ireland published on 20 December, 1972.

Downing Street Declaration   A communiqué issued jointly by the governments of Northern Ireland and the United Kingdom in August 1969 affirming, amongst other things, that the UK government had ultimate responsibility for the protection of the people and that both governments were committed to equal treatment for all citizens of Northern Ireland.

Fenian   A member of the Irish Republican Brotherhood, a revolutionary nationalist organization founded in the USA in 1858 by James Stephens. The word Fenian is derived from the name of an ancient Irish people.

Garda Siochana   The police force of the Irish Republic.

Gardiner Committee   A committee chaired by Lord Gardiner set up in 1975 to review measures for dealing with terrorism. Recommendations made by the committee included the termination of special category status for prisoners.

Guildford Four   The name given to Patrick Armstrong, Carole Richardson, Paul Hill and Gerard Conlon, all of whom were imprisoned

for their alleged involvement in the Guildford and Woolwich pub bombings in 1974. After 14 years imprisonment the Guildford Four were released in October 1989 following a review by the Court of Appeal.

Green Book   Compiled in 1980, the *Green Book* of the IRA is similar to the *Green Book* of Libyan leader, Colonel Qadhafi. It outlines the philosophy of the IRA cause, its history, and the means by which the IRA struggle is to be prosecuted.

H–Blocks   A prison block of 800 cells built in the form of an H to accommodate prisoners whose special category status was abolished in 1980.

Hillsborough Agreement   Another name for the 1985 Anglo–Irish Agreement.

home rule   The government of the whole of Ireland by its own people has formed the basis of the nationalist home rule movement ever since the English took control of Ireland, but between 1844 and 1914 the issue played a major part in British politics. After Gladstone's conversion in 1885 the Liberal Party gave its support to Irish home rule. They were opposed by the Conservative Party which endorsed the Unionist efforts to maintain the Union of 1801. Three Home Rule Bills were introduced to the British parliament between 1885 and 1913 before a Home Rule Act was finally passed in 1914.

Irish Independence Party   A political party formed in October 1977 to promote the ultimate independence of Northern Ireland from the United Kingdom.

Irish Nationalist Liberation Army (INLA)   The paramilitary arm of the left–wing Irish Republican Socialist Party formed in 1975 following a feud within the Official IRA. Initially centred on the Divis Flats in the Falls Road, Belfast, the INLA' was proscribed in 1979 following a series of terrorist actions which included the murder of the British politician Airey Neave in 1979.

Irish People's Liberation Organization   A breakaway faction of the INLA formed in 1987 after a struggle for power that resulted in the death of several well known terrorists.

Irish Republican Army (IRA) An Irish nationalist paramilitary organization committed to the expulsion of the British from Northern Ireland and the creation of a socialist republic encompassing all 32 Irish counties. Originally known as the Irish Volunteers, the IRA waged a violent guerrilla war against the British between 1919 and 1923. Banned in the Irish Republic in 1931, it launched a bombing campaign on the mainland of Britain in 1939. A limited campaign of violence was again carried out for six years (1956–62) but when civil rights disorders flared up in Northern Ireland during 1968–69 the guerrilla activities of the IRA were renewed with vigour. In 1970 a breakaway group calling itself the Provisional IRA was formed in the north and in 1975 another split in the IRA ranks took place with the formation of the Irish National Liberation Army (INLA). The Provisional IRA is the military wing of Sinn Féin (formerly the Provisional Sinn Féin) while the Official IRA is the military wing of the Workers' Party (formerly the Marxist Sinn Féin).

Irish Republican Socialist Party (IRSP) A left–wing republican political party set up in 1974 under the leadership of Seamus Costello and Bernadette McAliskey (née Devlin). The aim of the party is to achieve a united socialist republic in Ireland. In 1975 the INLA emerged as the military wing of this party.

Mickies A derogatory Ulster Protestant nickname for Irish Catholics.

New Ireland Forum A constitutional forum comprising the Catholic SDLP of Northern Ireland and the Fine Gael, Fianna Fail and Labour parties of the Irish Republic who held a series of meetings in Dublin Castle between April 1983 and May 1984 to examine the prospects for a united Ireland. The Unionists boycotted the forum whose finding gained little support from the British government.

Northern Ireland Civil Rights Association (NICRA) An organization founded in 1967 with the aim of emulating the American civil rights campaign by using non-violent protest to obtain equal rights for Catholics.

Operation Motorman The name given to a British Army offensive launched in July 1971 in a major motorized attempt to put an end to the so-called no-go areas of Derry and Belfast.

Orange Order A Protestant sectarian organization created in 1795 in opposition to the United Irishmen and other secret Catholic societies. The Orange Order was a revival of the Orange Institution which had been established in 1688 in support of William of Orange whose victory at the Battle of the Boyne in 1690 is celebrated by Protestant parades held every year on 12 July. Originally an Episcopalian peasant organization, the Orange Order extended its membership to Presbyterians in 1834. In 1885 the Order was used as a base for mobilizing opposition to the first Home Rule Bill. Since the formation of Northern Ireland in 1920, the Orange Order has played an important role in maintaining Protestant unity in the face of Irish nationalism and Catholicism.

Peace Movement A mass movement which began on 10 August 1976 when the three young children of Anne Maguire were accidentally killed during the pursuit of an IRA terrorist. A peace petition was organized by Mairead Corrigan and Betty Williams, both of whom were awarded the Nobel Peace Prize a year later in 1977.

People's Democracy An organization founded in 1968 by the (Trotskyist) International Socialists at Queen's University, Belfast. Until its leadership was taken over by the Official IRA in 1970, People's Democracy played a leading role in the Northern Ireland Civil Rights Association (founded in 1967).

Prevention of Terrorism (Temporary Provisions) Act Legislation passed by the British parliament in 1974 in the wake of the Birmingham pub bombings. Renewed every five years since then, the act allows police to arrest without warrant and detain for up to seven days those suspected of involvement with terrorist activities.

Provisional IRA (the "Provos") The military wing of Sinn Féin and the largest paramilitary guerrilla group in Europe, formed in 1970 following a split with the Official IRA. The Provisionals constitute the principal direct–action terrorist organization within the Irish republican movement.

Red Hand Commando An illegal Protestant paramilitary organization that played a significant role in the Belfast riots of August 1969.

right to silence The right of suspected terrorists to remain silent under police questioning or in court. This right was curtailed in November 1988 with the passing of the Criminal Evidence (Northern Ireland) Order.

Royal Ulster Constabulary (RUC) An armed police force of some 13 000 officers established in Northern Ireland in May 1922. The original force was permitted to recruit   3000 men , one–third of whom were to be Roman Catholic. Of the 1 100 former members of the Royal Irish Constabulary eventually accepted into the RUC, only 400 were Catholics. In 1977 the RUC assumed responsibility for law and order in Northern Ireland.

Saor Uladh ("Free Ulster") The military wing of the Fianna Uladh party which broke away from the IRA in 1953 under the leadership of Liam Kelly.

Shankill Butcher's Gang The name given to one of several Protestant death squads operating in the 1970s. In February 1979 eight of the "Butchers" were sentenced to a total of 42 life sentences for 19 deaths.

Sinn Féin ("we ourselves") An Irish nationalist party founded in 1905 by Arthur Griffith (1872–1922). Eamon de Valera, former President of the Irish Republic, was elected President of Sinn Féin in 1917. The IRA owes allegiance to Sinn Féin which gained representation in 17 out of 26 district councils in Northern Ireland in 1985.

Social Democratic and Labour Party (SDLP) A moderate Catholic political party formed in Northern Ireland in 1971.

Stalker Inquiry Following complaints by churchmen and nationalist leaders, John Stalker, Deputy Chief Constable of Greater Manchester, was appointed in May 1984 to head an investigation into reports of an RUC "Shoot to Kill" policy in Armagh. On 6 June 1986 John Stalker was replaced as leader of the inquiry by Colin Sampson, Chief Constable of West Yorkshire. His dismissal and subsequent suspension from duty aroused speculation that he had uncovered highly embarrassing information relating to the RUC.

Steelboys One of a number of secret 18th–century Catholic organizations which attempted to ensure that farm tenancies were prevented from passing into the hands of Protestants. The occasionally bloody fights waged by members of this and other groups eventually led to the formation of the Orange Order.

Sunningdale Agreement A 1973 agreement reiterating the Downing Street Declaration of 1969, announced at the conclusion of a conference between the British and Irish governments and representatives of some sections of Unionism, the Alliance Party and the Catholic Social Democratic and Labour Party (SDLP). The agreement affirmed that no change would be made in the status of Northern Ireland without the consent of the majority. It also envisaged the setting up of a power sharing Catholic–Protestant Executive in the North and an all–Ireland court procedure for combating terrorism.

supergrass system A system of obtaining information from terrorists who will testify against their colleagues in exchange for immunity from prosecution or other inducements. The supergrass system in Northern Ireland dates from the arrest of Christopher Black in the Ardoyne area of Belfast. His evidence led to the conviction of 35 members of the IRA. In the period November 1981–November 1983 at least seven Loyalist and 18 Republican supergrasses were responsible for over 590 people being arrested and charged with terrorist offences in Northern Ireland.

Ulster Defence Association (UDA) The principal paramilitary wing and fund raising organization of the Protestant loyalists. Founded in 1973 to defend Protestant communities from IRA attack, the Shankill–based UDA eventually attracted an estimated membership of some 15 000.

Ulster Defence Regiment (UDR) A military corps of 6 500 men and women, set up in April 1970 following advice given by Sir John Hunt's committee of inquiry into security in Northern Ireland.

Ulster Freedom Fighters (UFF) An extremist Protestant paramilitary organization associated with the UDA.

Ulster Independence Party A political party formed in October 1977 to promote the independence of Northern Ireland from the United Kingdom.

Ulster Loyalist Central Co-ordinating Committee A Protestant organization that grew out of the ad hoc committee responsible for organizing the Ulster Workers' Council strike of May 1974. Its function is to co-ordinate the activities of the Unionist paramilitary groups.

Ulster Unionist Party Allied to the British Conservative Party, the Ulster Unionist Party was formed in 1898 as the main voice of Irish Protestant unionists who subscribe to the maintenance of the Act of Union of 1800.

Ulster Volunteer Force (UVF) The loyalist equivalent of the IRA. Formed in 1912, it reappeared in 1966 as a Protestant paramilitary force.

Vanguard Unionist Party (VUP) A political party formed in 1973 by the former Northern Ireland Home Affairs Minister, William Craig. The party was eventually dissolved five years later in 1978.

Widgery Tribunal An inquiry into violence in Northern Ireland chaired by Lord Widgery whose report, published in April 1972, exonerated the British paratroopers charged with shooting the 13 Civil Rights demonstrators killed on Bloody Sunday.

Workers' Party Formerly known as the official (Marxist) Sinn Féin, the Workers' Party is the political wing of the Official IRA. Opposed to sectarian violence, the aim of the party is to unite the working class.

■ Further reading

P. Arthur and K. Jeffrey, *Northern Ireland Since 1968*, Basil Blackwell, Oxford, 1988

Patrick Bishop and Eamon Mallie, *The Provisional IRA*, Corgi, London, 1987

D.G. Boyce, *The Irish Question and British Politics, 1868–1986*, British History in Perspective, Macmillan Education, London, 1988

Steve Bruce, *God Save Ulster: The Religion and Politics of Paisleyism*, Clarendon, Oxford, 1989

Tim Pat Coogan, *The IRA*, Fontana/Collins, London, 1987

John Darby (ed.), *Northern Ireland: The Background to the Conflict*, Appletree Press, Belfast, 1983

Conor Cruise O'Brien, *States of Ireland*, Hutchinson, London, 1972

General Bibliography

Michael Banks (ed.), *Conflict in World Society*, Wheatsheaf Books (UK), 1984

Andrew Boyd (ed.), *An Atlas of World Affairs*, seventh edition, Methuen, London and New York, 1983

Gerald Butt, *The Arab World: A Personal View*, BBC Books, London, 1987

Gérard Chaliand and Jean–Pierre Rageau (eds.), *Strategic Atlas: World Geopolitics*, Penguin Books, London, 1986

H.C. Darby and Harold Fullard (eds.), *The New Cambridge Modern History Atlas*, Cambridge University Press, Cambridge, 1978

Alan J. Day (ed.), *Border and Territorial Disputes*, 2nd edition, Longman (UK), Harlow, 1987

Henry W. Degenhardt, *Treaties and Alliances of the World*, 4th edition, Longman (UK), Harlow, 1986

Henry W. Degenhardt, *Revolutionary and Dissident Movements*, Longman (UK), Harlow, 1988

Iewan Ll. Griffiths, *An Atlas of African Affairs*, Methuen, London, 1987

John Keegan and Andrew Wheatcroft, *Zones of Conflict*, Jonathan Cape, London, 1986

Minority Rights Group, *World Directory of Minorities*, Longman (UK), Harlow, 1989

Trevor Mostyn and Albert Hourani (eds.), *Cambridge Encyclopedia of the Middle East and North Africa*, Cambridge University Press, Cambridge, 1988

Alan Palmer, *Dictionary of Twentieth–Century History 1900–82*, Penguin Books (UK), London, 1985

Penguin Atlas of World History, Vol. II, Penguin Books (UK), London, 1986

Helen Schooley, *Conflict in Central America*, Longman (UK), Harlow, 1987

George Segal, *Guide to the World Today*, Simon & Schuster, London, 1987

Norman Stone (ed.), *The Times Atlas of World History*, 3rd edition, Guild Publishing, 1989

Paul Wilkinson and A.M. Stewart (eds.), *Contemporary Research on Terrorism*, Aberdeen University Press, Aberdeen, 1987

Gwyneth Williams and Brian Hackland, *The Dictionary of Contemporary Politics of Southern Africa*, Routledge, London, 1988